D0773091

DUMBARTON OAKS
MEDIEVAL LIBRARY

Jan M. Ziolkowski, General Editor

THE VULGATE BIBLE

VOLUME IIA

DOML 4

DUMBARTON OAKS MEDIEVAL LIBRARY

Jan M. Ziolkowski, General Editor
Danuta Shanzer, Medieval Latin Editor

Medieval Latin Editorial Board
Robert G. Babcock
B. Gregory Hays
Michael W. Herren
David Townsend
Winthrop Wetherbee III
Michael Winterbottom
Roger Wright

Medieval Latin Advisory Board
Walter Berschin
Peter Dronke
Ralph Hexter
Mayke de Jong
José Martínez Gázquez
Kurt Smolak
Francesco Stella
Jean-Yves Tilliette

The Vulgate Bible

VOLUME IIA

The Historical Books

DOUAY-RHEIMS TRANSLATION

Edited by

SWIFT EDGAR

DUMBARTON OAKS
MEDIEVAL LIBRARY

HARVARD UNIVERSITY PRESS
CAMBRIDGE, MASSACHUSETTS
LONDON, ENGLAND
2011

Copyright © 2011 by the President and Fellows of Harvard College

ALL RIGHTS RESERVED

Printed in the United States of America

Library of Congress Cataloging-in-Publication Data

Bible. English. Douai. 2011

The Vulgate Bible : Douay-Rheims translation / edited by Swift Edgar.

v. cm. — (Dumbarton Oaks medieval library ; DOML 4)

English and Latin text on facing pages.

Includes bibliographical references.

Contents: v. 1. The Pentateuch. v. 2a. The Historical Books, part a. v. 2b. The Historical Books, part b.

ISBN 978-0-674-05534-6 (v. 1 : alk. paper)

ISBN 978-0-674-99667-0 (v. 2a : alk. paper)

ISBN 978-0-674-06077-7 (v. 2b : alk. paper)

I. Edgar, Swift, 1985–   II. Dumbarton Oaks.   III. Title.

BS180 2010

222'.1047—dc22   2010015238

Contents

Introduction

The Vulgate Bible is a collection of Latin texts compiled and translated in large part by Saint Jerome (ca. 345–420) in the late fourth and early fifth centuries CE. Roughly speaking, Jerome translated the Old Testament—except for the books of Wisdom, Ecclesiasticus, Baruch and 1 and 2 Maccabees— and he revised existing Latin versions of the Psalms and the Gospels. Jerome's Bible was used widely in the Western European Christian (and later, specifically Catholic) tradition from the early Middle Ages through the twentieth century.

The adjective "Vulgate" (from the Latin verb *vulgare*, meaning "to disseminate") lacks the connotation of coarseness often inherent in its relative "vulgar," but both words imply commonness. Indeed, the Vulgate Bible was so widespread that its significance can hardly be overstated. It made critical contributions to literature, visual art, music and education during the Middle Ages and the Renaissance, and it informed much of the Western theological, intellectual, artistic and even political history of that period. Students of almost any aspect of European civilization from the seventh century (when the Latin Bible existed more or less in the form we know today) through the sixteenth century (when translations of scripture into various European vernaculars

became widely available to the public and acceptable to religious authorities) must refer frequently to the Vulgate Bible and have a thorough knowledge of it.

In this edition, the Latin is presented opposite the first English version of the Bible sanctioned by the Roman Catholic Church. This English Bible is typically referred to as the Douay-Rheims Version, after the present-day names of its places of publication. The New Testament was published in 1582 by the English College at Rheims, and the Old Testament (to call it the Hebrew Bible would be inaccurate, since it includes nine books that have never belonged to the Hebrew canon) was published in 1609 and 1610, in two volumes, by the English College at Douay. The entire Douay-Rheims Bible was revised several times, notably by Bishop Dr. Richard Challoner (1691–1781) in 1749 and 1750.

In this introduction, I use the terms "Catholic" and "Protestant" in their current senses. Adherents to the Church of England in the sixteenth century at times referred to themselves as Catholics and to those who followed the religious authorities in Rome as Popish or Papists. The members of the Roman Church called their Anglican rivals various names, such as heretics, Protestants, Lutherans and Calvinists, but they would not have called them Catholics.

Douay and Rheims were major centers of learning for English-speaking Catholics, who faced hostility in Protestant England. The English College, a prominent Catholic institution, was exiled from Douay to Rheims in 1578, near the beginning of the Eighty Years' War between the Netherlands (to which Douay at the time belonged) and Philip II of Spain, who had founded the college.[1] The exile lasted until 1593. The college undertook these translations of the Bi-

ble primarily in response to the English versions produced under the Church of England that did not treat Jerome's text as the ultimate authority. Protestant English translators did use the Vulgate, but they also consulted the German rendering by Martin Luther (1482–1546), the Greek Septuagint and New Testament, testimonia in Hebrew and other sources. In contrast, the Douay-Rheims Version was directly translated from the Latin Bible as it was known to the professors at the English College in 1582.

While the English College was working on its translations at Douay and Rheims, Pope Sixtus V (r. 1585–1590) called for the preparation of an authoritative Latin text. This Latin Bible was published in 1590, just prior to his death, but it contained errors and was soon suppressed for fear that Protestants would use them to attack the Catholic Church.[2] Three corrected printings followed, in 1592, 1593 and 1598, during the papacy of Clement VIII (r. 1592–1605). These four editions, substantially the same, are referred to collectively as the Sixto-Clementine Version. While it strongly resembles the Latin Bible that evidently served as the basis for the Douay-Rheims translation, the two are not identical. The Dumbarton Oaks Medieval Library (DOML) here presents a reconstructed Latin text of the lost Bible used by the professors at Douay and Rheims, and Challoner's revision of the English translation faces the Latin. Challoner's text, discussed in detail below ("The English Text of This Edition"), sometimes reflects the Sixto-Clementine Bible more closely than did the English College translations of 1582, 1609 and 1610, but many of the revision's features are not at all related to the Sixto-Clementine Bible, and some lead the translation even further from the Latin.

Although the Douay Old Testament was not published until 1609–1610, most of the work on the translation seems to have been completed much earlier, before any Sixto-Clementine edition. Despite its publication date, therefore, this section of the English translation still provides a valuable witness to a Latin text that predated the Sixto-Clementine Version. Most scholars accept the conclusion by Charles Dodd that "the work may be entirely ascribed to Mr. [Gregory] Martin [who died a decade before publication of the Sixto-Clementine edition] . . . He translated the whole Bible; tho' it was not publish'd all at one time."[3] There is good reason to believe that Dodd was right: an entry in the "Douay Diaries,"[4] records of the activities at the young English College, attests that Martin began translating the Bible in October 1578 and that he translated two chapters a day, which were revised by two other professors. Since there are 1,353 chapters in the Bible—including the Books of Tobit, Judith, Wisdom, Ecclesiasticus, Baruch, 1 and 2 Maccabees and 3 and 4 Ezra, and counting the Prayer of Manasseh as one chapter—the task would have taken Martin and his team slightly more than 676 days, far less time than the thirty years that elapsed between the project's commencement and the complete publication of the Bible. Indeed, this calculation is confirmed in the address "To the right vvelbeloved English reader" in the first volume of the Old Testament (1609), which states that the Bible was translated "about thirtie yeares since" (fifth page of the section). The translation thus almost certainly preceded the Sixto-Clementine text, which immediately became the standard edition upon its printing in 1592. The lag between translation and publication is explained on the first page of the

same section: "As for the impediments, which hitherto haue hindered this worke, they al proceded (as manie do know) of one general cause, our poore estate in banishment"—that is, the exile of the English College to Rheims.

The Douay-Rheims translation used here mostly follows the version printed in 1899, a slight revision of Challoner's editions, incorporating elements from the 1749, 1750 and 1752 printings. Challoner's principal contribution was to make the original Douay-Rheims easier to read by updating obscure phraseology and obsolete words. This volume modifies the 1899 version to bring the punctuation and the transliteration of proper nouns and adjectives into line with modern practice (see Alternate Spellings in the endmatter for this edition's policies regarding transliterations) and to restore some readings from Challoner's 1750 and 1752 editions that had been changed (mostly due to printers' errors) in the 1899 version. In addition, the whole text has been prepared according to the guidelines of the fifteenth edition of the *Chicago Manual of Style*. This policy has resulted in significant alterations to Challoner's edition, which superabounds in colons and commas, lacks quotation marks and begins each verse on a new line, sometimes making the text difficult to understand. In contrast to most English Bibles, this volume renders all of the text as prose, even the parts that were originally in verse, since neither the Latin nor the English is poetic. The Latin text has been punctuated according to the English translation to allow easy movement between the two languages. In the rare instances when they diverge, the text in each language has been punctuated according to its most natural meaning (see, for example, Gen 31:1–4).

Readers of the Dumbarton Oaks Medieval Library who wish to compare either the English or the Latin version presented here with another Bible should bear in mind that the versification in the Vulgate and the numbering of psalms differ from those in Bibles translated from languages other than Latin. Furthermore, the books in this volume have been selected and ordered according to Challoner's revisions, which follow the Sixto-Clementine Bible. This policy has resulted in the inclusion of some chapters and books commonly considered "apocryphal" or "deuterocanonical" (Tobit, Judith, Wisdom, Ecclesiasticus, Baruch, 1 and 2 Maccabees, Daniel 3:24–90, Daniel 13 and 14) and the omission of others that were relegated to appendices even in early printed versions of the Bible (3 and 4 Ezra and the Prayer of Mannaseh). The names of some books differ from the ones that may be familiar to many readers: for instance, 1 and 2 Kings in this volume are commonly called 1 and 2 Samuel; 3 and 4 Kings are usually 1 and 2 Kings; 1 and 2 Paralipomenon equate to 1 and 2 Chronicles; 1 Ezra is usually simply Ezra, while 2 Ezra is typically Nehemiah; the Canticle of Canticles is also known as the Song of Songs; Ecclesiasticus is Sirach and in some Latin Bibles is known as Iesu Filii Sirach; and, last, the Apocalypse of St. John the Apostle may be known to most readers as the Book of Revelation.

THE LATIN TEXT OF THIS EDITION

The Latin in this edition presents as closely as possible the text from which the Douay-Rheims translators worked. It would have been a version of the Bible known to many Europeans from the eighth through the sixteenth century. Be-

fore Jerome, translations of parts of the Bible into Latin existed; we call these disparate texts the Old Latin Bible. After Jerome finished his work, versions of his Vulgate proliferated. According to one count, a third of the biblical manuscripts we have today dating to about one hundred years after Jerome's death are from the Vulgate, and a century later "manuscripts of the Vulgate start to outnumber those of the Old Latin by about two to one. In the seventh century, the ratio has risen to about six to one."[5] The early ninth century brought the stabilization of a recension that was overseen by Alcuin, the schoolmaster from York who played a major role in the cultural revival promoted by Charlemagne. The so-called Alcuin Bibles, of which some thirty survive, became the standard text outside Italy during the Carolingian period. They were the products of monastic copy centers known as scriptoria. In the thirteenth century, the Alcuin Bibles gave way to the so-called Paris Bibles, which were written by professional scribes. The text of the Paris Bibles, a direct descendent of the Alcuin Bibles, was in turn closely related to the Sixto-Clementine Bibles of the late sixteenth century. In large part, the DOML text corresponds to Robert Weber's edition (2007). Most adjustments to bring the Latin closer to the English coincide with an edition of the Sixto-Clementine Bible (1959) that preserves the majority of the readings from the second Clementine edition (1593) and occasionally replaces that text with readings from the other two Clementine editions, which were very similar to each other. For consistency's sake, the spellings and inflections of adjustments based on the Sixto-Clementine Bible have been brought into line with Weber's text.

When neither the Weber nor the Sixto-Clementine text

provides the reading that the Douay-Rheims translators appear to have seen, the critical apparatuses in Weber and in Quentin's edition (1926–[1995]) have been consulted. Often the readings attested in early printed editions of the Bible, such as the famous "42-line Bible" printed by Johannes Gutenberg in 1454, come closest to the translation. In rare instances it has been necessary to print reconstructions of the text theoretically used by the translators, since neither the Sixto-Clementine, Weber and Quentin editions nor the citations in their apparatus provide a suitable reading. These reconstructions, often closer to the Greek Septuagint than to any Vulgate edition, follow the Old Latin Bible.

In trying to identify the Latin source or sources of the Douay-Rheims translation, some scholars have pointed to the Louvain Bible,[6] an early printed edition that strongly resembles the Sixto-Clementine Version. However, the readings in the Douay-Rheims Version do not support the conclusion that Martin based his translation on either the Louvain Bible of 1547 or the correction of that edition published at Rome in 1574. Furthermore, the preface of the Douay-Rheims Version addressed "To the right vvelbeloved English reader" states (and Greenslade accepts) that the editors of the Old Testament "conformed it to the most perfect Latin Edition"—presumably, given the publication date, the Sixto-Clementine Version.[7] To take just one illustration of the danger of assuming that the translators used a single identifiable source, consider Ex 16:29, which in the Douay translation reads in part, "and let none goe forth": of the many sources considered by Quentin (including the Louvain Bible), only two—both early printed editions and neither of them the Sixto-Clementine or the Louvain edition—begin

the relevant Latin clause with a conjunction. Moreover, while the translators claimed their work was "diligently conferred with the Hebrew, Greeke, and other Editions in diuers languages,"[8] the relative paucity of readings different from well-established Latin sources and the inconsistency in the nature of the divergences suggest that they were working with a now lost Latin text of idiosyncratic nature rather than a still extant one that they chose to ignore from time to time. Since several people collaborated on that translation, the translators may also have followed different editions of the Bible and therefore produced a translation for which there is no single surviving Latin source.

Unlike the Latin as edited by Weber, the Sixto-Clementine edition (to whose family the Douay-Rheims translation belongs) often regularizes the language found in earlier manuscripts. In general, the Sixto-Clementine rarely accepts the *lectio difficilior,* while most editors since the eighteenth century, including Weber, tend to choose the "more difficult reading" from among multiple possibilities. For example, at Gen 32:5, the Weber edition reads, "habeo boves et asinos oves et servos atque ancillas," while the Sixto-Clementine editors preferred to avoid the variations of asyndeton after *asinos* and of *atque,* so their text reads, "Habeo boves et asinos et oves et servos et ancillas." In this instance, the Douay-Rheims translators evidently saw a conjunction between *asinos* and *oves* and also between *servos* and *ancillas.* In this edition, an *et* has been inserted in the former case, but the *atque* has remained in the latter, because we cannot know which of the many options for the English "and" the translators encountered in their Latin.

At times, the translation reflects a base text closer to We-

ber's than to the Sixto-Clementine edition. For example, at Gen 1:14, Weber reads "fiant luminaria in firmamento caeli ut dividant diem ac noctem," while for *ut,* the Sixto-Clementine edition reads *et.* However, the Douay-Rheims translation (as revised by Challoner, but here retaining the grammatical construction of the original) reads, "Let there be lights made in the firmament of heaven to divide the day and the night," clearly translating *ut.* The Sixto-Clementine choice was probably made by analogy to verses like Gen 1:6, which reads in both editions "Fiat firmamentum in medio aquarum, et dividat."

The English Text of This Edition

The "Douay-Rheims Version" is an imperfect name for the translation of the Vulgate Bible used in this volume. Indeed, one anonymous scholar in 1836 went so far as to write that calling a translation similar to the one printed here "the Douay or Rhemish version is an abuse of terms."[9] The English here follows a text that was published in 1899. Although this text has been understood routinely as being the Douay-Rheims Version without any qualification, it in fact offers an English translation that derives not directly from the work of the English College of Douay and Rheims, but rather from a nineteenth-century form of a revision by Challoner. Challoner published at least five revisions of the New Testament and two of the Old (the New Testaments appeared in 1749, 1750, 1752, 1764 and 1772, the Old Testaments in 1750 and 1763–1764); after his death, others produced many more. Since the editions of 1582, 1609 and 1610, many subsequent revisions have purported to be simple reprints.

Indeed, the frontispiece to the 1899 edition has a message of approbation by James Cardinal Gibbons, then archbishop of Baltimore, who writes that the text "is an accurate reprint of the Rheims and Douay edition with Dr. Challoner's notes." But if we are to understand the "Rheims and Douay edition" to mean the translations originally printed in those cities in the late sixteenth and early seventeenth centuries, the text we have is by no means an accurate reprint of that.

Because the versions issued between 1610 and 1899 can be difficult to come by, and because the only work approaching a systematic collation of various "Douay-Rheims" Bibles is a bitterly anti-Catholic work from 1855,[10] many scholars regard the Douay-Rheims translation as a text that has barely changed (if at all) since its first printing. Some are aware of Challoner's extensive revisions in the mid-eighteenth century, which updated the language of the Douay-Rheims Version and toned down the polemical annotations, but few know the extent of his alterations, or that they make it more distant from the Latin Vulgate, or that they took place over several editions or that the editions published after his death often contain the work of other scholars.

Many factors complicate analysis of the modifications that the Douay-Rheims Version has undergone over the past four centuries. The most significant is the doctrinal conservatism of the Catholic Church. Owing to both the primacy of Jerome's Vulgate (another inadequate label, since Jerome hardly produced the Latin text by himself), recognized at the Council of Trent (1545–1563), and the desire of the Church to exert some control over access to scripture, the translation of the Bible into vernacular tongues was dis-

couraged. Yet after Protestant churches made the text of the Bible available to speakers of English and German, it became easier for reformist thinkers to disseminate their teachings. Some English-speaking Catholics then sought to produce their own translation, but since the point of this work was to regulate the message read by the flock, the translation required authorization to insure that it was appropriate. A letter of 1580 from William Allen, the president of the English College at Douay, to a colleague, Professor Jean de Vendeville, expresses the need for papal sanctioning of the translation: "We on our part will undertake, if His Holiness shall think proper, to produce a faithful, pure, and genuine version of the Bible in accordance with the version approved by the Church."[11] The printed edition was approved not by the pope but by three professors at Allen's own college (Douay-Rheims 1609, *Approbatio*).

Conservatism demanded the Church's approbation and made revision difficult. How could a reviser supplant something that had already been declared acceptable to the Church? Revisions required approval of their own, yet they could not directly contradict previously approved editions. For this reason, the only reference to a difference between Challoner's 1750 edition and the printings of 1582, 1609 and 1610 comes on the title page, which describes the work as "Newly revised and corrected, according to the Clementine Edition of the Scriptures." As the phrasing shows, Challoner was careful to note that his version derived from the Latin Bible first authorized by Pope Clement VIII in 1592, ten years after the Rheims New Testament, but he obscured the extent of his revisions. Despite the popularity of Challoner's revision and of the Bibles still in print that descend from it,

the English translations and revisions of scripture were not created under a directive from the Vatican. There is no single, indisputably "official" translation of the Latin Bible into English. All the translations lay claim to official status without criticizing other Catholic versions, and none of them has clear primacy.

This confusing (and confused) climate has misled modern readers into believing precisely what the editors and translators of English Catholic Bibles from the sixteenth through the nineteenth century wanted them to think: a single standard English translation of the Bible existed, and the reader in question was holding a copy of it. One well-respected medievalist cautioned against using the King James Version for medieval studies (because it lacks a close relationship to the Vulgate text), implying that the Douay-Rheims Version is preferable. While correct about the King James Version, he shows himself to be unaware of the Douay-Rheims's own modern tradition, writing, "The English translation of [the Vulgate] is the one known as the 'Douai-Rheims' translation . . . also available in many modern editions," and later quoting the translation of Ct 2:4 in the Douay-Rheims as "he set in order charity in me."[12] This quotation comes from Challoner's revision of the translation from 1750; the 1610 translation reads, "he hath ordered in me charitie."

The particular case of Ct 2:4 does not perfectly illustrate the danger of using Challoner's revision of the Douay-Rheims translation, because his rendering still matches the Vulgate text ("ordinavit in me caritatem"). But in many places (italicized in this edition) Challoner strayed from the Latin, usually to revise some particularly awkward phrasing

Rheims text primarily on the basis of literary sensibilities. His version significantly departs from the Douay-Rheims when that text is most stilted, and not infrequently in such instances, Challoner's revision closely matches the sense or wording (or both) of the King James Bible.

A word of caution should be issued to those who would accept the implication of the subtitle of Challoner's Bible: "Newly revised and corrected, according to the Clementine Edition of the Scriptures." This description suggests that Challoner updated the Douay-Rheims translation in light of the standard text of the Bible that had not been available to the translators at the English College. Through oversight, however, his revision skipped a few phrases that the Douay-Rheims translators had missed as well (mostly when similar Latin words appeared on different parts of the page, causing leaps of the eye).[15] These omissions suggest strongly that Challoner's primary task was to make the English of the Douay-Rheims version more readable; it was not a revision on textual grounds. Otherwise, a careful collation of the Douay-Rheims Version with the Sixto-Clementine Bible would have been essential. More often than not, Challoner appears simply to have read the Douay-Rheims and fixed the poor or awkward style, occasionally turning to the King James, Latin, Greek or possibly Hebrew texts for help. He does not seem to have compared the Douay-Rheims systematically with the Latin (or any other version).

If we are not prepared to credit the magnum opus of the Anglican Church as a major source for Challoner, we can say that many of his revisions came from Hebrew and Greek sources (the same texts that the King James editors read,

possibly accounting for the similarities). Why Challoner often turned to sources other than the Latin Vulgate, which had existed in stable and authorized form since 1592, is unclear, especially in view of his title-page statement that he had updated the Douay-Rheims according to the Sixto-Clementine Bible. The period in which Challoner published his first edition of the New Testament (1749) was one of lively productivity for biblical scholars. The monumental edition of the pre-Vulgate Latin Bible credited to Pierre Sabatier, a Benedictine monk, was in production (Rheims 1739, 1749; Paris 1751). This text was meant to reconstruct the Bible as it was known to the Church fathers writing in Latin before the general acceptance of Jerome's text, and it received the approbation of two vicars general and Sabatier's own abbot. It relies frequently on Greek and Hebrew sources, indicating that the study of those texts was not as distasteful to the Church elite in the eighteenth century as it had been in 1609, when the Douay-Rheims translators prefaced their edition with the following words:

> But here an other question may be proposed: VVhy we translate the Latin text, rather than the Hebrew, or Greke, which Protestantes preferre, as the fountaine tongues, wherin holie Scriptures were first written? To this we answer, that if in dede those first pure Editions were now extant, or if such as be extant, were more pure than the Latin, we would also preferre such fountaines before the riuers, in whatsoeuer they should be found to disagree. But the ancient best lerned Fathers, & Doctors of the Church, do much complaine, and

testifie to vs, that both the Hebrew and Greke Editions are fouly corrupted by Iewes, and Heretikes,
since the Latin was truly translated out of them,
whiles they were more pure.[16]

Indeed, by 1750 the Counter-Reformational motives of
the Douay-Rheims Version of 1582, 1609 and 1610 had become largely irrelevant, and the polemical annotations of
the first translation were either omitted or stripped of their
vehemence. Even the notes in the Old Testament of 1609–
1610 contain less vitriol than those in the 1582 New Testament. Strict adherence to the Vulgate Bible mattered less to
Challoner than to the original translators, although he still
evidently favored literalism in his renderings. Consequently,
he may have preferred to replace poorly worded translations
with a new literal translation of a different source, rather
than to print loose constructions of the Latin text. None-
theless, the translation on the whole adheres faithfully to
the Vulgate, the official Bible of the Catholic Church; after
all, Challoner wrote a pamphlet entitled "The Touchstone
of the New Religion: or, Sixty Assertions of Protestants,
try'd by their own Rule of Scripture alone, and condemned
by clear and express Texts of their own Bible" (London 1735).
Interestingly, this tract reveals Challoner's familiarity with,
or at least access to, the King James Version of the Bible. As
one scholar put it, "He sought to establish the Roman
Church's credentials out of the mouths of her enemies."[17]

It may be fitting that the DOML Bible is an artificial one.
After all, in whatever language or languages the texts collectively called the Bible are read, they are heterogeneous, cob-
bled together over centuries, having been composed (or re-

vealed) and varied by oral tradition throughout the preceding millennia. With only minor revisions, we use Challoner's edition of the Douay-Rheims Bible because his text preserves the character of the English translation that brings us closest to the end of the medieval period while still being fairly elegant and readable. This edition differs from the 1899 printing in restoring readings from the 1750 and 1752 editions which had been spuriously altered in the 1899 version and in updating the biblical names and the punctuation of the earlier edition. Challoner's notes have been excised, though his chapter summaries remain.

With its rich and somewhat thorny history, Challoner's English is important to scholars of many disciplines, and its proximity to the literal translation of the most important book of the medieval period—namely, the Latin Bible—makes it invaluable to English-speakers studying the Middle Ages.

A Note on the Translation

Every discussion of the Douay-Rheims translation—whether praising or condemning it, whether acknowledging or ignoring Challoner's contribution to the text—affirms its proximity to the Latin. The translation in this volume has, however, a few characteristics that are either difficult for contemporary English-speakers to understand or that make the English less literal than it could be.

Challoner's word choice may sometimes puzzle readers. In the service of literalism, the Douay-Rheims translators and Challoner usually rendered *postquam* by the now obsolete phrase "after that," regardless of whether the Latin

word was a conjunction or an adverb. For example, at Gen 24:22, the translation reads, "And after that the camels had drunk, the man took out golden earrings weighing two sicles and as many bracelets of ten sicles weight," whereas a natural, more modern rendering would eliminate the word "that." Possibly by analogy to the case of *postquam,* or possibly because in the seventeenth century there was little distinction between the meanings of "after" and "after that," the translators occasionally rendered other words as "after that" where the phrase makes little sense in modern usage; see, for example, the temporal *cum* at Gen 8:6. On the whole, though, Challoner avoided trying to fit the square peg of English translation into the round hole of the Latin text. He shied away from the Douay-Rheims tendency to translate Latin words with awkward cognates, such as "invocate" for forms of *invoco* (for example, Gen 4:26); he frequently rendered relative pronouns with a conjunction followed by a demonstrative (Gen 3:1 and elsewhere); and he and his antecedents were free with temporal constructions, rendering, to take one example, *de nocte* as "very early" at Ex 34:4. Furthermore, Challoner translated many conjunctions as "now" that literally mean "and," "but," "moreover" or "therefore" (for example, Gen 16:1 and 3 Rg 1:1); the King James translators were also liberal in their use of "now."

Challoner's breaches of the rule of strict (some have said excessive) literalism also occur in areas other than word choice. The most frequent deviations appear in the translation of participles, the passive voice and especially passive participles. The translation of Nm 20:6 illustrates this program: the verse in Latin begins, "Ingressusque Moses et Aaron dimissa multitudine Tabernaculum Foederis corruerunt"; the 1609 translation reads, "And Moyses and Aaron,

the multitude being dismissed, entering into the tabernacle of couenant, fel"; whereas Challoner, preferring not to employ the passive voice or more than one construction with a participle, rendered the verse (with my punctuation), "And Moses and Aaron leaving the multitude went into the Tabernacle of the Covenant and fell." The many ablatives absolute and other participial constructions that have been modified by Challoner to fit more neatly into his preferred English style have not been signaled by italics in this volume because they do not illuminate anything about the Latin text and because the renderings are not so loose as to make their relationship to the Latin difficult to perceive.

Another systematic abandonment of literal translations appears in Challoner's rendering of oath formulas and other invocations of God, especially those that begin in Latin *vivo* or *vivit Dominus* or that employ constructions similar to "haec faciat mihi Deus et haec addat." Usually the first two formulas are rendered by adding "as" in English before the subject of the verb, and if the next clause begins with a conjunction, it is excised in translation. See, for example, 1 Rg 14:39, which begins in Latin, "Vivit Dominus, salvator Israhel, quia si" and was translated in the 1609 edition as "Our Lord the sauiour of Israel liueth, that if," which was modified by Challoner to read, "As the Lord liveth who is the saviour of Israel, if." The constructions that substantially resemble "haec faciat mihi Deus et haec addat" as at 1 Rg 14:44 were translated predictably in 1609 as "These thinges doe God to me, and these thinges adde he." Challoner rendered the prayer as "May God do so and so to me and add still more." Both of these divergences from the Latin are anticipated in the English of the King James Version, and because such renderings are pervasive, they have

ard Challoner; Michael Herren and Danuta Shanzer for their careful reading and helpful suggestions; and especially Jan Ziolkowski, who conceived of the series, trusted me to see this project through, and supervised my work.

NOTES

1 See Carleton, *The Part of Rheims in the Making of the English Bible,* p. 13.

2 Quentin, *Mémoire sur l'établissement du texte de la Vulgate,* pp. 190–92.

3 Dodd, *The Church History of England,* vol. 2, p. 121, quoted in Pope and Bullough, *English Versions of the Bible,* p. 252.

4 Knox, *The First and Second Diaries of the English College,* p. 145, cited in Carleton, *The Part of Rheims in the Making of the English Bible,* p. 16.

5 de Hamel, *The Book: A History of the Bible,* p. 28.

6 Pope and Bullough, *English Versions of the Bible,* p. 295; Greenslade, *The Cambridge History of the Bible,* p. 163.

7 Greenslade, *The Cambridge History of the Bible,* p. 163.

8 Frontispiece, Douay-Rheims Bible, 1609.

9 A Catholic, "A new Version of the Four Gospels," p. 476, quoted in Cartmell, "English Spiritual Writers," p. 583. Cartmell erroneously cites the passage as appearing on page 276 but attributes it correctly to Nicholas Wiseman, though the review was published anonymously.

10 Cotton, *Rhemes and Doway.*

11 Translated from the Latin by Knox; see Carleton, *The Part of Rheims in the Making of the English Bible,* p. 15.

12 Kaske, *Medieval Christian Literary Imagery,* p. 6.

13 A Catholic, "A new Version of the Four Gospels," p. 476.

14 Duffy, *Challoner and His Church,* p. 6.

15 See Pope and Bullough, *English Versions of the Bible,* pp. 359–71.

16 "To the right vvelbeloved English reader," Douay-Rheims Bible, 1609.

17 Gilley, "Challoner as Controvertionalist," p. 93.

Abbreviations

Ecl	Ecclesiastes
Ct	Canticle of Canticles
Wis	Wisdom
Sir	Ecclesiasticus
Is	Isaiah
Jer	Jeremiah
Lam	Lamentations
Bar	Baruch
Ez	Ezekiel
Dn	Daniel
Hos	Hosea
Joel	Joel
Am	Amos
Ob	Obadiah
Jon	Jonah
Mi	Micah
Na	Nahum
Hab	Habakkuk
Zeph	Zephaniah
Hag	Haggai
Zech	Zechariah
Mal	Malachi
1 Mcc	1 Maccabees
2 Mcc	2 Maccabees
Mt	Matthew
Mk	Mark
Lk	Luke
John	John
Act	Acts of the Apostles

Rom	Romans
1 Cor	1 Corinthians
2 Cor	2 Corinthians
Gal	Galatians
Eph	Ephesians
Phlp	Philippians
Col	Colossians
1 Th	1 Thessalonians
2 Th	2 Thessalonians
1 Tim	1 Timothy
2 Tim	2 Timothy
Tit	Titus
Phlm	Philemon
Hbr	Hebrews
Ja	James
1 Pt	1 Peter
2 Pt	2 Peter
1 John	1 John
2 John	2 John
3 John	3 John
Jud	Jude
Apc	Apocalypse of St. John the Apostle

LATIN NAMES FOR BOOKS IN THE BIBLE

Gen	Genesis
Ex	Exodi
Lv	Levitici
Nm	Numerorum
Dt	Deuteronomii

Hbr	Ad Hebraeos
Iac	Epistula Iacobi
1 Pt	Epistula Petri 1
2 Pt	Epistula Petri 2
1 Io	Epistula Iohannis 1
2 Io	Epistula Iohannis 2
3 Io	Epistula Iohannis 3
Iud	Epistula Iudae
Apc	Apocalypsis Iohannis

JOSHUA

Caput 1

Et factum est post mortem Mosi, servi Domini, ut loqueretur Dominus ad Iosue, filium Nun, ministrum Mosi, et diceret ei, 2 "Moses, servus meus, mortuus est. Surge, et transi Iordanem istum, tu et omnis populus tecum, in terram quam ego dabo filiis Israhel. 3 Omnem locum quem calcaverit vestigium pedis vestri vobis tradam, sicut locutus sum Mosi. 4 A deserto et Libano usque ad fluvium magnum Eufraten, omnis terra Hettheorum usque ad Mare Magnum contra solis occasum erit terminus vester. 5 Nullus vobis poterit resistere cunctis diebus vitae tuae. Sicut fui cum Mose, ero et tecum: non dimittam nec derelinquam te.

6 "Confortare, et esto robustus, tu enim sorte divides populo huic terram pro qua iuravi patribus suis ut traderem eam illis. 7 Confortare igitur, et esto robustus valde ut custodias et facias omnem legem quam praecepit tibi Moses, servus meus. Ne declines ab ea ad dextram vel ad sinistram, ut intellegas cuncta quae agis. 8 Non recedat volumen legis

Chapter 1

Joshua, encouraged by the Lord, admonisheth the people to prepare themselves to pass over the Jordan.

Now it came to pass after the death of Moses, the servant of the Lord, that the Lord spoke to Joshua, the son of Nun, the minister of Moses, and said to him, 2 "Moses, my servant, is dead. Arise, and pass over this Jordan, thou and *thy* people with thee, into the land which I will give to the children of Israel. 3 I will deliver to you every place that the sole of your foot shall tread upon, as I have said to Moses. 4 From the desert and from Libanus unto the great river Euphrates, all the land of the Hittites unto the Great Sea toward the going down of the sun shall be your border. 5 No man shall be able to resist you all the days of thy life. As I have been with Moses, so will I be with thee: I will not leave thee nor forsake thee.

6 Take courage, and be strong, for thou shalt divide by lot to this people the land for which I swore to their fathers that I would deliver it to them. 7 Take courage therefore, and be very valiant that thou mayst observe and do all the law which Moses, my servant, hath commanded thee. Turn not from it to the right hand or to the left, that thou mayst understand all things which thou dost. 8 Let not the book of

Caput 2

Misit ergo Iosue, filius Nun, de Setthim duos viros ad explorandum in abscondito et dixit eis, "Ite, et considerate terram urbemque Hiericho." Qui pergentes ingressi sunt domum mulieris meretricis nomine Raab et quieverunt apud eam.

2 Nuntiatumque est regi Hiericho et dictum, "Ecce: viri ingressi sunt huc per noctem de filiis Israhel ut explorarent terram." 3 Misitque rex Hiericho ad Raab, dicens, "Educ viros qui venerunt ad te et ingressi sunt domum tuam, exploratores quippe sunt et omnem terram considerare venerunt."

4 Tollensque mulier viros abscondit et ait, "Fateor venerunt ad me, sed nesciebam unde essent, 5 cumque porta clauderetur in tenebris et illi pariter exierunt. Nescio quo abierunt. Persequimini cito, et conprehendetis eos." 6 Ipsa autem fecit ascendere viros in solarium domus suae operuitque eos lini stipula quae ibi erat.

7 Hii autem qui missi fuerant secuti sunt eos per viam quae ducit ad vadum Iordanis. Illisque egressis, statim porta clausa est. 8 Necdum obdormierant qui latebant, et ecce:

Chapter 2

Two spies are sent to Jericho who are received and concealed by Rahab.

And Joshua, the son of Nun, sent from Shittim two men to spy *secretly* and said to them, "Go, and view the land and the city of Jericho." They went and entered into the house of a woman that was a harlot named Rahab and lodged with her.

2 And it was told the king of Jericho and was said, "Behold: there are men come in hither by night of the children of Israel to spy the land." 3 And the king of Jericho sent to Rahab, saying, "Bring forth the men that came to thee and are entered into thy house, for they are spies and are come to view all the land."

4 And the woman taking the men hid them and said, "I confess they came to me, but I knew not whence they were, 5 and *at the time of shutting the gate* in the dark they also went out together. I know not whither they are gone. Pursue *after them* quickly, and you will overtake them." 6 But she made the men go up to the top of her house and covered them with the stalks of flax which was there.

7 Now they that were sent pursued after them by the way that leadeth to the *fords* of the Jordan. And as soon as they were gone out, the gate was presently shut. 8 The men that were hidden were not yet asleep, *when* behold: the woman

mulier ascendit ad eos et ait, 9 "Novi quod tradiderit Dominus vobis terram, etenim inruit in nos terror vester, et elanguerunt omnes habitatores terrae. 10 Audivimus quod siccaverit Dominus aquas Maris Rubri ad vestrum introitum quando egressi estis ex Aegypto et quae feceritis duobus Amorreorum regibus qui erant trans Iordanem, Seon et Og, quos interfecistis. 11 Et haec audientes, pertimuimus, et elanguit cor nostrum, nec remansit in nobis spiritus ad introitum vestrum, Dominus enim, Deus vester, ipse est Deus in caelo sursum et in terra deorsum. 12 Nunc ergo, iurate mihi per Dominum ut quomodo ego feci vobiscum misericordiam, ita et vos faciatis cum domo patris mei detisque mihi signum verum 13 ut salvetis patrem meum et matrem, fratres ac sorores meas et omnia quae eorum sunt et eruatis animas nostras de morte."

14 Qui responderunt ei, "Anima nostra sit pro vobis in mortem si tamen non prodideris nos. Cumque tradiderit nobis Dominus terram, faciemus in te misericordiam et veritatem."

15 Demisit ergo eos per funem de fenestra, domus enim eius herebat muro. 16 Dixitque ad eos, "Ad montana conscendite ne forte occurrant vobis revertentes, ibique latete diebus tribus donec redeant, et sic ibitis per viam vestram."

17 Qui dixerunt ad eam, "Innoxii erimus a iuramento hoc quo adiurasti nos 18 si, ingredientibus nobis terram, signum fuerit funiculus iste coccineus, et ligaveris eum in fenestra per quam nos dimisisti et patrem tuum ac matrem fratresque et omnem cognationem tuam congregaveris in domum tuam. 19 Qui ostium domus tuae egressus fuerit, sanguis ipsius erit in caput eius, et nos erimus alieni. Cunctorum

went up to them and said, 9 "I know that the Lord hath given this land to you, for the dread of you is fallen upon us, and all the inhabitants of the land have lost all strength. 10 We have heard that the Lord dried up the water of the Red Sea at your going in when you came out of Egypt and what things you did to the two kings of the Amorites that were beyond the Jordan, Sihon and Og, whom you slew. 11 And hearing these things, we were affrighted, and our heart fainted away, neither did there remain any spirit in us at your coming in, for the Lord, your God, he is God in heaven above and in the earth beneath. 12 Now therefore, swear ye to me by the Lord that as I have shewn mercy to you, so you also *will shew mercy to* my father's house and give me a true token 13 that you will save my father and mother, my brethren and sisters and all things that are theirs and deliver our souls from death."

14 They answered her, "Be our lives for you unto death only if thou betray us not. And when the Lord shall have delivered us the land, we will *show thee* mercy and truth."

15 Then she let them down with a cord out of a window, for her house joined close to the wall. 16 And she said to them, "Get ye up to the mountains lest perhaps they meet you as they return, and there lie ye hid three days till they come back, and so you shall go on your way."

17 And they said to her, "We shall be blameless of this oath which thou hast made us swear 18 if, when we come into the land, this scarlet cord be a sign, and thou tie it in the window by which thou hast let us down and gather together thy father and mother and brethren and all thy kindred into thy house. 19 Whosoever shall go out of the door of thy house, his blood shall be upon his own head, and we shall be quit.

autem sanguis qui tecum fuerint in domo redundabit in caput nostrum si eos aliquis tetigerit. 20 Quod si nos prodere
volueris et sermonem istum proferre in medium, erimus
mundi ab hoc iuramento quo adiurasti nos."

21 Et illa respondit, "Sicut locuti estis, ita fiat." Dimit-
tensque eos ut pergerent, adpendit funiculum coccineum in
fenestra.

22 Illi vero ambulantes pervenerunt ad montana et manserunt ibi tres dies donec reverterentur qui fuerant persecuti, quaerentes enim per omnem viam, non reppererunt
eos. 23 Quibus urbem ingressis, reversi sunt et descenderunt
exploratores de monte, et Iordane transmisso venerunt ad
Iosue, filium Nun, narraveruntque ei omnia quae acciderant
sibi 24 atque dixerunt, "Tradidit Dominus in manus nostras
omnem terram hanc, et timore prostrati sunt cuncti habitatores eius."

Caput 3

Igitur Iosue de nocte consurgens movit castra, egredien-
tesque de Setthim venerunt ad Iordanem, ipse et omnes filii
Israhel, et morati sunt ibi per tres dies. 2 Quibus evolutis,

But the blood of all that shall be with thee in the house shall light upon our head if any man touch them. 20 But if thou wilt betray us and utter this word abroad, we shall be quit of this oath which thou hast made us swear."

21 And she answered, "As you have spoken, so be it done." And sending them on their way, she hung the scarlet cord in the window.

22 But they went and came to the mountains and stayed there three days till they that pursued them were returned, for *having sought them* through all the way, they found them not. 23 And when they were gone back into the city, the spies returned and came down from the mountain, and passing over the Jordan they came to Joshua, the son of Nun, and told him all that befel them 24 and said, "The Lord hath delivered all this land into our hands, and all the inhabitants thereof are overthrown with fear."

Chapter 3

The river Jordan is miraculously dried up for the passage of the children of Israel.

And Joshua rose before daylight and removed the camp, and they departed from Shittim and came to the Jordan, he and all the children of Israel, and they abode there for three days. 2 After which, the heralds went through the midst of

transierunt praecones per castrorum medium 3 et clamare coeperunt, "Quando videritis Arcam Foederis Domini, Dei vestri, et sacerdotes stirpis Leviticae portantes eam, vos quoque consurgite, et sequimini praecedentes, 4 sitque inter vos et arcam spatium cubitorum duum milium ut procul videre possitis et nosse per quam viam ingrediamini, quia prius non ambulastis per eam, et cavete ne adpropinquetis ad arcam."

5 Dixitque Iosue ad populum, "Sanctificamini, cras enim faciet Dominus inter vos mirabilia." 6 Et ait ad sacerdotes, "Tollite Arcam Foederis, et praecedite populum." Qui iussa conplentes tulerunt et ambulaverunt ante eos.

7 Dixitque Dominus ad Iosue, "Hodie incipiam exaltare te coram omni Israhel ut sciant quod sicut cum Mosi fui, ita et tecum sim. 8 Tu autem praecipe sacerdotibus qui portant Arcam Foederis, et dic eis, 'Cum ingressi fueritis partem aquae Iordanis, state in ea.'"

9 Dixitque Iosue ad filios Israhel, "Accedite huc, et audite verbum Domini, Dei vestri." 10 Et rursum, "In hoc," inquit, "scietis quod Dominus, Deus vivens, in medio vestri est et disperdet in conspectu vestro Chananeum et Hettheum, Eveum et Ferezeum, Gergeseum quoque et Iebuseum et Amorreum. 11 Ecce! Arca Foederis Domini omnis terrae antecedet vos per Iordanem. 12 Parate duodecim viros de tribubus Israhel, singulos per singulas tribus. 13 Et cum posuerint vestigia pedum suorum sacerdotes qui portant arcam Domini, Dei universae terrae, in aquis Iordanis, aquae quae

the camp 3 and began to proclaim, "When you shall see the Ark of the Covenant of the Lord, your God, and the priests of the race of Levi carrying it, rise you up also, and follow them as they go before, 4 and let there be between you and the ark the space of two thousand cubits that you may see it afar off and know which way you must go, for you have not *gone this way* before, and take care you come not near the ark."

5 And Joshua said to the people, "Be ye sanctified, for tomorrow the Lord will do wonders among you." 6 And he said to the priests, "Take up the Ark of the Covenant, and go before the people." And they obeyed his commands and took it up and walked before them.

7 And the Lord said to Joshua, "This day will I begin to exalt thee before Israel that they may know that as I was with Moses, so I am with thee also. 8 And do thou command the priests that carry the Ark of the Covenant, and say to them, 'When you shall have entered into part of the water of the Jordan, stand in it.'"

9 And Joshua said to the children of Israel, "Come hither, and hear the word of the Lord, your God." 10 And again he said, "By this you shall know that the Lord, the living God, is in the midst of you and that he shall destroy before your sight the Canaanite and the Hittite, the Hivite and the Perizzite, the Girgashite also and the Jebusite and the Amorite. 11 Behold! The Ark of the Covenant of the Lord of all the earth shall go before you into the Jordan. 12 Prepare ye twelve men of the tribes of Israel, one of every tribe. 13 And when the priests that carry the ark of the Lord, the God of the whole earth, shall set the soles of their feet in the waters of the Jordan, the waters that are beneath shall run down

inferiores sunt decurrent atque deficient, quae autem desuper veniunt in una mole consistent."

14 Igitur egressus est populus de tabernaculis suis ut transirent Iordanem, et sacerdotes qui portabant Arcam Foederis pergebant ante eum. 15 Ingressisque eis Iordanem et pedibus eorum tinctis in parte aquae (Iordanis autem ripas alvei sui, tempore messis, impleverat), 16 steterunt aquae descendentes in uno loco, et instar montis intumescentes apparebant procul ab urbe quae vocatur Adom, usque ad locum Sarthan, quae autem inferiores erant in Mare Solitudinis (quod nunc vocatur Mortuum) descenderunt, usquequo omnino deficerent. 17 Populus autem incedebat contra Hiericho, et sacerdotes qui portabant Arcam Foederis Domini stabant super siccam humum in medio Iordanis accincti, omnisque populus per arentem alveum transiebat.

Caput 4

Quibus transgressis, dixit Dominus ad Iosue, 2 "Elige duodecim viros, singulos per singulas tribus, 3 et praecipe eis ut tollant de medio Iordanis alveo ubi steterunt sacerdotum

and go off, and those that come from above shall stand together upon a heap."

14 So the people went out of their tents to pass over the Jordan, and the priests that carried the Ark of the Covenant went on before them. 15 And as soon as they came into the Jordan and their feet were dipped in part of the water (now the Jordan, it being harvest time, had filled the banks of its channel), 16 the waters that came down from above stood in one place, and swelling up like a mountain *were seen* afar off from the city that is called Adam, to the place of Zarethan, but those that were beneath ran down into the Sea of the Wilderness (which now is called the Dead Sea), until they wholly failed. 17 And the people marched over against Jericho, and the priests that carried the Ark of the Covenant of the Lord stood girded upon the dry ground in the midst of the Jordan, and all the people passed over through the channel that was dried up.

Chapter 4

Twelve stones are taken out of the river to be set up for a monument of the miracle, and other twelve are placed in the midst of the river.

And when they were passed over, the Lord said to Joshua, 2 "Choose twelve men, one of every tribe, 3 and command them to take out of the *midst* of the Jordan where the feet

pedes duodecim durissimos lapides quos ponetis in loco castrorum ubi fixeritis hac nocte tentoria."

4 Vocavitque Iosue duodecim viros quos elegerat de filiis Israhel, singulos de tribubus singulis, 5 et ait ad eos, "Ite ante arcam Domini, Dei vestri, ad Iordanis medium, et portate inde singuli singulos lapides in umeris vestris iuxta numerum filiorum Israhel 6 ut sit signum inter vos, et quando interrogaverint vos filii vestri cras, dicentes, 'Quid sibi volunt isti lapides?' 7 respondebitis eis, 'Defecerunt aquae Iordanis ante Arcam Foederis Domini cum transiret eum, idcirco positi sunt lapides isti in monumentum filiorum Israhel usque in aeternum.'"

8 Fecerunt ergo filii Israhel sicut eis praecepit Iosue, portantes de medio Iordanis alveo duodecim lapides ut ei Dominus imperarat, iuxta numerum filiorum Israhel, usque ad locum in quo castrametati sunt, ibique posuerunt eos. 9 Alios quoque duodecim lapides posuit Iosue in medio Iordanis alveo ubi steterunt sacerdotes qui portabant Arcam Foederis, et sunt ibi usque in praesentem diem.

10 Sacerdotes autem qui portabant arcam stabant in Iordanis medio donec omnia conplerentur quae Iosue ut loqueretur ad populum praeceperat Dominus et dixerat ei Moses. Festinavitque populus et transiit. 11 Cumque transissent omnes, transivit et arca Domini, sacerdotesque pergebant

of the priests stood twelve very hard stones which you shall set in the place of the camp where you shall pitch your tents this night."

4 And Joshua called twelve men whom he had chosen out of the children of Israel, one out of every tribe, 5 and he said to them, "Go before the ark of the Lord, your God, to the midst of the Jordan, and carry from thence every man a stone on your shoulders according to the number of the children of Israel 6 that it may be a sign among you, and when your children shall ask you tomorrow, saying, 'What mean these stones?' 7 you shall answer them, 'The waters of the Jordan ran off before the Ark of the Covenant of the Lord when it passed over the same, therefore were these stones set for a monument of the children of Israel for ever.'"

8 The children of Israel therefore did as Joshua commanded them, carrying out of the *channel* of the Jordan twelve stones as the Lord had commanded him, according to the number of the children of Israel, unto the place wherein they camped, and there they set them. 9 And Joshua put other twelve stones in the midst of the channel of the Jordan where the priests stood that carried the Ark of the Covenant, and they are there until this present day.

10 Now the priests that carried the ark stood in the midst of the Jordan till all things were accomplished which the Lord had commanded Joshua to speak to the people and Moses had said to him. And the people made haste and passed over. 11 And when they had all passed over, the ark also of the Lord passed over, and the priests went before

ante populum. 12 Filii quoque Ruben et Gad et dimidiae tribus Manasse armati praecedebant filios Israhel sicut eis praeceperat Moses. 13 Et quadraginta pugnatorum milia per turmas et cuneos incedebant per plana atque campestria urbis Hiericho.

14 In illo die magnificavit Dominus Iosue coram omni Israhel ut timerent eum sicut timuerant Mosen dum adviveret. 15 Dixitque ad eum, 16 "Praecipe sacerdotibus qui portant Arcam Foederis ut ascendant de Iordane."

17 Qui praecepit eis, dicens, "Ascendite de Iordane." 18 Cumque ascendissent portantes Arcam Foederis Domini et siccam humum calcare coepissent, reversae sunt aquae in alveum suum et fluebant sicut ante consueverant. 19 Populus autem ascendit de Iordane decimo mensis primi die et castrametati sunt in Galgalis contra orientalem plagam urbis Hiericho. 20 Duodecim quoque lapides quos de Iordanis alveo sumpserant, posuit Iosue in Galgalis 21 et dixit ad filios Israhel, "Quando interrogaverint filii vestri cras patres suos et dixerint eis, 'Quid sibi volunt isti lapides?' 22 docebitis eos atque dicetis, 'Per arentem alveum transivit Israhel Iordanem istum, 23 siccante Domino, Deo vestro, aquas eius in conspectu vestro donec transiretis 24 sicut fecerat prius in Mari Rubro, quod siccavit donec transiremus, 25 ut discant omnes terrarum populi fortissimam Domini manum, ut et vos timeatis Dominum, Deum vestrum, omni tempore.'"

the people. 12 The children of Reuben also and Gad and *half the tribe* of Manasseh went armed before the children of Israel as Moses had commanded them. 13 And forty thousand fighting men by their troops and bands marched through the plains and fields of the city of Jericho.

14 In that day the Lord magnified Joshua in the sight of all Israel that they should fear him as they had feared Moses while he lived. 15 And he said to him, 16 "Command the priests that carry the Ark of the Covenant to come up out of the Jordan."

17 And he commanded them, saying, "Come ye up out of the Jordan." 18 And when they that carried the Ark of the Covenant of the Lord were come up and began to tread on the dry ground, the waters returned into their channel and ran as they were wont before. 19 And the people came up out of the Jordan the tenth day of the first month and camped in Gilgal over against the east side of the city of Jericho. 20 And the twelve stones which they had taken out of the channel of the Jordan, Joshua pitched in Gilgal 21 and said to the children of Israel, "When your children shall ask their fathers tomorrow and shall say to them, 'What mean these stones?' 22 you shall teach them and say, 'Israel passed over this Jordan through the dry channel, 23 the Lord, your God, drying up the waters thereof in your sight until you passed over 24 as he had done before in the Red Sea, which he dried up till we passed through, 25 that all the people of the earth may learn the most mighty hand of the Lord, that you also may fear the Lord, your God, for ever.'"

Caput 5

Postquam ergo audierunt omnes reges Amorreorum, qui habitabant trans Iordanem ad occidentalem plagam, et cuncti reges Chanaan, qui propinqua possidebant Magno Mari loca, quod siccasset Dominus fluenta Iordanis coram filiis Israhel donec transirent, dissolutum est cor eorum, et non remansit in eis spiritus, timentium introitum filiorum Israhel. 2 Eo tempore ait Dominus ad Iosue, "Fac tibi cultros lapideos, et circumcide secundo filios Israhel." 3 Fecit quod iusserat Dominus, et circumcidit filios Israhel in Colle Praeputiorum.

4 Haec autem causa est secundae circumcisionis: omnis populus qui egressus est ex Aegypto generis masculini, universi bellatores viri, mortui sunt in deserto per longissimos viae circuitus. 5 Qui omnes circumcisi erant, populus autem qui natus est in deserto 6 per quadraginta annos itineris latissimae solitudinis incircumcisus fuit donec consumerentur qui non audierant vocem Domini et quibus ante iuraverat ut non ostenderet eis terram lacte et melle manantem.

Chapter 5

The people are circumcised. They keep the pasch. The manna ceaseth. An angel appeareth to Joshua.

*N*ow *when* all the kings of the Amorites, who dwelt beyond the Jordan westward, and all the kings of Canaan, who possessed the places near the Great Sea, had heard that the Lord had dried up the waters of the Jordan before the children of Israel till they passed over, their heart failed *them,* and there remained no spirit in them, fearing the coming in of the children of Israel. 2 At that time the Lord said to Joshua, "Make thee knives of stone, and circumcise the second time the children of Israel." 3 He did what the Lord had commanded, and he circumcised the children of Israel in the Hill of the Foreskins.

4 Now this is the cause of the second circumcision: all the people that came out of Egypt *that were males,* all the men fit for war, died in the desert *during the time of the long going about in the way.* 5 Now these were all circumcised, but the people that were born in the desert 6 during the forty years of the journey in the wide wilderness were uncircumcised till *all* they were consumed that had not heard the voice of the Lord and to whom he had sworn before that he would not

7 Horum filii in locum successerunt patrum et circumcisi sunt ab Iosue, quia sicut nati fuerant in praeputio erant, nec eos in via aliquis circumciderat. 8 Postquam autem omnes circumcisi sunt, manserunt in eodem castrorum loco donec sanarentur. 9 Dixitque Dominus ad Iosue, "Hodie abstuli obprobrium Aegypti a vobis." Vocatumque est nomen loci illius Galgala usque in praesentem diem.

10 Manseruntque filii Israhel in Galgalis, et fecerunt Phase quartadecima die mensis ad vesperum in campestribus Hiericho, 11 et comederunt de frugibus terrae die altero azymos panes et pulentam eiusdem anni. 12 Defecitque manna postquam comederunt de frugibus terrae, nec usi sunt ultra illo cibo filii Israhel, sed comederunt de frugibus praesentis anni terrae Chanaan.

13 Cum autem esset Iosue in agro urbis Hiericho, levavit oculos et vidit virum stantem contra se evaginatum tenentem gladium, perrexitque ad eum et ait, "Noster es an adversariorum?"

14 Qui respondit, "Nequaquam, sed sum princeps exercitus Domini, et nunc venio."

15 Cecidit Iosue pronus in terram et, adorans, ait, "Quid Dominus meus loquitur ad servum suum?"

16 "Solve," inquit, "calciamentum tuum de pedibus tuis, locus enim in quo stas sanctus est." Fecitque Iosue ut sibi fuerat imperatum.

show them the land flowing with milk and honey. 7 The children of these succeeded in the place of their fathers and were circumcised by Joshua, for they were *uncircumcised* even as they were born, and no one had circumcised them in the way. 8 Now after they were all circumcised, they remained in the same place of the camp until they were healed. 9 And the Lord said to Joshua, "This day have I taken away from you the reproach of Egypt." And the name of that place was called Gilgal until *this* present day.

10 And the children of Israel abode in Gilgal, and they kept the Phase on the fourteenth day of the month at evening in the plains of Jericho, 11 and they ate on the next day unleavened bread of the corn of the land and frumenty of the same year. 12 And the manna ceased after they ate of the corn of the land, neither did the children of Israel use that food any more, but they ate of the corn of the present year of the land of Canaan.

13 And when Joshua was in the field of the city of Jericho, he lifted up his eyes and saw a man standing over against him holding a drawn sword, and he went to him and said, "Art thou one of ours or of our adversaries?"

14 And he answered, "No, but I am prince of the host of the Lord, and now I am come."

15 Joshua fell on his face to the ground and, worshipping, said, "What saith my Lord to his servant?"

16 "Loose," saith he, "thy *shoes from off* thy feet, for the place whereon thou standest is holy." And Joshua did as was commanded him.

Caput 6

Hiericho autem clausa erat atque munita timore filiorum Israhel, et nullus egredi audebat aut ingredi. 2 Dixitque Dominus ad Iosue, "Ecce! Dedi in manus tuas Hiericho et regem eius omnesque fortes viros. 3 Circuite urbem, cuncti bellatores, semel per diem; sic facietis sex diebus. 4 Septimo autem die sacerdotes tollant septem bucinas quarum usus est in iobeleo et praecedant Arcam Foederis, septiesque circuibitis civitatem, et sacerdotes clangent bucinis. 5 Cumque insonuerit vox tubae longior atque concisior et in auribus vestris increpuerit, conclamabit omnis populus vociferatione maxima, et muri funditus corruent civitatis, ingredienturque, singuli per locum contra quem steterint."

6 Vocavit ergo Iosue, filius Nun, sacerdotes et dixit ad eos, "Tollite Arcam Foederis, et septem alii sacerdotes tollant septem iobeleorum bucinas et incedant ante arcam Domini." 7 Ad populum quoque ait, "Vadite, et circuite civitatem armati, praecedentes arcam Domini." 8 Cumque Iosue verba finisset et septem sacerdotes septem bucinis clange-

Chapter 6

After seven days' processions, the priests sounding the trumpets, the walls of Jericho fall down, and the city is taken and destroyed.

Now Jericho was *close shut up* and fenced for fear of the children of Israel, and no man durst go out or come in. 2 And the Lord said to Joshua, "Behold! I have given into thy hands Jericho and the king thereof and all the valiant men. 3 Go round about the city, all ye fighting men, once a day; so shall ye do for six days. 4 And on the seventh day the priests shall take the seven trumpets which are used in the jubilee and shall go before the Ark of the Covenant, and you shall go about the city seven times, and the priests shall sound the trumpets. 5 And when the voice of the trumpet shall *give a longer and broken tune* and shall sound in your ears, all the people shall shout together with a very great shout, and the walls of the city shall fall to the ground, and they shall enter in, every one at the place against which they shall stand."

6 Then Joshua, the son of Nun, called the priests and said to them, "Take the Ark of the Covenant, and let seven other priests take the seven trumpets of the *jubilee* and march before the ark of the Lord." 7 And he said to the people, "Go, and compass the city armed, marching before the ark of the Lord." 8 And when Joshua had ended his words and the seven priests blew the seven trumpets before the

rent ante Arcam Foederis Domini 9 omnisque praecederet armatus exercitus, reliquum vulgus arcam sequebatur, ac bucinis omnia concrepabant. 10 Praeceperat autem Iosue populo, dicens, "Non clamabitis, nec audietur vox vestra, neque ullus sermo ex ore vestro egredietur donec veniat dies in quo dicam vobis, 'Clamate, et vociferamini!'"

11 Circuivit ergo arca Domini civitatem semel per diem et, reversa in castra, mansit ibi. 12 Igitur, Iosue de nocte consurgente, tulerunt sacerdotes arcam Domini 13 et septem ex eis septem bucinas quarum in iobeleo usus est, praecedebantque arcam Domini ambulantes atque clangentes, et armatus populus ibat ante eos, vulgus autem reliquum sequebatur arcam, et bucinis personabat. 14 Circumieruntque civitatem secundo die semel et reversi sunt in castra; sic fecerunt sex diebus. 15 Die autem septimo, diluculo consurgentes, circumierunt urbem sicut dispositum erat septies. 16 Cumque septimo circuitu clangerent bucinis sacerdotes, dixit Iosue ad omnem Israhel, "Vociferamini, tradidit enim vobis Dominus civitatem! 17 Sitque civitas haec anathema et omnia quae in ea sunt Domino. Sola Raab, meretrix, vivat cum universis qui cum ea in domo sunt, abscondit enim nuntios quos direximus. 18 Vos autem cavete ne de his quae praecepta sunt quippiam contingatis et sitis praevaricationis rei et omnia castra Israhel sub peccato sint atque turbentur. 19 Quicquid autem auri aut argenti fuerit et vasorum aeneorum ac ferri, Domino consecretur, repositum in thesauris eius."

Ark of the Covenant of the Lord 9 and all the armed *men* went before, the rest of the common people followed the ark, and the *sound of the trumpets was heard on all sides.* 10 But Joshua had commanded the people, saying, "You shall not shout, nor shall your voice be heard, nor any word go out of your mouth until the day come wherein I shall say to you, 'Cry, and shout!'"

11 So the ark of the Lord went about the city once a day and, returning into the camp, abode there. 12 And, Joshua rising before day, the priests took the ark of the Lord 13 and seven of them seven trumpets which are used in the jubilee, and they went before the ark of the Lord walking and sounding *the trumpets,* and the armed men went before them, and the rest of the common people followed the ark, and they blew the trumpets. 14 And they went round about the city the second day once and returned into the camp; so they did six days. 15 But the seventh day, rising up early, they went about the city as it was ordered seven times. 16 And when in the seventh going about the priests sounded with the trumpets, Joshua said to all Israel, "Shout, for the Lord hath delivered the city to you! 17 And let this city be an anathema and all things that are in it to the Lord. Let only Rahab, the harlot, live with all that are with her in the house, for she hid the messengers whom we sent. 18 But beware ye lest you touch ought of those things that are forbidden and you be guilty of transgression and all the camp of Israel be under sin and be troubled. 19 But whatsoever gold or silver there shall be *or* vessels of brass and iron, let it be consecrated to the Lord, laid up in his treasures."

20 Igitur omni vociferante populo et clangentibus tubis, postquam in aures multitudinis vox sonitusque increpuit, muri ilico corruerunt, et ascendit unusquisque per locum qui contra se erat, ceperuntque civitatem 21 et interfecerunt omnia quae erant in ea, a viro usque ad mulierem, ab infante usque ad senem. Boves quoque et oves et asinos in ore gladii percusserunt.

22 Duobus autem viris qui exploratores missi fuerant dixit Iosue, "Ingredimini domum mulieris meretricis, et producite eam omniaque quae illius sunt, sicut illi iuramento firmastis." 23 Ingressique iuvenes eduxerunt Raab et parentes eius, fratres quoque et cunctam supellectilem ac cognationem illius et extra castra Israhel manere fecerunt. 24 Urbem autem et omnia quae in ea inventa sunt succenderunt, absque auro et argento et vasis aeneis ac ferro, quae in aerarium Domini consecrarunt. 25 Raab vero, meretricem, et domum patris eius atque omnia quae habebat fecit Iosue vivere, et habitaverunt in medio Israhel usque in praesentem diem eo quod absconderit nuntios quos miserat ut explorarent Hiericho.

In tempore illo, inprecatus est Iosue, dicens, 26 "Maledictus vir coram Domino qui suscitaverit et aedificaverit civitatem Hiericho. In primogenito suo fundamenta illius iaciat et in novissimo liberorum ponat portas eius." 27 Fuit ergo Dominus cum Iosue, et nomen eius in omni terra vulgatum est.

20 So all the people making a shout and the trumpets sounding, *when* the voice and the sound thundered in the ears of the multitude, the walls forthwith fell down, and every man went up by the place that was over against him, and they took the city 21 and killed all that were in it, *man and woman, young and old.* The oxen also and the sheep and the asses they slew with the edge of the sword.

22 But Joshua said to the two men that had been sent for spies, "Go into the *harlot's* house, and bring her out and all things that are hers, as you assured her by oath." 23 And the young men went in and brought out Rahab and her parents, her brethren also and all her goods and her kindred and made them to stay without the *camp.* 24 But they burned the city and all things that *were* therein, except the gold and silver and vessels of brass and iron, which they consecrated into the treasury of the Lord. 25 But Joshua *saved* Rahab, the harlot, and her father's house and all she had, and they dwelt in the midst of Israel until this present day because she hid the messengers whom he had sent to spy out Jericho.

At that time, Joshua made an imprecation, saying, 26 "Cursed be the man before the Lord that shall raise up and build the city of Jericho. In his firstborn may he lay the foundation thereof and in the last of his children set up its gates." 27 And the Lord was with Joshua, and his name was noised throughout all the land.

Caput 7

Filii autem Israhel praevaricati sunt mandatum et usurpa-
verunt de anathemate, nam Achan, filius Charmi, filii Zabdi,
filii Zare, de tribu Iuda, tulit aliquid de anathemate, iratusque est Dominus contra filios Israhel. 2 Cumque mitteret
Iosue de Hiericho viros contra Ahi, quae est iuxta Bethaven
ad orientalem plagam oppidi Bethel, dixit eis, "Ascendite, et
explorate terram." Qui praecepta conplentes exploraverunt
Ahi.

3 Et reversi dixerunt ei, "Non ascendat omnis populus,
sed duo vel tria milia virorum pergant et deleant civitatem.
Quare omnis populus frustra vexabitur contra hostes aucis-
simos?" 4 Ascenderunt ergo tria milia pugnatores, qui statim
terga vertentes 5 percussi sunt a viris urbis Ahi, et corruerunt ex eis triginta et sex homines. Persecutique sunt eos
adversarii de porta usque Sabarim, et ceciderunt per prona
fugientes, pertimuitque cor populi et instar aquae liquefac-
tum est.

Chapter 7

For the sins of Achan, the Israelites are defeated at Ai. The offender is found out and stoned to death, and God's wrath is turned from them.

But the children of Israel transgressed the commandment and took to their own use of the anathema, for Achan, the son of Carmi, the son of Zabdi, the son of Zerah, of the tribe of Judah, took something of the anathema, and the Lord was angry against the children of Israel. 2 And when Joshua sent men from Jericho against Ai, which is beside Beth-aven on the east side of the town of Bethel, he said to them, "Go up, and view the country." And they fulfilled his *command* and viewed Ai.

3 And returning they said to him, "Let not all the people go up, but let two or three thousand men go and destroy the city. Why *should* all the people be troubled in vain against enemies that are very few?" 4 There went up therefore three thousand fighting men, who immediately turned their backs 5 and were defeated by the men of the city of Ai, and there fell of them six and thirty men. And the enemies pursued them from the gate as far as Shebarim, and they slew them as they fled by the descent, and the heart of the people was *struck with fear* and melted like water.

6 Iosue vero scidit vestimenta sua et cecidit pronus in terram coram arca Domini usque ad vesperum, tam ipse quam omnes senes Israhel, miseruntque pulverem super capita sua. 7 Et dixit Iosue, "Heu, Domine Deus, quid voluisti transducere populum istum Iordanem fluvium ut traderes nos in manus Amorrei et perderes? Utinam ut coepimus mansissemus trans Iordanem! 8 Mi Domine Deus, quid dicam, videns Israhelem hostibus suis terga vertentem? 9 Audient Chananei et omnes habitatores terrae, ac pariter conglobati circumdabunt nos atque delebunt nomen nostrum de terra, et quid facies magno nomini tuo?"

10 Dixitque Dominus ad Iosue, "Surge; cur iaces pronus in terra? 11 Peccavit Israhel et praevaricatus est pactum meum, tuleruntque de anathemate et furati sunt atque mentiti et absconderunt inter vasa sua. 12 Nec poterit Israhel stare ante hostes suos, eosque fugiet quia pollutus est anathemate. Non ero ultra vobiscum donec conteratis eum qui huius sceleris reus est. 13 Surge; sanctifica populum, et dic eis, 'Sanctificamini in crastinum, haec enim dicit Dominus, Deus Israhel, "Anathema in medio tui est, Israhel. Non poteris stare coram hostibus tuis donec deleatur ex te qui hoc contaminatus est scelere."' 14 Accedetisque mane, singuli per tribus vestras, et quamcumque tribum sors invenerit, accedet per cognationes suas et cognatio per domos domusque per viros. 15 Et quicumque ille in hoc facinore fuerit deprehensus, conburetur igni cum omni substantia sua quoniam praevaricatus est pactum Domini et fecit nefas in Israhel."

6 But Joshua rent his garments and fell flat on the ground before the ark of the Lord until the evening, both he and all the ancients of Israel, and they put dust upon their heads. 7 And Joshua said, "Alas, O Lord God, why wouldst thou bring this people over the river Jordan to deliver us into the hand of the Amorite and to destroy us? Would God we had stayed beyond the Jordan as we began! 8 My Lord God, what shall I say, seeing Israel turning their backs to their enemies? 9 The Canaanites and all the inhabitants of the land will hear of it, and being gathered together will surround us and cut off our name from the earth, and what wilt thou do to thy great name?"

10 And the Lord said to Joshua, "Arise; why liest thou flat on the ground? 11 Israel hath sinned and transgressed my covenant, and they have taken of the anathema and have stolen and lied and have hidden it among their goods. 12 Neither can Israel stand before his enemies, *but* he shall flee from them because he is defiled with the anathema. I will be no more with you till you destroy him that is guilty of this wickedness. 13 Arise; sanctify the people, and say to them, 'Be ye sanctified against tomorrow, for thus saith the Lord, God of Israel, "The anathema is in the midst of thee, O Israel. Thou canst not stand before thy enemies till he be destroyed out of thee that is defiled with this wickedness."' 14 And you shall come in the morning, every one by your tribes, and what tribe soever the lot shall find, it shall come by its kindreds and the kindred by its houses and the house by the men. 15 And whosoever he be that shall be found guilty of this fact, he shall be burnt with fire with all his substance because he hath transgressed the covenant of the Lord and hath done wickedness in Israel."

16 Surgens, itaque, Iosue mane, adplicavit Israhel per tribus suas. Et inventa est tribus Iuda, 17 quae cum iuxta familias suas esset oblata, inventa est familia Zarai. Illam quoque per domos offerens, repperit Zabdi. 18 Cuius domum in singulos dividens viros, invenit Achan, filium Charmi, filii Zabdi, filii Zare, de tribu Iuda. 19 Et ait Iosue ad Achan, "Fili mi, da gloriam Domino, Deo Israhel, et confitere, atque indica mihi quid feceris. Ne abscondas."

20 Responditque Achan Iosue et dixit ei, "Vere ego peccavi Domino, Deo Israhel, et sic et sic feci. 21 Vidi enim inter spolia pallium coccineum valde bonum et ducentos siclos argenti regulamque auream quinquaginta siclorum, et concupiscens abstuli et abscondi in terra contra medium tabernaculi mei, argentumque fossa humo operui."

22 Misit ergo Iosue ministros qui, currentes ad tabernaculum illius, reppererunt cuncta abscondita in eodem loco, et argentum simul. 23 Auferentesque de tentorio, tulerunt ea ad Iosue et ad omnes filios Israhel proieceruntque ante Dominum. 24 Tollens itaque Iosue Achan, filium Zare, argentumque et pallium et auream regulam, filios quoque et filias eius, boves et asinos et oves, ipsumque tabernaculum et cunctam supellectilem, et omnis Israhel cum eo duxerunt eos ad Vallem Achor, 25 ubi dixit Iosue, "Quia turbasti nos, exturbet te Dominus in die hac." Lapidavitque eum omnis Israhel. Et cuncta quae illius erant igne consumpta sunt. 26 Congregaveruntque super eum acervum magnum lapidum qui permanet usque in praesentem diem. Et aversus

16 Joshua, therefore, when he rose in the morning, made Israel to come by their tribes. And the tribe of Judah was found, 17 which being brought by its families, it was found to be the family of Zerah. Bringing that also by the houses, he found it to be Zabdi. 18 And *bringing* his house man by man, he found Achan, the son of Carmi, the son of Zabdi, the son of Zerah, of the tribe of Judah. 19 And Joshua said to Achan, "My son, give glory to the Lord, God of Israel, and confess, and tell me what thou hast done. Hide it not."

20 And Achan answered Joshua and said to him, "Indeed I have sinned against the Lord, the God of Israel, and thus and thus have I done. 21 For I saw among the spoils a scarlet garment exceeding good and two hundred sicles of silver and a golden rule of fifty sicles, and I coveted them and I took them away and hid them in the ground *in* the midst of my tent, and the silver I covered with the earth that *I dug* up."

22 Joshua therefore sent ministers who, running to his tent, found all hidden in the same place, together with the silver. 23 And taking them away out of the tent, they brought them to Joshua and to all the children of Israel and threw them down before the Lord. 24 Then Joshua *and all Israel with him took* Achan, the son of Zerah, and the silver and the garment and the golden rule, his sons also and his daughters, his oxen and asses and sheep, *the tent also* and all the goods, and brought them to the Valley of Achor, 25 where Joshua said, "Because thou hast troubled us, the Lord trouble thee this day." And all Israel stoned him. And all things that were his were consumed with fire. 26 And they gathered together upon him a great heap of stones which remaineth

est furor Domini ab eis, vocatumque est nomen loci illius Vallis Achor usque hodie.

Caput 8

Dixit autem Dominus ad Iosue, "Ne timeas, neque formides. Tolle tecum omnem multitudinem pugnatorum, et consurgens ascende in oppidum Ahi. Ecce: tradidi in manu tua regem eius et populum urbemque et terram. 2 Faciesque urbi Ahi et regi eius sicut fecisti Hiericho et regi illius, praedam vero et omnia animantia diripietis vobis. Pone insidias urbi post eam."

3 Surrexitque Iosue et omnis exercitus bellatorum cum eo ut ascenderent in Ahi, et electa triginta milia virorum fortium misit nocte 4 praecepitque eis, dicens, "Ponite insidias post civitatem, nec longius recedatis, et eritis omnes parati. 5 Ego autem et reliqua multitudo quae mecum est accedemus ex adverso contra urbem. Cumque exierint contra nos, sicut ante fecimus fugiemus et terga vertemus 6 donec, per-

until this present day. And the wrath of the Lord was turned away from them, and the name of that place was called the Valley of Achor until this day.

Chapter 8

Ai is taken and burnt, and all the inhabitants slain. An altar
is built, and sacrifices offered. The law is written on stones,
and the blessings and cursings are read before all the people.

And the Lord said to Joshua, "Fear not, nor be thou dismayed. Take with thee all the multitude of fighting men, arise, and go up to the town of Ai. Behold: I have delivered into thy hand the king thereof and the people and the city and the land. 2 And thou shalt do to the city of Ai and to the king thereof as thou hast done to Jericho and to the king thereof, but the spoils and all the cattle you shall take for a prey to yourselves. Lay an ambush for the city behind it."

3 And Joshua arose and all the army of the fighting men with him to go up against Ai, and he sent thirty thousand chosen valiant men in the night 4 and commanded them, saying, "Lay an ambush behind the city, and go not very far from it, and *be ye* all ready. 5 But I and the rest of the multitude which is with me will approach on the contrary side against the city. And when they shall come out against us, we will flee and turn our backs as we did before 6 till they,

sequentes, ab urbe longius protrahantur, putabunt enim fugere nos sicut prius. 7 Nobis ergo fugientibus et illis persequentibus, consurgetis de insidiis et vastabitis civitatem, tradetque eam Dominus, Deus vester, in manus vestras. 8 Cumque ceperitis, succendite eam, et sic omnia facietis ut iussi."

9 Dimisitque eos, et perrexerunt ad insidiarum locum sederuntque inter Bethel et Ahi, ad occidentalem plagam urbis Ahi. Iosue autem nocte illa in medio mansit populi, 10 surgensque diluculo recensuit socios et ascendit cum senioribus in fronte exercitus vallatus auxilio pugnatorum. 11 Cumque venissent et ascendissent ex adverso civitatis, steterunt ad septentrionalem urbis plagam inter quam et eos vallis media erat. 12 Quinque milia autem viros elegerat et posuerat in insidiis inter Bethel et Ahi, ex occidentali parte eiusdem civitatis, 13 omnis vero reliquus exercitus ad aquilonem aciem dirigebat, ita ut novissimi multitudinis occidentalem plagam urbis adtingerent. Abiit ergo Iosue nocte illa et stetit in vallis medio.

14 Quod cum vidisset rex Ahi, festinavit mane et egressus est cum omni exercitu civitatis direxitque aciem contra desertum, ignorans quod post tergum laterent insidiae. 15 Iosue vero et omnis Israhel cesserunt loco, simulantes metum et fugientes per viam solitudinis. 16 At illi, vociferantes pariter et se mutuo cohortantes, persecuti sunt eos. Cumque recessissent a civitate 17 et ne unus in urbe Ahi et Bethel remansisset qui non persequeretur Israhel, sicut eruperant aperta oppida relinquentes, 18 dixit Dominus ad Iosue, "Leva

pursuing us, be drawn farther from the city, for they will think that we flee as before. 7 And whilst we are fleeing and they pursuing, you shall arise out of the ambush and shall destroy the city, and the Lord, your God, will deliver it into your hands. 8 And when you shall have taken it, set it on fire, and you shall do all things so as I have commanded."

9 And he sent them away, and they went on to the place of the ambush and abode between Bethel and Ai, on the west side of the city of Ai. But Joshua stayed that night in the midst of the people, 10 and rising early in the morning he mustered his soldiers and went up with the ancients in the front of the army environed with the aid of the fighting men. 11 And when they were come and were gone up over against the city, they stood on the north side of the city between which and them there was a valley in the midst. 12 And he had chosen five thousand men and set them *to lie* in ambush between Bethel and Ai, on the west side of the same city, 13 but all the rest of the army went in battle array on the north side, so that the last of *that* multitude reached to the west side of the city. So Joshua went that night and stood in the midst of the valley.

14 And when the king of Ai saw this, he made haste in the morning and went out with all the army of the city and set it in battle array toward the desert, not knowing that there lay an ambush behind his back. 15 But Joshua and all Israel gave back, *making as if they were afraid* and fleeing by the way of the wilderness. 16 But they, shouting together and encouraging one another, pursued them. And when they were come from the city 17 and not one remained in the city of Ai and of Bethel that did not pursue after Israel, leaving the towns open as they had rushed out, 18 the Lord said to Joshua, "Lift

clypeum qui in manu tua est contra urbem Ahi, quoniam tibi tradam eam." 19 Cumque elevasset clypeum ex adverso civitatis, insidiae quae latebant surrexerunt confestim et pergentes ad civitatem ceperunt et succenderunt eam. 20 Viri autem civitatis qui persequebantur Iosue, respicientes et videntes fumum urbis ad caelum usque conscendere, non potuerunt ultra huc illucque diffugere, praesertim cum hii qui simulaverant fugam et tendebant ad solitudinem contra persequentes fortissime restitissent.

21 Vidensque Iosue et omnis Israhel quod capta esset civitas et fumus urbis ascenderet, reversus percussit viros Ahi. 22 Siquidem et illi qui ceperant et succenderant civitatem, egressi ex urbe contra suos, medios hostium ferire coeperunt, cum ergo ex utraque parte adversarii caederentur, ita ut nullus de tanta multitudine salvaretur. 23 Regem quoque urbis Ahi adprehendere viventem et obtulerunt Iosue. 24 Igitur omnibus interfectis qui Israhelem ad deserta tendentem fuerant persecuti et in eodem loco gladio corruentibus, reversi filii Israhel percusserunt civitatem. 25 Erant autem qui in eodem die conciderant, a viro usque ad mulierem, duodecim milia hominum, omnes urbis Ahi. 26 Iosue vero non contraxit manum quam in sublime porrexerat tenens clypeum donec interficerentur omnes habitatores Ahi.

27 Iumenta autem et praedam civitatis diviserunt sibi filii Israhel, sicut praeceperat Dominus Iosue, 28 qui succendit urbem, et fecit eam tumulum sempiternum, 29 regem quoque eius suspendit in patibulo usque ad vesperum et solis

up the shield that is in thy hand towards the city of Ai, for I will deliver it to thee." 19 And when he had lifted up his shield towards the city, the ambush that lay hid rose up immediately and going to the city took it and set it on fire. 20 And the men of the city that pursued after Joshua, looking back and seeing the smoke of the city rise up to heaven, had no more power to flee this way or that way, especially as they that had counterfeited flight and were going toward the wilderness turned back most valiantly against them that pursued.

21 So Joshua and all Israel, seeing that the city was taken and that the smoke of the city rose up, returned and slew the men of Ai. 22 And they also that had taken and set the city on fire, issuing out of the city *to meet* their own men, began *to cut off the enemies who were surrounded by them, so that* the enemies being cut off on both sides, not one of so great a multitude was saved. 23 And they took the king of the city of Ai alive and brought him to Joshua. 24 So all being slain that had pursued after Israel in his flight to the wilderness and falling by the sword in the same place, the children of Israel returned and laid waste the city. 25 And *the number of them* that fell *that* day, *both of* men *and* women, *was* twelve thousand persons, all of the city of Ai. 26 But Joshua drew not back his hand which he had stretched out on high holding the shield till all the inhabitants of Ai were slain.

27 And the children of Israel divided among them the cattle and the prey of the city, as the Lord had commanded Joshua, 28 and he burned the city, and made it a heap for ever, 29 and he hung the king thereof on a gibbet until the evening

occasum. Praecepitque, et deposuerunt cadaver eius de cruce proieceruntque in ipso introitu civitatis, congesto super eum magno acervo lapidum, qui permanet usque in praesentem diem.

30 Tunc aedificavit Iosue altare Domino, Deo Israhel, in Monte Hebal, 31 sicut praeceperat Moses, famulus Domini, filiis Israhel, et scriptum est in volumine legis Mosi: altare de lapidibus inpolitis quos ferrum non tetigit. Et obtulit super eo holocausta Domino immolavitque pacificas victimas. 32 Et scripsit super lapides Deuteronomium legis Mosi quod ille digesserat coram filiis Israhel. 33 Omnis autem populus et maiores natu ducesque ac iudices stabant ex utraque parte arcae in conspectu sacerdotum qui portabant Arcam Foederis Domini, ut advena ita et indigena, media eorum pars iuxta Montem Garizim, et media iuxta Montem Hebal, sicut praeceperat Moses, famulus Domini. Et primum quidem benedixit populo Israhel. 34 Post haec legit omnia verba benedictionis et maledictionis et cuncta quae scripta erant in legis volumine. 35 Nihil ex his quae Moses iusserat reliquit intactum, sed universa replicavit coram omni multitudine Israhel, mulieribus ac parvulis et advenis qui inter eos morabantur.

and the going down of the sun. *Then Joshua* commanded, and they took down his carcass from the gibbet and threw it in the very entrance of the city, heaping upon it a great heap of stones, which remaineth until this present day.

30 Then Joshua built an altar to the Lord, the God of Israel, in Mount Ebal, 31 as Moses, the servant of the Lord, had commanded the children of Israel, and it is written in the book of the law of Moses: an altar of unhewn stones which iron had not touched. And he offered upon it holocausts to the Lord and immolated victims of peace offerings. 32 And he wrote upon stones the Deuteronomy of the law of Moses which he had ordered before the children of Israel. 33 And all the people and the ancients and the princes and judges stood on both sides of the ark before the priests that carried the Ark of the Covenant of the Lord, *both* the stranger *and he that was born among them,* half of them by Mount Gerizim, and half by Mount Ebal, as Moses, the servant of the Lord, had commanded. And first he blessed the people of Israel. 34 After this he read all the words of the blessing and the cursing and all things that were written in the book of the law. 35 He left out nothing of those things which Moses had commanded, but he repeated all before all the people of Israel, with the women and children and strangers that dwelt among them.

Caput 9

Quibus auditis, cuncti reges trans Iordanem qui versabantur in montanis et campestribus, in maritimis ac litore Maris Magni, hii quoque qui habitabant iuxta Libanum, Hettheus et Amorreus, Chananeus, Ferezeus et Eveus et Iebuseus, 2 congregati sunt pariter ut pugnarent contra Iosue et Israhel uno animo eademque sententia. 3 At hii qui habitabant in Gabaon, audientes cuncta quae fecerat Iosue Hiericho et Ahi 4 callide cogitantes, tulerunt sibi cibaria, saccos veteres asinis inponentes et utres vinarios scissos atque consutos 5 calciamentaque perantiqua, quae ad indicium vetustatis pittaciis consuta erant, induti veteribus vestimentis, panes quoque quos portabant ob viaticum duri erant et in frusta comminuti. 6 Perrexeruntque ad Iosue, qui tunc morabatur in castris Galgalae, et dixerunt ei atque omni simul Israheli, "De terra longinqua venimus, pacem vobiscum facere cupientes."

Responderuntque viri Israhel ad eos atque dixerunt, 7 "Ne forsitan in terra quae nobis sorte debetur habitetis, et non possimus foedus inire vobiscum."

8 At illi ad Iosue, "Servi," inquiunt, "tui sumus."

Chapter 9

Joshua is deceived by the Gibeonites, who being detected
are condemned to be perpetual servants.

Now when these things were heard of, all the kings beyond the Jordan that dwelt in the mountains and in the
plains, in the places near the sea and on the *coasts* of the
Great Sea, they also that dwell by Libanus, the Hittite and
the Amorite, the Canaanite, the Perizzite and the Hivite
and the Jebusite, 2 gathered themselves together to fight
against Joshua and Israel with one mind and *one* resolution.
3 But they that dwelt in Gibeon, hearing all that Joshua had
done to Jericho and Ai, 4 cunningly devising, took for themselves provisions, laying old sacks upon their asses and wine
bottles rent and sewed up again 5 and very old shoes, which
for a show of age were clouted with patches, and old garments upon them, the loaves also which they carried for
provisions by the way were hard and broken into pieces.
6 And they went to Joshua, who then abode in the camp at
Gilgal, and said to him and to all Israel with him, "We are
come from a far country, desiring to make peace with you."

And the children of Israel answered them and said, 7 *"Perhaps* you dwell in the land which *falls to our lot; if so,* we can
make no league with you."

8 But they said to Joshua, "We are thy servants."

Quibus Iosue, "Quinam," ait, "estis? Et unde venistis?"

9 Responderunt, "De terra longinqua valde venerunt servi tui in nomine Domini, Dei tui. Audivimus enim famam potentiae eius, cuncta quae fecit in Aegypto 10 et duobus Amorreorum regibus qui fuerunt trans Iordanem, Seon, regi Esebon, et Og, regi Basan, qui erat in Astharoth, 11 dixeruntque nobis seniores et omnes habitatores terrae nostrae, 'Tollite in manibus cibaria ob longissimam viam, et occurrite eis, ac dicite, "Servi vestri sumus; foedus inite nobiscum."' 12 En: panes quando egressi sumus de domibus nostris ut veniremus ad vos calidos sumpsimus; nunc sicci facti sunt et vetustate nimia comminuti. 13 Utres vini novos implevimus; nunc rupti sunt et soluti. Vestes et calciamenta quibus induimur et quae habemus in pedibus ob longitudinem longioris viae trita sunt et paene consumpta." 14 Susceperunt igitur de cibariis eorum et os Domini non interrogaverunt. 15 Fecitque Iosue cum eis pacem et inito foedere pollicitus est quod non occiderentur; principes quoque multitudinis iuraverunt eis.

16 Post dies autem tres initi foederis, audierunt quod in vicino habitarent et inter eos futuri essent. 17 Moveruntque castra filii Israhel et venerunt in civitates eorum die tertio, quarum haec vocabula sunt Gabaon et Caphira et Beroth et Cariathiarim. 18 Et non percusserunt eos, eo quod iurassent eis principes multitudinis in nomine Domini, Dei Israhel. Murmuravit itaque omne vulgus contra principes. 19 Qui

Joshua said to *them,* "Who are you? And whence came you?"

9 They answered, "From a very far country thy servants are come in the name of the Lord, thy God. For we have heard the fame of his power, all the things that he did in Egypt 10 and to the two kings of the Amorites that were beyond the Jordan, Sihon, king of Heshbon, and Og, king of Bashan, that was in Ashtaroth, 11 and our ancients and all the inhabitants of our country said to us, 'Take *with you* victuals for a long way, and go meet them, and say, "We are your servants; make ye a league with us."' 12 Behold: *these* loaves we took hot when we set out from our houses to come to you; now they are become dry and broken in pieces *by being exceeding old.* 13 *These* bottles of wine *when* we filled them *were* new; now they are rent and burst. *These* garments we have on and the shoes we have on our feet by reason of the *very long* journey are worn out and almost consumed." 14 They took therefore of their victuals and consulted not the mouth of the Lord. 15 And Joshua made peace with them and entering into a league promised that they should not be slain; the princes also of the multitude swore to them.

16 Now three days after the league was made, they heard that they dwelt nigh and they should be among them. 17 And the children of Israel removed the camp and came into their cities on the third day, the *names of which are* Gibeon and Chephirah and Beeroth and Kiriath-jearim. 18 And they slew them not, because the princes of the multitude had sworn in the name of the Lord, the God of Israel. Then all the common people murmured against the princes. 19 And they an-

responderunt eis, "Iuravimus illis in nomine Domini, Dei Israhel, et idcirco non possumus eos contingere. 20 Sed hoc faciemus eis: reserventur quidem ut vivant ne contra nos ira Domini concitetur si peieraverimus. 21 Sed sic vivant ut in usus universae multitudinis ligna caedant aquasque conportent."

Quibus haec loquentibus, 22 vocavit Gabaonitas Iosue et dixit eis, "Cur nos decipere fraude voluistis ut diceretis, 'Procul valde habitamus a vobis,' cum in medio nostri sitis? 23 Itaque sub maledictione eritis, et non deficiet de stirpe vestra ligna caedens aquasque conportans in domum Dei mei."

24 Qui responderunt, "Nuntiatum est nobis, servis tuis, quod promisisset Dominus, Deus tuus, Mosi servo suo ut traderet vobis omnem terram et disperderet cunctos habitatores eius. Timuimus igitur valde et providimus animabus nostris vestro terrore conpulsi, et hoc consilium inivimus. 25 Nunc autem in manu tua sumus. Quod tibi bonum et rectum videtur fac nobis."

26 Fecit ergo Iosue ut dixerat et liberavit eos de manu filiorum Israhel ut non occiderentur, 27 decrevitque in illo die esse eos in ministerium cuncti populi et altaris Domini, caedentes ligna et aquas conportantes, usque in praesens tempus in loco quem Dominus elegisset.

swered them, "We have sworn to them in the name of the Lord, the God of Israel, and therefore we may not touch them. 20 But this we will do to them: let *their lives be saved* lest the wrath of the Lord be stirred up against us if we should be forsworn. 21 But so let them live as *to serve* the whole multitude *in hewing* wood and *bringing* in water."

As they were speaking these things, 22 Joshua called the Gibeonites and said to them, "Why would you *impose upon* us, *saying,* 'We dwell far off from you,' whereas you are in the midst of us? 23 Therefore you shall be under a curse, and *your race shall always be hewers of* wood and *carriers* of water unto the house of my God."

24 They answered, "It was told us, thy servants, that the Lord, thy God, had promised his servant Moses to give you all the land and to destroy all the inhabitants thereof. Therefore we feared exceedingly and provided for our lives compelled by the dread we had of you, and we took this counsel. 25 And now we are in thy hand. Deal with us as it seemeth good and right unto thee."

26 So Joshua did as he had said and delivered them from the hand of the children of Israel that they should not be slain, 27 and he gave orders in that day that they should be in the service of all the people and of the altar of the Lord, hewing wood and carrying water, until this present time in the place which the Lord hath chosen.

Caput 10

Quae cum audisset Adonisedec, rex Hierusalem, quod, scilicet, cepisset Iosue Ahi et subvertisset eam (sicut enim fecerat Hiericho et regi eius, sic fecit Ahi et regi illius) et quod transfugissent Gabaonitae ad Israhel et essent foederati eorum, 2 timuit valde, urbs enim magna erat Gabaon et una regalium civitatum et maior oppido Ahi, omnesque bellatores eius fortissimi. 3 Misit ergo Adonisedec, rex Hierusalem, ad Oham, regem Hebron, et ad Pharam, regem Hieremoth, ad Iaphie quoque, regem Lachis, et ad Dabir, regem Eglon, dicens, 4 "Ascendite ad me, et ferte praesidium ut expugnemus Gabaon quare transfugerit ad Iosue et ad filios Israhel." 5 Congregati igitur ascenderunt quinque reges Amorreorum—rex Hierusalem, rex Hebron, rex Hieremoth, rex Lachis, rex Eglon, simul cum exercitibus suis—et castrametati sunt circa Gabaon, obpugnantes eam.

6 Habitatores autem Gabaon urbis obsessae miserunt ad Iosue, qui tunc morabatur in castris apud Galgalam et dixerunt ei, "Ne retrahas manus tuas ab auxilio servorum tuo-

Chapter 10

Five kings war against Gibeon. Joshua defeateth them;
many are slain with hailstones. At the prayer of Joshua the
sun and moon stand still the space of one day. The five kings
are hanged. Divers cities are taken.

When Adoni-zedek, king of Jerusalem, had heard these things, to wit, that Joshua had taken Ai and had destroyed it (for as he had done to Jericho and the king thereof, so did he to Ai and its king) and that the Gibeonites were *gone over* to Israel and were their confederates, 2 he was exceedingly afraid, for Gibeon was a great city and one of the royal cities and greater than the town of Ai, and all its fighting men were most valiant. 3 Therefore Adoni-zedek, king of Jerusalem, sent to Hoham, king of Hebron, and to Piram, king of Jarmuth, and to Japhia, king of Lachish, and to Debir, king of Eglon, saying, 4 "Come up to me, and bring help that we may take Gibeon because it hath gone over to Joshua and to the children of Israel." 5 So the five kings of the Amorites being assembled together went up—the king of Jerusalem, the king of Hebron, the king of Jarmuth, the king of Lachish, the king of Eglon, *they and* their armies—and camped about Gibeon, laying siege to it.

6 But the inhabitants of the city of Gibeon which was besieged sent to Joshua, who then abode in the camp at Gilgal and said to him, "Withdraw not thy hands from helping thy

rum. Ascende cito, et libera nos, ferque praesidium, convenerunt enim adversum nos omnes reges Amorreorum qui habitant in montanis." 7 Ascenditque Iosue de Galgalis et omnis exercitus bellatorum cum eo, viri fortissimi.

8 Dixitque Dominus ad Iosue, "Ne timeas eos, in manus enim tuas tradidi illos. Nullus tibi ex eis resistere poterit." 9 Inruit itaque Iosue super eos repente tota ascendens nocte de Galgalis, 10 et conturbavit eos Dominus a facie Israhel, contrivitque plaga magna in Gabaon ac persecutus est eos per viam ascensus Bethoron et percussit usque Azeca et Maceda. 11 Cumque fugerent filios Israhel et essent in descensu Bethoron, Dominus misit super eos lapides magnos de caelo usque Azeca, et mortui sunt multo plures lapidibus grandinis quam quos gladio percusserant filii Israhel.

12 Tunc locutus est Iosue Domino in die qua tradidit Amorreum in conspectu filiorum Israhel, dixitque coram eis, "Sol, contra Gabaon ne movearis, et luna, contra vallem Ahialon." 13 Steteruntque sol et luna donec ulcisceretur se gens de inimicis suis. Nonne scriptum est hoc in Libro Iustorum? Stetit itaque sol in medio caeli et non festinavit occumbere spatio unius diei. 14 Non fuit ante et postea tam longa dies, oboediente Domino voci hominis et pugnante pro Israhel.

15 Reversusque est Iosue cum omni Israhel in castra Galgalae, 16 fugerant enim quinque reges et se absconderant in spelunca urbis Maceda. 17 Nuntiatumque est Iosue quod

servants. Come up quickly, and save us, and bring us succour, for all the kings of the Amorites who dwell in the mountains are gathered together against us." 7 And Joshua went up from Gilgal and all the army of the warriors with him, most valiant men.

8 And the Lord said to Joshua, "Fear them not, for I have delivered them into thy hands. None of them shall be able to stand against thee." 9 So Joshua going up from Gilgal all the night came upon them suddenly, 10 and the Lord troubled them at the sight of Israel, and he slew them with a great slaughter in Gibeon and pursued them by the way of the ascent to Beth-horon and cut them off all the way to Azekah and Makkedah. 11 And when they were fleeing from the children of Israel and were in the descent of Beth-horon, the Lord cast down upon them great stones from heaven as far as Azekah, and many more were killed with the hailstones than *were slain by the swords of the children* of Israel.

12 Then Joshua spoke to the Lord in the day that he delivered the Amorite in the sight of the children of Israel, and he said before them, "Move not, O sun, toward Gibeon, nor thou, O moon, toward the valley of Aijalon." 13 And the sun and the moon stood still till the people revenged themselves of their enemies. Is not this written in the Book of the Just? So the sun stood still in the midst of heaven and hasted not to go down the space of one day. 14 There was not before nor after so long a day, the Lord obeying the voice of a man and fighting for Israel.

15 And Joshua returned with all Israel into the camp of Gilgal, 16 for the five kings were fled and had hidden themselves in a cave of the city of Makkedah. 17 And it was told

inventi essent quinque reges latentes in spelunca urbis Maceda, 18 qui praecepit sociis et ait, "Volvite saxa ingentia ad os speluncae, et ponite viros industrios qui clausos custodiant, 19 vos autem nolite stare, sed persequimini hostes, et extremos quosque fugientium caedite, nec dimittatis eos urbium suarum intrare praesidia quos tradidit Dominus Deus in manus vestras."

20 Caesis igitur adversariis plaga magna et usque ad internicionem paene consumptis, hii qui Israhel effugere potuerunt ingressi sunt civitates munitas. 21 Reversusque est omnis exercitus ad Iosue in Maceda, ubi tunc erant castra, sani et integro numero, nullusque contra filios Israhel muttire ausus est. 22 Praecepitque Iosue, dicens, "Aperite os speluncae, et producite ad me quinque reges qui in ea latitant." 23 Feceruntque ministri ut sibi fuerat imperatum, et eduxerunt ad eum quinque reges de spelunca: regem Hierusalem, regem Hebron, regem Hieremoth, regem Lachis, regem Eglon. 24 Cumque educti essent ad eum, vocavit omnes viros Israhel et ait ad principes exercitus qui secum erant, "Ite, et ponite pedes super colla regum istorum." Qui cum perrexissent et subiectorum pedibus colla calcarent, 25 rursum ait ad eos, "Nolite timere, nec paveatis; confortamini, et estote robusti, sic enim faciet Dominus cunctis hostibus vestris adversum quos dimicatis." 26 Percussitque Iosue et interfecit eos atque suspendit super quinque stipites, fueruntque suspensi usque ad vesperum. 27 Cumque occumberet sol, praecepit sociis ut deponerent eos de patibulis. Qui depositos proiecerunt in speluncam in qua latuerant et posue-

Joshua that the five kings were found hidden in a cave of the city of Makkedah, 18 and he commanded them *that were with him, saying,* "Roll great stones to the mouth of the cave, and set careful men to keep them shut up, 19 and stay you not, but pursue after the enemies, and kill all the hindermost of them as they flee, and do not suffer them whom the Lord God hath delivered into your hands to *shelter themselves* in their cities."

20 So the enemies being slain with a great slaughter and almost utterly consumed, they that were able to escape from Israel entered into fenced cities. 21 And all the army returned to Joshua in Makkedah, where the camp then was, in good health and *without the loss of any one,* and no man durst *move his tongue* against the children of Israel. 22 And Joshua gave orders, saying, "Open the mouth of the cave, and bring forth to me the five kings that lie hid therein." 23 And the ministers did as they were commanded, and they brought out to him the five kings out of the cave: the king of Jerusalem, the king of Hebron, the king of Jarmuth, the king of Lachish, the king of Eglon. 24 And when they were brought out to him, he called all the men of Israel and said to the chiefs of the army that were with him, "Go, and set your feet on the necks of these kings." And when they had gone and *put their feet upon the necks* of them lying under them, 25 he said again to them, "Fear not, neither be ye dismayed; take courage, and be strong, for so will the Lord do to all your enemies against whom you fight." 26 And Joshua struck and slew them and hanged them upon five gibbets, and they hung until the evening. 27 And when the sun was down, he commanded the soldiers to take them down from the gibbets. And after they were taken down, they cast them into the

runt super os eius saxa ingentia, quae permanent usque in praesens.

28 Eodem die, Macedam cepit Iosue et percussit eam in ore gladii regemque illius interfecit et omnes habitatores eius. Non dimisit in ea saltim parvas reliquias. Fecitque regi Maceda sicut fecerat regi Hiericho.

29 Transivit autem cum omni Israhel de Maceda in Lebna et pugnabat contra eam, 30 quam tradidit Dominus cum rege suo in manus Israhel, percusseruntque urbem in ore gladii et omnes habitatores eius. Non dimiserunt in ea ullas reliquias. Feceruntque regi Lebna sicut fecerant regi Hiericho.

31 De Lebna transivit in Lachis cum omni Israhel et exercitu per gyrum disposito obpugnabat eam. 32 Tradiditque Dominus Lachis in manus Israhel, et cepit eam die altero atque percussit in ore gladii omnemque animam quae fuerat in ea, sicut fecerat Lebna. 33 Eo tempore ascendit Horam, rex Gazer, ut auxiliaretur Lachis quem percussit Iosue cum omni populo eius usque ad internicionem.

34 Transivitque de Lachis in Eglon et circumdedit 35 atque expugnavit eam eadem die percussitque in ore gladii omnes animas quae erant in ea, iuxta omnia quae fecerat Lachis.

36 Ascendit quoque cum omni Israhele de Eglon in Hebron et pugnavit contra eam, 37 cepit eam et percussit in ore gladii, regem quoque eius et omnia oppida regionis illius universasque animas quae in ea fuerant commoratae. Non reliquit in ea ullas reliquias. Sicut fecerat Eglon, sic fecit et Hebron, cuncta quae in ea repperit consumens gladio.

38 Inde reversus in Dabir, 39 cepit eam atque vastavit. Regem quoque eius et omnia per circuitum oppida percussit in

cave *where* they had lain hid and put great stones at the mouth thereof, which remain until this *day*.

28 The same day, Joshua took Makkedah and destroyed it with the edge of the sword and killed the king and all the inhabitants thereof. He left not in it the least remains. And he did to the king of Makkedah as he had done to the king of Jericho.

29 And he passed from Makkedah with all Israel to Libnah and fought against it, 30 and the Lord delivered it with the king thereof into the hands of Israel, and they destroyed the city with the edge of the sword and all the inhabitants thereof. They left not in it any remains. And they did to the king of Libnah as they had done to the king of Jericho.

31 From Libnah he passed unto Lachish with all Israel and *investing it with his army* besieged it. 32 And the Lord delivered Lachish into the hands of Israel, and he took it the following day and *put it to the sword* and every soul that was in it, as he had done to Libnah. 33 At that time Horam, king of Gezer, came up to succour Lachish, and Joshua slew him with all his people *so as to leave none alive*.

34 And he passed from Lachish to Eglon and surrounded it 35 and took it the same day and *put to the sword* all the souls that were in it, according to all that he had done to Lachish.

36 He went up also with all Israel from Eglon to Hebron and fought against it, 37 took it and destroyed it with the edge of the sword, the king also thereof and all the towns of that country and all the souls that dwelt in it. He left not therein any remains. As he had done to Eglon, so did he also to Hebron, *putting to the sword* all that he found in it.

38 Returning from thence to Debir, 39 he took it and destroyed it. The king also thereof and all the towns round

ore gladii. Non dimisit in ea ullas reliquias. Sicut fecerat Hebron et Lebna et regibus earum, sic fecit Dabir et regi illius.

40 Percussit itaque Iosue omnem terram montanam et meridianam atque campestrem et Asedoth cum regibus suis. Non dimisit in ea ullas reliquias, sed omne quod spirare poterat interfecit, sicut praeceperat ei Dominus, Deus Israhel, 41 a Cadesbarne usque Gazam, omnem terram Gosen usque Gabaon, 42 universosque reges et regiones eorum uno cepit impetu atque vastavit, Dominus enim, Deus Israhel, pugnabat pro eo.

43 Reversusque est cum omni Israhele ad locum castrorum in Galgala.

Caput 11

Quae cum audisset Iabin, rex Asor, misit ad Iobab, regem Madon, et ad regem Someron atque ad regem Acsaph, 2 ad reges quoque aquilonis qui habitabant in montanis et in planitie contra meridiem Cheneroth in campestribus quoque et in regionibus Dor iuxta mare, 3 Chananeum quoque ab oriente et occidente et Amorreum atque Hettheum ac

about he destroyed with the edge of the sword. He left not in it any remains. As he had done to Hebron and Libnah and to their kings, so did he to Debir and to the king thereof.

40 So Joshua conquered all the country of the hills and of the south and of the plain and of Asedoth with their kings. He left not any remains therein, but slew all that *breathed,* as the Lord, the God of Israel, had commanded him, 41 from Kadesh-barnea even to Gaza, all the land of Goshen even to Gibeon, 42 and all their kings and their lands he took and wasted at one onset, for the Lord, the God of Israel, fought for him.

43 And he returned with all Israel to the place of the camp in Gilgal.

Chapter II

The kings of the north are overthrown. The whole country is taken.

And when Jabin, king of Hazor, had heard these things, he sent to Jobab, king of Madon, and to the king of Shimron and to the king of Achshaph, 2 and to the kings of the north that dwelt in the mountains and in the plains over against the south side of Chinneroth and in the levels and the countries of Dor by the sea side, 3 *to the Canaanites* also on the east and on the west and the Amorite and the Hittite and

Ferezeum et Iebuseum in montanis, Eveum quoque qui habitabat ad radices Hermon in terra Masphe. 4 Egressique sunt omnes cum turmis suis, populus multus nimis sicut harena quae est in litore maris, equi quoque et currus inmensae multitudinis, 5 conveneruntque omnes reges isti in unum ad aquas Merom ut pugnarent contra Israhel.

6 Dixitque Dominus ad Iosue, "Ne timeas eos, cras enim hac eadem hora ego tradam omnes istos vulnerandos in conspectu Israhel. Equos eorum subnervabis, et currus igne conbures." 7 Venitque Iosue et omnis exercitus cum eo adversum illos ad aquas Merom subito et inruerunt super eos. 8 Tradiditque illos Dominus in manus Israhel, qui percusserunt eos et persecuti sunt usque ad Sidonem magnam et aquas Maserefoth campumque Masphe qui est ad orientalem illius partem. Ita percussit omnes ut nullas dimitteret ex eis reliquias. 9 Fecitque sicut praeceperat ei Dominus: equos eorum subnervavit currusque conbusit. 10 Reversusque statim, cepit Asor et regem eius percussit gladio (Asor enim antiquitus inter omnia regna haec principatum tenebat), 11 percussitque omnes animas quae ibidem morabantur. Non dimisit in ea ullas reliquias sed usque ad internicionem universa vastavit ipsamque urbem peremit incendio. 12 Et omnes per circuitum civitates regesque earum cepit, percussit atque delevit, sicut praeceperat ei Moses, famulus Dei, 13 absque urbibus quae erant in collibus et in tumulis sitae. Ceteras succendit Israhel; unam tantum Asor munitissimam flamma consumpsit. 14 Omnemque praedam istarum urbium ac iumenta diviserunt sibi filii Israhel, cunctis hominibus interfectis. 15 Sicut praeceperat Dominus Mosi, servo

the Perizzite and the Jebusite in the mountains, *to* the Hivite also who dwelt at the foot of Hermon in the land of Mizpah. 4 And they all came out with their troops, a people exceeding numerous as the sand that is on the sea shore, their horses also and chariots *a* very great multitude, 5 and all these kings assembled *together* at the waters of Merom to fight against Israel.

6 And the Lord said to Joshua, "Fear them not, for tomorrow at this same hour I will deliver all these to be slain in the sight of Israel. Thou shalt hamstring their horses, and thou shalt burn their chariots with fire." 7 And Joshua came and all the army with him against them to the waters of Merom on a sudden and fell upon them. 8 And the Lord delivered them into the hands of Israel, and they defeated them and chased them as far as the great Sidon and the waters of Misrephoth and the field of Mizpeh which is on the east side thereof. He slew them all so as to leave no remains of them. 9 And he did as the Lord had commanded him: he hamstringed their horses and burned their chariots. 10 And presently turning back, he took Hazor and slew the king thereof with the sword (now Hazor of old *was the head of all these kingdoms),* 11 and he *cut off* all the souls that abode there. He left not in it any remains but *utterly destroyed* all and *burned* the city itself with fire. 12 And he took *and put to the sword* and destroyed all the cities round about and their kings, as Moses, the servant of God, had commanded him, 13 except the cities that were on hills and high places. The rest Israel burned; *only* Hazor *that was very strong* he consumed with fire. 14 And the children of Israel divided among themselves all the spoil of these cities and the cattle, killing all the men. 15 As the Lord had commanded Moses, his servant, so did

suo, ita praecepit Moses Iosue, et ille universa conplevit. Non praeteriit de universis mandatis ne unum quidem verbum quod iusserat Dominus Mosi.

16 Cepit itaque Iosue omnem terram montanam et meridianam terramque Gosen et planitiem et occidentalem plagam montemque Israhel et campestria eius 17 et partem montis quae ascendit Seir usque Baalgad per planitiem Libani subter Montem Hermon. Omnes reges eorum cepit, percussit et occidit. 18 Multo tempore pugnavit Iosue contra reges istos. 19 Non fuit civitas quae se traderet filiis Israhel, praeter Eveum qui habitabat in Gabaon, omnes enim bellando cepit. 20 Domini enim sententia fuerat ut indurarentur corda eorum et pugnarent contra Israhel et caderent et non mererentur ullam clementiam ac perirent sicut praeceperat Dominus Mosi.

21 In tempore illo venit Iosue et interfecit Enacim de montanis, Hebron et Dabir et Anab et de omni monte Iuda et Israhel, urbesque eorum delevit. 22 Non reliquit ullum de stirpe Enacim in terra filiorum Israhel absque civitatibus Gaza et Geth et Azoto in quibus solis relicti sunt.

23 Cepit ergo Iosue omnem terram sicut locutus est Dominus ad Mosen et tradidit eam in possessionem filiis Israhel secundum partes et tribus suas. Quievitque terra a proeliis.

Moses command Joshua, and he accomplished all. He *left not one thing undone* of all the commandments which the Lord had commanded Moses.

16 So Joshua took all the country of the hills and of the south and the land of Goshen and the plains and the west country and the mountain of Israel and the plains thereof 17 and part of the mountain that goeth up to Seir as far as Baal-gad by the plain of Libanus under Mount Hermon. All their kings he took, smote and slew. 18 Joshua made war a long time against these kings. 19 There was not a city that delivered itself to the children of Israel, except the Hivite who dwelt in Gibeon, for he took all by fight. 20 For it was the sentence of the Lord that their hearts should be hardened and they should fight against Israel and fall and should not deserve any clemency and should be destroyed as the Lord had commanded Moses.

21 At that time Joshua came and cut off the Anakim from the mountains, from Hebron and Debir and Anab and from all the mountain of Judah and Israel, and destroyed their cities. 22 He left not any of the stock of the Anakim in the land of the children of Israel except the cities of Gaza and Gath and Ashdod in which alone they were left.

23 So Joshua took all the land as the Lord spoke to Moses and delivered it in possession to the children of Israel according to their divisions and tribes. And the land rested from wars.

Caput 12

Hii sunt reges quos percusserunt filii Israhel et possederunt terram eorum trans Iordanem ad solis ortum, a torrente
Arnon usque ad montem Hermon et omnem orientalem
plagam quae respicit solitudinem: 2 Seon, rex Amorreorum,
qui habitavit in Esebon, dominatus est ab Aroer, quae sita
est super ripam torrentis Arnon, et mediae partis in valle dimidiique Galaad usque ad torrentem Iaboc, qui est terminus
filiorum Ammon, 3 et a solitudine usque ad Mare Cheneroth
contra orientem et usque ad Mare Deserti, quod est Mare
Salsissimum, ad orientalem plagam per viam quae ducit
Bethesimoth, et ab australi parte quae subiacet Asedoth usque Phasga, 4 terminus Og, regis Basan, de reliquiis Rafaim
qui habitavit in Astharoth et in Edrain et dominatus est in
Monte Hermon et in Salacha atque in universa Basan usque
ad terminos 5 Gesuri et Machathi et dimidiae partis Galaad,
terminos Seon, regis Esebon. 6 Moses, famulus Domini, et
filii Israhel percusserunt eos, tradiditque terram eorum Moses in possessionem Rubenitis et Gadditis et dimidiae tribui
Manasse.

Chapter 12

These are the kings whom the children of Israel slew and possessed their land beyond the Jordan towards the rising of the sun, from the torrent Arnon unto Mount Hermon and all the east country that looketh towards the wilderness: 2 Sihon, king of the Amorites, who dwelt in Heshbon *and* had dominion from Aroer, which is seated upon the bank of the torrent Arnon, and of the middle part in the valley and of half Gilead as far as the torrent Jabbok, which is the border of the children of Ammon, 3 and from the wilderness to the Sea of Chinneroth towards the east and to the Sea of the Wilderness, which is the Most Salt Sea, on the east side by the way that leadeth to Beth-jeshimoth, and on the south side that lieth under *Asedoth, Pisgah,* 4 the border of Og, the king of Bashan, of the remnant of the Rephaim who dwelt in Ashtaroth and in Edrei and had dominion in Mount Hermon and in Salecah and in all Bashan unto the borders 5 of Geshur and Maacah and of half Gilead, the borders of Sihon, the king of Heshbon. 6 Moses, the servant of the Lord, and the children of Israel slew them, and Moses delivered their land in possession to the Reubenites and Gadites and the half-tribe of Manasseh.

7 Hii sunt reges terrae quos percussit Iosue et filii Israhel trans Iordanem ad occidentalem plagam a Baalgad in campo Libani, usque ad montem, cuius pars ascendit in Seir. Tradidit que eam Iosue in possessionem tribubus Israhel, singulis partes suas, 8 tam in montanis quam in planis atque campestribus (in Aseroth et in solitudine ac in meridie Hettheus fuit et Amorreus, Chananeus et Ferezeus, Eveus et Iebuseus): 9 rex Hiericho, unus; rex Ahi, quae est ex latere Bethel, unus; 10 rex Hierusalem, unus; rex Hebron, unus; 11 rex Hierimoth, unus; rex Lachis, unus; 12 rex Eglon, unus; rex Gazer, unus; 13 rex Dabir, unus; rex Gader, unus; 14 rex Herma, unus; rex Hered, unus; 15 rex Lebna, unus; rex Odollam, unus; 16 rex Maceda, unus; rex Bethel, unus; 17 rex Thaffua, unus; rex Afer, unus; 18 rex Afec, unus; rex Saron, unus; 19 rex Madon, unus; rex Asor, unus; 20 rex Someron, unus; rex Acsaph, unus; 21 rex Thenach, unus; rex Mageddo, unus; 22 rex Cades, unus; rex Iachanaem Chermeli, unus; 23 rex Dor et provinciae Dor, unus; rex gentium Galgal, unus; 24 rex Thersa, unus: omnes reges triginta unus.

7 These are the kings of the land whom Joshua and the children of Israel slew beyond the Jordan on the west side from Baal-gad in the field of Libanus, unto the mount, part of which goeth up into Seir. And Joshua delivered it in possession to the tribes of Israel, to every one their divisions, 8 as well in the mountains as in the plains and the champaign countries (in Asedoth and in the wilderness and in the south was the Hittite and the Amorite, the Canaanite and the Perizzite, the Hivite and the Jebusite): 9 the king of Jericho, one; the king of Ai, which is on the side of Bethel, one; 10 the king of Jerusalem, one; the king of Hebron, one; 11 the king of Jarmuth, one; the king of Lachish, one; 12 the king of Eglon, one; the king of Gezer, one; 13 the king of Debir, one; the king of Geder, one; 14 the king of Hormah, one; the king of Arad, one; 15 The king of Libnah, one; the king of Adullam, one; 16 the king of Makkedah, one; the king of Bethel, one; 17 the king of Tappuah, one; the king of Hepher, one; 18 the king of Aphek, one; the king of Lasharon, one; 19 the king of Madon, one; the king of Hazor, one; 20 the king of Shimron-meron, one; the king of Achshaph, one; 21 the king of Taanach, one; the king of Megiddo, one; 22 the king of Kedesh, one; the king of Jokneam of Carmel, one; 23 the king of Dor and of the province of Dor, one; the king of the nations of Gilgal, one; 24 the king of Tirzah, one: all the kings thirty *and* one.

Caput 13

Iosue senex provectaeque aetatis erat, et dixit Dominus ad eum, "Senuisti et longevus es, terraque latissima derelicta est quae necdum est sorte divisa, 2 omnis, videlicet, Galilea, Philisthim et universa Gesuri 3 a fluvio turbido qui inrigat Aegyptum usque ad terminos Accaron contra aquilonem, terra Chanaan, quae in quinque regulos Philisthim dividitur, Gazeos, Azotios, Ascalonitas, Gettheos et Accaronitas, 4 ad meridiem vero sunt Evei, omnis terra Chanaan et Maara Sidoniorum usque Afeca et terminos Amorrei 5 eiusque confinia, Libani quoque regio contra orientem a Baalgad sub Monte Hermon donec ingrediaris Emath, 6 omnium qui habitant in monte a Libano usque ad aquas Masrefoth universique Sidonii. Ego sum qui delebo eos a facie filiorum Israhel, veniat ergo in partem hereditatis Israhel, sicut praecepi tibi.

7 "Et nunc divide terram in possessionem novem tribubus et dimidiae tribui Manasse 8 cum qua Ruben et Gad possederunt terram quam tradidit eis Moses, famulus Domini, trans

Chapter 13

God commandeth Joshua to divide the land. The possessions of Reuben, Gad, and half the tribe of Manasseh beyond the Jordan.

Joshua was old and *far advanced* in *years,* and the Lord said to him, "Thou art grown old and advanced in age, and there is a very large country left which is not yet divided by lot, 2 to wit, all Galilee, Philistia and all Geshur 3 from the troubled river that watereth Egypt unto the borders of Ekron northward, the land of Canaan, which is divided among the *lords* of the Philistines, the Gazites, the Ashdodians, the Ashkelonites, the Gethites and the Ekronites, 4 and on the south side are the Hivites, all the land of Canaan and Mearah of the Sidonians as far as Aphek and the borders of the Amorite 5 and his confines, the country also of Libanus towards the east from Baal-gad under Mount Hermon *to the entering* into Hamath, 6 of all that dwell in the *mountains* from Libanus to the waters of Misrephoth and all the Sidonians. I am he that will cut them off from before the face of the children of Israel, so let their land come in *as a part* of the inheritance of Israel, as I have commanded thee.

7 "And now divide the land in possession to the nine tribes and to the half-tribe of Manasseh 8 with whom Reuben and Gad have possessed the land which Moses, the servant of the Lord, delivered to them beyond the river Jordan on the

fluenta Iordanis ad orientalem plagam 9 ab Aroer quae sita est in ripa torrentis Arnon et in vallis medio universaque campestria Medaba usque Dibon 10 et cunctas civitates Seon, regis Amorrei, qui regnavit in Esebon usque ad terminos filiorum Ammon 11 et Galaad ac terminum Gesuri et Machathi omnemque Montem Hermon et universam Basan usque Saleca, 12 omne regnum Og in Basan, qui regnavit in Astharoth et Edraim." Ipse fuit de reliquiis Rafaim. Percussitque eos Moses atque delevit, 13 nolueruntque disperdere filii Israhel Gesuri et Machathi, et habitaverunt in medio Israhel usque in praesentem diem.

14 Tribui autem Levi non dedit possessionem, sed sacrificia et victimae Domini Dei Israhel, ipsa est eius hereditas, sicut locutus est illi.

15 Dedit ergo Moses possessionem tribui filiorum Ruben iuxta cognationes suas, 16 fuitque terminus eorum ab Aroer, quae sita est in ripa torrentis Arnon et in valle eiusdem torrentis media, universam planitiem quae ducit Medaba, 17 et Esebon cunctosque viculos earum qui sunt in campestribus, Dibon quoque et Bamothbaal et oppidum Baalmaon 18 et Iessa et Cedmoth et Mepheeth 19 et Cariathaim et Sebama et Sarathasar in monte convallis, 20 Bethpheor et Asedoth, Phasga et Bethaisimoth 21 et omnes urbes campestres universaque regna Seon, regis Amorrei, qui regnavit in Esebon, quem percussit Moses cum principibus Madian, Eveum et Recem et Sur et Ur et Rabee, duces Seon, habitatores terrae; 22 et Balaam filium Beor, ariolum, occiderunt filii Israhel gladio cum ceteris interfectis. 23 Factusque est terminus

east side 9 from Aroer which is upon the bank of the torrent Arnon and in the midst of the valley and all the plains of Medeba as far as Dibon 10 and all the cities of Sihon, king of the *Amorites,* who reigned in Heshbon unto the borders of the children of Ammon 11 and Gilead and the borders of Geshur and Maacah and all Mount Hermon and all Bashan as far as Salecah, 12 all the kingdom of Og in Bashan, who reigned in Ashtaroth and Edrei." He was of the remains of the Rephaim. And Moses overthrew and destroyed them, 13 and the children of Israel would not destroy Geshur and Maacah, and they have dwelt in the midst of Israel until this present day.

14 But to the tribe of Levi he gave no possession, but the sacrifices and victims of the Lord God of Israel *are* his inheritance, as he spoke to him.

15 And Moses gave a possession to the children of Reuben according to their kindreds, 16 and their border was from Aroer, which is on the bank of the torrent Arnon and in the midst of the valley of the same torrent, all the plain that leadeth to Medeba, 17 and Heshbon and all their villages which are in the plains, Dibon also and Bamoth-baal and the town of Beth-baal-meon 18 and Jahaz and Kedemoth and Mephaath 19 and Kiriathaim and Sibmah and Zereth-shahar in the mountain of the valley, 20 Beth-peor and Asedoth, Pisgah and Beth-jeshimoth 21 and all the cities of the plain and all the kingdoms of Sihon, king of the Amorites, that reigned in Heshbon, whom Moses slew with the princes of Midian, Evi and Rekem and Zur and Hur and Reba, dukes of Sihon, inhabitants of the land; 22 Balaam also, the son of Beor, the soothsayer, the children of Israel slew with the sword among the rest that were slain. 23 And the river

filiorum Ruben Iordanis fluvius. Haec est possessio Rubeni-
tarum per cognationes suas urbium et viculorum.

24 Deditque Moses tribui Gad et filiis eius per cognationes suas possessionem, cuius haec divisio est: 25 terminus
Iazer et omnes civitates Galaad dimidiamque partem terrae
filiorum Ammon usque ad Aroer, quae est contra Rabba,
26 et ab Esebon usque Ramoth, Masphe et Batanim et a Manaim usque ad terminos Dabir 27 in valle quoque Betharaam
et Bethnemra et Soccoth et Saphon, reliquam partem regni
Seon, regis Esebon; huius quoque Iordanis finis est usque
ad extremam partem maris Chenereth trans Iordanem ad
orientalem plagam. 28 Haec est possessio filiorum Gad per
familias suas, civitates et villae earum.

29 Dedit et dimidiae tribui Manasse filiisque eius iuxta
cognationes suas possessionem, 30 cuius hoc principium est:
a Manaim universam Basan et cuncta regna Og, regis Basan,
omnesque vicos Air qui sunt in Basan, sexaginta oppida, 31 et
dimidiam partem Galaad et Astharoth et Edrai, urbes regni
Og in Basan filiis Machir, filii Manasse, dimidiae parti filiorum Machir iuxta cognationes suas. 32 Hanc possessionem
divisit Moses in campestribus Moab trans Iordanem contra
Hiericho ad orientalem plagam.

33 Tribui autem Levi non dedit possessionem, quoniam
Dominus, Deus Israhel, ipse est possessio eius, ut locutus
est illi.

Jordan *was* the border of the children of Reuben. This is the possession of the Reubenites by their kindreds of cities and villages.

24 And Moses gave to the tribe of Gad and to his children by their kindreds a possession, of which this is the division: 25 the border of Jazer and all the cities of Gilead and half the land of the children of Ammon as far as Aroer, which is over against Rabbah, 26 and from Heshbon unto Ramath, Mizpeh and Betonim and from Mahanaim unto the borders of Debir 27 and in the valley Beth-haram and Beth-nimrah and Succoth and Zaphon, the other part of the kingdom of Sihon, king of Heshbon; the limit of this also is the Jordan as far as the uttermost part of the sea of Cenereth beyond the Jordan on the east side. 28 This is the possession of the children of Gad by their families, their cities and villages.

29 He gave also to the half tribe of Manasseh and his children possession according to their kindreds, 30 the beginning whereof is this: from Mahanaim all Bashan and all the kingdoms of Og, king of Bashan, and all the villages of Jair which are in Bashan, threescore towns, 31 and half Gilead and Ashtaroth and Edrei, cities of the kingdom of Og in Bashan to the children of Machir, the son of Manasseh, to one half of the children of Machir according to their kindreds. 32 This possession Moses divided in the plains of Moab beyond the Jordan over against Jericho on the east side.

33 But to the tribe of Levi he gave no possession, because the Lord, the God of Israel, himself is their possession, as he spoke to them.

Caput 14

Hoc est quod possederunt filii Israhel in terra Chanaan quam dederunt eis Eleazar, sacerdos, et Iosue, filius Nun, et principes familiarum per tribus Israhel, 2 sorte omnia dividentes, sicut praeceperat Dominus in manu Mosi, novem tribubus et dimidiae tribui, 3 duabus enim tribubus et dimidiae dederat Moses trans Iordanem possessionem, absque Levitis, qui nihil terrae acceperunt inter fratres suos, 4 sed in eorum successerunt locum filii Ioseph in duas divisi tribus, Manasse et Ephraim, nec acceperunt Levitae aliam in terra partem nisi urbes ad habitandum et suburbana earum ad alenda iumenta et pecora sua. 5 Sicut praeceperat Dominus Mosi, ita fecerunt filii Israhel, et diviserunt terram.

6 Accesserunt itaque filii Iuda ad Iosue in Galgala, locutusque est ad eum Chaleb, filius Iepphonne, Cenezeus, "Nosti quid locutus sit Dominus ad Mosen, hominem Dei, de me et te in Cadesbarne. 7 Quadraginta annorum eram quando me misit Moses, famulus Domini, de Cadesbarne ut considerarem terram, nuntiavique ei quod mihi verum

Chapter 14

Caleb's petition. Hebron is given to him and to his seed.

This is what the children of Israel possessed in the land of Canaan which Eleazar, the priest, and Joshua, the son of Nun, and the princes of the families by the tribes of Israel gave to them, 2 dividing all by lot, as the Lord had commanded by the hand of Moses, to the nine tribes and the half-tribe, 3 for to two tribes and a half Moses had given possession beyond the Jordan, besides the Levites, who received no land among their brethren, 4 but in their place succeeded the children of Joseph divided into two tribes, of Manasseh and Ephraim, neither did the Levites receive other portion *of* land but cities to dwell in and their suburbs to feed their beasts and flocks. 5 As the Lord had commanded Moses, so did the children of Israel, and they divided the land.

6 Then the children of Judah came to Joshua in Gilgal, and Caleb, the son of Jephunneh, the Kenizzite, spoke to him, "Thou knowest what the Lord spoke to Moses, the man of God, concerning me and thee in Kadesh-barnea. 7 I was forty years old when Moses, the servant of the Lord, sent me from Kadesh-barnea to view the land, and I *brought*

videbatur. 8 Fratres autem mei qui ascenderant mecum dissolverunt cor populi, et nihilominus ego secutus sum Dominum, Deum meum. 9 Iuravitque Moses in die illo, dicens, 'Terram quam calcavit pes tuus erit possessio tua et filiorum tuorum in aeternum, quia secutus es Dominum, Deum meum.' 10 Concessit ergo Dominus vitam mihi sicut pollicitus est usque in praesentem diem. Quadraginta et quinque anni sunt ex quo locutus est Dominus verbum istud ad Mosen quando ambulabat Israhel per solitudinem. Hodie octoginta quinque annorum sum, 11 sic valens ut eo valebam tempore quando ad explorandum missus sum. Illius in me temporis fortitudo usque hodie perseverat, tam ad bellandum quam ad gradiendum. 12 Da ergo mihi montem istum quem pollicitus est Dominus te quoque audiente in quo Enacim sunt et urbes magnae atque munitae. Si forte sit Dominus mecum, et potuero delere eos sicut promisit mihi."

13 Benedixitque ei Iosue et tradidit ei Hebron in possessionem. 14 Atque ex eo fuit Hebron Chaleb, filio Iepphonne, Cenezeo, usque in praesentem diem, quia secutus est Dominum, Deum Israhel.

15 Nomen Hebron antea vocabatur Cariatharbe; Adam, maximus ibi inter Enacim, situs est, et terra cessavit a proeliis.

him word again as to me seemed true. 8 But my brethren that had gone up with me discouraged the heart of the people, and I nevertheless followed the Lord, my God. 9 And Moses swore in that day, saying, 'The land which thy foot hath trodden upon shall be thy possession and thy children's for ever, because thou hast followed the Lord, my God.' 10 The Lord therefore hath granted me life as he promised until this present day. It is forty and five years since the Lord spoke this word to Moses when Israel journeyed through the wilderness. This day I am eighty-five years old, 11 as strong as I was at that time when I was sent to view the land. The strength of that time continueth in me until this day, as well to fight as to march. 12 Give me therefore this mountain which the Lord promised in thy hearing also wherein are the Anakim and cities great and strong. If *so be, the Lord will be* with me, and I shall be able to destroy them as he promised me."

13 And Joshua blessed him and gave him Hebron in possession. 14 And from that time Hebron belonged to Caleb, the son of Jephunneh, the Kenizzite, until this present day, because he followed the Lord, the God of Israel.

15 The name of Hebron before was called Kiriath-arba; Adam, the greatest among the Anakim, was laid there, and the land rested from wars.

Caput 15

Igitur sors filiorum Iudae per cognationes suas ista fuit: a termino Edom usque desertum Sin contra meridiem et usque ad extremam partem australis plagae. 2 Initium eius a summitate Maris Salsissimi et a lingua eius quae respicit meridiem, 3 egrediturque contra ascensum Scorpionis et pertransit in Sina ascenditque in Cadesbarne et pervenit in Esrom, ascendens ad Addara et circumiens Caricaa, 4 atque inde pertransiens in Asemona et perveniens ad torrentem Aegypti, eruntque termini eius Mare Magnum. Hic erit finis meridianae plagae. 5 Ab oriente vero, erit initium Mare Salsissimum usque ad extrema Iordanis, et ea quae respiciunt ad aquilonem, a lingua maris usque ad eundem Iordanis fluvium. 6 Ascenditque terminus in Bethagla et transit ab aquilone in Betharaba ascendens ad Lapidem Boem, filii Ruben, 7 et tendens usque ad terminos Debera de Valle Achor, contra aquilonem respiciens Galgala quae est ex adverso ascensionis Adommim ab australi parte torrentis, transitque aquas quae vocantur Fons Solis, et erunt exitus eius ad fontem Rogel. 8 Ascenditque per Convallem Filii Ennom ex

Chapter 15

The borders of the lot of Judah. Caleb's portion and conquest. The cities of Judah.

Now the lot of the children of Judah by their kindreds was this: from the frontier of Edom to the desert of Zin southward and to the uttermost part of the south coast. 2 Its beginning was from the top of the Most Salt Sea and from the bay thereof that looketh to the south, 3 and it goeth out towards the ascent of the Scorpion and passeth on to Zin and ascendeth into Kadesh-barnea and reacheth into Hezron, going up to Addar and compassing Karka, 4 and from thence passing along into Azmon and reaching the torrent of Egypt, and the bounds thereof shall be the Great Sea. This shall be the limit of the south coast. 5 But on the east side, the beginning shall be the Most Salt Sea even to the end of the Jordan, and *towards* the north, from the bay of the sea unto the same river *Jordan*. 6 And the border goeth up into Beth-hogla and passeth by the north into Betharabah going up to the Stone of Bohan, the son of Reuben, 7 and reaching as far as the borders of Debir from the Valley of Achor, and so northward looking towards Gilgal which is opposite to the ascent of Adummim on the south side of the torrent, and *the border* passeth the waters that are called the Fountain of the Sun, and the goings out thereof shall be at the fountain Rogel. 8 And it goeth up by the Valley of the

latere Iebusei ad meridiem (haec est Hierusalem) et inde se erigens ad verticem montis qui est contra Gehennom ad occidentem in summitate Vallis Rafaim contra aquilonem. 9 Pertransitque a vertice montis usque ad fontem Aquae Nepthoa et pervenit usque ad vicos Montis Ephron, inclinaturque in Bala, quae est Cariathiarim, id est, "Urbs Silvarum." 10 Et circuit de Bala contra occidentem usque ad Montem Seir transitque iuxta latus Montis Iarim ad aquilonem in Cheslon et descendit in Bethsames transitque in Thamna. 11 Et pervenit contra aquilonem partis Accaron ex latere inclinaturque Sechrona et transit Montem Baala pervenitque in Iebnehel et Maris Magni contra occidentem fine concluditur. 12 Hii sunt termini filiorum Iuda per circuitum in cognationibus suis.

13 Chaleb, vero, filio Iepphonne, dedit partem in medio filiorum Iuda sicut praeceperat ei Dominus: Cariatharbe, patris Enach, ipsa est Hebron. 14 Delevitque ex ea Chaleb tres filios Enach, Sesai et Ahiman et Tholmai de stirpe Enach. 15 Atque inde conscendens venit ad habitatores Dabir quae prius vocabatur Cariathsepher, id est, "Civitas Litterarum," 16 dixitque Chaleb, "Qui percusserit Cariathsepher et ceperit eam, dabo illi Axam, filiam meam, uxorem." 17 Cepitque eam Othonihel, filius Cenez, frater Chaleb iunior, deditque ei Axam, filiam suam, uxorem.

Son of Hinnom on the side of the Jebusite towards the south (*the same* is Jerusalem) and thence *ascending* to the top of the mountain which is over against Geennom to the west in the end of the Valley of Rephaim northward. 9 And it passeth on from the top of the mountain to the fountain of the Water of Nephtoah and reacheth to the towns of Mount Ephron, and it bendeth *towards* Baalah, which is Kiriath-jearim, that is to say, "The City of the Woods." 10 And it compasseth from Baalah westward unto Mount Seir and passeth by the side of Mount Jaerim to the north into Chesalon and goeth down into Beth-shemesh and passeth into Timnah. 11 And it reacheth *northward to a part* of Ekron at the side and bendeth to Shikkeron and passeth Mount Baala and cometh into Jabneel and *is bounded westward with* the Great Sea. 12 These are the borders round about of the children of Judah in their kindreds.

13 But to Caleb, the son of Jephunneh, he gave a portion in the midst of the children of Judah as the Lord had commanded him: Kiriath-arba, the father of Anak, *which* is Hebron. 14 And Caleb destroyed out of it the three sons of Anak, Sheshai and Ahiman and Talmai of the race of Anak. 15 And going up from thence he came to the inhabitants of Debir which before was called Kiriath-sepher, that is to say, "The City of Letters," 16 and Caleb said, "He that shall smite Kiriath-sepher and take it, I will give him Achsah, my daughter, to wife." 17 And Othniel, the son of Kenaz, the younger brother of Caleb, took it, and he gave him Achsaha, his daughter, to wife.

18 Quae cum pergerent simul, suasa est a viro suo ut peteret a patre suo agrum, suspiravitque ut sedebat in asino. Cui Chaleb, "Quid habes?" inquit.

19 At illa respondit, "Da mihi benedictionem. Terram australem et arentem dedisti mihi; iunge et inriguam." Dedit itaque ei Chaleb inriguum superius et inferius.

20 Haec est possessio tribus filiorum Iuda per cognationes suas. 21 Erantque civitates ab extremis partibus filiorum Iuda iuxta terminos Edom a meridie Cabsehel et Eder et Iagur 22 et Cina et Dimona et Adeda 23 et Cedes et Asor et Iethnan, 24 Zif et Thelem et Baloth, 25 Asor Nova et Carioth, Hesrom, haec est Asor, 26 Aman, Same et Molada 27 et Asergadda et Asemon et Bethfeleth 28 et Asersual et Bersabee et Baziothia 29 et Bala et Hiim et Esem 30 et Heltholad et Exiil et Harma 31 et Siceleg et Medemena et Sensenna, 32 Lebaoth et Selim et Aen et Remmon: omnes civitates viginti novem, et villae earum. 33 In campestribus vero: Esthaul et Saraa et Asena 34 et Azanoe et Aengannim et Thaffua et Aenaim 35 et Hierimoth et Adulam, Soccho et Azeca 36 et Saraim et Adithaim et Gedera et Giderothaim: urbes quattuordecim et villae earum; 37 Sanan et Adesa et Magdalgad, 38 Delean et Mesfa et Iecthel, 39 Lachis et Bascath et Aglon, 40 Thebbon et Lehemas et Chethlis 41 et Gideroth et Bethdagon et Neema et Maceda: civitates sedecim et villae earum; 42 Labana et Aether et Asan, 43 Ieptha et Esna et Nesib 44 et Ceila et Achzib et Maresa: civitates novem et villae earum;

18 And as they were going together, she was moved by her husband to ask a field of her father, and she sighed as she sat on her ass. And Caleb said to her, "What aileth thee?"

19 But she answered, "Give me a blessing. Thou hast given me a southern and dry land; *give me also a land that is watered.*" And Caleb gave her the upper and the nether watery ground.

20 This is the possession of the tribe of the children of Judah by their kindreds. 21 And the cities from the uttermost parts of the children of Judah by the borders of Edom to the south were Kabzeel and Eder and Jagur 22 and Kinah and Dimonah and Adadah 23 and Kedesh and Hazor and Ithnan, 24 Ziph and Telem and Bealoth, 25 New Hazor and Kerioth, Hezron, which is Hazor, 26 Amam, Shema and Moladah 27 and Hazar-gaddah and Heshmon and Beth-pelet 28 and Hazar-shual and Beer-sheba and Biziothiah 29 and Baalah and Iim and Ezem 30 and Eltolad and Chesil and Hormah 31 and Ziklag and Madmannah and Sansannah, 32 Lebaoth and Shilhim and Ain and Rimmon: all the cities twenty-nine, and their villages. 33 But in the plains: Eshtaol and Zorah and Ashnah 34 and Zanoah and En-gannim and Tappuah and Enam 35 and Jarmuth and Adullam, Socoh and Azekah 36 and Shaaraim and Adithaim and Gederah and Gederothaim: fourteen cities and their villages; 37 Zenan and Hadashah and Migdal-gad, 38 Dilan and Mizpeh and Jokthe-el, 39 Lachish and Bozkath and Eglon, 40 Cabbon and Lahmam and Chitlish 41 and Gederoth and Beth-dagon and Naamah and Makkedah: sixteen cities and their villages; 42 Libnah and Ether and Ashan, 43 Iphtah and Ashnah and Nezib 44 and Keila and Achzib and Mareshah: nine cities and their

45 Accaron cum vicis et villulis suis, 46 ab Accaron usque ad mare, omnia quae vergunt ad Azotum et viculos eius, 47 Azotus cum vicis et villulis suis, Gaza cum viculis et villulis suis, usque ad torrentem Aegypti et Mare Magnum, terminus eius. 48 Et in monte Samir et Iether et Soccho 49 et Edenna et Cariathsenna (haec est Dabir), 50 Anab et Isthemo et Anim, 51 Gosen et Olon et Gilo: civitates undecim et villae earum; 52 Arab et Roma et Esaan 53 et Ianum et Bethafua et Afeca, 54 Ammatha et Cariatharbe (haec est Hebron) et Sior: civitates novem et villae earum; 55 Maon et Chermel et Zif et Iotae, 56 Iezrehel et Iucadam et Zanoe, 57 Accaim, Gebaa et Thamna: civitates decem et villae earum; 58 Alul et Bethsur et Gedor, 59 Mareth et Bethanoth et Elthecen: civitates sex et villae earum; 60 Cariathbaal (haec est Cariathiarim, Urbs Silvarum) et Arebba: civitates duae et villae earum. 61 In deserto Betharaba, Meddin et Schacha 62 et Anepsan et Civitas Salis et Engaddi: civitates sex et villae earum. 63 Iebuseum autem habitatorem Hierusalem non potuerunt filii Iuda delere, habitavitque Iebuseus cum filiis Iuda in Hierusalem usque in praesentem diem.

villages; 45 Ekron with the towns and villages thereof, 46 from Ekron even to the sea, all places that lie towards Ashdod and the villages thereof, 47 Ashdod with its towns and villages, Gaza with its towns and villages, even to the torrent of Egypt and the Great Sea *that is* the border thereof. 48 And in the mountain Shammir and Jattir and Socoh 49 and Dannah and Kiriath-sannah (this is Debir), 50 Anab and Eshtemoh and Anim, 51 Goshen and Holon and Giloh: eleven cities and their villages; 52 Arab and Dumah and Eshan 53 and Janim and Beth-tappuah and Aphekah, 54 Humtah and Kiriath-arba (this is Hebron) and Zior: nine cities and their villages; 55 Maon and Carmel and Ziph and Juttah, 56 Jezreel and Jokdeam and Zanoah, 57 Kain, Gibeah and Timnah: ten cities and their villages; 58 Halhul and Beth-zur and Gedor, 59 Maarath and Beth-anoth and Eltekon: six cities and their villages; 60 Kiriath-baal (the same is Kiriath-jearim, the City of Woods) and Rabbah: two cities and their villages. 61 In the desert Beth-arabah, Middin and Secacah 62 and Nibshan and the City of Salt and En-gedi: six cities and their villages. 63 But the children of Judah could not destroy the Jebusite that dwelt in Jerusalem, and the Jebusite dwelt with the children of Judah in Jerusalem until this present day.

Caput 16

Cecidit quoque sors filiorum Ioseph ab Iordane contra Hiericho et aquas eius ab oriente: solitudo quae ascendit de Hiericho ad montana Bethel 2 et egreditur de Bethel Luzam transitque terminum Archi Atharoth 3 et descendit ad occidentem iuxta terminum Ieflethi usque ad terminos Bethoron Inferioris et Gazer, finiunturque regiones eius Mari Magno. 4 Possederuntque filii Ioseph, Manasse et Ephraim. 5 Et factus est terminus filiorum Ephraim per cognationes suas, et possessio eorum contra orientem Atharothaddar usque Bethoron Superiorem, 6 egrediunturque confinia in mare, Machmethath vero aquilonem respicit, et circuit terminus contra orientem in Thanathselo et pertransit ab oriente Ianoe, 7 descenditque de Ianoe in Atharoth et Noaratha, et pervenit in Hiericho et egreditur ad Iordanem. 8 De Taffua pertransit contra mare in Vallem Harundineti, suntque egressus eius in Mare Salsissimum. Haec est possessio tribus filiorum Ephraim per familias suas, 9 urbesque quae separatae sunt filiis Ephraim in medio possessionis

Chapter 16

The lot of the sons of Joseph. The borders of the tribe of Ephraim.

And the lot of the sons of Joseph fell from the Jordan over against Jericho and the waters thereof on the east: the wilderness which goeth up from Jericho to the mountain of Bethel 2 and goeth out from Bethel to Luza and passeth the border of Archi to Ataroth 3 and goeth down westward by the border of Jephleti unto the borders of Beth-horon the Nether and to Gezer, and the countries of it are ended by the Great Sea. 4 And Manasseh and Ephraim, the children of Joseph, possessed it. 5 And the border of the children of Ephraim *was* according to their kindreds, and their possession towards the east was Ataroth-addar unto Beth-horon the Upper, 6 and the confines go out unto the sea, but Michmethath looketh to the north, and it goeth round the borders eastward into Taanath-shiloh and passeth along on the east side to Janoah, 7 and it goeth down from Janoah into Ataroth and Naarah, and it cometh to Jericho and goeth out to the Jordan. 8 From Tappuah it passeth on towards the sea into the Valley of Reeds, and the goings out thereof are at the Most Salt Sea. This is the possession of the tribe of the children of Ephraim by their families, 9 and there were cities with their villages separated for the children of Ephraim in

filiorum Manasse et villae earum, 10 et non interfecerunt filii Ephraim Chananeum qui habitabat in Gazer, habitavitque Chananeus in medio Ephraim usque in diem hanc tributarius.

Caput 17

Cecidit autem sors tribui Manasse (ipse est enim primogenitus Ioseph), Machir, primogenito Manasse, patri Galaad, qui fuit vir pugnator habuitque possessionem Galaad et Basan, 2 et reliquis filiorum Manasse iuxta familias suas, filiis Abiezer et filiis Elech et filiis Esrihel et filiis Sechem et filiis Epher et filiis Semida: isti sunt filii Manasse, filii Ioseph, mares, per cognationes suas.

3 Salphaad vero, filio Epher, filii Galaad, filii Machir, filii Manasse, non erant filii sed solae filiae, quarum ista sunt nomina: Maala et Noa et Egla et Melcha et Thersa. 4 Veneruntque in conspectu Eleazari, sacerdotis, et Iosue, filii Nun, et principum, dicentes, "Dominus praecepit per manum Mosi

the midst of the possession of the children of Manasseh, 10 and the children of Ephraim slew not the Canaanite who dwelt in Gezer, and the Canaanite dwelt in the midst of Ephraim until this day, paying tribute.

Chapter 17

The lot of the half-tribe of Manasseh.

And *this* lot fell to the tribe of Manasseh (for he is the firstborn of Joseph), to Machir, the firstborn of Manasseh, the father of Gilead, who was a warlike man and had for possession Gilead and Bashan, 2 and to the rest of the children of Manasseh according to their families, to the children of Abiezer and to the children of Helek and to the children of Asriel and to the children of Shechem and to the children of Hepher and to the children of Shemida: these are the male children of Manasseh, the son of Joseph, by their kindreds.

3 But Zelophehad, the son of Hepher, the son of Gilead, the son of Machir, the son of Manasseh, had no sons but only daughters, whose names are these: Mahlah and Noah and Hoglah and Milcah and Tirzah. 4 And they came in the presence of Eleazar, the priest, and of Joshua, the son of Nun, and of the princes, saying, "The Lord commanded by the hand of Moses that a possession should be given us in

ut daretur nobis possessio in medio fratrum nostrorum."
Deditque eis iuxta imperium Domini possessionem in medio fratrum patris earum.

5 Et ceciderunt funiculi Manasse decem absque terra Galaad et Basan trans Iordanem, 6 filiae enim Manasse possederunt hereditatem in medio filiorum eius, terra autem Galaad
cecidit in sortem filiorum Manasse qui reliqui erant. 7 Fuitque terminus Manasse, ab Aser, Machmathath quae respicit
Sychem, et egreditur ad dextram iuxta habitatores fontis
Taffuae, 8 etenim in sorte Manasse ceciderat terra Taffuae,
quae est iuxta terminos Manasse filiorum Ephraim. 9 Descenditque terminus Vallis Harundineti, in meridiem torrentis civitatum Ephraim, quae in medio sunt urbium Manasse. Terminus Manasse ab aquilone torrentis, et exitus
eius pergit ad mare, 10 ita ut ab austro sit possessio Ephraim
et ab aquilone Manasse, et utramque claudat mare, et co-
niungantur sibi in tribu Aser ab aquilone et in tribu Isachar
ab oriente. 11 Fuitque hereditas Manasse in Isachar et in
Aser Bethsan et viculi eius et Ieblaam cum villulis suis et habitatores Dor cum oppidis suis, habitatores quoque Hendor
cum villulis suis similiterque habitatores Thanach cum villulis suis et habitatores Mageddo cum viculis suis et tertia pars
urbis Nofeth. 12 Nec potuerunt filii Manasse has subvertere

the midst of our brethren." And he gave them according to the commandment of the Lord a possession amongst the brethren of their father.

5 And there fell ten portions to Manasseh beside the land of Gilead and Bashan beyond the Jordan, 6 for the daughters of Manasseh possessed inheritance in the midst of his sons, and the land of Gilead fell to the lot of the rest of the children of Manasseh. 7 And the border of Manasseh was, from Asher, Michmethath which looketh towards Shechem, and it goeth out on the right hand by the inhabitants of the fountain of Tappuah, 8 for *the lot of Manasseh took in the land* of Tappuah, which is on the borders of Manasseh *and belongs to the children* of Ephraim. 9 And *the border goeth down to the Valley of the Reeds,* to the south of the torrent of the cities of Ephraim, which are in the midst of the cities of Manasseh. The border of Manasseh is on the north side of the torrent, and the outgoings of it are at the sea, 10 so that the possession of Ephraim is on the south and on the north that of Manasseh, and the sea *is the border of* both, and they are joined together in the tribe of Asher on the north and in the tribe of Issachar on the east. 11 And the inheritance of Manasseh in Issachar and in Asher was Beth-shean and its villages and Ibleam with its villages and the inhabitants of Dor with the towns thereof, the inhabitants also of En-dor with the villages thereof and in like manner the inhabitants of Taanach with the villages thereof and the inhabitants of Megiddo with their villages and the third part of the city of Naphath. 12 Neither could the children of Manasseh over-

civitates, sed coepit Chananeus habitare in terra sua. 13 Postquam autem convaluerunt filii Israhel, subiecerunt Chananeos et fecerunt sibi tributarios, nec interfecerunt eos.

14 Locutique sunt filii Ioseph ad Iosue atque dixerunt, "Quare dedisti mihi possessionem sortis et funiculi unius, cum sim tantae multitudinis et benedixerit mihi Dominus?"

15 Ad quos Iosue ait, "Si populus multus es, ascende in silvam, et succide tibi spatia in terra Ferezei et Rafaim, quia angusta est tibi possessio montis Ephraim."

16 Cui responderunt filii Ioseph, "Non poterimus ad montana conscendere, cum ferreis curribus utantur Chananei qui habitant in terra campestri in qua sitae sunt Bethsan cum viculis suis et Iezrahel mediam possidens vallem."

17 Dixitque Iosue ad domum Ioseph, Ephraim et Manasse, "Populus multus es et magnae fortitudinis; non habebis sortem unam. 18 Sed transibis ad montem et succides tibi atque purgabis ad habitandum spatia et poteris ultra procedere cum subverteris Chananeum, quem dicis ferreos habere currus et esse fortissimum."

throw these cities, but the Canaanite began to dwell in his land. 13 But after that the children of Israel were grown strong, they subdued the Canaanites and made them their tributaries, and they did not kill them.

14 And the children of Joseph spoke to Joshua and said, "Why hast thou given me *but one lot and one portion to possess,* whereas I am of so great a multitude and the Lord hath blessed me?"

15 And Joshua said to them, "If thou be a great people, go up into the woodland, and cut down room for thyself in the land of the Perizzite and the Rephaim, because the possession of Mount Ephraim is *too* narrow for thee."

16 And the children of Joseph answered him, "We cannot go up to the mountains, for the Canaanites that dwell in the *low lands* wherein are situate Beth-shean with its towns and Jezreel *in* the midst of the valley *have* chariots of iron."

17 And Joshua said to the house of Joseph, to Ephraim and Manasseh, "Thou art a great people and of great strength; thou shalt not have one lot only. 18 But thou shalt pass to the mountain and shalt cut down *the wood* and make thyself room to dwell in and mayst proceed farther when thou hast destroyed the Canaanite, who as thou sayest have iron chariots and are very strong."

Caput 18

Congregatique sunt omnes filii Israhel in Silo, ibique fixerunt Tabernaculum Testimonii, et fuit eis terra subiecta. 2 Remanserant autem filiorum Israhel septem tribus quae necdum acceperant possessiones suas, 3 ad quos Iosue ait, "Usquequo marcetis ignavia et non intratis ad possidendam terram quam Dominus, Deus patrum vestrorum, dedit vobis? 4 Eligite de singulis tribubus ternos viros ut mittam eos et pergant atque circumeant terram et describant eam iuxta numerum uniuscuiusque multitudinis referantque ad me quod descripserint. 5 Dividite vobis terram in septem partes; Iudas sit in terminis suis ab australi plaga et domus Ioseph ab aquilone. 6 Mediam inter hos terram in septem partes describite, et huc venietis ad me ut coram Domino, Deo vestro, mittam vobis sortem, 7 quia non est inter vos pars Levitarum, sed sacerdotium Domini est eorum hereditas. Gad autem et Ruben et dimidia tribus Manasse iam acceperant possessiones suas trans Iordanem ad orientalem plagam quas dedit eis Moses, famulus Domini."

Chapter 18

Surveyors are sent to divide the rest of the land into seven tribes. The lot of Benjamin.

And all the children of Israel assembled together in Shiloh, and there they set up the Tabernacle of the Testimony, and the land was subdued before them. 2 But there remained seven tribes of the children of Israel which as yet had not received their possessions, 3 and Joshua said to them, "How long are you *indolent and slack* and go not in to possess the land which the Lord, the God of your fathers, hath given you? 4 Choose of every tribe three men that I may send them and they may go and compass the land and mark it out according to the number of each multitude and bring back to me what they have marked out. 5 Divide to yourselves the land into seven parts; let Judah be in his bounds on the south side and the house of Joseph on the north. 6 The land in the midst between these mark ye out into seven parts, and you shall come hither to me that I may cast *lots* for you before the Lord, your God, 7 for the Levites have no part among you, but the priesthood of the Lord is their inheritance. And Gad and Reuben and the half tribe of Manasseh have already received their possessions beyond the Jordan *eastward* which Moses, the servant of the Lord, gave them."

8 Cumque surrexissent viri ut pergerent ad describendam terram, praecepit eis Iosue, dicens, "Circuite terram, et describite eam, ac revertimini ad me ut hic coram Domino in Silo mittam vobis sortem."

9 Itaque perrexerunt et lustrantes eam in septem partes diviserunt, scribentes in volumine. Reversique sunt ad Iosue, in castra Silo. 10 Qui misit sortes coram Domino in Silo divisitque terram filiis Israhel in septem partes. 11 Et ascendit sors prima filiorum Beniamin per familias suas ut possiderent terram inter filios Iuda et filios Ioseph, 12 fuitque terminus eorum contra aquilonem ab Iordane pergens iuxta latus Hiericho septentrionalis plagae et inde contra occidentem ad montana conscendens et perveniens ad solitudinem Bethaven 13 atque pertransiens iuxta Luzam ad meridiem (ipsa est Bethel), descenditque in Atharothaddar in montem qui est ad meridiem Bethoron Inferioris, 14 et inclinatur circumiens contra mare ad meridiem montis qui respicit Bethoron contra africum, suntque exitus eius in Cariathbaal, quae vocatur et Cariathiarim, urbem filiorum Iuda. Haec est plaga contra mare ad occidentem. 15 A meridie autem ex parte Cariathiarim egreditur terminus contra mare et pervenit usque ad fontem aquarum Nepthoa, 16 descenditque in partem montis qui respicit Vallem Filiorum Ennom et est contra septentrionalem plagam in extrema parte Vallis Rafaim, descenditque in Gehennom, id est, Val-

8 And when the men were risen up to go to mark out the land, Joshua commanded them, saying, "Go round the land, and mark it out, and return to me *that* I may cast *lots* for you before the Lord in Shiloh."

9 So they went and surveying it divided it into seven parts, writing them down in a book. And they returned to Joshua, to the camp in Shiloh. 10 And he cast lots before the Lord in Shiloh and divided the land to the children of Israel into seven parts. 11 And first came up the lot of the children of Benjamin by their families to possess the land between the children of Judah and the children of Joseph, 12 and their border northward was from the Jordan going along by the side of Jericho on the north side and thence going up westward to the mountains and reaching to the wilderness of Beth-aven 13 and passing along southward by Luz (the same is Bethel), and it goeth down into Ataroth-addar to the mountain that is on the south of the Nether Beth-horon, 14 and it bendeth thence going round towards the sea south of the mountain that looketh towards Beth-horon to the southwest, and the outgoings thereof are into Kiriath-baal, which is called also Kiriath-jearim, a city of the children of Judah. This is their coast towards the sea westward. 15 But on the south side the border goeth out from part of Kiriath-jearim towards the sea and cometh to the fountain of the waters of Nephtoah, 16 and it goeth down to that part of the mountain that looketh on the Valley of the Children of Hinnom and is over against the north quarter in the furthermost part of the Valley of Rephaim, and it goeth down into Geennom, that is, the Valley of Hinnom, by the side of the

lis Ennom, iuxta latus Iebusei ad austrum et pervenit ad fontem Rogel, 17 transiens ad aquilonem et egrediens ad Aensemes, id est, "Fontem Solis." 18 Et pertransit usque ad tumulos qui sunt e regione ascensus Adommim, descenditque ad Abenboen, id est, Lapidem Boen, filii Ruben, et pertransit ex latere aquilonis ad campestria descenditque in planitiem, 19 et praetergreditur contra aquilonem Bethagla suntque exitus eius contra linguam Maris Salsissimi ab aquilone in fine Iordanis ad australem plagam, 20 qui est terminus illius ab oriente. Haec est possessio filiorum Beniamin per terminos suos in circuitu et familias suas, 21 fueruntque civitates eius Hiericho et Bethagla et Vallis Casis, 22 Betharaba et Semaraim et Bethel 23 et Avim et Affara et Ofra, 24 villa Emona et Ofni et Gabee: civitates duodecim et villae earum; 25 Gabaon et Rama et Beroth 26 et Mesfe et Cafera et Ammosa 27 et Recem, Iarafel et Tharala 28 et Sela, Eleph et Iebus (quae est Hierusalem), Gabaath et Cariath: civitates quattuordecim et villae earum. Haec est possessio filiorum Beniamin iuxta familias suas.

Jebusite to the south and cometh to the fountain of Rogel, 17 passing thence to the north and going out to En-shemesh, that is to say, "The Fountain of the Sun." 18 And it passeth along to the hills that are over against the ascent of Adummim, and it goeth down to Abenboen, that is, the Stone of Bohan, the son of Reuben, and it passeth on the north side to the champaign countries and goeth down into the plain, 19 and it passeth by Beth-hoglah northward, and the outgoings thereof are *towards the north* of the Most Salt Sea *at the south end* of the Jordan, 20 which is the border of it on the east side. This is the possession of the children of Benjamin by their borders round about and their families, 21 and their cities were Jericho and Beth-hoglah and Vale-Casis, 22 Betharabah and Zemaraim and Bethel 23 and Avvim and Parah and Ophrah, 24 the town Ammoni and Ophni and Geba: twelve cities and their villages; 25 Gibeah and Ramah and Beeroth 26 and Mizpeh and Chephirah and Mozah 27 and Rekem, Irpeel and Taralah 28 and Zela, Haeleph and Jebus (which is Jerusalem), Gibeah and Kiriath: fourteen cities and their villages. This is the possession of the children of Benjamin by their families.

Caput 19

Et egressa est sors secunda filiorum Symeon per cognationes suas, fuitque hereditas 2 eorum in medio possessionis filiorum Iuda, Bersabee et Sabee et Molada 3 et Asersual, Bala et Asem 4 et Heltholath, Bethul et Arma 5 et Seceleg et Bethmarchaboth et Asersusa 6 et Bethlebaoth et Saroen: civitates tredecim et villae earum; 7 Ahin et Remmon et Athar et Asan: civitates quattuor et villae earum; 8 omnes viculi per circuitum urbium istarum usque ad Balaath Ber Rameth contra australem plagam. Haec est hereditas filiorum Symeon iuxta cognationes suas 9 in funiculo et possessione filiorum Iuda, quia maior erat, et idcirco possederunt filii Symeon in medio hereditatis eorum.

10 Ceciditque sors tertia filiorum Zabulon per cognationes suas, et factus est terminus possessionis eorum usque Sarith, 11 ascenditque de mari et Medala ac pervenit in Debbaseth usque ad torrentem qui est contra Iecennam, 12 et revertitur de Sarith contra orientem in fines Ceseleththabor, et egreditur ad Dabereth ascenditque contra Iafie, 13 et inde pertransit ad orientalem plagam Getthefer et

Chapter 19

The lots of the tribes of Simeon, Zebulun, Issachar, Asher, Naphtali and Dan. A city is given to Joshua.

And the second lot came forth *for* the children of Simeon by their kindreds, and their inheritance was 2 in the midst of the possession of the children of Judah, Beer-sheba and Sheba and Moladah 3 and Hazar-shual, Balah and Ezem 4 and Eltolad, Bethul and Hormah 5 and Ziklag and Beth-marcaboth and Hazar-susah 6 and Beth-lebaoth and Shar-uhen: thirteen cities and their villages; 7 Ain and Rimmon and Ether and Ashan: four cities and their villages; 8 *and* all the villages round about these cities to Baalath Beer Ramath to the south quarter. This is the inheritance of the children of Simeon according to their kindreds 9 in the possession and lot of the children of Judah, because it was too great, and therefore the children of Simeon had their possession in the midst of their inheritance.

10 And the third lot fell *to* the children of Zebulun by their kindreds, and the border of their possession *was* unto Sarid, 11 and it went up from the sea and from Maralah and came to Dabbesheth as far as the torrent which is over against Jokneam, 12 and it returneth from Sarid eastward to the borders of Chiseloth-tabor, and it goeth out to Daberath and ascendeth towards Japhia, 13 and it passeth along from thence to the east side of Gath-hepher and Eth-kazin and

Thacasin, et egreditur in Remmon, Ampthar et Noa, 14 et circuit ad aquilonem Nathon, suntque egressus eius Vallis Iepthahel 15 et Catheth et Nehalal et Semron et Iedala et Bethleem: civitates duodecim et villae earum. 16 Haec est hereditas tribus filiorum Zabulon per cognationes suas, urbes et viculi earum.

17 Isachar egressa est sors quarta per cognationes suas, 18 fuitque eius hereditas Hiezrahel et Chasaloth et Sunem 19 et Afaraim et Seon et Anaarath 20 et Rabbith et Cesion, Abes 21 et Rameth et Engannim et Enadda et Bethfeses, 22 et pervenit terminus eius usque Thabor et Seesima et Bethsemes, erantque exitus eius Iordanes: civitates sedecim et villae earum. 23 Haec est possessio filiorum Isachar per cognationes suas, urbes et viculi earum.

24 Ceciditque sors quinta tribui filiorum Aser per cognationes suas, 25 fuitque terminus eorum Alchath et Oali et Beten et Axab 26 et Elmelech et Amaad et Messal, et pervenit usque ad Carmelum maris et Sior et Labanath, 27 ac revertitur contra orientem Bethdagon et pertransit usque Zabulon et Vallem Iepthahel contra aquilonem in Bethemech et Neihel, egrediturque ad levam Chabul 28 et Achran et Roob et Amon et Canae usque ad Sidonem Magnam, 29 revertiturque in Orma usque ad civitatem munitissimam Tyrum et usque Osa, eruntque exitus eius in mare de funiculo Acziba 30 et Amma et Afec et Roob: civitates viginti duae et villae earum. 31 Haec est possessio filiorum Aser per cognationes suas urbesque et viculi earum.

goeth out to Rimmon, Amthar and Neah, 14 and it turneth about to the north of Hannathon, and the outgoings thereof are the Valley of Iphtah-el 15 and Kattath and Nahalal and Shimron and Idalah and Bethlehem: twelve cities and their villages. 16 This is the inheritance of the tribe of the children of Zebulun by their kindreds, the cities and their villages.

17 The fourth lot came out to Issachar by their kindreds, 18 and his inheritance was Jezreel and Chesulloth and Shunem 19 and Hapharaim and Shion and Anaharath 20 and Rabbith and Kishion, Ebez 21 and Remeth and En-gannim and En-haddah and Beth-pazzez, 22 and the border thereof cometh to Tabor and Shahazumah and Beth-shemesh, and the outgoings thereof *shall be at* the Jordan: sixteen cities and their villages. 23 This is the possession of the sons of Issachar by their kindreds, the cities and their villages.

24 And the fifth lot fell to the tribe of the children of Asher by their kindreds, 25 and their border was Helkath and Hali and Beten and Achshaph 26 and Allammelech and Amad and Mishal, and it reacheth to Carmel by the sea and Shihor and Libnath, 27 and it returneth towards the east to Beth-dagon and passeth along to Zebulun and to the Valley of Iphtah-el towards the north to Beth-emek and Neiel, and it goeth out to the left side of Cabul 28 and to Ebron and Rehob and Hamon and Kanah as far as the Great Sidon, 29 and it returneth to Ramah to the strong city of Tyre and to Hosah, and the outgoings thereof shall be at the sea from the portion of Achzib 30 and Ummah and Aphek and Rehob: twenty-two cities and their villages. 31 This is the possession of the children of Asher by their kindreds and the cities and their villages.

32 Filiorum Nepthalim sexta sors cecidit per familias suas, 33 et coepit terminus de Heleb et Helon in Sananim et Adami, quae est Neceb, et Iebnahel usque Lecum et egressus eorum usque ad Iordanem, 34 revertiturque terminus contra occidentem in Aznoththabor atque inde egreditur in Ucoca et pertransit in Zabulon contra meridiem et in Aser contra occidentem et in Iuda ad Iordanem contra ortum solis. 35 Civitates munitissimae Aseddim, Ser et Ammath et Recchath et Chenereth 36 et Edema et Arama, Asor 37 et Cedes et Edrai, Nasor 38 et Ieron et Magdalel, Horem et Bethanath et Bethsemes: civitates decem et novem et villae earum. 39 Haec est possessio tribus filiorum Nepthali per cognationes suas, urbes et viculi earum.

40 Tribui filiorum Dan per familias suas egressa est sors septima, 41 et fuit terminus possessionis eius Saraa et Esthaol et Ahirsemes, id est, Civitas Solis, 42 Selebin et Ahialon et Iethela, 43 Helon et Themna et Acron, 44 Helthecen, Gebthon et Baalath, 45 et Iud et Bene et Barach et Gethremmon 46 et Meiarcon et Areccon cum termino qui respicit Ioppen 47 et ipso fine concluditur. Ascenderuntque filii Dan et pugnaverunt contra Lesem ceperuntque eam, et percusserunt eam in ore gladii ac possederunt et habitaverunt in ea, vocantes nomen eius Lesem Dan ex nomine Dan, patris sui. 48 Haec est possessio tribus filiorum Dan per cognationes suas, urbes et viculi earum.

49 Cumque conplesset terram sorte dividere singulis per tribus suas, dederunt filii Israhel possessionem Iosue, filio Nun, in medio sui 50 iuxta praeceptum Domini, urbem quam

32 The sixth lot came out *to* the sons of Naphtali by their families, 33 and the border began from Heleph and Elon to Zaanannim and Adami, which is Nekeb, and Jabneel even to Lakkum and their outgoings unto the Jordan, 34 and the border returneth westward to Azanoth-tabor and goeth out from thence to Hukkok and passeth along to Zebulun southward and to Asher westward and to Judah upon the Jordan towards the rising of the sun. 35 And the strong cities are Ziddim, Zer and Hamath and Rakkath and Chinnereth 36 and Adamah and Ramah, Hazor 37 and Kedesh and Edrei, En-hazor 38 and Iron and Migdal-el, Horem and Beth-anath and Beth-shemesh: nineteen cities and their villages. 39 This is the possession of the tribe of the children of Naphtali by their kindreds, the cities and their villages.

40 The seventh lot came out to the tribe of the children of Dan by their families, 41 and the border of their possession was Zorah and Eshtaol and Ir-shemesh, that is, the City of the Sun, 42 Shaalabbin and Aijalon and Ithlah, 43 Elon and Timnah and Ekron, 44 Eltekeh, Gibbethon and Baalath 45 and Jehud and Bene and Berak and Gath-rimmon 46 and Me-jarkon and Rakkon with the border that looketh towards Joppa 47 and is *terminated there.* And the children of Dan went up and fought against Leshem and took it, and they *put it to the sword* and possessed it and dwelt in it, calling the name of it Leshem Dan by the name of Dan, their father. 48 This is the possession of the tribe of the sons of Dan by their kindreds, the cities and their villages.

49 And when he had made an end of dividing the land by lot to each one by their tribes, the children of Israel gave a possession to Joshua, the son of Nun, in the midst of them 50 according to the commandment of the Lord, the city

postulavit, Thamnath Seraa, in Monte Ephraim, et aedificavit civitatem habitavitque in ea.

51 Hae sunt possessiones quas sorte diviserunt Eleazar,
sacerdos, et Iosue, filius Nun, et principes familiarum ac tribuum filiorum Israhel in Silo coram Domino ad ostium Tabernaculi Testimonii, partitique sunt terram.

Caput 20

Et locutus est Dominus ad Iosue, dicens, "Loquere filiis
Israhel, et dic eis, 2 'Separate urbes fugitivorum de quibus
locutus sum ad vos per manum Mosi 3 ut confugiat ad eas
quicumque animam percusserit nescius et possit evadere
iram proximi, qui ultor est sanguinis. 4 Cum ad unam harum
confugerit civitatum, stabit ante portam civitatis et loquetur
senioribus urbis illius ea quae se conprobent innocentem,
sicque suscipient eum et dabunt ei locum ad habitandum.
5 Cumque ultor sanguinis eum fuerit persecutus, non tradent in manus eius, quia ignorans percussit proximum eius
nec ante biduum triduumve eius probatur inimicus, 6 et habitabit in civitate illa donec stet ante iudicium causam red-

which he asked for, Timnath Serah, in Mount Ephraim, and he built up the city and dwelt in it.

51 These are the possessions which Eleazar, the priest, and Joshua, the son of Nun, and the princes of the families and of the tribes of the children of Israel distributed by lot in Shiloh before the Lord at the door of the Tabernacle of the Testimony, and they divided the land.

Chapter 20

The cities of refuge are appointed for casual manslaughter.

And the Lord spoke to Joshua, saying, "Speak to the children of Israel, and say to them, 2 *Appoint* cities of *refuge* of which I spoke to you by the hand of Moses 3 that whosoever shall kill a *person* unawares may flee to them and may escape the wrath of the kinsman, who is the avenger of blood. 4 And when he shall flee to one of these cities, he shall stand before the gate of the city and shall speak to the ancients of that city *such things* as prove him innocent, and so shall they receive him and give him a place to dwell in. 5 And when the avenger of blood shall pursue him, they shall not deliver him into his hands, because he slew his neighbour unawares and is not proved to have been his enemy two or three days before, 6 and he shall dwell in that city till he stand before judgment *to give an account* of his fact and till *the death of the high*

dens facti sui et moriatur sacerdos magnus qui fuerit in illo tempore. Tunc revertetur homicida et ingredietur civitatem et domum suam de qua fugerat.'"

7 Decreveruntque Cedes in Galilea Montis Nepthali et Sychem in Monte Ephraim et Cariatharbe (ipsa est Hebron) in monte Iuda. 8 Et trans Iordanem contra orientalem plagam Hiericho, statuerunt Bosor, quae sita est in campestri solitudine de tribu Ruben, et Ramoth in Galaad de tribu Gad et Gaulon in Basan de tribu Manasse. 9 Hae civitates constitutae sunt cunctis filiis Israhel et advenis qui habitabant inter eos, ut fugeret ad eas qui animam nescius percussisset et non moreretur in manu proximi effusum sanguinem vindicare cupientis donec staret ante populum expositurus causam suam.

Caput 21

Accesseruntque principes familiarum Levi ad Eleazar, sacerdotem, et Iosue, filium Nun, et ad duces cognationum per singulas tribus filiorum Israhel, 2 locutique sunt ad eos in Silo terrae Chanaan atque dixerunt, "Dominus praecepit

priest who shall be at that time. Then shall the manslayer return and go into his own city and house from whence he fled.'"

7 And they appointed Kedesh in Galilee of Mount Naphtali and Shechem in Mount Ephraim and Kiriath-arba (the same is Hebron) in the mountain of Judah. 8 And beyond the Jordan to the east of Jericho, they appointed Bezer, which is upon the plain of the wilderness of the tribe of Reuben, and Ramoth in Gilead of the tribe of Gad and Golan in Bashan of the tribe of Manasseh. 9 These cities were appointed for all the children of Israel and for the strangers that dwelt among them, that *whosoever* had killed a person unawares might flee to them and not die by the hand of the kinsman coveting to revenge the blood that was shed until he should stand before the people to lay open his cause.

Chapter 21

Cities with their suburbs are assigned for the priests and Levites.

Then the princes of the families of Levi came to Eleazar, the priest, and to Joshua, the son of Nun, and to the princes of the kindreds *of* all the tribes of the children of Israel, 2 and they spoke to them in Shiloh in the land of Canaan and said, "The Lord commanded by the hand of Moses that cities

per manum Mosi ut darentur nobis urbes ad habitandum et suburbana earum ad alenda iumenta."

3 Dederuntque filii Israhel de possessionibus suis, iuxta imperium Domini, civitates et suburbana earum. 4 Egressaque est sors in familiam Caath filiorum Aaron, sacerdotis, de tribubus Iuda et Symeon et Beniamin, civitates tredecim, 5 et reliquis filiorum Caath, id est, Levitis qui superfuerant de tribubus Ephraim et Dan et dimidia tribu Manasse, civitates decem, 6 porro filiis Gerson egressa est sors ut acciperent de tribubus Isachar et Aser et Nepthalim dimidiaque tribu Manasse in Basan civitates numero tredecim, 7 et filiis Merari per cognationes suas, de tribubus Ruben et Gad et Zabulon, urbes duodecim. 8 Dederuntque filii Israhel Levitis civitates et suburbana earum sicut praecepit Dominus per manum Mosi, singulis sorte tribuentes.

9 De tribubus filiorum Iuda et Symeon, dedit Iosue civitates quarum ista sunt nomina: 10 filiis Aaron per familias Caath Levitici generis, prima enim sors illis egressa est, 11 Cariatharbe, patris Enach, quae vocatur Hebron, in monte Iuda et suburbana eius per circuitum. 12 Agros vero et villas eius dederat Chaleb, filio Iepphonne, ad possidendum. 13 Dedit ergo filiis Aaron, sacerdotis, Hebron, confugii civitatem, ac suburbana eius et Lebnam cum suburbanis suis 14 et Iether et Isthimon 15 et Helon et Dabir 16 et Ahin et

should be given us to dwell in and their suburbs to feed our cattle."

3 And the children of Israel gave out of their possessions, according to the commandment of the Lord, cities and their suburbs. 4 And the lot came out *for* the family of Kohath of the children of Aaron, the priest, out of the tribes of Judah and of Simeon and of Benjamin, thirteen cities, 5 and to the rest of the children of Kohath, that is, to the Levites who remained out of the tribes of Ephraim and of Dan and the half-tribe of Manasseh, ten cities, 6 and the lot came out to the children of Gershon that they should take of the tribes of Issachar and of Asher and of Naphtali and of the half-tribe of Manasseh in Bashan *thirteen cities,* 7 and to the sons of Merari by their kindreds, of the tribes of Reuben and of Gad and of Zebulun, twelve cities. 8 And the children of Israel gave to the Levites the cities and their suburbs as the Lord commanded by the hand of Moses, giving to every one by lot.

9 Of the tribes of the children of Judah and of Simeon, Joshua gave cities whose names are these: 10 to the sons of Aaron of the families of Kohath of the race of Levi, for the first lot came out for them, 11 *the city of Arba,* the father of Anak, which is called Hebron, in the mountain of Judah and the suburbs thereof round about. 12 But the fields and the villages thereof he had given to Caleb, the son of Jephunneh, for his possession. 13 He gave therefore to the children of Aaron, the priest, Hebron, a city of refuge, and the suburbs thereof and Libnah with the suburbs thereof 14 and Jattir and Eshtemoa 15 and Holon and Dabir 16 and Ain and Jut-

Iethan et Bethsemes cum suburbanis suis: civitates novem de tribubus, ut dictum est, duabus. 17 De tribu autem filiorum Beniamin, Gabaon et Gabee 18 et Anathoth et Almon cum suburbanis suis: civitates quattuor. 19 Omnes simul civitates filiorum Aaron, sacerdotis, tredecim cum suburbanis suis.

20 Reliquis vero per familias filiorum Caath Levitici generis haec est data possessio: 21 de tribu Ephraim, urbes confugii Sychem, cum suburbanis suis in Monte Ephraim, et Gazer 22 et Cebsain et Bethoron cum suburbanis suis: civitates quattuor. 23 De tribu quoque Dan, Elthece et Gebbethon 24 et Ahialon et Gethremmon cum suburbanis suis: civitates quattuor. 25 Porro de dimidia tribu Manasse, Thanach et Gethremmon cum suburbanis suis: civitates duae. 26 Omnes civitates decem et suburbana earum datae sunt filiis Caath inferioris gradus.

27 Filiis quoque Gerson, Levitici generis, dedit de dimidia tribu Manasse, confugii civitates Gaulon in Basan, et Bosram cum suburbanis suis: civitates duas. 28 Porro de tribu Isachar, Cesion et Dabereth 29 et Iaramoth et Engannim cum suburbanis suis: civitates quattuor. 30 De tribu autem Aser, Masal et Abdon 31 et Elacoth et Roob cum suburbanis suis: civitates quattuor. 32 De tribu quoque Nepthali, civitates confugii Cedes in Galilea, et Ammothdor et Charthan cum suburba-

tah and Beth-shemesh with their suburbs: nine cities out of the two tribes, as hath been said. 17 And out of the tribe of the children of Benjamin, Gibeon and Geba 18 and Anathoth and Almon with their suburbs: four cities. 19 All the cities together of the children of Aaron, the priest, were thirteen with their suburbs.

20 And to the rest of the families of the children of Kohath of the race of Levi was given this possession: 21 of the tribe of Ephraim, Shechem, *one of* the cities of refuge, with the suburbs thereof in Mount Ephraim, and Gezer 22 and Kibzaim and Beth-horon with their suburbs: four cities. 23 And of the tribe of Dan, Elteke and Gibbethon 24 and Aijalon and Gath-rimmon with their suburbs: four cities. 25 And of the half-tribe of Manasseh, Taanach and Gath-rimmon with their suburbs: two cities. 26 All the cities *were ten with their suburbs which* were given to the children of Kohath of the inferior degree.

27 To the children of Gershon also, of the race of Levi, *out* of the half-tribe of Manasseh, Golan in Bashan, *one of* the cities of refuge, and Bosra with their suburbs: two cities. 28 And of the tribe of Issachar, Kishion and Daberath 29 and Jamuth and En-gannim with their suburbs: four cities. 30 And of the tribe of Asher, Mishal and Abdon 31 and Helkath and Rehob with their suburbs: four cities. 32 Of the tribe also of Naphtali, Kedesh in Galilee, *one of* the cities of refuge, and Hammoth-dor and Kartan with their suburbs:

nis suis: civitates tres. 33 Omnes urbes familiarum Gerson tredecim cum suburbanis suis.

34 Filiis autem Merari, Levitis inferioris gradus, per familias suas data est de tribu Zabulon, Iechenam et Chartha 35 et Damna et Nalol: civitates quattuor cum suburbanis suis. 36 De tribu Ruben ultra Iordanem contra Hiericho, ciuitates confugii Bosor in solitudine, Misor et Iaser et Iethson et Mephaath: ciuitates quattuor cum suburbanis suis. 37 Et de tribu Gad, civitates confugii Ramoth in Galaad, et Manaim et Esebon et Iazer: civitates quattuor cum suburbanis suis. 38 Omnes urbes filiorum Merari per familias et cognationes suas duodecim.

39 Itaque universae civitates Levitarum in medio possessionis filiorum Israhel fuerunt quadraginta octo 40 cum suburbanis suis, singulae per familias distributae. 41 Dedit-que Dominus Deus Israheli omnem terram quam traditurum se patribus eorum iuraverat, et possederunt illam atque habitaverunt in ea. 42 Dataque est ab eo pax in omnes per circuitum nationes, nullusque eis hostium resistere ausus est sed cuncti in eorum dicionem redacti sunt. 43 Ne unum quidem verbum quod illis praestaturum se esse promiserat irritum fuit, sed rebus expleta sunt omnia.

three cities. 33 All the cities of the families of Gershon were thirteen with their suburbs.

34 And to the children of Merari, Levites of the inferior degree, by their families *were* given of the tribe of Zebulun, Jokneam and Kartah 35 and Dimnah and Nahalal, four cities with their suburbs. 36 Of the tribe of Reuben beyond the Jordan over against Jericho, Bezer in the wilderness, *one of* the cities of refuge, Misor and Jahzah and Jethson and Mephaath: four cities with their suburbs. 37 Of the tribe of Gad, Ramoth in Gilead, *one of* the cities of refuge, and Mahanaim and Heshbon and Jazer: four cities with their suburbs. 38 All the cities of the children of Merari by their families and kindreds were twelve.

39 So all the cities of the Levites *within* the possession of the children of Israel were forty-eight 40 with their suburbs, each distributed by the families. 41 And the Lord God gave to Israel all the land that he had sworn to give to their fathers, and they possessed it and dwelt in it. 42 And he gave them peace *from* all nations round about, and none of their enemies durst stand against them but all were brought *under* their dominion. 43 Not so much as one word which he had promised to perform unto them was made void, but *all came to pass.*

Caput 22

Eodem tempore vocavit Iosue Rubenitas et Gadditas et dimidiam tribum Manasse 2 dixitque ad eos, "Fecistis omnia quae vobis praecepit Moses, famulus Domini; mihi quoque in omnibus oboedistis, 3 nec reliquistis fratres vestros longo tempore usque in praesentem diem, custodientes imperium Domini, Dei vestri. 4 Quia, igitur, dedit Dominus, Deus vester, fratribus vestris quietem ac pacem sicut pollicitus est, revertimini, et ite in tabernacula vestra et in terram possessionis vestrae quam tradidit vobis Moses, famulus Domini, trans Iordanem, 5 ita dumtaxat ut custodiatis adtente et opere conpleatis mandatum et legem quam praecepit vobis Moses, servus Domini: ut diligatis Dominum, Deum vestrum, et ambuletis in omnibus viis eius et observetis mandata illius adhereatisque ei ac serviatis in omni corde et in omni anima vestra." 6 Benedixitque eis Iosue et dimisit eos, qui reversi sunt in tabernacula sua.

Chapter 22

The tribes of Reuben and Gad and half the tribe of Manasseh return to their possessions. They build an altar by
the side of the Jordan, which alarms the other tribes. An
embassage is sent to them, to which they give a satisfactory
answer.

At the same time Joshua called the Reubenites and the
Gadites and the half-tribe of Manasseh 2 and said to them,
"You have done all that Moses, the servant of the Lord, commanded you; you have also obeyed me in all things, 3 neither
have you left your brethren this long time until this present day, keeping the commandment of the Lord, your God.
4 Therefore as the Lord, your God, hath given your brethren
rest and peace as he promised, return, and go to your dwellings and to the land of your possession which Moses, the
servant of the Lord, gave you beyond the Jordan, 5 yet so
that you observe attentively and in work fulfill the commandment and the law which Moses, the servant of the
Lord, commanded you: that you love the Lord, your God,
and walk in all his ways and keep *all* his commandments and
cleave to him and serve him with all your heart and with all
your soul." 6 And Joshua blessed them and sent them away,
and they returned to their dwellings.

7 Tribui autem Manasse mediae, possessionem Moses dederat in Basan, et idcirco mediae quae superfuit, dedit Iosue sortem inter ceteros fratres suos trans Iordanem ad occidentalem plagam. Cumque dimitteret eos in tabernacula sua et benedixisset illis, 8 dixit ad eos, "In multa substantia atque divitiis revertimini ad sedes vestras, cum argento et auro, aere ac ferro et veste multiplici. Dividite praedam hostium cum fratribus vestris." 9 Reversique sunt et abierunt filii Ruben et filii Gad et dimidia tribus Manasse a filiis Israhel de Silo, quae sita est in Chanaan, ut intrarent Galaad, terram possessionis suae, quam obtinuerant iuxta imperium Domini in manu Mosi.

10 Cumque venissent ad tumulos Iordanis in terram Chanaan, aedificaverunt iuxta Iordanem altare infinitae magnitudinis. 11 Quod cum audissent filii Israhel et ad eos certi nuntii detulissent aedificasse filios Ruben et Gad et dimidiae tribus Manasse altare in terra Chanaan super Iordanis tumulos contra filios Israhel, 12 convenerunt omnes in Silo ut ascenderent et dimicarent contra eos. 13 Et interim, miserunt ad illos in terram Galaad Finees, filium Eleazar, sacerdotis, 14 et decem principes cum eo, singulos de tribubus singulis, 15 qui venerunt ad filios Ruben et Gad et dimidiae tribus Manasse in terram Galaad dixeruntque ad eos, 16 "Haec mandat omnis populus Domini: 'Quae est ista transgressio? Cur reliquistis Dominum, Deum Israhel, aedificantes altare sacrilegum et a cultu illius recedentes? 17 An parum vobis est quod peccastis in Beelphegor et usque

7 Now to half the tribe of Manasseh, Moses had given a possession in Bashan, and therefore to the half that remained, Joshua gave a lot among the rest of their brethren beyond the Jordan *to the west*. And when he sent them away to their dwellings and had blessed them, 8 he said to them, "With much substance and riches you return to your settlements, with silver and gold, brass and iron and variety of raiment. Divide the prey of your enemies with your brethren." 9 *So* the children of Reuben and the children of Gad and the half-tribe of Manasseh returned and parted from the children of Israel in Shiloh, which is in Canaan, to go into Gilead, the land of their possession, which they had obtained according to the commandment of the Lord by the hand of Moses.

10 And when they were come to the banks of the Jordan in the land of Canaan, they built an altar *immensely great* near the Jordan. 11 And when the children of Israel had heard of it and certain messengers had *brought them an account* that the children of Reuben and of Gad and the half-tribe of Manasseh had built an altar in the land of Canaan upon the banks of the Jordan over against the children of Israel, 12 they all assembled in Shiloh to go up and fight against them. 13 And in the mean time, they sent to them into the land of Gilead Phinehas, the son of Eleazar, the priest, 14 and ten princes with him, one of every tribe, 15 who came to the children of Reuben and of Gad and the half-tribe of Manasseh into the land of Gilead and said to them, 16 "Thus saith all the people of the Lord: 'What *meaneth* this transgression? Why have you forsaken the Lord, the God of Israel, building a sacrilegious altar and revolting from the worship of him? 17 Is it a small thing to you that you sinned with

in praesentem diem macula huius sceleris in nobis permanet multique de populo corruerunt? 18 Et vos hodie reliquistis Dominum, et cras in universum Israhel eius ira desaeviet. 19 Quod si putatis inmundam esse terram possessionis vestrae, transite ad terram in qua tabernaculum Domini est, et habitate inter nos, tantum ut a Domino et a nostro consortio non recedatis aedificato altari praeter altare Domini, Dei nostri. 20 Nonne Achan, filius Zare, praeteriit mandatum Domini et super omnem populum Israhel ira eius incubuit, et ille erat unus homo? Atque utinam solus perisset in scelere suo!'"

21 Responderuntque filii Ruben et Gad et dimidiae tribus Manasse principibus legationis Israhel, 22 "Fortissimus Deus, Dominus, fortissimus Deus, Dominus, ipse novit, et Israhel simul intelleget: si praevaricationis animo hoc altare construximus, non custodiat nos, sed puniat nos in praesenti. 23 Et si ea mente fecimus ut holocausta et sacrificium et pacificas victimas super eo inponeremus, ipse quaerat et iudicet, 24 et non ea magis cogitatione atque tractatu, ut diceremus, 'Cras dicent filii vestri filiis nostris, "Quid vobis et Domino, Deo Israhel? 25 Terminum posuit Dominus inter nos et vos, o filii Ruben et filii Gad, Iordanem fluvium, et idcirco partem non habetis in Domino."' Et per hanc occasionem avertent filii vestri filios nostros a timore Domini.

"Putavimus itaque melius 26 et diximus, 'Extruamus nobis altare, non in holocausta, neque ad victimas offerendas, 27 sed in testimonium inter nos et vos, et subolem nostram

Beelphegor and the stain of that crime remaineth in us to this day and many of the people perished? 18 And you have forsaken the Lord today, and tomorrow his wrath will rage against all Israel. 19 But if you think the land of your possession to be unclean, pass over to the land wherein is the tabernacle of the Lord, and dwell among us. Only *depart* not from the Lord and from our society by building an altar beside the altar of the Lord, our God. 20 Did not Achan, the son of Zerah, transgress the commandment of the Lord and his wrath lay upon all the people of Israel, and he was but one man? And would to God he alone had perished in his wickedness!'"

21 And the children of Reuben and of Gad and of the half-tribe of Manasseh answered the princes of the embassage of Israel, 22 "The Lord, the most mighty God, the Lord, the most mighty God, he knoweth, and Israel *also* shall understand: if with the design of transgression we have set up this altar, let him not save us, but punish us immediately. 23 And if we did it with that mind that we might lay upon it holocausts and sacrifice and victims of peace offerings, let him require and judge, 24 and not rather with this thought and design, that we should say, 'Tomorrow your children will say to our children, "What have you to do with the Lord, the God of Israel? 25 The Lord hath put the River Jordan for a border between us and you, O ye children of Reuben and ye children of Gad, and therefore you have no part in the Lord."' And by this occasion your children shall turn away our children from the fear of the Lord.

"We therefore thought it *best* 26 and said, 'Let us build us an altar, not for holocausts, nor to offer victims, 27 but for a testimony between us and you, and our posterity and *yours,*

vestramque progeniem, ut serviamus Domino et iuris nostri sit offerre et holocausta et victimas et pacificas hostias et nequaquam dicant cras filii vestri filiis nostris, "Non est vobis pars in Domino." 28 Quod si voluerint dicere, respondebunt eis, "Ecce altare Domini quod fecerunt patres nostri, non in holocausta neque in sacrificium, sed in testimonium vestrum ac nostrum."'

29 Absit a nobis hoc scelus ut recedamus a Domino et eius vestigia relinquamus extructo altari ad holocausta et sacrificia et victimas offerendas praeter altare Domini, Dei nostri, quod extructum est ante tabernaculum eius."

30 Quibus auditis Finees, sacerdos, et principes legationis Israhel qui erant cum eo, placati sunt, et verba filiorum Ruben et Gad et dimidiae tribus Manasse libentissime susceperunt. 31 Dixitque Finees, filius Eleazari, sacerdos, ad eos, "Nunc scimus quod nobiscum sit Dominus, quoniam alieni estis a praevaricatione hac et liberastis filios Israhel de manu Domini."

32 Reversusque est cum principibus a filiis Ruben et Gad de terra Galaad in terram Chanaan ad filios Israhel et rettulit eis. 33 Placuitque sermo cunctis audientibus. Et laudaverunt Deum filii Israhel, et nequaquam ultra dixerunt ut ascenderent contra eos atque pugnarent et delerent terram possessionis eorum. 34 Vocaveruntque filii Ruben et filii Gad altare quod extruxerant Testimonium Nostrum quod Dominus ipse sit Deus.

that we may serve the Lord and that we may have a right to offer both holocausts and victims and sacrifices of peace offerings and that your children tomorrow may not say to our children, "You have no part in the Lord." 28 And if they will say so, they shall answer them, "Behold the altar of the Lord which our fathers made, not for holocausts nor for sacrifice, but for a testimony between us and you.'"

29 "God keep us from *any* such wickedness that we should revolt from the Lord and leave *off following* his steps by building an altar to offer holocausts and sacrifices and victims beside the altar of the Lord, our God, which is erected before his tabernacle."

30 And when Phinehas, the priest, and the princes of the embassage who were with him had heard this, they were satisfied, and they admitted most willingly the words of the children of Reuben and Gad and of the half-tribe of Manasseh. 31 And Phinehas, the priest, the son of Eleazar, said to them, "Now we know that the Lord is with us, because you are not guilty of this revolt and you have delivered the children of Israel from the hand of the Lord."

32 And he returned with the princes from the children of Reuben and Gad out of the land of Gilead into the land of Canaan to the children of Israel and *brought* them *word again*. 33 And the saying pleased all that heard it. And the children of Israel praised God, and they no longer said that they would go up against them and fight and destroy the land of their possession. 34 And the children of Reuben and the children of Gad called the altar which they had built Our Testimony that the Lord is God.

Caput 23

Evoluto autem multo tempore postquam pacem Dominus dederat Israheli, subiectis in gyro nationibus universis et Iosue iam longevo et persenilis aetatis, 2 vocavit Iosue omnem Israhelem maioresque natu et principes ac iudices et magistros dixitque ad eos, "Ego senui et progressioris aetatis sum, 3 vosque cernitis omnia quae fecerit Dominus, Deus vester, cunctis per circuitum nationibus, quomodo pro vobis ipse pugnaverit, 4 et nunc, quia vobis sorte divisit omnem terram ab orientali parte Iordanis usque ad Mare Magnum, multaeque adhuc supersunt nationes, 5 Dominus, Deus vester, disperdet eas et auferet a facie vestra, et possidebitis terram sicut vobis pollicitus est. 6 Tantum confortamini, et estote solliciti ut custodiatis cuncta quae scripta sunt in volumine legis Mosi, et non declinetis ab eis nec ad dextram nec ad sinistram 7 ne postquam intraveritis ad Gentes quae inter vos futurae sunt, iuretis in nomine deorum earum et serviatis eis et adoretis illos. 8 Sed adhereatis Domino, Deo vestro, quod fecistis usque in diem hanc. 9 Et tunc auferet Dominus Deus in conspectu vestro gentes mag-

Chapter 23

Joshua being old admonisheth the people to keep God's commandments and to avoid marriages and all society with the Gentiles for fear of being brought to idolatry.

And when a long time was passed after that the Lord had given peace to Israel, all the nations round about being subdued and Joshua being now old and *far advanced in years,* 2 Joshua called for all Israel and for the elders and for the princes and for the judges and for the masters and said to them, "I am old and *far advanced in years,* 3 and you see all that the Lord, your God, hath done to all the nations round about, how he himself hath fought for you, 4 and now, since he hath divided to you by lot all the land from the *east* of the Jordan unto the Great Sea, and many nations yet remain, 5 the Lord, your God, will destroy them and take them away from before your face, and you shall possess the land as he hath promised you. 6 Only take courage, and be careful to observe all things that are written in the book of the law of Moses, and turn not aside from them neither to the right hand nor to the left 7 lest after that you are come in *among* the Gentiles who will *remain* among you, you should swear by the name of their gods and serve them and adore them. 8 But cleave ye unto the Lord, your God, as you have done until this day. 9 And then the Lord God will take away before your eyes nations that are great and very strong, and no man

nas et robustissimas, et nullus vobis resistere poterit. 10 Unus e vobis persequetur hostium mille viros quia Dominus, Deus vester, pro vobis ipse pugnabit sicut pollicitus est. 11 Hoc tantum diligentissime praecavete, ut diligatis Dominum, Deum vestrum.

12 "Quod si volueritis gentium harum quae inter vos habitant erroribus adherere et cum eis miscere conubia atque amicitias copulare, 13 iam nunc scitote quod Dominus, Deus vester, non eas deleat ante faciem vestram, sed sint vobis in foveam ac laqueum et offendiculum ex latere vestro et sudes in oculis vestris donec vos auferat atque disperdat de terra hac optima quam tradidit vobis.

14 "En! Ego hodie ingredior viam universae terrae, et toto animo cognoscetis quod de omnibus verbis quae se Dominus praestaturum vobis esse pollicitus est unum non praeterierit in cassum. 15 Sicut ergo implevit opere quod promisit et prospera cuncta venerunt, sic adducet super vos quicquid malorum comminatus est donec vos auferat atque disperdat de terra hac optima quam tradidit vobis 16 eo quod praeterieritis pactum Domini, Dei vestri, quod pepigit vobiscum et servieritis diis alienis et adoraveritis eos. Cito atque velociter consurget in vos furor Domini, et auferemini de terra hac optima quam tradidit vobis."

shall be able to resist you. 10 One of you shall chase a thousand men of the enemies because the Lord, your God, himself will fight for you as he hath promised. 11 This only take care of with all diligence, that you love the Lord, your God.

12 "But if you will embrace the errors of these nations that dwell among you and make marriages with them and join friendships, 13 know ye *for a certainty* that the Lord, your God, will not destroy them before your face, but they shall be a pit and a snare *in your way* and a stumbling block at your side and stakes in your eyes till he take you away and destroy you from off this excellent land which he hath given you.

14 "Behold! This day I am going into the way of all the earth, and you shall know with all your mind that of all the words which the Lord promised to perform for you not one hath *failed.* 15 Therefore as he hath fulfilled in deed what he promised and all things prosperous have come, so will he bring upon you *all the evils* he hath threatened till he take you away and destroy you from off this excellent land which he hath given you 16 *when* you shall have transgressed the covenant of the Lord, your God, which he hath made with you and shall have served strange gods and adored them. Then shall the indignation of the Lord rise up quickly and speedily against you, and you shall be taken away from this excellent land which he hath delivered to you."

Caput 24

Congregavitque Iosue omnes tribus Israhel in Sychem et vocavit maiores natu ac principes et iudices et magistros, steteruntque in conspectu Domini, 2 et ad populum sic locutus est, "Haec dicit Dominus, Deus Israhel: 'Trans fluvium habitaverunt patres vestri ab initio, Thare, pater Abraham, et Nahor, servieruntque diis alienis. 3 Tuli ergo patrem vestrum Abraham de Mesopotamiae finibus et adduxi eum in terram Chanaan, multiplicavique semen eius 4 et dedi ei Isaac, illique rursum dedi Iacob et Esau. E quibus Esau dedi Montem Seir ad possidendum, Iacob vero et filii eius descenderunt in Aegyptum. 5 Misique Mosen et Aaron, et percussi Aegyptum multis signis atque portentis. 6 Eduxique vos et patres vestros de Aegypto, et venistis ad mare, persecutique sunt Aegyptii patres vestros cum curribus et equitatu usque ad Mare Rubrum. 7 Clamaverunt autem ad Dominum filii Israhel, qui posuit tenebras inter vos et Aegyptios et adduxit super eos mare et operuit illos. Viderunt oculi vestri cuncta quae in Aegypto fecerim, et habitastis in solitudine multo tempore. 8 Et introduxi vos in terram Amorrei qui habitabat trans Iordanem. Cumque pugnarent contra

Chapter 24

Joshua assembleth the people, and reneweth the covenant between them and God. His death and burial.

And Joshua gathered together all the tribes of Israel in Shechem and called for the ancients and the princes and the judges and the masters, and they stood in the sight of the Lord, 2 and he spoke thus to the people, "Thus saith the Lord, the God of Israel: 'Your fathers dwelt *of old* on the other side of the river, Terah, the father of Abraham, and Nahor, and they served strange gods. 3 And I took your father Abraham from the borders of Mesopotamia and brought him into the land of Canaan, and I multiplied his seed 4 and gave him Isaac, and to him again I gave Jacob and Esau. *And* I gave to Esau Mount Seir *for his possession,* but Jacob and his children went down into Egypt. 5 And I sent Moses and Aaron, and I struck Egypt with many signs and wonders. 6 And I brought you and your fathers out of Egypt, and you came to the sea, and the Egyptians pursued your fathers with chariots and horsemen as far as the Red Sea. 7 And the children of Israel cried to the Lord, and he put darkness between you and the Egyptians and brought the sea upon them and covered them. Your eyes saw all that I did in Egypt, and you dwelt in the wilderness a long time. 8 And I brought you into the land of the Amorite who dwelt beyond the Jordan. And when they fought against you, I de-

vos, tradidi eos in manus vestras, et possedistis terram eorum atque interfecistis illos. 9 Surrexit autem Balac, filius
Sepphor, rex Moab, et pugnavit contra Israhelem. Misitque
et vocavit Balaam, filium Beor, ut malediceret vobis. 10 Et
ego nolui audire eum, sed e contrario per illum benedixi vobis, et liberavi vos de manu eius. 11 Transistisque Iordanem,
et venistis ad Hiericho. Pugnaveruntque contra vos viri civitatis eius, Amorreus et Ferezeus et Chananeus et Hettheus
et Gergeseus et Eveus et Iebuseus, et tradidi illos in manus
vestras. 12 Misique ante vos crabrones, et eieci eos de locis
suis, duos reges Amorreorum, non in gladio et arcu tuo.
13 Dedique vobis terram in qua non laborastis et urbes quas
non aedificastis ut habitaretis in eis, vineas et oliveta quae
non plantastis. 14 Nunc ergo timete Dominum, et servite ei
perfecto corde atque verissimo, et auferte deos quibus servierunt patres vestri in Mesopotamia et in Aegypto, ac servite Domino.'

15 "Sin autem malum vobis videtur ut Domino serviatis,
optio vobis datur: eligite hodie quod placet, cui potissimum
servire debeatis, utrum diis quibus servierunt patres vestri
in Mesopotamia, an diis Amorreorum in quorum terra habitatis. Ego autem et domus mea serviemus Domino."

16 Responditque populus et ait, "Absit a nobis ut relinquamus Dominum et serviamus diis alienis. 17 Dominus, Deus
noster, ipse eduxit nos et patres nostros de terra Aegypti, de
domo servitutis, fecitque videntibus nobis signa ingentia et
custodivit nos in omni via per quam ambulavimus et in cunc-

livered them into your hands, and you possessed their land and slew them. 9 And Balak, son of Zippor, king of Moab, arose and fought against Israel. And he sent and called for Balaam, son of Beor, to curse you. 10 And I would not hear him, but on the contrary I blessed you by him, and I delivered you out of his hand. 11 And you passed over the Jordan, and you came to Jericho. And the men of that city fought against you, the Amorite and the Perizzite and the Canaanite and the Hittite and the Girgashite and the Hivite and the Jebusite, and I delivered them into your hands. 12 And I sent before you hornets, and I drove them out from their places, the two kings of the Amorites, not *with* thy sword *nor with thy* bow. 13 And I gave you a land in which you had not laboured and cities to dwell in which you built not, vineyards and oliveyards which you planted not. 14 Now therefore fear the Lord, and serve him with a perfect and most sincere heart, and put away the gods which your fathers served in Mesopotamia and in Egypt, and serve the Lord.'

15 "But if it seem evil to you to serve the Lord, *you have your choice:* choose this day that which pleaseth you, *whom you would rather* serve, whether the gods which your fathers served in Mesopotamia, or the gods of the Amorites in whose land you dwell. But *as for me* and my house, we will serve the Lord."

16 And the people answered and said, "God forbid we should leave the Lord and serve strange gods. 17 The Lord, our God, he brought us and our fathers out of the land of Egypt, out of the house of bondage, and did very great signs in our sight and preserved us in all the way by which we journeyed and among all the people through whom we

tis populis per quos transivimus, 18 et eiecit universas gentes, Amorreum, habitatorem terrae quam nos intravimus. Serviemus igitur Domino, quia ipse est Deus noster."

19 Dixitque Iosue ad populum, "Non poteritis servire Domino, Deus enim sanctus et fortis aemulator est nec ignoscet sceleribus vestris atque peccatis. 20 Si dimiseritis Dominum et servieritis diis alienis, convertet se et adfliget vos atque subvertet postquam vobis praestiterit bona."

21 Dixitque populus ad Iosue, "Nequaquam ita ut loqueris erit, sed Domino serviemus."

22 Et Iosue ad populum, "Testes," inquit, "vos estis quia ipsi elegeritis vobis Dominum ut serviatis ei."

Responderuntque, "Testes."

23 "Nunc ergo," ait, "auferte deos alienos de medio vestrum, et inclinate corda vestra ad Dominum, Deum Israhel."

24 Dixitque populus ad Iosue, "Domino, Deo nostro, serviemus, et oboedientes erimus praeceptis eius."

25 Percussit igitur Iosue in die illo foedus et proposuit populo praecepta atque iudicia in Sychem. 26 Scripsit quoque omnia verba haec in volumine legis Domini, et tulit lapidem pergrandem posuitque eum subter quercum quae erat in sanctuario Domini, 27 et dixit ad omnem populum, "En: lapis iste erit vobis in testimonium quod audierit omnia verba Domini quae locutus est vobis ne forte postea negare velitis et mentiri Domino, Deo vestro."

28 Dimisitque populum, singulos in possessionem suam. 29 Et post haec mortuus est Iosue, filius Nun, servus Domini, centum et decem annorum. 30 Sepelieruntque eum in

passed, 18 and he hath cast out all the nations, the Amorite, the inhabitant of the land into which we are come. Therefore, we will serve the Lord, for he is our God."

19 And Joshua said to the people, "You will not be able to serve the Lord, for he is a holy God and *mighty and jealous* and will not forgive your wickedness and sins. 20 If you leave the Lord and serve strange gods, he will *turn* and will afflict you and will destroy you after *all the good he hath done you*."

21 And the people said to Joshua, "No, it shall not be so as thou sayest, but we will serve the Lord."

22 And Joshua said to the people, "You are witnesses that you yourselves have chosen you the Lord to serve him."

And they answered, "We are witnesses."

23 "Now therefore," said he, "put away strange gods from among you, and incline your hearts to the Lord, the God of Israel."

24 And the people said to Joshua, "We will serve the Lord, our God, and we will be obedient to his commandments."

25 Joshua therefore on that day made a covenant and set before the people commandments and judgments in Shechem. 26 And he wrote all these things in the volume of the law of the Lord, and he took a great stone and set it under the oak that was in the sanctuary of the Lord, 27 and he said to all the people, "Behold: this stone shall be a testimony unto you that it hath heard all the words of the Lord which he hath spoken to you lest perhaps hereafter you will deny it and lie to the Lord, your God."

28 And he sent the people away, every one to their own possession. 29 And after these things Joshua, the son of Nun, the servant of the Lord, died, being a hundred and ten years old. 30 And they buried him in the border of his posses-

finibus possessionis suae in Thamnathsare, quae sita est in Monte Ephraim, a septentrionali parte Montis Gaas. 31 Servivitque Israhel Domino cunctis diebus Iosue et seniorum qui longo vixerunt tempore post Iosue et qui noverant omnia opera Domini quae fecerat in Israhel. 32 Ossa quoque Ioseph quae tulerant filii Israhel de Aegypto sepelierunt in Sychem, in parte agri quem emerat Iacob a filiis Emmor, patris Sychem, centum novellis ovibus, et fuit in possessione filiorum Ioseph. 33 Eleazar quoque, filius Aaron, mortuus est, et sepelierunt eum in Gaab Finees, filii eius, quae data est ei in Monte Ephraim.

sion in Timnath-serah, which is situate in Mount Ephraim, on the north side of Mount Gaash. 31 And Israel served the Lord all the days of Joshua and of the ancients that lived a long time after Joshua and that had known all the works of the Lord which he had done in Israel. 32 And the bones of Joseph which the children of Israel had taken out of Egypt they buried in Shechem, in that part of the field which Jacob had bought of the sons of Hamor, the father of Shechem, for a hundred young ewes, and it was in the possession of the sons of Joseph. 33 Eleazar also, the son of Aaron, died, and they buried him in Gibeah *that belonged to* Phinehas, his son, which was given him in Mount Ephraim.

JUDGES

Caput 1

Post mortem Iosue, consuluerunt filii Israhel Dominum, dicentes, "Quis ascendet ante nos contra Chananeum et erit dux belli?"

2 Dixitque Dominus, "Iudas ascendet. Ecce: tradidi terram in manus eius."

3 Et ait Iudas Symeoni, fratri suo, "Ascende mecum in sortem meam, et pugna contra Chananeum ut et ego pergam tecum in sortem tuam." Et abiit cum eo Symeon. 4 Ascenditque Iudas, et tradidit Dominus Chananeum ac Ferezeum in manus eorum, et percusserunt in Bezec decem milia virorum. 5 Inveneruntque Adonibezec in Bezec et pugnaverunt contra eum, ac percusserunt Chananeum et Ferezeum. 6 Fugit autem Adonibezec, quem persecuti conprehenderunt caesis summitatibus manuum eius ac pedum.

7 Dixitque Adonibezec, "Septuaginta reges, amputatis manuum ac pedum summitatibus, colligebant sub mensa mea ciborum reliquias. Sicut feci, ita reddidit mihi Deus." Adduxeruntque eum in Hierusalem, et ibi mortuus est.

Chapter 1

The expedition and victory of Judah against the Canaanites,
who are tolerated in many places.

After the death of Joshua, the children of Israel consulted
the Lord, saying, "Who shall go up before us against the Canaanite and shall be the leader of the war?"

2 And the Lord said, "Judah shall go up. Behold: I have delivered the land into his hands."

3 And Judah said to Simeon, his brother, "Come up with
me into my lot, and fight against the Canaanite that I also
may go along with thee into thy lot." And Simeon went with
him. 4 And Judah went up, and the Lord delivered the Canaanite and the Perizzite into their hands, and they slew *of
them* in Bezek ten thousand men. 5 And they found Adoni-
bezek in Bezek and fought against him, and they defeated
the Canaanite and the Perizzite. 6 And Adoni-bezek fled,
and they pursued after him and took him and cut off his fingers and toes.

7 And Adoni-bezek said, "Seventy kings, having their fingers and toes cut off, gathered up the leavings of the meat
under my table. As I have done, so hath God requited me."
And they brought him to Jerusalem, and he died there.

8 Obpugnantes ergo filii Iuda Hierusalem ceperunt eam et percusserunt in ore gladii tradentes cunctam incendio civitatem. 9 Et postea, descendentes pugnaverunt contra Chananeum qui habitabat in montanis et ad meridiem et in campestribus. 10 Pergensque Iudas contra Chananeum qui habitabat in Hebron (cuius nomen fuit antiquitus Cariatharbe) percussit Sisai et Ahiman et Tholmai. 11 Atque inde profectus abiit ad habitatores Dabir, cuius nomen vetus erat Cariathsepher, id est, Civitas Litterarum. 12 Dixitque Chaleb, "Qui percusserit Cariathsepher et vastaverit eam, dabo ei Axam filiam meam uxorem." 13 Cumque cepisset eam Othonihel, filius Cenez, frater Chaleb minor, dedit ei Axam, filiam suam, coniugem.

14 Quam pergentem in itinere, monuit vir suus ut peteret a patre suo agrum. Quae cum suspirasset sedens asino, dixit ei Chaleb, "Quid habes?"

15 At illa respondit, "Da mihi benedictionem, quia terram arentem dedisti mihi; da et inriguam aquis." Dedit ergo ei Chaleb inriguum superius et inriguum inferius.

16 Filii autem Cinei, cognati Mosi, ascenderunt de Civitate Palmarum cum filiis Iuda in desertum sortis eius, quod est ad meridiem Arad, et habitaverunt cum eo. 17 Abiit autem Iudas cum Symeone, fratre suo, et percusserunt simul Chananeum qui habitabat in Sephath et interfecerunt eum. Vocatumque est nomen urbis Horma, id est, Anathema. 18 Cepitque Iudas Gazam cum finibus suis et Ascalonem atque Accaron cum terminis suis. 19 Fuitque Dominus cum Iuda, et montana possedit nec potuit delere habitatores val-

8 And the children of Judah besieging Jerusalem took it and *put it to* the sword and set the whole city on fire. 9 And afterwards, they went down and fought against the Canaanite who dwelt in the mountains and in the south and in the plains. 10 And Judah going forward against the Canaanite that dwelt in Hebron (the name whereof was in former times Kiriath-arba) slew Sheshai and Ahiman and Talmai. 11 And departing from thence he went to the inhabitants of Debir, the ancient name of which was Kiriath-sepher, that is, the City of Letters. 12 And Caleb said, "He that shall take Kiriath-sepher and lay it waste, to him will I give my daughter Achsah to wife." 13 And Othniel, the son of Kenaz, the younger brother of Caleb, *having taken* it, he gave him Achsah, his daughter, to wife.

14 And as she was going on her way, her husband admonished her to ask a field of her father. And as she sighed sitting on her ass, Caleb said to her, "What aileth thee?"

15 But she answered, "Give me a blessing, for thou hast given me a dry land; give me also a watery land." So Caleb gave her the upper and the nether watery ground.

16 And the children of the Kenite, the kinsman of Moses, went up from the City of Palms with the children of Judah into the wilderness of his lot, which is at the south side of Arad, and they dwelt with him. 17 And Judah went with Simeon, his brother, and they together defeated the *Canaanites* that dwelt in Zephath and slew them. And the name of the city was called Hormah, that is, Anathema. 18 And Judah took Gaza with its confines and Ashkelon and Ekron with their confines. 19 And the Lord was with Judah, and he possessed the hill country but was not able to destroy the inhabitants of the valley because they had many chariots

lis quia falcatis curribus abundabant. 20 Dederuntque Chaleb Hebron, sicut dixerat Moses, qui delevit ex ea tres filios Enach.

21 Iebuseum autem, habitatorem Hierusalem, non deleverunt filii Beniamin, habitavitque Iebuseus cum filiis Beniamin in Hierusalem usque in praesentem diem.

22 Domus quoque Ioseph ascendit in Bethel, fuitque Dominus cum eis, 23 nam cum obsiderent urbem, quae prius Luza vocabatur, 24 viderunt hominem egredientem de civitate, dixeruntque ad eum, "Ostende nobis introitum civitatis, et faciemus tecum misericordiam." 25 Qui cum ostendisset eis, percusserunt urbem in ore gladii, hominem autem illum et omnem cognationem eius dimiserunt, 26 qui dimissus abiit in terram Etthim et aedificavit ibi civitatem vocavitque eam Luzam, quae ita appellatur usque in praesentem diem.

27 Manasses quoque non delevit Bethsan et Thanach cum viculis suis, et habitatores Dor et Ieblaam et Mageddo cum viculis suis, coepitque Chananeus habitare cum eis. 28 Postquam autem confortatus est Israhel, fecit eos tributarios et delere noluit. 29 Ephraim etiam non interfecit Chananeum qui habitabat in Gazer, sed habitavit cum eo. 30 Zabulon non delevit habitatores Cetron et Naalon, sed habitavit Chananeus in medio eius factusque est ei tributarius. 31 Aser quoque non delevit habitatores Achcho et Sidonis, Alab et Achazib et Alba et Afec et Roob, 32 habitavitque in medio Chananei, habitatoris illius terrae, nec interfecit eum. 33 Nepthali non delevit habitatores Bethsemes et Beth-

armed with scythes. 20 And they gave Hebron to Caleb, as Moses had said, who destroyed out of it the three sons of Anak.

21 But the sons of Benjamin did not destroy the *Jebusites that inhabited* Jerusalem, and the Jebusite hath dwelt with the sons of Benjamin in Jerusalem until this present day.

22 The house of Joseph also went up against Bethel, and the Lord was with them, 23 for when they were besieging the city, which before was called Luz, 24 they saw a man coming out of the city, and they said to him, "Show us the entrance into the city, and we will show thee mercy." 25 And when he had shown them, they smote the city with the edge of the sword, but that man and all his kindred they let go, 26 who being sent away went into the land of Hethim and built there a city and called it Luz, which is so called until this day.

27 Manasseh also did not destroy Beth-shean and Taanach with their villages, *nor* the inhabitants of Dor and Ibleam and Megiddo with their villages, and the Canaanite began to dwell with them. 28 But after Israel was grown strong, he made them tributaries and would not destroy them. 29 Ephraim also did not slay the Canaanite that dwelt in Gezer, but dwelt with him. 30 Zebulun destroyed not the inhabitants of Kitron and Nahalol, but the Canaanite dwelt *among them* and became their tributary. 31 Asher also destroyed not the inhabitants of Acco and of Sidon, of Ahlab and of Achzib and of Helbah and of Aphik and of Rehob, 32 and he dwelt in the midst of the *Canaanites, the inhabitants* of that land, and did not slay them. 33 Naphtali also destroyed not the inhabitants of Beth-shemesh and of Beth-

anath, et habitavit inter Chananeum, habitatorem terrae, fueruntque ei Bethsemitae et Bethanitae tributarii.

34 Artavitque Amorreus filios Dan in monte nec dedit eis locum ut ad planiora descenderent, 35 habitavitque in monte Hares, quod interpretatur, "testaceo," in Ahilon et Salabim. Et adgravata est manus domus Ioseph, factusque est ei tributarius. 36 Fuit autem terminus Amorrei ab ascensu Scorpionis, petra et superiora loca.

Caput 2

Ascenditque angelus Domini de Galgal ad Locum Flentium et ait, "Eduxi vos de Aegypto et introduxi in terram pro qua iuravi patribus vestris, et pollicitus sum ut non facerem irritum pactum meum vobiscum in sempiternum 2 ita dumtaxat ut non feriretis foedus cum habitatoribus terrae huius sed aras eorum subverteretis, et noluistis audire vocem

anath, and he dwelt in the midst of the Canaanites, the inhabitants of the land, and the Beth-shemites and Beth-anites were tributaries to him.

34 And the Amorite straitened the children of Dan in the mountain and gave them not place to go down to the plain, 35 and he dwelt in the mountain Harheres, that is, "of potsherds," in Aijalon and Shaalbim. And the hand of the house of Joseph was heavy *upon him,* and he became tributary to him. 36 And the border of the Amorite was from the ascent of the Scorpion, the rock and the higher places.

Chapter 2

An angel reproveth Israel. They weep for their sins. After the death of Joshua, they often fall and repenting are delivered from their afflictions, but still fall worse and worse.

And an angel of the Lord went up from Gilgal to the Place of Weepers and said, "I *made you go* out of Egypt and have brought you into the land for which I swore to your fathers, and I promised that I would not make void my covenant with you for ever 2 on condition that you should not make a league with the inhabitants of this land but should throw down their altars, and you would not hear my voice.

meam. Cur hoc fecistis? 3 Quam ob rem nolui delere eos a facie vestra, ut habeatis hostes et dii eorum sint vobis in ruinam."

4 Cumque loqueretur angelus Domini verba haec ad omnes filios Israhel, elevaverunt vocem suam et fleverunt, 5 et vocatum est nomen loci illius Locus Flentium (sive Lacrimarum), immolaveruntque ibi hostias Domino. 6 Dimisit ergo Iosue populum, et abierunt filii Israhel unusquisque in possessionem suam ut obtinerent eam, 7 servieruntque Domino cunctis diebus eius et seniorum qui longo post eum vixerunt tempore et noverant omnia opera Domini quae fecerat cum Israhel.

8 Mortuus est autem Iosue, filius Nun, famulus Domini, centum et decem annorum, 9 et sepelierunt eum in finibus possessionis suae in Thamnathsare in Monte Ephraim a septentrionali plaga Montis Gaas. 10 Omnisque illa generatio congregata est ad patres suos, et surrexerunt alii qui non noverant Dominum et opera quae fecerat cum Israhel. 11 Feceruntque filii Israhel malum in conspectu Domini, et servierunt Baalim. 12 Ac dimiserunt Dominum, Deum patrum suorum, qui eduxerat eos de terra Aegypti, et secuti sunt deos alienos deosque populorum qui habitabant in circuitu eorum, et adoraverunt eos, et ad iracundiam concitaverunt Dominum, 13 dimittentes eum et servientes Baal et Astharoth.

14 Iratusque Dominus contra Israhel tradidit eos in manus diripientium qui ceperunt eos et vendiderunt hostibus qui habitabant per gyrum. Nec potuerunt resistere adversa-

Why have you done this? 3 Wherefore I would not destroy them from before your face, that you may have enemies and their gods may be your ruin."

4 And when the angel of the Lord spoke these words to all the children of Israel, they lifted up their voice and wept, 5 and the name of that place was called The Place of Weepers (or of Tears), and there they offered sacrifices to the Lord. 6 And Joshua sent away the people, and the children of Israel went every one to his own possession to hold it, 7 and they served the Lord all his days and the days of the ancients that lived a long time after him and *who* knew all the works of the Lord which he had done for Israel.

8 And Joshua, the son of Nun, the servant of the Lord, died being a hundred and ten years old, 9 and they buried him in the borders of his possession in Timnath-heres in Mount Ephraim on the north side of Mount Gaash. 10 And all that generation was gathered to their fathers, and there arose others that knew not the Lord and the works which he had done for Israel. 11 And the children of Israel did evil in the sight of the Lord, and they served Baalim. 12 And they left the Lord, the God of their fathers, who had brought them out of the land of Egypt, and they followed strange gods and the gods of the people that dwelt round about them, and they adored them, and they provoked the Lord to anger, 13 forsaking him and serving Baal and Astarte.

14 And the Lord being angry against Israel delivered them into the hands of plunderers who took them and sold them to their enemies that dwelt round about. Neither could they

riis suis, 15 sed quocumque pergere voluissent, manus Domini erat super eos, sicut locutus est et iuravit eis, et vehementer adflicti sunt. 16 Suscitavitque Dominus iudices qui liberarent eos de vastantium manibus, sed nec illos audire voluerunt, 17 fornicantes cum diis alienis et adorantes eos. Cito deseruerunt viam per quam ingressi fuerant patres eorum, et audientes mandata Domini omnia fecere contraria.

18 Cumque Dominus iudices suscitaret, in diebus eorum flectebatur misericordia et audiebat adflictorum gemitus et liberabat eos de caede vastantium. 19 Postquam autem mortuus esset iudex, revertebantur et multo peiora faciebant quam fecerant patres sui, sequentes deos alienos, servientes eis et adorantes illos. Non dimiserunt adinventiones suas et viam durissimam per quam ambulare consueverunt. 20 Iratusque est furor Domini in Israhel, et ait, "Quia irritum fecit gens ista pactum meum, quod pepigeram cum patribus eorum, et vocem meam audire contempsit. 21 Et ego non delebo gentes quas dimisit Iosue et mortuus est, 22 ut in ipsis experiar Israhel, utrum custodiant viam Domini et ambulent in ea sicut custodierunt patres eorum, an non." 23 Dimisit ergo Dominus omnes has nationes et cito subvertere noluit, nec tradidit in manibus Iosue.

stand against their enemies, 15 but whithersoever they meant to go, the hand of the Lord was upon them, as he had said and *as he had* sworn to them, and they were greatly distressed. 16 And the Lord raised up judges to deliver them from the hands of those that oppressed them, but they would not hearken to them, 17 committing fornication with strange gods and adoring them. They quickly forsook the way in which their fathers had walked, and hearing the commandments of the Lord they did all things contrary.

18 And when the Lord raised them up judges, in their days he was moved *to* mercy and heard the groanings of the afflicted and delivered them from the slaughter of the oppressors. 19 But after the judge was dead, they returned and did much worse things than their fathers had done, following strange gods, serving them and adoring them. They left not their own inventions and the stubborn way by which they were accustomed to walk. 20 And the wrath of the Lord was kindled against Israel, and he said, "*Behold:* this nation hath made void my covenant, which I had made with their fathers, and hath despised to hearken to my voice. 21 I also will not destroy the nations which Joshua left *when* he died, 22 that through them I may try Israel, whether they will keep the way of the Lord and walk in it as their fathers kept it, or not." 23 The Lord therefore left all these nations and would not quickly destroy them, neither did he deliver them into the hands of Joshua.

Caput 3

Hae sunt gentes quas Dominus dereliquit ut erudiret in eis Israhelem et omnes qui non noverant bella Chananeorum 2 ut postea discerent filii eorum certare cum hostibus et habere consuetudinem proeliandi: 3 quinque satrapas Philisthinorum omnemque Chananeum et Sidonium atque Eveum qui habitabat in Monte Libano, de Monte Baalhermon usque ad introitum Emath. 4 Dimisitque eos ut in ipsis experiretur Israhelem, utrum audiret mandata Domini quae praeceperat patribus eorum per manum Mosi, an non. 5 Itaque filii Israhel habitaverunt in medio Chananei et Hetthei et Amorrei et Ferezei et Evei et Iebusei, 6 et duxerunt uxores filias eorum, ipsique filias suas eorum filiis tradiderunt, et servierunt diis eorum. 7 Feceruntque malum in conspectu Domini, et obliti sunt Dei sui servientes Baalim et Astharoth.

8 Iratusque Dominus contra Israhel tradidit eos in manus Chusan Rasathaim, regis Mesopotamiae, servieruntque ei octo annis. 9 Et clamaverunt ad Dominum, qui suscitavit eis salvatorem et liberavit eos, Othonihel, videlicet, filium Cenez,

Chapter 3

The people falling into idolatry are oppressed by their enemies, but repenting are delivered by Othniel, Ehud and Shamgar.

These are the nations which the Lord left that by them he might instruct Israel and all that had not known the wars of the Canaanites 2 that afterwards their children might learn to fight with their enemies and to be *trained up* to war: 3 the five princes of the Philistines and all the *Canaanites* and the *Sidonians* and the *Hivites* that dwelt in Mount Libanus, from Mount Baal-hermon to the entering into Hamath. 4 And he left them that he might try Israel by them, whether they would hear the commandments of the Lord which he had commanded their fathers by the hand of Moses, or not. 5 So the children of Israel dwelt in the midst of the Canaanite and the Hittite and the Amorite and the Perizzite and the Hivite and the Jebusite, 6 and they took their daughters to wives, and they gave their own daughters to their sons, and they served their gods. 7 And they did evil in the sight of the Lord, and they forgot their God and served Baalim and Asherah.

8 And the Lord being angry with Israel delivered them into the hands of Cushan Rishathaim, king of Mesopotamia, and they served him eight years. 9 And they cried to the Lord, who raised them up a saviour and delivered them, to wit, Othniel, the son of Kenaz, the younger brother of

fratrem Chaleb minorem. 10 Fuitque in eo spiritus Domini, et iudicavit Israhel. Egressusque est ad pugnam, et tradidit Dominus in manus eius Chusan Rasathaim, regem Syriae, et oppressit eum. 11 Quievitque terra quadraginta annis, et mortuus est Othonihel, filius Cenez.

12 Addiderunt autem filii Israhel facere malum in conspectu Domini, qui confortavit adversum eos Eglon, regem Moab, quia fecerunt malum in conspectu eius. 13 Et copulavit ei filios Ammon et Amalech, abiitque et percussit Israhel atque possedit Urbem Palmarum. 14 Servieruntque filii Israhel Eglon, regi Moab, decem et octo annis, 15 et postea clamaverunt ad Dominum, qui suscitavit eis salvatorem vocabulo Ahoth, filium Gera, filii Iemini, qui utraque manu utebatur pro dextera. Miseruntque filii Israhel per illum munera Eglon, regi Moab. 16 Qui fecit sibi gladium ancipitem, habentem in medio capulum longitudinis palmae manus et accinctus est eo subter sagum in dextro femore. 17 Obtulitque munera Eglon, regi Moab.

Erat autem Eglon crassus nimis, 18 cumque obtulisset ei munera, prosecutus est socios qui cum eo venerant. 19 Et, reversus de Galgalis, ubi erant idola, dixit ad regem, "Verbum secretum habeo ad te, o rex." Et ille imperavit silentium. Egressisque omnibus qui circa eum erant, 20 ingressus est Ahoth ad eum (sedebat autem in aestivo cenaculo solus), dixitque, "Verbum Dei habeo ad te." Qui statim surrexit de throno, 21 extenditque Ahoth manum sinistram et tulit sicam de dextro femore suo infixitque eam in ventre eius 22 tam valide ut capulus ferrum sequeretur in vulnere ac pin-

Caleb. 10 And the spirit of the Lord was in him, and he judged Israel. And he went out to fight, and the Lord delivered into his hands Cushan Rishathaim, king of Syria, and he overthrew him. 11 And the land rested forty years, and Othniel, the son of Kenaz, died.

12 And the children of Israel did evil again in the sight of the Lord, who strengthened against them Eglon, king of Moab, because they did evil in his sight. 13 And he joined to him the children of Ammon and Amalek, and he went and overthrew Israel and possessed the City of Palm Trees. 14 And the children of Israel served Eglon, king of Moab, eighteen years, 15 and afterwards they cried to the Lord, who raised them up a saviour called Ehud, the son of Gera, the son of Jemini, who used *the left hand as well as* the right. And the children of Israel sent presents to Eglon, king of Moab, by him. 16 And he made himself a two-edged sword, with a haft in the midst of the length of the palm of the hand and was girded therewith under his garment on the right thigh. 17 And he presented the gifts to Eglon, king of Moab.

Now Eglon was exceeding fat, 18 and when he had presented the gifts unto him, he followed his companions that came along with him. 19 Then, returning from Gilgal, where the idols were, he said to the king, "I have a secret message to thee, O king." And he commanded silence. And all being gone out that were about him, 20 Ehud went in to him (now he was sitting in a summer parlour alone), and he said, "I have a word from God to thee." And he forthwith rose up from his throne, 21 and Ehud put forth his left hand and took the dagger from his right thigh and thrust it into his belly 22 with such force that the haft *went in after* the blade

guissimo adipe stringeretur, nec eduxit gladium, sed ita ut percusserat reliquit in corpore.

Statimque per secreta naturae, alvi stercora proruperunt, 23 Ahoth autem, clausis diligentissime ostiis cenaculi et obfirmatis sera, 24 per posticam egressus est. Servique regis ingressi viderunt clausas fores cenaculi, atque dixerunt, "Forsitan purgat alvum in aestivo cubiculo." 25 Expectantesque diu donec erubescerent, et videntes quod nullus aperiret, tulerunt clavem, et aperientes, invenerunt dominum suum iacentem in terra mortuum.

26 Ahoth autem dum illi turbarentur effugit et pertransiit Locum Idolorum unde reversus fuerat. Venitque in Seirath, 27 et statim insonuit bucina in Monte Ephraim, descenderuntque cum eo filii Israhel, ipso in fronte gradiente. 28 Qui dixit ad eos, "Sequimini me, tradidit enim Dominus inimicos nostros Moabitas in manus nostras." Descenderuntque post eum et occupaverunt vada Iordanis, quae transmittunt in Moab, et non dimiserunt transire quemquam, 29 sed percusserunt Moabitas in tempore illo, circiter decem milia, omnes robustos et fortes viros. Nullus eorum evadere potuit. 30 Humiliatusque est Moab die illo sub manu Israhel, et quievit terra octoginta annis.

31 Post hunc fuit Samgar, filius Anath, qui percussit de Philisthim sescentos viros vomere, et ipse quoque defendit Israhel.

into the wound and was closed up with the abundance of fat, *so that he did not* draw out the dagger, but left it in his body as he had struck it in.

And forthwith by the secret parts of nature, the excrements of the belly came out, 23 but Ehud, carefully shutting the doors of the parlour and locking them, 24 went out by a postern door. And the king's servants going in saw the doors of the parlour shut, and they said, "Perhaps he *is easing nature* in his summer parlour." 25 And waiting a long time till they were ashamed, and seeing that no man opened *the door,* they took a key, and opening, they found their lord lying dead on the ground.

26 But Ehud while they were in confusion escaped and passed by the Place of the Idols from whence he had returned. And he came to Seirath, 27 and forthwith he sounded the trumpet in Mount Ephraim, and the children of Israel went down with him, he himself going in the front. 28 And he said to them, "Follow me, for the Lord hath delivered our enemies the Moabites into our hands." And they went down after him and seized upon the fords of the Jordan, which are in the way to Moab, and they suffered no man to pass over, 29 but they slew of the Moabites at that time, about ten thousand, all strong and valiant men. None of them could escape. 30 And Moab was humbled that day under the hand of Israel, and the land rested eighty years.

31 After him was Shamgar, the son of Anath, who slew of the Philistines six hundred men with a ploughshare, and he also defended Israel.

Caput 4

Addideruntque filii Israhel facere malum in conspectu Domini post mortem Ahoth, 2 et tradidit illos Dominus in manus Iabin, regis Chanaan, qui regnavit in Asor. Habuitque ducem exercitus sui nomine Sisaram, ipse autem habitabat in Aroseth Gentium. 3 Clamaveruntque filii Israhel ad Dominum, nongentos enim habebat falcatos currus et per viginti annos vehementer oppresserat eos.

4 Erat autem Debbora, prophetis, uxor Lapidoth, quae iudicabat populum in illo tempore, 5 et sedebat sub palma quae nomine illius vocabatur inter Rama et Bethel in Monte Ephraim, ascendebantque ad eam filii Israhel in omne iudicium. 6 Quae misit et vocavit Barac, filium Abinoem, de Cedes Nepthalim, dixitque ad eum, "Praecepit tibi Dominus, Deus Israhel, 'Vade, et duc exercitum in Montem Thabor, tollesque tecum decem milia pugnatorum de filiis Nepthalim et de filiis Zabulon, 7 ego autem ducam ad te in loco torrentis Cison Sisaram, principem exercitus Iabin, et currus eius atque omnem multitudinem et tradam eos in manu tua.'"

8 Dixitque ad eam Barac, "Si venis mecum, vadam. Si nolueris venire mecum, non pergam."

Chapter 4

Deborah and Barak deliver Israel from Jabin and Sisera. Jael killeth Sisera.

And the children of Israel again did evil in the sight of the Lord after the death of Ehud, 2 and the Lord delivered them up into the hands of Jabin, king of Canaan, who reigned in Hazor. And he had a general of his army named Sisera, and he dwelt in Harosheth of the Gentiles. 3 And the children of Israel cried to the Lord, for he had nine hundred chariots set with scythes and for twenty years had grievously oppressed them.

4 And there was at that time Deborah, a prophetess, the wife of Lappidoth, who judged the people, 5 and she sat under a palm tree which was called by her name between Ramah and Bethel in Mount Ephraim, and the children of Israel came up to her for all judgment. 6 And she sent and called Barak, the son of Abinoam, out of Kedesh in Naphtali, and she said to him, "The Lord, God of Israel, hath commanded thee, 'Go, and lead an army to mount Tabor, and thou shalt take with thee ten thousand fighting men of the children of Naphtali and of the children of Zebulun, 7 and I will bring unto thee in the place of the torrent Kishon Sisera, the general of Jabin's army, and his chariots and all his multitude and will deliver them into thy hand.'"

8 And Barak said to her, "If thou wilt come with me, I will go. If thou wilt not come with me, I will not go."

9 Quae dixit ad eum, "Ibo quidem tecum, sed in hac vice tibi victoria non reputabitur quia in manu mulieris tradetur Sisara." Surrexit itaque Debbora et perrexit cum Barac in Cedes. 10 Qui accitis Zabulon et Nepthalim ascendit cum decem milibus pugnatorum, habens Debboram in comitatu suo.

11 Aber autem, Cineus, recesserat quondam a ceteris Cineis, fratribus suis, filiis Obab, cognati Mosi, et tetenderat tabernacula usque ad vallem quae vocatur Sennim et erat iuxta Cedes. 12 Nuntiatumque est Sisarae quod ascendisset Barac, filius Abinoem, in Montem Thabor, 13 et congregavit nongentos falcatos currus omnemque exercitum de Aroseth Gentium ad torrentem Cison. 14 Dixitque Debbora ad Barac, "Surge, haec est enim dies in qua tradidit Dominus Sisaram in manus tuas. En: ipse ductor est tuus." Descendit itaque Barac de Monte Thabor et decem milia pugnatorum cum eo.

15 Perterruitque Dominus Sisaram et omnes currus eius universamque multitudinem in ore gladii ad conspectum Barac in tantum ut Sisara de curru desiliens pedibus fugeret. 16 Et Barac persequeretur fugientes currus et exercitum usque ad Aroseth Gentium, et omnis hostium multitudo usque ad internicionem caderet. 17 Sisara autem fugiens pervenit ad tentorium Iahel, uxoris Aber, Cinei, erat enim pax inter Iabin, regem Asor, et domum Aber, Cinei. 18 Egressa igitur Iahel in occursum Sisarae dixit ad eum, "Intra ad me, domine mi. Intra; ne timeas."

Qui ingressus tabernaculum eius et opertus ab ea pallio 19 dixit ad eam, "Da mihi, obsecro, paululum aquae, quia

9 She said to him, "I will go indeed with thee, but at this time the victory shall not be attributed to thee because Sisera shall be delivered into the hand of a woman." Deborah therefore arose and went with Barak to Kedesh. 10 And he called unto him Zebulun and Naphtali and went up with ten thousand fighting men, having Deborah in his company.

11 Now Heber, the Kenite, had some time before departed from the rest of the Kenites, his brethren, the sons of Hobab, the kinsman of Moses, and had pitched his tents unto the valley which is called Zaanannim and was near Kedesh. 12 And it was told Sisera that Barak, the son of Abinoam, was gone up to Mount Tabor, 13 and he gathered together his nine hundred chariots armed with scythes and all his army from Haroseth of the Gentiles to the torrent Kishon. 14 And Deborah said to Barak, "Arise, for this is the day wherein the Lord hath delivered Sisera into thy hands. Behold: he is thy leader." And Barak went down from Mount Tabor and ten thousand fighting men with him.

15 And the Lord struck a terror into Sisera and all his chariots and all his multitude with the edge of the sword at the sight of Barak insomuch that Sisera leaping down from off his chariot fled away on foot. 16 And Barak pursued after the fleeing chariots and the army unto Haroseth of the Gentiles, and all the multitude of the enemies was utterly destroyed. 17 But Sisera fleeing came to the tent of Jael, the wife of Heber, the Kenite, for there was peace between Jabin, the king of Hazor, and the house of Heber, the Kenite. 18 *And* Jael went forth to meet Sisera and said to him, "Come in to me, my lord. Come in; fear not."

He went in to her tent and being covered by her with a cloak 19 said to her, "Give me, I beseech thee, a little water,

valde sitio." Quae aperuit utrem lactis et dedit ei bibere et operuit illum. 20 Dixitque Sisara ad eam, "Sta ante ostium tabernaculi, et cum venerit aliquis, interrogans te et dicens, 'Numquid hic est aliquis?' dices, 'Nullus est.'"

21 Tulit itaque Iahel, uxor Aber, clavum tabernaculi adsumens pariter et malleum et ingressa abscondite et cum silentio, posuit supra tempus capitis eius clavum percussumque malleo defixit in cerebrum usque ad terram, qui soporem morti consocians, defecit et mortuus est.

22 Et ecce: Barac sequens Sisaram veniebat, egressaque Iahel in occursum eius dixit ei, "Veni, et ostendam tibi virum quem quaeris." Qui cum intrasset ad eam vidit Sisaram iacentem mortuum et clavum infixum in tempora eius. 23 Humiliavit ergo Deus in die illo Iabin, regem Chanaan, coram filiis Israhel, 24 qui crescebant cotidie et forti manu opprimebant Iabin, regem Chanaan, donec delerent eum.

Caput 5

Cecineruntque Debbora et Barac, filius Abinoem, in die illo, dicentes, 2 "Qui sponte obtulistis de Israhel animas vestras ad periculum, benedicite Domino. 3 Audite, reges; per-

for I am very thirsty." She opened a bottle of milk and gave him to drink and covered him. 20 And Sisera said to her, "Stand before the door of the tent, and when any shall come *and inquire of thee,* saying, 'Is there any man here?' thou shalt say, 'There is none.'"

21 So Jael, Heber's wife, took a nail of the tent, and, taking *also* a hammer and going in softly and with silence, she put the nail upon the temples of his head and striking it with the hammer drove it through his brain fast into the ground, *and so passing from* deep sleep *to* death, he fainted away and died.

22 And behold: Barak came pursuing after Sisera, and Jael went out to meet him and said to him, "Come, and I will show thee the man whom thou seekest." And when he came into *her tent* he saw Sisera lying dead and the nail fastened in his temples. 23 So God that day humbled Jabin, the king of Canaan, before the children of Israel, 24 who grew daily stronger and with a mighty hand overpowered Jabin, king of Canaan, till they quite destroyed him.

Chapter 5

The canticle of Deborah and Barak after their victory.

In that day Deborah and Barak, son of Abinoam, sung *and said,* 2 "O you of Israel that have willingly offered your lives to danger, bless the Lord. 3 Hear, O ye kings; give ear, ye

cipite auribus, principes: ego sum, ego sum quae Domino canam. Psallam Domino, Deo Israhel.

4 "Domine, cum exires de Seir et transires per regiones Edom, terra mota est, caelique ac nubes distillaverunt aquis. 5 Montes fluxerunt a facie Domini et Sinai a facie Domini, Dei Israhel.

6 "In diebus Samgar, filii Anath, in diebus Iahel, quieverunt semitae, et qui ingrediebantur per eas ambulaverunt per calles devios. 7 Cessaverunt fortes in Israhel et quieverunt donec surgeret Debbora; surgeret mater in Israhel. 8 Nova bella elegit Dominus, et portas hostium ipse subvertit, clypeus et hasta si apparuerint in quadraginta milibus Israhel.

9 "Cor meum diligit principes Israhel. Qui propria voluntate obtulistis vos discrimini, benedicite Domino. 10 Qui ascenditis super nitentes asinos et sedetis in iudicio et ambulatis in via, loquimini. 11 Ubi conlisi sunt currus et hostium est suffocatus exercitus, ibi narrentur iustitiae Domini et clementia in fortes Israhel. Tunc descendit populus Domini ad portas et obtinuit principatum.

12 "Surge, surge, Debbora, surge, surge, et loquere canticum. Surge, Barac, et adprehende captivos tuos, fili Abinoem. 13 Salvatae sunt reliquiae populi; Dominus in fortibus dimicavit. 14 Ex Ephraim delevit eos in Amalech, et post eum ex Beniamin in populos tuos, o Amalech. De Machir principes descenderunt, et de Zabulon qui exercitum ducerent ad bellandum. 15 Duces Isachar fuere cum Debbora et

princes: it is I, it is I that will sing to the Lord. I will sing to the Lord, the God of Israel.

4 "O Lord, when thou wentest out of Seir and passedst by the regions of Edom, the earth trembled, and the *heavens* dropped water. 5 The mountains melted before the face of the Lord and Sinai before the face of the Lord, the God of Israel.

6 "In the days of Shamgar, the son of Anath, in the days of Jael, the paths rested, and they that went by them walked through by-ways. 7 The valiant men ceased and rested in Israel until Deborah arose; a mother arose in Israel. 8 The Lord chose new wars, and he himself overthrew the gates of the enemies. *A shield and spear was not seen* among forty thousand of Israel.

9 "My heart loveth the princes of Israel. O you that of your own good will offered yourselves to danger, bless the Lord. 10 Speak, you that ride upon fair asses and you that sit in judgment and walk in the way. 11 Where the chariots were dashed together and the army of the enemies was choked, there let the justices of the Lord be rehearsed and his clemency towards the brave men of Israel. Then the people of the Lord went down to the gates and obtained the sovereignty.

12 "Arise, arise, O Deborah, arise, arise, and utter a canticle. Arise, Barak, and take hold of thy captives, O son of Abinoam. 13 The remnants of the people are saved; the Lord hath fought among the valiant ones. 14 Out of Ephraim he destroyed them into Amalek, and after him out of Benjamin into thy people, O Amalek. Out of Machir there came down princes, and out of Zebulun they that led the army to fight. 15 The captains of Issachar were with Deborah and

Barac vestigia sunt secuti, qui quasi in praeceps ac baratrum se discrimini dedit. Diviso contra se Ruben, magnanimorum repperta contentio est. 16 Quare habitas inter duos terminos, ut audias sibilos gregum? Diviso contra se Ruben, magnanimorum repperta contentio est. 17 Galaad trans Iordanem quiescebat, et Dan vacabat navibus. Aser habitabat in litore maris et in portibus morabatur. 18 Zabulon vero et Nepthalim obtulerunt animas suas morti in regione Merome.

19 "Venerunt reges et pugnaverunt; pugnaverunt reges Chanaan in Thanach iuxta aquas Mageddo, et tamen nihil tulere praedantes. 20 De caelo dimicatum est contra eos: stellae manentes in ordine et cursu suo adversum Sisaram pugnaverunt. 21 Torrens Cison traxit cadavera eorum, torrens Cadumim, torrens Cison. Conculca, anima mea, robustos. 22 Ungulae equorum ceciderunt fugientibus impetu et per praeceps ruentibus fortissimis hostium.

23 "'Maledicite terrae Meroz,' dixit angelus Domini, 'Maledicite habitatoribus eius quia non venerunt ad auxilium Domini, in adiutorium fortissimorum eius. 24 Benedicta inter mulieres Iahel, uxor Aber, Cinei, et benedicatur in tabernaculo suo.'

25 "Aquam petenti lac dedit et in fiala principum obtulit butyrum. 26 Sinistram manum misit ad clavum et dexteram ad fabrorum malleos, percussitque Sisaram, quaerens in capite vulneri locum et tempus valide perforans. 27 Inter pedes eius ruit. Defecit, et mortuus est. Ante pedes illius volvebatur, et iacebat exanimis et miserabilis. 28 Per fenestram pro-

followed the steps of Barak, who exposed himself to danger as one going *headlong and into* a pit. Reuben being divided against himself, there was found a strife of courageous men. 16 Why dwellest thou between two borders, that thou mayest hear the bleatings of the flocks? Reuben being divided against himself, there was found a strife of courageous men. 17 Gilead rested beyond the Jordan, and Dan applied himself to ships. Asher dwelt on the sea shore and abode in the havens. 18 But Zebulun and Naphtali offered their lives to death in the region of Merome.

19 "The kings came and fought; the kings of Canaan fought in Taanach by the waters of Megiddo, and yet they took no spoils. 20 War from heaven was made against them: the stars remaining in their order and *courses* fought against Sisera. 21 The torrent of Kishon dragged their carcasses, the torrent of Cadumim, the torrent of Kishon. Tread thou, my soul, upon the strong ones. 22 The hoofs of the horses were broken whilst the stoutest of the enemies fled amain and fell headlong down.

23 "'Curse ye the land of Meroz,' said the angel of the Lord, 'Curse the inhabitants thereof because they came not to the help of the Lord, to help his most valiant men. 24 Blessed among women be Jael, the wife of Heber, the Kenite, and blessed be she in her tent.'

25 "*He asked her water, and* she gave him milk and offered him butter in a dish fit for princes. 26 She put her left hand to the nail and her right hand to the workman's hammer, and she struck Sisera, seeking in his head a place for the wound and strongly piercing through his *temples.* 27 Between her feet he fell. He fainted, and he died. He rolled before her feet, and he lay lifeless and wretched. 28 His mother

spiciens ululabat mater eius, et de cenaculo loquebatur, 'Cur moratur regredi currus eius? Quare tardaverunt pedes quadrigarum illius?'

29 "Una sapientior ceteris uxoribus eius haec socrui verba respondit: 30 'Forsitan nunc dividit spolia, et pulcherrima feminarum eligitur ei. Vestes diversorum colorum Sisarae traduntur in praedam, et supellex varia ad ornanda colla congeritur.'

31 "Sic pereant omnes inimici tui, Domine, qui autem diligunt te, sicut sol in ortu suo splendet, ita rutilent."

32 Quievitque terra per quadraginta annos.

Caput 6

Fecerunt autem filii Israhel malum in conspectu Domini, qui tradidit eos in manu Madian septem annis, 2 et oppressi sunt valde ab eis. Feceruntque sibi antra et speluncas in montibus et munitissima ad repugnandum loca. 3 Cumque sevisset Israhel, ascendebat Madian et Amalech et ceteri orientalium nationum 4 et apud eos figentes tentoria sicut erant in herbis cuncta vastabant usque ad introitum Gazae.

looked *out at* a window and howled, and she spoke from the dining room, 'Why *is* his chariot *so long in coming* back? Why are the feet of his horses *so* slow?'

29 "One that was wiser than the rest of his wives returned this answer to her mother-in-law: 30 'Perhaps he is now dividing the spoils, and the fairest of the women is chosen out for him. Garments of divers colours are given to Sisera for his prey, and furniture of different kinds is heaped together to adorn the necks.'

31 "So let all thy enemies perish, O Lord, but let them that love thee shine as the sun shineth in his rising."

32 And the land rested for forty years.

Chapter 6

The people for their sins are oppressed by the Midianites.
Gideon is called to deliver them.

And the children of Israel *again* did evil in the sight of the Lord, and he delivered them into the hand of Midian seven years, 2 and they were grievously oppressed by them. And they made themselves dens and caves in the mountains and strong holds to resist. 3 And when Israel had sown, Midian and Amalek and the rest of the eastern nations came up 4 and pitching their tents among them wasted all things as they were in the blade even to the entrance of Gaza. And

Nihilque omnino ad vitam pertinens relinquebant in Israhel, non oves, non boves, non asinos, 5 ipsi enim et universi greges eorum veniebant cum tabernaculis suis et instar lucustarum universa conplebant, innumera multitudo hominum et camelorum, quicquid tetigerant devastantes.

6 Humiliatusque est Israhel valde in conspectu Madian, 7 et clamavit ad Dominum postulans auxilium contra Madianitas. 8 Qui misit ad eos virum prophetam, et locutus est, "Haec dicit Dominus, Deus Israhel, 'Ego vos feci conscendere de Aegypto et eduxi de domo servitutis 9 et liberavi de manu Aegyptiorum et omnium inimicorum qui adfligebant vos, eiecique eos ad introitum vestrum et tradidi vobis terram eorum. 10 Et dixi, "Ego Dominus, Deus vester; ne timeatis deos Amorreorum in quorum terra habitatis." Et noluistis audire vocem meam.'"

11 Venit autem angelus Domini et sedit sub quercu quae erat in Ephra et pertinebat ad Ioas, patrem familiae Ezri. Cumque Gedeon, filius eius, excuteret atque purgaret frumenta in torculari ut fugeret Madian, 12 apparuit ei angelus Domini et ait, "Dominus tecum, virorum fortissime."

13 Dixitque ei Gedeon, "Obsecro, mi Domine, si Dominus nobiscum est, cur adprehenderunt nos haec omnia mala? Ubi sunt mirabilia eius quae narraverunt patres nostri, atque dixerunt, 'De Aegypto eduxit nos Dominus'? Nunc autem dereliquit nos Dominus et tradidit in manu Madian."

14 Respexitque ad eum Dominus et ait, "Vade in hac fortitudine tua, et liberabis Israhel de manu Madian. Scito quod miserim te."

they left nothing at all in Israel *for sustenance of* life, *nor* sheep *nor* oxen *nor* asses, 5 for they and all their flocks came with their tents and like locusts filled all places, an innumerable multitude of men and of camels, wasting whatsoever they touched.

6 And Israel was humbled exceedingly in the sight of Midian, 7 and he cried to the Lord desiring help against the Midianites. 8 And he sent unto them a prophet, and he spoke, "Thus saith the Lord, the God of Israel, 'I made you to come up out of Egypt and brought you out of the house of bondage 9 and delivered you out of the *hands* of the Egyptians and of all the enemies that afflicted you, and I cast them out at your coming in and gave you their land. 10 And I said, "I am the Lord, your God; fear not the gods of the Amorites in whose land you dwell." And you would not hear my voice.'"

11 And an angel of the Lord came and sat under an oak that was in Ophrah and belonged to Joash, the father of the family of Abiezer. And when Gideon, his son, was threshing and cleansing wheat by the winepress to flee from Midian, 12 the angel of the Lord appeared to him and said, "The Lord is with thee, O most valiant of men."

13 And Gideon said to him, "I beseech thee, my Lord, if the Lord be with us, why have these evils fallen upon us? Where are his miracles which our fathers have told us of, *saying,* 'The Lord brought us out of Egypt'? But now the Lord hath forsaken us and delivered us into the hands of Midian."

14 And the Lord looked upon him and said, "Go in this thy strength, and thou shalt deliver Israel out of the hand of Midian. Know that I have sent thee."

15 Qui respondens ait, "Obsecro, Domine mi, in quo liberabo Israhel? Ecce: familia mea infima est in Manasse, et ego minimus in domo patris mei."

16 Dixitque ei Dominus, "Ego ero tecum, et percuties Madian quasi unum virum."

17 Et ille, "Si inveni," inquit, "gratiam coram te, da mihi signum quod tu sis qui loquaris ad me, 18 nec recedas hinc donec revertar ad te portans sacrificium et offerens tibi."

Qui respondit, "Ego praestolabor adventum tuum."

19 Ingressus est itaque Gedeon et coxit hedum et de farinae modio azymos panes, carnesque ponens in canistro et ius carnium mittens in ollam tulit omnia sub quercum et obtulit ei. 20 Cui dixit angelus Domini, "Tolle carnes et panes azymos, et pone super petram illam, et ius desuper funde." Cumque fecisset ita, 21 extendit angelus Domini summitatem virgae quam tenebat in manu et tetigit carnes et azymos panes, ascenditque ignis de petra et carnes azymosque panes consumpsit, angelus autem Domini evanuit ex oculis eius.

22 Vidensque Gedeon quod esset angelus Domini ait, "Heu, mi Domine Deus, quia vidi angelum Domini facie ad faciem."

23 Dixitque ei Dominus, "Pax tecum. Ne timeas; non morieris."

24 Aedificavitque ibi Gedeon altare Domino vocavitque illud Domini Pax usque in praesentem diem. Cumque adhuc esset in Ephra, quae est familiae Ezri, 25 nocte illa dixit Dominus ad eum, "Tolle taurum patris tui et alterum taurum

15 He answered and said, "I beseech thee, my lord, wherewith shall I deliver Israel? Behold: my family is the meanest in Manasseh, and I am the least in my father's house."

16 And the Lord said to him, "I will be with thee, and thou shalt cut off Midian as one man."

17 And he said, "If I have found grace before thee, give me a sign that it is thou that speakest to me, 18 and depart not hence till I return to thee and bring a sacrifice and offer it to thee."

And he answered, "I will wait thy coming."

19 So Gideon went in and boiled a kid and made unleavened loaves of a measure of flour, and putting the flesh in a basket *and the broth* of the flesh into a pot he carried all under the oak and presented to him. 20 And the angel of the Lord said to him, "Take the flesh and the unleavened loaves, and lay them upon that rock, and pour out the broth thereon." And when he had done so, 21 the angel of the Lord put forth the tip of the rod which he held in his hand and touched the flesh and the unleavened loaves, and there arose a fire from the rock and consumed the flesh and the unleavened loaves, and the angel of the Lord vanished out of his sight.

22 And Gideon seeing that it was the angel of the Lord said, "Alas, my Lord God, for I have seen the angel of the Lord face to face."

23 And the Lord said to him, "Peace be with thee. Fear not; thou shalt not die."

24 And Gideon built there an altar to the Lord and called it The Lord's Peace until this present day. And when he was yet in Ophrah, which is of the family of Abiezer, 25 that night the Lord said to him, "Take a bullock of thy father's and an-

annorum septem, destruesque aram Baal, quae est patris tui, et nemus quod circa aram est succide. 26 Et aedificabis altare Domino, Deo tuo, in summitate petrae huius super quam sacrificium ante posuisti, tollesque taurum secundum et offeres holocaustum super lignorum struem quae de nemore succideris."

27 Adsumptis igitur Gedeon decem viris de servis suis fecit sicut praeceperat ei Dominus. Timens autem domum patris sui et homines illius civitatis, per diem id facere noluit sed omnia nocte conplevit. 28 Cumque surrexissent viri oppidi eius mane, viderunt destructam aram Baal lucumque succisum et taurum alterum inpositum super altare quod tunc aedificatum erat. 29 Dixeruntque ad invicem, "Quis hoc fecit?"

Cumque perquirerent auctorem facti, dictum est, "Gedeon, filius Ioas, fecit haec omnia."

30 Et dixerunt ad Ioas, "Produc filium tuum huc ut moriatur quia destruxit aram Baal et succidit nemus."

31 Quibus ille respondit, "Numquid ultores estis Baal ut pugnetis pro eo? Qui adversarius eius est, moriatur antequam lux crastina veniat. Si deus est, vindicet se de eo qui suffodit aram eius."

32 Ex illo die vocatus est Gedeon Hierobbaal eo quod dixisset Ioas, "Ulciscatur se de eo Baal qui suffodit altare eius."

33 Igitur omnis Madian et Amalech et orientales populi congregati sunt simul et transeuntes Iordanem castrametati sunt in valle Iezrahel. 34 Spiritus autem Domini induit Ge-

other bullock of seven years, and thou shalt destroy the altar of Baal, which is thy father's, and cut down the grove that is about the altar. 26 And thou shalt build an altar to the Lord, thy God, in the top of this rock whereupon thou didst lay the sacrifice before, and thou shalt take the second bullock and shalt offer a holocaust upon a pile of the wood which thou shalt cut down out of the grove."

27 Then Gideon taking ten men of his servants did as the Lord had commanded him. But, fearing his father's house and the men of that city, he would not do it by day but did all by night. 28 And when the men of that town were risen in the morning, they saw the altar of Baal destroyed and the grove cut down and the second bullock laid upon the altar which then was built. 29 And they said one to another, "Who hath done this?"

And when they inquired for the author of the fact, it was said, "Gideon, the son of Joash, did all *this.*"

30 And they said to Joash, "Bring out thy son hither that he may die because he hath destroyed the altar of Baal and hath cut down his grove."

31 He answered them, "Are you the avengers of Baal that you fight for him? He that is his adversary, let him die before tomorrow light appear. If he be a god, let him revenge himself on him that hath cast down his altar."

32 From that day Gideon was called Jerubbaal because Joash had said, "Let Baal revenge himself on him that hath cast down his altar."

33 Now all Midian and Amalek and the eastern people were gathered together and passing over the Jordan camped in the Valley of Jezreel. 34 But the spirit of the Lord came upon Gideon, and he sounded the trumpet and called to-

deon, qui clangens bucina convocavit domum Abiezer ut sequeretur se. 35 Misitque nuntios in universum Manassen, qui et ipse secutus est eum, et alios nuntios in Aser et Zabulon et Nepthalim, qui occurrerunt ei. 36 Dixitque Gedeon ad Deum, "Si salvum facis per manum meam Israhel, sicut locutus es, 37 ponam vellus hoc lanae in area; si ros in solo vellere fuerit et in omni terra siccitas, sciam quod per manum meam, sicut locutus es, liberabis Israhel." 38 Factumque est ita. Et, de nocte consurgens, expresso vellere, concam rore conplevit. 39 Dixitque rursus ad Deum, "Ne irascatur furor tuus contra me si adhuc semel temptavero, signum quaerens in vellere. Oro ut solum vellus siccum sit et omnis terra rore madens." 40 Fecitque Deum nocte illa ut postulaverat, et fuit siccitas in solo vellere, et ros in omni terra.

Caput 7

Igitur Hierobbaal, qui est et Gedeon, de nocte consurgens et omnis populus cum eo, venit ad fontem qui vocatur Arad. Erant autem castra Madian in valle ad septentrionalem plagam collis excelsi, 2 dixitque Dominus ad Gedeon, "Multus tecum est populus, nec tradetur Madian in manus eius ne

gether the house of Abiezer to follow him. 35 And he sent messengers into all Manasseh, and they also followed him, and other messengers into Asher and Zebulun and Naphtali, and they *came to meet* him. 36 And Gideon said to God, "If thou *wilt save* Israel by my hand, as thou hast said, 37 I will put this fleece of wool on the floor; if there be dew on the fleece only and *it be dry* on all the ground beside, I shall know that by my hand, as thou hast said, thou wilt deliver Israel." 38 And it *was* so. And, rising *before day,* wringing the fleece, he filled a vessel with the dew. 39 And he said again to God, "Let not thy wrath be kindled against me if I try once more, seeking a sign in the fleece. I pray that the fleece only may be dry and all the ground wet with dew." 40 And God did that night as he had requested, and *it was dry* on the fleece only, and there was dew on all the ground.

Chapter 7

Gideon, with three hundred men, by stratagem defeateth the Midianites.

Then Jerubbaal, who is *the same as* Gideon, rising up early and all the people with him, came to the fountain that is called Harod. Now the camp of Midian was in the valley on the north side of the high hill, 2 and the Lord said to Gideon, "The people that are with thee are many, and Midian shall

glorietur contra me Israhel et dicat, 'Meis viribus liberatus sum.' 3 Loquere ad populum, et cunctis audientibus praedica, 'Qui formidolosus et timidus est, revertatur.'" Recesseruntque de Monte Galaad et reversa sunt viginti duo milia virorum, et tantum decem milia remanserunt.

4 Dixitque Dominus ad Gedeon, "Adhuc populus multus est. Duc eos ad aquas, et ibi probabo illos, et de quo dixero tibi ut tecum vadat ipse, pergat; quem ire prohibuero, revertatur."

5 Cumque descendisset populus ad aquas, dixit Dominus ad Gedeon, "Qui lingua lambuerint aquas, sicut solent canes lambere, separabis eos seorsum, qui autem curvatis genibus biberint in altera parte erunt." 6 Fuit itaque numerus eorum qui manu ad os proiciente aquas lambuerant trecenti viri, omnis autem reliqua multitudo flexo poplite biberat.

7 Et ait Dominus ad Gedeon, "In trecentis viris qui lambuerunt aquas liberabo vos et tradam Madian in manu tua, omnis autem reliqua multitudo revertatur in locum suum." 8 Sumptis itaque pro numero cibariis et tubis, omnem reliquam multitudinem abire praecepit ad tabernacula sua, et ipse cum trecentis se certamini dedit.

Castra autem Madian erant subter in valle. 9 Eadem nocte dixit Dominus ad eum, "Surge, et descende in castra quia tradidi eos in manu tua. 10 Sin autem solus ire formidas, descendat tecum Phara, puer tuus. 11 Et cum audieris quid loquantur, tunc confortabuntur manus tuae, et securior ad

not be delivered into their hands lest Israel should glory against me and say, 'I was delivered by my own strength.' 3 Speak to the people, and proclaim in the hearing of all, '*Whosoever* is fearful and timorous, let him return.'" So two and twenty thousand men went away from Mount Gilead and returned *home,* and only ten thousand remained.

4 And the Lord said to Gideon, "The people are still *too many.* Bring them to the waters, and there I will try them, and of whom I shall say to thee, '*This shall go with thee,*' let him go; whom I shall forbid to go, let him return."

5 And when the people were come down to the waters, the Lord said to Gideon, "They that shall lap the water with their tongues, as dogs are wont to lap, thou shalt set apart by themselves, but they that shall drink bowing down their knees shall be on the other side." 6 And the number of them that had lapped water, *casting it with the hand* to their mouth, was three hundred men, and all the rest of the multitude had drunk kneeling. 7 And the Lord said to Gideon, "By the three hundred men that lapped water I will save you and deliver Midian into thy hand, but let all the rest of the people return to their place." 8 So taking victuals and trumpets according to their number, he ordered all the rest of the multitude to depart to their tents, and he with the three hundred gave himself to the battle.

Now the camp of Midian was beneath *him* in the valley. 9 The same night the Lord said to him, "Arise, and go down into the camp because I have delivered them into thy hand. 10 But if thou be afraid to go alone, let Purah, thy servant, go down with thee. 11 And when thou shalt hear what they are saying, then shall thy hands be strengthened, and thou shalt

hostium castra descendes." Descendit ergo ipse et Phara, puer eius, in partem castrorum ubi erant armatorum vigiliae.

12 Madian autem et Amalech et omnes orientales populi fusi iacebant in valle ut lucustarum multitudo; cameli quoque innumerabiles erant sicut harena quae iacet in litore maris. 13 Cumque venisset Gedeon, narrabat aliquis somnium proximo suo et in hunc modum referebat quod viderat: "Vidi somnium, et videbatur mihi quasi subcinericius panis ex hordeo volvi et in Madian castra descendere, cumque pervenisset ad tabernaculum percussit illud atque subvertit et terrae funditus coaequavit."

14 Respondit is cui loquebatur, "Non est hoc aliud nisi gladius Gedeonis, filii Ioas, viri Israhelitae. Tradidit enim Dominus in manus eius Madian et omnia castra eius."

15 Cumque audisset Gedeon somnium et interpretationem eius, adoravit et reversus est ad castra Israhel et ait, "Surgite, tradidit enim Dominus in manus nostras castra Madian." 16 Divisitque trecentos viros in tres partes et dedit tubas in manibus eorum lagoenasque vacuas ac lampadas in medio lagoenarum. 17 Et dixit ad eos, "Quod me facere videritis, hoc facite. Ingrediar partem castrorum, et quod fecero sectamini. 18 Quando personaverit tuba in manu mea, vos quoque per castrorum circuitum clangite, et conclamate, 'Domino et Gedeoni!'"

19 Ingressusque est Gedeon et trecenti viri qui erant cum eo in partem castrorum incipientibus vigiliis noctis mediae, et, custodibus suscitatis, coeperunt bucinis clangere et conplodere inter se lagoenas. 20 Cumque per gyrum cas-

go down more secure to the enemies' camp." And he went down with Purah, his servant, into part of the camp where was the watch of men in arms.

12 But Midian and Amalek and all the eastern people lay scattered in the valley as a multitude of locusts; their camels also were innumerable as the sand that lieth on the sea shore. 13 And when Gideon was come, one told his neighbour a dream and in this manner related what he had seen: "I dreamt a dream, and it seemed to me as if a hearth-cake of barley bread rolled and came down into the camp of Midian, and when it was come to a tent it struck it and beat it down flat to the ground."

14 He to whom he spoke answered, "This is nothing else but the sword of Gideon, the son of Joash, a man of Israel, for the Lord hath delivered Midian and all their camp into his *hand.*"

15 And when Gideon had heard the dream and the interpretation thereof, he adored and returned to the camp of Israel and said, "Arise, for the Lord hath delivered the camp of Midian into our hands." 16 And he divided the three hundred men into three parts and gave them trumpets in their hands and empty pitchers and lamps within the pitchers. 17 And he said to them, "What you shall see me do, do you *the same.* I will go into one part of the camp, and *do you as I shall do.* 18 When the trumpet shall sound in my hand, do you also blow the trumpets *on every side of the camp.*"

19 And Gideon and the three hundred men that were with him went into part of the camp at the beginning of the midnight watch, and, the watchmen being alarmed, they began to sound their trumpets and to clap the pitchers one against another. 20 And when they sounded *their trumpets* in three

trorum in tribus personarent locis et hydrias confregis-
sent, tenuerunt sinistris manibus lampadas et dextris sonan-
tes tubas, clamaveruntque, "Gladius Domini et Gedeonis!"
21 stantes singuli in loco suo per circuitum castrorum hosti-
lium. Omnia itaque castra turbata sunt et vociferantes ulu-
lantesque fugerunt. 22 Et nihilominus insistebant trecenti
viri bucinis personantes. Inmisitque Dominus gladium in
omnibus castris, et mutua se caede truncabant, 23 fugientes
usque Bethseta et crepidinem Abelmeula in Tebbath.
Conclamantes autem viri Israhel de Nepthali et Aser et
omni Manasse persequebantur Madian.

24 Misitque Gedeon nuntios in omnem Montem Ephraim,
dicens, "Descendite in occursum Madian, et praeoccupate
aquas usque Bethbera atque Iordanem." Clamavitque omnis
Ephraim et praeoccupavit aquas atque Iordanem usque
Bethbera. 25 Adprehensosque duos viros Madian, Oreb et
Zeb, interfecit Oreb in Petra Oreb, Zeb vero in Torculari
Zeb. Et persecuti sunt Madian, capita Oreb et Zeb portan-
tes ad Gedeon trans fluenta Iordanis.

places round about the camp and had broken their pitchers, they held their lamps in their left hands and with their right hands the trumpets *which they blew,* and they cried out, "The sword of the Lord and of Gideon!" 21 standing every man in his place round about the enemies' camp. So all the camp was troubled, and crying out and howling they fled away. 22 And the three hundred men nevertheless persisted sounding the trumpets. And the Lord sent the sword into all the camp, and they killed one another, 23 fleeing as far as Beth-shittah and the border of Abel-meholah in Tabbath. But the men of Israel shouting from Naphtali and Asher and from all Manasseh pursued after Midian.

24 And Gideon sent messengers into all Mount Ephraim, saying, "Come down to meet Midian, and take the waters before them to Beth-barah and the Jordan." And all Ephraim shouted and took the waters before them and the Jordan as far as Beth-barah. 25 And having taken two men of Midian, Oreb and Zeeb, Oreb *they* slew in the Rock of Oreb, and Zeeb in the Winepress of Zeeb. And they pursued Midian, carrying the heads of Oreb and Zeeb to Gideon beyond the waters of the Jordan.

Caput 8

Dixeruntque ad eum viri Ephraim, "Quid est hoc quod facere voluisti ut non nos vocares cum ad pugnam pergeres contra Madian?" iurgantes fortiter et prope vim inferentes.

2 Quibus ille respondit, "Quid enim tale facere potui quale vos fecistis? Nonne melior est racemus Ephraim vindemiis Abiezer? 3 In manus vestras tradidit Dominus principes Madian, Oreb et Zeb; quid tale facere potui quale vos fecistis?" Quod cum locutus esset, requievit spiritus eorum quo tumebant contra eum.

4 Cumque venisset Gedeon ad Iordanem, transivit eum cum trecentis viris qui secum erant, et prae lassitudine fugientes persequi non poterant. 5 Dixitque ad viros Soccoth, "Date, obsecro, panes populo qui mecum est, quia valde defecerunt, ut possimus persequi Zebee et Salmana, reges Madian."

6 Responderunt principes Soccoth, "Forsitan palmae manuum Zebee et Salmana in manu tua sunt, et idcirco postulas ut demus exercitui tuo panes."

Chapter 8

Gideon appeaseth the Ephraimites, taketh Zebah and Zalmunna, destroyeth Succoth and Penuel, refuseth to be king, maketh an ephod of the gold of the prey and dieth in a good old age. The people return to idolatry.

$\mathbf{A}$nd the men of Ephraim said to him, "What is this that thou meanest to do that thou wouldst not call us when thou wentest to fight against Midian?" *And they chid* him sharply and almost offered violence.

2 And he answered them, *"What* could I have done like to that which you have done? Is not one bunch of grapes of Ephraim better than the vintages of Abiezer? 3 The Lord hath delivered into your hands the princes of Midian, Oreb and Zeeb; what could I have done like to what you have done?" And when he had said this, their spirit was appeased with which they swelled against him.

4 And when Gideon was come to the Jordan, he passed over it with the three hundred men that were with him, *who were so weary that* they could not pursue after them that fled. 5 And he said to the men of Succoth, "Give, I beseech you, bread to the people that is with me, for they are *faint,* that we may pursue Zebah and Zalmunna, the kings of Midian."

6 The princes of Succoth answered, "Peradventure the palms of the hands of Zebah and Zalmunna are in thy hand, and therefore thou demandest that we should give bread to thy army."

7 Quibus ille ait, "Cum ergo tradiderit Dominus Zebee et Salmana in manus meas, conteram carnes vestras cum spinis tribulisque deserti."

8 Et inde conscendens, venit in Phanuhel, locutusque est ad viros eius loci similia. Cui et illi responderunt sicut responderant viri Soccoth. 9 Dixit itaque et eis, "Cum reversus fuero victor in pace, destruam turrem hanc."

10 Zebee autem et Salmana requiescebant cum omni exercitu suo, quindecim milia enim viri remanserant ex omnibus turmis orientalium populorum, caesis centum viginti milibus bellatorum et educentium gladium. 11 Ascendensque Gedeon per viam eorum qui in tabernaculis morabantur ad orientalem partem Nobee et Iecbaa percussit castra hostium, qui securi erant et nihil adversi suspicabantur. 12 Fugeruntque Zebee et Salmana, quos persequens Gedeon conprehendit, turbato omni exercitu eorum.

13 Revertensque de bello ante solis ortum 14 adprehendit puerum de viris Soccoth, interrogavitque eum nomina principum et seniorum Soccoth, et descripsit septuaginta septem viros. 15 Venitque ad Soccoth et dixit eis, "En Zebee et Salmana, super quibus exprobrastis mihi, dicentes, 'Forsitan manus Zebee et Salmana in manibus tuis sunt, et idcirco postulas ut demus viris qui lassi sunt et defecerunt panes.'" 16 Tulit ergo seniores civitatis et spinas deserti ac tribulos et contrivit cum eis, atque comminuit viros Soccoth. 17 Turrem quoque Phanuhel subvertit occisis habitatoribus civitatis.

7 And he said to them, "When the Lord therefore shall have delivered Zebah and Zalmunna into my hands, I will thresh your flesh with the thorns and briers of the desert."

8 And going up from thence, he came to Penuel, and he spoke the like things to the men of that place. And they also answered him as the men of Succoth had answered. 9 He said therefore to them also, "When I shall return a conqueror in peace, I will destroy this tower."

10 But Zebah and Zalmunna were resting with all their army, for fifteen thousand men were left of all the troops of the eastern people, and one hundred and twenty thousand warriors *that* drew the sword were slain. 11 And Gideon went up by the way of them that dwelt in tents on the *east* of Nobah and Jogbehah and smote the camp of the enemies, who were secure and suspected no hurt. 12 And Zebah and Zalmunna fled, and Gideon pursued and took them, all their host being put in confusion.

13 And returning from the battle before the sun rising 14 he took a boy of the men of Succoth, and he asked him the names of the princes and ancients of Succoth, and he described *unto him* seventy-seven men. 15 And he came to Succoth and said to them, "Behold Zebah and Zalmunna, concerning whom you upbraided me, saying, 'Peradventure the hands of Zebah and Zalmunna are in thy hands, and therefore thou demandest that we should give bread to the men that are weary and faint.'" 16 So he took the ancients of the city and thorns and briers of the desert and tore them with the same, and cut in pieces the men of Succoth. 17 And he demolished the tower of Penuel and slew the men of the city.

18 Dixitque ad Zebee et Salmana, "Quales fuerunt viri quos occidistis in Thabor?"

Qui responderunt, "Similes tui, et unus ex eis quasi filius regis."

19 Quibus ille respondit, "Fratres mei fuerunt, filii matris meae. Vivit Dominus, si servassetis eos, non vos occiderem."

20 Dixitque Ietther, primogenito suo, "Surge, et interfice eos." Qui non eduxit gladium, timebat enim, quia adhuc puer erat.

21 Dixeruntque Zebee et Salmana, "Tu surge, et inrue in nos, quia iuxta aetatem robur est hominis." Surrexit Gedeon et interfecit Zebee et Salmana, et tulit ornamenta ac bullas quibus colla regalium camelorum decorari solent.

22 Dixeruntque omnes viri Israhel ad Gedeon, "Dominare nostri tu et filius tuus et filius filii tui, quia liberasti nos de manu Madian."

23 Quibus ille ait, "Non dominabor vestri, nec dominabitur in vos filius meus, sed dominabitur vobis Dominus." 24 Dixitque ad eos, "Unam petitionem postulo a vobis: date mihi inaures ex praeda vestra," inaures enim aureas Ismahelitae habere consuerant.

25 Qui responderunt, "Libentissime dabimus." Expandentesque super terram pallium, proiecerunt in eo inaures de praeda, 26 et fuit pondus postulatarum inaurium mille septingenti auri sicli absque ornamentis et monilibus et veste purpurea quibus Madian reges uti soliti erant et praeter torques aureos camelorum. 27 Fecitque ex eo Gedeon ephod et posuit illud in civitate sua Ephra. Fornicatusque

18 And he said to Zebah and Zalmunna, "What manner of men were they whom you slew in Tabor?"

They answered, "They were like thee, and one of them as the son of a king."

19 He answered them, "They were my brethren, the sons of my mother. *As* the Lord liveth, *if* you had saved them, I would not kill you."

20 And he said to Jether, his eldest son, "Arise, and slay them." But he drew not his sword, for he was afraid, being but yet a boy.

21 And Zebah and Zalmunna said, "Do thou rise, and run upon us, because the strength of a man is according to his age." Gideon rose up and slew Zebah and Zalmunna, and he took the ornaments and bosses with which the necks of the camels of kings are wont to be adorned.

22 And all the men of Israel said to Gideon, "Rule thou over us and thy son and thy son's son, because thou hast delivered us from the hand of Midian."

23 And he said to them, "I will not rule over you, neither shall my son rule over you, but the Lord shall rule over you." 24 And he said to them, "I desire one request of you: give me the earlets of your spoils," for the Ishmaelites were accustomed to wear golden earlets.

25 They answered, "We will give them most willingly." And spreading a mantle on the ground, they cast upon it the earlets of the spoils, 26 and the weight of the earlets that he requested was a thousand seven hundred sicles of gold besides the ornaments and jewels and purple raiment which the kings of Midian were wont to use and besides the golden chains *that were about the camels' necks.* 27 And Gideon made an ephod thereof and put it in his city Ophrah. And all

est omnis Israhel in eo, et factum est Gedeoni et omni domui eius in ruinam. 28 Humiliatus est autem Madian coram filiis Israhel, nec potuerunt ultra elevare cervices, sed quievit terra per quadraginta annos quibus praefuit Gedeon.

29 Abiit itaque Hierobbaal, filius Ioas, et habitavit in domo sua, 30 habuitque septuaginta filios qui egressi sunt de femore eius, eo quod plures haberet uxores. 31 Concubina autem illius quam habebat in Sychem genuit ei filium nomine Abimelech. 32 Mortuusque est Gedeon, filius Ioas, in senectute bona et sepultus in sepulchro Ioas patris sui in Ephra de familia Ezri.

33 Postquam autem mortuus est Gedeon, aversi sunt filii Israhel et fornicati cum Baalim. Percusseruntque cum Baal foedus ut esset eis in deum, 34 nec recordati sunt Domini, Dei sui, qui eruit eos de manibus omnium inimicorum suorum per circuitum, 35 nec fecerunt misericordiam cum domo Hierobbaal Gedeon, iuxta omnia bona quae fecerat Israheli.

Israel committed fornication with it, and it became a ruin to Gideon and to all his house. 28 But Midian was humbled before the children of Israel, neither could they any more lift up their heads, but the land rested for forty years while Gideon presided.

29 So Jerubbaal, the son of Joash, went and dwelt in his own house, 30 and he had seventy sons who came out of his thigh, for he had many wives. 31 And his concubine that he had in Shechem bore him a son whose name was Abimelech. 32 And Gideon, the son of Joash, died in a good old age and was buried in the sepulchre of his father in Ophrah of the family of Abiezer.

33 But after Gideon was dead, the children of Israel turned again and committed fornication with Baalim. And they made a covenant with Baal that he should be their god, 34 and they remembered not the Lord, their God, who delivered them out of the hands of all their enemies round about, 35 neither did they show mercy to the house of Jerubbaal Gideon, according to all the good things he had done to Israel.

Caput 9

Abiit autem Abimelech, filius Hierobbaal, in Sychem ad fratres matris suae et locutus est ad eos et ad omnem cognationem domus patris matris suae, dicens, 2 "Loquimini ad omnes viros Sychem, 'Quid vobis est melius, ut dominentur vestri septuaginta viri, omnes filii Hierobbaal, an ut dominetur vobis unus vir?' Simulque considerate quia os vestrum et caro vestra sum." 3 Locutique sunt fratres matris eius de eo ad omnes viros Sychem universos sermones istos, et inclinaverunt cor eorum post Abimelech, dicentes, "Frater noster est." 4 Dederuntque illi septuaginta pondo argenti de fano Baalbrith qui conduxit sibi ex eo viros inopes et vagos, secutique sunt eum. 5 Et venit in domum patris sui in Ephra et occidit fratres suos, filios Hierobbaal, septuaginta viros, super lapidem unum, remansitque Ioatham, filius Hierobbaal minimus, et absconditus est. 6 Congregati sunt autem omnes viri Sychem et universae familiae urbis Mello, abieruntque et constituerunt regem Abimelech iuxta quercum quae stabat in Sychem.

Chapter 9

Abimelech killeth his brethren. Jotham's parable. Gaal conspireth with the Shechemites against Abimelech but is overcome. Abimelech destroyeth Shechem but is killed at Thebez.

And Abimelech, the son of Jerubbaal, went to Shechem to his mother's brethren and spoke to them and to all the *kindred* of his mother's father, saying, 2 "Speak to all the men of Shechem, 'Whether is better for you, that seventy men, all the sons of Jerubbaal, should rule over you, or that one man should rule over you?' And withal consider that I am your bone and your flesh." 3 And his mother's brethren spoke of him to all the men of Shechem all these words, and they inclined their *hearts* after Abimelech, saying, "He is our brother." 4 And they gave him seventy weight of silver out of the temple of Baal-berith *wherewith* he hired to himself men that were needy and vagabonds, and they followed him. 5 And he came to his father's house in Ophrah and slew his brethren, the sons of Jerubbaal, seventy men, upon one stone, and there remained *only* Jotham, the youngest son of Jerubbaal, *who* was hidden. 6 And all the men of Shechem were gathered together and all the families of the city of Millo, and they went and made Abimelech king by the oak that stood in Shechem.

7 Quod cum nuntiatum esset Ioatham, ivit et stetit in vertice Montis Garizim, elevataque voce clamavit et dixit, "Audite me, viri Sychem; ita audiat vos Deus. 8 Ierunt ligna ut unguerent super se regem, dixeruntque olivae, 'Impera nobis.' 9 Quae respondit, 'Numquid possum deserere pinguedinem meam, qua et dii utuntur et homines, et venire ut inter ligna promovear?' 10 Dixeruntque ligna ad arborem ficum, 'Veni, et super nos regnum accipe.' 11 Quae respondit eis, 'Numquid possum deserere dulcedinem meam fructusque suavissimos et ire ut inter cetera ligna promovear?' 12 Locutaque sunt ligna ad vitem, 'Veni, et impera nobis.' 13 Quae respondit eis, 'Numquid possum deserere vinum meum quod laetificat Deum et homines et inter ligna cetera promoveri?' 14 Dixeruntque omnia ligna ad ramnum, 'Veni, et impera super nos.' 15 Quae respondit eis, 'Si vere me regem vobis constituitis, venite, et sub mea umbra requiescite, sin autem non vultis, egrediatur ignis de ramno et devoret cedros Libani.' 16 Nunc igitur si recte et absque peccato constituistis super vos regem Abimelech et bene egistis cum Hierobbaal et cum domo eius et reddidistis vicem beneficiis eius qui pugnavit pro vobis 17 et animam suam dedit periculis ut erueret vos de manu Madian 18 qui nunc surrexistis contra domum patris mei et interfecistis filios eius, septuaginta viros, super unum lapidem et constituistis regem Abimelech, filium ancillae eius, super habitatores Sychem eo quod frater vester sit, 19 si ergo recte et absque vitio egistis cum Hierobbaal et domo eius, hodie laetamini in Abimelech, et ille laetetur in vobis. 20 Sin autem perverse, egredia-

7 This being told to Jotham, he went and stood on the top of Mount Gerizim, and lifting up his voice he cried and said, "Hear me, ye men of Shechem; so may God hear you. 8 The trees went to anoint a king over them, and they said to the olive tree, 'Reign thou over us.' 9 And it answered, 'Can I leave my fatness, which both gods and men make use of, *to* come to be promoted among the trees?' 10 And the trees said to the fig tree, 'Come thou, and *reign* over us.' 11 And it answered them, 'Can I leave my sweetness and my delicious fruits and go to be promoted among the other trees?' 12 And the trees said to the vine, 'Come thou, and reign over us.' 13 And it answered them, 'Can I forsake my wine that cheereth God and men and be promoted among the other trees?' 14 And all the trees said to the bramble, 'Come thou, and reign over us.' 15 And it answered them, 'If indeed you mean to make me *king,* come ye, and rest under my shadow, but if you mean it not, let fire come out from the bramble and devour the cedars of Libanus.' 16 Now therefore if you have *done* well and without sin *in appointing* Abimelech king over you and have dealt well with Jerubbaal and with his house and have made a suitable return for the benefits of him who fought for you 17 and exposed his life to dangers to deliver you from the hand of Midian 18 and you are now risen up against my father's house and have killed his sons, seventy men, upon one stone and have made Abimelech, the son of his handmaid, king over the inhabitants of Shechem because he is your brother, 19 if therefore you have dealt well and without fault with Jerubbaal and his house, rejoice ye this day in Abimelech, and may he rejoice in you. 20 But if

tur ignis ex eo et consumat habitatores Sychem et oppidum Mello, egrediaturque ignis de viris Sychem et de oppido Mello et devoret Abimelech." 21 Quae cum dixisset fugit et abiit in Bera habitavitque ibi ob metum Abimelech, fratris sui.

22 Regnavit itaque Abimelech super Israhel tribus annis, 23 misitque Dominus spiritum pessimum inter Abimelech et habitatores Sychem qui coeperunt eum detestari 24 et scelus interfectionis septuaginta filiorum Hierobbaal et effusionem sanguinis eorum conferre in Abimelech, fratrem suum, et in ceteros Sycimarum principes qui eum adiuverant. 25 Posueruntque insidias adversum eum in montium summitate, et dum illius praestolabantur adventum, exercebant latrocinia, agentes praedas de praetereuntibus, nuntiatumque est Abimelech. 26 Venit autem Gaal, filius Obed, cum fratribus suis et transivit in Sycimam, ad cuius adventum erecti habitatores Sychem 27 egressi sunt in agros, vastantes vineas uvasque calcantes, et factis cantantium choris ingressi sunt fanum dei sui, et inter epulas et pocula maledicebant Abimelech, 28 clamante Gaal filio Obed, "Quis est Abimelech, et quae est Sychem, ut serviamus ei? Numquid non est filius Hierobbaal et constituit principem Zebul, servum suum, super viros Emmor, patris Sychem? Cur igitur serviemus ei? 29 Utinam daret aliquis populum istum sub manu mea ut auferrem de medio Abimelech."

Dictumque est Abimelech, "Congrega exercitus multitudinem, et veni," 30 Zebul enim, princeps civitatis, auditis

unjustly, let fire come out from him and consume the inhabitants of Shechem and the town of Millo, and let fire come out from the men of Shechem and from the town of Millo and devour Abimelech." 21 And when he had said thus he fled and went into Beer and dwelt there for fear of Abimelech, his brother.

22 So Abimelech reigned over Israel for three years, 23 and the Lord sent a very evil spirit between Abimelech and the inhabitants of Shechem who began to detest him 24 and to leave the crime of the murder of the seventy sons of Jerubbaal and the shedding of their blood upon Abimelech, their brother, and upon the rest of the princes of the Shechemites who aided him. 25 And they set an ambush against him on the top of the mountains, and while they waited for his coming, they committed robberies, taking spoils of *all* that passed by, and it was told Abimelech. 26 And Gaal, the son of Ebed, came with his brethren and went over to Shechem, and the inhabitants of Shechem taking courage at his coming 27 went out into the fields, wasting the vineyards and treading down the grapes, and *singing and dancing* they went into the temple of their god, and in their banquets and cups they cursed Abimelech, 28 *and* Gaal, the son of Ebed, *cried,* "Who is Abimelech, and what is Shechem, that we should serve him? Is he not the son of Jerubbaal and hath made Zebul, his servant, ruler over the men of Hamor, the father of Shechem? Why then shall we serve him? 29 Would to God that some man would put this people under my hand that I might remove Abimelech out of the way."

And it was said to Abimelech, "Gather together the multitude of an army, and come," 30 for Zebul, the ruler of the

sermonibus Gaal, filii Obed, iratus est valde 31 et misit clam
ad Abimelech nuntios, dicens, "Ecce: Gaal, filius Obed, venit in Sycimam cum fratribus suis et obpugnat adversum te
civitatem. 32 Surge itaque nocte cum populo qui tecum est,
et latita in agro, 33 et primo mane oriente sole inrue super
civitatem. Illo autem egrediente adversum te cum populo
suo, fac ei quod potueris."

34 Surrexit itaque Abimelech cum omni exercitu suo
nocte et tetendit insidias iuxta Sycimam in quattuor locis.
35 Egressusque est Gaal, filius Obed, et stetit in introitu portae civitatis. Surrexit autem Abimelech et omnis exercitus
cum eo de insidiarum loco. 36 Cumque vidisset populum
Gaal, dixit ad Zebul, "Ecce: de montibus multitudo descendit."

Cui ille respondit, "Umbras montium vides quasi hominum capita, et hoc errore deciperis."

37 Rursumque Gaal ait, "Ecce: populus de umbilico terrae
descendit, et unus cuneus venit per viam quae respicit quercum."

38 Cui dixit Zebul, "Ubi est nunc os tuum quo loquebaris,
'Quis est Abimelech ut serviamus ei?' Nonne iste est populus quem despiciebas? Egredere, et pugna contra eum."

39 Abiit ergo Gaal spectante Sycimarum populo et pugnavit contra Abimelech, 40 qui persecutus est eum fugientem et in urbem conpulit, cecideruntque ex parte eius plurimi usque ad portam civitatis. 41 Et Abimelech sedit in

city, hearing the words of Gaal, the son of Ebed, was very angry 31 and sent messengers privately to Abimelech, saying, "Behold: Gaal, the son of Ebed, is come into Shechem with his brethren and endeavoureth to set the city against thee. 32 Arise therefore in the night with the people that is with thee, and lie hid in the field, 33 and betimes in the morning at sun rising set upon the city. And when he shall come out against thee with his people, do to him what thou shalt be able."

34 Abimelech therefore arose with all his army by night and laid ambushes near Shechem in four places. 35 And Gaal, the son of Ebed, went out and stood in the entrance of the gate of the city. And Abimelech rose up and all his army with him from the *places* of the ambushes. 36 And when Gaal saw the people, he said to Zebul, "Behold: a multitude cometh down from the mountains."

And he answered him, "Thou seest the shadows of the mountains as if they were the heads of men, and *this is thy mistake.*"

37 Again Gaal said, "Behold: there cometh people down from the middle of the land, and one troop cometh by the way that looketh towards the oak."

38 And Zebul said to him, "Where is now thy mouth wherewith thou saidst, 'Who is Abimelech that we should serve him?' Is not this the people which thou didst despise? Go out, and fight against him."

39 So Gaal went out in the sight of the people of Shechem and fought against Abimelech, 40 who chased *and put him to flight* and drove him to the city, and many were slain of his *people* even to the gate of the city. 41 And Abimelech sat down

Ruma, Zebul autem Gaal et socios eius expulit de urbe nec in ea passus est commorari.

⁴²Sequenti ergo die egressus est populus in campum, quod cum nuntiatum esset Abimelech, ⁴³tulit exercitum suum et divisit in tres turmas tendens insidias in agris. Vidensque quod egrederetur populus de civitate, surrexit et inruit in eos ⁴⁴cum cuneo suo, obpugnans et obsidens civitatem, duae autem turmae palantes per campum adversarios persequebantur. ⁴⁵Porro Abimelech omni illo die obpugnabat urbem quam cepit interfectis habitatoribus eius ipsaque destructa ita ut sal in ea dispergeret. ⁴⁶Quod cum audissent qui habitabant in turre Sycimorum, ingressi sunt fanum dei sui Berith ubi foedus cum eo pepigerant, et ex eo locus nomen acceperat, qui erat valde munitus.

⁴⁷Abimelech quoque audiens viros turris Sycimorum pariter conglobatos ⁴⁸ascendit in Montem Selmon cum omni populo suo, et arrepta securi praecidit arboris ramum, inpositumque ferens umero dixit ad socios, "Quod me videtis facere, cito facite." ⁴⁹Igitur certatim ramos de arboribus praecidentes sequebantur ducem. Qui circumdantes praesidium succenderunt, atque ita factum est ut fumo et igne mille hominum necarentur, viri pariter ac mulieres, habitatorum turris Sychem.

⁵⁰Abimelech autem inde proficiscens venit ad oppidum Thebes, quod circumdans obsidebat exercitu. ⁵¹Erat autem turris excelsa in media civitate ad quam confugerant viri simul ac mulieres et omnes principes civitatis, clausa firmis-

in Arumah, but Zebul drove Gaal and his companions out of the city and would not suffer them to abide in it.

42 So the day following the people went out into the field, *and it was* told Abimelech, 43 *and* he took his army and divided it into three companies and laid ambushes in the fields. And seeing that the people came out of the city, he arose and set upon them 44 with his own company, assaulting and besieging the city *whilst* the two other companies chased the enemies that were scattered about the field. 45 And Abimelech assaulted the city all that day and took it and killed the inhabitants thereof and demolished it so that he sowed salt in it. 46 And when they who dwelt in the tower of Shechem had heard this, they went into the temple of their god Berith where they had made a covenant with him, and from thence the place had taken its name, and it was exceeding strong.

47 Abimelech also hearing that the men of the tower of Shechem were gathered together 48 went up into Mount Zalmon, *he and all his people with him,* and taking an axe he cut down the bough of a tree, and laying it on his shoulder and carrying it he said to his companions, "What you see me do, do you out of hand." 49 So they cut down boughs from the trees, *every man as fast as he could,* and followed their leader. And surrounding the fort they set it on fire, and so it came to pass that with the smoke and with the fire a thousand persons were killed, men and women together, of the inhabitants of the tower of Shechem.

50 Then Abimelech departing from thence came to the town of Thebez, which he surrounded and besieged with his army. 51 And there was in the midst of the city a high tower to which both the men and the women were fled together and all the princes of the city, *and having shut and strongly*

sime ianua et super turris tectum stantes per propugnacula. ⁵²Accedensque Abimelech iuxta turrem pugnabat fortiter et adpropinquans ostio ignem subponere nitebatur, ⁵³et ecce: una mulier fragmen molae desuper iaciens inlisit capiti Abimelech, et confregit cerebrum eius. ⁵⁴Qui vocavit cito armigerum suum et ait ad eum, "Evagina gladium tuum, et percute me ne forte dicatur quod a femina interfectus sim." Qui iussa perficiens interfecit eum.

⁵⁵Illoque mortuo omnes qui cum eo erant de Israhel reversi sunt in sedes suas. ⁵⁶Et reddidit Deus malum quod fecerat Abimelech contra patrem suum, interfectis septuaginta fratribus suis. ⁵⁷Sycimitis quoque quod operati erant retributum est, et venit super eos maledictio Ioatham, filii Hierobbaal.

Caput 10

Post Abimelech, surrexit dux in Israhel, Thola, filius Phoa, patrui Abimelech, vir de Isachar, qui habitavit in Sanir Montis Ephraim, ²et iudicavit Israhel viginti et tribus annis,

barred the gate they stood upon the battlements of the tower to defend themselves. 52 And Abimelech coming near the tower fought stoutly and approaching to the gate endeavoured to set fire to it, 53 and behold: a certain woman casting a piece of a millstone from above dashed it against the head of Abimelech, and broke his skull. 54 And he called hastily to his armourbearer and said to him, "Draw thy sword, and kill me lest it should be said that I was slain by a woman." He did as he was commanded and slew him.

55 And when he was dead, all the men of Israel that were with him returned to their homes. 56 And God repaid the evil that Abimelech had done against his father, killing his seventy brethren. 57 The Shechemites also were rewarded for what they had done, and the curse of Jotham, the son of Jerubbaal, came upon them.

Chapter 10

Tola ruleth Israel twenty-three years and Jair twenty-two.
The people fall again into idolatry and are afflicted again by
the Philistines and Ammonites. They cry to God for help,
who upon their repentance hath compassion on them.

After Abimelech, there arose a ruler in Israel, Tola, son of Phua, the uncle of Abimelech, a man of Issachar, who dwelt in Shamir of Mount Ephraim, 2 and he judged Israel three

mortuusque ac sepultus est in Sanir. 3 Huic successit Iair, Galaadites, qui iudicavit Israhel per viginti et duos annos 4 habens triginta filios sedentes super triginta pullos asinarum et principes triginta civitatum, quae ex nomine eius appellatae sunt Avoth Iair, id est, "oppida Iair," usque in praesentem diem in terra Galaad.

5 Mortuusque est Iair ac sepultus in loco cui est vocabulum Camon, 6 filii autem Israhel, peccatis veteribus iungentes nova, fecerunt malum in conspectu Domini et servierunt idolis, Baalim et Astharoth, et diis Syriae ac Sidonis et Moab et filiorum Ammon et Philisthim, dimiseruntque Dominum et non colebant eum. 7 Contra quos Dominus iratus tradidit eos in manus Philisthim et filiorum Ammon. 8 Adflictique sunt et vehementer oppressi per annos decem et octo, omnes qui habitabant trans Iordanem in terra Amorrei quae est in Galaad, 9 in tantum ut filii Ammon Iordane transmisso vastarent Iudam et Beniamin et Ephraim. Adflictusque est Israhel nimis, 10 et clamantes ad Dominum dixerunt, "Peccavimus tibi quia dereliquimus Dominum, Deum nostrum, et servivimus Baalim."

11 Quibus locutus est Dominus, "Numquid non Aegyptii et Amorrei filiique Ammon et Philisthim, 12 Sidonii quoque et Amalech et Chanaan oppresserunt vos, et clamastis ad me, et erui vos de manu eorum? 13 Et tamen reliquistis me et coluistis deos alienos, idcirco non addam ut ultra vos liberem. 14 Ite, et invocate deos quos elegistis. Ipsi vos liberent in tempore angustiae."

15 Dixeruntque filii Israhel ad Dominum, "Peccavimus;

and twenty years, and he died and was buried in Shamir. 3 To him succeeded Jair, the Gileadite, who judged Israel for two and twenty years 4 having thirty sons that rode on thirty ass-colts and were princes of thirty cities, which from his name were called Havvoth Jair, that is, "the towns of Jair," until this present day in the land of Gilead.

5 And Jair died and was buried in the place which was called Kamon, 6 but the children of Israel, adding new sins to their old ones, did evil in the sight of the Lord and served idols, Baalim and Astarte, and the gods of Syria and of Sidon and of Moab and of the children of Ammon and of the Philistines, and they left the Lord and did not serve him. 7 And the Lord being angry with them delivered them into the hands of the Philistines and of the children of Ammon. 8 And they were afflicted and grievously oppressed for eighteen years, all they that dwelt beyond the Jordan in the land of the Amorite *who* is in Gilead, 9 insomuch that the children of Ammon passing over the Jordan wasted Judah and Benjamin and Ephraim. And Israel was distressed exceedingly, 10 and they cried to the Lord and said, "We have sinned against thee because we have forsaken the Lord, our God, and have served Baalim."

11 And the Lord said to them, "Did not the Egyptians and the Amorites and the children of Ammon and the Philistines, 12 the Sidonians also and Amalek and Canaan oppress you, and you cried to me, and I delivered you out of their hand? 13 And yet you have forsaken me and have worshipped strange gods, therefore I will *deliver* you no more. 14 Go, and call upon the gods which you have chosen. Let them deliver you in the time of distress."

15 And the children of Israel said to the Lord, "We have

redde tu nobis quicquid tibi placet; tantum nunc libera nos."
16 Quae dicentes, omnia de finibus suis alienorum deorum
idola proiecerunt et servierunt Domino Deo, qui doluit super miseriis eorum. 17 Itaque filii Ammon conclamantes in
Galaad fixere tentoria contra quos congregati filii Israhel in
Maspha castrametati sunt. 18 Dixeruntque principes Galaad
singuli ad proximos suos, "Qui primus e nobis contra filios
Ammon coeperit dimicare, erit dux populi Galaad."

Caput 11

Fuit illo tempore Iepthae, Galaadites, vir fortissimus atque pugnator, filius meretricis mulieris, qui natus est de Galaad. 2 Habuit autem Galaad uxorem de qua suscepit filios
qui postquam creverant eiecerunt Iepthae, dicentes, "Heres
in domo patris nostri esse non poteris quia de altera matre
generatus es." 3 Quos ille fugiens atque devitans habitavit in
terra Tob, congregatique sunt ad eum viri inopes et latroci-
nantes et quasi principem sequebantur.

sinned; do thou unto us whatsoever pleaseth thee; only deliver us this time." 16 And saying these things, they cast away out of their coasts all the idols of strange gods and served the Lord, *their* God, and he was touched with their miseries. 17 And the children of Ammon shouting together pitched their tents in Gilead against whom the children of Israel assembled themselves together and camped in Mizpah. 18 And the princes of Gilead said *one to another,* "*Whosoever* of us shall first begin to fight against the children of Ammon, he shall be the leader of the people of Gilead."

Chapter 11

Jephthah is made ruler of the people of Gilead. He first
pleads their cause against the Ammonites, then making a
vow obtains a signal victory. He performs his vow.

There was at that time Jephthah, the Gileadite, a most valiant man and a warrior, the son of a woman that was a harlot, *and his father was Gilead.* 2 Now Gilead had a wife of whom he had sons who after they were grown up thrust out Jephthah, saying, "Thou canst not *inherit* in the house of our father because thou art born of another mother." 3 Then he fled and avoided them and dwelt in the land of Tob, and there were gathered to him needy men and robbers and they followed him as their prince.

4 In illis diebus pugnabant filii Ammon contra Israhel, 5 quibus acriter instantibus, perrexerunt maiores natu de Galaad ut tollerent in auxilium sui Iepthae de terra Tob, 6 dixeruntque ad eum, "Veni, et esto princeps noster, et pugna contra filios Ammon."

7 Quibus ille respondit, "Nonne vos estis qui odistis me et eiecistis de domo patris mei, et nunc venistis ad me necessitate conpulsi?"

8 Dixeruntque principes Galaad ad Iepthae, "Ob hanc igitur causam nunc ad te venimus: ut proficiscaris nobiscum et pugnes contra filios Ammon sisque dux omnium qui habitant in Galaad."

9 Iepthae quoque dixit eis, "Si vere venistis ad me, ut pugnem pro vobis contra filios Ammon, tradideritque eos Dominus in manus meas, ego ero princeps vester?"

10 Qui responderunt ei, "Dominus qui haec audit, ipse mediator ac testis est quod nostra promissa faciemus."

11 Abiit itaque Iepthae cum principibus Galaad, fecitque eum omnis populus principem sui. Locutusque est Iepthae omnes sermones suos coram Domino in Maspha. 12 Et misit nuntios ad regem filiorum Ammon qui ex persona sua dicerent, "Quid mihi et tibi est quia venisti contra me ut vastares terram meam?"

13 Quibus ille respondit, "Quia tulit Israhel terram meam quando ascendit de Aegypto a finibus Arnon usque Iaboc atque Iordanem, nunc, igitur, cum pace redde mihi eam."

14 Per quos rursum mandavit Iepthae et imperavit eis ut

4 In those days the children of Ammon made war against Israel, 5 and as they pressed hard upon them, the ancients of Gilead went to fetch Jephthah out of the land of Tob to help them, 6 and they said to him, "Come thou, and be our prince, and fight against the children of Ammon."

7 And he answered them, "Are not you the men that hated me and cast me out of my father's house, and now you are come to me constrained by necessity?"

8 And the princes of Gilead said to Jephthah, "For this cause we are now come to thee: that thou mayst go with us and fight against the children of Ammon and be head over all *the inhabitants of* Gilead."

9 Jephthah also said to them, "If you be come to me sincerely, that I should fight for you against the children of Ammon, and the Lord shall deliver them into my *hand,* shall I be your prince?"

10 They answered him, "The Lord who heareth these things, he himself is mediator and witness that we will do as we have promised."

11 Jephthah therefore went with the princes of Gilead, and all the people made him their prince. And Jephthah spoke all his words before the Lord in Mizpah. 12 And he sent messengers to the king of the children of Ammon to say in his name, "What *hast thou to do with me* that thou art come against me to waste my land?"

13 And he answered them, "Because Israel took away my land when he came up out of Egypt from the confines of the Arnon unto the Jabbok and the Jordan, now, therefore, restore the same peaceably to me."

14 And Jephthah again sent word by them and com-

dicerent regi Ammon, 15 "Haec dicit Iepthae, 'Non tulit Israhel terram Moab nec terram filiorum Ammon, 16 sed
quando de Aegypto conscenderunt, ambulavit per solitudinem usque ad mare Rubrum et venit in Cades. 17 Misitque
nuntios ad regem Edom, dicens, "Dimitte me ut transeam
per terram tuam." Qui noluit adquiescere precibus eius. Misit quoque ad regem Moab, qui et ipse transitum praebere
contempsit. Mansit itaque in Cades 18 et circuivit ex latere
terram Edom et terram Moab venitque contra orientalem
plagam terrae Moab et castrametatus est trans Arnon, nec
voluit intrare terminos Moab. Arnon quippe confinium est
terrae Moab. 19 Misit itaque Israhel nuntios ad Seon, regem
Amorreorum, qui habitabat in Esebon, et dixerunt ei, "Dimitte ut transeam per terram tuam usque ad fluvium." 20 Qui
et ipse Israhel verba despiciens non dimisit eum transire per
terminos suos sed infinita multitudine congregata egressus
est contra eum in Iassa et fortiter resistebat. 21 Tradiditque
eum Dominus in manus Israhel cum omni exercitu suo, qui
percussit eum et possedit omnem terram Amorrei, habitatoris regionis illius, 22 et universos fines eius de Arnon usque
Iaboc et de solitudine usque ad Iordanem. 23 Dominus ergo,
Deus Israhel, subvertit Amorreum, pugnante contra illum
populo suo Israhel, et tu nunc vis possidere terram eius?
24 Nonne ea quae possedit Chamos deus tuus tibi iure de-
bentur? Quae autem Dominus, Deus noster, victor obtinuit
in nostram cedent possessionem, 25 nisi forte melior es Balac, filio Sepphor, rege Moab aut docere potes quod iurgatus

manded them to say to the king of Ammon, 15 "Thus saith Jephthah, 'Israel did not take away the land of Moab nor the land of the children of Ammon, 16 but when they came up out of Egypt, he walked through the desert to the Red Sea and came into Kadesh. 17 And he sent messengers to the king of Edom, saying, "Suffer me to pass through thy land." But he would not condescend to his *request.* He sent also to the king of Moab, who likewise refused to give him passage. He abode therefore in Kadesh 18 and went round the land of Edom at the side and the land of Moab and came over against the east coast of the land of Moab and camped on the other side of the Arnon, and he would not enter the bounds of *Moab.* 19 So Israel sent messengers to Sihon, king of the Amorites, who dwelt in Heshbon, and they said to him, "Suffer me to pass through thy land to the river." 20 But he also despising the words of Israel suffered him not to pass through his borders but gathering an infinite multitude went out against him to Jahaz and *made strong opposition.* 21 And the Lord delivered him with all his army into the hands of Israel, and he slew him and possessed all the land of the Amorite, the inhabitant of that country, 22 and all the coasts thereof from the Arnon to the Jabbok and from the wilderness to the Jordan. 23 So the Lord, the God of Israel, destroyed the Amorite, his people of Israel fighting against him, and wilt thou now possess this land? 24 Are not those things which thy god Chemosh *possesseth* due to thee by right? But what the Lord, our God, hath obtained *by con-quest* shall *be* our possession, 25 unless perhaps thou art better than Balak, the son of Zippor, king of Moab or canst

sit contra Israhel et pugnaverit contra eum, 26 quando habitavit in Esebon et viculis eius et in Aroer et villis illius vel in cunctis civitatibus iuxta Iordanem per trecentos annos. Quare tanto tempore nihil super hac repetitione temptastis? 27 Igitur non ego pecco in te, sed tu contra me male agis indicens mihi bella non iusta. Iudicet Dominus arbiter huius diei inter Israhel et inter filios Ammon.'"

28 Noluitque adquiescere rex filiorum Ammon verbis Iepthae quae per nuntios mandaverat. 29 Factus est ergo super Iepthae spiritus Domini, et circumiens Galaad et Manasse, Maspha quoque Galaad et inde transiens ad filios Ammon, 30 votum vovit Domino, dicens, "Si tradideris filios Ammon in manus meas, 31 quicumque primus fuerit egressus de foribus domus meae mihique occurrerit revertenti cum pace a filiis Ammon, eum holocaustum offeram Domino."

32 Transivitque Iepthae ad filios Ammon ut pugnaret contra eos, quos tradidit Dominus in manus eius. 33 Percussitque ab Aroer usque dum venias in Mennith viginti civitates, et usque ad Abel quae est vineis consita plaga magna nimis, humiliatique sunt filii Ammon a filiis Israhel. 34 Revertente autem Iepthae in Maspha domum suam, occurrit ei unigenita filia cum tympanis et choris, non enim habebat alios liberos. 35 Qua visa, scidit vestimenta sua et ait, "Heu me! Filia mi, decepisti me, et ipsa decepta es, aperui enim os meum ad Dominum et aliud facere non potero."

36 Cui illa respondit, "Pater mi, si aperuisti os tuum ad

show that he strove against Israel and fought against him, 26 whereas he hath dwelt in Heshbon and the villages thereof and in Aroer and its villages *and* in all the cities near the Jordan for three hundred years. Why have you for so long a time attempted nothing about this claim? 27 Therefore I do not trespass against thee, but thou wrongest me by declaring an unjust war against me. The Lord be judge *and decide this day* between Israel and the children of Ammon.'"

28 And the king of the children of Ammon would not hearken to the words of Jephthah which he sent him by the messengers. 29 Therefore the spirit of the Lord came upon Jephthah, and going round Gilead and Manasseh and Mizpah of Gilead and passing over from thence to the children of Ammon, 30 he made a vow to the Lord, saying, "If thou wilt deliver the children of Ammon into my hands, 31 whosoever shall first come forth out of the doors of my house and shall meet me when I return in peace from the children of Ammon, *the same* will I offer a holocaust to the Lord."

32 And Jephthah passed over to the children of Ammon to fight against them, and the Lord delivered them into his hands. 33 And he smote *them* from Aroer till you come to Minnith, twenty cities, and as far as Abel which is set with vineyards with a very great slaughter, and the children of Ammon were humbled by the children of Israel. 34 And when Jephthah returned into Mizpah to his house, his only daughter met him with timbrels and with dances, for he had no other children. 35 And when he saw her, he rent his garments and said, "*Alas!* My daughter, thou hast deceived me, and thou thyself art deceived, for I have opened my mouth to the Lord and I can do no other thing."

36 And she answered him, "My father, if thou hast opened

Dominum, fac mihi quodcumque pollicitus es, concessa tibi ultione atque victoria de hostibus tuis." 37 Dixitque ad patrem, "Hoc solum mihi praesta quod deprecor: dimitte me ut duobus mensibus circumeam montes et plangam virginitatem meam cum sodalibus meis."

38 Cui ille respondit, "Vade." Et dimisit eam duobus mensibus. Cumque abisset cum sociis ac sodalibus suis, flebat virginitatem suam in montibus. 39 Expletisque duobus mensibus, reversa est ad patrem suum, et fecit ei sicut voverat, quae ignorabat virum. Exinde mos increbuit in Israhel, et consuetudo servata est, 40 ut post anni circulum conveniant in unum filiae Israhel et plangant filiam Iepthae, Galaaditae, diebus quattuor.

Caput 12

Ecce autem: in Ephraim orta seditio est, nam transeuntes contra aquilonem, dixerunt ad Iepthae, "Quare vadens ad pugnam contra filios Ammon vocare nos noluisti ut pergeremus tecum? Igitur incendemus domum tuam."

thy mouth to the Lord, do unto me whatsoever thou hast promised, since the victory hath been granted to thee and revenge of thy enemies." 37 And she said to her father, "Grant me only this which I desire: let me go that I may go about the mountains for two months and may bewail my virginity with my companions."

38 And he answered her, "Go." And he sent her away for two months. And when she was gone with her comrades and companions, she mourned her virginity in the mountains. 39 And the two months being expired, she returned to her father, and he did to her as he had vowed, and she knew no man. From thence came a fashion in Israel, and a custom has been kept, 40 that *from year to year* the daughters of Israel assemble together and lament the daughter of Jephthah, the Gileadite, for four days.

Chapter 12

The Ephraimites quarrel with Jephthah; forty-two thousand of them are slain. Ibzan, Elon and Abdon are judges.

But behold: there arose a sedition in Ephraim. *And* passing towards the north, they said to Jephthah, "When thou wentest to fight against the children of Ammon, why wouldst thou not call us that we might go with thee? Therefore we will burn thy house."

2 Quibus ille respondit, "Disceptatio erat mihi et populo meo contra filios Ammon vehemens, vocavique vos ut mihi praeberetis auxilium, et facere noluistis. 3 Quod cernens, posui in manibus meis animam meam transivique ad filios Ammon, et tradidit eos Dominus in manus meas. Quid commerui ut adversum me consurgatis in proelium?"

4 Vocatis itaque ad se cunctis viris Galaad, pugnabat contra Ephraim, percusseruntque viri Galaad Ephraim quia dixerat, "Fugitivus est Galaad de Ephraim et habitat in medio Ephraim et Manasse."

5 Occupaveruntque Galaaditae vada Iordanis per quae Ephraim reversurus erat. Cumque venisset ad ea de Ephraim numero fugiens atque dixisset, "Obsecro ut me transire permittatis," dicebant ei Galaaditae, "Numquid Ephrateus es?" Quo dicente, "Non sum," 6 interrogabant eum, "Dic ergo, 'Sebboleth,'" quod interpretatur, "Spica." Qui respondebat, "Tebboleth," eadem littera spicam exprimere non valens. Statimque adprehensum iugulabant in ipso Iordanis transitu. Et ceciderunt in illo tempore de Ephraim quadraginta duo milia.

7 Iudicavit itaque Iepthae, Galaadites, Israhel sex annis, et mortuus est ac sepultus in civitate sua Galaad. 8 Post hunc iudicavit Israhel Abessan de Bethleem. 9 Qui habuit triginta filios et totidem filias quas emittens foras maritis dedit et eiusdem numeri filiis suis accepit uxores, introducens in domum suam. Qui septem annis iudicavit Israhel, 10 mortuusque est ac sepultus in Bethleem. 11 Cui successit Ahialon, Zabulonites, et iudicavit Israhelem decem annis, 12 mortuusque est ac sepultus in Zabulon. 13 Post hunc iudicavit Israhel Abdon, filius Hellel, Farathonites, 14 qui habuit quad-

2 And he answered them, "I and my people were at great strife with the children of Ammon, and I called you to assist me, and you would not do it. 3 And when I saw this, I put my life in my own hands and passed over against the children of Ammon, and the Lord delivered them into my hands. What have I deserved that you should rise up *to fight* against me?"

4 Then calling to him all the men of Gilead, he fought against Ephraim, and the men of Gilead defeated Ephraim because he had said, "Gilead is a fugitive of Ephraim and dwelleth in the midst of Ephraim and Manasseh."

5 And the Gileadites secured the fords of the Jordan by which Ephraim was to return. And when any one of the number of Ephraim came thither in the flight and said, "I beseech you, let me pass," the Gileadites said to him, "Art thou not an Ephraimite?" If he said, "I am not," 6 they asked him, "Say then, 'Shibboleth,'" which is interpreted, "An ear of corn." But he answered, "Sibboleth," not being able to express an ear of corn by the same letter. Then presently they took him and killed him in the very passage of the Jordan. And there fell at that time of Ephraim two and forty thousand.

7 And Jephthah, the Gileadite, judged Israel six years, and he died and was buried in his city of Gilead. 8 After him Ibzan of Bethlehem judged Israel. 9 He had thirty sons and as many daughters whom he sent abroad and gave to husbands and took wives for his sons of the same number, bringing them into his house. And he judged Israel seven years, 10 and he died and was buried in Bethlehem. 11 To him succeeded Elon, a Zebulunite, and he judged Israel ten years, 12 and he died and was buried in Zebulun. 13 After him Abdon, the son of Hillel, a Pirathonite, judged Israel, 14 and

raginta filios et triginta ex eis nepotes ascendentes super septuaginta pullos asinarum, et iudicavit Israhel octo annis, 15 mortuusque est ac sepultus in Farathon terrae Ephraim in monte Amalech.

Caput 13

Rursumque filii Israhel fecerunt malum in conspectu Domini, qui tradidit eos in manus Philisthinorum quadraginta annis. 2 Erat autem vir quidam de Saraa et de stirpe Dan nomine Manue, habens uxorem sterilem. 3 Cui apparuit angelus Domini et dixit ad eam, "Sterilis es et absque liberis, sed concipies et paries filium. 4 Cave ergo nec vinum bibas ac siceram, nec inmundum quicquam comedas, 5 quia concipies et paries filium, cuius non tanget caput novacula, erit enim Nazareus Dei ab infantia sua et ex matris utero, et ipse incipiet liberare Israhel de manu Philisthinorum."

6 Quae cum venisset ad maritum dixit ei, "Vir Dei venit ad me, habens vultum angelicum, terribilis nimis. Quem cum interrogassem quis esset et unde venisset et quo nom-

he had forty sons and of them thirty grandsons mounted upon seventy ass-colts, and he judged Israel eight years, 15 and he died and was buried in Pirathon in the land of Ephraim in the mount of Amalek.

Chapter 13

The people fall again into idolatry and are afflicted by the Philistines. An angel foretelleth the birth of Samson.

And the children of Israel did evil again in the sight of the Lord, and he delivered them into the hands of the Philistines forty years. 2 Now there was a certain man of Zorah and of the race of Dan *whose name was* Manoah, *and his wife was barren.* 3 And an angel of the Lord appeared to her and *said,* "Thou art barren and without children, but thou shalt conceive and bear a son. 4 Now therefore beware, *and drink no wine nor* strong drink, and eat not any unclean thing, 5 because thou shalt conceive and bear a son, and no razor shall touch his head, for he shall be a Nazirite of God from his infancy and from his mother's womb, and he shall begin to deliver Israel from the hands of the Philistines."

6 And when she was come to her husband she said to him, "A man of God came to me, having the countenance of an angel, very awful. And when I asked him who he was and whence he came and by what name he was called, he would

ine vocaretur, noluit mihi dicere, 7 sed hoc respondit: 'Ecce: concipies et paries filium. Cave ne vinum bibas nec siceram et ne aliquo vescaris inmundo, erit enim puer Nazareus Dei ab infantia sua, et ex utero matris usque ad diem mortis suae.'"

8 Oravit itaque Manue Dominum et ait, "Obsecro, Domine, ut vir Dei quem misisti veniat iterum et doceat nos quid debeamus facere de puero qui nasciturus est."

9 Exaudivitque Dominus precantem Manue, et apparuit rursum angelus Domini uxori eius sedenti in agro, Manue autem, maritus eius, non erat cum ea. Quae cum vidisset angelum, 10 festinavit et cucurrit ad virum suum nuntiavitque ei, dicens, "Ecce! Apparuit mihi vir quem ante videram."

11 Qui surrexit et secutus est uxorem suam veniensque ad virum dixit ei, "Tu es qui locutus es mulieri?"

Et ille respondit, "Ego sum."

12 Cui Manue, "Quando," inquit, "sermo tuus fuerit expletus, quid vis ut faciat puer, aut a quo se observare debebit?"

13 Dixitque angelus Domini ad Manue, "Ab omnibus quae locutus sum uxori tuae, abstineat se. 14 Et quicquid ex vinea nascitur non comedat, vinum et siceram non bibat; nullo vescatur inmundo, et quod ei praecepi, impleat atque custodiat."

15 Dixitque Manue ad angelum Domini, "Obsecro te ut adquiescas precibus meis et faciamus tibi hedum de capris."

16 Cui respondit angelus, "Si me cogis, non comedam

not tell me, 7 but he answered *thus:* 'Behold: thou shalt conceive and bear a son. Beware thou drink no wine nor strong drink nor eat any unclean thing, for the child shall be a Nazirite of God from his infancy, *from* his mother's womb until the day of his death.'"

8 Then Manoah prayed to the Lord and said, "I beseech thee, O Lord, that the man of God whom thou didst send may come again and teach us what we ought to do concerning the child that shall be born."

9 And the Lord heard *the prayer of* Manoah, and the angel of the Lord appeared again to his wife as she was sitting in the field, but Manoah, her husband, was not with her. And when she saw the angel, 10 she made haste and ran to her husband and told him, saying, "Behold! The man hath appeared to me whom I saw before."

11 He rose up and followed his wife and coming to the man said to him, "Art thou he that spoke to the woman?"

And he answered, "I am."

12 And Manoah said to him, "When thy word shall come to pass, what wilt thou that the child should do, or from what shall he keep himself?"

13 And the angel of the Lord said to Manoah, "From all the things I have spoken of to thy wife, let *her* refrain *herself.* 14 And let *her* eat nothing that cometh of the vine, *neither* let *her* drink wine or strong drink nor eat any unclean thing, and whatsoever I have commanded her, let *her* fulfill and observe."

15 And Manoah said to the angel of the Lord, "I beseech thee to consent to my request, and let us dress a *kid* for thee."

16 And the angel answered him, "If thou press me, I will

panes tuos. Sin autem vis holocaustum facere, offer illud Domino."

Et nesciebat Manue quod angelus Domini esset, 17 dixitque ad eum, "Quod est tibi nomen ut, si sermo tuus fuerit expletus, honoremus te?"

18 Cui ille respondit, "Cur quaeris nomen meum, quod est mirabile?"

19 Tulit itaque Manue hedum de capris et libamenta et posuit super petram, offerens Domino qui facit mirabilia, ipse autem et uxor eius intuebantur. 20 Cumque ascenderet flamma altaris in caelum, angelus Domini in flamma pariter ascendit. Quod cum vidisset Manue et uxor eius, proni ceciderunt in terram. 21 Et ultra non eis apparuit angelus Domini, statimque intellexit Manue angelum esse Domini, 22 et dixit ad uxorem suam, "Morte moriemur, quia vidimus Deum."

23 Cui respondit mulier, "Si Dominus nos vellet occidere, de manibus nostris holocaustum et libamenta non suscepisset, nec ostendisset nobis haec omnia neque ea quae sunt ventura dixisset." 24 Peperit itaque filium et vocavit nomen eius Samson. Crevitque puer, et benedixit ei Dominus, 25 coepitque spiritus Domini esse cum eo in Castris Dan inter Saraa et Esthaol.

not eat of thy bread. But if thou wilt offer a holocaust, offer it to the Lord."

And Manoah knew not it was the angel of the Lord, 17 and he said to him, "What is thy name that, if thy word shall come to pass, we may honour thee?"

18 And he answered him, "Why askest thou my name, which is wonderful?"

19 Then Manoah took a kid of the flocks and the libations and put them upon a rock, offering to the Lord who doth wonderful things, and he and his wife looked on. 20 And when the flame from the altar went up towards heaven, the angel of the lord ascended also in the flame. And when Manoah and his wife saw this, they fell flat on the ground. 21 And the angel of the Lord appeared to them no more, and forthwith Manoah understood that it was an angel of the Lord, 22 and he said to his wife, "We shall *certainly* die, because we have seen God."

23 And his wife answered him, "If the Lord had a mind to kill us, he would not have received a holocaust and libations at our hands, neither would he have showed us all these things nor have told us the things that are to come." 24 And she bore a son and called his name Samson. And the child grew, and the Lord blessed him, 25 and the spirit of the Lord began to be with him in the camp of Dan between Zorah and Eshtaol.

Caput 14

Descendit igitur Samson in Thamnatha, vidensque ibi mulierem de filiabus Philisthim 2 ascendit et nuntiavit patri suo et matri suae, dicens, "Vidi mulierem in Thamnatha de filiabus Philisthinorum, quam quaeso ut mihi accipiatis uxorem."

3 Cui dixerunt pater et mater sua, "Numquid non est mulier in filiabus fratrum tuorum et in omni populo meo, quia vis accipere uxorem de Philisthim qui incircumcisi sunt?"

Dixitque Samson ad patrem suum, "Hanc mihi accipe, quia placuit oculis meis." 4 Parentes autem eius nesciebant quod res a Domino fieret et quaereret occasionem contra Philisthim, eo enim tempore Philisthim dominabantur Israheli.

5 Descendit itaque Samson cum patre suo et matre in Thamnatha. Cumque venissent ad vineas oppidi, apparuit catulus leonis, saevus et rugiens, et occurrit ei. 6 Inruit autem spiritus Domini in Samson, et dilaceravit leonem

Chapter 14

Samson desireth a wife of the Philistines. He killeth a lion in whose mouth he afterwards findeth honey. His marriage feast and riddle, which is discovered by his wife. He killeth and strippeth thirty Philistines. His wife taketh another man.

Then Samson went down to Timnah, and seeing there a woman of the daughters of the Philistines 2 he came up and told his father and his mother, saying, "I saw a woman in Timnah of the daughters of the Philistines. I beseech you, take *her* for me to wife."

3 And his father and mother said to him, "Is there no woman among the daughters of thy brethren or among all my people, that thou wilt take a wife of the Philistines who are uncircumcised?"

And Samson said to his father, "Take this woman for me, for she hath pleased my eyes." 4 Now his parents knew not that the thing was done by the Lord and that he sought an occasion against the Philistines, for at that time the Philistines had dominion over Israel.

5 Then Samson went down with his father and mother to Timnah. And when they were come to the vineyards of the town, *behold: a young lion met him,* raging and roaring. 6 And the spirit of the Lord came upon Samson, and he tore the

quasi hedum in frusta concerperet, nihil omnino habens in manu, et hoc patri et matri noluit indicare. 7 Descenditque et locutus est mulieri quae placuerat oculis eius. 8 Et post aliquot dies revertens ut acciperet eam, declinavit ut videret cadaver leonis, et ecce: examen apium in ore leonis erat ac favus mellis. 9 Quem cum sumpsisset in manibus, comedebat in via, veniensque ad patrem suum et matrem, dedit eis partem, qui et ipsi comederunt, nec tamen eis voluit indicare quod mel de corpore leonis adsumpserat.

10 Descendit itaque pater eius ad mulierem et fecit filio suo Samson convivium, sic enim iuvenes facere consuerant. 11 Cum igitur cives loci illius vidissent eum, dederunt ei sodales triginta qui essent cum eo. 12 Quibus locutus est Samson, "Proponam vobis problema quod si solveritis mihi intra septem dies convivii, dabo vobis triginta sindones et totidem tunicas, 13 sin autem non potueritis solvere, vos dabitis mihi triginta sindones et eiusdem numeri tunicas."

Qui responderunt ei, "Propone problema ut audiamus."

14 Dixitque eis, "De comedente exivit cibus, et de forte est egressa dulcedo." Nec potuerunt per tres dies propositionem solvere.

15 Cumque adesset dies septimus, dixerunt ad uxorem Samson, "Blandire viro tuo, et suade ei ut indicet tibi quid

lion as he would have torn a kid in pieces, having nothing at all in his hand, and he would not tell this to his father and mother. 7 And he went down and spoke to the woman that had pleased his eyes. 8 And after some days returning to take her, he went aside to see the carcass of the lion, and behold: there was a swarm of bees in the mouth of the lion and a honeycomb. 9 And when be had taken it in his hands, he *went on eating,* and coming to his father and mother, he gave them *of it, and they* ate, but he would not tell them that he had taken the honey from the body of the lion.

10 So his father went down to the woman and made a feast for his son Samson, for so the young men used to do. 11 And when the citizens of that place saw him, they brought him thirty companions to be with him. 12 And Samson said to them, "I will propose to you a riddle which if you declare unto me within the seven days of the feast, I will give you thirty shirts and as many coats, 13 but if you shall not be able to declare it, you shall give me thirty shirts and the same number of coats."

They answered him, "Put forth the riddle that we may hear it."

14 And he said to them, "Out of the eater came forth meat, and out of the strong came forth sweetness." And they could not in three days expound the riddle.

15 And when the seventh day came, they said to the wife of Samson, "Soothe thy husband, and persuade him to tell

significet problema. Quod si facere nolueris, incendemus te et domum patris tui. An idcirco nos vocastis ad nuptias ut spoliaretis?"

16 Quae fundebat apud Samson lacrimas et querebatur, dicens, "Odisti me et non diligis, idcirco problema quod proposuisti filiis populi mei non vis mihi exponere."

At ille respondit, "Patri meo et matri nolui dicere, et tibi indicare potero?"

17 Septem igitur diebus convivii flebat apud eum, tandemque die septimo cum ei molesta esset, exposuit. Quae statim indicavit civibus suis. 18 Et illi dixerunt ei die septimo ante solis occubitum, "Quid dulcius melle? Et quid leone fortius?"

Qui ait ad eos, "Si non arassetis in vitula mea, non invenissetis propositionem meam."

19 Inruit itaque in eo spiritus Domini, descenditque Ascalonem et percussit ibi triginta viros quorum ablatas vestes dedit his qui problema solverant. Iratusque nimis ascendit in domum patris sui. 20 Uxor autem eius accepit maritum unum de amicis eius et pronubis.

thee what the riddle meaneth. But if thou wilt not do it, we will burn thee and thy father's house. Have you called us to the wedding on purpose to strip us?"

16 *So she wept* before Samson and complained, saying, "Thou hatest me and dost not love me, therefore thou wilt not expound to me the riddle which thou hast proposed to the sons of my people."

But he answered, "I would not tell it to my father and mother, and *how* can I tell it to thee?"

17 So she wept before him the seven days of the feast, and at length on the seventh day as she was troublesome to him, he expounded it. And she immediately told her countrymen. 18 And they on the seventh day before the sun went down said to him, "What is sweeter than honey? And what is stronger than a lion?"

And he said to them, "If you had not ploughed with my heifer, you had not found out my riddle."

19 And the spirit of the Lord came upon him, and he went down to Ashkelon and slew there thirty men whose garments he took away and gave to them that had declared the riddle. And being exceeding angry he went up to his father's house. 20 But his wife took one of his friends and bridal companions for her husband.

Caput 15

Post aliquantum autem temporis, cum dies triticeae messis instarent, venit Samson, invisere volens uxorem suam, et adtulit ei hedum de capris. Cumque cubiculum eius solito vellet intrare, prohibuit eum pater illius, dicens, 2 "Putavi quod odisses eam, et ideo tradidi illam amico tuo. Sed habet sororem quae iunior et pulchrior illa est; sit tibi pro ea uxor."

3 Cui respondit Samson, "Ab hac die non erit culpa in me contra Philistheos, faciam enim vobis mala."

4 Perrexitque et cepit trecentas vulpes caudasque earum iunxit ad caudas et faces ligavit in medio. 5 Quas igne succendens dimisit ut huc illucque discurrerent. Quae statim perrexerunt in segetes Philisthinorum, quibus succensis, et conportatae iam fruges et adhuc stantes in stipula, concrematae sunt in tantum ut vineas quoque et oliveta flamma consumeret. 6 Dixeruntque Philisthim, "Quis fecit hanc rem?"

Quibus dictum est, "Samson, gener Thamnathei, quia tulit uxorem eius et alteri tradidit haec operatus est." Ascenderuntque Philisthim et conbuserunt tam mulierem quam patrem eius.

Chapter 15

Samson is denied his wife. He burns the corn of the Philistines and kills many of them.

And a while after, when the days of the wheat harvest were at hand, Samson came, meaning to visit his wife, and he brought her a kid of the flock. And when he would have gone into her chamber as usual, her father *would not suffer* him, saying, 2 "I thought thou hadst hated her, and therefore I gave her to thy friend. But she hath a sister who is younger and fairer than she; *take her to wife* instead of her."

3 And Samson answered him, "From this day *I shall be blameless in what I do* against the Philistines, for I will do you evils."

4 And he went and caught three hundred foxes and coupled them tail to tail and fastened torches *between the tails.* 5 And setting them on fire he let *the foxes* go that they might run about hither and thither. And they presently went into the standing corn of the Philistines, which being set on fire, both the corn that was already carried together and that which was yet *standing,* was all burnt insomuch that the flame consumed also the vineyards and the oliveyards. 6 Then the Philistines said, "Who hath done this thing?"

And it was *answered,* "Samson, the son-in-law of the Thamnathite, because he took away his wife and gave her to another hath done these things." And the Philistines went up and burnt both the woman and her father.

7 Quibus ait Samson, "Licet haec feceritis, tamen adhuc ex vobis expetam ultionem, et tunc quiescam." 8 Percussitque eos ingenti plaga ita ut stupentes suram femori inponerent. Et descendens habitavit in spelunca petrae Aetham.

9 Igitur ascendentes Philisthim in terram Iuda castrametati sunt in loco qui postea vocatus est Lehi, id est, "Maxilla," ubi eorum est effusus exercitus. 10 Dixeruntque ad eos de tribu Iuda, "Cur ascendistis adversum nos?"

Qui responderunt, "Ut ligemus Samson venimus et reddamus ei quae in nos operatus est."

11 Descenderunt ergo tria milia virorum de Iuda ad specum silicis Aetham dixeruntque ad Samson, "Nescis quod Philisthim imperent nobis? Quare hoc facere voluisti?"

Quibus ille ait, "Sicut fecerunt mihi, sic feci eis."

12 "Ligare," inquiunt, "te venimus et tradere in manus Philisthinorum."

"Iurate," ait, "et spondete mihi quod non me occidatis."

13 Dixerunt, "Non te occidemus, sed vinctum trademus." Ligaveruntque eum duobus novis funibus et tulerunt de petra Aetham.

14 Qui cum venisset ad locum Maxillae et Philisthim vociferantes occurrissent ei, inruit spiritus Domini in eum, et sicut solent ad odorem ignis lina consumi, ita vincula quibus ligatus erat dissipata sunt et soluta. 15 Inventamque maxillam, id est, mandibulam asini, quae iacebat, arripiens, inter-

7 But Samson said to them, "Although you have done this, yet will I *be revenged* of you, and then I will be quiet." 8 And he made a great slaughter of them so that in astonishment they laid the calf of the leg upon the thigh. And going down he dwelt in a cavern of the rock Etam.

9 Then the Philistines going up into the land of Judah camped in the place which afterwards was called Lehi, that is, "the Jawbone," where their army was spread. 10 And the men of the tribe of Judah said to them, "Why are you come up against us?"

They answered, "We are come to bind Samson and to *pay him for what* he hath done against us."

11 Wherefore three thousand men of Judah went down to the cave of the rock Etam and said to Samson, "Knowest thou not that the Philistines rule over us? Why wouldst thou do thus?"

And he said to them, "As they did to me, so have I done to them."

12 And they said to him, "We are come to bind thee and to deliver thee into the hands of the Philistines."

And Samson said to them, "Swear to me and promise me that you will not kill me."

13 They said, "We will not kill thee, but we will deliver thee up bound." And they bound him with two new cords and brought him from the rock Etam.

14 Now when he was come to the place of the Jawbone and the Philistines shouting went to meet him, the spirit of the Lord came strongly upon him, and as the flax is wont to be consumed at the approach of fire, so the bands with which he was bound were broken and loosed. 15 And finding a jawbone, even the jawbone of an ass, which lay there,

cumdederunt eum, positis in porta civitatis custodibus et ibi tota nocte cum silentio praestolantes ut facto mane exeuntem occiderent. 3 Dormivit autem Samson usque ad noctis medium, et inde consurgens adprehendit ambas portae fores cum postibus suis et sera inpositasque umeris portavit ad verticem montis qui respicit Hebron.

4 Post haec, amavit mulierem quae habitabat in valle Sorech, et vocabatur Dalila. 5 Veneruntque ad eam principes Philisthinorum atque dixerunt, "Decipe eum, et disce ab illo in quo tantam habeat fortitudinem et quomodo eum superare valeamus et vinctum adfligere, quod si feceris, dabimus tibi singuli mille et centum argenteos."

6 Locuta est ergo Dalila ad Samson, "Dic mihi, obsecro, in quo sit tua maxima fortitudo et quid sit quo ligatus erumpere nequeas."

7 Cui respondit Samson, "Si septem nerviceis funibus necdum siccis, et adhuc humentibus, ligatus fuero, infirmus ero ut ceteri homines." 8 Adtuleruntque ad eam satrapae Philisthinorum septem funes, ut dixerat, quibus vinxit eum, 9 latentibus apud se insidiis et in cubiculo finem rei expectantibus, clamavitque ad eum, "Philisthim super te, Samson!" Qui rupit vincula quomodo si rumpat quis filum de stuppae tortum sputamine cum odorem ignis acceperit, et non est cognitum in quo esset fortitudo eius.

10 Dixitque ad eum Dalila, "Ecce! Inlusisti mihi et falsum locutus es, saltim nunc indica mihi quo ligari debeas."

11 Cui ille respondit, "Si ligatus fuero novis funibus qui

come into the city, they surrounded him, setting guards at the gate of the city and watching there all the night in silence that in the morning they might kill him as he went out. 3 But Samson slept till midnight, and then rising he took both the doors of the gate with the posts thereof and the bolt and laying them on his shoulders carried them up to the top of the hill which looketh towards Hebron.

4 After this, he loved a woman who dwelt in the valley of Sorek, and she was called Delilah. 5 And the princes of the Philistines came to her and said, "Deceive him, and learn of him wherein *his great strength lieth* and how we may be able to overcome him, *to bind and afflict* him, which if thou shalt do, we will give thee every one *of us* eleven hundred pieces of silver."

6 And Delilah said to Samson, "Tell me, I beseech thee, wherein thy greatest strength *lieth* and what it is wherewith *if thou wert* bound thou couldst not break loose."

7 And Samson answered her, "If I shall be bound with seven cords made of sinews not yet dry, but still moist, I shall be weak like other men." 8 And the princes of the Philistines brought unto her seven cords, such as he spoke of, with which she bound him, 9 men lying privately in wait with her and in the chamber expecting the event of the thing, and she cried out to him, "The Philistines are upon thee, Samson!" And he broke the bands as a man would break a thread of tow twined with spittle when it *smelleth* the fire, *so* it was not known wherein his strength *lay*.

10 And Delilah said to him, "Behold! Thou hast mocked me and hast told me a false thing, but now at least tell me wherewith thou mayest be bound."

11 And he answered her, "If I shall be bound with new

numquam fuerunt in opere, infirmus ero et aliorum hominum similis."

12 Quibus rursum Dalila vinxit eum et clamavit, "Philisthim super te, Samson!" in cubiculo insidiis praeparatis. Qui
ita rupit vincula quasi fila telarum.

13 Dixitque Dalila rursum ad eum, "Usquequo decipis me
et falsum loqueris? Ostende quo vinciri debeas."

Cui Samson respondit, "Si septem crines capitis mei cum
licio plexueris et clavum his circumligatum terrae fixeris, infirmus ero."

14 Quod cum fecisset Dalila, dixit ad eum, "Philisthim super te, Samson!" Qui consurgens de somno extraxit clavum
cum crinibus et licio. 15 Dixitque ad eum Dalila, "Quomodo
dicis quod ames me cum animus tuus non sit mecum? Per
tres vices mentitus es mihi et noluisti dicere in quo sit tua
maxima fortitudo." 16 Cumque molesta ei esset et per multos dies iugiter adhereret spatium ad quietem non tribuens,
defecit anima eius et ad mortem usque lassata est.

17 Tunc aperiens veritatem rei, dixit ad eam, "Ferrum
numquam ascendit super caput meum, quia Nazareus, id
est, consecratus Deo sum de utero matris meae. Si rasum
fuerit caput meum, recedet a me fortitudo mea, et deficiam
eroque ut ceteri homines."

18 Vidensque illa quod confessus ei esset omnem ani-
mum suum, misit ad principes Philisthinorum atque mandavit, "Aascendite adhuc semel, quia nunc mihi aperuit cor
suum." Qui ascenderunt adsumpta pecunia quam promise-

ropes that were never in work, I shall be weak and like other men."

12 Delilah bound him again with these and cried out, "The Philistines are upon thee, Samson!" there being an ambush prepared for him in the chamber. But he broke the bands like threads of webs.

13 And Delilah said to him again, "How long dost thou deceive me and tell me lies? Show me wherewith thou mayest be bound."

And Samson answered her, "If thou plattest the seven locks of my head with a lace and tying them round about a nail fastenest it in the ground, I shall be weak."

14 And when Delilah had done this, she said to him, "The Philistines are upon thee, Samson!" And awaking out of his sleep he drew out the nail with the hairs and the lace. 15 And Delilah said to him, "How dost thou say thou lovest me when thy mind is not with me? Thou hast *told me lies* these three times and wouldst not tell me wherein thy great strength *lieth.*" 16 And when she *pressed* him *much* and continually hung upon him for many days giving him no time to rest, his soul fainted away and was wearied even until death.

17 Then opening the truth of the thing, he said to her, "The razor hath never come upon my head, for I am a Nazirite, that is to say, consecrated to God from my mother's womb. If my head be shaven, my strength shall depart from me, and I shall become weak and shall be like other men."

18 Then seeing that he had discovered to her all his mind, she sent to the princes of the Philistines, *saying,* "Come up this once more, for now he hath opened his heart to me." And they went up taking with them the money which they

Samson. 28 At ille, invocato Domino, ait, "Domine Deus, memento mei, et redde nunc mihi pristinam fortitudinem, Deus meus, ut ulciscar me de hostibus meis, et pro amissione duorum luminum unam ultionem recipiam." 29 Et adprehendens ambas columnas quibus innitebatur domus, alteramque earum dextera et alteram leva tenens, 30 ait, "Moriatur anima mea cum Philisthim." Concussisque fortiter columnis, cecidit domus super omnes principes et ceteram multitudinem quae ibi erat, multoque plures interfecit moriens quam ante vivus occiderat. 31 Descendentes autem fratres eius et universa cognatio tulerunt corpus eius et sepelierunt inter Saraa et Esthaol in sepulchro patris, Manue, iudicavitque Israhel viginti annis.

Caput 17

Fuit eo tempore vir quidam de Monte Ephraim nomine Michas, 2 qui dixit matri suae, "Mille et centum argenteos quos separaveras tibi et super quibus me audiente iuraveras—ecce—ego habeo, et apud me sunt."

part of the house were beholding Samson's play. 28 But he called upon the Lord, *saying,* "O Lord God, remember me, and restore to me now my former strength, O my God, that I may revenge myself on my enemies, and for the loss of my two eyes I may take one revenge." 29 And laying hold on both the pillars on which the house rested, and holding the one with his right hand and the other with his left, 30 he said, "Let *me* die with the Philistines." And when he had strongly shook the pillars, the house fell upon all the princes and the rest of the multitude that was there, and he killed many more at his death than he had killed before in his life. 31 And his brethren and all his kindred going down took his body and buried it between Zorah and Eshtaol in the burying-place of his father, Manoah, and he judged Israel twenty years.

Chapter 17

The history of the idol of Micah and the young Levite.

There was at that time a man of Mount Ephraim whose name was Micah, 2 who said to his mother, "The eleven hundred pieces of silver which thou hadst put aside for thyself and concerning which thou didst swear in my hearing—behold—I have, and they are with me."

Cui illa respondit, "Benedictus filius meus Domino."
3 Reddidit ergo eos matri suae, quae dixerat ei, "Consecravi
et vovi argentum hoc Domino ut de manu mea suscipiat filius meus et faciat sculptile atque conflatile, et nunc trado
illud tibi. 4 Reddidit igitur matri suae, quae tulit ducentos
argenteos et dedit eos argentario ut faceret ex eis sculptile
atque conflatile quod fuit in domo Micha. 5 Qui aediculam
quoque in ea Deo separavit et fecit ephod ac therafin, id est,
vestem sacerdotalem, et idola, implevitque unius filiorum
suorum manum et factus est ei sacerdos.

6 In diebus illis non erat rex in Israhel, sed unusquisque
quod sibi rectum videbatur hoc faciebat. 7 Fuit quoque alter
adulescens de Bethleem Iuda ex cognatione eius, eratque
ipse Levites et habitabat ibi. 8 Egressusque de civitate Bethleem peregrinari voluit ubicumque sibi commodum reppe-
risset. Cumque venisset in Montem Ephraim iter faciens et
declinasset parumper in domum Micha, 9 interrogatus est
ab eo unde venisset. Qui respondit, "Levita sum de Bethleem Iuda, et vado ut habitem ubi potuero et utile mihi esse
perspexero."

10 Dixitque Michas, "Mane apud me, et esto mihi parens
ac sacerdos, daboque tibi per annos singulos decem argenteos ac vestem duplicem et quae ad victum necessaria sunt."
11 Adquievit et mansit apud hominem fuitque illi quasi unus
de filiis. 12 Implevitque Micha manum eius et habuit apud se
puerum sacerdotem, 13 "Nunc scio," dicens, "quod benefaciet mihi Deus, habenti levitici generis sacerdotem."

And she said to him, "Blessed be my son by the Lord."
3 So he restored them to his mother, who said to him, "I
have consecrated and vowed this silver to the Lord that my
son may receive it at my hand and make a graven and a molten god, *so* now I deliver it to thee. 4 And he restored them
to his mother, and she took two hundred pieces of silver and
gave them to the silversmith to make of them a graven and a
molten god which was in the house of Micah. 5 And he separated also therein a little temple for the *god* and made an
ephod and theraphim, that is to say, a priestly garment, and
idols, and he filled the hand of one of his sons and he became his priest.

6 In those days there was no king in Israel, but every one
did that which seemed right to himself. 7 There was also
another young man of Bethlehem Judah of the kindred
thereof, and he was a Levite and dwelt there. 8 Now he went
out from the city of Bethlehem and desired to sojourn
wheresoever he should find it convenient for him. And when
he was come to Mount Ephraim as he was on his journey
and had turned aside a little into the house of Micah, 9 he
was asked by him whence he came. And he answered, "I am
a Levite of Bethlehem Judah, and I am going to dwell where
I can and where I shall find *a place* to my advantage."

10 And Micah said, "Stay with me, and be unto me a father and a priest, and I will give thee every year ten pieces of
silver and a double suit of apparel and *thy victuals.*" 11 He was
content and abode with the man and was unto him as one of
his sons. 12 And Micah filled his hand and had the young
man with him for his priest, saying, 13 "Now I know God will
do me good, since I have a priest of the race of the Levites."

Caput 18

In diebus illis non erat rex in Israhel, et tribus Dan quaerebat possessionem sibi ut habitaret in ea, usque ad illum enim diem inter ceteras tribus sortem non acceperat. 2 Miserunt igitur filii Dan stirpis et familiae suae quinque viros fortissimos de Saraa et Esthaol ut explorarent terram et diligenter inspicerent, dixeruntque eis, "Ite, et considerate terram." Qui cum pergentes venissent in Montem Ephraim et intrassent domum Micha, requieverunt ibi. 3 Et agnoscentes vocem adulescentis, Levitae, utentesque illius diversorio, dixerunt ad eum, "Quis te huc adduxit? Quid hic agis? Quam ob causam huc venire voluisti?"

4 Qui respondit eis, "Haec et haec praestitit mihi Michas et me mercede conduxit ut sim ei sacerdos." 5 Rogaveruntque eum ut consuleret Dominum ut scire possent an prospero itinere pergerent et res haberet effectum. 6 Qui respondit eis, "Ite in pace; Dominus respicit viam vestram et iter quo pergitis."

7 Euntes igitur quinque viri venerunt Lais, videruntque populum habitantem in ea absque ullo timore iuxta Sidoniorum consuetudinem, securum et quietum, nullo eis penitus resistente, magnarumque opum et procul a Sidone atque a cunctis hominibus separatum. 8 Reversique ad fratres suos

Chapter 18

The expedition of the men of Dan against Laish. In their way they rob Micah of his priest and his gods.

In those days there was no king in Israel, and the tribe of Dan sought them an inheritance to dwell in, for unto that day they had not received their lot among the other tribes. 2 So the children of Dan sent five most valiant men of their stock and family from Zorah and Eshtaol to spy out the land and to view it diligently, and they said to them, "Go, and view the land." They went on their way, and when they came to Mount Ephraim, *they went into* the house of Micah *and* rested there. 3 And knowing the voice of the young man, the Levite, and *lodging with him,* they said to him, "Who brought thee hither? What dost thou here? Why wouldst thou come hither?"

4 He answered them, "Micah hath done such and such things for me and hath hired me to be his priest." 5 Then they desired him to consult the Lord that they might know whether *their journey should be prosperous* and the thing should have effect. 6 He answered them, "Go in peace; the Lord looketh on your way and the journey that you go."

7 So the five men going on came to Laish, and they saw *how* the people *dwelt* therein without any fear according to the custom of the Sidonians, secure and easy, having no man at all to oppose them, being very rich and *living* separated at a distance from Sidon and from all men. 8 And they returned

in Saraa et Esthaol, et quid egissent sciscitantibus responderunt, 9 "Surgite, et ascendamus ad eos, vidimus enim terram
valde opulentam et uberem. Nolite neglegere; nolite cessare;
eamus et possideamus eam; nullus erit labor. 10 Intrabimus
ad securos, in regionem latissimam, tradetque nobis Dominus locum in quo nullius rei est penuria eorum quae gignun-
tur in terra." 11 Profecti igitur sunt de cognatione Dan, id
est, de Saraa et Esthaol, sescenti viri accincti armis bellicis,
12 ascendentesque manserunt in Cariathiarim Iudae, qui locus ex eo tempore Castrorum Dan nomen accepit et est
post tergum Cariathiarim.

13 Inde transierunt in Montem Ephraim, cumque venissent ad domum Micha, 14 dixerunt quinque viri qui prius
missi fuerant ad considerandam terram Lais ceteris fratribus
suis, "Nostis quod in domibus istis sit ephod et therafin et
sculptile atque conflatile; videte quid vobis placeat." 15 Et
cum paululum declinassent, ingressi sunt domum adulescentis, Levitae qui erat in domo Micha, salutaveruntque
eum verbis pacificis. 16 Sescenti autem viri ita ut erant armati stabant ante ostium. 17 At illi qui ingressi fuerant domum iuvenis sculptile et ephod et therafin atque conflatile
tollere nitebantur, et sacerdos stabat ante ostium, sescentis
viris fortissimis haut procul expectantibus.

18 Tulerunt igitur qui intraverant sculptile, ephod et idola
atque conflatile, quibus dixit sacerdos, "Quid facitis?"

to their brethren in Zorah and Eshtaol, *who asked them what they had done, to whom they answered,* 9 "Arise, and let us go up to them, for we have seen the land which is exceeding rich and fruitful. Neglect not; lose no time; let us go and possess it; there will be no difficulty. 10 We shall come to *a people that is* secure, into a spacious country, and the Lord will deliver the place to us in which there is no want of *any thing* that groweth on the earth." 11 There went therefore of the kindred of Dan, to wit, from Zorah and Eshtaol, six hundred men furnished with arms for war, 12 and going up they lodged in Kiriath-jearim of Judah, which place from that time *is called* the Camp of Dan and is behind Kiriath-jearim.

13 From thence they passed into Mount Ephraim, and when they were come to the house of Micah, 14 the five men that before had been sent to view the land of Laish said to the rest of their brethren, "You know that in these houses there is an ephod and theraphim and a graven and a molten god; see what you are pleased to do." 15 And when they had turned a little aside, they went into the house of the young man, the Levite who was in the house of Micah, and they saluted him with words of peace. 16 And the six hundred men stood before the door, *appointed with their arms.* 17 But they that were gone into the house of the young man went about to take away the graven god and the ephod and the theraphim and the molten god, and the priest stood before the door, the six hundred valiant men waiting not far off.

18 So they that were gone in took away the graven thing, the ephod and the idols and the molten god, and the priest said to them, "What are you doing?"

19 Cui responderunt, "Tace, et pone digitum super os tuum, venique nobiscum ut habeamus te patrem et sacerdotem. Quid tibi melius est, ut sis sacerdos in domo unius viri an in una tribu et familia in Israhel?" 20 Quod cum audisset, adquievit sermonibus eorum et tulit ephod et idola ac sculptile et cum eis profectus est. 21 Qui cum pergerent et ante se ire fecissent parvulos et iumenta et omne quod erat pretiosum 22 iamque a domo Michae essent procul, viri qui habitabant in aedibus Michae conclamantes secuti sunt 23 et post tergum clamare coeperunt. Qui cum respexissent dixerunt ad Micham, "Quid tibi vis? Cur clamas?"

24 Qui respondit, "Deos meos quos mihi feci tulistis et sacerdotem et omnia quae habeo, et dicitis, 'Quid tibi est?'"

25 Dixeruntque ei filii Dan, "Cave ne ultra loquaris ad nos et veniant ad te viri animo concitati, et ipse cum omni domo tua pereas." 26 Et sic coepto itinere perrexerunt, videns autem Micha quod fortiores se essent reversus est in domum suam. 27 Sescenti autem viri tulerunt sacerdotem et quae supra diximus veneruntque in Lais, ad populum quiescentem atque securum, et percusserunt eos in ore gladii, urbemque incendio tradiderunt, 28 nullo penitus ferente praesidium eo quod procul habitarent a Sidone et cum nullo hominum haberent quicquam societatis ac negotii. Erat autem civitas sita in regione Roob, quam rursum extruentes habitaverunt in ea, 29 vocato nomine civitatis Dan iuxta vocabulum patris sui, quem genuerat Israhel, quae prius Lais dicebatur. 30 Posueruntque sibi sculptile, et Ionathan, filium

19 And they said to him, "Hold thy peace, and put thy finger on thy mouth, and come with us that we may have thee for a father and a priest. Whether is better for thee, to be a priest in the house of one man or in a tribe and family in Israel?" 20 When he had heard this, he agreed to their words and took the ephod and the idols and the graven god and departed with them. 21 And when they were going forward and had *put* before them the children and the cattle and all that was valuable 22 and were now at a distance from the house of Micah, the men that dwelt in the houses of Micah gathering together followed them 23 and began to shout out after them. They looked back and said to Micah, "What aileth thee? Why dost thou cry?"

24 And he answered, "You have taken away my gods which I have made me and the priest and all that I have, and do you say, 'What aileth thee?'"

25 And the children of Dan said to him, "See thou say no more to us *lest* men *enraged* come upon thee, and thou perish with all thy house." 26 And so they went on the journey they had begun, but Micah seeing that they were stronger than he returned to his house. 27 And the six hundred men took the priest and the things we spoke of before and came to Laish, to a people that was quiet and secure, and smote them with the edge of the sword, and *the city was burnt with fire,* 28 there being no man at all who brought them any succour because they dwelt far from Sidon and had no society or business with any man. And the city was in the land of Rehob, and they rebuilt it and dwelt therein, 29 calling the name of the city Dan after the name of their father, *who was the son of Israel,* which before was called Laish. 30 And they set up to themselves the graven idol, and Jonathan, the son

Gersan, filii Mosi, ac filios eius sacerdotes in tribu Dan usque ad diem captivitatis suae. 31 Mansitque apud eos idolum Michae omni tempore quo fuit domus Dei in Silo.

In diebus illis non erat rex in Israhel.

Caput 19

Fuit quidam vir Levites habitans in latere Montis Ephraim, qui accepit uxorem de Bethleem Iuda, 2 quae reliquit eum et reversa est in domum patris sui in Bethleem mansitque apud eum quattuor mensibus. 3 Secutusque est eam vir suus, volens ei reconciliari atque blandiri et secum reducere, habens in comitatu puerum et duos asinos. Quae suscepit eum et introduxit in domum patris sui. Quod cum audisset socer eius eumque vidisset, occurrit ei laetus 4 et amplexatus est hominem. Mansitque gener in domo soceri tribus diebus, comedens cum eo et bibens familiariter. 5 Die autem quarto

of Gershom, the son of Moses, *he* and his sons were priests in the tribe of Dan until the day of their captivity. 31 And the idol of Micah remained with them all the time that the house of God was in Shiloh.

In those days there was no king in Israel.

Chapter 19

A Levite bringing home his wife is lodged by an old man at Gibeah in the tribe of Benjamin. His wife is there abused by wicked men and in the morning found dead. Her husband cutteth her body in pieces and sendeth to every tribe of Israel, requiring them to revenge the wicked fact.

There was a certain *Levite who dwelt* on the side of Mount Ephraim, who took a wife of Bethlehem Judah, 2 and she left him and returned to her father's house in Bethlehem and abode with him four months. 3 And her husband followed her, willing to be reconciled with her and to speak kindly to her and to bring her back with him, having *with him* a servant and two asses. And she received him and brought him into her father's house. And when his father-in-law had heard this and had seen him, he met him *with joy* 4 and embraced the man. And the son-in-law tarried in the house of his father in law three days, eating with him and drinking familiarly. 5 But on the fourth day arising early in the morn-

de nocte consurgens proficisci voluit. Quem tenuit socer et ait ad eum, "Gusta prius pauxillum panis, et conforta stomachum, et sic proficisceris." 6 Sederuntque simul et comederunt ac biberunt. Dixitque pater puellae ad generum suum, "Quaeso te ut hodie hic maneas, pariterque laetemur." 7 At ille consurgens coepit velle proficisci. Et nihilominus obnixe eum socer tenuit et apud se fecit manere. 8 Mane autem facto, parabat Levites iter. Cui rursum socer, "Oro te," inquit, "ut paululum cibi capias et adsumptis viribus donec increscat dies postea proficiscaris." Comederunt ergo simul. 9 Surrexitque adulescens ut pergeret cum uxore sua et puero, cui rursum locutus est socer, "Considera quod dies ad occasum declivior sit et propinquet ad vesperum. Mane apud me etiam hodie, et duc laetum diem, et cras proficisceris ut vadas in domum tuam." 10 Noluit gener adquiescere sermonibus eius, sed statim perrexit et venit contra Iebus, quae altero nomine vocatur Hierusalem, ducens secum duos asinos onustos et concubinam.

11 Iamque aderant iuxta Iebus, et dies mutabatur in noctem, dixitque puer ad dominum suum, "Veni, obsecro; declinemus ad urbem Iebuseorum et maneamus in ea."

12 Cui respondit dominus, "Non ingrediar oppidum gentis alienae quae non est de filiis Israhel, sed transibo usque Gabaa. 13 Et cum illuc pervenero, manebimus in ea, aut certe in urbe Rama."

ing he desired to depart. But his father-in-law kept him and said to him, "Taste first a little bread, and strengthen thy stomach, and so thou shalt depart." 6 And they sat down together and ate and drank. And the father of the young woman said to his son-in-law, "I beseech thee to stay here today, and let us make merry together." 7 But he rising up began to be for departing. And nevertheless his father-in-law earnestly *pressed* him and made him stay with him. 8 But when morning was come, the Levite prepared *to go on* his journey. And his father in law said to him again, "I beseech thee to take a little meat, and strengthening thyself till the day be farther advanced afterwards thou mayest depart." And they ate together. 9 And the young man arose to set forward with his wife and servant, and his father-in-law spoke to him again, "Consider that the day is *declining* and draweth toward evening. Tarry with me today also, and spend the day in mirth, and tomorrow thou shalt depart that thou mayest go into thy house." 10 His son-in-law would not consent to his words, but forthwith went forward and came over against Jebus, which by another name is called Jerusalem, leading with him two asses laden and his concubine.

11 And now they were come near Jebus, and the day *was far spent,* and the servant said to his master, "Come, I beseech thee; let us turn into the city of the Jebusites and lodge there."

12 His master answered him, "I will not go into the town of another nation *who are* not of the children of Israel, but I will pass over to Gibeah. 13 And when I shall come thither, we will lodge there, or at least in the city of Ramah."

14 Transierunt igitur Iebus et coeptum carpebant iter, occubuitque eis sol iuxta Gabaa, quae est in tribu Beniamin, 15 deverteruntque ad eam ut manerent ibi. Quo cum intrassent sedebant in platea civitatis, et nullus eos recipere volebat hospitio. 16 Et ecce: apparuit homo senex revertens de agro et de opere suo vespere, qui et ipse erat de Monte Ephraim et peregrinus habitabat in Gabaa, homines autem regionis illius erant filii Iemini. 17 Elevatisque oculis vidit senex sedentem hominem cum sarcinulis suis in platea civitatis et dixit ad eum, "Unde venis? Et quo vadis?"

18 Qui respondit ei, "Profecti sumus de Bethleem Iuda, et pergimus ad locum nostrum qui est in latere Montis Ephraim unde ieramus in Bethleem, et nunc vadimus ad domum Dei, nullusque nos sub tectum suum vult recipere. 19 Habentes paleas et faenum in asinorum pabulum et panem ac vinum in meos et ancillae tuae usus et pueri qui mecum est; nulla re indigemus nisi hospitio."

20 Cui respondit senex, "Pax tecum sit. Ego praebebo omnia quae necessaria sunt. Tantum, quaeso, ne in platea maneas." 21 Introduxitque eum in domum suam et pabulum asinis praebuit, ac postquam laverunt pedes suos, recepit eos in convivium. 22 Illis epulantibus et post laborem itineris cibo ac potu reficientibus corpora, venerunt viri civitatis illius, filii Belial (id est "absque iugo"), et circumdantes domum senis fores pulsare coeperunt, clamantes ad dominum domus atque dicentes, "Educ virum qui ingressus est domum tuam ut abutamur eo."

14 So they passed by Jebus and went on their *journey,* and the sun went down upon them *when they were by* Gibeah, which is in the tribe of Benjamin, 15 and they turned into it to lodge there. And when they were come in they sat in the street of the city, *for* no man would receive them *to lodge.* 16 And behold: *they saw* an old man returning out of the field and from his work in the evening, and he also was of Mount Ephraim and dwelt as a stranger in Gibeah, but the men of that country were the children of Jemini. 17 And the old man lifting up his eyes saw the man sitting with his bundles in the street of the city and said to him, "Whence comest thou? And whither goest thou?"

18 He answered him, "We came out from Bethlehem Judah, and we are going to our home which is on the side of Mount Ephraim from whence we went to Bethlehem, and now we go to the house of God, and none will receive us under his roof. 19 We have straw and hay for provender of the asses and bread and wine for the use of myself and of thy handmaid and of the servant that is with me; we want nothing but lodging."

20 And the old man answered him, "Peace be with thee. I will furnish all things that are necessary. Only, I beseech thee, stay not in the street." 21 And he brought him into his house and gave provender to his asses, and after they had washed their feet, he entertained them with a feast. 22 While they were making merry and refreshing their bodies with meat and drink after the labour of the journey, the men of that city, sons of Belial (that is, "without yoke"), came and beset the old man's house and began to knock at the door, calling to the master of the house and saying, "Bring forth the man that came into thy house that we may abuse him."

23 Egressusque est ad eos senex et ait, "Nolite, fratres; nolite facere malum hoc, quia ingressus est homo hospitium meum, et cessate ab hac stultitia. 24 Habeo filiam virginem, et hic homo habet concubinam; educam eas ad vos ut humilietis eas et vestram libidinem conpleatis. Tantum, obsecro, ne scelus hoc contra naturam operemini in virum."

25 Nolebant adquiescere sermonibus eius, quod cernens homo eduxit ad eos concubinam suam et eis tradidit inludendam, qua cum tota nocte abusi essent, dimiserunt eam mane. 26 At mulier recedentibus tenebris venit ad ostium domus ubi manebat dominus suus et ibi corruit. 27 Mane facto surrexit homo et aperuit ostium ut coeptam expleret viam, et ecce: concubina eius iacebat ante ostium sparsis in limine manibus. 28 Cui ille, putans eam quiescere, loquebatur, "Surge, et ambulemus." Qua nihil respondente, intellegens quod erat mortua tulit eam et inposuit asino reversusque est in domum suam. 29 Quam cum esset ingressus arripuit gladium et cadaver uxoris cum ossibus suis in duodecim partes ac frusta concidens misit in omnes terminos Israhel. 30 Quod cum vidissent singuli, conclamabant, "Numquam res talis facta est in Israhel ex eo die quo ascenderunt patres nostri de Aegypto usque in praesens tempus. Ferte sententiam, et in commune decernite quid facto opus sit."

23 And the old man went out to them and said, "Do not so, my brethren; do not *so wickedly,* because this man is come into my lodging, and cease, *I pray you,* from this folly. 24 I have a maiden daughter, and this man hath a concubine; I will bring them out to you, *and* you may humble them and satisfy your lust. Only, I beseech you, commit not this crime against nature on the man."

25 They would not be satisfied with his words, which the man seeing brought out his concubine to them and *abandoned her to their wickedness,* and when they had abused her all the night, they let her go in the morning. 26 But the woman *at the dawning of the day* came to the door of the house where her lord lodged and there fell down. 27 And *in the morning* the man arose and opened the door that he might end the journey he had begun, and behold: his concubine lay before the door with her hands spread on the threshold. 28 He, thinking she was taking her rest, said to her, "Arise, and let us be going." But as she made no answer, perceiving she was dead he took her up and laid her upon his ass and returned to his house. 29 *And when he was come home* he took a sword and divided the dead body of his wife with her bones into twelve parts and sent the pieces into all the borders of Israel. 30 And when every one had seen this, they all cried out, "There was never such a thing done in Israel from the day that our fathers came up out of Egypt until this day. Give sentence, and decree in common what ought to be done."

Caput 20

Egressi sunt itaque omnes filii Israhel et pariter congregati quasi vir unus de Dan usque Bersabee et terra Galaad ad Dominum in Maspha, 2 omnesque anguli populorum et cunctae tribus Israhel in ecclesiam populi Dei convenerunt, quadringenta milia peditum pugnatorum, 3 nec latuit filios Beniamin quod ascendissent filii Israhel in Maspha. Interrogatusque Levita, maritus mulieris interfectae, quomodo tantum scelus perpetratum esset 4 respondit, "Veni in Gabaa Beniamin cum uxore mea, illucque deverti, 5 et ecce: homines civitatis illius circumdederunt nocte domum in qua manebam, volentes me occidere, et uxorem meam incredibili libidinis furore vexantes denique mortua est. 6 Quam arreptam in frusta concidi misique partes in omnes terminos possessionis vestrae, quia numquam tantum nefas et tam grande piaculum factum est in Israhel. 7 Adestis omnes, filii Israhel; decernite quid facere debeatis."

8 Stansque omnis populus quasi unius hominis sermone respondit, "Non recedemus in tabernacula nostra, nec suam quisquam intrabit domum, 9 sed hoc contra Gabaa in commune faciemus: 10 decem viri eligantur e centum ex omnibus

Chapter 20

The Israelites warring against Benjamin are twice defeated, but in the third battle the Benjamites are all slain, saving six hundred men.

Then all the children of Israel went out and gathered together as one man from Dan to Beer-sheba *with* the land of Gilead to the Lord in Mizpah, 2 and all the *chiefs* of the people and all the tribes of Israel met together in the assembly of the people of God, four hundred thousand footmen *fit for war,* 3 nor were the children of Benjamin ignorant that the children of Israel were come up to Mizpah. And the Levite, the husband of the woman that was killed, being asked how so great a wickedness had been committed 4 answered, "I came into Gibeah of Benjamin with my wife, and there I lodged, 5 and behold: the men of that city in the night beset the house wherein I *was,* intending to kill me, and abused my wife with an incredible fury of lust so that at last she died. 6 And I took her and cut her in pieces and sent the parts into all the borders of your possession, because there never was so heinous a crime and so great an abomination committed in Israel. 7 You are all here, O children of Israel; determine what you ought to do."

8 And all the people standing answered as by the voice of one man, "We will not return to our tents, neither shall any one of us go into his own house, 9 but this we will do in common against Gibeah: 10 *we will take ten men* of a hundred out

tribubus Israhel et centum de mille et mille de decem milibus ut conportent exercitui cibaria et possimus pugnare contra Gabaa Beniamin et reddere ei pro scelere quod meretur." 11 Convenitque universus Israhel ad civitatem quasi unus homo eadem mente unoque consilio. 12 Et miserunt nuntios ad omnem tribum Beniamin qui dicerent, "Cur tantum nefas in vobis reppertum est? 13 Tradite homines de Gabaa qui hoc flagitium perpetrarunt ut moriantur et auferatur malum de Israhel." Qui noluerunt fratrum suorum, filiorum Israhel, audire mandatum, 14 sed ex cunctis urbibus quae suae sortis erant convenerunt in Gabaa ut illis ferrent auxilium et contra universum Israhel populum dimicarent. 15 Inventique sunt viginti quinque milia de Beniamin educentium gladium praeter habitatores Gabaa, 16 qui septingenti erant viri fortissimi ita sinistra ut dextra proeliantes et sic fundis ad certum iacientes lapides ut capillum quoque possent percutere et nequaquam in alteram partem ictus lapidis deferretur. 17 Virorum quoque Israhel, absque filiis Beniamin, inventa sunt quadringenta milia educentium gladios et paratorum ad pugnam.

18 Qui surgentes venerunt in domum Dei, hoc est, in Silo, consulueruntque Deum atque dixerunt, "Quis erit in exercitu nostro princeps certaminis contra filios Beniamin?"

Quibus respondit Dominus, "Iudas sit dux vester." 19 Statimque filii Israhel surgentes mane castrametati sunt iuxta Gabaa 20 et inde procedentes ad pugnam contra Beniamin

of all the tribes of Israel and a hundred out of a thousand and a thousand out of ten thousand to bring victuals for the army and that we might fight against Gibeah of Benjamin and render to it for its wickedness what it deserveth." 11 And all Israel were gathered together against the city as one man with *one* mind and one counsel. 12 And they sent messengers to all the tribe of Benjamin to say *to them,* "Why hath so great an abomination been found among you? 13 Deliver up the men of Gibeah that have committed this heinous crime that they may die and the evil may be taken away out of Israel." But they would not hearken to the proposition of their brethren, the children of Israel, 14 but out of all the cities which were of their lot they gathered themselves together into Gibeah to aid them and to fight against the whole people of Israel. 15 And there were found of Benjamin five and twenty thousand men that drew the sword besides the inhabitants of Gibeah, 16 who were seven hundred most valiant men fighting with the left hand as well as with the right and slinging stones so sure that they could hit even a hair and *not miss by the stone's going on either side.* 17 Of the men of Israel also, beside the children of Benjamin, were found four hundred thousand that drew swords and were prepared to fight.

18 And they arose and came to the house of God, that is, to Shiloh, and they consulted God and said, "Who shall be in our army the first *to go to the battle* against the children of Benjamin?"

And the Lord answered them, "Let Judah be your leader." 19 And forthwith the children of Israel rising in the morning camped by Gibeah 20 and going out from thence to fight

urbem obpugnare coeperunt. 21 Egressique filii Beniamin de Gabaa occiderunt de filiis Israhel die illo viginti et duo milia viros. 22 Rursum filii Israhel et fortitudine et numero confidentes in eodem loco in quo prius certaverant aciem direxerunt, 23 ita tamen ut prius ascenderent et flerent coram Domino usque ad noctem consulerentque eum et dicerent, "Debeo ultra procedere ad dimicandum contra filios Beniamin, fratres meos, an non?"

Quibus ille respondit, "Ascendite ad eos, et inite certamen."

24 Cumque filii Israhel altero die contra filios Beniamin ad proelium processissent, 25 eruperunt filii Beniamin de portis Gabaa, et occurrentes eis tanta in illos caede baccati sunt ut decem et octo milia virorum educentium gladium prosternerent. 26 Quam ob rem omnes filii Israhel venerunt in domum Dei et sedentes flebant coram Domino, ieiunaveruntque illo die usque ad vesperam et obtulerunt ei holocausta et pacificas victimas 27 et super statu suo interrogaverunt. Eo tempore ibi erat Arca Foederis Domini, 28 et Finees, filius Eleazari, filii Aaron, praepositus domus. Consuluerunt igitur Dominum atque dixerunt, "Exire ultra debemus ad pugnam contra filios Beniamin, fratres nostros, an quiescere?"

Quibus ait Dominus, "Ascendite, cras enim tradam eos in manus vestras."

29 Posueruntque filii Israhel insidias per circuitum urbis Gabaa, 30 et tertia vice sicut semel et bis contra Beniamin exercitum produxerunt. 31 Sed et filii Beniamin audacter

against Benjamin began to assault the city. 21 And the children of Benjamin coming out of Gibeah slew of the children of Israel that day two and twenty thousand men. 22 Again *Israel* trusting in their strength and their number set their army in array in the same place where they had fought before, 23 yet so that they first went up and wept before the Lord until night and consulted him and said, "Shall I go out any more to fight against the children of Benjamin, my brethren, or not?"

And he answered them, "Go up against them, and join battle."

24 And when the children of Israel went out the next day to fight against the children of Benjamin, 25 the children of Benjamin sallied forth out of the gates of Gibeah, and meeting them *made* so great a slaughter of them as to kill eighteen thousand men that drew the sword. 26 Wherefore all the children of Israel came to the house of God and sat and wept before the Lord, and they fasted that day till the evening and offered to him holocausts and victims of peace offerings 27 and inquired of him concerning their state. At that time the Ark of the Covenant of the Lord was there, 28 and Phinehas, the son of Eleazar, the son of Aaron, was over the house. So they consulted the Lord and said, "Shall we go out any more to fight against the children of Benjamin, our brethren, or shall we cease?"

And the Lord said to them, "Go up, for tomorrow I will deliver them into your hands."

29 And the children of Israel set ambushes round about the city of Gibeah, 30 and they drew up their army against Benjamin the third time as they had done the first and second. 31 *And* the children of *Benjamin* boldly issued out of the

eruperunt de civitate et fugientes adversarios longius persecuti sunt ita ut vulnerarent ex eis sicut primo et secundo die
et caederent per duas semitas terga vertentes quarum una
ferebat in Bethel et altera in Gabaa, atque prosternerent triginta circiter viros, 32 putaverunt enim solito eos more ce-
dere. Qui, fugam arte simulantes, iniere consilium ut abs-
traherent eos de civitate et quasi fugientes ad supradictas
semitas perducerent. 33 Omnes itaque filii Israhel surgentes
de sedibus suis, tetenderunt aciem in loco qui vocatur Baal-
thamar. Insidiae quoque quae circa urbem erant paulatim se
aperire coeperunt 34 et ab occidentali urbis parte procedere.
Sed et alia decem milia virorum de universo Israhel habitatores urbis ad certamina provocabant, ingravatumque est
bellum contra filios Beniamin et non intellexerunt quod ex
omni parte illis instaret interitus. 35 Percussitque eos Dominus in conspectu filiorum Israhel, et interfecerunt ex eis in
illo die viginti quinque milia et centum viros, omnes bellatores et educentes gladium.

36 Filii autem Beniamin cum se inferiores esse vidissent
coeperunt fugere, quod cernentes filii Israhel, dederunt eis
ad fugiendum locum ut ad praeparatas insidias devenirent
quas iuxta urbem posuerant. 37 Qui cum repente de latibulis
surrexissent et, Beniamin terga caedentibus daret, ingressi
sunt civitatem et percusserunt eam in ore gladii.

38 Signum autem dederant filii Israhel his quos in insidiis
conlocaverant ut postquam urbem cepissent ignem accen-
derent ut ascendente in altum fumo captam urbem demons-

city and *seeing their enemies flee pursued them* a long way so as
to wound and kill some of them as they had done the first
and second day *whilst they fled* by two highways whereof one
goeth up to Bethel and the other to Gibeah, and they slew
about thirty men, 32 for they thought *to cut them off, as they
did before.* But they, artfully feigning a flight, designed to
draw them away from the city and *by their seeming to flee* to
bring them to the highways aforesaid. 33 Then all the children of Israel rising up out of *the places where they were,* set
their army in battle array in the place which is called Baal-
tamar. The ambushes also which were about the city began
by little and little to come forth 34 and to march from the
west side of the city. *And* other ten thousand men *chosen* out
of all Israel *attacked* the inhabitants of the city, and the battle grew hot against the children of Benjamin, and they understood not that present death threatened them on every
side. 35 And the Lord defeated them before the children of
Israel, and they slew of them in that day five and twenty
thousand and one hundred, all fighting men and that drew
the sword.

36 But the children of Benjamin when they saw themselves to be too weak began to flee, which the children of
Israel seeing, gave them place to flee that they might come
to the ambushes that were prepared which they had set near
the city. 37 And *they that were in ambush* arose on a sudden out
of their coverts and, whilst Benjamin turned their backs to
the slayers, went into the city and smote it with the edge of
the sword.

38 Now the children of Israel had given a sign to them
whom they had laid in ambushes that after they had taken
the city they should make a fire that by the smoke rising on

trarent. 39 Quod cum cernerent filii Israhel in ipso certamine positi (putaverunt enim filii Beniamin eos fugere et instantius persequebantur, caesis de exercitu eorum triginta viris) 40 et viderent quasi columnam fumi de civitate conscendere, Beniamin quoque retro aspiciens cum captam cerneret civitatem et flammas in sublime ferri, 41 qui prius simulaverant fugam, versa facie fortius resistebant, quod cum vidissent filii Beniamin in fugam versi sunt 42 et ad viam deserti ire coeperunt, illuc quoque eos adversariis persequentibus. Sed et hii qui urbem succenderant occurrerunt eis. 43 Atque ita factum est ut ex utraque parte ab hostibus caederentur, nec erat ulla morientium requies. Ceciderunt atque prostrati sunt ad orientalem plagam urbis Gabaa. 44 Fuerunt autem qui in eodem loco interfecti sunt decem et octo milia virorum, omnes robustissimi pugnatores. 45 Quod cum vidissent qui remanserant de Beniamin, fugerunt in solitudinem et pergebant ad petram cuius vocabulum est Remmon. In illa quoque fuga, palantes et in diversa tendentes, occiderunt quinque milia viros. Et cum ultra tenderent, persecuti sunt eos et interfecerunt etiam alia duo milia. 46 Et sic factum est ut omnes qui ceciderant de Beniamin in diversis locis essent viginti quinque milia pugnatores, ad bella promptissimi. 47 Remanserunt itaque de omni numero Beniamin qui evadere potuerant et fugere in solitudinem sescenti viri, sederuntque in petra Remmon mensibus quattuor. 48 Regressi autem filii Israhel omnes reliquias civitatis, a viris usque ad iumenta, gladio percusserunt, cunctasque urbes et viculos Beniamin vorax flamma consumpsit.

high they might show that the city was taken. 39 And when the children of Israel saw this *in the battle* (for the children of Benjamin thought they fled and pursued them vigorously, killing thirty men of their army) 40 and perceived as it were a pillar of smoke rise up from the city, and Benjamin looking back *saw* that the city was taken and that the flames ascended on high, 41 they that before had made as if they fled, turning their faces stood bravely against them, which the children of Benjamin seeing *turned their backs* 42 and began to go towards the way of the desert, the enemy pursuing them thither also. *And* they that fired the city *came* also *out to meet* them. 43 And so it was that they were slain on both sides by the enemies, and there was no rest of their men dying. They fell and were beaten down on the east side of the city Gibeah. 44 And they that were slain in the same place were eighteen thousand men, all most valiant soldiers. 45 And when they that remained of Benjamin saw this, they fled into the wilderness and made towards the rock *that is called* Rimmon. In that flight also, as they were straggling and going different ways, they slew of them five thousand men. And as they went farther, they still pursued them and slew also other two thousand. 46 And so it came to pass that all that were slain of Benjamin in divers places were five and twenty thousand fighting men, most valiant for war. 47 And there remained of all the number of Benjamin only six hundred men that were able to escape and flee to the wilderness, and they abode in the rock Rimmon four months. 48 But the children of Israel returning put all the remains of the city to the sword, *both* men *and* beasts, and all the cities and villages of Benjamin *were consumed with devouring flames.*

Caput 21

Iuraverunt quoque filii Israhel in Maspha, et dixerunt, "Nullus nostrum dabit filiis Beniamin de filiabus suis uxorem." 2 Veneruntque omnes ad domum Dei in Silo et in conspectu eius sedentes usque ad vesperam levaverunt vocem et magno ululatu coeperunt flere, dicentes, 3 "Quare, Domine Deus Israhel, factum est hoc malum in populo tuo ut hodie una tribus auferretur ex nobis?" 4 Altera autem die diluculo consurgentes, extruxerunt altare obtuleruntque ibi holocausta et pacificas victimas, et dixerunt, 5 "Quis non ascendit in exercitu Domini de universis tribubus Israhel?" Grandi enim se iuramento constrinxerant cum essent in Maspha interfici eos qui defuissent. 6 Ductique paenitentia filii Israhel super fratre suo Beniamin coeperunt dicere, "Ablata est una tribus de Israhel. 7 Unde uxores accipient? Omnes enim in commune iuravimus non daturos nos his filias nostras." 8 Idcirco dixerunt, "Quis est de universis tribubus Israhel qui non ascendit ad Dominum in Maspha?" Et ecce: inventi sunt habitatores Iabis Galaad in illo exercitu non fuisse. 9 (Eo quoque tempore cum essent in Silo nullus ex eis ibi reppertus est). 10 Miserunt itaque decem milia vi-

Chapter 21

The tribe of Benjamin is saved from being utterly extinct by
providing wives for the six hundred that remained.

Now the children of Israel had also sworn in Mizpah, *say-ing*, "None of us shall give of his daughters to the children of
Benjamin to wife." 2 And they all came to the house of God
in Shiloh and abiding before him till the evening lifted up
their voices and *began to lament and weep*, saying, 3 "O Lord
God of Israel, why is *so great an* evil come to pass in thy people that this day one tribe should be taken away from among
us?" 4 And rising early the next day, they built an altar and
offered there holocausts and victims of peace, and they said,
5 "Who *is there* among all the tribes of Israel *that* came not
up with the army of the Lord?" For they had bound themselves with a great oath when they were in Mizpah that *whosoever* were wanting should be slain. 6 And the children of
Israel being moved with repentance for their brother Benjamin began to say, "One tribe is taken away from Israel.
7 Whence shall they take wives? For we have all in general
sworn not to give our daughters to them." 8 Therefore they
said, "Who is there of all the tribes of Israel that came not
up to the Lord to Mizpah?" And behold: the inhabitants of
Jabesh Gilead were found not to have been in that army.
9 (At that time also when they were in Shiloh no one of them
was found there). 10 So they sent ten thousand of the most

ros robustissimos et praeceperunt eis, "Ite, et percutite habitatores Iabis Galaad in ore gladii tam uxores quam parvulos eorum. 11 Et hoc erit quod observare debebitis: omne generis masculini et mulieres quae cognoverunt viros interficite, virgines autem reservate." 12 Inventaeque sunt de Iabis Galaad quadringentae virgines quae nescierunt viri torum, et adduxerunt eas ad castra in Silo, in terram Chanaan. 13 Miseruntque nuntios ad filios Beniamin qui erant in petra Remmon et praeceperunt eis ut eos in pace susciperent. 14 Veneruntque filii Beniamin in illo tempore, et datae sunt eis uxores de filiabus Iabis Galaad, alias autem non reppererunt quas simili modo traderent. 15 Universusque Israhel valde doluit et egit paenitudinem super interfectione unius tribus ex Israhel.

16 Dixeruntque maiores natu, "Quid faciemus reliquis qui non acceperunt uxores, omnes enim in Beniamin feminae conciderunt? 17 Et magna nobis cura ingentique studio providendum est ne una tribus deleatur ex Israhel, 18 filias enim nostras eis dare non possumus, constricti iuramento et maledictione qua diximus, 'Maledictus qui dederit de filiabus suis uxorem Beniamin.'" 19 Ceperuntque consilium atque dixerunt, "Ecce: sollemnitas Domini est in Silo anniversaria," quae sita est ad septentrionem urbis Bethel et ad orientalem plagam viae quae de Bethel tendit ad Sycimam et ad meridiem oppidi Lebona. 20 Praeceperuntque filiis Beniamin atque dixerunt, "Ite, et latete in vineis, 21 cumque videritis filias Silo ad ducendos choros, ex more, procedere, exite repente de vineis, et rapite ex eis singuli uxores singulas, et

valiant men and commanded them, *saying,* "Go, and *put* the inhabitants of Jabesh Gilead *to the sword with* their wives *and* their children. 11 And this is what you shall observe: every male and all women that have known men you shall kill, but the virgins you shall save." 12 And there were found of Jabesh Gilead four hundred virgins that had not known the bed of a man, and they brought them to the camp in Shiloh, into the land of Canaan. 13 And they sent messengers to the children of Benjamin that were in the rock Rimmon and commanded them to receive them in peace. 14 And the children of Benjamin came at that time, and wives were given them of the daughters of Jabesh Gilead, but they found no others whom they might give in like manner. 15 And all Israel was very sorry and repented for the destroying of one tribe out of Israel.

16 And the ancients said, "What shall we do with the rest that have not received wives, for all the women in Benjamin are dead? 17 And we must *use all care and* provide with great diligence that one tribe be not destroyed out of Israel, 18 for *as to* our own daughters, we cannot give *them,* being bound with an oath and a curse whereby we said, 'Cursed be he that shall give Benjamin any of his daughters to wife.'" 19 So they took counsel and said, "Behold: there is a yearly solemnity of the Lord in Shiloh," which is situate on the north of the city of Bethel and on the east side of the way that goeth from Bethel to Shechem and on the south of the town of Lebonah. 20 And they commanded the children of Benjamin and said, "Go, and lie hid in the vineyards, 21 and when you shall see the daughters of Shiloh come out, as the custom is, to dance, come ye on a sudden out of the vineyards, and catch you every man his wife among them, and go into the

pergite in terram Beniamin. 22 Cumque venerint patres earum ac fratres et adversum vos queri coeperint atque iurgari, dicemus eis, 'Miseremini eorum, non enim rapuerunt eas iure bellantium atque victorum, sed rogantibus ut acciperent non dedistis, et a vestra parte peccatum est.'" 23 Feceruntque filii Beniamin ut sibi fuerat imperatum, et iuxta numerum suum rapuerunt sibi de his quae ducebant choros uxores singulas, abieruntque in possessionem suam aedificantes urbes et habitantes in eis. 24 Filii quoque Israhel reversi sunt per tribus et familias in tabernacula sua.

In diebus illis non erat rex in Israhel, sed unusquisque quod sibi rectum videbatur hoc faciebat.

land of Benjamin. 22 And when their fathers and their brethren shall come and shall begin to complain against you and to chide, we will say to them, 'Have pity on them, for they took them not away as by the right of *war or conquest,* but when they asked to have them, you gave them not, and the fault was committed on your part.'" 23 And the children of Benjamin did as they had been commanded, and according to their number they carried off for themselves every man his wife of them that were dancing, and they went into their possession and built up their cities and dwelt in them. 24 The children of Israel also returned by their tribes and families to their dwellings.

In those days there was no king in Israel, but every one did that which seemed right to himself.

RUTH

Caput 1

In diebus unius iudicis, quando iudices praeerant, facta est fames in terra, abiitque homo de Bethleem Iuda ut peregrinaretur in regione Moabitide cum uxore sua ac duobus liberis. 2 Ipse vocabatur Helimelech, et uxor eius, Noemi, et duo filii, alter Maalon et alter Chellion, Ephrathei de Bethleem Iuda. Ingressique regionem Moabitidem, morabantur ibi. 3 Et mortuus est Helimelech, maritus Noemi, remansitque ipsa cum filiis. 4 Qui acceperunt uxores Moabitidas, quarum una vocabatur Orpha, altera vero Ruth. Manseruntque ibi decem annis. 5 Et ambo mortui sunt, Maalon, videlicet, et Chellion, remansitque mulier, orbata duobus liberis ac marito. 6 Et surrexit ut in patriam pergeret cum utraque nuru sua de regione Moabitide, audierat enim quod respexisset Dominus populum suum et dedisset eis escas. 7 Egressa est itaque de loco peregrinationis suae cum utraque nuru, et

Chapter 1

Elimelech of Bethlehem, going with his wife Naomi and
two sons into the land of Moab, dieth there. His sons marry
wives of that country and die without issue. Naomi returneth home with her daughter-in-law Ruth, who refuseth to
part with her.

I n the days of one *of the judges,* when the judges ruled, there
came a famine in the land, and a *certain* man of Bethlehem
Judah went to sojourn in the land of Moab with his wife
and his two sons. 2 He was named Elimelech, and his wife,
Naomi, and his two sons, the one Mahlon and the other
Chilion, Ephrathites of Bethlehem Judah. And entering into
the country of Moab, they abode there. 3 And Elimelech,
the husband of Naomi, died, and she remained with her
sons. 4 And they took wives of the women of Moab, of which
one was called Orpah and the other Ruth. And they dwelt
there ten years. 5 And they both died, to wit, Mahlon and
Chilion, and the woman *was left alone,* having lost both her
sons and her husband. 6 And she arose to go from the land of
Moab to her own country with both her daughters-in-law,
for she had heard that the Lord had looked upon his people
and had given them food. 7 Wherefore she went forth out of
the place of her sojournment with both her daughters-in-

iam in via posita revertendi in terram Iuda, 8 dixit ad eas, "Ite in domum matris vestrae; faciat Dominus vobiscum misericordiam, sicut fecistis cum mortuis et mecum. 9 Det vobis invenire requiem in domibus virorum quos sortiturae estis." Et osculata est eas.

Quae elevata voce flere coeperunt 10 et dicere, "Tecum pergemus ad populum tuum."

11 Quibus illa respondit, "Revertimini, filiae mi. Cur venitis mecum? Num ultra habeo filios in utero meo, ut viros ex me sperare possitis? 12 Revertimini filiae mi, et abite, iam enim senectute confecta sum nec apta vinculo coniugali. Etiam si possem hac nocte concipere et parere filios, 13 si eos expectare velitis donec crescant et annos impleant pubertatis, ante eritis vetulae quam nubatis. Nolite, quaeso, filiae mi, quia vestra angustia me magis premit et egressa est manus Domini contra me."

14 Elevata igitur voce rursum flere coeperunt. Orpha osculata socrum est ac reversa; Ruth adhesit socrui suae. 15 Cui dixit Noemi, "En: reversa est cognata tua ad populum suum et ad deos suos; vade cum ea."

16 Quae respondit, "Ne adverseris mihi ut relinquam te et abeam, quocumque enim perrexeris, pergam, et ubi morata fueris, et ego pariter morabor. Populus tuus populus meus, et Deus tuus Deus meus. 17 Quae te morientem terra susceperit, in ea moriar, ibique locum accipiam sepulturae. Haec mihi faciat Deus et haec addat, si non sola mors me et te separaverit."

18 Videns ergo Noemi quod obstinato Ruth animo decrevisset secum pergere, adversari noluit nec ultra ad suos redi-

law, and being now in the way to return into the land of Judah, 8 she said to them, "Go ye *home to your mothers;* the Lord deal mercifully with you, as you have dealt with the dead and with me. 9 May he grant you to find rest in the houses of the husbands which you shall take." And she kissed them.

And they lifted up their voice and began to weep 10 and to say, "We will go on with thee to thy people."

11 But she answered them, "Return, my daughters. Why come ye with me? Have I any more sons in my womb, that you may hope for husbands of me? 12 Return *again,* my daughters, and go your ways, for I am now spent with age and not fit for wedlock. Although I might conceive this night and bear children, 13 if you would wait till they were grown up and *come to man's estate,* you would be old women before you marry. Do not so, my daughters, I beseech you, for I am grieved the more for your distress and the hand of the Lord is gone out against me."

14 And they lifted up their voice and began to weep again. Orpah kissed her mother-in-law and returned; Ruth stuck close to her mother-in-law. 15 And Naomi said to her, "Behold: thy kinswoman is returned to her people and to her gods; go thou with her."

16 She answered, "Be not against me *to desire* that I should leave thee and depart, for whithersoever thou shalt go, I will go, and where thou shalt dwell, I also will dwell. Thy people shall be my people, and thy God, my God. 17 The land that shall receive thee dying, in the same will I die, and there *will I be buried.* The Lord do so and so to me and add more also, if *aught but death* part me and thee."

18 Then Naomi, seeing that Ruth was *steadfastly* determined to go with her, would not be against it nor per-

tum persuadere, [19] profectaeque sunt simul et venerunt in Bethleem. Quibus urbem ingressis, velox apud cunctos fama percrebuit, dicebantque mulieres, "Haec est illa Noemi."

[20] Quibus ait, "Ne vocetis me Noemi,"—id est, pulchram —"sed vocate me Mara,"—hoc est, amaram—"quia valde me amaritudine replevit Omnipotens. [21] Egressa sum plena, et vacuam reduxit me Dominus. Cur igitur vocatis me Noemi, quam humiliavit Dominus et adflixit Omnipotens?"

[22] Venit ergo Noemi cum Ruth, Moabitide, nuru sua, de terra peregrinationis suae ac reversa est in Bethleem quando primum hordea metebantur.

Caput 2

Erat autem viro, Helimelech, consanguineus, homo potens et magnarum opum, nomine Booz. [2] Dixitque Ruth, Moabitis, ad socrum suam, "Si iubes, vadam in agrum et colligam spicas quae metentium fugerint manus ubicumque clementis in me patris familias repperero gratiam."

Cui illa respondit, "Vade, filia mi."

[3] Abiit itaque et colligebat spicas post terga metentium.

suade her any more to return to her friends, 19 *so* they went together and came to Bethlehem. And when they were come into the city, the report was quickly spread among all, and the women said, "This is that Naomi."

20 But she said to them, "Call me not Naomi,"—that is, beautiful—"but call me Mara,"—that is, bitter—"for the Almighty hath quite filled me with bitterness. 21 I went out full, and the Lord hath brought me back empty. Why then do you call me Naomi, whom the Lord hath humbled and the Almighty hath afflicted?"

22 So Naomi came with Ruth, the Moabitess, her daughter-in-law, from the land of her sojournment and returned into Bethlehem *in the beginning of the barley harvest.*

Chapter 2

Ruth gleaneth in the field of Boaz, who showeth her favour.

Now her husband, Elimelech, had a kinsman, a powerful man and very rich, whose name was Boaz. 2 And Ruth, the Moabitess, said to her mother-in-law, "If thou *wilt,* I will go into the field and glean the ears of corn that escape the hands of the reapers wheresoever I shall find grace with a householder that will be favourable to me."

And she answered her, "Go, my daughter."

3 She went therefore and gleaned the ears of corn *after*

Accidit autem ut ager ille haberet dominum Booz, qui erat de cognatione Helimelech. 4 Et ecce: ipse veniebat de Bethleem dixitque messoribus, "Dominus vobiscum."

Qui responderunt ei, "Benedicat tibi Dominus."

5 Dixitque Booz iuveni qui messoribus praeerat, "Cuius est haec puella?"

6 Cui respondit, "Haec est Moabitis quae venit cum Noemi, de regione Moabitide, 7 et rogavit ut spicas colligeret remanentes, sequens messorum vestigia, et de mane usque nunc stat in agro et ne ad momentum quidem domum reversa est."

8 Et ait Booz ad Ruth, "Audi, filia; ne vadas ad colligendum in alterum agrum, nec recedas ab hoc loco, sed iungere puellis meis, 9 et ubi messuerint sequere, mandavi enim pueris meis ut nemo tibi molestus sit, sed etiam si sitieris, vade ad sarcinulas, et bibe aquas de quibus et pueri bibunt."

10 Quae cadens in faciem suam et adorans super terram dixit ad eum, "Unde mihi hoc, ut invenirem gratiam ante oculos tuos et nosse me dignareris peregrinam mulierem?"

11 Cui ille respondit, "Nuntiata sunt mihi omnia quae feceris socrui tuae post mortem viri tui et quod dereliqueris parentes tuos et terram in qua nata es et veneris ad populum quem ante nesciebas. 12 Reddat tibi Dominus pro opere tuo, et plenam mercedem recipias a Domino, Deo Israhel, ad quem venisti et sub cuius confugisti alas."

13 Quae ait, "Inveni gratiam apud oculos tuos, domine mi,

the reapers. And it happened that the owner of that field was Boaz, who was of the kindred of Elimelech. 4 And behold: he came out of Bethlehem and said to the reapers, "The Lord be with you."

And they answered him, "The Lord bless thee."

5 And Boaz said to the young man that was set over the reapers, "Whose maid is this?"

6 And he answered him, "This is the Moabitess who came with Naomi, from the land of Moab, 7 and she desired leave to glean the ears of corn that remain, following the steps of the reapers, and she *hath been* in the field from morning till now and hath not gone home for one moment."

8 And Boaz said to Ruth, "Hear *me,* daughter; do not go to glean in *any* other field, and do not depart from this place, but keep with my maids, 9 and follow where they reap, for I have charged my young men *not to* molest thee, *and* if thou art thirsty, go to the vessels, and drink of the waters whereof the servants *drink."*

10 She fell on her face and worshipping upon the ground said to him, "Whence cometh this to me, that I should find grace before thy eyes and that thou shouldst vouchsafe to take notice of me a woman of another country?"

11 And he answered her, "All hath been told me that thou hast done to thy mother-in-law after the death of thy husband and *how* thou hast left thy parents and the land wherein thou wast born and art come to a people which thou knewest not heretofore. 12 The Lord render unto thee for thy work, and mayest thou receive a full reward of the Lord, the God of Israel, to whom thou art come and under whose wings thou art fled."

13 And she said, "I have found grace in thy eyes, my lord,

qui consolatus es me et locutus es ad cor ancillae tuae, quae non sum similis unius puellarum tuarum."

14 Dixitque ad eam Booz, "Quando hora vescendi fuerit, veni huc, et comede panem, et intingue buccellam tuam in aceto." Sedit itaque ad messorum latus, et congessit pulentam sibi comeditque et saturata est et tulit reliquias. 15 Atque inde surrexit ut spicas ex more colligeret. Praecepit autem Booz pueris suis, dicens, "Etiam si vobiscum metere voluerit, ne prohibeatis eam, 16 et de vestris quoque manipulis proicite de industria, et remanere permittite ut absque rubore colligat, et colligentem nemo corripiat." 17 Collegit ergo in agro usque ad vesperam, et quae collegerat virga caedens et excutiens, invenit hordei quasi oephi mensuram, id est, tres modios, 18 quos portans reversa est in civitatem et ostendit socrui suae. Insuper, protulit et dedit ei de reliquiis cibi sui quo saturata fuerat.

19 Dixitque ei socrus, "Ubi hodie collegisti, et ubi fecisti opus? Sit benedictus qui misertus est tui." Indicavitque ei apud quem esset operata, et nomen dixit viri, quod Booz vocaretur. 20 Cui respondit Noemi, "Benedictus sit a Domino quoniam eandem gratiam quam praebuerat vivis, servavit et mortuis." Rursumque, "Propinquus," ait, "noster est homo."

21 Et Ruth, "Hoc quoque," inquit, "praecepit mihi ut tamdiu messoribus eius iungerer donec omnes segetes meterentur."

22 Cui dixit socrus, "Melius est, filia mi, ut cum puellis eius exeas ad metendum, ne in alieno agro quispiam resis-

who hast comforted me and hast spoken to the heart of thy handmaid, who am not like to one of thy maids."

14 And Boaz said to her, *"At mealtime,* come thou hither, and eat of the bread, and dip thy morsel in the vinegar." So she sat at the side of the reapers, and she heaped to herself frumenty and ate and was filled and took the leavings. 15 And she arose from thence to glean the ears of corn as before. And Boaz commanded his servants, saying, "If she would even reap with you, hinder her not, 16 and *let fall some of your handfuls* of purpose, and *leave them* that she may gather them without shame, and let no man rebuke her when she gathereth them." 17 She gleaned therefore in the field till evening, and beating out with a rod and threshing what she had gleaned, she found about the measure of an ephi of barley, that is, three bushels, 18 which she took up and returned into the city and showed it to her mother-in-law. Moreover, she brought out and gave her of the remains of her meat wherewith she had been filled.

19 And her mother-in-law said to her, "Where hast thou gleaned today, and where hast thou wrought? Blessed be he that hath had pity on thee." And she told her with whom she had wrought, and she told the man's name, that he was called Boaz. 20 And Naomi answered her, "Blessed be he of the Lord because the same kindness which he showed to the living, he hath kept also to the dead." And again she said, "The man is our kinsman."

21 And Ruth said, *"He* also charged me that I should keep close to his reapers till all the corn should be reaped."

22 And her mother-in-law said to her, "It is better *for thee,* my daughter, *to go* out to reap with his maids, lest in another

tat tibi." 23 Iuncta est itaque puellis Booz et tamdiu cum eis messuit donec hordea et triticum in horreis conderentur.

Caput 3

Postquam autem reversa est ad socrum suam, audivit ab ea, "Filia mi, quaeram tibi requiem et providebo ut bene sit tibi. 2 Booz iste, cuius puellis in agro iuncta es, propinquus est noster, et hac nocte aream hordei ventilat. 3 Lava igitur, et unguere, et induere cultioribus vestimentis, ac descende in aream, non te videat homo donec esum potumque finierit. 4 Quando autem ierit ad dormiendum, nota locum in quo dormiat, veniesque et discoperies pallium quo operitur a parte pedum et proicies te et ibi iacebis, ipse autem dicet tibi quid agere debeas."

5 Quae respondit, "Quicquid praeceperis, faciam."

6 Descenditque in aream et fecit omnia quae sibi imperaverat socrus. 7 Cumque comedisset Booz et bibisset et fac-

man's field some one may resist thee." 23 So she kept close to the maids of Boaz and *continued to glean* with them till all the barley and the wheat were laid up in the barns.

Chapter 3

Ruth, instructed by her mother-in-law, lieth at Boaz's feet, claiming him for her husband by the law of affinity. She receiveth a good answer and six measures of barley.

After she was returned to her mother-in-law, *Naomi said to her,* "My daughter, I will seek rest for thee and will provide that it may be well with thee. 2 This Boaz, with whose maids thou wast joined in the field, is our near kinsman, and *behold:* this night he winnoweth *barley in the threshingfloor.* 3 Wash thyself therefore, and anoint thee, and put on thy best garments, and go down to the barnfloor, but let not the man see thee till he shall have done eating and drinking. 4 And when he shall go to sleep, mark the place wherein he sleepeth, and thou shalt go in and lift up the *clothes* wherewith he is covered towards his feet and shalt *lay thyself down* there, and he will tell thee what thou must do."

5 She answered, "Whatsoever thou shalt command, I will do."

6 And she went down to the barnfloor and did all that her mother-in-law had bid her. 7 And when Boaz had eaten and

tus esset hilarior issetque ad dormiendum iuxta acervum manipulorum, venit abscondite et, discoperto a pedibus eius pallio, se proiecit. 8 Et ecce: nocte iam media, expavit homo et conturbatus est, viditque mulierem iacentem ad pedes suos, 9 et ait illi, "Quae es?"

Illaque respondit, "Ego sum Ruth, ancilla tua. Expande pallium tuum super famulam tuam, quia propinquus es."

10 Et ille, "Benedicta," inquit, "es a Domino, filia mi, et priorem misericordiam posteriore superasti, quia non es secuta iuvenes pauperes sive divites. 11 Noli, ergo, metuere, sed quicquid dixeris mihi faciam tibi, scit enim omnis populus qui habitat intra portas urbis meae mulierem te esse virtutis. 12 Nec abnuo me propinquum, sed est alius me propinquior. 13 Quiesce hac nocte, et facto mane, si te voluerit propinquitatis iure retinere, bene res acta est, sin autem ille noluerit, ego te absque ulla dubitatione suscipiam. Vivit Dominus. Dormi usque mane."

14 Dormivit itaque ad pedes eius usque ad noctis abscessum, surrexit itaque antequam homines se cognoscerent mutuo, et dixit Booz, "Cave ne quis noverit quod huc veneris." 15 Et rursum, "Expande," inquit, "palliolum tuum quo operiris, et tene utraque manu." Qua extendente et tenente, mensus est sex modios hordei et posuit super eam.

Quae portans ingressa est civitatem 16 et venit ad socrum suam, quae dixit ei, "Quid egisti, filia?"

drunk and *was merry, he* went to sleep by the heap of sheaves, *and* she came softly and, *uncovering his feet,* laid herself down. 8 And behold: when it was now midnight, the man was afraid and troubled, and he saw a woman lying at his feet, 9 and he said to her, "Who art thou?"

And she answered, "I am Ruth, thy handmaid. Spread thy coverlet over thy servant, for thou art a near kinsman."

10 And he said, "Blessed art thou of the Lord, my daughter, and *thy latter kindness has surpassed the former,* because thou hast not followed young men either poor or rich. 11 Fear not, therefore, but whatsoever thou shalt say to me I will do to thee, for all the people that dwell within the gates of my city know that thou art a virtuous woman. 12 Neither do I deny myself to be near of kin, but there is another nearer than I. 13 Rest thou this night, and when morning is come, if he will take thee by the right of kindred, *all is well,* but if he will not, I will undoubtedly take thee *as* the Lord liveth. Sleep till the morning."

14 So she slept at his feet till the night was going off, and she arose before men could know one another, and Boaz said, "Beware lest any man know that thou camest hither." 15 And again he said, "Spread thy mantle wherewith thou art covered, and hold it with both hands." And when she spread it and held it, he measured six measures of barley and laid it upon her.

And she carried it and went into the city 16 and came to her mother-in-law, who said to her, "What hast thou done, daughter?"

Narravitque ei omnia quae sibi fecisset homo, 17 et ait, "Ecce! Sex modios hordei dedit mihi, et ait, 'Nolo vacuam te reverti ad socrum tuam.'"

18 Dixitque Noemi, "Expecta, filia, donec videamus quem res exitum habeat, neque enim cessabit homo nisi conpleverit quod locutus est."

Caput 4

Ascendit ergo Booz ad portam et sedit ibi. Cumque vidisset propinquum praeterire de quo prius sermo habitus est, dixit ad eum, "Declina paulisper, et sede hic," vocans eum nomine suo. Qui devertit et sedit. 2 Tollens autem Booz decem viros de senioribus civitatis, dixit ad eos, "Sedete hic." 3 Quibus residentibus, locutus est ad propinquum, "Partem agri fratris nostri Helimelech vendet Noemi, quae reversa est de regione Moabitide. 4 Quod audire te volui et tibi dicere coram cunctis sedentibus et maioribus natu de populo meo: si vis possidere iure propinquitatis, eme, et posside, sin autem tibi displicet, hoc ipsum indica mihi, ut

And she told her all that the man had done to her, 17 and she said, "Behold! He hath given me six measures of barley, *for* he said, 'I will not have thee return empty to thy mother-in-law.'"

18 And Naomi said, "Wait, *my* daughter, till we see what end the thing will have, for the man will not rest until he have accomplished what he hath said."

Chapter 4

Upon the refusal of the nearer kinsman, Boaz marrieth
Ruth, who bringeth forth Obed, the grandfather of David.

Then Boaz went up to the gate and sat there. And when he had seen the kinsman going by of whom *he had spoken* before, he said to him, calling him by his name, "Turn aside for a little while, and sit down here." He turned aside and sat down. 2 And Boaz, taking ten men of the ancients of the city, said to them, "Sit ye down here." 3 They sat down, and he spoke to the kinsman, "Naomi, who is returned from the country of Moab, will sell a parcel of land that belonged to our brother Elimelech. 4 I would have thee to understand this and would tell thee before all that sit *here* and before the ancients of my people: if thou wilt take possession of it by the right of kindred, buy it, and possess it, but if it please thee not, tell me *so,* that I may know what I have to

sciam quid facere debeam. Nullus est enim propinquus excepto te, qui prior es, et me, qui secundus sum."

At ille respondit, "Ego agrum emam."

5 Cui dixit Booz, "Quando emeris agrum de manu mulieris, Ruth quoque, Moabitidem, quae uxor defuncti fuit, debes accipere ut suscites nomen propinqui tui in hereditate sua."

6 Qui respondit, "Cedo iure propinquitatis, neque enim posteritatem familiae meae delere debeo. Tu meo utere privilegio, quo me libenter carere profiteor."

7 Hic autem erat mos antiquitus in Israhel inter propinquos, ut si quando alter alteri suo iure cedebat, ut esset firma concessio, solvebat homo calciamentum suum et dabat proximo suo. Hoc erat testimonium cessionis in Israhel. 8 Dixit ergo propinquo suo Booz, "Tolle calciamentum." Quod statim solvit de pede suo. 9 At ille maioribus natu et universo populo, "Testes," inquit, "vos estis hodie quod possederim omnia quae fuerunt Helimelech et Chellion et Maalon tradente Noemi 10 et Ruth, Moabitidem, uxorem Maalon, in coniugium sumpserim ut suscitem nomen defuncti in hereditate sua ne vocabulum eius de familia sua ac fratribus et populo deleatur. Vos, inquam, huius rei testes estis."

11 Respondit omnis populus qui erat in porta et maiores natu, "Nos testes sumus. Faciat Dominus hanc mulierem quae ingreditur domum tuam sicut Rachel et Liam, quae aedificaverunt domum Israhel, ut sit exemplum virtutis in Ephrata et habeat celebre nomen in Bethleem 12 fiatque do-

do. For there is no near kinsman besides thee, who art first, and me, who am second."

But he answered, "I will buy the field."

5 And Boaz said to him, "When thou shalt buy the field at the woman's hand, thou must take also Ruth, the Moabitess, who was the wife of the deceased, to raise up the name of thy kinsman in his inheritance."

6 He answered, "I yield up my right of next akin, for I must not cut off the posterity of my own family. Do thou make use of my privilege, which I profess I do willingly forego."

7 Now this in former times was the manner in Israel between kinsmen, that if at any time one yielded his right to another, that the grant might be sure, the man put off his shoe and gave it to his neighhour. This was a testimony of cession *of right* in Israel. 8 So Boaz said to his kinsman, "Put off thy shoe." And immediately he took it off from his foot. 9 *And* he said to the ancients and to all the people, "You are witnesses this day that I have bought all that was Elimelech's and Chilion's and Mahlon's *of the hand of Naomi* 10 and have taken to wife Ruth, the Moabitess, the wife of Mahlon, to raise up the name of the deceased in his inheritance lest his name be *cut off* from among his family and his brethren and his people. You, I say, are witnesses of this thing."

11 Then all the people that were in the gate and the ancients answered, "We are witnesses. The Lord make this woman who cometh into thy house like Rachel and Leah, who built up the house of Israel, that she may be an example of virtue in Ephrathah and may have a famous name in Bethlehem 12 and that thy house may be as the house of

mus tua sicut domus Phares quem Thamar peperit Iudae de semine quod dederit Dominus tibi ex hac puella."

13 Tulit itaque Booz Ruth et accepit uxorem ingressusque est ad eam, et dedit illi Dominus ut conciperet et pareret filium. 14 Dixeruntque mulieres ad Noemi, "Benedictus Dominus, qui non est passus ut deficeret successor familiae tuae, ut vocaretur nomen eius in Israhel. 15 Et habeas qui consoletur animam tuam et enutriat senectutem, de nuru enim tua natus est quae te diligit et multo tibi est melior quam si septem haberes filios."

16 Susceptumque Noemi puerum posuit in sinu suo, et nutricis ac gerulae officio fungebatur. 17 Vicinae autem mulieres, congratulantes ei et dicentes, "Natus est filius Noemi," vocaverunt nomen eius Obed; hic est pater Isai, patris David.

18 Hae sunt generationes Phares: Phares genuit Esrom; 19 Esrom genuit Aram; Aram genuit Aminadab; 20 Aminadab genuit Naasson; Naasson genuit Salma; 21 Salma genuit Booz; Booz genuit Obed; 22 Obed genuit Isai; Isai genuit David.

Perez whom Tamar bore unto Judah of the seed which the Lord shall give thee of this young woman."

13 Boaz therefore took Ruth and married her and went in unto her, and the Lord gave her to conceive and to bear a son. 14 And the women said to Naomi, "Blessed be the Lord, who hath not suffered thy family to want a successor, that his name should be preserved in Israel. 15 And thou shouldst have one to comfort thy soul and cherish thy old age, for he is born of thy daughter-in-law who loveth thee and is much better to thee than if thou hadst seven sons."

16 And Naomi taking the child laid it in her bosom, and *she carried it and was a nurse unto it.* 17 And the women, her neighbours, congratulating with her and saying, "There is a son born to Naomi," called his name Obed; he is the father of Jesse, the father of David.

18 These are the generations of Perez: Perez begot Hezron; 19 Hezron begot Ram; Ram begot Amminadab; 20 Amminadab begot Nahshon; Nahshon begot Salmon; 21 Salmon begot Boaz; Boaz begot Obed; 22 Obed begot Jesse; Jesse begot David.

1 KINGS

Caput 1

Fuit vir unus de Ramathaimsophim de Monte Ephraim, et nomen eius Helcana, filius Hieroam, filii Heliu, filii Thau, filii Suph, Ephratheus, 2 et habuit duas uxores: nomen uni Anna, et nomen secundae Fenenna. Fueruntque Fenennae filii, Annae autem non erant liberi. 3 Et ascendebat vir ille de civitate sua statutis diebus ut adoraret et sacrificaret Domino exercituum in Silo. Erant autem ibi duo filii Heli, Ofni et Finees, sacerdotes Domini.

4 Venit ergo dies, et immolavit Helcana deditque Fenennae, uxori suae, et cunctis filiis eius et filiabus partes, 5 Annae autem dedit partem unam tristis, quia Annam diligebat Dominus autem concluserat vulvam eius. 6 Adfligebat quoque eam aemula eius et vehementer angebat, in tantum ut exprobraret quod conclusisset Dominus vulvam eius. 7 Sicque faciebat per singulos annos cum redeunte tempore ascenderent templum Domini, et sic provocabat eam. Porro

Chapter 1

Hannah, the wife of Elkanah, being barren, by vow and prayer obtaineth a son whom she calleth Samuel and presenteth him to the service of God in Shiloh according to her vow.

There was a man of Ramathaim-zophim of Mount Ephraim, and his name was Elkanah, the son of Jeroham, the son of Elihu, the son of Tohu, the son of Zuph, an Ephraimite, 2 and he had two wives: the name of one was Hannah, and the name of the other Peninnah. Peninnah had children, but Hannah had no children. 3 And this man went up out of his city upon the appointed days to adore and to offer sacrifice to the Lord of hosts in Shiloh. And the two sons of Eli, Hophni and Phinehas, were there priests of the Lord.

4 Now the day came, and Elkanah offered sacrifice and gave to Peninnah, his wife, and to all her sons and daughters portions, 5 but to Hannah he gave one portion with sorrow, because he loved Hannah and the Lord had shut up her womb. 6 Her rival also afflicted her and troubled her exceedingly, insomuch that she upbraided her that the Lord had shut up her womb. 7 And thus she did every year when the time returned that they went up to the temple of the Lord,

illa flebat et non capiebat cibum. 8 Dixit ergo ei Helcana, vir suus, "Anna, cur fles? Et quare non comedis? Et quam ob rem adfligitur cor tuum? Numquid non ego melior sum tibi quam decem filii?"

9 Surrexit autem Anna postquam comederat in Silo et biberat, et Heli, sacerdote, sedente super sellam ante postes templi Domini 10 cum esset Anna amaro animo, oravit ad Dominum, flens largiter, 11 et votum vovit, dicens, "Domine exercituum, si respiciens videris adflictionem famulae tuae et recordatus mei fueris nec oblitus ancillae tuae dederisque servae tuae sexum virilem, dabo eum Domino omnes dies vitae eius, et novacula non ascendet super caput eius."

12 Factum est autem cum illa multiplicaret preces coram Domino ut Heli observaret os eius. 13 Porro Anna loquebatur in corde suo, tantumque labia illius movebantur, et vox penitus non audiebatur. Aestimavit igitur eam Heli temulentam 14 dixitque ei, "Usquequo ebria eris? Digere paulisper vinum quo mades."

15 Respondens Anna, "Nequaquam," inquit, "domine mi: nam mulier infelix nimis ego sum vinumque et omne quod inebriare potest non bibi, sed effudi animam meam in conspectu Domini. 16 Ne reputes ancillam tuam quasi unam de filiabus Belial, quia ex multitudine doloris et maeroris mei locuta sum usque in praesens."

17 Tunc Heli ait ei, "Vade in pace, et Deus Israhel det tibi petitionem tuam quam rogasti eum."

18 Et illa dixit, "Utinam inveniat ancilla tua gratiam in oculis tuis." Et abiit mulier in viam suam et comedit, vultusque eius non sunt amplius in diversa mutati. 19 Et surrexe-

and thus she provoked her. But Hannah wept and *did not eat.* 8 Then Elkanah, her husband, said to her, "Hannah, why weepest thou? And why dost thou not eat? And why dost thou afflict thy heart? Am not I better to thee than ten children?"

9 So Hannah arose after she had eaten and drunk in Shiloh, and Eli, the priest, sitting upon a stool before the door of the temple of the Lord 10 as Hannah had her heart full of grief, she prayed to the Lord, *shedding many tears,* 11 and she made a vow, saying, "O Lord of hosts, if thou wilt *look down on* the affliction of thy servant and wilt be mindful of me and not forget thy handmaid and wilt give to thy servant a man-child, I will give him to the Lord all the days of his life, and no razor shall come upon his head."

12 And it came to pass as she multiplied prayers before the Lord that Eli observed her mouth. 13 Now Hannah spoke in her heart, and only her lips moved, *but* her voice was not heard at all. Eli therefore thought her to be drunk 14 and said to her, "How long wilt thou be drunk? Digest a little the wine *of which thou hast taken too much."*

15 Hannah answering, said, "Not so, my lord: for I am an exceeding unhappy woman and have drunk neither wine *nor any strong drink,* but I have poured out my soul before the Lord. 16 Count not thy handmaid for one of the daughters of Belial, for out of the abundance of my sorrow and grief have I spoken till now."

17 Then Eli said to her, "Go in peace, and the God of Israel grant thee thy petition which thou hast asked of him."

18 And she said, "Would to God thy handmaid may find grace in thy eyes." *So* the woman went on her way and ate, and her countenance was no more *changed.* 19 And they rose

runt mane et adoraverunt coram Domino, reversique sunt et venerunt in domum suam Ramatha. Cognovit autem Helcana Annam, uxorem suam, et recordatus est eius Dominus. 20 Et factum est post circulum dierum, concepit Anna et peperit filium vocavitque nomen eius Samuhel, eo quod a Domino postulasset eum. 21 Ascendit autem vir eius, Helcana, et omnis domus eius ut immolaret Domino hostiam sollemnem et votum suum, 22 et Anna non ascendit, dixit enim viro suo, "Non vadam donec ablactetur infans et ducam eum, ut appareat ante conspectum Domini et maneat ibi iugiter."

23 Et ait ei Helcana, vir suus, "Fac quod bonum tibi videtur, et mane donec ablactes eum, precorque ut impleat Dominus verbum suum." Mansit ergo mulier et lactavit filium suum donec amoveret eum a lacte. 24 Et adduxit eum secum postquam ablactaverat in vitulis tribus et tribus modiis farinae et amphora vini, et adduxit eum ad domum Domini in Silo.

Puer autem erat adhuc infantulus, 25 et immolaverunt vitulum, et obtulerunt puerum Heli, 26 et ait Anna, "Obsecro, mi domine, vivit anima tua, domine; ego sum illa mulier quae steti coram te hic orans Dominum. 27 Pro puero isto oravi, et dedit Dominus mihi petitionem meam quam postulavi eum. 28 Idcirco et ego commodavi eum Domino cunctis diebus quibus fuerit accommodatus Domino." Et adoraverunt ibi Dominum.

Et oravit Anna et ait:

in the morning and worshipped before the Lord, and they returned and came into their house at Ramah. And Elkanah knew Hannah, his wife, and the Lord remembered her. 20 And it came to pass *when the time was come about,* Hannah conceived and bore a son and called his name Samuel, because she had asked him of the Lord. 21 And Elkanah, her husband, went up and all his house to offer to the Lord the solemn sacrifice and his vow, 22 *but* Hannah went not up, for she said to her husband, "I will not go till the child be weaned and till I may carry him, that he may appear before the Lord and may abide always there."

23 And Elkanah, her husband, said to her, "Do what seemeth good to thee, and stay till thou wean him, and I pray that the Lord may fulfill his word." So the woman stayed at home and gave her son suck till she weaned him. 24 And after she had weaned him, she carried him with her with three calves and three bushels of flour and a bottle of wine, and she brought him to the house of the Lord in Shiloh.

Now the child was as yet very young, 25 and they immolated a calf, and offered the child to Eli, 26 and Hannah said, "I beseech thee, my lord, as thy soul liveth, my lord, I am that woman who stood before thee here praying to the Lord. 27 For this child did I pray, and the Lord hath granted me my petition which I asked of him. 28 Therefore I also have lent him to the Lord; all the days *of his life he shall be lent* to the Lord." And they adored the Lord there.

And Hannah prayed and said:

Caput 2

"Exultavit cor meum in Domino; et exaltatum est cornu meum in Deo meo. Dilatatum est os meum super inimicos meos, quia laetata sum in salutari tuo.

2 "Non est sanctus ut est Dominus, neque enim est alius extra te, et non est fortis sicut Deus noster.

3 "Nolite multiplicare loqui sublimia, gloriantes. Recedant vetera de ore vestro, quoniam Deus scientiarum Dominus est et ipsi praeparantur cogitationes.

4 "Arcus fortium superatus est, et infirmi accincti sunt robore. 5 Saturati prius pro pane se locaverunt, et famelici saturati sunt donec sterilis peperit plurimos et quae multos habebat filios infirmata est.

6 "Dominus mortificat et vivificat; deducit ad infernum et reducit. 7 "Dominus pauperem facit et ditat; humiliat et sublevat. 8 Suscitat de pulvere egenum et de stercore elevat pauperem ut sedeat cum principibus et solium gloriae teneat, Domini enim sunt cardines terrae et posuit super eos orbem. 9 Pedes sanctorum suorum servabit, et impii in tenebris conticescent, quia non in fortitudine sua roborabitur vir.

Chapter 2

The canticle of Hannah. The wickedness of the sons of Eli for which they are not duly corrected by their father. A prophecy against the house of Eli.

"My heart hath rejoiced in the Lord, and my horn is exalted in my God. My mouth is enlarged over my enemies, because I have joyed in thy salvation.

2 "There is none holy as the Lord is, for there is no other beside thee, and there is none strong like our God.

3 "Do not multiply to speak lofty things, boasting. Let old matters depart from your mouth, for the Lord is a God of all knowledge and to him are thoughts prepared.

4 "The bow of the mighty is overcome, and the weak are girt with strength. 5 They that were full before have hired out themselves for bread, and the hungry are filled *so that* the barren hath borne many and she that had many children is weakened.

6 "The Lord killeth and maketh alive; he bringeth down to hell and bringeth back again. 7 The Lord maketh poor and maketh rich; he humbleth and he exalteth. 8 He raiseth up the needy from the dust and lifteth up the poor from the dunghill that he may sit with princes and hold the throne of glory, for the poles of the earth are the Lord's and upon them he hath set the world. 9 He will keep the feet of his saints, and the wicked shall be silent in darkness, because no man shall prevail by his own strength.

10 "Dominum formidabunt adversarii eius, et super ipsos in caelis tonabit. Dominus iudicabit fines terrae, et dabit imperium regi suo et sublimabit cornu Christi sui."

11 Et abiit Helcana Ramatha, in domum suam, puer autem erat minister in conspectu Domini ante faciem Heli, sacerdotis. 12 Porro filii Heli filii Belial, nescientes Dominum 13 neque officium sacerdotum ad populum, sed quicumque immolasset victimam, veniebat puer sacerdotis dum coquerentur carnes et habebat fuscinulam tridentem in manu sua 14 et mittebat eam in lebetem vel in caldariam aut in ollam sive in caccabum, et omne quod levabat fuscinula, tollebat sacerdos sibi. Sic faciebant universo Israheli venientium in Silo. 15 Etiam antequam adolerent adipem, veniebat puer sacerdotis et dicebat immolanti, "Da mihi carnem ut coquam sacerdoti, non enim accipiam a te carnem coctam, sed crudam."

16 Dicebatque illi immolans, "Incendatur primum iuxta morem hodie adeps, et tolle tibi quantumcumque desiderat anima tua."

Qui respondens aiebat ei, "Nequaquam, nunc enim dabis, alioquin tollam vi." 17 Erat ergo peccatum puerorum grande nimis coram Domino quia detrahebant homines sacrificio Domini.

18 Samuhel autem ministrabat ante faciem Domini, puer accinctus ephod lineo. 19 Et tunicam parvam faciebat ei mater sua, quam adferebat statutis diebus, ascendens cum viro suo ut immolaret hostiam sollemnem. 20 Et benedixit Heli Helcanae et uxori eius, dixitque ei, "Reddat Dominus tibi

10 "The adversaries of the Lord shall fear him, and upon them shall he thunder in the heavens. The Lord shall judge the ends of the earth, and he shall give empire to his king and shall exalt the horn of his Christ."

11 And Elkanah went to Ramah, to his house, but the child ministered in the sight of the Lord before the face of Eli, the priest. 12 Now the sons of Eli were children of Belial, not knowing the Lord 13 nor the office of the priests to the people, but whosoever had offered a sacrifice, the servant of the priest came while the flesh was in boiling *with* a flesh-hook of three teeth in his hand 14 and thrust it into the kettle or into the caldron or into the pot or into the pan, and all that the fleshhook brought up, the priest took to himself. Thus did they to all Israel that came to Shiloh. 15 Also before they burnt the fat, the servant of the priest came and said to the man that sacrificed, "Give me flesh to boil for the priest, for I will not take of thee sodden flesh, but raw."

16 And he that sacrificed said to him, "Let the fat first be burnt today according to the custom, and *then* take as much as thy soul desireth."

But he answered and said to him, "Not so, *but* thou shalt give it me now, or else I will take it by force." 17 Wherefore the sin of the young men was exceeding great before the Lord because they withdrew men from the sacrifice of the Lord.

18 But Samuel ministered before the face of the Lord, being a child girded with a linen ephod. 19 And his mother made him a little coat, which she brought to him on the appointed days, when she went up with her husband to offer the solemn sacrifice. 20 And Eli blessed Elkanah and his wife, and he said to him, "The Lord give thee seed of this woman

semen de muliere hac pro fenore quod commodasti Domino." Et abierunt in locum suum. 21 Visitavit ergo Dominus Annam, et concepit et peperit tres filios et duas filias, et magnificatus est puer Samuhel apud Dominum.

22 Heli autem erat senex valde, et audivit omnia quae faciebant filii sui universo Israheli et quomodo dormiebant cum mulieribus quae observabant ad ostium tabernaculi, 23 et dixit eis, "Quare facitis res huiuscemodi quas ego audio, res pessimas, ab omni populo? 24 Nolite, filii mi, non enim est bona fama quam ego audio, ut transgredi faciatis populum Domini. 25 Si peccaverit vir in virum, placari ei potest Deus, si autem in Domino peccaverit vir, quis orabit pro eo?" Et non audierunt vocem patris sui, quia voluit Dominus occidere eos. 26 Puer autem Samuhel proficiebat atque crescebat et placebat tam Domino quam hominibus.

27 Venit autem vir Dei ad Heli et ait ad eum, "Haec dicit Dominus, 'Numquid non aperte revelatus sum domui patris tui cum essent in Aegypto in domo Pharaonis? 28 Et elegi eum ex omnibus tribubus Israhel mihi in sacerdotem, ut ascenderet altare meum et adoleret mihi incensum et portaret ephod coram me, et dedi domui patris tui omnia de sacrificiis filiorum Israhel. 29 Quare calce abiecistis victimam meam et munera mea quae praecepi ut offerrentur in templo, et magis honorasti filios tuos quam me, ut comederetis primitias omnis sacrificii Israhel, populi mei?' 30 Propterea ait Dominus, Deus Israhel, 'Loquens locutus sum ut domus tua et domus patris tui ministraret in conspectu meo usque in sempiternum. Nunc autem dicit Dominus, "Absit hoc a me, sed quicumque glorificaverit me, glorificabo eum, qui autem contemnunt me erunt ignobiles. 31 Ecce! Dies ve-

for the loan thou hast lent to the Lord." And they went to their own home. 21 And the Lord visited Hannah, and she conceived and bore three sons and two daughters, and the child Samuel became great before the Lord.

22 Now Eli was very old, and he heard all that his sons did to all Israel and how they lay with the women that waited at the door of the tabernacle, 23 and he said to them, "Why do ye these kinds of things which I hear, very wicked things, from all the people? 24 Do not so, my sons, for it is no good report that I hear, that you make the people of the Lord to transgress. 25 If *one* man shall sin against *another,* God may be appeased in his behalf, but if a man shall sin against the Lord, who shall pray for him?" And they hearkened not to the voice of their father, because the Lord would slay them. 26 But the child Samuel advanced and grew on and pleased both the Lord and men.

27 And there came a man of God to Eli and said to him, "Thus saith the Lord, 'Did I not plainly appear to thy father's house when they were in Egypt in the house of Pharaoh? 28 And I chose him out of all the tribes of Israel to be my priest, to go up to my altar and burn incense to me and to wear the ephod before me, and I gave to thy father's house *of all* the sacrifices of the children of Israel. 29 Why have you *kicked away my victims* and my gifts which I commanded to be offered in the temple, and thou hast rather honoured thy sons than me, to eat the firstfruits of every sacrifice of my people, Israel?' 30 Wherefore *thus* saith the Lord, the God of Israel, '*I said indeed* that thy house and the house of thy father should minister in my sight for ever. But now saith the Lord, "Far be this from me, but whosoever shall glorify me, him will I glorify, but they that despise me shall be *despised.* 31 Behold! The days come, and I will cut off

niunt, et praecidam brachium tuum et brachium domus patris tui ut non sit senex in domo tua. 32 Et videbis aemulum tuum in templo in universis prosperis Israhel, et non erit senex in domo tua omnibus diebus. 33 Verumtamen, non auferam penitus virum ex te ab altari meo sed ut deficiant oculi tui et tabescat anima tua, et pars magna domus tuae morietur cum ad virilem aetatem venerit. 34 Hoc autem erit tibi signum quod venturum est duobus filiis tuis, Ofni et Finees: in die uno morientur ambo. 35 Et suscitabo mihi sacerdotem fidelem qui iuxta cor meum et animam meam faciet, et aedificabo ei domum fidelem, et ambulabit coram christo meo cunctis diebus. 36 Futurum est autem ut quicumque remanserit in domo tua veniet ut oretur pro eo et offerat nummum argenteum et tortam panis dicatque, 'Dimitte me, obsecro, ad unam partem sacerdotalem, ut comedam buccellam panis.'""

Caput 3

Puer autem Samuhel ministrabat Domino coram Heli. Et sermo Domini erat pretiosus in diebus illis: non erat visio manifesta. 2 Factum est ergo in die quadam Heli iacebat in

thy arm and the arm of thy father's house that there shall not be an old man in thy house. 32 And thou shalt see thy rival in the temple in all the prosperity of Israel, and there shall not be an old man in thy house for ever. 33 However, I will not altogether take away a man of thee from my altar but that thy eyes may faint and thy soul be spent, and a great part of thy house shall die when they come to man's estate. 34 And this shall be a sign to thee that shall come upon thy two sons, Hophni and Phinehas: in one day they shall both of them die. 35 And I will raise me up a faithful priest who shall do according to my heart and my soul, and I will build him a faithful house, and he shall walk all days before my anointed. 36 And it shall come to pass that whosoever shall remain in thy house shall come that he may be prayed for and shall offer a piece of silver and a roll of bread and shall say, 'Put me, I beseech thee, to *somewhat of the priestly office,* that I may eat a morsel of bread.'"'"

Chapter 3

Samuel is four times called by the Lord, who revealeth to him the evil that shall fall on Eli and his house.

Now the child Samuel ministered to the Lord before Eli. And the word of the Lord was precious in those days: there was no manifest vision. 2 And it came to pass one day *when*

loco suo et oculi eius caligaverant nec poterat videre. 3 Lucerna Dei antequam extingueretur, Samuhel dormiebat in templo Domini ubi erat arca Dei, 4 et vocavit Dominus Samuhel. Qui respondens ait, "Ecce ego," 5 et cucurrit ad Heli et dixit, "Ecce ego, vocasti enim me."

Qui dixit, "Non vocavi; revertere, et dormi." Et abiit et dormivit.

6 Et adiecit Dominus vocare rursum Samuhel, consurgensque Samuhel abiit ad Heli et dixit, "Ecce ego, quia vocasti me."

Qui respondit, "Non vocavi te, fili mi; revertere, et dormi."

7 Porro Samuhel necdum sciebat Dominum, neque revelatus fuerat ei sermo Domini. 8 Et adiecit Dominus et vocavit adhuc Samuhel tertio, qui consurgens abiit ad Heli 9 et ait, "Ecce ego, quia vocasti me."

Intellexit igitur Heli quia Dominus vocaret puerum, et ait ad Samuhel, "Vade, et dormi, et si deinceps vocaverit te, dices, 'Loquere, Domine, quia audit servus tuus.'" Abiit ergo Samuhel et dormivit in loco suo.

10 Et venit Dominus et stetit, et vocavit sicut vocaverat secundo, "Samuhel, Samuhel."

Et ait Samuhel, "Loquere, Domine, quia audit servus tuus."

11 Et dixit Dominus ad Samuhel, "Ecce: ego facio verbum in Israhel, quod quicumque audierit, tinnient ambae aures eius. 12 In die illo suscitabo adversum Heli omnia quae locutus sum super domum eius. Incipiam, et conplebo. 13 Praedixi enim ei quod iudicaturus essem domum eius in aeter-

Eli lay in his place and his eyes were grown dim that he could not see. 3 Before the lamp of God went out, Samuel slept in the temple of the Lord where the ark of God was, 4 and the Lord called Samuel. And he *answered,* "Here am I," 5 and he ran to Eli and said, "Here am I, for thou didst call me."

He said, "I did not call; go back, and sleep." And he went and slept.

6 And the Lord called Samuel again, and Samuel arose and went to Eli and said, "Here am I, for thou calledst me."

He answered, "I did not call thee, my son; return, and sleep."

7 Now Samuel did not yet know the Lord, neither had the word of the Lord been revealed to him. 8 And the Lord called Samuel again the third time, and he arose up and went to Eli 9 and said, "Here am I, for thou didst call me."

Then Eli understood that the Lord called the child, and he said to Samuel, "Go, and sleep, and if he shall call thee any more, thou shalt say, 'Speak, Lord, for thy servant heareth.'" So Samuel went and slept in his place.

10 And the Lord came and stood, and he called as he had called *the other times,* "Samuel, Samuel."

And Samuel said, "Speak, Lord, for thy servant heareth."

11 And the Lord said to Samuel, "Behold: I do a thing in Israel, and whosoever shall hear it, both his ears shall tingle. 12 In that day I will raise up against Eli all the things I have spoken concerning his house. I will begin, and I will make an end. 13 For I have foretold unto him that I will judge his

num propter iniquitatem, eo quod noverat indigne agere filios suos et non corripuit eos. 14 Idcirco iuravi domui Heli quod non expietur iniquitas domus eius victimis et muneribus usque in aeternum."

15 Dormivit autem Samuhel usque mane aperuitque ostia domus Domini, et Samuhel timebat indicare visionem Heli. 16 Vocavit ergo Heli Samuhelem et dixit, "Samuhel, fili mi."

Qui respondens ait, "Praesto sum."

17 Et interrogavit eum, "Quis est sermo quem locutus est Dominus ad te? Oro te ne celaveris me. Haec faciat tibi Deus et haec addat, si absconderis a me sermonem ex omnibus verbis quae dicta sunt tibi."

18 Indicavit itaque ei Samuhel universos sermones et non abscondit ab eo. Et ille respondit, "Dominus est. Quod bonum est in oculis suis faciat."

19 Crevit autem Samuhel, et Dominus erat cum eo, et non cecidit ex omnibus verbis eius in terram. 20 Et cognovit universus Israhel a Dan usque Bersabee quod fidelis Samuhel propheta esset Domini. 21 Et addidit Dominus ut appareret in Silo, quoniam revelatus fuerat Dominus Samuheli in Silo iuxta verbum Domini. Et evenit sermo Samuhelis universo Israheli.

house for ever for iniquity because he knew that his sons did wickedly and did not chastise them. 14 Therefore have I sworn to the house of Eli that the iniquity of his house shall not be expiated with victims nor offerings for ever."

15 And Samuel slept till morning and opened the doors of the house of the Lord, and Samuel feared to tell the vision to Eli. 16 Then Eli called Samuel and said, "Samuel, my son."

And he *answered,* "Here am I."

17 And he asked him, "What is the word that the Lord hath spoken to thee? I beseech thee hide it not from me. May God do so and so to thee and add so and so, if thou hide from me one word of all that were said to thee."

18 So Samuel told him all the words and did not hide them from him. And he answered, "It is the Lord. Let him do what is good in his sight."

19 And Samuel grew, and the Lord was with him, and *not one* of his words fell to the ground. 20 And all Israel from Dan to Beer-sheba knew that Samuel was a faithful prophet of the Lord. 21 And the Lord again appeared in Shiloh, for the Lord *revealed himself* to Samuel in Shiloh according to the word of the Lord. And the word of Samuel came to pass to all Israel.

Caput 4

Et factum est in diebus illis convenerunt Philisthim in pugnam, et egressus est Israhel obviam Philisthim in proelium et castrametatus est iuxta Lapidem Adiutorii. Porro Philisthim venerunt in Afec 2 et instruxerunt aciem contra Israhel. Inito autem certamine, terga vertit Israhel Philistheis, et caesa sunt in illo certamine passim per agros quasi quattuor milia virorum.

3 Et reversus est populus ad castra, dixeruntque maiores natu de Israhel, "Quare percussit nos Dominus hodie coram Philisthim? Adferamus ad nos de Silo Arcam Foederis Domini, et veniat in medium nostri ut salvet nos de manu inimicorum nostrorum." 4 Misit ergo populus in Silo, et tulerunt inde Arcam Foederis Domini exercituum sedentis super cherubin, erantque duo filii Heli cum Arca Foederis Dei, Ofni et Finees.

5 Cumque venisset Arca Foederis Domini in castra, vociferatus est omnis Israhel clamore grandi, et personuit terra. 6 Et audierunt Philisthim vocem clamoris, dixeruntque, "Quaenam haec est vox clamoris magni in castris Hebraeo-

Chapter 4

The Israelites being overcome by the Philistines send for
the ark of God, but they are beaten again; the sons of Eli are
killed, and the ark taken. Upon the hearing of the news, Eli
falleth backward and dieth.

And it came to pass in those days that the Philistines
gathered themselves together to fight, and Israel went out
to war against the Philistines and camped by the Stone of
Help. And the Philistines came to Aphek 2 and put their
army in array against Israel. And when they had joined battle, Israel turned their backs to the Philistines, and there
was slain in that fight here and there in the fields about four
thousand men.

3 And the people returned to the camp, and the ancients
of Israel said, "Why hath the Lord defeated us today before
the Philistines? Let us fetch unto us the Ark of the Covenant of the Lord from Shiloh, and let it come in the midst of
us that it may save us from the hand of our enemies." 4 So
the people sent to Shiloh, and they brought from thence the
Ark of the Covenant of the Lord of hosts sitting upon the
cherubims, and the two sons of Eli, Hophni and Phinehas,
were with the Ark of the Covenant of God.

5 And when the Ark of the Covenant of the Lord was
come into the camp, all Israel shouted with a great shout,
and the earth rang *again*. 6 And the Philistines heard the
noise of the shout, and they said, "What is this noise of a

rum?" Et cognoverunt quod arca Domini venisset in castra.
7 Timueruntque Philisthim, dicentes, "Venit Deus in castra." Et ingemuerunt, dicentes, 8 "Vae nobis, non enim fuit
tanta exultatio heri et nudius tertius. Vae nobis! Quis nos
servabit de manu deorum sublimium istorum? Hii sunt dii
qui percusserunt Aegyptum omni plaga in deserto. 9 Confortamini, et estote viri, Philisthim, ne serviatis Hebraeis sicut
et illi servierunt vobis. Confortamini, et bellate." 10 Pugnaverunt ergo Philisthim, et caesus est Israhel, et fugit unusquisque in tabernaculum suum, et facta est plaga magna nimis, et ceciderunt de Israhel triginta milia peditum. 11 Et
arca Dei capta est, duo quoque filii Heli mortui sunt, Ofni
et Finees.

12 Currens autem vir de Beniamin ex acie venit in Silo in
die illo scissa veste et conspersus pulvere caput. 13 Cumque
ille venisset, Heli sedebat super sellam contra viam, aspectans, erat enim cor eius pavens pro arca Dei. Vir autem ille
postquam ingressus est, nuntiavit urbi, et ululavit omnis civitas. 14 Et audivit Heli sonitum clamoris, dixitque, "Quis
est hic sonitus tumultus huius?" At ille festinavit et venit et
adnuntiavit Heli.

15 Heli autem erat nonaginta et octo annorum, et oculi
eius caligaverant, et videre non poterat. 16 Et dixit ad Heli,
"Ego sum qui veni de proelio et ego qui de acie fugi hodie."

Cui ille ait, "Quid actum est, fili mi."

17 Respondens autem qui nuntiabat, "Fugit," inquit, "Israhel coram Philisthim, et ruina magna facta est in populo.

great shout in the camp of the Hebrews?" And they understood that the ark of the Lord was come into the camp. 7 And the Philistines were afraid, saying, "God is come into the camp." And sighing, they said, 8 "Woe to us, for there was no such great joy yesterday and the day before. Woe to us! Who shall deliver us from the hand of these high gods? These are the gods that struck Egypt with *all the plagues* in the desert. 9 Take courage, and *behave like* men, ye Philistines, lest you come to be servants to the Hebrews as they have served you. Take courage, and fight." 10 So the Philistines fought, and Israel was overthrown, and every man fled to his own dwelling, and there was an exceeding great slaughter, *for* there fell of Israel thirty thousand footmen. 11 And the ark of God was taken, and the two sons of Eli, Hophni and Phinehas, were slain.

12 And there ran a man of Benjamin out of the army and came to Shiloh the same day with his clothes rent and his head strewed with dust. 13 And when he was come, Eli sat upon a stool over against the way, watching, for his heart was fearful for the ark of God. And when *the man was come into the city, he told it,* and all the city cried out. 14 And Eli heard the noise of the cry, and he said, "What *meaneth the noise* of this uproar?" But he made haste and came and told Eli.

15 Now Eli was ninety and eight years old, and his eyes were dim, and he could not see. 16 And he said to Eli, "I am he that came from the battle and *have fled* out of the field this day."

And he said to him, "What is there done, my son?"

17 And he *that* brought the news answered and said, "Israel has fled before the Philistines, and there has been a great slaughter *of* the people. Moreover thy two sons,

Insuper et duo filii tui mortui sunt, Ofni et Finees, et arca Dei capta est." 18 Cumque ille nominasset arcam Dei, cecidit de sella retrorsum iuxta ostium et fractis cervicibus mortuus est, senex enim erat vir et grandevus, et ipse iudicavit Israhel quadraginta annis. 19 Nurus autem eius, uxor Finees, praegnans erat vicinaque partui, et audito nuntio quod capta esset arca Dei et mortuus socer suus et vir suus, incurvavit se et peperit, inruerant enim in eam dolores subiti.

20 In ipso autem momento mortis eius, dixerunt ei quae stabant circa eam, "Ne timeas, quia filium peperisti."

Quae non respondit eis neque animadvertit, 21 et vocavit puerum Hicabod, dicens, "Translata est gloria de Israhel quia capta est arca Dei," et pro socero suo et pro viro suo, 22 et ait, "Translata est gloria ab Israhel eo quod capta esset arca Dei."

Caput 5

Philisthim autem tulerunt arcam Dei et asportaverunt eam a Lapide Adiutorii in Azotum. 2 Tuleruntque Philisthim arcam Dei et intulerunt eam in templum Dagon et statue-

Hophni and Phinehas, are dead, and the ark of God is taken." 18 And when he had named the ark of God, he fell from his stool backwards by the door and broke his neck and died, for he was an old man and far advanced in years, and he judged Israel forty years. 19 And his daughter-in-law, the wife of Phinehas, was big with child and near her time, and hearing the news that the ark of God was taken and her father-in-law and her husband were dead, she bowed herself and *fell in labour*, for her pains came upon her on a sudden.

20 And when she was upon the point of *death*, they that stood about her said to her, "Fear not, for thou hast borne a son."

She answered them not nor gave heed to them, 21 and she called the child Ichabod, saying, "The glory is gone from Israel because the ark of God was taken," and for her father-in-law and her husband, 22 and she said, "The glory is departed from Israel because the ark of God was taken."

Chapter 5

Dagon twice falleth down before the ark. The Philistines
are grievously afflicted wherever the ark cometh.

And the Philistines took the ark of God and carried it from the Stone of Help into Ashdod. 2 And the Philistines took the ark of God and brought it into the temple of Da-

runt eam iuxta Dagon. 3 Cumque surrexissent diluculo Azotii altera die, ecce: Dagon iacebat pronus in terram ante arcam Domini, et tulerunt Dagon et restituerunt eum in
locum suum. 4 Rursumque mane die altera consurgentes invenerunt Dagon iacentem super faciem suam in terram coram arca Domini, caput autem Dagon et duae palmae manuum eius abscisae erant super limen, 5 porro Dagon truncus
solus remanserat in loco suo. Propter hanc causam non cal-
cant sacerdotes Dagon et omnes qui ingrediuntur templum
eius super limen Dagon in Azoto usque in hodiernum diem.

6 Adgravata autem est manus Domini super Azotios, et
demolitus est eos et percussit in secretiori parte natium
Azotum et fines eius. Et ebullierunt villae et agri in medio
regionis illius, et nati sunt mures, et facta est confusio mortis magnae in civitate. 7 Videntes autem viri Azotii huiuscemodi plagam dixerunt, "Non maneat arca Dei Israhel apud
nos, quoniam dura est manus eius super nos et super Dagon,
deum nostrum. 8 Et mittentes, congregaverunt omnes satrapas Philisthinorum ad se et dixerunt, "Quid faciemus de
arca Dei Israhel?"

Responderuntque Getthei, "Circumducatur arca Dei Israhel." Et circumduxerunt arcam Dei Israhel. 9 Illis autem
circumducentibus eam, fiebat manus Domini per singulas
civitates interfectionis magnae nimis, et percutiebat viros
uniuscuiusque urbis, a parvo usque ad maiorem, et conpu-
trescebant prominentes extales eorum. Inieruntque Gethaei
consilium et fecerunt sibi sedes pelliceas.

gon and set it by Dagon. 3 And when the Ashdodians arose early the next day, behold: Dagon lay *upon his face* on the ground before the ark of the Lord, and they took Dagon and set him again in his place. 4 And the next day again, when they rose in the morning they found Dagon lying upon his face on the earth before the ark of the Lord, and the head of Dagon and both the palms of his hands were cut off upon the threshold, 5 and only the stump of Dagon remained in its place. For this cause *neither* the priests of Dagon *nor any* that go into *the* temple tread on the threshold of Dagon in Ashdod unto this day.

6 And the hand of the Lord was heavy upon the Ashdodians, and he destroyed them and afflicted Ashdod and the coasts thereof *with emerods.* And *in the villages and fields* in the midst of that country *there came forth a multitude of mice,* and there was the confusion of a great mortality in the city. 7 And the men of Ashdod seeing this kind of plague said, "The ark of the God of Israel *shall* not stay with us, for his hand is heavy upon us and upon Dagon, our god." 8 And sending, they gathered together all the lords of the Philistines to them and said, "What shall we do with the ark of the God of Israel?"

And the Gathites answered, "Let the ark of the God of Israel be carried about." And they carried the ark of the God of Israel about. 9 And while they were carrying it about, the hand of the Lord came upon every city with an exceeding great slaughter, and he smote the men of every city, *both* small *and* great, and *they had emerods in their secret parts.* And the Gathites consulted together and made themselves seats of skins.

10 Miserunt ergo arcam Dei in Accaron, cumque venisset arca Dei in Accaron, exclamaverunt Accaronitae, dicentes, "Adduxerunt ad nos arcam Dei Israhel ut interficiat nos et populum nostrum." 11 Miserunt, itaque, et congregaverunt omnes satrapas Philisthinorum, qui dixerunt, "Dimittite arcam Dei Israhel, et revertatur in locum suum et non interficiat nos cum populo nostro," 12 fiebat enim pavor mortis in singulis urbibus, et gravissima valde manus Dei. Viri quoque qui mortui non fuerant percutiebantur in secretiori parte natium, et ascendebat ululatus uniuscuiusque civitatis in caelum.

Caput 6

Fuit ergo arca Domini in regione Philisthinorum septem mensibus. 2 Et vocaverunt Philisthim sacerdotes et divinos, dicentes, "Quid faciemus de arca Domini? Indicate nobis quomodo remittamus eam in locum suum."

Qui dixerunt, 3 "Si remittitis arcam Dei Israhel, nolite dimittere eam vacuam, sed quod debetis reddite ei pro peccato, et tunc curabimini, et scietis quare non recedat manus eius a vobis."

10 Therefore they sent the ark of God into Ekron, and when the ark of God was come into Ekron, the Ekronites cried out, saying, "They have brought the ark of the God of Israel to us to kill us and our people." 11 They sent, therefore, and gathered together all the lords of the Philistines, and they said, "Send away the ark of the God of Israel, and let it return into its own place and not kill us *and* our people," 12 for there was the fear of death in every city, and the hand of God was exceeding heavy. The men also that did not die were afflicted *with the emerods,* and the cry of every city went up to heaven.

Chapter 6

The ark is sent back to Beth-shemesh, where many are slain for looking through curiosity into it.

Now the ark of God was in the land of the Philistines seven months. 2 And the Philistines called for the priests and the diviners, saying, "What shall we do with the ark of the Lord? Tell us how we are to send it back to its place."

And they said, 3 "If you send back the ark of the God of Israel, send it not away empty, but render unto him what you owe for sin, and then you shall be healed, and you shall know why his hand departeth not from you."

4 Qui dixerunt, "Quid est quod pro delicto reddere debeamus ei?"

Responderuntque illi, 5 "Iuxta numerum provinciarum Philisthim, quinque anos aureos facietis et quinque mures aureos, quia plaga una fuit omnibus vobis et satrapis vestris. Facietisque similitudines anorum vestrorum et similitudines murium qui demoliti sunt terram, et dabitis Deo Israhel gloriam si forte relevet manum suam a vobis et a diis vestris et a terra vestra. 6 Quare gravatis corda vestra, sicut adgravavit Aegyptus et Pharao cor suum? Nonne postquam percussus est tunc dimisit eos, et abierunt? 7 Nunc, ergo, arripite, et facite plaustrum novum unum, et duas vaccas fetas quibus non est inpositum iugum iungite in plaustro, et recludite vitulos earum domi. 8 Tolletisque arcam Domini et ponetis in plaustro, et vasa aurea quae exsolvistis ei pro delicto ponetis in capsellam ad latus eius, et dimittite eam ut vadat. 9 Et aspicietis, et si quidem per viam finium suorum ascenderit contra Bethsames, ipse fecit nobis malum hoc grande, sin autem minime, sciemus quia nequaquam manus eius tetigit nos, sed casu accidit."

10 Fecerunt ergo illi hoc modo, et tollentes duas vaccas quae lactabant vitulos, iunxerunt ad plaustrum vitulosque earum concluserunt domi. 11 Et posuerunt arcam Dei super plaustrum et capsellam quae habebat mures aureos et similitudines anorum. 12 Ibant autem in directum vaccae per viam quae ducit Bethsames, et itinere uno gradiebantur, pergentes et mugientes, et non declinabant, neque ad dextram ne-

4 They answered, "What is it we ought to render unto him for sin?"

And they answered, 5 "According to the number of the provinces of the Philistines, you shall make five golden emerods and five golden mice, for the same plague hath been upon you all and upon your lords. And you shall make the likeness of your emerods and the likeness of the mice that have destroyed the land, and you shall give glory to the God of Israel *to see if* he will take off his hand from you and from your gods and from your land. 6 Why do you harden your hearts, as Egypt and Pharaoh hardened their hearts? Did not he after he was struck then let them go, and they departed? 7 Now, therefore, take, and make a new cart, and two kine that have calved on which there hath come no yoke tie to the cart, and shut up their calves at home. 8 And you shall take the ark of the Lord and lay it on the cart, and the vessels of gold which you have paid him for sin you shall put into a little box at the side thereof, and send it away that it may go. 9 And you shall look, and *if* it go up by the way of his own coasts towards Beth-shemesh, then he hath done us this great evil, but if not, we shall know that it is not his hand hath touched us, but it hath happened by chance."

10 They did therefore in this manner, and taking two kine that had suckling calves, they yoked them to the cart and shut up their calves at home. 11 And they laid the ark of God upon the cart and the little box that had in it the golden mice and the likeness of the emerods. 12 And the kine took the straight way that leadeth to Beth-shemesh, and they went *along the* way, lowing as they went, and turned not aside, neither to the right hand nor to the left, *and* the lords

que ad sinistram, sed et satrapae Philisthinorum sequebantur usque ad terminos Bethsames.

13 Porro Bethsamitae metebant triticum in valle, et ele-
vantes oculos viderunt arcam et gavisi sunt cum vidissent.
14 Et plaustrum venit in agrum Iosue, Bethsamitae, et stetit
ibi. Erat autem ibi lapis magnus, et conciderunt ligna plaus-
tri vaccasque inposuerunt super ea, holocaustum Domino.
15 Levitae autem deposuerunt arcam Dei et capsellam quae
erat iuxta eam in qua erant vasa aurea, et posuerunt super
lapidem grandem. Viri autem Bethsamitae obtulerunt holocausta et immolaverunt victimas in die illa Domino. 16 Et
quinque satrapae Philisthinorum viderunt, et reversi sunt in
Accaron in die illa.

17 Hii sunt autem ani aurei quos reddiderunt Philisthim
pro delicto Domino—Azotus unum, Gaza unum, Ascalon
unum, Geth unum, Accaron unum—18 et mures aureos secundum numerum urbium Philisthim quinque provinciarum ab urbe murata usque ad villam quae erat absque muro
et usque ad Abel magnum super quem posuerunt arcam Domini, quae erat usque in illa die in agro Iosue, Bethsamitis.

19 Percussit autem de viris bethsamitibus eo quod vidissent arcam Domini, et percussit de populo septuaginta viros et quinquaginta milia plebis. Luxitque populus quod
percussisset Dominus plebem plaga magna. 20 Et dixerunt
viri Bethsamitae, "Quis poterit stare in conspectu Domini,
Dei sancti huius? Et ad quem ascendet a nobis?" 21 Miserunt-

of the Philistines followed them as far as the borders of Beth-shemesh.

13 Now the Beth-shemites were reaping wheat in the valley, and lifting up their eyes they saw the ark and rejoiced *to see* it. 14 And the cart came into the field of Joshua, a Beth-shemite, and stood there. And there was a great stone, and they cut in pieces the wood of the cart and laid the kine upon it a holocaust to the Lord. 15 And the Levites took down the ark of God and the little box that was at the side of it wherein were the vessels of gold, and they put them upon the great stone. The men also of Beth-shemesh offered holocausts and sacrificed victims that day to the Lord. 16 And the five princes of the Philistines saw, and they returned to Ekron *the same* day.

17 And these are the golden emerods which the Philistines returned for sin to the Lord—for Ashdod one, for Gaza one, for Ashkelon one, for Gath one, for Ekron one— 18 and the golden mice according to the number of the cities of the Philistines of the five provinces from the fenced city to the village that was without wall and to the great Abel *(the stone)* whereon they set down the ark of the Lord, which was till that day in the field of Joshua, the Beth-shemite.

19 But he slew of the men of Beth-shemesh because they had seen the ark of the Lord, and he slew of the people seventy men and fifty thousand of the common people. And the people lamented because the Lord had smitten the *people* with a great slaughter. 20 And the men of Beth-shemesh said, "Who shall be able to stand before the Lord, this holy God? And to whom shall he go up from us?" 21 And they sent

que nuntios ad habitatores Cariathiarim, dicentes, "Reduxerunt Philisthim arcam Domini; descendite, et reducite eam ad vos."

Caput 7

Venerunt ergo viri Cariathiarim et reduxerunt arcam Domini et intulerunt eam in domum Abinadab in Gabaa, Eleazarum autem, filium eius, sanctificaverunt ut custodiret arcam Domini. 2 Et factum est ex qua die mansit arca Domini in Cariathiarim, multiplicati sunt dies (erat quippe iam annus vicesimus), et requievit omnis domus Israhel post Dominum. 3 Ait autem Samuhel ad universam domum Israhel, dicens, "Si in toto corde vestro revertimini ad Dominum, auferte deos alienos de medio vestri, Baalim et Astharoth, et praeparate corda vestra Domino, et servite ei soli, et eruet vos de manu Philisthim." 4 abstulerunt ergo filii Israhel Baalim et Astharoth et servierunt Domino soli.

5 Dixit autem Samuhel, "Congregate universum Israhel in Masphat ut orem pro vobis Dominum." 6 Et convenerunt in

messengers to the inhabitants of Kiriath-jearim, saying, "The Philistines have brought back the ark of the Lord; come ye down, and fetch it *up* to you."

Chapter 7

The ark is brought to Kiriath-jearim. By Samuel's exhortation the people cast away their idols and serve God alone. The Lord defeateth the Philistines while Samuel offereth sacrifice.

And then men of Kiriath-jearim came and fetched *up* the ark of the Lord and carried it into the house of Abinadab in Gibeah, and they sanctified Eleazar, his son, to keep the ark of the Lord. 2 And it came to pass that from the day the ark of the Lord abode in Kiriath-jearim, days were multiplied (for it was now the twentieth year), and all the house of Israel rested, following the Lord. 3 And Samuel spoke to all the house of Israel, saying, "If you turn to the Lord *with* all your heart, put away the strange gods *from among* you, Baalim and Astarte, and prepare your hearts unto the Lord, and serve him only, and he will deliver you out of the hand of the Philistines." 4 Then the children of Israel put away Baalim and Astarte and served the Lord only.

5 And Samuel said, "Gather all Israel to Mizpah that I may pray to the Lord for you." 6 And they gathered together

Masphat, hauseruntque aquam et effuderunt in conspectu Domini, et ieiunaverunt in die illa, et dixerunt ibi, "Peccavimus Domino." Iudicavitque Samuhel filios Israhel in Masphat.

7 Et audierunt Philisthim quod congregati essent filii Israhel in Masphat, et ascenderunt satrapae Philisthinorum ad Israhel. Quod cum audissent filii Israhel, timuerunt a facie Philisthinorum, 8 dixeruntque ad Samuhel, "Ne cesses pro nobis clamare ad Dominum, Deum nostrum, ut salvet nos de manu Philisthinorum." 9 Tulit autem Samuhel agnum lactentem unum et obtulit illum holocaustum integrum Domino, et clamavit Samuhel ad Dominum pro Israhel, et exaudivit eum Dominus. 10 Factum est autem cum Samuhel offerret holocaustum Philistheos inire proelium contra Israhel, intonuit autem Dominus fragore magno in die illa super Philisthim et exterruit eos, et caesi sunt a facie Israhel. 11 Egressique viri Israhel de Masphat persecuti sunt Philistheos et percusserunt eos usque ad locum qui erat subter Bethchar. 12 Tulit autem Samuhel lapidem unum et posuit eum inter Masphat et inter Sen, et vocavit nomen loci illius Lapis Adiutorii, dixitque, "Hucusque auxiliatus est nobis Dominus." 13 Et humiliati sunt Philisthim, nec adposuerunt ultra ut venirent in terminos Israhel. Facta est itaque manus Domini super Philistheos cunctis diebus Samuhel. 14 Et redditae sunt urbes quas tulerant Philisthim ab Israhel Israheli, ab Accaron usque Geth, et terminos suos, liberavitque Israhel de manu Philisthinorum, eratque pax inter Israhel et Amorreum. 15 Iudicabat quoque Samuhel Israhel cunctis diebus vitae suae, 16 et ibat per singulos annos circumiens Bethel et Galgal et Masphat, et iudicabat Israhelem in su-

to Mizpah, and they drew water and poured it out before the Lord, and they fasted on that day, and they said there, "We have sinned against the Lord." And Samuel judged the children of Israel in Mizpah.

7 And the Philistines heard that the children of Israel were gathered together to Mizpah, and the lords of the Philistines went up against Israel. And when the children of Israel heard this, they were afraid *of* the Philistines, 8 and they said to Samuel, "Cease not to cry to the Lord, our God, for us, that he may save us out of the hand of the Philistines." 9 And Samuel took a sucking lamb and offered it whole for a holocaust to the Lord, and Samuel cried to the Lord for Israel, and the Lord heard him. 10 And it came to pass when Samuel was offering the holocaust, the Philistines began the battle against Israel, but the Lord thundered with a great thunder on that day upon the Philistines and terrified them, and they were *overthrown* before the face of Israel. 11 And the men of Israel going out of Mizpah pursued after the Philistines and made slaughter of them *till they came* under Bethcar. 12 And Samuel took a stone and laid it between Mizpah and Shen, and he called *the* place the Stone of Help, and he said, "Thus far the Lord hath helped us." 13 And the Philistines were humbled, and they did not come any more into the borders of Israel. And the hand of the Lord was against the Philistines all the days of Samuel. 14 And the cities which the Philistines had taken from Israel were restored to Israel, from Ekron to Gath, and their borders, and he delivered Israel from the hand of the Philistines, and there was peace between Israel and the Amorites. 15 And Samuel judged Israel all the days of his life, 16 and he went every year about to Bethel and to Gilgal and to Mizpah, and he judged

pradictis locis. 17 Revertebaturque in Ramatha, ibi enim erat domus eius et ibi iudicabat Israhelem. Aedificavit etiam ibi altare Domino.

Caput 8

Factum est autem cum senuisset Samuhel posuit filios suos iudices Israhel. 2 Fuitque nomen filii eius primogeniti Iohel, et nomen secundi Abia, iudicum in Bersabee. 3 Et non ambulaverunt filii illius in viis eius, sed declinaverunt post avaritiam acceperuntque munera et perverterunt iudicium. 4 Congregati ergo universi maiores natu Israhel venerunt ad Samuhel, in Ramatha. 5 Dixeruntque ei, "Ecce: tu senuisti, et filii tui non ambulant in viis tuis. Constitue nobis regem ut iudicet nos, sicut et universae habent nationes."

6 Displicuitque sermo in oculis Samuhelis eo quod dixissent, "Da nobis regem ut iudicet nos," et oravit Samuhel ad Dominum. 7 Dixit autem Dominus ad Samuhel, "Audi vocem populi in omnibus quae loquuntur tibi, non enim te abiecerunt, sed me, ne regnem super eos. 8 Iuxta omnia opera sua quae fecerunt a die qua eduxi eos de Aegypto usque ad diem hanc. Sicut dereliquerunt me et servierunt diis

Israel in the aforesaid places. 17 And he returned to Ramah, for there was his house and there he judged Israel. He built also there an altar to the Lord.

Chapter 8

Samuel growing old and his sons not walking in his ways, the people desire a king.

And it came to pass when Samuel was old that he appointed his sons to be judges over Israel. 2 Now the name of his firstborn son was Joel, and the name of the second was Abijah, judges in Beer-sheba. 3 And his sons walked not in his ways, but they turned aside after lucre and took bribes and perverted judgment. 4 Then all the ancients of Israel, being assembled, came to Samuel, to Ramah. 5 And they said to him, "Behold: thou art old, and thy sons walk not in thy ways. Make us a king to judge us, *as* all nations have."

6 And the word was displeasing in the eyes of Samuel *that they should say,* "Give us a king to judge us," and Samuel prayed to the Lord. 7 And the Lord said to Samuel, "Hearken to the voice of the people in all that they say to thee, for they have not rejected thee, but me, that I should not reign over them. 8 According to all their works they have done from the day that I brought them out of Egypt until this day. As they have forsaken me and served strange gods, so do

alienis, sic faciunt etiam tibi. 9 Nunc, ergo, audi vocem eorum, verumtamen contestare eos, et praedic eis ius regis qui regnaturus est super eos."

10 Dixit itaque Samuhel omnia verba Domini ad populum qui petierat a se regem 11 et ait, "Hoc erit ius regis qui imperaturus est vobis: filios vestros tollet et ponet in curribus suis facietque sibi equites et praecursores quadrigarum suarum, 12 et constituet sibi tribunos et centuriones et aratores agrorum suorum et messores segetum et fabros armorum et curruum suorum. 13 Filias quoque vestras faciet sibi unguentarias et focarias et panificas. 14 Agros quoque vestros et vineas et oliveta optima tollet et dabit servis suis. 15 Sed et segetes vestras et vinearum reditus addecimabit ut det eunuchis et famulis suis. 16 Servos etiam vestros et ancillas et iuvenes optimos et asinos auferet et ponet in opere suo. 17 Greges quoque vestros addecimabit, vosque eritis ei servi. 18 Et clamabitis in die illa a facie regis vestri quem elegistis vobis, et non exaudiet vos Dominus in die illa, quia petistis vobis regem."

19 Noluit autem populus audire vocem Samuhel, sed dixerunt, "Nequaquam, rex enim erit super nos. 20 Et erimus nos quoque sicut omnes gentes, et iudicabit nos rex noster et egredietur ante nos et pugnabit bella nostra pro nobis."

21 Et audivit Samuhel omnia verba populi et locutus est ea in auribus Domini, 22 dixit autem Dominus ad Samuhel, "Audi vocem eorum, et constitue super eos regem."

Et ait Samuhel ad viros Israhel, "Vadat unusquisque in civitatem suam."

they also unto thee. 9 Now, therefore, hearken to their voice, but yet testify to them, and foretell them the right of the king that shall reign over them."

10 Then Samuel told all the words of the Lord to the people that had desired a king of him 11 and said, "This will be the right of the king that shall reign over you: he will take your sons and put them in his chariots and will make them his horsemen and his running footmen *to run* before his chariots, 12 and he will appoint *of* them to be his tribunes and centurions and to plough his fields and to reap his corn and to make him arms and chariots. 13 Your daughters also he will *take to make him ointments and to be* his cooks and bakers. 14 And he will take your fields and your vineyards and your best oliveyards and give them to his servants. 15 Moreover, he will take the tenth of your corn and of the revenues of your vineyards to give his eunuchs and servants. 16 Your servants also and handmaids and your goodliest young men and your asses he will take away and put them to his work. 17 Your flocks also he will tithe, and you shall be his servants. 18 And you shall cry out in that day from the face of the king whom you have chosen to yourselves, and the Lord will not hear you in that day, because you desired unto yourselves a king."

19 But the people would not hear the voice of Samuel, *and* they said, "Nay, *but* there shall be a king over us. 20 And we also will be like all nations, and our king shall judge us and go out before us and fight our battles for us."

21 And Samuel heard all the words of the people and rehearsed them in the ears of the Lord, 22 and the Lord said to Samuel, "Hearken to their voice, and *make them* a king."

And Samuel said to the men of Israel, "Let every man go to his city."

sportulam non habemus ut demus homini Dei, nec quicquam aliud."

8 Rursum puer respondit Sauli et ait, "Ecce: inventa est in manu mea quarta pars sicli argenti. Demus homini Dei ut indicet nobis viam nostram."

9 (Olim in Israhel sic loquebatur unusquisque vadens consulere Deum: "Venite, et eamus ad videntem," qui enim propheta dicitur hodie vocabatur olim videns.)

10 Et dixit Saul ad puerum suum, "Optimus sermo tuus; veni; eamus." Et ierunt in civitatem in qua erat vir Dei.

11 Cumque ascenderent clivum civitatis, invenerunt puellas egredientes ad hauriendam aquam, et dixerunt eis, "Num hic est videns?"

12 Quae respondentes dixerunt illis, "Hic est. Ecce: ante te. Festina nunc, hodie enim venit in civitatem, quia sacrificium est hodie populo in excelso. 13 Ingredientes urbem, statim invenietis eum antequam ascendat excelsum ad vescendum, neque enim comesurus est populus donec ille veniat quia ipse benedicit hostiae, et deinceps comedunt qui vocati sunt. Nunc, ergo, conscendite, quia hodie repperietis eum."

14 Et ascenderunt in civitatem. Cumque illi ambularent in medio urbis, apparuit Samuhel egrediens obviam eis ut ascenderet in excelsum. 15 Dominus autem revelaverat auriculam Samuhel ante unam diem quam veniret Saul, dicens, 16 "Hac ipsa quae nunc est hora cras mittam ad te virum de terra Beniamin, et ungues eum ducem super populum meum Israhel, et salvabit populum meum de manu Philisthinorum,

our bags, and we have no present to make to the man of God, nor any thing at all."

8 The servant answered Saul again and said, "Behold: there is found in my hand the fourth part of a sicle of silver. Let us give it to the man of God that he may tell us our way."

9 (Now in time past, in Israel when a man went to consult God he spoke thus: "Come; *let* us go to the seer," for he that is now called a prophet in time past was called a seer.)

10 And Saul said to his servant, "Thy word is very good; come; let us go." And they went into the city *where* the man of God was.

11 And when they went up the ascent *to* the city, they found maids coming out to draw water, and they said to them, "Is the seer here?"

12 They answered and said to them, "*He is*. Behold: he is before you. Make haste now, for he came today into the city, for there is a sacrifice of the people today in the high place. 13 *As soon as you come* into the city, you shall immediately find him before he go up to the high place to eat, for the people will not eat till he come because he blesseth the victim, and afterwards they eat that are invited. Now, therefore, go up, for today you shall find him."

14 And they went up into the city. And when they were walking in the midst of the city, *behold: Samuel was coming* out over against them to go up to the high place. 15 Now the Lord had revealed to the ear of Samuel the day before Saul came, saying, 16 "Tomorrow *about this same hour* I will send thee a man of the land of Benjamin, and thou shalt anoint him to be ruler over my people Israel, and he shall save my people out of the hand of the Philistines, for I have looked

quia respexi populum meum venit enim clamor eorum ad me." 17 Cumque aspexisset Samuhel Saulem, Dominus ait ei, "Ecce: vir quem dixeram tibi, iste dominabitur populo meo."

18 Accessit autem Saul ad Samuhelem in medio portae et ait, "Indica, oro, mihi, ubi est domus videntis?"

19 Et respondit Samuhel Sauli, dicens, "Ego sum videns; ascende ante me in excelsum ut comedatis mecum hodie, et dimittam te mane et omnia quae sunt in corde tuo indicabo tibi, 20 et de asinis quas perdidisti nudius tertius, ne sollicitus sis, quia inventae sunt. Et cuius erunt optima quaeque Israhel? Nonne tibi et omni domui patris tui?"

21 Respondens autem Saul ait, "Numquid non filius Iemini ego sum, de minima tribu Israhel, et cognatio mea novissima inter omnes familias de tribu Beniamin? Quare ergo locutus es mihi sermonem istum?"

22 Adsumens itaque Samuhel Saulem et puerum eius, introduxit eos in triclinium et dedit eis locum in capite eorum qui fuerant invitati, erant enim quasi triginta viri. 23 Dixitque Samuhel coco, "Da partem quam dedi tibi et praecepi ut reponeres seorsum apud te." 24 Levavit autem cocus armum et posuit ante Saul. Dixitque Samuhel, "Ecce quod remansit; pone ante te, et comede, quia de industria servatum est tibi quando populum vocavi." Et comedit Saul cum Samuhel in die illa.

25 Et descenderunt de excelso in oppidum, et locutus est cum Saul in solario, stravitque Saul in solario, et dormivit. 26 Cumque mane surrexissent et iam dilucesceret, vocavit

down upon my people because their cry is come to me."
17 And when Samuel saw Saul, the Lord said to him, "Behold:
the man of whom I spoke to thee, this man shall reign over
my people."

18 And Saul came to Samuel in the midst of the gate and
said, "Tell me, I pray thee, where is the house of the seer?"

19 And Samuel answered Saul, saying, "I am the seer; go
up before me to the high place that you may eat with me today, and I will let thee go in the morning and tell thee all
that is in thy heart, 20 and as for the asses which were lost
three days ago, be not solicitous, because they are found.
And for whom shall be all the best things of Israel? Shall
they not be for thee and for all thy father's house?"

21 And Saul answering said, "Am not I a son of Jemini, of
the least tribe of Israel, and my kindred the last among all
the families of the tribe of Benjamin? Why then hast thou
spoken this word to me?"

22 Then Samuel, taking Saul and his servant, brought
them into the parlour and gave them a place at the head of
them that were invited, for there were about thirty men.
23 And Samuel said to the cook, "Bring the portion which
I gave thee and commanded thee to set it apart by thee."
24 And the cook took up the shoulder and set it before Saul.
And Samuel said, "Behold what is left; set it before thee, and
eat, because it was kept of purpose for thee when I invited
the people." And Saul ate with Samuel that day.

25 And they went down from the high place into the town,
and he spoke with Saul upon the top of the house, and he
prepared a bed for Saul on the top of the house, and he slept.
26 And when they were risen in the morning and it began

Samuhel Saul in solarium, dicens, "Surge ut dimittam te." Et surrexit Saul, egressique sunt, ambo, ipse, videlicet, et Samuhel. 27 Cumque descenderent in extrema parte civitatis, Samuhel dixit ad Saul, "Dic puero ut antecedat nos et transeat, tu autem subsiste paulisper ut indicem tibi verbum Domini."

Caput 10

Tulit autem Samuhel lenticulam olei et effudit super caput eius et deosculatus est eum et ait, "Ecce: unxit te Dominus super hereditatem suam in principem, et liberabis populum suum de manibus inimicorum eius qui in circitu eius sunt. Et hoc tibi signum quia unxit te Deus in principem: 2 cum abieris hodie a me, invenies duos viros iuxta sepulchrum Rachel in finibus Beniamin in meridie, dicentque tibi, 'Inventae sunt asinae ad quas ieras perquirendas, et intermissis pater tuus asinis sollicitus est pro vobis et dicit, "Quid faciam de filio meo?"' 3 Cumque abieris inde et ultra

now to be light, Samuel called Saul on the top of the house, saying, "Arise that I may let thee go." And Saul arose, and they went out, both of them, to wit, he and Samuel. 27 And as they were going down in the end of the city, Samuel said to Saul, "Speak to the servant to go before us and pass on, but stand thou still a while that I may tell thee the word of the Lord."

Chapter 10

Saul is anointed. He prophesieth and is changed into another man. Samuel calleth the people together to make a king; the lot falleth on Saul.

And Samuel took a little vial of oil and poured it upon his head and kissed him and said, "Behold: the Lord hath anointed thee to be prince over his inheritance, and thou shalt deliver his people out of the hands of their enemies that are round about them. And this shall be a sign unto thee that God hath anointed thee to be prince: 2 when thou shalt depart from me this day, thou shalt find two men by the sepulchre of Rachel in the borders of Benjamin to the south, and they shall say to thee, 'The asses are found which thou wentest to seek, and thy father thinking no more of the asses is concerned for you and saith, "What shall I do *for* my son?"' 3 And when thou shalt depart from thence and go far-

transieris et veneris ad quercum Thabor, invenient te ibi tres viri ascendentes ad Deum, in Bethel, unus portans tres hedos et alius tres tortas panis et alius portans lagoenam vini. 4 Cumque te salutaverint dabunt tibi duos panes, et accipies de manu eorum. 5 Post haec venies in collem Dei, ubi est statio Philisthinorum, et cum ingressus fueris ibi urbem, obviam habebis gregem prophetarum descendentium de excelso, et ante eos psalterium et tympanum et tibiam et citharam, ipsosque prophetantes. 6 Et insiliet in te spiritus Domini, et prophetabis cum eis et mutaberis in virum alium. 7 Quando ergo evenerint signa haec omnia tibi, fac quaecumque invenerit manus tua, quia Dominus tecum est. 8 Et descendes ante me in Galgala (ego quippe descendam ad te) ut offeras oblationem et immoles victimas pacificas. Septem diebus expectabis donec veniam ad te, et ostendam tibi quae facias." 9 Itaque cum avertisset umerum suum ut abiret a Samuhele, inmutavit ei Deus cor aliud, et venerunt omnia signa haec in die illa.

10 Veneruntque ad praedictum collem, et ecce: cuneus prophetarum obvius ei, et insilivit super eum spiritus Domini, et prophetavit in medio eorum. 11 Videntes autem omnes qui noverant eum heri et nudius tertius quod esset cum prophetis et prophetaret, dixerunt ad invicem, "Quaenam res accidit filio Cis? Num et Saul in prophetis?" 12 Responditque alius ad alterum, dicens, "Et quis pater eorum?" Propterea versum est in proverbium: "Num et Saul inter prophetas?"

ther on and shalt come to the oak of Tabor, there shall meet thee three men going up to God, to Bethel, one carrying three kids and another three loaves of bread and another carrying a bottle of wine. 4 And *they will salute thee and* will give thee two loaves, and thou shalt take them at their hand. 5 After *that* thou shalt come to the hill of God, where the garrison of the Philistines is, and when thou shalt be come there into the city, thou shalt meet a company of prophets coming down from the high place *with* a psaltery and a timbrel and a pipe and a harp before them, and they shall be prophesying. 6 And the spirit of the Lord shall come upon thee, and thou shalt prophesy with them and shalt be changed into another man. 7 When therefore *these* signs shall happen to thee, do whatsoever thy hand shall find, for the Lord is with thee. 8 And thou shalt go down before me to Gilgal (for I will come down to thee) that thou mayest offer an oblation and sacrifice victims of peace. Seven days shalt thou wait till I come to thee, and I will show thee what thou art to do." 9 So when he had turned his back to go from Samuel, God gave unto him another heart, and all these *things* came to pass that day.

10 And they came to the foresaid hill, and behold: a company of prophets met him, and the spirit of the Lord came upon him, and he prophesied in the midst of them. 11 And all that had known him yesterday and the day before, seeing that he was with the prophets and prophesied, said to each other, "What *is this that* hath happened to the son of Kish? Is Saul also among the prophets?" 12 And one answered another, saying, "And who is their father?" Therefore it became a proverb: "Is Saul also among the prophets?"

13 Cessavit autem prophetare et venit ad excelsum, 14 dixit-que patruus Saul ad eum et ad puerum eius, "Quo abistis?"

Qui responderunt, "Quaerere asinas, quas cum non rep-perissemus venimus ad Samuhelem."

15 Et dixit ei patruus suus, "Indica mihi quid dixerit tibi Samuhel."

16 Et ait Saul ad patruum suum, "Indicavit nobis quia in-ventae essent asinae." De sermone autem regni non indica-vit ei, quem locutus illi fuerat Samuhel.

17 Et convocavit Samuhel populum ad Dominum in Mas-pha, 18 et ait ad filios Israhel, "Haec dicit Dominus, Deus Is-rahel, 'Ego eduxi Israhel de Aegypto et erui vos de manu Aegyptiorum et de manu omnium regum qui adfligebant vos. 19 Vos autem hodie proiecistis Deum vestrum qui solus salvavit vos de universis malis et tribulationibus vestris, et dixistis, "Nequaquam, sed regem constitue super nos." Nunc, ergo, state coram Domino per tribus vestras et per familias'"

20 Et adplicuit Samuhel omnes tribus Israhel, et cecidit sors super tribum Beniamin. 21 Et adplicuit tribum Benia-min et cognationes eius, et cecidit cognatio Metri, et perve-nit usque ad Saul, filium Cis. Quaesierunt ergo eum, et non est inventus. 22 Et consuluerunt post haec Dominum utrum-nam venturus esset illuc. Responditque Dominus, "Ecce: absconditus est domi."

23 Cucurrerunt itaque et tulerunt eum inde, stetitque in medio populi, et altior fuit universo populo ab umero et sur-sum. 24 Et ait Samuhel ad omnem populum, "Certe videtis

13 And *when he had made an end of prophesying, he* came to the high place, 14 and Saul's uncle said to him and to his servant, "Whither went you?"

They answered, "To seek the asses, and not finding them we went to Samuel."

15 And his uncle said to him, "Tell me what Samuel said to thee."

16 And Saul said to his uncle, "He told us that the asses were found." But of the matter of the kingdom of which Samuel had spoken to him, he told him not.

17 And Samuel called together the people to the Lord in Mizpah, 18 and he said to the children of Israel, "Thus saith the Lord, the God of Israel, 'I brought up Israel out of Egypt and delivered you from the hand of the Egyptians and from the hand of all the kings who afflicted you. 19 But you this day have rejected your God who only hath saved you out of all your evils and your tribulations, and you have said, "Nay, but set a king over us." Now, therefore, stand before the Lord by your tribes and by your families.'"

20 And Samuel brought to him all the tribes of Israel, and the lot fell on the tribe of Benjamin. 21 And he brought the tribe of Benjamin and the kindreds thereof, and the lot fell upon the kindred of Matri, and it came to Saul, the son of Kish. They sought him therefore, and he was not found. 22 And after this they consulted the Lord whether he would come thither. And the Lord answered, "Behold: he is hidden at home."

23 And they ran and fetched him thence, and he stood in the midst of the people, and he was higher than any of the people from the shoulders and upward. 24 And Samuel said

quem elegit Dominus, quoniam non sit similis ei in omni populo."

Et clamavit cunctus populus et ait, "Vivat rex." 25 Locutus est autem Samuhel ad populum legem regni, et scripsit in libro et reposuit coram Domino, et dimisit Samuhel omnem populum, singulos in domum suam.

26 Sed et Saul abiit in domum suam in Gabaath, et abiit cum eo pars exercitus quorum tetigerat Deus corda. 27 Filii vero Belial dixerunt, "Num salvare nos poterit iste?" Et despexerunt eum et non adtulerunt ei munera, ille vero dissimulabat se audire.

Caput 11

Et factum est quasi post mensem ascendit Naas, Ammonites, et pugnare coepit adversus Iabes Galaad. Dixeruntque omnes viri Iabes ad Naas, "Habeto nos foederatos, et serviemus tibi." 2 Et respondit ad eos Naas, Ammonites, "In hoc feriam vobiscum foedus: ut eruam omnium vestrum oculos dextros ponamque vos obprobrium in universo Israhel."

3 Et dixerunt ad eum seniores Iabes, "Concede nobis sep-

to all the people, "Surely you see him whom the Lord hath chosen, that there is none like him among all the people."

And all the people cried and said, "God save the king." 25 And Samuel told the people the law of the kingdom, and wrote it in a book and laid it up before the Lord, and Samuel sent away all the people, every one to his own house.

26 Saul also departed to his own house in Gibeah, and there went with him a part of the army whose hearts God had touched. 27 But the children of Belial said, "Shall this fellow be able to save us?" And they despised him and brought him no presents, but he dissembled as though he heard not.

Chapter 11

Saul defeateth the Ammonites and delivereth Jabesh Gilead.

And it came to pass about a month after *this* that Nahash, the Ammonite, came up and began to fight against Jabesh Gilead. And all the men of Jabesh said to Nahash, "Make a covenant with us, and we will serve thee." 2 And Nahash, the Ammonite, answered them, "On this condition will I make a covenant with you: that I may pluck out all your right eyes and make you a reproach in all Israel."

3 And the ancients of Jabesh said to him, "Allow us seven

tem dies ut mittamus nuntios ad universos terminos Israhel, et si non fuerit qui defendat nos, egrediemur ad te." 4 Venerunt ergo nuntii in Gabaath Saulis, et locuti sunt verba haec audiente populo, et levavit omnis populus vocem suam et flevit.

5 Et ecce: Saul veniebat sequens boves de agro, et ait, "Quid habet populus quod plorat?" Et narraverunt ei verba virorum Iabes, 6 et insilivit spiritus Domini in Saul cum audisset verba haec, et iratus est furor eius nimis. 7 Et adsumens utrumque bovem concidit in frusta misitque in omnes terminos Israhel per manum nuntiorum, dicens, "Quicumque non exierit secutusque fuerit Saul et Samuhelem, sic fiet bubus eius." Invasit ergo timor Domini populum, et egressi sunt quasi vir unus.

8 Et recensuit eos in Bezec, fueruntque filiorum Israhel trecenta milia virorum autem Iuda triginta milia. 9 Et dixerunt nuntiis qui venerant, "Sic dicetis viris qui sunt in Iabes Galaad, 'Cras erit vobis salus, cum incaluerit sol.'"

Venerunt ergo nuntii et adnuntiaverunt viris Iabes, qui laetati sunt, 10 et dixerunt, "Mane exibimus ad vos, et facietis nobis omne quod placuerit vobis." 11 Et factum est cum venisset dies crastinus constituit Saul populum in tres partes, et ingressus est media castra in vigilia matutina, et percussit Ammon usque dum incalesceret dies, reliqui autem dispersi sunt ita ut non relinquerentur in eis duo pariter. 12 Et ait populus ad Samuhel, "Quis est iste qui dixit, 'Saul num regnabit super nos?' Date nobis viros, et interficiemus eos."

days that we may send messengers to all the coasts of Israel, and if there be no one to defend us, we will come out to thee." 4 The messengers therefore came to Gibeah of Saul, and they spoke these words in the hearing of the people, and all the people lifted up their voices and wept.

5 And behold: Saul came following oxen out of the field, and he said, "What aileth the people that they weep?" And they told him the words of the men of Jabesh, 6 and the spirit of the Lord came upon Saul when he had heard these words, and his anger was exceedingly kindled. 7 And taking both the oxen he cut them in pieces and sent them into all the coasts of Israel by messengers, saying, "Whosoever shall not come forth and follow Saul and Samuel, so shall it be done to his oxen." And the fear of the Lord fell upon the people, and they went out as one man.

8 And he numbered them in Bezek, and there were of the children of Israel three hundred thousand and of the men of Judah thirty thousand. 9 And they said to the messengers that came, "Thus shall you say to the men *of* Jabesh Gilead, 'Tomorrow, when the sun shall be hot, you shall have relief.'"

The messengers therefore came and told the men of Jabesh, and they were glad, 10 and they said, "In the morning we will come out to you, and you shall do *what* you please with us." 11 And it came to pass when the morrow was come that Saul put the people in three companies, and he came into the midst of the camp in the morning watch, and he slew the Ammonites until the day grew hot, and the rest were scattered so that *two of them were not left together.* 12 And the people said to Samuel, "Who is he that said, 'Shall Saul reign over us?' *Bring* the men, and we will kill them."

13 Et ait Saul, "Non occidetur quisquam in die hac, quia hodie fecit Dominus salutem in Israhel."

14 Dixit autem Samuhel ad populum, "Venite, et eamus in Galgala, et innovemus ibi regnum." 15 Et perrexit omnis populus in Galgala, et fecerunt ibi regem Saul coram Domino in Galgala, et immolaverunt ibi victimas pacificas coram Domino. Et laetatus est ibi Saul et cuncti viri Israhel nimis.

Caput 12

Dixit autem Samuhel ad universum Israhel, "Ecce: audivi vocem vestram iuxta omnia quae locuti estis ad me et constitui super vos regem. 2 Et nunc rex graditur ante vos, ego autem senui et incanui, porro filii mei vobiscum sunt. Itaque conversatus coram vobis ab adulescentia mea usque ad diem hanc, ecce: praesto sum. 3 Loquimini de me coram Domino et coram christo eius utrum bovem cuiusquam tulerim an asinum, si quempiam calumniatus sum, si oppressi aliquem, si de manu cuiusquam munus accepi, et contemnam illud hodie restituamque vobis."

4 Et dixerunt, "Non es calumniatus nos neque oppressisti neque tulisti de manu alicuius quippiam."

13 And Saul said, "No man shall be killed this day, because the Lord this day hath wrought salvation in Israel."

14 And Samuel said to the people, "Come, and let us go to Gilgal, and let us renew the kingdom there." 15 And all the people went to Gilgal, and there they made Saul king before the Lord in Gilgal, and they sacrificed there victims of peace before the Lord. And there Saul and all the men of Israel rejoiced exceedingly.

Chapter 12

Samuel's integrity is acknowledged. God showeth by a sign
from heaven that they had done ill in asking for a king.

And Samuel said to all Israel, "Behold: I have hearkened to your voice in all that you said to me and have made a king over you. 2 And now the king goeth before you, but I am old and greyheaded, and my sons are with you. Having then conversed with you from my youth unto this day, behold: here I am. 3 Speak of me before the Lord and before his anointed whether I have taken any man's ox or ass, if I have wronged any man, if I have oppressed any man, if I have taken a bribe at any man's hand, and I will despise it this day and will restore it to you."

4 And they said, "Thou hast not wronged us nor oppressed us nor taken ought at any man's hand."

5 Dixitque ad eos, "Testis Dominus adversus vos, et testis christus eius in die hac, quia non inveneritis in manu mea quippiam."

Et dixerunt, "Testis."

6 Et ait Samuhel ad populum, "Dominus qui fecit Mosen et Aaron et eduxit patres nostros de terra Aegypti. 7 Nunc, ergo, state ut iudicio contendam adversum vos coram Domino de omnibus misericordiis Domini quas fecit vobiscum et cum patribus vestris, 8 quomodo ingressus est Iacob in Aegyptum et clamaverunt patres vestri ad Dominum et misit Dominus Mosen et Aaron et eduxit patres vestros ex Aegypto et conlocavit eos in loco hoc. 9 Qui obliti sunt Domini, Dei sui, et tradidit eos in manu Sisarae, magistri militiae Asor, et in manu Philisthinorum et in manu regis Moab, et pugnaverunt adversum eos. 10 Postea autem clamaverunt ad Dominum et dixerunt, 'Peccavimus quia dereliquimus Dominum et servivimus Baalim et Astharoth, nunc ergo erue nos de manu inimicorum nostrorum, et serviemus tibi.' 11 Et misit Dominus Hierobaal et Bedan et Ieptha et Samuhel et eruit vos de manu inimicorum vestrorum per circuitum, et habitastis confidenter. 12 Videntes autem quod Naas, rex filiorum Ammon, venisset adversum vos, dixistis mihi, 'Nequaquam, sed rex imperabit nobis,' cum Dominus, Deus vester, regnaret in vobis. 13 Nunc ergo praesto est rex vester, quem elegistis et petistis. Ecce: dedit vobis Dominus regem. 14 Si timueritis Dominum et servieritis ei et audieritis vocem eius et non exasperaveritis os Domini, eritis et vos et rex qui imperat vobis sequentes Domi-

5 And he said to them, "The Lord is witness against you, and his anointed is witness this day, that you have not found any thing in my hand."

And they said, "He is witness."

6 And Samuel said to the people, "It is the Lord who made Moses and Aaron and brought our fathers out of the land of Egypt. 7 Now, therefore, stand up that I may plead in judgment against you before the Lord concerning all the kindness of the Lord which he hath *shown to* you and *to* your fathers, 8 how Jacob went into Egypt and your fathers cried to the Lord and the Lord sent Moses and Aaron and brought your fathers out of Egypt and *made them dwell* in this place. 9 And they forgot the Lord, their God, and he delivered them into the hand of Sisera, captain of the army of Hazor, and into the *hands* of the Philistines and into the hand of the king of Moab, and they fought against them. 10 But afterwards they cried to the Lord and said, 'We have sinned because we have forsaken the Lord and have served Baalim and Astarte, *but now* deliver us from the hand of our enemies, and we will serve thee.' 11 And the Lord sent Jerubbaal and Bedan and Jephthah and Samuel and delivered you from the hand of your enemies round about, and you dwelt securely. 12 But seeing that Nahash, king of the children of Ammon, was come against you, you said to me, 'Nay, but a king shall reign over us,' whereas the Lord, your God, *was your king.* 13 Now therefore your king is here, whom you have chosen and desired. Behold: the Lord hath given you a king. 14 If you will fear the Lord and serve him and hearken to his voice and not provoke the mouth of the Lord, then shall both you and the king who reigneth over you be followers of

num, Deum vestrum. 15 Si autem non audieritis vocem Domini sed exasperaveritis sermones eius, erit manus Domini super vos et super patres vestros. 16 Sed et nunc state, et videte rem istam grandem quam facturus est Dominus in conspectu vestro. 17 Numquid non messis tritici est hodie? Invocabo Dominum, et dabit voces et pluvias, et scietis et videbitis quia grande malum feceritis vobis in conspectu Domini petentes super vos regem."

18 Et clamavit Samuhel ad Dominum, et dedit Dominus voces et pluviam in die illa. 19 Et timuit omnis populus nimis Dominum et Samuhelem, dixitque universus populus ad Samuhel, "Ora pro servis tuis ad Dominum, Deum tuum, ut non moriamur, addidimus enim universis peccatis nostris malum, ut peteremus nobis regem."

20 Dixit autem Samuhel ad populum, "Nolite timere; vos fecistis universum malum hoc, verumtamen nolite recedere a tergo Domini, sed servite Domino in omni corde vestro, 21 et nolite declinare post vana quae non proderunt vobis neque eruent vos, quia vana sunt. 22 Et non derelinquet Dominus populum suum propter nomen suum magnum, quia iuravit Dominus facere vos sibi populum. 23 Absit autem a me hoc peccatum in Domino, ut cessem orare pro vobis, et docebo vos viam bonam et rectam. 24 Igitur timete Dominum, et servite ei in veritate et ex toto corde vestro, vidistis enim magnifica quae in vobis gesserit. 25 Quod si perseveraveritis in malitia, et vos et rex vester pariter peribitis."

the Lord, your God. 15 But if you will not hearken to the voice of the Lord but will rebel against his words, the hand of the Lord shall be upon you and upon your fathers. 16 *Now then,* stand, and see this great thing which the Lord will do in your sight. 17 Is it not wheat harvest today? I will call upon the Lord, and he shall *send thunder* and rain, and you shall know and see that you *yourselves* have done a great evil in the sight of the Lord in desiring a king over you."

18 And Samuel cried unto the Lord, and the Lord *sent thunder* and rain that day. 19 And all the people greatly feared the Lord and Samuel, and all the people said to Samuel, "Pray for thy servants to the Lord, thy God, that we may not die, for we have added to all our sins *this* evil, to ask for a king."

20 And Samuel said to the people, "Fear not; you have done all this evil, but yet depart not from *following* the Lord, but serve the Lord with all your heart, 21 and turn not aside after vain things which shall *never* profit you nor deliver you, because they are vain. 22 And the Lord will not forsake his people for his great name's sake, because the Lord hath sworn to make you his people. 23 And far from me be this sin against the Lord, that I should cease to pray for you, and I will teach you the good and right way. 24 Therefore fear the Lord, and serve him in truth and with your whole heart, for you have seen the great works which he hath done among you. 25 But if you will *still do wickedly,* both you and your king shall perish together."

Caput 13

Filius unius anni Saul cum regnare coepisset, duobus autem annis regnavit super Israhel. 2 Et elegit sibi Saul tria milia de Israhel, et erant cum Saul duo milia in Machmas et in Monte Bethel mille autem cum Ionathan in Gabaath Beniamin, porro ceterum populum remisit unumquemque in tabernacula sua. 3 Et percussit Ionathan stationem Philisthim quae erat in Gabaa. Quod cum audissent Philisthim, Saul cecinit bucina in omni terra, dicens, "Audiant Hebraei." 4 Et universus Israhel audivit huiuscemodi famam: "Percussit Saul stationem Philisthinorum, et erexit se Israhel adversum Philisthim." Clamavit ergo populus post Saul in Galgala.

5 Et Philisthim congregati sunt ad proeliandum contra Israhel, triginta milia curruum et sex milia equitum et reliquum vulgus, sicut harena quae est in litore maris plurima. Et ascendentes castrametati sunt in Machmas ad orientem Bethaven. 6 Quod cum vidissent viri Israhel, se in arto sitos, (adflictus est enim populus), absconderunt se in speluncis et in abditis, in petris quoque et in antris et in cisternis. 7 Hebraei autem transierunt Iordanem in terram Gad et Galaad,

Chapter 13

The war between Saul and the Philistines. The distress of
the Israelites. Saul offereth sacrifice before the coming of
Samuel, for which he is reproved.

Saul was a child of one year when he began to reign, and he
reigned two years over Israel. 2 And Saul chose him three
thousand men of Israel, and two thousand were with Saul in
Michmash and in Mount Bethel and a thousand with Jonathan in Gibeah of Benjamin, and the rest of the people he
sent back every man to their dwellings. 3 And Jonathan
smote the garrison of the Philistines which was in Geba.
And when the Philistines had heard of it, Saul sounded *the
trumpet over* all the land, saying, "Let the Hebrews hear."
4 And all Israel heard *this report:* "Saul hath smitten the garrison of the Philistines, and Israel took courage against the
Philistines." *And the people were called together* after Saul to
Gilgal.

5 The Philistines also were assembled to fight against Israel, thirty thousand chariots and six thousand horsemen
and a *multitude of people besides,* like the sand on the sea shore
for number. And going up they camped in Michmash at the
east of Beth-aven. 6 And when the men of Israel saw *that
they were straitened* (for the people were distressed), they hid
themselves in caves and in thickets and in rocks and in dens
and in pits. 7 And *some of* the Hebrews passed over the Jordan into the land of Gad and Gilead, and when Saul was

cumque adhuc esset Saul in Galgal universus populus perterritus est qui sequebatur eum. 8 Et expectavit septem diebus iuxta placitum Samuhel, et non venit Samuhel in Galgala, dilapsusque est populus ab eo. 9 Ait ergo Saul, "Adferte mihi holocaustum et pacifica." Et obtulit holocaustum. 10 Cumque conplesset offerens holocaustum—ecce—Samuhel veniebat, et egressus est Saul obviam ei ut salutaret eum.

11 Locutusque est ad eum Samuhel, "Quid fecisti?"

Respondit Saul, "Quia vidi quod dilaberetur populus a me et tu non veneras iuxta placitos dies porro Philisthim congregati fuerant in Machmas, 12 dixi, 'Nunc descendent Philisthim ad me in Galgala, et faciem Domini non placavi.' Necessitate conpulsus, obtuli holocaustum."

13 Dixitque Samuhel ad Saul, "Stulte egisti nec custodisti mandata Domini, Dei tui, quae praecepit tibi. Quod si non fecisses, iam nunc praeparasset Dominus regnum tuum super Israhel in sempiternum. 14 Sed nequaquam regnum tuum ultra consurget. Quaesivit sibi Dominus virum iuxta cor suum, et praecepit ei Dominus ut esset dux super populum suum, eo quod non servaveris quae praecepit Dominus."

15 Surrexit autem Samuhel et ascendit de Galgalis in Gabaa Beniamin. Et reliqui populi ascenderunt post Saul obviam populo qui expugnabant eos, venientes de Galgala in Gabaa in colle Beniamin. Et recensuit Saul populum qui in-

yet in Gilgal all the people that followed him were greatly afraid. 8 And he waited seven days according to the appointment of Samuel, and Samuel came not to Gilgal, and the people slipt away from him. 9 Then Saul said, "Bring me the holocaust and the peace offerings." And he offered the holocaust. 10 And when he had made an end of offering the holocaust—behold—Samuel came, and Saul went forth to meet him *and* salute him.

11 And Samuel said to him, "What hast thou done?"

Saul answered, "Because I saw that the people slipt from me and thou wast not come according to the days appointed and the Philistines were gathered together in Michmash, 12 I said, 'Now will the Philistines come down upon me to Gilgal, and I have not appeased the face of the Lord.' Forced by necessity, I offered the holocaust."

13 And Samuel said to Saul, "Thou hast done foolishly and hast not kept the commandments of the Lord, thy God, which he commanded thee. *And* if thou hadst not done *thus,* the Lord would now have established thy kingdom over Israel for ever. 14 But thy kingdom shall *not continue.* The Lord hath sought him a man according to his own heart, and him hath the Lord commanded to be prince over his people, because thou hast not observed that which the Lord commanded."

15 And Samuel arose and went up from Gilgal to Gibeah of Benjamin. And the rest of the people went up after Saul to meet the people who fought against them, going from Gilgal to Gibeah in the hill of Benjamin. And Saul numbered the people that were found with him, about six hundred

venti fuerant cum eo, quasi sescentos viros. 16 Et Saul et Ionathan, filius eius, populusque qui inventus fuerat cum eis
erat in Gabaa Beniamin, porro Philisthim consederant in
Machmas. 17 Et egressi sunt ad praedandum de castris Philisthim tres cunei: unus cuneus pergebat contra viam Ephra
ad terram Saul; 18 porro alius ingrediebatur per viam Bethoron; tertius autem verterat se ad iter termini, inminentis
valli Seboim contra desertum. 19 Porro faber ferrarius non
inveniebatur in omni terra Israhel, caverant enim Philisthim
ne forte facerent Hebraei gladium aut lanceam, 20 descendebat ergo omnis Israhel ad Philisthim ut exacueret unusquisque vomerem suum et ligonem et securim et sarculum, 21 re-
tunsae itaque erant acies vomerum et ligonum et tridentum
et securium, usque ad stimulum corrigendum. 22 Cumque
venisset dies proelii, non est inventus ensis et lancea in manu
totius populi qui erat cum Saul et Ionathan, excepto Saul et
Ionathan, filio eius. 23 Egressa est autem statio Philisthim ut
transcenderet in Machmas.

men. 16 And Saul and Jonathan, his son, and the people that were *present* with them were in Geba of Benjamin, but the Philistines encamped in Michmash. 17 And there went out of the camp of the Philistines three companies to plunder: one company went towards the way of Ophrah to the land of Shual; 18 and another went by the way of Beth-horon; and the third *turned* to the way of the border, above the valley of Zeboim towards the desert. 19 Now there was no *smith* to be found in all the land of Israel, for the Philistines had taken this precaution lest the Hebrews should make *them swords or spears,* 20 so all Israel went down to the Philistines to sharpen every man his ploughshare and his spade and his axe and his rake, 21 so that *their shares and their spades and their forks and their axes* were blunt, even to the goad which was to be mended. 22 And when the day of battle was come, there was neither sword nor spear found in the hand of *any* of the people that were with Saul and Jonathan, except Saul and Jonathan, his son. 23 And the army of the Philistines went out in order to advance further in Michmash.

Caput 14

Et accidit quadam die ut diceret Ionathan, filius Saul, ad adulescentem, armigerum suum, "Veni, et transeamus ad stationem Philisthim quae est trans locum illum." Patri autem suo hoc ipsum non indicavit. 2 Porro Saul morabatur in extrema parte Gabaa sub malogranato quae erat in Magron, et erat populus cum eo quasi sescentorum virorum. 3 Et Ahias, filius Achitob, fratris Ichabod, filii Finees, qui ortus fuerat ex Heli, sacerdote Domini in Silo, portabat ephod. Sed et populus ignorabat quo isset Ionathan.

4 Erant autem inter ascensus per quos nitebatur Ionathan transire ad stationem Philisthinorum eminentes petrae ex utraque parte et quasi in modum dentium scopuli hinc inde praerupti; nomen uni Boses, et nomen alteri Sene, 5 unus scopulus prominens ad aquilonem ex adverso Machmas, et alter ad meridiem contra Gabaa. 6 Dixit autem Ionathan ad adulescentem, armigerum suum, "Veni; transeamus ad stationem incircumcisorum horum, si forte faciat Dominus pro nobis quia non est Domino difficile salvare vel in multis vel in paucis."

Chapter 14

Jonathan attacketh the Philistines. A miraculous victory.
Saul's unadvised oath by which Jonathan is put in danger of
his life but is delivered by the people.

N ow it came to pass one day that Jonathan, the son of
Saul, said to the young man *that bore his armour,* "Come, and
let us go over to the garrison of the Philistines which is on
the other side of yonder place." But he told not this to his
father. 2 And Saul abode in the uttermost part of Gibeah
under the pomegranate tree which was in Migron, and the
people with him were about six hundred men. 3 And Ahijah,
the son of Ahitub, brother to Ichabod, the son of Phinehas, *the son* of Eli, the priest of the Lord in Shiloh, wore
the ephod. *And* the people knew not whither Jonathan was
gone.

4 Now there were between the ascents by which Jonathan
sought to go over to the garrison of the Philistines rocks
standing up on both sides and steep cliffs like teeth on *the
one side and on the other;* the name of the one was Bozez, and
the name of the other was Seneh. 5 One rock *stood* out towards the north over against Michmash, and the other to
the south over against Geba. 6 And Jonathan said to the
young man *that bore his armour,* "Come let us go over to the
garrison of these uncircumcised. *It may be* the Lord will do
for us because it is *easy* for the Lord to save either by many
or by few."

7 Dixitque ei armiger suus, "Fac omnia quae placent animo tuo. Perge quo cupis, et ero tecum ubicumque volueris."

8 Et ait Ionathan, "Ecce: nos transimus ad viros istos. Cumque apparuerimus eis, 9 si taliter locuti fuerint ad nos: 'Manete donec veniamus ad vos,' stemus in loco nostro nec ascendamus ad eos, 10 si autem dixerint, 'Ascendite ad nos,' ascendamus, quia tradidit eos Dominus in manibus nostris. Hoc erit nobis signum."

11 Apparuit igitur uterque stationi Philisthinorum, dixeruntque Philisthim, "En: Hebraei egrediuntur de cavernis in quibus absconditi fuerant."

12 Et locuti sunt viri de statione ad Ionathan et ad armigerum eius dixeruntque, "Ascendite ad nos, et ostendemus vobis rem."

Et ait Ionathan ad armigerum suum, "Ascendamus; sequere me, tradidit enim eos Dominus in manus Israhel." 13 Ascendit autem Ionathan reptans manibus et pedibus et armiger eius post eum. Itaque alii cadebant ante Ionathan; alios armiger eius interficiebat sequens eum. 14 Et facta est plaga prima qua percussit Ionathan et armiger eius quasi viginti virorum in media parte iugeri, quam par boum in die arare consuevit. 15 Et factum est miraculum in castris per agros, sed et omnis populus stationis eorum qui ierant ad praedandum obstipuit, et conturbata est terra, et accidit quasi miraculum a Deo. 16 Et respexerunt speculatores Saul qui erant in Gabaa Beniamin, et ecce: multitudo prostrata et huc illucque diffugiens.

7 And his armourbearer said to him, "Do all that pleaseth thy mind. Go whither thou wilt, and I will be with thee wheresoever thou hast a mind."

8 And Jonathan said, "Behold: we will go over to these men. And when we shall *be seen by* them, 9 if they shall speak thus to us: 'Stay till we come to you,' let us stand *still* in our place and not go up to them, 10 but if they shall say, 'Come up to us,' let us go up, because the Lord hath delivered them into our hands. This shall be a sign unto us."

11 So both of them discovered themselves to the garrison of the Philistines, and the Philistines said, "Behold: the Hebrews come forth out of the holes wherein they were hid."

12 And the men of the garrison spoke to Jonathan and to his armourbearer and said, "Come up to us, and we will show you a thing."

And Jonathan said to his armourbearer, "Let us go up; follow me, for the Lord hath delivered them into the hands of Israel." 13 And Jonathan went up creeping on his hands and feet and his armourbearer after him. And some fell before Jonathan; others his armourbearer slew as he followed him. 14 And the first slaughter which Jonathan and his armourbearer made was of about twenty men within half an acre *of land,* which a yoke of oxen is wont to plough in a day. 15 And there was a miracle in the camp through the fields, yea, and all the people of their garrison who had gone out to plunder were amazed, and the earth trembled, and it happened as a miracle from God. 16 And the watchmen of Saul who were in Gibeah of Benjamin looked, and behold: a multitude overthrown and fleeing this way and that.

17 Et ait Saul populo qui erat cum eo, "Requirite, et videte quis abierit ex nobis." Cumque requisissent, reppertum est non adesse Ionathan et armigerum eius. 18 Et ait Saul ad Ahiam, "Adplica arcam Dei," erat enim ibi arca Dei in die illa cum filiis Israhel. 19 Cumque loqueretur Saul ad sacerdotem tumultus magnus exortus est in castris Philisthinorum, crescebatque paulatim et clarius reboabat. Et ait Saul ad sacerdotem, "Contrahe manum tuam." 20 Conclamavit ergo Saul et omnis populus qui erat cum eo, et venerunt usque ad locum certaminis, et ecce: versus fuerat gladius uniuscuiusque ad proximum suum, et caedes magna nimis. 21 Sed et Hebraei qui fuerant cum Philisthim heri et nudius tertius ascenderantque cum eis in castris reversi sunt ut essent cum Israhele qui erant cum Saul et Ionathan. 22 Omnes quoque Israhelitae qui se absconderant in Monte Ephraim, audientes quod fugissent Philisthim, sociaverunt se cum suis in proelio. Et erant cum Saul quasi decem milia virorum. 23 Et salvavit Dominus in die illa Israhel, pugna autem pervenit usque Bethaven.

24 Et viri Israhel sociati sibi sunt in die illa, adiuravit autem Saul populum, dicens, "Maledictus vir qui comederit panem usque ad vesperam donec ulciscar de inimicis meis." Et non manducavit universus populus panem, 25 omneque terrae vulgus venit in saltum in quo erat mel super faciem agri. 26 Ingressus est itaque populus saltum, et apparuit fluens mel, nullusque adplicuit manum ad os suum, timebat enim populus iuramentum.

17 And Saul said to the people that were with him, "Look, and see who is gone from us." And when they had sought, it was found that Jonathan and his armourbearer were not there. 18 And Saul said to Ahijah, "Bring the ark of the Lord," for the ark of God was there that day with the children of Israel. 19 And while Saul spoke to the priest there arose a great uproar in the camp of the Philistines, and it increased by degrees and *was heard* more clearly. And Saul said to the priest, "Draw in thy hand." 20 Then Saul and all the people that were with him shouted together, and they came to the place of the fight, and behold: every man's sword was turned upon his neighbour, and there was a very great slaughter. 21 Moreover, the Hebrews that had been with the Philistines yesterday and the day before and went up with them into the camp returned to be with the Israelites who were with Saul and Jonathan. 22 And all the Israelites that had hid themselves in Mount Ephraim, hearing that the Philistines fled, joined themselves with their *countrymen* in the fight. And there were with Saul about ten thousand men. 23 And the Lord saved Israel that day, and the fight went on as far as Beth-aven.

24 And the men of Israel were joined together that day, and Saul adjured the people, saying, "Cursed be the man that shall eat food till evening till I be revenged of my enemies." *So none of the people tasted any food,* 25 and all the common *people* came into a forest in which there was honey upon the *ground.* 26 *And when* the people came into the forest, *behold: the honey dropped, but* no man put his hand to his mouth, for the people feared the oath.

27 Porro Ionathan non audierat cum adiuraret pater eius populum, extenditque summitatem virgae quam habebat in manu et intinxit in favum mellis, et convertit manum suam ad os suum, et inluminati sunt oculi eius. 28 Respondensque unus de populo ait, "Iureiurando constrinxit pater tuus populum, dicens, 'Maledictus vir qui comederit panem hodie.'"

Defecerat autem populus, 29 dixitque Ionathan, "Turbavit pater meus terram. Vidistis ipsi quia inluminati sunt oculi mei eo quod gustaverim paululum de melle isto. 30 Quanto magis si comedisset populus de praeda inimicorum suorum quam repperit? Nonne maior facta fuisset plaga in Philisthim?" 31 Percusserunt ergo in die illa Philistheos a Machmis usque in Ahialon, defatigatus est autem populus nimis. 32 Et versus ad praedam, tulit oves et boves et vitulos et mactaverunt in terra, comeditque populus cum sanguine.

33 Nuntiaverunt autem Saul, dicentes quod populus peccasset Domino, comedens cum sanguine, qui ait, "Praevaricati estis. Volvite ad me iam nunc saxum grande." 34 Et dixit Saul, "Dispergimini in vulgus, et dicite eis ut adducat ad me unusquisque bovem suum et arietem, et occidite super istud, et vescimini, et non peccabitis Domino comedentes cum sanguine." Adduxit itaque omnis populus unusquisque bovem in manu sua usque ad noctem et occiderunt ibi. 35 Aedificavit autem Saul altare Domino, tuncque primum coepit aedificare altare Domino.

27 But Jonathan had not heard when his father adjured the people, and he put forth the end of the rod which he had in his hand and dipt it in a honeycomb, and he carried his hand to his mouth, and his eyes were enlightened. 28 And one of the people answering, said, "Thy father hath bound the people with an oath, saying, 'Cursed be the man that shall eat *any food* this day.'"

And the people were faint, 29 and Jonathan said, "My father hath troubled the land. You have seen yourselves that my eyes are enlightened because I tasted a little of this honey. 30 How much more if the people had eaten of the prey of their enemies which they found? Had there not been made a greater slaughter among the Philistines?" 31 So they smote that day the Philistines from Michmash to Aijalon, and the people were wearied exceedingly. 32 And falling upon the spoils, they took sheep and oxen and calves and slew them on the ground, and the people ate them with the blood.

33 And they told Saul *that* the people had sinned against the Lord, eating with the blood, and he said, "You have transgressed. Roll here to me now a great stone." 34 And Saul said, "Disperse yourselves among the people, and tell them to bring me every man his ox and his ram, and slay them upon this *stone,* and eat, and you shall not sin against the Lord in eating with the blood." So all the people brought every man his ox *with him* till the night and slew them there. 35 And Saul built an altar to the Lord, and he then first began to build an altar to the Lord.

36 Et dixit Saul, "Inruamus super Philisthim nocte et vastemus eos usque dum inlucescat mane, nec relinquamus de eis virum."

Dixitque populus, "Omne quod bonum videtur in oculis tuis fac."

Et ait sacerdos, "Accedamus huc ad Deum."

37 Et consuluit Saul Dominum, "Num persequar Philisthim? Si trades eos in manus Israhel?" Et non respondit ei in die illa. 38 Dixitque Saul, "Adplicate huc universos angulos populi, et scitote et videte per quem acciderit peccatum hoc hodie. 39 Vivit Dominus, salvator Israhel, quia si per Ionathan, filium meum, factum est, absque retractatione morietur." Ad quod nullus contradixit ei de omni populo, 40 et ait ad universum Israhel, "Separamini vos in partem unam, et ego cum Ionathan, filio meo, ero in parte altera."

Responditque populus ad Saul, "Quod bonum videtur in oculis tuis fac."

41 Et dixit Saul ad Dominum, "Domine, Deus Israhel, da indicium." Et deprehensus est Ionathan et Saul, populus autem exivit. 42 Et ait Saul, "Mittite sortem inter me et inter Ionathan, filium meum." Et captus est Ionathan. 43 Dixit autem Saul ad Ionathan, "Indica mihi quid feceris."

Et indicavit ei Ionathan et ait, "Gustans gustavi in summitate virgae quae erat in manu mea paululum mellis, et ecce: ego morior."

44 Et ait Saul, "Haec faciat mihi Deus et haec addat, quia morte morieris, Ionathan."

45 Dixitque populus ad Saul, "Ergone Ionathan morietur

36 And Saul said, "Let us fall upon the Philistines by night and destroy them till *the morning light,* and let us not leave a man of them."

And the people said, "Do all that seemeth good in thy eyes."

And the priest said, "Let us draw near hither unto God."

37 And Saul consulted the Lord, "Shall I pursue after the Philistines? Wilt thou deliver them into the hands of Israel?" And he answered him not that day. 38 And Saul said, "Bring hither all the corners of the people, and know and see by whom this sin hath happened today. 39 As the Lord liveth *who is* the saviour of Israel, if it was done by Jonathan, my son, he shall *surely* die." In this none of *the* people gainsaid him, 40 and he said to all Israel, "Be you *on* one side, and I with Jonathan, my son, will be on the other side."

And the people answered Saul, "Do what seemeth good in thy eyes."

41 And Saul said to the Lord, "O Lord, God of Israel, give a sign *by which we may know what the meaning is that thou answerest not thy servant today. If this iniquity be in me or in my son Jonathan, give a proof, or if this iniquity be in thy people, give holiness."* And Jonathan and Saul were taken, and the people escaped. 42 And Saul said, "Cast *lots* between me and Jonathan, my son." And Jonathan was taken. 43 And Saul said to Jonathan, "Tell me what thou hast done."

And Jonathan told him and said, *"I did but taste* a little honey with the end of the rod which was in my hand, and behold: I *must* die."

44 And Saul said, "May God do so and so to me and add still more, for dying thou shalt die, O Jonathan."

45 And the people said to Saul, "Shall Jonathan then die

qui fecit salutem hanc magnam in Israhel? Hoc nefas est. Vivit Dominus, si ceciderit capillus de capite eius in terram, quia cum Deo operatus est hodie." Liberavit ergo populus Ionathan ut non moreretur.

46 Recessitque Saul nec persecutus est Philisthim, porro Philisthim abierunt in loca sua. 47 Et Saul, confirmato regno super Israhel, pugnabat per circuitum adversum omnes inimicos eius, contra Moab et filios Ammon et Edom et reges Suba et Philistheos, et quocumque se verterat superabat. 48 Congregatoque exercitu, percussit Amalech et eruit Israhel de manu vastatorum eius.

49 Fuerunt autem filii Saul Ionathan et Iesui et Melchisua. Et nomina duarum filiarum eius, nomen primogenitae Merob, et nomen minoris Michol. 50 Et nomen uxoris Saul Ahinoem, filia Ahimaas, et nomen principis militiae eius Abner, filius Ner, patruelis Saul. 51 Porro Cis fuerat pater Saul et Ner; pater Abner filius Abihel.

52 Erat autem bellum potens adversum Philistheos omnibus diebus Saul, nam quemcumque viderat Saul virum fortem et aptum ad proelium sociabat eum sibi.

who hath wrought this great salvation in Israel? *This must not be.* As the Lord liveth, there shall not *one* hair of his head fall to the ground, for he hath wrought with God this day." So the people delivered Jonathan that he should not die.

46 And Saul went back and did not pursue after the Philistines, and the Philistines went to their own places. 47 And Saul, having his kingdom established over Israel, fought against all his enemies round about, against Moab and against the children of Ammon and Edom and the kings of Zobah and the Philistines, and whithersoever he turned himself he overcame. 48 And gathering together an army, he defeated Amalek and delivered Israel from the hand of them that spoiled them.

49 And the sons of Saul were Jonathan and Ishvi and Malchishua. And the names of his two daughters, the name of the firstborn was Merab, and the name of the younger Michal. 50 And the name of Saul's wife was Ahinoam, the daughter of Ahimaaz, and the name of the captain of his army was Abner, the son of Ner, the cousin-german of Saul, 51 for Kish was the father of Saul and Ner; the father of Abner was son of Abiel.

52 And there was a great war against the Philistines all the days of Saul, for whomsoever Saul saw to be a valiant man and fit for war he took him to himself.

Caput 15

Et dixit Samuhel ad Saul, "Me misit Dominus ut unguerem te in regem super populum eius, Israhel; nunc, ergo, audi vocem Domini. 2 Haec dicit Dominus exercituum: 'Recensui quaecumque fecit Amalech Israheli, quomodo restitit ei in via cum ascenderet de Aegypto. 3 Nunc, igitur, vade, et percute Amalech, et demolire universa eius. Non parcas ei, et non concupiscas ex rebus ipsius aliquid, sed interfice a viro usque ad mulierem et parvulum atque lactentem, bovem et ovem, camelum et asinum.'"

4 Praecepit itaque Saul populo et recensuit eos quasi agnos, ducenta milia peditum et decem milia virorum Iuda. 5 Cumque venisset Saul usque ad civitatem Amalech, tetendit insidias in torrente. 6 Dixitque Saul Cineo, "Abite; recedite, atque descendite ab Amalech ne forte involvam te cum eo, tu enim fecisti misericordiam cum omnibus filiis Israhel cum ascenderent de Aegypto." Et recessit Cineus de medio Amalech. 7 Percussitque Saul Amalech ab Evila donec venias Sur, quae est e regione Aegypti. 8 Et adprehendit Agag, regem Amalech, vivum, omne autem vulgus interfecit in ore gladii. 9 Et pepercit Saul et populus Agag et optimis gregibus

Chapter 15

Saul is sent to destroy Amalek. He spareth their king and the best of their cattle, for which disobedience he is cast off by the Lord.

And Samuel said to Saul, "The Lord sent me to anoint thee king over his people, Israel; now, therefore, hearken thou unto the voice of the Lord. 2 Thus saith the Lord of hosts: 'I have reckoned up *all that* Amalek hath done to Israel, how he opposed them in the way when they came up out of Egypt. 3 Now, therefore, go, and smite Amalek, and *utterly* destroy all that he hath. Spare him not, nor covet any thing *that is his,* but slay *both* man *and* woman, *child* and suckling, ox and sheep, camel and ass.'"

4 So Saul commanded the people and numbered them as lambs, two hundred thousand footmen and ten thousand of the men of Judah. 5 And when Saul was come to the city of Amalek, he laid ambushes in the torrent. 6 And Saul said to the Kenite, "Go; depart, and get ye down from Amalek lest *I destroy* thee with him, for thou hast shown kindness to all the children of Israel when they came up out of Egypt." And the Kenite departed from the midst of Amalek. 7 And Saul smote Amalek from Havilah until thou comest to Shur, which is over against Egypt. 8 And he took Agag, the king of Amalek, alive, but all the common people he slew with the edge of the sword. 9 And Saul and the people spared Agag

ovium et armentorum et vestibus et arietibus et universis quae pulchra erant nec voluerunt disperdere ea, quicquid vero vile fuit et reprobum, hoc demoliti sunt.

10 Factum est autem verbum Domini ad Samuhel, dicens, 11 "Paenitet me quod constituerim Saul regem, quia dereliquit me et verba mea opere non implevit." Contristatusque est Samuhel, et clamavit ad Dominum tota nocte.

12 Cumque de nocte surrexisset Samuhel ut iret ad Saul mane, nuntiatum est Samuheli quod venisset Saul in Carmelum et erexisset sibi fornicem triumphalem et reversus transisset descendissetque in Galgala. Venit ergo Samuhel ad Saul, et Saul offerebat holocaustum Domino de initiis praedarum quae adtulerat ex Amalech. 13 Et cum venisset Samuhel ad Saul, dixit ei Saul, "Benedictus tu Domino; implevi verbum Domini."

14 Dixitque Samuhel, "Et quae est haec vox gregum quae resonat in auribus meis et armentorum quam ego audio?"

15 Et ait Saul, "De Amalech adduxerunt ea, pepercit enim populus melioribus ovibus et armentis ut immolarentur Domino, Deo tuo, reliqua vero occidimus."

16 Dixit autem Samuhel ad Saul, "Sine me, et indicabo tibi quae locutus sit Dominus ad me nocte."

Dixitque ei, "Loquere."

17 Et ait Samuhel, "Nonne, cum parvulus esses in oculis tuis, caput in tribubus Israhel factus es? Unxitque te Domi-

and the best *of the* flocks of sheep and of the herds and the garments and the rams and all that was beautiful and would not destroy them, but every thing that was vile and *good for nothing,* that they destroyed.

10 And the word of the Lord *came* to Samuel, saying, 11 "It repenteth me that I have made Saul king, for he hath forsaken me and hath not *executed my commandments."* And Samuel was grieved, and he cried unto the Lord all night.

12 And when Samuel rose early to go to Saul in the morning, it was told Samuel that Saul was come to Carmel and had erected for himself a triumphant arch and returning had passed on and gone down to Gilgal. And Samuel came to Saul, and Saul was offering a holocaust to the Lord out of the *choicest* of the spoils which he had brought from Amalek. 13 And when Samuel was come to Saul, Saul said to him, "Blessed be thou of the Lord; I have fulfilled the word of the Lord."

14 And Samuel said, "What meaneth then this *bleating* of the flocks which soundeth in my ears and the *lowing* of the herds which I hear?"

15 And Saul said, "They have brought them from Amalek, for the people spared the *best of the* sheep and of the herds that they might be sacrificed to the Lord, thy God, but the rest we have slain."

16 And Samuel said to Saul, "Suffer me, and I will tell thee what the Lord hath said to me *this* night."

And he said to him, "Speak."

17 And Samuel said, "When thou wast a little one in thy own eyes, wast thou not made the head of the tribes of Israel? And the Lord anointed thee to be king over Israel.

nus regem super Israhel. 18 Et misit te Dominus in via et ait, 'Vade, et interfice peccatores Amalech, et pugnabis contra eos usque ad internicionem eorum.' 19 Quare ergo non audisti vocem Domini sed versus ad praedam es et fecisti malum in oculis Domini?"

20 Et ait Saul ad Samuhelem, "Immo, audivi vocem Domini et ambulavi in via per quam misit me Dominus et adduxi Agag, regem Amalech, et Amalech interfeci. 21 Tulit autem populus de praeda oves et boves primitias eorum quae caesa sunt ut immolet Domino, Deo suo, in Galgalis."

22 Et ait Samuhel, "Numquid vult Dominus holocausta et victimas et non potius ut oboediatur voci Domini? Melior est enim oboedientia quam victimae, et auscultare magis quam offerre adipem arietum. 23 Quoniam quasi peccatum ariolandi est repugnare et quasi scelus idolatriae nolle adquiescere. Pro eo, ergo, quod abiecisti sermonem Domini, abiecit te Dominus ne sis rex."

24 Dixitque Saul ad Samuhel, "Peccavi quia praevaricatus sum sermonem Domini et verba tua, timens populum et oboediens voci eorum. 25 Sed nunc porta, quaeso, peccatum meum, et revertere mecum ut adorem Dominum."

26 Et ait Samuhel ad Saul, "Non revertar tecum, quia proiecisti sermonem Domini et proiecit te Dominus ne sis rex super Israhel." 27 Et conversus est Samuhel ut abiret, ille

18 And the Lord sent thee on the way and said, 'Go, and kill the sinners of Amalek, and thou shalt fight against them until *thou hast utterly destroyed them.*' 19 Why then didst thou not hearken to the voice of the Lord but hast turned to the prey and hast done evil in the eyes of the Lord?"

20 And Saul said to Samuel, "Yea, I have hearkened to the voice of the Lord and have walked in the way by which the Lord sent me and have brought Agag, the king of Amalek, and Amalek I have slain. 21 But the people took of the spoils sheep and oxen as the firstfruits of those things that were slain to offer sacrifice to the Lord, their God, in Gilgal."

22 And Samuel said, "Doth the Lord desire holocausts and victims and not rather that the voice of the Lord should be obeyed? For obedience is better than sacrifices, and to hearken rather than to offer the fat of rams. 23 Because it is like the sin of witchcraft to rebel and like the crime of idolatry to refuse to obey. Forasmuch, therefore, as thou hast rejected the word of the Lord, the Lord hath also rejected thee from being king."

24 And Saul said to Samuel, "I have sinned because I have transgressed the commandment of the Lord and thy words, fearing the people and obeying their voice. 25 But now bear, I beseech thee, my sin, and return with me that I may adore the Lord."

26 And Samuel said to Saul, "I will not return with thee, because thou hast rejected the word of the Lord and the Lord hath rejected thee from being king over Israel." 27 And Samuel turned about to go away, but he laid hold upon the

autem adprehendit summitatem pallii eius, quae et scissa est, 28 et ait ad eum Samuhel, "Scidit Dominus regnum Israhel a te hodie et tradidit illud proximo tuo meliori te. 29 Porro triumphator in Israhel non parcet et paenitudine non flectetur, neque enim homo est ut agat paenitentiam."

30 At ille ait, "Peccavi, sed nunc honora me coram senibus populi mei et coram Israhel, et revertere mecum ut adorem Dominum, Deum tuum." 31 Reversus ergo Samuhel secutus est Saulem, et adoravit Saul Dominum.

32 Dixitque Samuhel, "Adducite ad me Agag, regem Amalech."

Et oblatus est ei Agag pinguissimus, tremens. Et dixit Agag, "Sicine separat amara mors?"

33 Et ait Samuhel, "Sicut fecit absque liberis mulieres gladius tuus, sic absque liberis erit inter mulieres mater tua." Et in frusta concidit eum Samuhel coram Domino in Galgalis. 34 Abiit autem Samuhel in Ramatha, Saul vero ascendit in domum suam in Gabaath. 35 Et non vidit Samuhel ultra Saul usque ad diem mortis suae. Verumtamen lugebat Samuhel Saul quoniam Dominum paenitebat quod constituisset eum regem super Israhel.

skirt of his mantle, *and it* rent, 28 and Samuel said to him, "The Lord hath rent the kingdom of Israel from thee this day and hath given it to thy neighbour who is better than thee. 29 But the triumpher in Israel will not spare and will not be moved to repentance, for he is not a man that he should repent."

30 Then he said, "I have sinned, yet honour me now before the ancients of my people and before Israel, and return with me that I may adore the Lord, thy God." 31 So Samuel turned again after Saul, and Saul adored the Lord.

32 And Samuel said, "Bring hither to me Agag, the king of Amalek."

And Agag was presented to him very fat *and* trembling. And Agag said, "Doth bitter death separate in this manner?"

33 And Samuel said, "As thy sword hath made women childless, so shall thy mother be childless among women." And Samuel hewed him in pieces before the Lord in Gilgal. 34 And Samuel departed to Ramah, but Saul went up to his house in Gibeah. 35 And Samuel saw Saul no more till the day of his death. Nevertheless Samuel mourned for Saul because the Lord repented that he had made him king over Israel.

Caput 16

Dixitque Dominus ad Samuhel, "Usquequo tu luges Saul, cum ego proiecerim eum ne regnet super Israhel? Imple cornu tuum oleo, et veni, ut mittam te ad Isai, Bethleemitem, providi enim in filiis eius mihi regem."

2 Et ait Samuhel, "Quomodo vadam? Audiet enim Saul, et interficiet me."

Et ait Dominus, "Vitulum de armento tolles in manu tua, et dices, 'Ad immolandum Domino veni,' 3 et vocabis Isai ad victimam, et ego ostendam tibi quid facias, et ungues quemcumque monstravero tibi."

4 Fecit ergo Samuhel sicut locutus est ei Dominus, venitque in Bethleem, et admirati sunt seniores civitatis, occurrentes ei dixeruntque, "Pacificus ingressus tuus?"

5 Et ait, "Pacificus. Ad immolandum Domino veni. Sanctificamini, et venite mecum ut immolem." Sanctificavit ergo Isai et filios eius et vocavit eos ad sacrificium.

6 Cumque ingressi essent, vidit Heliab et ait, "Num coram Domino est christus eius?"

Chapter 16

Samuel is sent to Bethlehem where he anointeth David, who is taken into Saul's family.

And the Lord said to Samuel, "How long wilt thou mourn for Saul, *whom* I have rejected from reigning over Israel? Fill thy horn with oil, and come, that I may send thee to Jesse, the Bethlehemite, for I have provided me a king among his sons."

2 And Samuel said, "How shall I go? For Saul will hear of it, and he will kill me."

And the Lord said, "Thou shalt take *with thee* a calf of the herd, and thou shalt say, 'I am come to sacrifice to the Lord,' 3 and thou shalt call Jesse to the sacrifice, and I will show thee what thou art to do, and thou shalt anoint him whom I shall show to thee."

4 Then Samuel did as the Lord had said to him, and he came to Bethlehem, and the ancients of the city wondered, and meeting him they said, "Is thy coming hither peaceable?"

5 And he said, "It is peaceable. I am come to offer sacrifice to the Lord. Be ye sanctified, and come with me *to the sacrifice.*" And he sanctified Jesse and his sons and called them to the sacrifice.

7 Et dixit Dominus ad Samuhel, "Ne respicias vultum eius neque altitudinem staturae eius, quoniam abieci eum nec iuxta intuitum hominis iudico, homo enim videt ea quae parent Dominus autem intuetur cor."

8 Et vocavit Isai Abinadab et adduxit eum coram Samuhel, qui dixit, "Nec hunc elegit Dominus." 9 Adduxit autem Isai Samma, de quo ait, "Etiam hunc non elegit Dominus." 10 Adduxit itaque Isai septem filios suos coram Samuhel, et ait Samuhel ad Isai, "Non elegit Dominus ex istis." 11 Dixitque Samuhel ad Isai, "Numquid iam conpleti sunt filii?"

Qui respondit, "Adhuc reliquus est parvulus, et pascit oves."

Et ait Samuhel ad Isai, "Mitte, et adduc eum, nec enim discumbemus priusquam ille huc venerit." 12 Misit ergo et adduxit eum.

Erat autem rufus et pulcher aspectu decoraque facie, et ait Dominus, "Surge, et ungue eum, ipse est enim."

13 Tulit igitur Samuhel cornu olei et unxit eum in medio fratrum eius, et directus est spiritus Domini in David a die illa et deinceps, surgensque Samuhel abiit in Ramatha. 14 Spiritus autem Domini recessit a Saul, et exagitabat eum spiritus nequam a Domino. 15 Dixeruntque servi Saul ad eum, "Ecce! Spiritus Dei malus exagitat te. 16 Iubeat dominus noster, et servi tui qui coram te sunt quaerent hominem

6 And when they were come in, he saw Eliab and said, "Is the Lord's anointed before him?"

7 And the Lord said to Samuel, "Look not on his countenance nor on the height of his stature, because I have rejected him nor do I judge according to the look of man, for man seeth those things that appear but the Lord beholdeth the heart."

8 And Jesse called Abinadab and brought him before Samuel, and he said, "Neither hath the Lord chosen this." 9 And Jesse brought Shammah, and he said of him, "Neither hath the Lord chosen this." 10 Jesse therefore brought his seven sons before Samuel, and Samuel said to Jesse, "The Lord hath not chosen any one of these." 11 And Samuel said to Jesse, *"Are here all thy sons?"*

He answered, "There remaineth yet a young one *who* keepeth the sheep."

And Samuel said to Jesse, "Send, and fetch him, for we will not sit down till he come hither." 12 He sent therefore and brought him.

Now he was ruddy and beautiful to behold and of a comely face, and the Lord said, "Arise, and anoint him, for this is he."

13 Then Samuel took the horn of oil and anointed him in the midst of his brethren, and the spirit of the Lord *came* upon David from that day forward, and Samuel rose up and went to Ramah. 14 But the spirit of the Lord departed from Saul, and an evil spirit from the Lord troubled him. 15 And the servants of Saul said to him, "Behold! *Now* an evil spirit from God troubleth thee. 16 Let our lord give orders, and thy servants who are before thee will seek out a man skillful

scientem psallere cithara, ut quando arripuerit te spiritus Domini malus, psallat manu sua, et levius feras."

17 Et ait Saul ad servos suos, "Providete ergo mihi aliquem bene psallentem, et adducite eum ad me."

18 Et respondens unus de pueris ait, "Ecce: vidi filium Isai, Bethleemitem, scientem psallere et fortissimum robore et virum bellicosum et prudentem in verbis et virum pulchrum, et Dominus est cum eo."

19 Misit ergo Saul nuntios ad Isai, dicens, "Mitte ad me David, filium tuum, qui est in pascuis." 20 Tulit itaque Isai asinum plenum panibus et lagoenam vini et hedum de capris unum et misit per manum David, filii sui, Saul. 21 Et venit David ad Saul et stetit coram eo, at ille dilexit eum nimis et factus est eius armiger. 22 Misitque Saul ad Isai, dicens, "Stet David in conspectu meo, invenit enim gratiam in oculis meis." 23 Igitur quandocumque spiritus Domini malus arripiebat Saul, tollebat David citharam et percutiebat manu sua, et refocilabatur Saul et levius habebat, recedebat enim ab eo spiritus malus.

in playing on the harp, that when the evil spirit from the Lord *is upon* thee, he may play with his hand, and thou mayest bear it more easily."

17 And Saul said to his servants, "Provide me then some man that *can play* well, and bring him to me."

18 And one of the servants answering said, "Behold: I have seen a son of Jesse, the Bethlehemite, a skillful player and one of great strength and a man fit for war and prudent in his words and a comely person, and the Lord is with him."

19 Then Saul sent messengers to Jesse, saying, "Send me David, thy son, who is in the pastures." 20 And Jesse took an ass laden with bread and a bottle of wine and a kid of the flock and sent them by the hand of David, his son, to Saul. 21 And David came to Saul and stood before him, *and* he loved him exceedingly and made him his armourbearer. 22 And Saul sent to Jesse, saying, "Let David stand before me, for he hath found favour in my *sight.*" 23 So whensoever the evil spirit from the Lord *was upon* Saul, David took his harp and *played* with his hand, and Saul was refreshed and was better, for the evil spirit departed from him.

eum vos servi eritis et servietis nobis." 10 Et aiebat Philistheus, "Ego exprobravi agminibus Israhelis hodie. Date mihi virum, et ineat mecum singulare certamen." 11 Audiens autem Saul et omnes Israhelitae sermones Philisthei huiuscemodi stupebant et metuebant nimis.

12 David autem erat filius viri Ephrathei de quo supra dictum est de Bethleem Iuda, cui erat nomen Isai qui habebat octo filios et erat vir in diebus Saul senex et grandevus inter viros. 13 Abierunt autem tres filii eius maiores post Saul in proelium, et nomina trium filiorum eius qui perrexerunt ad bellum Heliab, primogenitus, et secundus Abinadab tertiusque Samma, 14 David autem erat minimus. Tribus ergo maioribus secutis Saulem, 15 abiit David et reversus est a Saul ut pasceret gregem patris sui in Bethleem. 16 Procedebat vero Philistheus mane et vespere et stabat quadraginta diebus. 17 Dixit autem Isai ad David, filium suum, "Accipe fratribus tuis oephi pulentae et decem panes istos, et curre in castra ad fratres tuos. 18 Et decem formellas casei has deferes ad tribunum, et fratres tuos visitabis si recte agant, et cum quibus ordinati sint disce." 19 Saul autem et illi et omnes filii Israhel in valle Terebinthi pugnabant adversum Philisthim. 20 Surrexit itaque David mane et commendavit gregem custodi et onustus abiit sicut praeceperat ei Isai. Et venit ad locum Magala et ad exercitum qui egressus ad pugnam vociferatus erat in certamine, 21 direxerat enim aciem Israhel sed et Philisthim ex adverso fuerant praeparati. 22 Derelinquens ergo David vasa quae adtulerat sub manu custodis ad sarcinas cucurrit ad locum certaminis et interrogabat si omnia

shall be servants and shall serve us." 10 And the Philistine said, "I have defied the bands of Israel this day. Give me a man, and let him fight with me *hand to hand.*" 11 And Saul and all the Israelites hearing *these* words of the Philistine were dismayed and greatly afraid.

12 Now David was the son of *that* Ephrathite of Bethlehem Judah *before mentioned* whose name was Jesse, who had eight sons and was an old man in the days of Saul and of great age among men. 13 And his three eldest sons *followed* Saul to the battle, and the names of his three sons that went to the battle were Eliab, the firstborn, and the second Abinadab and the third Shammah, 14 but David was the youngest. So the three eldest having followed Saul, 15 David went and returned from Saul to feed his father's flock at Bethlehem. 16 Now the Philistine came out morning and evening and *presented himself* forty days. 17 And Jesse said to David, his son, "Take for thy brethren an ephi of frumenty and these ten loaves, and run to the camp to thy brethren. 18 And *carry* these ten little cheeses to the tribune, and *go see* thy brethren if they are well, and learn with whom they are placed." 19 But Saul and they and all the children of Israel *were* in the valley of Terebinth *fighting* against the Philistines. 20 David therefore arose in the morning and gave the charge of the flock to the keeper and went away loaded as Jesse had commanded him. And he came to the place of Magala and to the army which was going out to fight and shouted for the battle, 21 for Israel had put themselves in array and the Philistines who stood against them were prepared. 22 And David, leaving the vessels which he had brought under the care of the keeper of the baggage, ran to the place of the battle and

recte agerentur erga fratres suos. 23 Cumque adhuc ille loqueretur eis, apparuit vir ille spurius ascendens, Goliath nomine, Philistheus de Geth, ex castris Philisthinorum, et loquente eo haec eadem verba audivit David. 24 Omnes autem Israhelitae cum vidissent virum fugerunt a facie eius, timentes eum valde.

25 Et dixit unus quispiam de Israhel, "Num vidistis virum hunc qui ascendit? Ad exprobrandum enim Israheli ascendit, virum ergo qui percusserit eum ditabit rex divitiis magnis et filiam suam dabit ei et domum patris eius faciet absque tributo in Israhel."

26 Et ait David ad viros qui stabant secum, dicens, "Quid dabitur viro qui percusserit Philistheum hunc et tulerit obprobrium de Israhel, quis est enim hic Philistheus incircumcisus qui exprobravit acies Dei viventis?"

27 Referebat autem ei populus eundem sermonem, dicens, "Haec dabuntur viro qui percusserit eum."

28 Quod cum audisset Heliab, frater eius maior, loquente eo cum aliis, iratus est contra David et ait, "Quare venisti? Et quare dereliquisti pauculas oves illas in deserto? Ego novi superbiam tuam et nequitiam cordis tui quia ut videres proelium descendisti."

29 Et dixit David, "Quid feci? Numquid non verbum est?" 30 Et declinavit paululum ab eo ad alium dixitque eundem sermonem. Et respondit ei populus verbum sicut prius.

31 Audita sunt autem verba quae locutus est David et adnuntiata in conspectu Saul. 32 Ad quem cum fuisset adductus

asked if all things went well with his brethren. 23 And as he talked with them, that baseborn man whose name was Goliath, the Philistine of Gath, *showed himself* coming up from the camp of the Philistines, and he spoke according to the same words, and David heard them. 24 And all the Israelites when they saw the man fled from his face, fearing him exceedingly.

25 And some one of Israel said, "Have you seen this man that is come up? For he is come up to defy Israel, and the man that shall slay him the king will enrich with great riches and will give him his daughter and will make his father's house free from tribute in Israel."

26 And David spoke to the men that stood by him, saying, "What shall be given to the man that shall kill this Philistine and shall take away the reproach from Israel, for who is this uncircumcised Philistine that he should defy the armies of the living God?"

27 And the people answered him the same *words,* saying, "These things shall be given to the man that shall slay him."

28 *Now* when Eliab, his eldest brother, heard this when he was speaking with others, he was angry with David and said, "Why camest thou *hither?* And why didst thou leave those few sheep in the desert? I know thy pride and the wickedness of thy heart that thou art come down to see the battle."

29 And David said, "What have I done? Is there not *cause to speak?"* 30 And he turned a little aside from him to another and said the same word. And the people answered him as before.

31 And the words which David spoke were heard and were *rehearsed before* Saul. 32 And when he was brought to him he

locutus est ei, "Non concidat cor cuiusquam in eo. Ego, servus tuus, vadam et pugnabo adversus Philistheum."

33 Et ait Saul ad David, "Non vales resistere Philistheo isti nec pugnare adversum eum, quia puer es hic autem vir bellator ab adulescentia sua."

34 Dixitque David ad Saul, "Pascebat servus tuus patris sui gregem, et veniebat leo vel ursus tollebatque arietem de medio gregis, 35 et persequebar eos et percutiebam eruebamque de ore eorum, et illi consurgebant adversum me, et adprehendebam mentum eorum, et suffocabam interficiebamque eos, 36 nam et leonem et ursum interfeci ego, servus tuus, erit igitur et Philistheus hic incircumcisus quasi unus ex eis. Nunc vadam et auferam opprobrium populi, quoniam quis est iste Philisthaeus incircumcisus qui ausus est maledicere exercitum Dei viventis?" 37 Et ait David, "Dominus, qui eripuit me de manu leonis et de manu ursi, ipse liberabit me de manu Philisthei huius."

Dixit autem Saul ad David, "Vade, et Dominus tecum sit."

38 Et induit Saul David vestimentis suis et inposuit galeam aeream super caput eius et vestivit eum lorica. 39 Accinctus ergo David gladio eius super veste sua coepit temptare si armatus posset incedere, non enim habebat consuetudinem. Dixitque David ad Saul, "Non possum sic incedere, quia nec usum habeo." Et deposuit ea, 40 et tulit baculum suum, quem semper habebat in manibus, et elegit sibi quinque limpidissimos lapides de torrente et misit eos in peram pastoralem quam habebat secum, et fundam manu tulit et processit adversum Philistheum. 41 Ibat autem Philistheus incedens et adpropinquans adversum David et armiger eius ante eum.

42 Cumque inspexisset Philistheus et vidisset David, de-

said to him, "Let not any man's heart be dismayed in him. I, thy servant, will go and will fight against the Philistine."

33 And Saul said to David, "Thou art not able to withstand this Philistine nor to fight against him, for thou art *but* a boy but he is a warrior from his youth."

34 And David said to Saul, "Thy servant kept his father's sheep, and there came a lion or a bear and took a ram out of the midst of the flock, 35 and I pursued after them and struck them and delivered it out of their mouth, and they rose up against me, and I caught *them by the throat,* and I strangled and killed them, 36 for I, thy servant, have killed both a lion and a bear, and this uncircumcised Philistine shall be also as one of them. I will go now and take away the reproach of the people, for who is this uncircumcised Philistine who hath dared to curse the army of the living God?" 37 And David said, "The Lord, who delivered me out of the paw of the lion and out of the paw of the bear, he will deliver me out of the hand of this Philistine."

And Saul said to David, "Go, and the Lord be with thee."

38 And Saul clothed David with his garments and put a helmet of brass upon his head and armed him with a coat of mail. 39 And David, having girded his sword upon his armour, began to try if he could walk in armour, for he was not accustomed to it. And David said to Saul, "I cannot go thus, for I am not used to it." And he laid them off, 40 and he took his staff, which he had always in his hands, and chose him five *smooth* stones out of the brook, and put them into the shepherd's scrip which he had with him, and he took a sling in his hand and went forth against the Philistine. 41 And the Philistine came on and drew nigh against David and his armourbearer before him.

42 And when the Philistine looked and beheld David, he

spexit eum, erat enim adulescens, rufus et pulcher aspectu. 43 Et dixit Philistheus ad David, "Numquid ego canis sum quod tu venis ad me cum baculo?" Et maledixit Philistheus David in diis suis, 44 dixitque ad David, "Veni ad me, et dabo carnes tuas volatilibus caeli et bestiis terrae."

45 Dixit autem David ad Philistheum, "Tu venis ad me cum gladio et hasta et clypeo, ego autem venio ad te in nomine Domini exercituum, Dei agminum Israhel quibus exprobrasti 46 hodie, et dabit te Dominus in manu mea, et percutiam te et auferam caput tuum a te, et dabo cadavera castrorum Philisthim hodie volatilibus caeli et bestiis terrae, ut sciat omnis terra quia est Deus in Israhel. 47 Et noverit universa ecclesia haec quia non in gladio nec in hasta salvat Dominus, ipsius est enim bellum et tradet vos in manus nostras."

48 Cum ergo surrexisset Philistheus et veniret et adpropinquaret contra David, festinavit David et cucurrit ad pugnam ex adverso Philisthei. 49 Et misit manum suam in peram tulitque unum lapidem et funda iecit et circumducens percussit Philistheum in fronte, et infixus est lapis in fronte eius, et cecidit in faciem suam super terram. 50 Praevaluitque David adversus Philistheum in funda et lapide, percussumque Philistheum interfecit. Cumque gladium non haberet in manu David, 51 cucurrit et stetit super Philistheum et tulit gladium eius et eduxit de vagina sua et interfecit eum praeciditque caput eius. Videntes autem Philisthim quod mortuus esset fortissimus eorum fugerunt. 52 Et consurgentes viri Israhel et Iuda vociferati sunt et persecuti Philistheos usque dum venirent in vallem et usque ad portas Accaron, cecideruntque vulnerati de Philisthim in via Sarim

despised him, for he was a young man, ruddy and of a comely countenance. 43 And the Philistine said to David, "Am I a dog that thou comest to me with a staff?" And the Philistine cursed David by his gods, 44 and he said to David, "Come to me, and I will give thy flesh to the birds of the air and to the beasts of the earth."

45 And David said to the Philistine, "Thou comest to me with a sword and with a spear and with a shield, but I come to thee in the name of the Lord of hosts, the God of the armies of Israel which thou hast defied 46 this day, and the Lord will deliver thee into my hand, and I will slay thee and take away thy head from thee, and I will give the carcasses of the *army* of the Philistines this day to the birds of the air and to the beasts of the earth, that all the earth may know that there is a God in Israel. 47 And all this assembly shall know that the Lord saveth not with sword and spear, for it is his battle and he will deliver you into our hands."

48 And when the Philistine arose and was coming and drew nigh *to meet* David, David made haste and ran to the fight *to meet* the Philistine. 49 And he put his hand into his scrip and took a stone and cast it with the sling and fetching it about struck the Philistine in the forehead, and the stone was fixed in his forehead, and he fell on his face upon the earth. 50 And David prevailed over the Philistine with a sling and a stone, and he struck and slew the Philistine. And as David had no sword in his hand, 51 he ran and stood over the Philistine and took his sword and drew it out of the sheath and slew him and cut off his head. And the Philistines, seeing that their *champion* was dead, fled away. 52 And the men of Israel and Judah rising up shouted and pursued after the Philistines till they came to the valley and to the gates of Ekron, and there fell *many* wounded of the Philistines in

usque ad Geth et usque Accaron. 53 Et revertentes filii Israhel postquam persecuti fuerant Philistheos invaserunt
castra eorum. 54 Adsumens autem David caput Philisthei
adtulit illud in Hierusalem, arma vero eius posuit in tabernaculo suo.

55 Eo autem tempore quo viderat Saul David egredientem
contra Philistheum, ait ad Abner, principem militiae, "De
qua stirpe descendit hic adulescens, Abner?"

Dixitque Abner, "Vivit anima tua, rex, si novi."

56 Et ait rex, "Interroga tu cuius filius sit iste puer." 57 Cumque regressus esset David percusso Philistheo, tulit eum
Abner et introduxit coram Saul caput Philisthei habentem
in manu. 58 Et ait ad eum Saul, "De qua progenie es, o adulescens?"

Dixitque David, "Filius servi tui Isai, Bethleemitae, ego
sum."

Caput 18

Et factum est cum conplesset loqui ad Saul anima Ionathan conligata est animae David, et dilexit eum Ionathan
quasi animam suam. 2 Tulitque eum Saul in die illa et non

the way of Shaaraim and as far as Gath and as far as Ekron. 53 And the children of Israel, returning after they had pursued the Philistines, fell upon their camp. 54 And David, taking the head of the Philistine, brought it to Jerusalem, but his armour he put in his tent.

55 Now at the time that Saul saw David going out against the *Philistines,* he said to Abner, the captain of the army, "Of what family is this young man descended, Abner?"

And Abner said, "As thy soul liveth, O king, I know not."

56 And the king said, "Inquire thou whose son this man is." 57 And when David was returned after the Philistine was slain, Abner took him and brought him in before Saul *with* the head of the Philistine in his hand. 58 And Saul said to him, "Young man, of what family art thou?"

And David said, "I am the son of thy servant Jesse, the Bethlehemite."

Chapter 18

The friendship of Jonathan and David. The envy of Saul and his design upon David's life. He marrieth him to his daughter Michal.

And it came to pass when he had made an end of speaking to Saul the soul of Jonathan was knit with the soul of David, and Jonathan loved him as his own soul. 2 And Saul took

concessit ei ut reverteretur in domum patris sui. 3 Inierunt autem Ionathan et David foedus, diligebat enim eum quasi animam suam, 4 nam expoliavit se Ionathan tunicam qua erat vestitus et dedit eam David et reliqua vestimenta sua, usque ad gladium et arcum suum et usque ad balteum. 5 Egrediebatur quoque David ad omnia quocumque misisset eum Saul, et prudenter se agebat, posuitque eum Saul super viros belli, et acceptus erat in oculis universi populi maximeque in conspectu famulorum Saul.

6 Porro cum reverteretur percusso Philistheo David, egressae sunt mulieres de universis urbibus Israhel, cantantes chorosque ducentes in occursum Saul Regis in tympanis laetitiae et in sistris. 7 Et praecinebant mulieres ludentes atque dicentes, "Percussit Saul mille, et David decem milia."

8 Iratus est autem Saul nimis, et displicuit in oculis eius iste sermo, dixitque, "Dederunt David decem milia, et mihi dederunt mille. Quid ei superest nisi solum regnum?" 9 Non rectis ergo oculis Saul aspiciebat David ex die illa et deinceps. 10 Post diem autem alteram, invasit spiritus Dei malus Saul, et prophetabat in medio domus suae. David autem psallebat manu sua sicut per singulos dies, tenebatque Saul lanceam 11 et misit eam, putans quod configere posset David cum pariete, et declinavit David a facie eius secundo. 12 Et timuit Saul David eo quod esset Dominus cum eo et a se recessisset. 13 Amovit ergo eum Saul a se et fecit eum tribunum super mille viros, et egrediebatur et intrabat in conspectu populi.

14 In omnibus quoque viis suis David prudenter agebat, et Dominus erat cum eo. 15 Vidit itaque Saul quod prudens

him that day and would not *let* him return to his father's house. 3 And David and Jonathan made a covenant, for he loved him as his own soul. 4 *And* Jonathan stripped himself of the coat with which he was clothed and gave it to David and the rest of his garments, even to his sword and to his bow and to his girdle. 5 And David went out to *whatsoever business* Saul sent him, and he behaved himself prudently, and Saul set him over the soldiers, and he was acceptable in the eyes of all the people and especially in the eyes of Saul's servants.

6 Now when David returned after he slew the Philistine, the women came out of all the cities of Israel, singing and dancing to meet King Saul with timbrels of joy and cornets. 7 And the women sung as they played, and they said, "Saul slew *his thousands,* and David *his ten thousands."*

8 And Saul was exceeding angry, and this word was displeasing in his eyes, and he said, "They have given David ten thousands, and to me they have given *but* a thousand. What *can he have more but* the kingdom?" 9 And Saul did not look on David with *a good eye* from that day and forward. 10 And the day after, the evil spirit from God came upon Saul, and he prophesied in the midst of his house. And David played with his hand as *at other times,* and Saul held a spear *in his hand* 11 and threw it, thinking *to* nail David to the wall, and David *stept aside out of his presence twice.* 12 And Saul feared David because the Lord was with him and was departed from himself. 13 Therefore Saul removed him from him and made him a captain over a thousand men, and he went out and came in before the people.

14 And David behaved wisely in all his ways, and the Lord was with him. 15 And Saul saw that he was exceeding pru-

esset nimis et coepit cavere eum. 16 Omnis autem Israhel et Iuda diligebat David, ipse enim egrediebatur et ingrediebatur ante eos. 17 Dixit autem Saul ad David, "Ecce filia mea maior, Merob; ipsam dabo tibi uxorem. Tantummodo esto vir fortis, et proeliare bella Domini." Saul autem reputabat, dicens, "Non sit manus mea in eo, sed sit super illum manus Philisthinorum."

18 Ait autem David ad Saul, "Quis ego sum, aut quae est vita mea aut cognatio patris mei in Israhel, ut fiam gener regis?"

19 Factum est autem tempus cum deberet dari Merob, filia Saul, David; data est Hadrihel, Molathitae, uxor. 20 Dilexit autem Michol, filia Saul altera, David. Et nuntiatum est Saul, et placuit ei. 21 Dixitque Saul, "Dabo eam illi ut fiat ei in scandalum et sit super eum manus Philisthinorum." Dixitque Saul ad David, "In duabus rebus gener meus eris hodie."

22 Et mandavit Saul servis suis, "Loquimini ad David clam me, dicentes, 'Ecce: places regi, et omnes servi eius diligunt te. Nunc, ergo, esto gener regis. 23 Et locuti sunt servi Saul in auribus David omnia verba haec.

Et ait David, "Num parum vobis videtur generum esse regis? Ego autem sum vir pauper et tenuis."

24 Et renuntiaverunt servi Saul, dicentes, "Huiuscemodi verba locutus est David."

25 Dixit autem Saul, "Sic loquimini ad David: 'Non habet necesse rex sponsalia, nisi tantum centum praeputia Philisthinorum ut fiat ultio de inimicis regis.'" Porro Saul cogita-

dent and began to beware of him. 16 But all Israel and Judah loved David, for he came in and went out before them. 17 And Saul said to David, "Behold my elder daughter, Merab; her will I give thee to wife. Only be a valiant man, and fight the battles of the Lord." *Now* Saul *said within himself,* "Let not my hand be upon him, but let the hands of the Philistines be upon him."

18 And David said to Saul, "Who am I, or what is my life or my father's family in Israel, that I should be son-in-law of the king?"

19 And *it came to pass at the time* when Merab, the daughter of Saul, should have been given to David that she was given to Adriel, the Meholathite, to wife. 20 But Michal, the other daughter of Saul, loved David. And it was told Saul, and it pleased him. 21 And Saul said, "I will give her to him that she may be a stumblingblock to him and that the hand of the Philistines may be upon him." And Saul said to David, "In two things thou shalt be my son-in-law this day."

22 And Saul commanded his servants *to speak* to David *privately,* saying, "Behold: thou pleasest the king, and all his servants love thee. Now, therefore, be the king's son-in-law. 23 And the servants of Saul spoke all these words in the ears of David.

And David said, "Doth it seem to you a small matter to be the king's son-in-law? But I am a poor man and of small ability."

24 And the servants of Saul told *him,* saying, "Such words as these hath David spoken."

25 And Saul said, "Speak thus to David: 'The king *desireth* not any dowry, but only a hundred foreskins of the Philistines *to be avenged* of the king's enemies.'" Now Saul thought

407

bat tradere David in manus Philisthinorum, 26 cumque re-
nuntiassent servi eius David verba quae dixerat Saul, placuit
sermo in oculis David ut fieret gener regis. 27 Et post dies
paucos surgens David abiit cum viris qui sub eo erant, et
percussit ex Philisthim ducentos viros et adtulit praeputia
eorum et adnumeravit ea regi ut esset gener eius. Dedit itaque ei Saul Michol, filiam suam, uxorem. 28 Et vidit Saul et
intellexit quia Dominus esset cum David, Michol autem, filia Saul, diligebat eum. 29 Et Saul magis coepit timere David, factusque est Saul inimicus David cunctis diebus. 30 Et
egressi sunt principes Philisthinorum, a principio autem
egressionis eorum, prudentius se gerebat David quam omnes servi Saul, et celebre factum est nomen eius nimis.

Caput 19

Locutus est autem Saul ad Ionathan, filium suum, et ad
omnes servos suos ut occiderent David. Porro Ionathan, filius Saul, diligebat David valde. 2 Et indicavit Ionathan David, dicens, "Quaerit Saul, pater meus, occidere te, quapropter observa te, quaeso, mane, et manebis clam et absconderis.

to deliver David into the hands of the Philistines, 26 and when his servants had told David the words that Saul had said, the word was pleasing in the eyes of David to be the king's son-in-law. 27 And after a few days David rose up and went with the men that were under him, and he slew of the Philistines two hundred men and brought their foreskins and numbered them out to the king that he might be his son-in-law. Saul therefore gave him Michal, his daughter, to wife. 28 And Saul saw and understood that the Lord was with David, and Michal, the daughter of Saul, loved him. 29 And Saul began to fear David more, and Saul became David's enemy *continually*. 30 And the princes of the Philistines went forth, and from the beginning of their going forth, David behaved himself more wisely than all the servants of Saul, and his name became very famous.

Chapter 19

Other attempts of Saul upon David's life. He cometh to Samuel. Saul's messengers and Saul himself prophesy.

And Saul spoke to Jonathan, his son, and to all his servants that they should kill David. But Jonathan, the son of Saul, loved David exceedingly. 2 And Jonathan told David, saying, "Saul, my father, seeketh to kill thee, wherefore look to thyself, I beseech thee, in the morning, and thou shalt

3 Ego autem egrediens stabo iuxta patrem meum in agro ubicumque fuerit, et ego loquar de te ad patrem meum, et quodcumque videro nuntiabo tibi." 4 Locutus est ergo Ionathan de David bona ad Saul, patrem suum, dixitque ad eum, "Ne pecces, rex, in servum tuum David, quia non peccavit tibi et opera eius bona sunt tibi valde 5 et posuit animam suam in manu sua et percussit Philistheum et fecit Dominus salutem magnam universo Israhel. Vidisti et laetatus es. Quare ergo peccas in sanguine innoxio interficiens David, qui est absque culpa?"

6 Quod cum audisset Saul placatus voce Ionathae iuravit, "Vivit Dominus, quia non occidetur." 7 Vocavit itaque Ionathan David et indicavit ei omnia verba haec, et introduxit Ionathan David ad Saul, et fuit ante eum sicut fuerat heri et nudius tertius. 8 Motum est autem rursus bellum, et egressus David pugnavit adversus Philisthim percussitque eos plaga magna, et fugerunt a facie eius. 9 Et factus est spiritus Domini malus in Saul, sedebat autem in domo sua et tenebat lanceam, porro David psallebat manu sua. 10 Nisusque est Saul configere lancea David in pariete, et declinavit David a facie Saul, lancea autem casso vulnere perlata est in parietem, et David fugit et salvatus est nocte illa.

11 Misit ergo Saul satellites suos in domum David ut custodirent eum et interficeretur mane, quod cum adnuntiasset David Michol, uxor sua, dicens, "Nisi salvaveris te nocte hac, cras morieris," 12 deposuit eum per fenestram, porro ille abiit et aufugit atque salvatus est.

abide *in a secret place* and shalt be hid. 3 And I will go out and stand beside my father in the field *where thou art,* and I will speak of thee to my father, and whatsoever I shall see I will tell thee." 4 And Jonathan spoke good things of David to Saul, his father, and said to him, "Sin not, O king, against thy servant David, because he hath not sinned against thee and his works are very good towards thee 5 and he put his life in his hand and slew the Philistine and the Lord wrought great salvation for all Israel. Thou sawest it and didst rejoice. Why therefore *wilt* thou sin against innocent blood by killing David, who is without fault?"

6 And when Saul heard this he was appeased with the *words* of Jonathan and swore, "As the Lord liveth, he shall not be slain." 7 Then Jonathan called David and told him all these words, and Jonathan brought in David to Saul, and he was before him as he had been yesterday and the day before. 8 And the war began again, and David went out and fought against the Philistines and defeated them with a great slaughter, and they fled from his face. 9 And the evil spirit from the Lord came upon Saul, and he sat in his house and held a spear *in his hand,* and David played with his hand. 10 And Saul endeavoured to nail David to the wall with his spear, and David slipt away *out of the presence* of Saul, and the spear *missed him and* was fastened in the wall, and David fled and *escaped* that night.

11 Saul therefore sent his guards to David's house to watch him *that* he might be killed in the morning, and when Michal, *David's wife, had told him* this, saying, "Unless thou save thyself this night, tomorrow thou wilt die," 12 she let him down through a window, and he went and fled away and *escaped.*

13 Tulit autem Michol statuam et posuit eam super lectum et pellem pilosam caprarum posuit ad caput eius et operuit eam vestimentis. 14 Misit autem Saul apparitores qui raperent David, et responsum est quod aegrotaret. 15 Rursumque misit Saul nuntios ut viderent David, dicens, "Adferte eum ad me in lecto ut occidatur." 16 Cumque venissent nuntii, inventum est simulacrum super lectum et pellis caprarum ad caput eius. 17 Dixitque Saul ad Michol, "Quare sic inlusisti mihi et dimisisti inimicum meum ut fugeret?"

Et respondit Michol ad Saul, "Quia ipse locutus est mihi, 'Dimitte me, alioquin interficiam te.'" 18 David autem fugiens salvatus est et venit ad Samuhel in Ramatha et nuntiavit ei omnia quae fecerat sibi Saul, et abierunt ipse et Samuhel et morati sunt in Nahioth.

19 Nuntiatum est autem Sauli a dicentibus, "Ecce: David in Nahioth in Rama." 20 Misit ergo Saul lictores ut raperent David, qui cum vidissent cuneum prophetarum vaticinantium et Samuhel stantem super eos, factus est etiam in illis spiritus Domini, et prophetare coeperunt etiam ipsi. 21 Quod cum nuntiatum esset Sauli, misit alios nuntios, prophetaverunt autem et illi. Et rursum Saul misit tertios nuntios, qui et ipsi prophetaverunt. Et iratus iracundia Saul 22 abiit etiam ipse in Ramatha et venit usque ad cisternam magnam quae est in Soccho, et interrogavit et dixit, "In quo loco sunt Samuhel et David?"

Dictumque est ei, "Ecce! In Nahioth sunt in Rama." 23 Et abiit in Nahioth in Rama, et factus est etiam super eum spiritus Domini, et ambulabat ingrediens et prophetabat usque

13 And Michal took an image and laid it on the bed and put a *goat's skin with the hair* at the head of it and covered it with clothes. 14 And Saul sent officers to seize David, and it was answered that he was sick. 15 And again Saul *sent* to see David, saying, "Bring him to me in the bed that he may be slain." 16 And when the messengers were come in, they found an image upon the bed and *a goat's skin* at its head. 17 And Saul said to Michal, "Why hast thou deceived me so and let my enemy go *and* flee away?"

And Michal answered Saul, "Because he said to me, 'Let me go, or else I will kill thee.'" 18 But David fled and *escaped* and came to Samuel in Ramah and told him all that Saul had done to him, and he and Samuel went and dwelt in Naioth.

19 And it was told Saul by some saying, "Behold: David is in Naioth in Ramah." 20 So Saul sent officers to take David, and when they saw a company of prophets prophesying and Samuel presiding over them, the spirit of the Lord came also upon them, and they likewise began to prophesy. 21 And when this was told Saul, he sent other messengers, but they also prophesied. And again Saul sent messengers *the third time,* and they prophesied also. And Saul being *exceedingly* angry 22 went also himself to Ramah and came as far as the great cistern which is in Socoh, and he asked and said, "In what place are Samuel and David?"

And it was told him, "Behold! They are in Naioth in Ramah." 23 And he went to Naioth in Ramah, and the spirit of the Lord came upon him also, and he *went on* and prophe-

dum veniret in Nahioth in Rama. 24 Et expoliavit se etiam ipse vestimentis suis et prophetavit cum ceteris coram Samuhel et cecidit nudus tota die illa et nocte. Unde et exivit proverbium: "Num et Saul inter prophetas?"

Caput 20

Fugit autem David de Nahioth, quae est in Rama, veniensque locutus est coram Ionathan, "Quid feci? Quae est iniquitas mea, et quod peccatum meum in patrem tuum, quia quaerit animam meam?"

2 Qui dixit ei, "Absit; non morieris, neque enim faciet pater meus quicquam grande vel parvum nisi prius indicaverit mihi. Hunc ergo celavit me pater meus sermonem tantummodo? Nequaquam erit istud."

3 Et iuravit rursum David. Et ille ait, "Scit profecto pater tuus quia inveni gratiam in conspectu tuo, et dicet, 'Nesciat hoc Ionathan ne forte tristetur.' Quinimmo vivit Dominus et vivit anima tua, quia uno tantum (ut ita dicam) gradu ego morsque dividimur."

4 Et ait Ionathan ad David, "Quodcumque dixerit mihi anima tua faciam tibi."

sied till he came to Naioth in Ramah. 24 And he stripped himself also of his garments and prophesied with the rest before Samuel and lay down naked all that day and night. This gave occasion to a proverb: "What, is Saul too among the prophets?"

Chapter 20

Saul being obstinately bent upon killing David, he is sent away by Jonathan.

But David fled from Naioth, which is in Ramah, and came and said to Jonathan, "What have I done? What is my iniquity, and what is my sin against thy father, that he seeketh my life?"

2 And he said to him, "God forbid; thou shalt not die, for my father will do nothing great or little without first telling me. Hath then my father hid this word only from me? No, this shall not be."

3 And he swore again to David. And *David* said, "Thy father certainly knoweth that I have found grace in thy sight, and he will say, 'Let not Jonathan know this lest he be grieved.' But truly as the Lord liveth and thy soul liveth, *there is but one step* (as I *may* say) *between me and death."*

4 And Jonathan said to David, "Whatsoever thy soul shall say to me I will do for thee."

5 Dixit autem David ad Ionathan, "Ecce: kalendae sunt crastino, et ego ex more sedere soleo iuxta regem ad vescendum. Dimitte ergo me ut abscondar in agro usque ad vesperam diei tertiae. 6 Si respiciens requisierit me pater tuus, respondebis ei, 'Rogavit me David ut iret celeriter in Bethleem, civitatem suam, quia victimae sollemnes ibi sunt universis contribulibus eius.' 7 Si dixerit, 'Bene,' pax erit servo tuo, si autem fuerit iratus, scito quia conpleta est malitia eius. 8 Fac ergo misericordiam in servum tuum, quia foedus Domini me, famulum tuum, tecum inire fecisti. Si autem est in me aliqua iniquitas, tu me interfice, et ad patrem tuum ne introducas me."

9 Et ait Ionathan, "Absit hoc a te, neque enim fieri potest ut si certo cognovero conpletam patris mei esse malitiam contra te, non adnuntiem tibi."

10 Responditque David ad Ionathan, "Quis nuntiabit mihi si quid forte responderit tibi pater tuus dure de me?"

11 Et ait Ionathan ad David, "Veni, et egrediamur foras in agrum." Cumque exissent ambo in agrum, 12 ait Ionathan ad David, "Domine, Deus Israhel, si investigavero sententiam patris mei crastino vel perendie et aliquid boni fuerit super David et non statim misero ad te et notum tibi fecero, 13 haec faciat Dominus Ionathan et haec addat. Si autem perseveraverit patris mei malitia adversum te, revelabo aurem tuam et dimittam te ut vadas in pace et sit Dominus tecum sicut fuit cum patre meo. 14 Et si vixero, facies mihi misericordiam Domini, si vero mortuus fuero, 15 non aufe-

5 And David said to Jonathan, "Behold: tomorrow *is the new moon,* and I according to custom am wont to sit beside the king to eat. Let me go then that I may be hid in the field till the evening of the third day. 6 If thy father look and inquire for me, thou shalt answer him, 'David asked me that he might run to Bethlehem, his own city, because there are solemn sacrifices there for all his tribe.' 7 If he shall say, 'It is well,' thy servant shall have peace, but if he be angry, know that his malice is *come to its height.* 8 Deal mercifully then with thy servant, for thou hast brought me, thy servant, into a covenant of the Lord with thee. But if there be any iniquity in me, do thou kill me, and bring me not in to thy father."

9 And Jonathan said, "Far be this from thee, for if I should certainly know that evil is determined by my father against thee, *I could do no otherwise than* tell thee."

10 And David answered Jonathan, "Who shall bring me word if thy father should answer thee harshly concerning me?"

11 And Jonathan said to David, "Come, and let us go *out* into the field." And when they were both of them gone out into the field, 12 Jonathan said to David, "O Lord, God of Israel, if I shall discover my father's mind tomorrow or the day after and there be any thing good for David and I send not immediately to thee and make it known to thee, 13 may the Lord do so and so to Jonathan and add still more. But if my father shall continue in malice against thee, I will discover *it* to thy ear and will send thee away that thou mayest go in peace and the Lord be with thee as he hath been with my father. 14 And if I live, thou shalt show me the kindness of the Lord, but if I die, 15 thou shalt not take away thy kind-

res misericordiam tuam a domo mea usque in sempiternum;
quando eradicaverit Dominus inimicos David, unumquemque de terra, auferat Ionathan de domo sua, et requirat Dominus de manu inimicorum David." 16 Pepigit ergo foedus
Ionathan cum domo David, et requisivit Dominus de manu
inimicorum David. 17 Et addidit Ionathan deierare David
eo quod diligeret illum, sicut animam enim suam ita diligebat eum. 18 Dixitque ad eum Ionathan, "Cras kalendae sunt,
et requireris, 19 requiretur enim sessio tua usque perendie.
Descendes ergo festinus et venies in locum ubi celandus es
in die qua operari licet, et sedebis iuxta lapidem cui est nomen Ezel. 20 Et ego tres sagittas mittam iuxta eum et iaciam
quasi exercens me ad signum. 21 Mittam quoque et puerum,
dicens ei, 'Vade, et adfer mihi sagittas.' 22 Si dixero puero,
'Ecce: sagittae intra te sunt; tolle eas,' tu veni ad me, quia
pax tibi est et nihil est mali: vivit Dominus. Si autem sic locutus fuero puero, 'Ecce: sagittae ultra te sunt,' vade in pace,
quia dimisit te Dominus. 23 De verbo autem quod locuti
sumus ego et tu, sit Dominus inter me et te usque in sempiternum."

24 Absconditus est ergo David in agro, et venerunt kalendae, et sedit rex ad comedendum panem. 25 Cumque sedisset rex super cathedram suam secundum consuetudinem
quae erat iuxta parietem, surrexit Ionathan, et sedit Abner
ex latere Saul, vacuusque apparuit locus David. 26 Et non est
locutus Saul quicquam in die illa, cogitabat enim quod forte
evenisset ei ut non esset mundus nec purificatus. 27 Cumque inluxisset dies secunda post kalendas, rursum vacuus

ness from my house for ever; when the Lord shall have rooted out the enemies of David, every one of them from the earth, may he take away Jonathan from his house, and may the Lord require it at the *hands* of David's enemies." 16 Jonathan therefore made a covenant with the house of David, and the Lord required it at the *hands* of David's enemies. 17 And Jonathan swore again to David because he loved him, for he loved him as his own soul. 18 And Jonathan said to him, "Tomorrow *is the new moon,* and thou wilt be *missed,* 19 for thy seat will be *empty* till after tomorrow. So thou shalt go down quickly and come to the place where thou must be hid on the day when it is lawful to work, and thou shalt *remain* beside the stone which is called Ezel. 20 And I will shoot three arrows near it and will shoot as if I were exercising myself at a mark. 21 *And* I will send a boy, saying to him, 'Go, and fetch me the arrows.' 22 If I shall say to the boy, 'Behold: the arrows are on this side of thee; take them up,' come thou to me, because there is peace to thee and there is no evil as the Lord liveth. But if I shall speak thus to the boy: 'Behold: the arrows are beyond thee,' go in peace, for the Lord hath sent thee away. 23 And concerning the word which I and thou have spoken, the Lord be between thee and me for ever."

24 So David was hid in the field, and the *new moon* came, and the king sat down to eat bread. 25 And when the king sat down upon his chair according to custom which was beside the wall, Jonathan arose, and Abner sat by Saul's side, and David's place appeared empty. 26 And Saul said nothing that day, for he thought it might have happened to him that he was not clean nor purified. 27 And when the second day after

apparuit locus David. Dixitque Saul ad Ionathan, filium suum, "Cur non venit filius Isai nec heri nec hodie ad vescendum?"

28 Et respondit Ionathan Sauli, "Rogavit me obnixe ut iret in Bethleem, 29 et ait, 'Dimitte me, quoniam sacrificium sollemne est in civitate; unus de fratribus meis accersivit me, nunc ergo si inveni gratiam in oculis tuis, vadam cito et videbo fratres meos.' Ob hanc causam non venit ad mensam regis."

30 Iratus autem Saul adversus Ionathan dixit ei, "Fili mulieris virum ultro rapientis, numquid ignoro quia diligis filium Isai in confusionem tuam et in confusionem ignominiosae matris tuae? 31 Omnibus enim diebus quibus filius Isai vixerit super terram, non stabilieris tu neque regnum tuum. Itaque iam nunc mitte, et adduc eum ad me, quia filius mortis est."

32 Respondens autem Ionathan Sauli, patri suo, ait, "Quare morietur? Quid fecit?" 33 Et arripuit Saul lanceam ut percuteret eum. Et intellexit Ionathan quod definitum esset a patre suo ut interficeret David. 34 Surrexit ergo Ionathan a mensa in ira furoris et non comedit in die kalendarum secunda panem, contristatus est enim super David eo quod confudisset eum pater suus.

35 Cumque inluxisset mane, venit Ionathan in agrum, iuxta placitum David, et puer parvulus cum eo, 36 et ait ad puerum suum, "Vade, et adfer mihi sagittas quas ego iacio." Cumque puer cucurrisset, iecit aliam sagittam trans puerum. 37 Venit itaque puer ad locum iaculi quod miserat Ionathan, et clamavit Ionathan post tergum pueri et ait, "Ecce: ibi est sagitta porro ultra te." 38 Clamavitque iterum Iona-

the *new moon was come,* David's place appeared empty again. And Saul said to Jonathan, his son, "Why cometh not the son of Jesse to meat neither yesterday nor today?"

28 And Jonathan answered Saul, "He asked leave of me earnestly to go to Bethlehem, 29 and he said, 'Let me go, for there is a solemn sacrifice in the city; one of my brethren hath sent for me, and now if I have found favour in thy eyes, I will go quickly and see my brethren.' For this cause he came not to the king's table."

30 Then Saul being angry against Jonathan said to him, "Thou son of a woman *that* is the ravisher of a man, do I not know that thou lovest the son of Jesse to thy own confusion and to the confusion of thy shameless mother? 31 For *as long as* the son of Jesse liveth upon earth, thou shalt not be established nor thy kingdom. Therefore now presently send, and fetch him to me, for he is the son of death."

32 And Jonathan answering Saul, his father, said, "Why shall he die? What hath he done?" 33 And Saul caught up a spear to strike him. And Jonathan understood that it was determined by his father to kill David. 34 So Jonathan rose from the table in *great anger* and did not eat bread on the second day *after the new moon,* for he was grieved for David because his father had put him to confusion.

35 And when the morning came, Jonathan went into the field, according to the appointment with David, and a little boy with him, 36 and he said to his boy, "Go, and fetch me the arrows which I shoot." And when the boy ran, he shot another arrow beyond the boy. 37 The boy therefore came to the place of the arrow which Jonathan had shot, and Jonathan cried after the boy and said, "Behold: the arrow is there further beyond thee." 38 And Jonathan cried again after the

than post tergum pueri, dicens, "Festina velociter; ne stete-
ris." Collegit autem puer Ionathae sagittas et adtulit ad
dominum suum, 39 et quid ageretur penitus ignorabat, tantummodo enim Ionathan et David rem noverant. 40 Dedit
igitur Ionathan arma sua puero et dixit ei, "Vade, et defer in
civitatem."

41 Cumque abisset puer, surrexit David de loco qui verge-
bat ad austrum et cadens pronus in terram adoravit tertio,
et osculantes alterutrum fleverunt pariter, David autem amplius. 42 Dixit ergo Ionathan ad David, "Vade in pace, quaecumque iuravimus ambo in nomine Domini, dicentes, 'Dominus sit inter me et te et inter semen meum et semen tuum
usque in sempiternum.'" 43 Et surrexit David et abiit, sed et
Ionathan ingressus est civitatem.

Caput 21

Venit autem David in Nobe ad Ahimelech, sacerdotem,
et obstipuit Ahimelech eo quod venisset David. Et dixit ei,
"Quare tu solus et nullus est tecum?"

2 Et ait David ad Ahimelech, sacerdotem, "Rex praecepit
mihi sermonem et dixit, 'Nemo sciat rem propter quam a
me missus es et cuiusmodi tibi praecepta dederim, nam et

boy, saying "Make haste speedily; stand not." And Jonathan's boy gathered up the arrows and brought them to his master, 39 and he knew not at all what was doing, for only Jonathan and David knew the matter. 40 Jonathan therefore gave his arms to the boy and said to him, "Go, and carry them into the city."

41 And when the boy was gone, David rose out of his place which was towards the south and falling on his face to the ground adored thrice, and kissing one another they wept together, but David more. 42 And Jonathan said to David, "Go in peace, *and let all stand that* we have sworn both of us in the name of the Lord, saying, 'The Lord be between me and thee and between my seed and thy seed for ever.'" 43 *And* David arose and departed, and Jonathan went into the city.

Chapter 21

David receiveth holy bread of Ahimelech, the priest, and feigneth himself mad before Achish, king of Gath.

And David came to Nob to Ahimelech, the priest, and Ahimelech was astonished *at David's coming*. And he said to him, "Why art thou alone and no man *with* thee?"

2 And David said to Ahimelech, the priest, "The king hath commanded me a business and said, 'Let no man know the thing for which thou art sent by me and what manner of

pueris condixi in illum et illum locum.' 3 Nunc, igitur, si quid habes ad manum, vel quinque panes, da mihi, aut quicquid inveneris."

4 Et respondens sacerdos David ait, "Non habeo panes laicos ad manum sed tantum panem sanctum, si mundi sunt pueri, maxime a mulieribus."

5 Et respondit David sacerdoti et dixit ei, "Equidem, si de mulieribus agitur, continuimus nos ab heri et nudius tertius quando egrediebamur et fuerunt vasa puerorum sancta. Porro via haec polluta est, sed et ipsa hodie sanctificabitur in vasis."

6 Dedit ergo ei sacerdos sanctificatum panem, neque enim erat ibi panis nisi tantum panes propositionis qui sublati fuerant a facie Domini ut ponerentur panes calidi. 7 Erat autem ibi vir quidam de servis Saul in die illa intus in tabernaculo Domini, et nomen eius Doec, Idumeus, potentissimus pastorum Saul. 8 Dixit autem David ad Ahimelech, "Si habes hic ad manum hastam aut gladium, quia gladium meum et arma mea non tuli mecum, sermo enim regis urguebat."

9 Et dixit sacerdos, "Ecce: hic gladius Goliath, Philisthei quem percussisti in valle Terebinthi, est involutus pallio post ephod. Si istum vis tollere, tolle, neque enim est alius hic absque eo."

Et ait David, "Non est huic alter similis; da mihi eum." 10 Surrexit itaque David et fugit in die illa a facie Saul et venit ad Achis, regem Geth.

11 Dixeruntque ei servi Achis, cum vidissent David, "Numquid non iste est David, rex terrae? Nonne huic canta-

commands I have given thee, *and* I have appointed my servants to such and such a place.' 3 Now, therefore, if thou have any thing at hand, though it were but five loaves, give me, or whatsoever thou canst find."

4 And the priest answered David, saying, "I have no common bread at hand but only holy bread, if the young men be clean, especially from women."

5 And David answered the priest and said to him, "Truly, *as to what concerneth women,* we have refrained ourselves from yesterday and the day before when we came out and the vessels of the young men were holy. Now this way is defiled, but it shall also be sanctified this day in the vessels."

6 The priest therefore gave him hallowed bread, for there was no bread there but only the loaves of proposition which had been taken away from *before* the face of the Lord that hot loaves might be set up. 7 Now a certain man of the servants of Saul was there that day within the tabernacle of the Lord, and his name was Doeg, an Edomite, the chiefest of Saul's herdsmen. 8 And David said to Ahimelech, "Hast thou here at hand a spear or a sword? For I brought not my own sword nor my own weapons with me, for the king's business required haste."

9 And the priest said, "Lo: here is the sword of Goliath, the Philistine whom thou slewest in the valley of Terebinth, wrapped up in a cloth behind the ephod, if thou wilt take this, take it, for here is no other but this."

And David said, "There is none like that; give it me." 10 And David arose and fled that day from the face of Saul and came to Achish, the king of Gath.

11 And the servants of Achish when they saw David said to him, "Is not this David, the king of the land? Did they not

bant per choros, dicentes, 'Percussit Saul mille et David decem milia.'?"

12 Posuit autem David sermones istos in corde suo et extimuit valde a facie Achis, regis Geth. 13 Et inmutavit os suum coram eis et conlabebatur inter manus eorum, et inpingebat in ostia portae, defluebantque salivae eius in barbam. 14 Et ait Achis ad servos suos, "Vidistis hominem insanum; quare adduxistis eum ad me? 15 An desunt nobis furiosi quod introduxistis istum ut fureret me praesente? Hicine ingredietur domum meam?"

Caput 22

Abiit ergo inde David et fugit in speluncam Odollam. Quod cum audissent fratres eius et omnis domus patris eius, descenderunt ad eum illuc, 2 et convenerunt ad eum omnes qui erant in angustia constituti et oppressi aere alieno et amaro animo, et factus est eorum princeps, fueruntque cum eo quasi quadringenti viri.

3 Et profectus est David inde in Maspha, quae est Moab,

sing to him in their dances, saying, 'Saul hath slain *his thousands* and David *his ten thousands.'?*"

12 But David laid up these words in his heart and was exceedingly afraid at the face of Achish, the king of Gath. 13 And he changed his countenance before them and slipt down between their hands, and he stumbled against the doors of the gate, and his spittle ran down upon his beard. 14 And Achish said to his servants, "You saw the man was mad; why have you brought him to me? 15 Have we need of madmen that you have brought in this fellow to play the madman in my presence? Shall this fellow come into my house?"

Chapter 22

Many resort to David. Doeg accuseth Ahimelech to Saul.
He ordereth him and all the other priests of Nob to be slain.
Abiathar escapeth.

David therefore went from thence and fled to the cave of Adullam. And when his brethren and all his father's house had heard of it, they went down to him thither, 2 and all that were in distress and oppressed with debt and *under affliction of* mind gathered themselves unto him, and he became their prince, and there were with him about four hundred men.

3 And David departed from thence into Mizpah *of* Moab,

et dixit ad regem Moab, "Maneat, oro, pater meus et mater mea vobiscum donec sciam quid faciat mihi Deus." 4 Et reliquit eos ante faciem regis Moab, manseruntque apud eum cunctis diebus quibus David fuit in praesidio.

5 Dixitque Gad, propheta, ad David, "Noli manere in praesidio; proficiscere, et vade in terram Iuda." Et profectus est David et venit in saltum Hareth.

6 Et audivit Saul quod apparuisset David et viri qui erant cum eo. Saul autem cum maneret in Gabaa et esset in nemore quod est in Rama, hastam manu tenens cunctique servi eius circumstarent eum, 7 ait ad servos suos qui adsistebant ei, "Audite me nunc, filii Iemini: numquid omnibus vobis dabit filius Isai agros et vineas et universos vos faciet tribunos et centuriones 8 quoniam coniurastis omnes adversum me et non est qui mihi renuntiet, maxime cum et filius meus foedus inierit cum filio Isai? Non est qui vicem meam doleat ex vobis nec qui adnuntiet mihi, eo quod suscitaverit filius meus servum meum adversum me, insidiantem mihi usque hodie."

9 Respondens autem Doec, Idumeus, qui adsistebat et erat primus inter servos Saul, "Vidi," inquit, "filium Isai, in Nobe apud Ahimelech, filium Achitob, sacerdotem. 10 Qui consuluit pro eo Dominum et cibaria dedit ei, sed et gladium Goliath, Philisthei, dedit illi."

11 Misit ergo rex ad accersiendum Ahimelech, filium Achitob, sacerdotem, et omnem domum patris eius, sacerdotum qui erant in Nobe, qui venerunt universi ad regem. 12 Et ait Saul ad Achimelech, "Audi, fili Achitob."

Qui respondit, "Praesto sum, domine."

and he said to the king of Moab, "Let my father and my mother tarry with you, I beseech thee, till I know what God will do for me." 4 And he left them *under the eyes* of the king of Moab, and they abode with him all the days that David was in the hold.

5 And Gad, the prophet, said to David, "Abide not in the hold; depart, and go into the land of Judah." And David departed and came into the forest of Hereth.

6 And Saul heard that David was seen and the men that were with him. Now whilst Saul abode in Gibeah and was in the wood which is *by* Rama, having his spear in his hand and all his servants were standing about him, 7 he said to his servants that stood about him, "Hear me now, ye sons of Jemini: will the son of Jesse give everyone of you fields and vineyards and make you all tribunes and centurions 8 that all of you have conspired against me and there is no one to inform me, especially when even my son hath entered into league with the soil of Jesse? There is not one of you that pitieth my case nor that *giveth* me *any information,* because my son hath raised up my servant against me, plotting against me to this day."

9 And Doeg, the Edomite, who stood by and was the chief among the servants of Saul, answering said, "I saw the son of Jesse, in Nob with Ahimelech, the son of Ahitub, the priest. 10 And he consulted the Lord for him and gave him victuals *and* gave him the sword of Goliath, the Philistine."

11 Then the king sent to call for Ahimelech, the priest, the son of Ahitub, and all his father's house, the priests that were in Nob, and they came all of them to the king. 12 And Saul said to Ahimelech, "Hear, thou son of Ahitub."

He answered, "Here I am, my lord."

13 Dixitque ad eum Saul, "Quare coniurastis adversum me, tu et filius Isai, et dedisti ei panes et gladium et consuluisti pro eo Dominum ut consurgeret adversum me, insidiator usque hodie permanens?"

14 Respondensque Ahimelech regi ait, "Et quis in omnibus servis tuis sicut David fidelis et gener regis et pergens ad imperium tuum et gloriosus in domo tua? 15 Num hodie coepi consulere pro eo Deum? Absit hoc a me. Ne suspicetur rex adversus servum suum rem huiuscemodi in universa domo patris mei, non enim scivit servus tuus quicquam super hoc negotio vel modicum vel grande."

16 Dixitque rex, "Morte morieris, Ahimelech, tu et omnis domus patris tui."

17 Et ait rex emissariis qui circumstabant eum, "Convertimini, et interficite sacerdotes Domini, nam manus eorum cum David est, scientes quod fugisset et non indicaverunt mihi." Noluerunt autem servi regis extendere manus suas in sacerdotes Domini. 18 Et ait rex ad Doec, "Convertere tu, et inrue in sacerdotes." Conversusque Doec, Idumeus, inruit in sacerdotes et trucidavit in die illa octoginta quinque viros vestitos ephod lineo. 19 Nobe autem, civitatem sacerdotum, percussit in ore gladii, viros et mulieres, parvulos et lactantes bovemque et asinum et ovem in ore gladii.

20 Evadens autem unus filius Ahimelech, filii Achitob, cuius nomen erat Abiathar, fugit ad David 21 et adnuntiavit ei quod occidisset Saul sacerdotes Domini. 22 Et ait David ad Abiathar, "Sciebam in die illa quod cum ibi esset Doec,

13 And Saul said to him, "Why have you conspired against me, thou and the son of Jesse, and thou hast given him bread and a sword and hast consulted the Lord for him that he should rise up against me, continuing a traitor to this day?"

14 And Ahimelech answering the king said, "And who amongst all thy servants is so faithful as David, *who is* the king's son-in-law and goeth forth at thy bidding and is honourable in thy house? 15 Did I begin today to consult the Lord for him? Far be this from me. Let not the king suspect such a thing against his servant *or any one* in all my father's house, for thy servant knew nothing of this matter either little or great."

16 And the king said, "Dying thou shalt die, Ahimelech, thou and all thy father's house."

17 And the king said to the messengers that stood about him, "Turn, and kill the priests of the Lord, for their hand is with David, because they knew that he was fled and they told it not to me." And the king's servants would not put forth their hands against the priests of the Lord. 18 And the king said to Doeg, "Turn thou, and fall upon the priests." And Doeg, the Edomite, turned and fell upon the priests and slew in that day eighty-five men that wore the linen ephod. 19 And Nob, the city of the priests, he smote with the edge of his sword, *both* men and women, children and sucklings and ox and ass and sheep with the edge of the sword.

20 But one of the sons of Ahimelech, the son of Ahitub, whose name was Abiathar, escaped, and fled to David 21 and told him that Saul had slain the priests of the Lord. 22 And David said to Abiathar, "I knew that day when Doeg, the

Idumeus, procul dubio adnuntiaret Saul, 'Ego sum reus omnium animarum patris tui.' 23 Mane mecum; ne timeas: si quis quaesierit animam meam, quaeret et animam tuam, mecumque servaberis."

Caput 23

Et nuntiaverunt David, dicentes, "Ecce: Philisthim obpugnant Ceila, et diripiunt areas."

2 Consuluit igitur David Dominum, dicens, "Num vadam et percutiam Philistheos istos?"

Et ait Dominus ad David, "Vade, et percuties Philistheos et salvabis Ceila."

3 Et dixerunt viri qui erant cum David ad eum, "Ecce: nos hic in Iudaea consistentes timemus: quanto magis si ierimus in Ceila adversum agmina Philisthinorum?"

4 Rursum ergo David consuluit Dominum, qui respondens ei ait, "Surge, et vade in Ceila, ego enim tradam Philistheos in manu tua." 5 Abiit ergo David et viri eius in Ceila et pugnavit adversum Philistheos et abegit iumenta eorum

Edomite, was there that without doubt he would tell Saul, 'I *have been the occasion of the death* of all the souls of thy father's house.' 23 Abide thou with me; fear not, *for he that seeketh* my life seeketh thy life also, and with me thou shalt be saved."

Chapter 23

David relieveth Keilah, besieged by the Philistines. He fleeth into the desert of Ziph. Jonathan and he confirm their former covenant. The Ziphites discover him to Saul, who pursuing close after him is called away by an invasion from the Philistines.

And they told David, saying, "Behold: the Philistines fight against Keilah, and they rob the barns."

2 Therefore David consulted the Lord, saying, "Shall I go and smite these Philistines?"

And the Lord said to David, "Go, and thou shalt smite the Philistines and shalt save Keilah."

3 And the men that were with David said to him, "Behold: we are in fear here in Judea how much more if we go to Keilah against the bands of the Philistines?"

4 Therefore David consulted the Lord again, and he answered and said to him, "Arise, and go to Keilah, for I will deliver the Philistines into thy hand." 5 David therefore and his men went to Keilah and fought against the Philistines

et percussit eos plaga magna, et salvavit David habitatores Ceilae.

6 Porro eo tempore quo fugiebat Abiathar, filius Ahimelech, ad David, in Ceila, ephod secum habens descenderat. 7 Nuntiatum est autem Saul quod venisset David in Ceila, et ait Saul, "Tradidit eum Deus in manus meas, conclususque est, introgressus urbem in qua portae et serae." 8 Et praecepit Saul omni populo ut ad pugnam descenderet in Ceila et obsideret David et viros eius.

9 Quod cum rescisset David quia praepararet ei Saul clam malum, dixit ad Abiathar, sacerdotem, "Adplica ephod." 10 Et ait David, "Domine, Deus Israhel, audivit famam servus tuus quod disponat Saul venire in Ceila ut evertat urbem propter me. 11 Si tradent me viri Ceila in manus eius? Et si descendet Saul, sicut audivit servus tuus? Domine, Deus Israhel, indica servo tuo."

Et ait Dominus, "Descendet."

12 Dixitque David, "Si tradent viri Ceilae me et viros qui sunt mecum in manus Saul?"

Et dixit Dominus, "Tradent."

13 Surrexit ergo David et viri eius, quasi sescenti, et egressi de Ceila huc atque illuc vagabantur incerti, nuntiatumque est Saul quod fugisset David de Ceila et salvatus esset, quam ob rem dissimulavit exire. 14 Morabatur autem David in deserto in locis firmissimis, mansitque in monte solitudinis Ziph, in monte opaco. Quaerebat tamen eum Saul cunctis diebus, et non tradidit eum Deus in manus eius. 15 Et vidit David quod egressus esset Saul ut quaereret animam eius.

and brought away their cattle and *made a great slaughter of them,* and David saved the inhabitants of Keilah.

6 Now at that time when Abiathar, the son of Ahimelech, fled to David, to Keilah, he came down having an ephod with him. 7 And it was told Saul that David was come to Keilah, and Saul said, "The Lord hath delivered him into my hands, and he is shut up, being come into a city that hath gates and bars." 8 And Saul commanded all the people to go down to fight against Keilah and to besiege David and his men.

9 Now when David understood that Saul secretly prepared evil against him, he said to Abiathar, the priest, "Bring hither the ephod." 10 And David said, "O Lord, God of Israel, thy servant hath heard a report that Saul designeth to come to Keilah to destroy the city for my sake. 11 Will the men of Keilah deliver me into his hands? And will Saul come down, as thy servant hath heard? O Lord, God of Israel, tell thy servant."

And the Lord said, "He will come down."

12 And David said, "Will the men of Keilah deliver me and my men into the hands of Saul?"

And the Lord said, "They will deliver thee up."

13 Then David and his men, *who were* about six hundred, arose and departing from Keilah wandered up and down uncertain *where they should stay,* and it was told Saul that David was fled from Keilah and had *escaped,* wherefore he *forbore* to go out. 14 But David abode in the desert in *strong holds,* and he remained in a mountain of the desert of Ziph, in a *woody* hill. And Saul sought him always, *but* the Lord delivered him not into his hands. 15 And David saw that Saul was come out

Porro David erat in deserto Ziph, in silva. 16 Et surrexit Ionathan, filius Saul, et abiit ad David in silvam et confortavit
manus eius in Deo, dixitque ei, 17 "Ne timeas, neque enim
inveniet te manus Saul, patris mei, et tu regnabis super Israhel, et ego ero tibi secundus, sed et pater meus scit hoc."
18 Percussit igitur uterque foedus coram Domino, mansitque David in silva, Ionathas autem reversus est in domum
suam.

19 Ascenderunt autem Ziphei ad Saul in Gabaa, dicentes,
"Nonne, ecce, David latitat apud nos in locis tutissimis silvae, in Colle Achilae, quae est ad dexteram deserti? 20 Nunc,
ergo, sicut desideravit anima tua ut descenderes, descende,
nostrum autem erit ut tradamus eum in manus regis."

21 Dixitque Saul, "Benedicti vos a Domino, quia doluistis
vicem meam. 22 Abite, ergo, oro, et diligentius praeparate, et
curiosius agite, et considerate locum ubi sit pes eius vel quis
viderit eum ibi, recogitat enim de me quod callide insidier
ei. 23 Considerate, et videte omnia latibula eius in quibus
absconditur, et revertimini ad me ad rem certam ut vadam
vobiscum. Quod si etiam in terram se abstruserit, perscruta-
bor eum in cunctis milibus Iuda."

24 At illi surgentes abierunt in Ziph ante Saul, David
autem et viri eius erant in deserto Maon, in campestribus ad
dextram Iesimuth. 25 Ivit ergo Saul et socii eius ad quaerendum eum, et nuntiatum est David, statimque descendit ad
petram et versabatur in deserto Maon, quod cum audisset
Saul persecutus est David in deserto Maon. 26 Et ibat Saul ad
latus montis ex parte una, David autem et viri eius erant

to seek his life. *And* David was in the desert of Ziph, in a wood. 16 And Jonathan, the son of Saul, arose and went to David into the wood and strengthened his hands in God, and he said to him, 17 "Fear not, for the hand of my father, Saul, shall not find thee, and thou shalt reign over Israel, and I shall be next to thee, yea, and my father knoweth this." 18 And the two made a covenant before the Lord, and David abode in the wood, but Jonathan returned to his house.

19 And the Ziphites went up to Saul in Gibeah, saying, "Lo: doth not David lie hid with us in the *strong holds* of the wood, in Mount Hachilah, which is on the right hand of the desert? 20 Now, therefore, come down, as thy soul hath desired to come down, and it shall be our business to deliver him into the king's hands."

21 And Saul said, "Blessed be ye of the Lord, for you have pitied my case. 22 Go, therefore, I pray you, and *use all diligence,* and curiously inquire, and consider the place where his foot is *and* who hath seen him there, for he thinketh of me that I lie craftily in wait for him. 23 Consider, and see all his lurking holes wherein he is hid, and return to me with the certainty of the thing that I may go with you. And if he should even *go down* into the earth *to hide* himself, I will search him out in all the thousands of Judah."

24 And they arose and went to Ziph before Saul, and David and his men were in the desert of Maon, in the *plain* at the right hand of Jeshimon. 25 Then Saul and his men went to seek him, and it was told David, and forthwith he went down to the rock and abode in the wilderness of Maon, and when Saul had heard of it he pursued after David in the wilderness of Maon. 26 And Saul went on this side of the mountain, and David and his men were on the other side of the

in latere montis ex parte altera, porro David desperabat se posse evadere a facie Saul, itaque Saul et viri eius in modum coronae cingebant David et viros eius ut caperent eos. 27 Et nuntius venit ad Saul, dicens, "Festina, et veni, quoniam infuderunt se Philisthim super terram." 28 Reversus est ergo Saul, desistens persequi David, et perrexit in occursum Philisthinorum; propter hoc vocaverunt locum illum Petram Dividentem.

Caput 24

Ascendit ergo David inde et habitavit in locis tutissimis Engaddi. 2 Cumque reversus esset Saul postquam persecutus est Philistheos nuntiaverunt ei, dicentes, "Ecce: David in deserto est Engaddi." 3 Adsumens ergo Saul tria milia electorum virorum ex omni Israhel perrexit ad investigandum David et viros eius, etiam super abruptissimas petras quae solis hibicibus perviae sunt. 4 Et venit ad caulas ovium quae se offerebant vianti, eratque ibi spelunca quam ingressus est Saul ut purgaret ventrem; porro David et viri eius in interiori parte speluncae latebant.

5 Et dixerunt servi David ad eum, "Ecce dies de qua locu-

mountain, and David despaired of being able to escape from the face of Saul, and Saul and his men encompassed David and his men *round about* to take them. 27 And a messenger came to Saul, saying, "Make haste *to* come, for the Philistines have poured in themselves upon the land." 28 Wherefore Saul returned, leaving the pursuit of David, and went to meet the Philistines; for this cause they called that place the Rock *of Division.*

Chapter 24

Saul seeketh David in the wilderness of En-gedi. He goeth into a cave where David hath him in his power.

Then David went up from thence and dwelt in *strong holds* of En-gedi. 2 And when Saul was returned *from following* the Philistines they told him, saying, "Behold: David is in the desert of En-gedi." 3 Saul therefore took three thousand chosen men out of all Israel and went out to seek after David and his men, even upon the most craggy rocks which are accessible only to wild goats. 4 And he came to the sheep-cotes which *were in his way,* and there was a cave into which Saul went to *ease nature;* now David and his men lay hid in the inner part of the cave.

5 And the servants of David said to him, "Behold the day

tus est Dominus ad te, 'Ego tradam tibi inimicum tuum ut facias ei sicut placuerit in oculis tuis.'"

Surrexit ergo David et praecidit oram clamydis Saul silenter; 6 post haec percussit cor suum David, eo quod abscidisset oram clamydis Saul, 7 dixitque ad viros suos, "Propitius mihi sit Dominus, ne faciam hanc rem domino meo, christo Domini, ut mittam manum meam in eum, quoniam christus Domini est." 8 Et confregit David viros suos sermonibus et non permisit eos ut consurgerent in Saul. Porro Saul, exsurgens de spelunca, pergebat coepto itinere. 9 Surrexit autem et David post eum et egressus de spelunca clamavit post tergum Saul, dicens, "Domine mi, rex!" Et respexit Saul post se, et inclinans se David pronus in terram adoravit 10 dixitque ad Saul, "Quare audis verba hominum loquentium David quaerit malum adversum te? 11 Ecce: hodie viderunt oculi tui quod tradiderit te Dominus in manu mea in spelunca, et cogitavi ut occiderem te, sed pepercit tibi oculus meus, dixi enim, 'Non extendam manum meam in domino meo, quia christus Domini est.' 12 Quin potius, pater mi, vide, et cognosce, oram clamydis tuae in manu mea quoniam cum praeciderem summitatem clamydis tuae nolui extendere manum meam in te. Animadverte, et vide quoniam non est in manu mea malum neque iniquitas, neque peccavi in te, tu autem insidiaris animae meae ut auferas eam. 13 Iudicet Dominus inter me et te, et ulciscatur me Dominus ex te, manus autem mea non sit in te. 14 Sicut et in proverbio antiquo dicitur, 'Ab impiis egredietur impietas,' manus ergo mea non sit in te. 15 Quem persequeris, rex Israhel? Quem persequeris? Canem mortuum persequeris et

of which the Lord said to thee, 'I will deliver thy enemy unto thee that thou mayest do to him as it shall seem good in thy eyes.'"

Then David arose and *secretly* cut off the hem of Saul's robe, 6 after *which* David's heart struck him, because he had cut off the hem of Saul's robe, 7 and he said to his men, "The Lord be merciful unto me, that I may do no such thing to my master, the Lord's anointed, as to lay my hand upon him, because he is the Lord's anointed." 8 And David stopped his men with his words and suffered them not to rise against Saul. But Saul, rising up out of the cave, went on his *way*. 9 And David also rose up after him and going out of the cave cried after Saul, saying, "My lord, the king!" And Saul looked behind him, and David bowing himself down to the ground worshipped 10 and said to Saul, "Why dost thou hear the words of men that say David seeketh *thy hurt?* 11 Behold: this day thy eyes have seen that the Lord hath delivered thee into my hand in the cave, and I had a thought to kill thee, but my eye hath spared thee, for I said, 'I will not put out my hand against my lord, because he is the Lord's anointed.' 12 Moreover, see, and know, O my father, the hem of thy robe in my hand that when I cut off the hem of thy robe I would not put out my hand against thee. Reflect, and see that there is no evil in my hand nor iniquity, neither have I sinned against thee, but thou liest in wait for my life to take it away. 13 The Lord judge between me and thee, and the Lord revenge me of thee, but *my hand shall not be* upon thee. 14 As also it is said in the old proverb, 'From the wicked shall wickedness come forth,' therefore *my hand shall not be* upon thee. 15 *After* whom dost thou *come out,* O king of Israel? *After* whom dost thou pursue? *After* a dead dog; *after* a

pulicem unum. 16 Sit Dominus iudex, et iudicet inter me et te, et videat, et diiudicet causam meam, et eruat me de manu tua."

17 Cum autem conplesset David loquens sermones huiuscemodi ad Saul, dixit Saul, "Numquid vox haec tua est, fili mi David?" Et levavit Saul vocem suam et flevit. 18 Dixitque ad David, "Iustior tu es quam ego, tu enim tribuisti mihi bona, ego autem reddidi tibi mala. 19 Et tu indicasti hodie quae feceris mihi bona, quomodo tradiderit me Dominus in manum tuam et non occideris me, 20 quis enim cum invenerit inimicum suum dimittet eum in via bona? Sed Dominus reddat tibi vicissitudinem hanc, pro eo quod hodie operatus es in me. 21 Et nunc quia scio quod certissime regnaturus sis et habiturus in manu tua regnum Israhel, 22 iura mihi in Domino ne deleas semen meum post me neque auferas nomen meum de domo patris mei." 23 Et iuravit David Sauli, abiit ergo Saul in domum suam, et David et viri eius ascenderunt ad tutiora loca.

flea. 16 Be the Lord judge, and judge between me and thee, and see, and judge my cause, and deliver me out of thy hand."

17 And when David had made an end of speaking *these* words to Saul, Saul said, "Is this thy voice, my son David?" And Saul lifted up his voice and wept. 18 And he said to David, "Thou art more just than I, for thou hast done good to me, and I have rewarded thee with evil. 19 And thou hast shown this day what good things thou hast done to me, how the Lord delivered me into thy hand and thou hast not killed me, 20 for who when he hath found his enemy will let him go *well away?* But the Lord reward thee for this good turn, for what thou hast done to me this day. 21 And now as I know that thou shalt surely be king and have the kingdom of Israel in thy hand, 22 swear to me by the Lord that thou wilt not destroy my seed after me nor take away my name from the house of my father." 23 And David swore to Saul, so Saul went home, and David and his men went up into safer places.

Caput 25

Mortuus est autem Samuhel, et congregatus est universus Israhel, et planxerunt eum et sepelierunt in domo sua in Rama. Consurgensque David descendit in desertum Pharan. 2 Erat autem vir quispiam in solitudine Maon, et possessio eius in Carmelo, et homo ille magnus nimis, erantque ei oves tria milia et mille caprae, et accidit ut tonderetur grex eius in Carmelo. 3 Nomen autem viri illius erat Nabal, et nomen uxoris eius Abigail. Eratque mulier illa prudentissima et speciosa, porro vir eius durus et pessimus et malitiosus, erat autem de genere Chaleb. 4 Cum ergo audisset David in deserto quod tonderet Nabal gregem suum, 5 misit decem iuvenes et dixit eis, "Ascendite in Carmelum, et venietis ad Nabal, et salutabitis eum ex nomine meo pacifice, 6 et dicetis, 'Sit fratribus meis et tibi pax, et domui tuae pax, et omnibus quaecumque habes sit pax. 7 Audivi quod tonderent pastores tui qui erant nobiscum in deserto. Numquam eis molesti fuimus, nec aliquando defuit eis quicquam de grege omni tempore quo fuerunt nobiscum in Carmelo. 8 Interroga pueros tuos, et indicabunt tibi. Nunc, ergo, inveniant pueri tui gratiam in oculis tuis, in die enim bona venimus. Quodcumque invenerit manus tua da servis tuis et filio tuo

Chapter 25

The death of Samuel. David, provoked by Nabal, threateneth to destroy him but is appeased by Abigail.

And Samuel died, and all Israel was gathered together, and they mourned for him and buried him in his house in Ramah. And David rose and went down into the wilderness of Paran. 2 Now there was a certain man in the wilderness of Maon, and his *possessions were* in Carmel, and the man was very great, and he had three thousand sheep and a thousand goats, and it happened that he was shearing his *sheep* in Carmel. 3 Now the name of the man was Nabal, and the name of his wife was Abigail. And she was a *prudent and very comely* woman, but her husband was churlish and very bad and ill-natured, and he was of the house of Caleb. 4 And when David heard in the wilderness that Nabal was shearing his sheep, 5 he sent ten young men and said to them, "Go up to Carmel, and *go* to Nabal, and *salute* him in my name with peace, 6 and you shall say, 'Peace be to my brethren and to thee, and peace to thy house, and peace to all that thou hast. 7 I heard that thy shepherds that were with us in the desert were shearing. We never molested them, neither was there ought missing to them of the flock at any time all the while they were with us in Carmel. 8 Ask thy servants, and they will tell thee. Now, therefore, let thy servants find favour in thy eyes, for we are come in a good day. Whatsoever thy

David.'" 9 Cumque venissent pueri David, locuti sunt ad Nabal omnia verba haec ex nomine David et siluerunt.

10 Respondens autem Nabal pueris David ait, "Quis est David? Et quis est filius Isai? Hodie increverunt servi qui fugiunt dominos suos. 11 Tollam ergo panes meos et aquas meas et carnes pecorum, quae occidi tonsoribus meis, et dabo viris quos nescio unde sint?" 12 Regressi sunt itaque pueri David per viam suam et reversi venerunt et nuntiaverunt ei omnia verba quae dixerat.

13 Tunc David ait pueris suis, "Accingatur unusquisque gladio suo." Et accincti sunt singuli gladio suo. Accinctusque est et David ense suo, et secuti sunt David quasi quadringenti viri, porro ducenti remanserunt ad sarcinas.

14 Abigail autem, uxori Nabal, nuntiavit unus de pueris suis, dicens, "Ecce: misit David nuntios de deserto ut benedicerent domino nostro, et aversatus est eos. 15 Homines isti boni satis fuerunt nobis et non molesti, nec quicquam aliquando periit omni tempore quo sumus conversati cum eis in deserto. 16 Pro muro erant nobis tam in nocte quam in die; omnibus diebus quibus pavimus apud eos greges. 17 Quam ob rem considera, et recogita quid facias, quoniam conpleta est malitia adversum virum tuum et adversus domum tuam, et ipse filius est Belial, ita ut nemo ei possit loqui.

18 Festinavit igitur Abigail et tulit ducentos panes et duos utres vini et quinque arietes coctos et quinque sata pulentae et centum ligaturas uvae passae et ducentas massas carica-

hand shall find give to thy servants and to thy son David.'"
9 And when David's servants came, they spoke to Nabal all these words in David's name and then held their peace.

10 But Nabal, answering the servants of David, said, "Who is David? And what is the son of Jesse? Servants are multiplied nowadays who flee from their masters. 11 Shall I then take my bread and my water and the flesh of my cattle, which I have killed for my shearers, and give to men whom I know not whence they are?" 12 So the servants of David went back their way and returning came and told him all the words that he said.

13 Then David said to his young men, "Let every man gird on his sword." And they girded on every man his sword, and David also girded on his sword, and there followed David about four hundred men, and two hundred remained with the baggage.

14 But one of the servants told Abigail, the wife of Nabal, saying, "Behold: David sent messengers out of the wilderness to salute our master, and he rejected them. 15 These men were *very* good to us and *gave us no trouble,* neither did we ever lose any thing all the time that we conversed with them in the desert. 16 They were a wall unto us both by night and day; all the while we *were* with them *keeping the sheep.* 17 Wherefore consider, and think what thou hast to do, for evil is determined against thy husband and against thy house, and he is a son of Belial, so that no man can speak to him."

18 Then Abigail made haste and took two hundred loaves and two vessels of wine and five sheep ready dressed and five measures of parched corn and a hundred clusters of raisins and two hundred cakes of dry figs and laid them upon

rum et inposuit super asinos, 19 dixitque pueris suis, "Praecedite me. Ecce: ego post tergum sequar vos," viro autem
suo, Nabal, non indicavit.

20 Cum ergo ascendisset asinum et descenderet ad radices
montis, David et viri eius descendebant in occursum eius,
quibus et illa occurrit. 21 Et ait David, "Vere frustra servavi
omnia quae huius erant in deserto, et non periit quicquam
de cunctis quae ad eum pertinebant, et reddidit mihi malum
pro bono. 22 Haec faciat Deus inimicis David et haec addat
si reliquero de omnibus quae ad eum pertinent usque mane
mingentem ad parietem."

23 Cum autem vidisset Abigail David festinavit et descendit de asino et procidit coram David super faciem suam et
adoravit super terram. 24 Et cecidit ad pedes eius et dixit,
"In me sit, domine mi, haec iniquitas; loquatur, obsecro, ancilla tua in auribus tuis, et audi verba famulae tuae. 25 Ne ponat, oro, dominus meus, rex, cor suum super virum istum
iniquum Nabal, quia secundum nomen suum stultus est, et
est stultitia cum eo, ego autem, ancilla tua, non vidi pueros
tuos, domine mi, quos misisti. 26 Nunc, ergo, domine mi, vivit Dominus, et vivit anima tua, qui prohibuit te ne venires
in sanguine et salvavit manum tuam tibi. Et nunc fiant sicut
Nabal inimici tui et qui quaerunt domino meo malum.
27 Quapropter, suscipe benedictionem hanc quam adtulit
ancilla tua tibi, domino meo, et da pueris qui sequuntur te,
dominum meum. 28 Aufer iniquitatem famulae tuae, faciens
enim faciet tibi Dominus domino meo domum fidelem, quia
proelia Domini, domine mi, tu proeliaris. Malitia, ergo, non
inveniatur in te omnibus diebus vitae tuae. 29 Si enim sur-
rexerit aliquando homo persequens te et quaerens animam

asses, 19 and she said to her servants, "Go before me. Behold: I will follow *after you,*" but she told not her husband, Nabal.

20 And when she had gotten upon an ass and was coming down to the foot of the mountain, David and his men came down over against her, and she met them. 21 And David said, "Truly in vain have I kept all that belonged to this man in the wilderness, and nothing was lost of all that pertained unto him, and he hath returned me evil for good. 22 May God do so and so and add more to the foes of David if I leave of all that belong to him till the morning any that pisseth against the wall."

23 And when Abigail saw David she made haste and lighted off the ass and fell before David on her face and adored upon the ground. 24 And she fell at his feet and said, "Upon me let this iniquity be, my lord; let thy handmaid speak, I beseech thee, in thy ears, and hear the words of thy servant. 25 Let not my lord, the king, I pray, *regard* this naughty man Nabal, for according to his name he is a fool, and folly is with him, but I, thy handmaid, did not see thy servants, my lord, whom thou sentest. 26 Now, therefore, my lord, the Lord liveth, and thy soul liveth, who hath withholden thee from coming to blood and hath saved thy hand to thee. And now let thy enemies be as Nabal and *all* they that seek evil to my lord. 27 Wherefore, receive this blessing which thy handmaid hath brought to thee, my lord, and give it to the young men that follow thee, my lord. 28 Forgive the iniquity of thy handmaid, for the Lord will *surely* make for my lord a faithful house, because thou, my lord, fightest the battles of the Lord. Let not evil, therefore, be found in thee all the days of thy life. 29 For if a man at any time shall rise and persecute thee and seek thy life, the soul of my lord shall

tuam, erit anima domini mei custodita quasi in fasciculo viventium apud Dominum, Deum tuum, porro anima inimicorum tuorum rotabitur quasi in impetu et circulo fundae. 30 Cum ergo fecerit tibi Dominus, domino meo, omnia quae locutus est bona de te et constituerit te ducem super Israhel, 31 non erit tibi hoc in singultum et in scrupulum cordis domino meo quod effuderis sanguinem innoxium aut ipse te ultus fueris. Et cum benefecerit Dominus domino meo, recordaberis ancillae tuae."

32 Et ait David ad Abigail, "Benedictus Dominus, Deus Israhel, qui misit te hodie in occursum meum, et benedictum eloquium tuum, 33 et benedicta tu quae prohibuisti me hodie ne irem ad sanguinem et ulciscerer me manu mea. 34 Alioquin, vivit Dominus, Deus Israhel, qui prohibuit me ne malum facerem tibi, nisi cito venisses in occursum mihi, non remansisset Nabal usque ad lucem matutinam mingens ad parietem." 35 Suscepit ergo David de manu eius omnia quae adtulerat ei dixitque ei, "Vade pacifice in domum tuam. Ecce: audivi vocem tuam et honoravi faciem tuam."

36 Venit autem Abigail ad Nabal, et ecce: erat ei convivium in domo eius quasi convivium regis, et cor Nabal iucundum, erat enim ebrius nimis, et non indicavit ei verbum pusillum aut grande usque in mane. 37 Diluculo autem cum digessisset vinum Nabal, indicavit ei uxor sua verba haec, et emortuum est cor eius intrinsecus, et factus est quasi lapis. 38 Cumque pertransissent decem dies, percussit Dominus Nabal, et mortuus est. 39 Quod cum audisset David mortuum Nabal, ait, "Benedictus Dominus, qui iudicavit causam obprobrii mei de manu Nabal et servum suum custodivit a malo,

be kept as in the bundle of the living with the Lord, thy God, but the *souls* of thy enemies shall be whirled as with the violence and whirling of a sling. 30 And when the Lord shall have done to thee, my lord, all the good that he hath spoken concerning thee and shall have made thee prince over Israel, 31 This shall not be an occasion of *grief* to thee and a scruple of heart to my lord that thou hast shed innocent blood or hast revenged thyself. And when the Lord shall have done well by my lord, thou shalt remember thy handmaid."

32 And David said to Abigail, "Blessed be the Lord, the God of Israel, who sent thee this day to meet me, and blessed be thy speech, 33 and blessed be thou who hast kept me today from coming to blood and revenging me with my own hand. 34 Otherwise, as the Lord liveth, the God of Israel, who hath withholden me from doing thee any evil, if thou hadst not quickly come to meet me, there had not been left to Nabal by the morning light any that pisseth against the wall." 35 And David received at her hand all that she had brought him and said to her, "Go in peace into thy house. Behold: I have heard thy voice and have honoured thy face."

36 And Abigail came to Nabal, and behold: he had a feast in his house like the feast of a king, and Nabal's heart was merry, for he was very drunk, and she told him nothing less or more until morning. 37 But early in the morning when Nabal had digested his wine, his wife told him these words, and his heart died within him, and he became as a stone. 38 And after ten days had passed, the Lord struck Nabal, and he died. 39 And when David had heard that Nabal was dead, he said, "Blessed be the Lord, who hath judged the cause of my reproach at the hand of Nabal and hath kept his servant

et malitiam Nabal reddidit Dominus in caput eius." Misit ergo David et locutus est ad Abigail ut sumeret eam sibi in uxorem.

40 Et venerunt pueri David ad Abigail in Carmelum et locuti sunt ad eam, dicentes, "David misit nos ad te ut accipiat te sibi in uxorem."

41 Quae consurgens adoravit prona in terram et ait, "Ecce: famula tua sit in ancillam ut lavet pedes servorum domini mei." 42 Et festinavit et surrexit Abigail et ascendit super asinum, et quinque puellae ierunt cum ea, pedisequae eius, et secuta est nuntios David et facta est illi uxor. 43 Sed et Ahinoem accepit David de Iezrahel, et fuit utraque uxor eius. 44 Saul autem dedit Michol, filiam suam, uxorem David, Falti, filio Lais, qui erat de Gallim.

Caput 26

Et venerunt Ziphei ad Saul in Gabaa, dicentes, "Ecce: David absconditus est in colle Achilae, quae est ex adverso solitudinis."

from evil, and the Lord hath returned the wickedness of Nabal upon his head." Then David sent and *treated with* Abigail that he might take her to himself for a wife.

40 And David's servants came to Abigail to Carmel and spoke to her, saying, "David hath sent us to thee to take thee to himself for a wife."

41 And she arose and bowed herself down with her face to the earth and said, "Behold: let thy servant be a handmaid to wash the feet of the servants of my lord." 42 And Abigail arose and made haste and got upon an ass, and five damsels went with her, her waiting maids, and she followed the messengers of David and became his wife. 43 Moreover David took also Ahinoam of Jezreel, and they were both of them his wives. 44 But Saul gave Michal, his daughter, David's wife, to Palti, the son of Laish, who was of Gallim.

Chapter 26

Saul goeth out again after David, who cometh by night
where Saul and his men are asleep but suffereth him not to
be touched. Saul again confesseth his fault and promiseth
peace.

And the men of Ziph came to Saul in Gibeah, saying, "Behold: David is hid in the hill of Hachilah, which is over against the wilderness."

2 Et surrexit Saul et descendit in desertum Ziph et cum eo tria milia virorum de electis Israhel ut quaereret David in deserto Ziph. 3 Et castrametatus est Saul in Gabaa Achilae quae erat ex adverso solitudinis in via, David autem habitabat in deserto. Videns autem quod venisset Saul post se in desertum, 4 misit exploratores et didicit quod illuc venisset certissime. 5 Et surrexit David clam et venit ad locum ubi erat Saul, cumque vidisset locum in quo dormiebat Saul et Abner, filius Ner, princeps militiae eius, et Saulem dormientem in tentorio et reliquum vulgus per circuitum eius, 6 ait David ad Ahimelech, Cettheum, et Abisai, filium Sarviae, fratrem Ioab, dicens, "Quis descendet mecum ad Saul in castra?"

Dixitque Abisai, "Ego descendam tecum." 7 Venerunt ergo David et Abisai ad populum nocte et invenerunt Saul iacentem et dormientem in tentorio et hastam fixam in terra ad caput eius Abner autem et populum dormientes in circuitu eius. 8 Dixitque Abisai ad David, "Conclusit Deus hodie inimicum tuum in manus tuas. Nunc ergo perfodiam eum lancea in terra semel, et secundo opus non erit."

9 Et dixit David ad Abisai, "Ne interficias eum, quis enim extendet manum suam in christum Domini et innocens erit?" 10 Et dixit David, "Vivit Dominus, quia nisi Dominus percusserit eum aut dies eius venerit ut moriatur aut in proelium descendens perierit, 11 propitius mihi sit Dominus ne extendam manum meam in christum Domini. Nunc, igitur, tolle hastam quae est ad caput eius et scyphum aquae, et abeamus." 12 Tulit ergo David hastam et scyphum aquae qui erat ad caput Saul, et abierunt, et non erat quisquam qui

2 And Saul arose and went down to the wilderness of Ziph having with him three thousand chosen men of Israel to seek David in the wilderness of Ziph. 3 And Saul encamped in Gibeah Hachilah which was over against the wilderness in the way, and David abode in the wilderness. And seeing that Saul was come after him into the wilderness, 4 he sent spies and learned that he was most certainly come thither. 5 And David arose secretly and came to the place where Saul was, and when he had beheld the place wherein Saul slept and Abner, the son of Ner, the captain of his army, and Saul sleeping in a tent and the rest of the multitude round about him, 6 David spoke to Ahimelech, the Hittite, and Abishai, the son of Zeruiah, the brother of Joab, saying, "Who will go down with me to Saul into the camp?"

And Abishai said, "I will go with thee." 7 So David and Abishai came to the people by night and found Saul lying and sleeping in the tent and his spear fixed in the ground at his head and Abner and the people sleeping round about him. 8 And Abishai said to David, "God hath shut up thy enemy this day into thy hands. Now then I will run him through with my spear *even to* the earth at once, and there shall be no need of a second time."

9 And David said to Abishai, "Kill him not, for who shall put forth his hand against the Lord's anointed and shall be guiltless?" 10 And David said, "As the Lord liveth, unless the Lord shall strike him or his day shall come to die or he shall go down to battle and perish, 11 the Lord be merciful unto me that I extend not my hand upon the Lord's anointed. But now take the spear which is at his head and the cup of water, and let us go." 12 So David took the spear and the cup of water which was at Saul's head, and they went away, and no man

videret et intellegeret aut vigilaret, sed omnes dormiebant, quia sopor Domini inruerat super eos.

13 Cumque transisset David ex adverso et stetisset in vertice montis de longe et esset grande intervallum inter eos, 14 clamavit David ad populum et ad Abner, filium Ner, dicens, "Nonne respondebis, Abner?"

Et respondens Abner ait, "Quis es tu qui clamas et inquietas regem?"

15 Et ait David ad Abner, "Numquid non vir tu es? Et quis similis tui in Israhel? Quare ergo non custodisti dominum tuum, regem? Ingressus est enim unus de turba ut interficeret regem, dominum tuum. 16 Non est bonum hoc quod fecisti. Vivit Dominus, quoniam filii mortis estis vos qui non custodistis dominum vestrum, christum Domini. Nunc ergo vide ubi sit hasta regis et ubi sit scyphus aquae qui erat ad caput eius."

17 Cognovit autem Saul vocem David et dixit, "Num vox tua est haec, fili mi David?"

Et ait David, "Vox mea, domine mi, rex."

18 Et ait, "Quam ob causam dominus meus persequitur servum suum? Quid feci? Aut quod est in manu mea malum? 19 Nunc, ergo, audi, oro, domine mi, rex, verba servi tui: si Dominus incitat te adversum me, odoretur sacrificium, si autem filii hominum, maledicti sunt in conspectu Domini qui eiecerunt me hodie ut non habitem in hereditate Domini, dicentes, 'Vade; servi diis alienis.' 20 Et nunc non effundatur sanguis meus in terra coram Domino, quia egressus est rex Israhel ut quaerat pulicem unum sicut persequitur perdix in montibus."

21 Et ait Saul, "Peccavi; revertere, fili mi David, nequaquam enim ultra male tibi faciam eo quod pretiosa fuerit

saw it *or* knew it or awaked, but they were all asleep, for a deep sleep from the Lord was fallen upon them.

13 And when David was gone over to the other side and stood on the top of the hill afar off and a good space was between them, 14 David cried to the people and to Abner, the son of Ner, saying, "Wilt thou not answer, Abner?"

And Abner answering said, "Who art thou that criest and disturbest the king?"

15 And David said to Abner, "Art not thou a man? And who is like thee in Israel? Why then hast thou not kept thy lord, the king? For there came one of the people in to kill the king, thy lord. 16 This thing is not good that thou hast done. As the Lord liveth, you are the sons of death who have not kept your master, the Lord's anointed. And now *where* is the king's spear and *the cup of water* which was at his head?"

17 And Saul knew David's voice and said, "Is this thy voice, my son David?"

And David said, "It is my voice, my lord, the king."

18 And he said, "Wherefore doth my lord persecute his servant? What have I done? Or what evil is there in my hand? 19 Now, therefore, hear, I pray thee, my lord, the king, the words of thy servant: if the Lord stir thee up against me, let *him accept* of sacrifice, but if the sons of men, they are cursed in the sight of the Lord who have cast me out this day that I should not dwell in the inheritance of the Lord, saying, 'Go; serve strange gods.' 20 And now let not my blood be shed upon the earth before the Lord, for the king of Israel is come out to seek a flea as the partridge is hunted in the mountains."

21 And Saul said, "I have sinned; return, my son David, for I will no more do thee harm because my life hath been pre-

anima mea in oculis tuis hodie; apparet enim quod stulte egerim et ignoraverim multa nimis."

22 Et respondens David ait, "Ecce hasta regis: transeat unus de pueris regis et tollat eam. 23 Dominus autem retribuet unicuique secundum iustitiam suam et fidem, tradidit enim te Dominus hodie in manum meam, et nolui extendere manum meam in christum Domini. 24 Et sicuti magnificata est anima tua hodie in oculis meis, sic magnificetur anima mea in oculis Domini, et liberet me de omni angustia."

25 Ait ergo Saul ad David, "Benedictus tu, fili mi David, et quidem faciens facies, et potens poteris." Abiit autem David in viam suam, et Saul reversus est in locum suum.

Caput 27

Et ait David in corde suo, "Aliquando incidam uno die in manus Saul; nonne melius est ut fugiam et salver in terra Philisthinorum ut desperet Saul cessetque me quaerere in cunctis finibus Israhel? Fugiam ergo manus eius." 2 Et surrexit David et abiit, ipse et sescenti viri cum eo ad Achis, fi-

cious in thy eyes this day, for it appeareth that I have done foolishly and have been ignorant in very many things."

22 And David answering said, "Behold the king's spear: let one of the king's servants come over and fetch it. 23 And the Lord will reward every one according to his justice and his faithfulness, for the Lord hath delivered thee this day into my hand, and I would not put forth my hand against the Lord's anointed. 24 And as thy life hath been *much set by* this day in my eyes, so let my life be *much set by* in the eyes of the Lord, and let him deliver me from all distress."

25 Then Saul said to David, "Blessed art thou, my son David, and truly doing thou shalt do, and prevailing thou shalt prevail." And David went on his way, and Saul returned to his place.

Chapter 27

David goeth again to Achish, king of Gath, and obtaineth of him the city of Ziklag.

And David said in his heart, "I shall *one day or other* fall into the hands of Saul; is it not better for me to flee and to be saved in the land of the Philistines that Saul may despair *of me* and cease to seek me in all the coasts of Israel? I will flee then out of his hands." 2 And David arose and went away, *both* he and the six hundred men that were with him, to Ach-

lium Mahoc, regem Geth. 3 Et habitavit David cum Achis in Geth, ipse et viri eius, vir et domus eius, et duae uxores eius, Ahinoem, Iezrahelites, et Abigail, uxor Nabal Carmeli. 4 Et nuntiatum est Saul quod fugisset David in Geth, et non addidit ultra ut quaereret eum.

5 Dixit autem David ad Achis, "Si inveni gratiam in oculis tuis, detur mihi locus in una urbium regionis huius ut habitem ibi, cur enim manet servus tuus in civitate regis tecum?" 6 Dedit itaque ei Achis in die illa Siceleg, propter quam causam facta est Siceleg regum Iuda usque in diem hanc. 7 Fuit autem numerus dierum quibus habitavit David in regione Philisthinorum quattuor mensuum. 8 Et ascendit David et viri eius et agebant praedas de Gesuri et de Gedri et de Amalechitis, hii enim pagi habitabantur in terra antiquitus euntibus Sur usque ad terram Aegypti. 9 Et percutiebat David omnem terram nec relinquebat viventem virum et mulierem tollensque oves et boves et asinos et camelos et vestes revertebatur et veniebat ad Achis.

10 Dicebat autem ei Achis, "In quem inruisti hodie?"

Respondebat David, "Contra meridiem Iudae et contra meridiem Hiramel et contra meridiem Ceni." 11 Virum et mulierem non vivificabat David, nec adducebat in Geth, dicens, "Ne forte loquantur adversum nos." Haec fecit David, et hoc erat decretum illi omnibus diebus quibus habitavit in regione Philisthinorum.

12 Credidit ergo Achis David, dicens, "Multa mala operatus est contra populum suum Israhel, erit igitur mihi servus sempiternus."

ish, the son of Maoch, king of Gath. 3 And David dwelt with Achish at Gath, he and his men, every man *with* his household *and David with* his two wives, Ahinoam, the Jezreelitess, and Abigail, the wife of Nabal of Carmel. 4 And it was told Saul that David was fled to Gath, and he sought no more after him.

5 And David said to Achish, "If I have found favour in thy sight, let a place be given me in one of the cities of this country that I may dwell there, for why should thy servant dwell in the royal city with thee?" 6 Then Achish gave him Ziklag that day, for which reason Ziklag *belongeth to* the kings of Judah unto this day. 7 And the *time* that David dwelt in the country of the Philistines was four months. 8 And David and his men went up and *pillaged* Geshur and Gerzi and the Amalekites, for these were of old the inhabitants of the *countries* as men go to Shur even to the land of Egypt. 9 And David wasted all the land and left neither man *nor* woman *alive* and took away the sheep and the oxen and the asses and the camels and the apparel and returned and came to Achish.

10 And Achish said to him, "Whom hast thou gone against today?"

David answered, "Against the south of Judah and against the south of Jerahmeel and against the south of Ceni." 11 And David *saved* neither man nor woman, neither brought he any of them to Gath, saying, "Lest they should speak against us." So did David, and *such was his proceeding* all the days that he dwelt in the country of the Philistines.

12 And Achish believed David, saying, "He hath done *much harm* to his people Israel, therefore he shall be my servant for ever."

Caput 28

Factum est autem in diebus illis congregaverunt Philisthim agmina sua ut praepararentur ad bellum contra Israhel. Dixitque Achis ad David, "Sciens nunc scito quoniam mecum egredieris in castris, tu et viri tui."

2 Dixitque David ad Achis, "Nunc scies quae facturus est servus tuus."

Et ait Achis ad David, "Et ego custodem capitis mei ponam te cunctis diebus."

3 Samuhel autem mortuus est, planxitque eum omnis Israhel et sepelierunt eum in Rama, urbe sua. Et Saul abstulit magos et ariolos de terra, 4 congregatique sunt Philisthim et venerunt et castrametati sunt in Sunam. Congregavit autem et Saul universum Israhel et venit in Gelboe. 5 Et vidit Saul castra Philisthim et timuit, et expavit cor eius nimis, 6 consuluitque Dominum, et non respondit ei, neque per somnia neque per sacerdotes neque per prophetas. 7 Dixitque Saul servis suis, "Quaerite mihi mulierem habentem pythonem, et vadam ad eam et sciscitabor per illam."

Et dixerunt servi eius ad eum, "Est mulier habens pythonem in Aendor."

Chapter 28

The Philistines go out to war against Israel. Saul being forsaken by God hath recourse to a witch. Samuel appeareth to him.

And it came to pass in those days that the Philistines gathered together their armies to be prepared for war against Israel. And Achish said to David, "Know thou now *assuredly* that thou shalt go out with me *to the war,* thou and thy men."

2 And David said to Achish, "Now thou shalt know what thy servant will do."

And Achish said to David, "And I will appoint thee *to guard my life* for ever."

3 Now Samuel was dead, and all Israel mourned for him and buried him in Ramah, his city. And Saul had put away all the magicians and soothsayers out of the land, 4 and the Philistines were gathered together and came and camped in Shunem. And Saul also gathered together all Israel and came to Gilboa. 5 And Saul saw the *army* of the Plilistines and was afraid, and his heart was very much dismayed, 6 and he consulted the Lord, and he answered him not, neither by dreams nor by priests nor by prophets. 7 And Saul said to his servants, "Seek me a woman that hath a divining spirit, and I will go to her and inquire by her."

And his servants said to him, "There is a woman that hath a divining spirit at Endor."

8 Mutavit ergo habitum suum vestitusque est aliis vestimentis, et abiit ipse et duo viri cum eo, veneruntque ad mulierem nocte, et ait illi, "Divina mihi in pythone, et suscita
mihi quem dixero tibi."

9 Et ait mulier ad eum, "Ecce: tu nosti quanta fecerit Saul
et quomodo eraserit magos et ariolos de terra. Quare ergo
insidiaris animae meae ut occidar?"

10 Et iuravit ei Saul in Domino, dicens, "Vivit Dominus,
quia non eveniet tibi quicquam mali propter hanc rem."

11 Dixitque ei mulier, "Quem suscitabo tibi?"

Qui ait, "Samuhelem suscita mihi."

12 Cum autem vidisset mulier Samuhelem, exclamavit
voce magna et dixit ad Saul, "Quare inposuisti mihi? Tu es
enim Saul."

13 Dixitque ei rex, "Noli timere; quid vidisti?"

Et ait mulier ad Saul, "Deos vidi ascendentes de terra."

14 Dixitque ei, "Qualis est forma eius?"

Quae ait, "Vir senex ascendit, et ipse amictus est pallio."

Et intellexit Saul quod Samuhel esset, et inclinavit se super faciem suam in terra et adoravit. 15 Dixit autem Samuhel
ad Saul, "Quare inquietasti me ut suscitarer?"

Et ait Saul, "Coartor nimis, siquidem Philisthim pugnant
adversum me, et Deus recessit a me et exaudire me noluit,

8 Then he *disguised himself* and put on other clothes, and he went and two men with him, and they came to the woman by night, and he said to her, "Divine to me by *thy divining* spirit, and bring me up him whom I shall tell thee."

9 And the woman said to him, "Behold: thou knowest *all that* Saul hath done and how he hath rooted out the magicians and soothsayers from the land. Why then dost thou lay a snare for my life to cause me to be put to death?"

10 And Saul swore unto her by the Lord, saying, "As the Lord liveth, there shall no evil happen to thee for this thing."

11 And the woman said to him, "Whom shall I bring up to thee?"

And he said, "Bring me up Samuel."

12 And when the woman saw Samuel, she cried out with a loud voice and said to Saul, "Why hast thou deceived me? For thou art Saul."

13 And the king said to her, "Fear not; what hast thou seen?"

And the woman said to Saul, "I saw gods ascending out of the earth."

14 And he said to her, "What form is he of?"

And she said, "An old man cometh up, and he is covered with a mantle."

And Saul understood that it was Samuel, and he bowed himself *with* his face *to* the ground and adored. 15 And Samuel said to Saul, "Why hast thou disturbed *my rest* that I should be brought up?"

And Saul said, "I am in great distress, for the Philistines fight against me, and God is departed from me and would not hear me, neither by the hand of prophets nor by dreams.

neque in manu prophetarum neque per somnia. Vocavi ergo te ut ostenderes mihi quid faciam."

16 Et ait Samuhel, "Quid interrogas me, cum Dominus recesserit a te et transierit ad aemulum tuum? 17 Faciet enim Dominus tibi sicut locutus est in manu mea, et scindet regnum tuum de manu tua et dabit illud proximo tuo David 18 quia non oboedisti voci Domini, neque fecisti iram furoris eius in Amalech. Idcirco quod pateris fecit tibi Dominus hodie. 19 Et dabit Dominus etiam Israhel tecum in manus Philisthim, cras autem tu et filii tui mecum eritis, sed et castra Israhel tradet Dominus in manus Philisthim."

20 Statimque Saul cecidit porrectus in terram, extimuerat enim verba Samuhel, et robur non erat in eo, quia non comederat panem tota die illa. 21 Ingressa est itaque mulier illa ad Saul, conturbatus enim erat valde, dixitque ad eum, "Ecce! Oboedivit ancilla tua voci tuae, et posui animam meam in manu mea, et audivi sermones tuos quos locutus es ad me. 22 Nunc, igitur, audi et tu vocem ancillae tuae, et ponam coram te buccellam panis ut comedens convalescas et possis iter agere."

23 Qui rennuit et ait, "Non comedam." Coegerunt autem eum servi sui et mulier, et tandem audita voce eorum surrexit de terra et sedit super lectum. 24 Mulier autem illa habebat vitulum pascualem in domo, et festinavit et occidit

Therefore I have called thee that thou mayest show me what I shall do."

16 And Samuel said, "Why askest thou me, seeing the Lord has departed from thee and is gone over to thy rival? 17 For the Lord will do to thee as he spoke *by me,* and he will rend thy kingdom out of thy hand and will give it to thy neighbour David 18 because thou didst not obey the voice of the Lord, neither didst thou execute the wrath of his indignation upon Amalek. Therefore hath the Lord done to thee what thou sufferest this day. 19 And the Lord also will deliver Israel with thee into the hands of the Philistines, and tomorrow thou and thy sons shall be with me, *and* the Lord will also deliver the *army* of Israel into the hands of the Philistines."

20 And forthwith Saul fell all along on the ground, for he was frightened with the words of Samuel, and there was no strength in him, for he had eaten no bread all that day. 21 And the woman came to Saul, for he was very much troubled, and said to him, "Behold! Thy handmaid hath obeyed thy voice, and I have put my life in my hand, and I hearkened unto the words which thou spokest to me. 22 Now, therefore, hear thou also the voice of thy handmaid, and let me set before thee a morsel of bread that thou mayest eat and recover strength and be able to go on thy journey."

23 But he refused and said, "I will not eat." But his servants and the woman forced him, and at length hearkening to their voice he arose from the ground and sat upon the bed. 24 Now the woman had a fatted calf in the house, and she made haste and killed it and taking meal kneaded it and

nostris? 5 Nonne iste est David cui cantabant in choris, dicentes, 'Percussit Saul in milibus suis et David in decem milibus suis'?"

6 Vocavit ergo Achis David et ait ei, "Vivit Dominus, quia rectus es tu et bonus in conspectu meo, et exitus tuus et introitus tuus mecum est in castris, et non inveni in te quicquam mali ex die qua venisti ad me usque ad diem hanc, sed satrapis non places. 7 Revertere, ergo, et vade in pace, et non offendas oculos satraparum Philisthim."

8 Dixitque David ad Achis, "Quid enim feci, et quid invenisti in me, servo tuo, a die qua fui in conspectu tuo usque in diem hanc ut non veniam et pugnem contra inimicos domini mei, regis?"

9 Respondens autem Achis locutus est ad David, "Scio quia bonus es tu in oculis meis sicut angelus Dei, sed principes Philisthim dixerunt, 'Non ascendet nobiscum in proelium.' 10 Igitur consurge mane, tu et servi domini tui, qui venerunt tecum, et cum de nocte surrexeritis et coeperit dilucescere, pergite." 11 Surrexit itaque de nocte David ipse et viri eius ut proficiscerentur mane et reverterentur ad terram Philisthim, Philisthim autem ascenderunt in Iezrahel.

master but with our heads? 5 Is not this David to whom they sung in their dances, saying, 'Saul slew his thousands and David his ten thousands'?"

6 Then Achish called David and said to him, "As the Lord liveth, thou art upright and good in my sight, and *so* is thy going out and thy coming in with me in the *army,* and I have not found any evil in thee since the day that thou camest to me unto this day, but thou pleasest not the lords. 7 Return, therefore, and go in peace, and offend not the eyes of the princes of the Philistines."

8 And David said to Achish, *"But* what have I done, and what hast thou found in me, thy servant, from the day that I have been in thy sight until this day that I may not go and fight against the enemies of my lord, the king?"

9 And Achish answering said to David, "I know that thou art good in my *sight* as an angel of God, but the princes of the Philistines have said, 'He shall not go up with us to the battle.' 10 Therefore arise in the morning, thou and the servants of thy lord, who came with thee, and when you are up before day and it shall begin to be light, go on your way." 11 So *David and his men arose* in the night that they might set forward in the morning and return to the land of the Philistines, and the Philistines went up to Jezreel.

Caput 30

Cumque venissent David et viri eius in Siceleg die tertia, Amalechitae impetum fecerant ex parte australi in Siceleg et percusserant Siceleg et succenderant eam igni 2 et captivas duxerant mulieres ex ea, a minimo usque ad magnum, et non interfecerant quemquam sed secum duxerant et pergebant in itinere suo. 3 Cum ergo venissent David et viri eius ad civitatem et invenissent eam succensam igni et uxores suas et filios suos et filias ductas esse captivas, 4 levaverunt David et populus qui erat cum eo voces suas et planxerunt donec deficerent in eis lacrimae, 5 siquidem et duae uxores David captivae ductae fuerant, Ahinoem, Iezrahelites, et Abigail, uxor Nabal Carmeli. 6 Et contristatus est David valde, volebat enim eum populus lapidare, quia amara erat anima uniuscuiusque viri super filiis suis et filiabus, confortatus est autem David in Domino, Deo suo, 7 et ait ad Abiathar, sacerdotem, filium Ahimelech, "Adplica ad me ephod." Et adplicuit Abiathar ephod ad David, 8 et consuluit David Dominum, dicens, "Persequar latrunculos hos, et conprehendam eos, an non?"

Dixitque ei Dominus, "Persequere, absque dubio enim conprehendes eos et excuties praedam."

Chapter 30

The Amalekites burn Ziklag and carry off the prey. David
pursueth after them and recovereth all out of their hands.

Now when David and his men were come to Ziklag on
the third day, the Amalekites had made an invasion on the
south side upon Ziklag and had smitten Ziklag and burnt it
with fire 2 and had taken the women captives *that were in*
it, *both* little *and* great, and they had not killed any person
but had carried them with them and went on their way. 3 So
when David and his men came to the city and found it burnt
with fire and that their wives and their sons and their daughters were taken captives, 4 David and the people that were
with him lifted up their voices and wept till they had no
more tears, 5 for the two wives also of David were taken captives, Ahinoam, the Jezreelitess, and Abigail, the wife of
Nabal of Carmel. 6 And David was greatly afflicted, for the
people had a mind to stone him, for the soul of every man
was bitterly *grieved* for his sons and daughters, but David
took courage in the Lord, his God, 7 and he said to Abiathar,
the priest, the son of Ahimelech, *"Bring me hither* the ephod."
And Abiathar brought the ephod to David, 8 and David consulted the Lord, saying, "Shall I pursue *after* these robbers,
and shall I overtake them, or not?"

And the Lord said to him, "Pursue *after them,* for thou
shalt surely overtake them and recover the prey."

9 Abiit ergo David, ipse et sescenti viri qui erant cum eo, et venerunt usque ad Torrentem Besor, et lassi quidam substiterunt. 10 Persecutus est autem David, ipse et quadringenti viri, substiterant enim ducenti qui lassi transire non poterant Torrentem Besor. 11 Et invenerunt virum Aegyptium in agro et adduxerunt eum ad David, dederuntque ei panem ut comederet et ut biberet aquam, 12 sed et fragmen massae caricarum et duas ligaturas uvae passae. Quae cum comedisset, reversus est spiritus eius, et refocilatus est, non enim comederat panem neque biberat aquam tribus diebus et tribus noctibus. 13 Dixit itaque ei David, "Cuius es tu? Vel unde? Et quo pergis?"

Qui ait, "Puer Aegyptius ego sum, servus viri Amalechitae, dereliquit autem me dominus meus quia aegrotare coepi nudius tertius, 14 siquidem nos erupimus ad australem plagam Cerethi et contra Iudam et ad meridiem Chaleb, et Siceleg succendimus igni."

15 Dixitque ei David, "Potes me ducere ad istum cuneum?"

Qui ait, "Iura mihi per Deum quod non occidas me et non tradas me in manus domini mei, et ducam te ad cuneum istum." Et iuravit ei David.

16 Qui cum duxisset eum, ecce: illi discumbebant super faciem universae terrae, comedentes et bibentes et quasi festum celebrantes diem pro cuncta praeda et spoliis quae ceperant de terra Philisthim et de terra Iuda. 17 Et percussit eos David a vespere usque ad vesperam alterius diei, et non evasit ex eis quisquam nisi quadringenti viri adulescentes qui ascenderant camelos et fugerant. 18 Eruit ergo David

9 So David went, he and the six hundred men that were with him, and they came to the Torrent Besor, and some being weary stayed there. 10 But David pursued, he and four hundred men, for two hundred stayed who being weary could not go over the Torrent Besor. 11 And they found an Egyptian in the field and brought him to David, and they gave him bread to eat and water to drink, 12 *as* also a piece of a cake of figs and two bunches of raisins. And when he had eaten them, his spirit returned, and he was refreshed, for he had not eaten bread nor drunk water three days and three nights. 13 And David said to him, "To whom dost thou belong? Or whence *dost thou come? And* whither art thou going?"

He said, "I am a young man of Egypt, the servant of an Amalekite, and my master left me because I began to be sick three days ago, 14 for we made an invasion on the south side of Cherethites and upon Judah and upon the south of Caleb, and we burnt Ziklag with fire."

15 And David said to him, "Canst thou bring me to this company?"

And he said, "Swear to me by God that thou wilt not kill me nor deliver me into the hands of my master, and I will bring thee to this company." And David swore to him.

16 And when he had brought him, behold: they were lying spread upon all the ground, eating and drinking and as it were keeping a festival day for all the prey and the spoils which they had taken out of the land of the Philistines and out of the land of Judah. 17 And David slew them from the evening unto the evening of the next day, and there escaped not a man of them but four hundred young men who had gotten upon camels and fled. 18 So David recovered all that

omnia quae tulerant Amalechitae, et duas uxores suas eruit, 19 nec defuit quicquam a parvo usque ad magnum, tam de filiis quam de filiabus, et de spoliis et quaecumque rapuerant. Omnia reduxit David. 20 Et tulit universos greges et armenta et minavit ante faciem suam, dixeruntque, "Haec est praeda David."

21 Venit autem David ad ducentos viros qui lassi substiterant nec sequi potuerant David, et residere eos iusserat in Torrente Besor, qui egressi sunt obviam David et populo qui erat cum eo, accedens autem David ad populum salutavit eos pacifice. 22 Respondensque omnis vir pessimus et iniquus de viris qui ierant cum David dixit, "Quia non venerunt nobiscum, non dabimus eis quicquam de praeda quam eruimus, sed sufficiat unicuique uxor sua et filii quos cum acceperint recedant."

23 Dixit autem David, "Non sic facietis, fratres mei, de his quae tradidit Dominus nobis, et custodivit nos et dedit latrunculos qui eruperant adversum nos in manus nostras. 24 Nec audiet vos quisquam super sermone hoc, aequa enim pars erit descendentis ad proelium et remanentis ad sarcinas, et similiter divid=ent." 25 Et factum est hoc ex die illa et deinceps constitutum et praefinitum et quasi lex in Israhel usque ad diem hanc.

26 Venit ergo David in Siceleg et misit dona de praeda senioribus Iuda, proximis suis, dicens, "Accipite benedictionem de praeda hostium Domini," 27 his qui erant in Bethel et qui in Ramoth ad meridiem et qui in Iether 28 et qui in

the Amalekites had taken, and he rescued his two wives, 19 and there was nothing missing small *or* great, *neither* of their sons *or* their daughters, nor of the spoils and whatsoever they had taken. David recovered all. 20 And he took all the flocks and the herds and made them go before him, and they said, "This is the prey of David."

21 And David came to the two hundred men who being weary had stayed and were not able to follow David, and he had ordered them to abide at the Torrent Besor, and they came out to meet David and the people that were with him, and David coming to the people saluted them peaceably. 22 Then *all the* wicked and unjust *men* that had gone with David answering said, "Because they came not with us, we will not give them any thing of the prey which we have recovered, but *let every man take his wife and his children and be contented with them and go his way.*"

23 But David said, "You shall not do so, my brethren, *with* these things which the Lord hath given us, *who* hath kept us and hath delivered the robbers that *invaded* us into our hands. 24 And no man shall hearken to you in this matter, *but* equal shall be the portion of him that went down to battle and of him that abode at the baggage, and they shall divide alike." 25 And this hath been done from that day *forward and since* was made a statute and an ordinance and as a law in *Israel.*

26 Then David came to Ziklag and sent presents of the prey to the ancients of Judah, his neighbours, saying, "Receive a blessing of the prey of the enemies of the Lord," 27 to them that were in Bethel and that were in Ramoth to the south and *to* them that were in Jattir 28 and *to* them that were

Aroer et qui in Sefamoth et qui in Esthama 29 et qui in Rachal et qui in urbibus Ierameli et qui in urbibus Ceni 30 et qui in Arama et qui in lacu Asan et qui in Athac 31 et qui in Hebron et reliquis qui erant in his locis in quibus commoratus fuerat David et viri eius.

Caput 31

Philisthim autem pugnabant adversum Israhel, et fugerunt viri Israhel ante faciem Philisthim et ceciderunt interfecti in Monte Gelboe. 2 Inrueruntque Philisthim in Saul et in filios eius, et percusserunt Ionathan et Abinadab et Melchisue, filios Saul. 3 Totumque pondus proelii versum est in Saul, et consecuti sunt eum viri sagittarii, et vulneratus est vehementer a sagittariis. 4 Dixitque Saul ad armigerum suum, "Evagina gladium tuum, et percute me ne forte veniant incircumcisi isti et interficiant me inludentes mihi." Et noluit armiger eius, fuerat enim nimio timore perterritus. Arripuit itaque Saul gladium et inruit super eum. 5 Quod cum vidisset armiger eius, videlicet, quod mortuus esset Saul, inruit etiam ipse super gladium suum et mortuus est

in Aroer and that were in Siphmoth and that were in Eshtemoa 29 and that were in Racal and that were in the cities of
Jerahmeel and that were in the cities of Ceni 30 and that
were in Hormah and that were in the lake Ashan and that
were in Athach 31 and that were in Hebron and to the rest
that were in those places in which David had abode *with* his
men.

Chapter 31

Israel is defeated by the Philistines. Saul and his sons are
slain.

And the Philistines fought against Israel, and the men of
Israel fled from before the *Philistines* and fell down slain in
Mount Gilboa. 2 And the Philistines fell upon Saul and upon
his sons, and they slew Jonathan and Abinadab and Malchishua, the sons of Saul. 3 And the whole weight of the battle
was turned upon Saul, and the archers overtook him, and he
was grievously wounded by the archers. 4 Then Saul said to
his armourbearer, "Draw thy sword, and kill me lest these
uncircumcised come and slay me and mock at me." And his
armourbearer would not, for he was struck with exceeding
great fear. Then Saul took his sword and fell upon it. 5 And
when his armourbearer saw this, to wit, that Saul was dead,

cum eo. 6 Mortuus est ergo Saul et tres filii eius et armiger illius et universi viri eius in die illa pariter.

7 Videntes autem viri Israhel qui erant trans vallem et trans Iordanem quod fugissent viri Israhelitae et quod mortuus esset Saul et filii eius reliquerunt civitates suas et fugerunt. Veneruntque Philisthim et habitaverunt ibi. 8 Facta autem die altera, venerunt Philisthim ut spoliarent interfectos, et invenerunt Saul et tres filios eius iacentes in Monte Gelboe. 9 Et praeciderunt caput Saul et expoliaverunt eum armis et miserunt in terram Philisthinorum per circuitum ut adnuntiaretur in templo idolorum et in populis. 10 Et posuerunt arma eius in templo Astharoth, corpus vero eius suspenderunt in muro Bethsan. 11 Quod cum audissent habitatores Iabes Galaad quaecumque fecerant Philisthim Saul, 12 surrexerunt omnes viri fortissimi et ambulaverunt tota nocte et tulerunt cadaver Saul et cadavera filiorum eius de muro Bethsan, veneruntque Iabes Galaad et conbuserunt ea ibi, 13 et tulerunt ossa eorum et sepelierunt in nemore Iabes et ieiunaverunt septem diebus.

he also fell upon his sword and died with him. 6 So Saul died and his three sons and his armourbearer and all his men that same day together.

7 And the men of Israel that were beyond the valley and beyond the Jordan, seeing that the Israelites were fled and that Saul was dead and his sons, forsook their cities and fled. And the Philistines came and dwelt there. 8 And on the morrow, the Philistines came to strip the slain, and they found Saul and his three sons lying in Mount Gilboa. 9 And they cut off Saul's head and stripped him of his armour and sent into the land of the Philistines round about to *publish* it in the temples of their idols and among their people. 10 And they put his armour in the temple of Astarte, but his body they hung on the wall of Beth-shan. 11 Now when the inhabitants of Jabesh Gilead had heard all that the Philistines had done to Saul, 12 all the most valiant men arose and walked all the night and took the body of Saul and the bodies of his sons from the wall of Beth-shan, and they came to Jabesh Gilead and burnt them there, 13 and they took their bones and buried them in the wood of Jabesh and fasted seven days.

2 KINGS

Caput 1

Factum est autem postquam mortuus est Saul ut David reverteretur a caede Amalech et maneret in Siceleg dies duos. 2 In die autem tertia apparuit homo veniens de castris Saul veste conscissa et pulvere aspersus caput, et ut venit ad David cecidit super faciem suam et adoravit. 3 Dixitque ad eum David, "Unde venis?"

Qui ait ad eum, "De castris Israhel fugi."

4 Et dixit ad eum David, "Quod est verbum quod factum est? Indica mihi."

Qui ait, "Fugit populus e proelio, et multi corruentes e populo mortui sunt. Sed et Saul et Ionathan, filius eius, interierunt."

5 Dixitque David ad adulescentem qui nuntiabat ei, "Unde scis quia mortuus est Saul et Ionathan, filius eius?"

6 Et ait adulescens qui narrabat ei, "Casu veni in Montem Gelboe, et Saul incumbebat super hastam suam, porro cur-

Chapter 1

David mourneth for the death of Saul and Jonathan. He ordereth the man to be slain who pretended he had killed Saul.

Now it came to pass after Saul was dead that David returned from the slaughter of *the Amalekites* and abode two days in Ziklag. 2 And on the third day there appeared a man who came out of Saul's camp with his garments rent and dust strewed on his head, and when he came to David he fell upon his face and adored. 3 And David said to him, "From whence comest thou?"

And he said to him, "I am fled out of the camp of Israel."

4 And David said unto him, "What is the matter that is come to pass? Tell me."

He said, "The people are fled from the battle, and many of the people are fallen and dead. Moreover, Saul and Jonathan, his son, are slain."

5 And David said to the young man that told him, "How knowest thou that Saul and Jonathan, his son, are dead?"

6 And the young man that told him said, "I came by chance upon Mount Gilboa, and Saul leaned upon his spear,

rus et equites adpropinquabant ei, 7 et conversus post tergum suum vidensque me vocavit. Cui cum respondissem,
'Adsum,' 8 dixit mihi, 'Quisnam es tu?' Et aio ad eum, 'Amale-
chites sum.' 9 Et locutus est mihi, 'Sta super me, et interfice
me, quoniam tenent me angustiae et adhuc tota anima mea
in me est.' 10 Stansque super eum occidi illum, sciebam enim
quod vivere non poterat post ruinam, et tuli diadema quod
erat in capite eius et armillam de brachio illius et adtuli ad
te, dominum meum, huc."

11 Adprehendens autem David vestimenta sua scidit, omnesque viri qui erant cum eo. 12 Et planxerunt et fleverunt et
ieiunaverunt usque ad vesperam super Saul et super Ionathan, filium eius, et super populum Domini et super domum
Israhel, quod corruissent gladio. 13 Dixitque David ad iuve-
nem qui nuntiaverat ei, "Unde es?"

Qui respondit, "Filius hominis advenae Amalechitae ego
sum."

14 Et ait ad eum David, "Quare non timuisti mittere manum tuam ut occideres christum Domini?" 15 Vocansque
David unum de pueris suis ait, "Accedens inrue in eum." Qui
percussit illum et mortuus est. 16 Et ait ad eum David, "Sanguis tuus super caput tuum, os enim tuum locutum est adversum te, dicens, 'Ego interfeci christum Domini.'" 17 Planxit autem David planctum huiuscemodi super Saul et super
Ionathan, filium eius. 18 (Et praecepit ut docerent filios Iuda
arcum, sicut scriptum est in Libro Iustorum.)

and the chariots and horsemen drew nigh unto him, 7 and looking behind him and seeing me he called me. *And I answered, 'Here am I.'* 8 *And* he said to me, 'Who art thou?' And I said to him, 'I am an Amalekite.' 9 And he said to me, 'Stand over me, and kill me, for *anguish is come upon* me and as yet my whole life is in me.' 10 So standing over him I killed him, for I knew that he could not live after the fall, and I took the diadem that was on his head and the bracelet *that was on* his arm and have brought them hither to thee, my lord."

11 *Then* David took hold of his garments and rent them, and *likewise* all the men that were with him. 12 And they mourned and wept and fasted until evening for Saul and for Jonathan, his son, and for the people of the Lord and for the house of Israel, because they were fallen by the sword. 13 And David said to the young man that told him, "Whence art thou?"

He answered, "I am the son of a stranger of Amalek."

14 *David* said to him, "Why didst thou not fear to put out thy hand to kill the Lord's anointed?" 15 And David calling one of his servants said, "Go near, and fall upon him." And he struck him *so that* he died. 16 And David said to him, "Thy blood be upon thy own head, for thy own mouth hath spoken against thee, saying, 'I have slain the Lord's anointed.'" 17 And David made this kind of lamentation over Saul and over Jonathan, his son. 18 (Also he commanded that they should teach the children of Judah the use of the bow, as it is written in the Book of the Just.)

Et ait, "Considera, Israel, pro his qui mortui sunt, super excelsa tua vulnerati. 19 Incliti Israhel super montes tuos interfecti sunt. Quomodo ceciderunt fortes? 20 Nolite adnuntiare in Geth; neque adnuntietis in conpetis Ascalonis ne forte laetentur filiae Philisthim, ne exultent filiae incircumcisorum.

21 "Montes Gelboe, nec ros nec pluvia veniant super vos, neque sint agri primitiarum, quia ibi abiectus est clypeus fortium, clypeus Saul, quasi non esset unctus oleo. 22 A sanguine interfectorum, ab adipe fortium, sagitta Ionathan numquam rediit retrorsum et gladius Saul non est reversus inanis. 23 Saul et Ionathan, amabiles et decori in vita sua, in morte quoque non sunt divisi. Aquilis velociores, leonibus fortiores.

24 "Filiae Israhel, super Saul flete, qui vestiebat vos coccino in deliciis, qui praebebat ornamenta aurea cultui vestro. 25 Quomodo ceciderunt fortes in proelio? Ionathan in excelsis tuis occisus? 26 Doleo super te, frater mi Ionathan, decore nimis et amabilis super amorem mulierum. Sicut mater unicum amat filium suum, ita ego te diligebam.

27 "Quomodo ceciderunt robusti et perierunt arma bellica?"

And he said, "Consider, O Israel, for them that are dead, wounded on thy high places. 19 The illustrious of Israel are slain upon thy mountains. How are the valiant fallen? 20 Tell it not in Gath; publish it not in the streets of Ashkelon *lest* the daughters of the Philistines rejoice, lest the daughters of the uncircumcised triumph.

21 "Ye mountains of Gilboa, let neither dew nor rain come upon you, neither be they fields of firstfruits, for there was cast away the shield of the valiant, the shield of Saul, as though he had not been anointed with oil. 22 From the blood of the slain, from the fat of the valiant, the arrow of Jonathan never turned back and the sword of Saul did not return empty. 23 Saul and Jonathan, lovely and comely in their life, even in death they were not divided. They were swifter than eagles, stronger than lions.

24 "Ye daughters of Israel, weep over Saul, who clothed you with scarlet in delights, who gave ornaments of gold for your attire. 25 How are the valiant fallen in battle? *How was* Jonathan slain in the high places? 26 I grieve for thee, my brother Jonathan, exceeding beautiful and amiable *to me* above the love of women. As the mother loveth her only son, so did I love thee.

27 "How are the valiant fallen and the weapons of war perished?"

Caput 2

Igitur post haec consuluit David Dominum, dicens, "Num ascendam in unam de civitatibus Iuda?"

Et ait Dominus ad eum, "Ascende."

Dixitque David, "Quo ascendam?"

Et respondit ei, "In Hebron."

2 Ascendit ergo David et duae uxores eius, Ahinoem, Iezrahelites, et Abigail, uxor Nabal Carmeli. 3 Sed et viros qui erant cum eo duxit David, singulos cum domo sua, et manserunt in oppidis Hebron. 4 Veneruntque viri Iuda et unxerunt ibi David ut regnaret super domum Iuda. Et nuntiatum est David quod viri Iabes Galaad sepelissent Saul. 5 Misit ergo David nuntios ad viros Iabes Galaad, dixitque ad eos, "Benedicti vos Domino, qui fecistis misericordiam hanc cum domino vestro Saul et sepelistis eum. 6 Et nunc retribuet quidem vobis Dominus misericordiam et veritatem, sed et ego reddam gratiam eo quod feceritis verbum istud. 7 Confortentur manus vestrae, et estote viri fortitudinis, licet enim mortuus sit dominus vester Saul, tamen me unxit domus Iuda regem sibi."

Chapter 2

David is received and anointed king of Judah. Ish-bosheth, the son of Saul, reigneth over the rest of Israel. A battle between Abner and Joab.

And after these things David consulted the Lord, saying, "Shall I go up into one of the cities of Judah?"

And the Lord said to him, "Go up."

And David said, "Whither shall I go up?"

And he answered him, "Into Hebron."

2 So David went up and his two wives, Ahinoam, the Jezreelitess, and Abigail, the wife of Nabal of Carmel. 3 *And* the men also that were with him David brought up, every man with his household, and they abode in the towns of Hebron. 4 And the men of Judah came and anointed David there to be king over the house of Judah. And it was told David that the men of Jabesh Gilead had buried Saul. 5 David therefore sent messengers to the men of Jabesh Gilead, and said to them, "Blessed be you to the Lord, who have shewn this mercy to your master Saul and have buried him. 6 And now the Lord surely will render you mercy and truth, *and* I also will requite you *for this* good turn because you have done this thing. 7 Let your hands be strengthened, and be ye men of valour, for although your master Saul be dead, yet the house of Judah hath anointed me to be their king."

8 Abner autem, filius Ner, princeps exercitus Saul, tulit Hisboseth, filium Saul, et circumduxit eum per castra 9 regemque constituit super Galaad et super Gesuri et super Iezrahel et super Ephraim et super Beniamin et super Israhel universum. 10 Quadraginta annorum erat Hisboseth, filius Saul, cum regnare coepisset super Israhel, et duobus annis regnavit, sola autem domus Iuda sequebatur David. 11 Et fuit numerus dierum quos commoratus est David imperans in Hebron super domum Iuda septem annorum et sex mensuum.

12 Egressusque Abner, filius Ner, et pueri Hisboseth, filii Saul, de castris in Gabaon. 13 Porro Ioab, filius Sarviae, et pueri David egressi sunt et occurrerunt eis iuxta piscinam Gabaon. Et cum in unum convenissent, e regione sederunt, hii ex una parte piscinae et illi ex altera. 14 Dixitque Abner ad Ioab, "Surgant pueri et ludant coram nobis."

Et respondit Ioab, "Surgant." 15 Surrexerunt ergo et transierunt numero duodecim de Beniamin ex parte Hisboseth, filii Saul, et duodecim de pueris David. 16 Adprehensoque unusquisque capite conparis sui defixit gladium in latus contrarii, et ceciderunt simul. Vocatumque est nomen loci illius Ager Robustorum, in Gabaon. 17 Et ortum est bellum durum satis in die illa, fugatusque est Abner et viri Israhel a pueris David.

18 Erant autem ibi tres filii Sarviae, Ioab et Abisai et Asahel. Porro Asahel cursor velocissimus fuit, quasi unus ex capreis quae morantur in silvis. 19 Persequebatur autem Asahel Abner et non declinavit ad dexteram sive ad sinistram omit-

8 But Abner, the son of Ner, general of Saul's army, took Ish-bosheth, the son of Saul, and led him about through the camp 9 and made him king over Gilead and over Gessuri and over Jezreel and over Ephraim and over Benjamin and over all Israel. 10 Ish-bosheth, the son of Saul, was forty years old when he began to reign over Israel, and he reigned two years, and only the house of Judah followed David. 11 And the number of the days that David abode reigning in Hebron over the house of Judah was seven years and six months.

12 And Abner, the son of Ner, and the servants of Ish-bosheth, the son of Saul, went out from the camp to Gibeon. 13 And Joab, the son of Zeruiah, and the servants of David went out and met them by the pool of Gibeon. And when they were come together, they sat down over against one another, *the one* on the one side of the pool and *the other* on the other side. 14 And Abner said to Joab, "Let the young men rise and play before us."

And Joab answered, "Let them rise." 15 Then there arose and went over twelve in number of Benjamin of the part of Ish-bosheth, the son of Saul, and twelve of the servants of David. 16 And every one catching his fellow by the head thrust his sword into the side of his adversary, and they fell down together. And the name of the place was called the Field of the Valiant, in Gibeon. 17 And there was a very fierce battle that day, and Abner was put to flight with the men of Israel by the servants of David.

18 And there were the three sons of Zeruiah there, Joab and Abishai and Asahel. Now Asahel was a most swift runner, like one of the roes that abide in the woods. 19 And Asahel pursued after Abner and turned not to the right hand

tens persequi Abner. 20 Respexit itaque Abner post tergum suum et ait, "Tune es Asahel?"

Qui respondit, "Ego sum."

21 Dixitque ei Abner, "Vade ad dextram sive ad sinistram, et adprehende unum de adulescentibus, et tolle tibi spolia eius." Noluit autem Asahel omittere quin urgueret eum. 22 Rursumque locutus est Abner ad Asahel, "Recede, et noli me sequi, ne conpellar confodere te in terra, et levare non potero faciem meam ad Ioab, fratrem tuum." 23 Qui audire contempsit et noluit declinare; percussit ergo eum Abner aversa hasta in inguine et transfodit, et mortuus est in eodem loco, omnesque qui transiebant per locum illum in quo ceciderat Asahel et mortuus erat subsistebant.

24 Persequentibus autem Ioab et Abisai fugientem Abner, sol occubuit et venerunt usque ad collem aquaeductus qui est ex adverso vallis itineris deserti in Gabaon. 25 Congregatique sunt filii Beniamin ad Abner, et conglobati in unum cuneum steterunt in summitate tumuli unius. 26 Et exclamavit Abner ad Ioab et ait, "Num usque ad internicionem tuus mucro desaeviet? An ignoras quod periculosa sit desperatio? Usquequo non dicis populo ut omittat persequi fratres suos?"

27 Et ait Ioab, "Vivit Dominus, si locutus fuisses, mane recessisset populus persequens fratres suos." 28 Insonuit ergo Ioab bucina, et stetit omnis exercitus nec persecuti sunt ultra Israhel neque iniere certamen. 29 Abner autem et viri eius

nor to the left *from following* Abner. 20 And Abner looked behind him and said, "Art thou Asahel?"

And he answered, "I am."

21 And Abner said to him, "Go to the right hand or to the left, and lay hold on one of the young men, and take thee his spoils." But Asahel would not leave off following him close. 22 And again Abner said to Asahel, "Go off, and do not follow me, lest I be obliged to stab thee to the ground, and I shall not be able to hold up my face to Joab, thy brother." 23 But he refused to hearken to him and would not turn aside, wherefore Abner struck him with his spear with a back stroke in the groin and thrust him through, and he died upon the spot, and all that came to the place where Asahel fell down and died stood still.

24 Now while Joab and Abishai pursued after *Abner,* the sun went down and they came as far as the hill of the aqueduct that *lieth* over against the valley by the way of the wilderness in Gibeon. 25 And the children of Benjamin gathered themselves together to Abner, and being joined in one body they stood on the top of a hill. 26 And Abner cried out to Joab and said, "Shall thy sword rage unto utter destruction? Knowest thou not that it is dangerous *to drive people to despair?* How long dost thou defer to bid the people cease from pursuing after their brethren?"

27 And Joab said, "As the Lord liveth, if thou hadst spoke *sooner, even* in the morning the people should have retired from pursuing after their brethren." 28 Then Joab sounded the trumpet, and all the army stood still and did not pursue after Israel any farther nor *fight any more.* 29 And Abner and

abierunt per campestria tota nocte illa et transierunt Iordanem et lustrata omni Bethoron venerunt ad castra.

30 Porro Ioab reversus omisso Abner congregavit omnem
populum, et defuerunt de pueris David decem et novem
viri excepto Asahele. 31 Servi autem David percusserunt de
Beniamin et de viris qui erant cum Abner trecentos sexaginta, qui et mortui sunt. 32 Tuleruntque Asahel et sepelierunt eum in sepulchro patris sui in Bethleem, et ambulaverunt tota nocte Ioab et viri qui erant cum eo, et in ipso
crepusculo pervenerunt in Hebron.

Caput 3

Facta est ergo longa concertatio inter domum Saul et inter
domum David, David proficiens et semper se ipso robustior
domus autem Saul decrescens cotidie. 2 Natique sunt filii
David in Hebron, fuitque primogenitus eius Amnon de Ahi-
noem, Iezrahelitide, 3 et post eum Chelaab de Abigail, uxore
Nabal Carmeli, porro tertius Absalom, filius Maacha, filiae
Tholomai, regis Gessur 4 quartus autem Adonias, filius
Aggith, et quintus Safathia, filius Abital, 5 sextus quoque

his men walked all that night through the plains, and they passed the Jordan and having gone through all Beth-horon came to the camp.

30 And Joab returning after he had left Abner assembled all the people, and there were wanting of David's servants nineteen men beside Asahel. 31 But the servants of David had killed of Benjamin and of the men that were with Abner three hundred and sixty, who *all* died. 32 And they took Asahel and buried him in the sepulchre of his father in Bethlehem, and Joab and the men that were with him marched all the night, and they came to Hebron at *break of day.*

Chapter 3

David groweth daily stronger. Abner cometh over to him.
He is treacherously slain by Joab.

Now there was a long war between the house of Saul and the house of David, David prospering and *growing* always *stronger and stronger* but the house of Saul decaying daily. 2 And sons were born to David in Hebron, and his firstborn was Amnon of Ahinoam, the Jezreelitess, 3 and *his second* Chileab of Abigail, the wife of Nabal of Carmel, and the third Absalom, the son of Maacah, the daughter of Talmai, king of Geshur, 4 and the fourth Adonijah, the son of Haggith, and the fifth Shephatiah, the son of Abital, 5 and the

Iethraam de Agla, uxore David. Hii nati sunt David in Hebron.

6 Cum ergo esset proelium inter domum Saul et domum David, Abner, filius Ner, regebat domum Saul. 7 Fuerat autem Sauli concubina nomine Respha, filia Ahia. Dixitque Hisboseth ad Abner, 8 Quare ingressus es ad concubinam patris mei?"

Qui iratus nimis propter verba Hisboseth ait, "Numquid caput canis ego sum adversum Iuda hodie, qui fecerim misericordiam super domum Saul, patris tui, et super fratres et proximos eius et non tradidi te in manus David? Et tu requisisti in me quod argueres pro muliere hodie? 9 Haec faciat Deus Abner et haec addat ei nisi quomodo iuravit Dominus David sic faciam cum eo, 10 ut transferatur regnum de domo Saul et elevetur thronus David super Israhel et super Iudam a Dan usque Bersabee."

11 Et non potuit respondere ei quicquam, quia metuebat illum. 12 Misit ergo Abner nuntios ad David pro se, dicentes, "Cuius est terra?" Et ut loquerentur, "Fac mecum amicitias, et erit manus mea tecum, et reducam ad te universum Israhel."

13 Qui ait, "Optime, ego faciam tecum amicitias, sed unam rem peto a te, dicens, 'Non videbis faciem meam antequam adduxeris Michol, filiam Saul,' et sic venies et videbis me."

14 Misit autem David nuntios ad Hisboseth, filium Saul, dicens, "Redde uxorem meam Michol, quam despondi mihi centum praeputiis Philisthim." 15 Misit ergo Hisboseth et tulit eam a viro suo Faltihel, filio Lais.

sixth Ithream of Eglah, the wife of David. These were born to David in Hebron.

6 Now while there was war between the house of Saul and the house of David, Abner, the son of Ner, ruled the house of Saul. 7 And Saul had a concubine named Rizpah, the daughter of Aiah. And Ish-bosheth said to Abner, 8 "Why didst thou go in to my father's concubine?"

And he was exceedingly angry for the words of Ish-bosheth and said, "Am I a dog's head against Judah this day, who have shewn mercy to the house of Saul, thy father, and to his brethren and *friends* and have not delivered thee into the hands of David? And hast thou sought this day against me to charge me *with a matter concerning* a woman? 9 So do God to Abner and more also unless as the Lord hath sworn to David so I do to him, 10 that the kingdom be translated from the house of Saul and the throne of David be set up over Israel and over Judah from Dan to Beer-sheba."

11 And he could not answer him *a word,* because he feared him. 12 Abner therefore sent messengers to David for himself, saying, "Whose is the land?" And that they should say, "Make *a league* with me, and my hand shall be with thee, and I will bring all Israel to thee."

13 And he said, "Very well, I will make a league with thee, but one thing I require of thee, saying, 'Thou shalt not see my face before thou bring Michal, the daughter of Saul,' and so thou shalt come and see me."

14 And David sent messengers to Ish-bosheth, the son of Saul, saying, "Restore my wife Michal, whom I espoused to me for a hundred foreskins of the Philistines." 15 And Ish-bosheth sent and took her from her husband Paltiel, the son of Laish.

16 Sequebaturque eam vir suus, plorans usque Baurim, et dixit ad eum Abner, "Vade, et revertere." Qui reversus est.

17 Sermonem quoque intulit Abner ad seniores Israhel, dicens, "Tam heri quam nudius tertius quaerebatis David ut regnaret super vos. 18 Nunc ergo, facite, quoniam Dominus locutus est ad David, dicens, 'In manu servi mei David salvabo populum meum Israhel de manu Philisthim et omnium inimicorum eius.'" 19 Locutus est autem Abner etiam ad Beniamin. Et abiit ut loqueretur ad David in Hebron omnia quae placuerant Israhel et universo Beniamin.

20 Venitque ad David in Hebron cum viginti viris, et fecit David Abner et viris eius qui venerant cum eo convivium. 21 Et dixit Abner ad David, "Surgam ut congregem ad te, dominum meum, regem, omnem Israhel et ineam tecum foedus et imperes omnibus sicut desiderat anima tua."

Cum ergo deduxisset David Abner et ille isset in pace, 22 statim pueri David et Ioab venerunt caesis latronibus cum praeda magna nimis, Abner autem non erat cum David in Hebron, quia iam dimiserat eum et profectus fuerat in pace. 23 Et Ioab et omnis exercitus qui erat cum eo postea venerant, nuntiatum est itaque Ioab a narrantibus, "Venit Abner, filius Ner, ad regem, et dimisit eum, et abiit in pace."

24 Et ingressus est Ioab ad regem et ait, "Quid fecisti? Ecce: venit Abner ad te. Quare dimisisti eum, et abiit et recessit? 25 Ignoras Abner, filium Ner, quoniam ad hoc venit ad te, ut deciperet te et sciret exitum tuum et introitum tuum et nosset omnia quae agis?" 26 Egressus itaque Ioab a

16 And her husband followed her, weeping as far as Bahurim, and Abner said to him, "Go, and return." And he returned.

17 Abner also spoke to the ancients of Israel, saying, "Both yesterday and the day before you sought for David that he might reign over you. 18 Now then do it, because the Lord hath spoken to David, saying, 'By the hand of my servant David I will save my people Israel from the *hands* of the Philistines and of all their enemies.'" 19 And Abner spoke also to Benjamin. And he went to speak to David in Hebron all that seemed good to Israel and to all Benjamin.

20 And he came to David in Hebron with twenty men, and David made a feast for Abner and his men that came with him. 21 And Abner said to David, "I will rise that I may gather all Israel unto thee, my lord, the king, and may enter into a league with thee and that thou mayst reign over all as thy soul desireth."

Now when David bad brought Abner on his way and he was gone in peace, 22 immediately David's servants and Joab came after having slain the robbers with an exceeding great booty, and Abner was not with David in Hebron, for he had now sent him away and he was gone in peace. 23 And Joab and all the army that was with him came afterwards, and it was told Joab *that* Abner, the son of Ner, came to the king and he hath sent him away and he is gone in peace.

24 And Joab went in to the king and said, "What hast thou done? Behold: Abner came to thee. Why didst thou send him away, and he is gone and departed? 25 Knowest thou not Abner, the son of Ner, that to this end he came to thee: that he might deceive thee and to know thy going out and thy coming in and to know all thou dost?" 26 Then Joab going

David misit nuntios post Abner et reduxit eum a cisterna Sira, ignorante David.

27 Cumque redisset Abner in Hebron, seorsum abduxit eum Ioab ad medium portae ut loqueretur ei in dolo, et percussit illum ibi in inguine, et mortuus est in ultionem sanguinis Asahel, fratris eius. 28 Quod cum audisset David rem iam gestam, ait, "Mundus ego sum et regnum meum apud Dominum usque in sempiternum a sanguine Abner, filii Ner, 29 et veniat super caput Ioab et super omnem domum patris eius, nec deficiat de domo Ioab fluxum seminis sustinens et leprosus et tenens fusum et cadens gladio et indigens pane." 30 Igitur Ioab et Abisai, frater eius, interfecerunt Abner eo quod occidisset Asahel, fratrem eorum, in Gabaon in proelio. 31 Dixit autem David ad Ioab et ad omnem populum qui erat cum eo, "Scindite vestimenta vestra, et accingimini saccis, et plangite ante exequias Abner." Porro Rex David sequebatur feretrum. 32 Cumque sepelissent Abner in Hebron, levavit Rex David vocem suam et flevit super tumulum Abner, flevit autem et omnis populus. 33 Plangensque rex et lugens Abner ait, "Nequaquam ut mori solent ignavi mortuus est Abner. 34 Manus tuae non sunt ligatae et pedes tui non sunt conpedibus adgravati, sed sicut solent cadere coram filiis iniquitatis, sic corruisti." Congeminansque omnis populus flevit super eum. 35 Cumque venisset universa multitudo cibum capere cum David clara adhuc die, iuravit David, dicens, "Haec faciat mihi Deus et haec addat, si ante occasum solis gustavero panem vel aliud quicquam."

out from David sent messengers after Abner and brought him back from the cistern of Sirah, David knowing nothing of it.

27 And when Abner was returned to Hebron, Joab took him aside to the middle of the gate to speak to him treacherously, and he stabbed him there in the groin, and he died in revenge of the blood of Asahel, his brother. 28 And when David heard of it after the thing was now done, he said, "I and my kingdom are innocent before the Lord for ever of the blood of Abner, the son of Ner, 29 and may it come upon the head of Joab and upon all his father's house, and let there not fail from the house of Joab one that hath an issue of seed *or* that is a leper *or* that holdeth the distaff *or* that falleth by the sword *or* that wanteth bread." 30 So Joab and Abishai, his brother, slew Abner because he had killed their brother Asahel at Gibeon in the battle. 31 And David said to Joab and to all the people that were with him, "Rend your garments, and gird yourselves with sackcloths, and mourn before the funeral of Abner." *And* King David *himself* followed the bier. 32 And when they had buried Abner in Hebron, King David lifted up his voice and wept at the grave of Abner, and all the people also wept. 33 And the king mourning and lamenting over Abner said, "Not as cowards are wont to die hath Abner died. 34 Thy hands were not bound nor thy feet laden with fetters, but as men fall before the children of iniquity, so didst thou fall." And all the people repeating it wept over him. 35 And when all the people came to take meat with David while it was yet broad day, David swore, saying, "So do God to me and more also, if I taste bread or any thing else before sunset."

36 Omnisque populus audivit, et placuerunt eis cuncta quae fecit rex in conspectu totius populi. 37 Et cognovit omne vulgus et universus Israhel in die illa quoniam non actum fuisset a rege ut occideretur Abner, filius Ner. 38 Dixit quoque rex ad servos suos, "Num ignoratis quoniam princeps et maximus cecidit hodie in Israhel? 39 Ego autem adhuc delicatus, et unctus rex. Porro viri isti, filii Sarviae, duri mihi sunt. Retribuat Dominus facienti malum iuxta malitiam suam."

Caput 4

Audivit autem Isboseth filius Saul quod cecidisset Abner in Hebron, et dissolutae sunt manus eius, omnisque Israhel perturbatus est. 2 Duo autem viri principes latronum erant filio Saul. Nomen uni Baana, et nomen alteri Rechab, filii Remmon, Berothitae de filiis Beniamin, siquidem et Beroth reputata est in Beniamin. 3 Et fugerunt Berothitae in Getthaim fueruntque ibi advenae usque in tempus illud. 4 Erat autem Ionathan, filio Saul, filius debilis pedibus, quinquennis enim fuit quando venit nuntius de Saul et Ionathan ex Iezrahel, tollens itaque eum nutrix sua fugit, cumque fes-

36 And all the people heard, *and they were pleased,* and all that the king did seemed good in the sight of all the people. 37 And all the people and all Israel understood that day that it was not the king's doing that Abner, the son of Ner, was slain. 38 The king also said to his servants, "Do you not know that a prince and great man is slain this day in Israel? 39 But I as yet am tender, though anointed king. And these men, the sons of Zeruiah, are too hard for me. The Lord reward him that doth evil according to his wickedness."

Chapter 4

Ish-bosheth is murdered by two of his servants. David punisheth the murderers.

And Ish-bosheth, the son of Saul, heard that Abner was slain in Hebron, and his hands were weakened, and all Israel was troubled. 2 Now the son of Saul had two men captains of his bands. The name of the one was Baanah, and the name of the other Rechab, the sons of Rimmon, a Beerothite of the children of Benjamin, for Beeroth also was reckoned in Benjamin. 3 And the Beerothites fled into Gittaim and were sojourners there until that time. 4 And Jonathan, the son of Saul, had a son that was lame of his feet, for he was five years old when the tidings came of Saul and Jonathan from Jezreel, and his nurse took him up and fled, and as she made

tinaret ut fugeret, cecidit et claudus effectus est. Habuitque vocabulum Mifiboseth.

5 Venientes igitur filii Remmon, Berothitae, Rechab et Baana, ingressi sunt fervente die domum Hisboseth, qui dormiebat super stratum suum meridie. 6 Ingressi sunt autem domum latenter adsumentes spicas tritici, et percusserunt eum in inguine Rechab et Baana, frater eius, et fugerunt, 7 cum autem ingressi fuissent domum ille dormiebat super lectulum suum in conclavi, et percutientes interfecerunt eum. Sublatoque capite eius abierunt per viam deserti tota nocte. 8 Et adtulerunt caput Hisboseth ad David, in Hebron, dixeruntque ad regem, "Ecce caput Hisboseth, filii Saul, inimici tui qui quaerebat animam tuam, et dedit Dominus domino meo, regi, ultionem hodie de Saul et de semine eius."

9 Respondens autem David Rechab et Baana, fratri eius, filiis Remmon, Berothitae, dixit ad eos, "Vivit Dominus qui eruit animam meam de omni angustia, 10 quoniam eum qui adnuntiaverat mihi et dixerat, 'Mortuus est Saul,' qui putabat se prospera nuntiare, tenui et occidi eum in Siceleg cui oportebat me dare mercedem pro nuntio. 11 Quanto magis nunc cum homines impii interfecerint virum innoxium in domo sua, super lectulum suum? Non quaeram sanguinem eius de manu vestra et auferam vos de terra?" 12 Praecepit itaque David pueris suis, et interfecerunt eos praecidentesque manus et pedes eorum suspenderunt eos super piscinam in Hebron, caput autem Hisboseth tulerunt et sepelierunt in sepulchro Abner, in Hebron.

haste to flee, he fell and became lame. And his name was Mephibosheth.

5 And the sons of Rimmon, the Beerothite, Rechab and Baanah, coming went into the house of Ish-bosheth in the heat of the day, and he was sleeping upon his bed at noon. *And the doorkeeper of the house, who was cleansing wheat, was fallen asleep.* 6 And they entered into the house secretly taking ears of corn, and Rechab and Baanah, his brother, stabbed him in the groin, and fled away, 7 *for* when they came into the house he was sleeping upon his bed in a parlour, and they struck him and killed him. And taking away his head they went off by the way of the wilderness, *walking* all night. 8 And they brought the head of Ish-bosheth to David, to Hebron, and they said to the king, "Behold the head of Ish-bosheth, the son of Saul, thy enemy who sought thy life, and the Lord hath revenged my lord, the king, this day of Saul and of his seed."

9 But David answered Rechab and Baanah, his brother, the sons of Rimmon, the Beerothite, and said to them, "As the Lord liveth who hath delivered my soul out of all distress, 10 the man that told me and said, 'Saul is dead,' who thought he *brought good tidings,* I apprehended and slew him in Ziklag *who should have been rewarded* for his news. 11 How much more now when wicked men have slain an innocent man in his own house, upon his bed? Shall I not require his blood at your hand and take you away from the earth?" 12 And David commanded his servants, and they slew them and cutting off their hands and feet hanged them up over the pool in Hebron, but the head of Ish-bosheth they took and buried in the sepulchre of Abner, in Hebron.

Caput 5

Et venerunt universae tribus Israhel ad David in Hebron, dicentes, "Ecce: nos os tuum et caro tua sumus. 2 Sed et heri et nudius tertius, cum esset Saul rex super nos, tu eras educens et reducens Israhel, dixit autem Dominus ad te, 'Tu pasces populum meum Israhel, et tu eris dux super Israhel.'"

3 Venerunt quoque et senes de Israhel ad regem, in Hebron, et percussit cum eis Rex David foedus in Hebron coram Domino, unxeruntque David in regem super Israhel. 4 Triginta annorum erat David cum regnare coepisset, et quadraginta annis regnavit. 5 In Hebron regnavit super Iudam septem annis et sex mensibus, in Hierusalem autem regnavit triginta tribus annis super omnem Israhel et Iudam.

6 Et abiit rex et omnes viri qui erant cum eo in Hierusalem, ad Iebuseum, habitatorem terrae, dictumque est ad David ab eis, "Non ingredieris huc nisi abstuleris caecos et claudos, dicentes, 'Non ingredietur David huc.'" 7 Cepit autem David arcem Sion, haec est civitas David, 8 proposuerat enim David in die illa praemium qui percussisset Iebuseum et tetigisset domatum fistulas et abstulisset claudos et

Chapter 5

David is anointed king of all Israel. He taketh Jerusalem and dwelleth there. He defeateth the Philistines.

Then all the tribes of Israel came to David in Hebron, saying, "Behold: we are thy bone and thy flesh. 2 Moreover yesterday also and the day before, when Saul was king over us, thou wast he that did lead out and bring in Israel, and the Lord said to thee, 'Thou shalt feed my people Israel, and thou shalt be prince over Israel.'"

3 The ancients also of Israel came to the king, to Hebron, and King David made a league with them in Hebron before the Lord, and they anointed David to be king over Israel. 4 David was thirty years old when he began to reign, and he reigned forty years. 5 In Hebron he reigned over Judah seven years and six months, and in Jerusalem he reigned three and thirty years over all Israel and Judah.

6 And the king and all the men that were with him went to Jerusalem, to the *Jebusites, the inhabitants* of the land, and they said to David, "Thou shalt not come in hither unless thou take away the blind and the lame that say, 'David shall not come in hither.'" 7 But David took the castle of Zion, *the same* is the city of David, 8 for David had offered that day a reward *to whosoever* should strike the *Jebusites* and get up to the gutters of the tops of the houses and take away the blind

caecos odientes animam David. Idcirco dicitur in proverbio, "Caecus et claudus non intrabunt ad templum."

9 Habitavit autem David in arce et vocavit eam civitatem David et aedificavit per gyrum a Mello et intrinsecus. 10 Et ingrediebatur proficiens atque succrescens, et Dominus Deus exercituum erat cum eo. 11 Misit quoque Hiram, rex Tyri, nuntios ad David et ligna cedrina et artifices lignorum artificesque lapidum ad parietes, et aedificaverunt domum David. 12 Et cognovit David quoniam confirmasset eum Dominus regem super Israhel et quoniam exaltasset regnum eius super populum suum Israhel. 13 Accepit ergo David adhuc concubinas et uxores de Hierusalem postquam venerat de Hebron, natique sunt David et alii filii et filiae, 14 et haec nomina eorum qui nati sunt ei in Hierusalem: Samua et Sobab et Nathan et Salomon 15 et Ibaar et Helisua et Nepheg 16 et Iafia et Helisama et Helida et Helifeleth.

17 Audierunt ergo Philisthim quod unxissent David regem super Israhel, et ascenderunt universi ut quaererent David. Quod cum audisset David, descendit in praesidium. 18 Philisthim autem venientes diffusi sunt in Valle Raphaim 19 et consuluit David Dominum, dicens, "Si ascendam ad Philisthim, et si dabis eos in manum meam?"

Et dixit Dominus ad David, "Ascende, quia tradens dabo Philisthim in manu tua."

20 Venit ergo David in Baal Pharasim et percussit eos ibi, et dixit, "Divisit Dominus inimicos meos coram me sicut dividuntur aquae." Propterea vocatum est nomen loci illius

and the lame that hated the soul of David. Therefore it is said in the proverb, "The blind and the lame shall not come into the temple."

9 And David dwelt in the castle and called it the city of David and built round about from Millo and inwards. 10 And he went on prospering and growing up, and the Lord God of hosts was with him. 11 And Hiram, the king of Tyre, sent messengers to David and cedar trees and carpenters and masons for walls, and they built a house for David. 12 And David knew that the Lord had confirmed him king over Israel and that he had exalted his kingdom over his people Israel. 13 And David took more concubines and wives of Jerusalem after he was come from Hebron, and there were born to David other sons also and daughters, 14 and these are the names of them that were born to him in Jerusalem: Shammua and Shobab and Nathan and Solomon 15 and Ibhar and Elishua and Nepheg 16 and Japhia and Elishama and Eliada and Eliphelet.

17 And the Philistines heard that they had anointed David to be king over Israel, and they all came to seek David. And when David heard of it, he went down to a strong hold. 18 And the Philistines coming spread themselves in the Valley of Rephaim. 19 And David consulted the Lord, saying, "Shall I go up to the Philistines, and wilt thou deliver them into my hand?"

And the Lord said to David, "Go up, for I will *surely* deliver the Philistines *into* thy hand."

20 And David came to Baal Perazim and defeated them there, and he said, "The Lord hath divided my enemies before me as waters are divided." Therefore the name of the

Baalpharasim. 21 Et reliquerunt ibi sculptilia sua, quae tulit David et viri eius.

22 Et addiderunt adhuc Philisthim ut ascenderent et diffusi sunt in Valle Raphaim. 23 Consuluit autem David Dominum, "Si ascendam contra Philistheos, et trades eos in manus meas?"

Qui respondit, "Non ascendas contra eos, sed gyra post tergum eorum, et venies ad eos ex adverso pirorum. 24 Et cum audieris sonitum gradientis in cacumine pirorum, tunc inibis proelium, quia tunc egredietur Dominus ante faciem tuam ut percutiat castra Philisthim." 25 Fecit itaque David sicut ei praeceperat Dominus, et percussit Philisthim de Gabee usque dum venias Gezer.

Caput 6

Congregavit autem rursum David omnes electos ex Israhel, triginta milia. 2 Surrexitque David et abiit et universus populus qui erat cum eo de viris Iuda ut adducerent arcam Dei super quam invocatum est nomen Domini exercituum,

place was called Baal Perazim. 21 And they left there their idols, which David and his men took away.

22 And the Philistines came up *again* and spread themselves in the Valley of Rephaim. 23 And David consulted the Lord, "Shall I go up against the Philistines, and wilt thou deliver them into my hands?"

He answered, "Go not up against them, but fetch a compass behind them, and thou shalt come upon them over against the pear trees. 24 And when thou shalt hear the sound of one going in the *tops* of the pear trees, then shalt thou join battle, for then will the Lord go out before thy face to strike the *army* of the Philistines." 25 And David did as the Lord had commanded him, and he smote the Philistines from Gibeah until thou come to Gezer.

Chapter 6

David fetcheth the ark from Kiriath-jearim. Uzzah is struck dead for touching it. It is deposited in the house of Obed-edom and from thence carried to David's house.

And David again gathered together all the chosen men of Israel, thirty thousand. 2 And David arose and went *with* all the people that were with him of the men of Judah to fetch the ark of God upon which the name of the Lord of hosts is invoked, who sitteth over it upon the cheru-

sedentis in cherubin super eam. 3 Et inposuerunt arcam Dei super plaustrum novum tuleruntque eam de domo Abinadab, qui erat in Gabaa, Oza autem et Haio, filii Abinadab, minabant plaustrum novum. 4 Cumque tulissent eam de domo Abinadab, qui erat in Gabaa, custodiens arcam Dei Haio praecedebat arcam. 5 David autem et omnis Israhel ludebant coram Domino in omnibus lignis fabrefactis, et citharis et lyris et tympanis et sistris et cymbalis. 6 Postquam autem venerunt ad aream Nachon, extendit manum Oza ad arcam Dei et tenuit eam quoniam calcitrabant boves et declinaverunt eam. 7 Iratusque est indignatione Dominus contra Ozam, et percussit eum super temeritate, qui mortuus est ibi iuxta arcam Dei. 8 Contristatus autem est David eo quod percussisset Dominus Ozam, et vocatum est nomen loci illius Percussio Oza usque in diem hanc.

9 Et extimuit David Dominum in die illa, dicens, "Quomodo ingredietur ad me arca Domini?" 10 Et noluit devertere ad se arcam Domini in civitatem David, sed devertit eam in domum Obededom Getthei 11 et habitavit arca Domini in domo Obededom, Getthei, tribus mensibus, et benedixit Dominus Obededom et omnem domum eius. 12 Nuntiatumque est Regi David quod benedixisset Dominus Obededom et omnia eius propter arcam Dei, abiit ergo David et adduxit arcam Dei de domo Obededom in civitatem David cum gaudio. 13 cumque transcendissent qui portabant arcam Domini sex passus, immolabat bovem et arietem, 14 et David saltabat totis viribus ante Dominum, porro

bims. 3 And they laid the ark of God upon a new cart and took it out of the house of Abinadab, who was in Gibeah, and Uzzah and Ahio, the sons of Abinadab, drove the new cart. 4 And when they had taken it out of the house of Abinadab, who was in Gibeah, Ahio having care of the ark of God went before the ark. 5 But David and all Israel played before the Lord on all *manner of instruments made of* wood, *on* harps and lutes and timbrels and cornets and cymbals. 6 And *when* they came to the floor of Nacon, Uzzah put forth his hand to the ark of God and took hold of it because the oxen kicked and made it lean aside. 7 And the indignation of the Lord was enkindled against Uzzah, and he struck him for his rashness, and he died there before the ark of God. 8 And David was grieved because the Lord had struck Uzzah, and the name of that place was called the Striking of Uzzah to this day.

9 And David was afraid of the Lord that day, saying, "How shall the ark of the Lord come to me?" 10 And he would not have the ark of the Lord *brought in* to himself into the city of David, but he caused it to *be carried* into the house of Obed-edom, the Gittite. 11 And the ark of the Lord abode in the house of Obed-edom, the Gittite, three months, and the Lord blessed Obed-edom and all his household. 12 And it was told King David that the Lord had blessed Obed-edom and all that he had because of the ark of God, so David went and brought away the ark of God out of the house of Obed-edom into the city of David with joy. *And there were with David seven choirs and calves for victims.* 13 And when they that carried the ark of the Lord had gone six paces, he sacrificed an ox and a ram, 14 and David danced with all his might be-

David erat accinctus ephod lineo. 15 Et David et omnis domus Israhel ducebant Arcam Testamenti Domini in iubilo et in clangore bucinae.

16 Cumque intrasset arca Domini in civitatem David, Michol, filia Saul, prospiciens per fenestram vidit Regem David subsilientem atque saltantem coram Domino, et despexit eum in corde suo. 17 Et introduxerunt arcam Domini et posuerunt eam in loco suo in medio tabernaculi quod tetenderat ei David, et obtulit David holocausta coram Domino et pacifica. 18 Cumque conplesset offerens holocausta et pacifica, benedixit populo in nomine Domini exercituum, 19 et partitus est multitudini universae Israhel, tam viro quam mulieri, singulis, collyridam panis unam et assaturam bubulae carnis unam et similam frixam oleo, et abiit omnis populus, unusquisque in domum suam.

20 Reversusque est David ut benediceret domui suae, et egressa Michol, filia Saul, in occursum David ait, "Quam gloriosus fuit hodie rex Israhel, discoperiens se ante ancillas servorum suorum, et nudatus est quasi si nudetur unus de scurris!"

21 Dixitque David ad Michol, "Ante Dominum, qui elegit me potius quam patrem tuum et quam omnem domum eius et praecepit mihi ut essem dux super populum Domini in Israhel, 22 et ludam et vilior fiam plus quam factus sum, et ero humilis in oculis meis, et cum ancillis de quibus locuta es gloriosior apparebo." 23 Igitur Michol, filiae Saul, non est natus filius usque ad diem mortis suae.

fore the Lord, and David was girded with a linen ephod. 15 And David and all the house of Israel brought the Ark of the Covenant of the Lord *with joyful shouting* and with sound of trumpet.

16 And when the ark of the Lord was come into the city of David, Michal, the daughter of Saul, looking out through a window saw King David leaping and dancing before the Lord, and she despised him in her heart. 17 And they brought the ark of the Lord and set it in its place in the midst of the tabernacle which David had pitched for it, and David offered holocausts and peace offerings before the Lord. 18 And when he had made an end of offering holocausts and peace offerings, he blessed the people in the name of the Lord of hosts, 19 and he distributed to all the multitude of Israel, both men and women, to every one, a cake of bread and a piece of roasted beef and fine flour fried with oil, and all the people departed, every one to his house.

20 And David returned to bless his own house, and Michal, the daughter of Saul, coming out to meet David said, "How glorious was the king of Israel today, uncovering himself before the handmaids of his servants, and was naked as if one of the buffoons should be naked!"

21 And David said to Michal, "Before the Lord, who chose me rather than thy father and than all his house and commanded me to be ruler over the people of the Lord in Israel, 22 I will both play and make myself meaner than I have done, and I will be little in my own eyes, and with the handmaids of whom thou speakest I shall appear more glorious." 23 Therefore Michal, the daughter of Saul, had no child to the day of her death.

Caput 7

Factum est autem cum sedisset rex in domo sua et Dominus dedisset ei requiem undique ab universis inimicis suis, 2 dixit ad Nathan, prophetam, "Videsne quod ego habitem in domo cedrina et arca Dei posita sit in medio pellium?"

3 Dixitque Nathan ad regem, "Omne quod est in corde tuo—vade—fac, quia Dominus tecum est."

4 Factum est autem in nocte illa, et ecce: sermo Domini ad Nathan, dicens, 5 "Vade, et loquere ad servum meum David, 'Haec dicit Dominus, "Numquid tu aedificabis mihi domum ad habitandum? 6 Neque enim habitavi in domo ex die qua eduxi filios Israhel de terra Aegypti usque in diem hanc sed ambulabam in tabernaculo et in tentorio. 7 Per cuncta loca quae transivi cum omnibus filiis Israhel, numquid loquens locutus sum ad unam de tribubus Israhel, cui praecepi ut pasceret populum meum Israhel, dicens, 'Quare non aedificastis mihi domum cedrinam?'"' 8 Et nunc haec dices servo meo David, 'Haec dicit Dominus exercituum: "Ego tuli te de pascuis sequentem greges ut esses dux super populum meum Israhel, 9 et fui tecum ubicumque ambulasti et interfeci universos inimicos tuos a facie tua, fecique tibi no-

Chapter 7

David's purpose to build a temple is rewarded with the
promise of great blessings in his seed. His prayer and
thanksgiving.

And it came to pass when the king sat in his house and
the Lord had given him rest on every side from all his enemies, 2 he said to Nathan, the prophet, "Dost thou see that I
dwell in a house of cedar and the ark of God is lodged within
skins?"

3 And Nathan said to the king, "Go; do all that is in thy
heart, because the Lord is with thee."

4 But it came to pass that *night* that the word of the Lord
came to Nathan, saying, 5 "Go, and say to my servant David,
'Thus saith the Lord, "Shalt thou build me a house to dwell
in? 6 *Whereas* I have not dwelt in a house from the day that I
brought the children of Israel out of the land of Egypt even
to this day but have walked in a tabernacle and in a tent. 7 In
all the places that I have gone through with all the children
of Israel, did ever I speak *a word* to *any* one of the tribes of
Israel, whom I commanded to feed my people Israel, saying,
'Why have you not built me a house of cedar?'"' 8 And now
thus shalt thou speak to my servant David, 'Thus saith the
Lord of hosts: "I took thee out of the pastures *from* following the sheep to be ruler over my people Israel, 9 and I have
been with thee wheresoever thou hast walked and have slain

men grande, iuxta nomen magnorum qui sunt in terra, 10 et ponam locum populo meo Israhel, et plantabo eum, et habitabit sub eo et non turbabitur amplius. Nec addent filii iniquitatis ut adfligant eum sicut prius 11 ex die qua constitui iudices super populum meum Israhel, et requiem dabo tibi ab omnibus inimicis tuis. Praedicitque tibi Dominus quod domum faciat tibi Dominus. 12 Cumque conpleti fuerint dies tui et dormieris cum patribus tuis, suscitabo semen tuum post te quod egredietur de utero tuo, et firmabo regnum eius. 13 Ipse aedificabit domum nomini meo, et stabiliam thronum regni eius usque in sempiternum. 14 Ego ero ei in patrem, et ipse erit mihi in filium. Qui si inique aliquid gesserit, arguam eum in virga virorum et in plagis filiorum hominum. 15 Misericordiam autem meam non auferam ab eo sicut abstuli a Saul, quem amovi a facie tua. 16 Et fidelis erit domus tua et regnum tuum usque in aeternum ante faciem tuam, et thronus tuus erit firmus iugiter.""'"

17 Secundum omnia verba haec et iuxta universam visionem istam, sic locutus est Nathan ad David. 18 Ingressus est autem rex David et sedit coram Domino et dixit, "Quis ego sum, Domine Deus, et quae domus mea quia adduxisti me hucusque? 19 Sed et hoc parum visum est in conspectu tuo, Domine Deus, nisi loquereris etiam de domo servi tui in longinquum, ista est enim lex Adam, Domine Deus. 20 Quid ergo addere poterit adhuc David ut loquatur ad te? Tu enim scis servum tuum, Domine Deus. 21 Propter verbum tuum et secundum cor tuum fecisti omnia magnalia haec ita ut

all thy enemies from before thy face, and I have made thee a great name, like unto the name of the great ones that are on the earth, 10 and I will appoint a place for my people Israel, and I will plant them, and they shall dwell *therein* and shall be disturbed no more. Neither shall the children of iniquity afflict them any more as they did before 11 from the day that I appointed judges over my people Israel, and I will give thee rest from all thy enemies. And the Lord foretelleth to thee that the Lord will make thee a house. 12 And when thy days shall be fulfilled and thou shalt sleep with thy fathers, I will raise up thy seed after thee which shall proceed out of thy bowels, and I will establish his kingdom. 13 He shall build a house to my name, and I will establish the throne of his kingdom for ever. 14 I will be to him *a* father, and he shall be to me *a* son. And if he commit any iniquity, I will correct him with the rod of men and with the stripes of the children of men. 15 But my mercy I will not take away from him as I took it from Saul, whom I removed from before *my* face. 16 And thy house shall be faithful and thy kingdom for ever before thy face, and thy throne shall be firm for ever."'"

17 According to all these words and according to all this vision, so did Nathan speak to David. 18 And David went in and sat before the Lord and said, "Who am I, O Lord God, and what is my house that thou hast brought me thus far? 19 But yet this hath seemed little in thy sight, O Lord God, unless thou didst also speak of the house of thy servant for a long time to come, for this is the law of Adam, O Lord God. 20 And what can David say more unto thee? For thou knowest thy servant, O Lord God. 21 For thy word's sake and according to thy own heart thou hast done all these great things so that thou wouldst make it known to thy ser-

notum faceres servo tuo. 22 Idcirco magnificatus es, Domine Deus, quia non est similis tui, neque est Deus extra te, in omnibus quae audivimus auribus nostris.

23 "Quae est autem ut populus tuus Israhel gens in terra, propter quam ivit Deus ut redimeret eam sibi in populum et poneret sibi nomen faceretque eis magnalia et horribilia super terram a facie populi tui, quem redemisti tibi ex Aegypto, gentibus et diis earum? 24 Firmasti enim tibi populum tuum Israhel in populum sempiternum, et tu, Domine Deus, factus es eis in Deum.

25 "Nunc ergo, Domine Deus, verbum quod locutus es super servum tuum et super domum eius suscita in sempiternum, et fac sicut locutus es, 26 ut magnificetur nomen tuum usque in sempiternum atque dicatur, 'Dominus exercituum Deus super Israhel.' Et domus servi tui David erit stabilita coram Domino 27 quia tu, Domine exercituum, Deus Israhel, revelasti aurem servi tui, dicens, 'Domum aedificabo tibi.' Propterea invenit servus tuus cor suum ut oraret te oratione hac.

28 "Nunc ergo, Domine Deus, tu es Deus, et verba tua erunt vera, locutus es enim ad servum tuum bona haec. 29 Incipe igitur, et benedic domui servi tui ut sit in sempiternum coram te quia tu, Domine Deus, locutus es, et benedictione tua benedicetur domus servi tui in sempiternum."

vant. 22 Therefore thou art magnified, O Lord God, because there is none like to thee, neither is there any God besides thee, in all the things that we have heard with our ears.

23 "And what nation is there upon earth as thy people Israel, *whom* God went to redeem for a people to himself and to make him a name and to do for them great and terrible things upon the earth before the face of thy people, whom thou redeemedst to thyself out of Egypt, from the nations and their gods? 24 For thou hast confirmed to thyself thy people Israel to be an everlasting people, and thou, O Lord God, art become their God.

25 "And now, O Lord God, raise up for ever the word that thou hast spoken concerning thy servant and concerning his house, and do as thou hast spoken 26 that thy name may be magnified for ever and it may be said, 'The Lord of hosts is God over Israel.' And the house of thy servant David shall be established before the Lord 27 because thou, O Lord of hosts, God of Israel, hast revealed to the ear of thy servant, saying, 'I will build thee a house.' Therefore hath thy servant found *in* his heart to pray this prayer to thee.

28 "And now, O Lord God, thou art God, and thy words shall be true, for thou hast spoken to thy servant these good things. 29 *And now* begin, and bless the house of thy servant that it may *endure* for ever before thee because thou, O Lord God, hast spoken it, and with thy blessing let the house of thy servant be blessed for ever."

Caput 8

Factum est autem post haec percussit David Philisthim et humiliavit eos, et tulit David frenum tributi de manu Philisthim. 2 Et percussit Moab et mensus est eos funiculo, coaequans terrae, mensus est autem duos funiculos, unum ad occidendum et unum ad vivificandum, factusque est Moab David serviens sub tributo. 3 Et percussit David Adadezer, filium Roob, regem Soba, quando profectus est ut dominaretur super flumen Eufraten. 4 Et captis David ex parte eius mille septingentis equitibus et viginti milibus peditum subnervavit omnes iugales curruum dereliquit autem ex eis centum currus. 5 Venit quoque Syria Damasci ut praesidium ferret Adadezer, regi Soba, et percussit David de Syria viginti duo milia virorum. 6 Et posuit David praesidium in Syria Damasci, factaque est Syria David serviens sub tributo, servavitque Dominus David in omnibus, ad quaecumque profectus est. 7 Et tulit David arma aurea quae habebant servi Adadezer et detulit ea in Hierusalem. 8 Et de Bete et de Beroth, civitatibus Adadezer, tulit Rex David aes multum nimis.

Chapter 8

David's victories and his chief officers.

And it came to pass after *this* that David defeated the Philistines and brought them down, and David took the bridle of tribute out of the hand of the Philistines. 2 And he defeated Moab and measured them with a line, casting them down to the earth, and he measured with two lines, one to put to death and one to save alive, and Moab was made to serve David under tribute. 3 David defeated also Hadadezer, the son of Rehob, king of Zobah, when he went to *extend his* dominion over the river Euphrates. 4 And David took from him a thousand and seven hundred horsemen and twenty thousand footmen and houghed all the chariot horses and *only reserved* of them *for* one hundred chariots. 5 And the *Syrians* of Damascus came to succour Hadadezer, the king of Zobah, and David slew of the *Syrians* two and twenty thousand men. 6 And David put *garrisons* in Syria of Damascus, and Syria *served* David under tribute, and the Lord preserved David in all his enterprises, whithersoever he went. 7 And David took the arms of gold which the servants of Hadadezer wore and brought them to Jerusalem. 8 And out of Betah and out of Berothai, cities of Hadadezer, King David took an exceeding great quantity of brass.

9 Audivit autem Thou, rex Emath, quod percussisset David omne robur Adadezer, 10 et misit Thou Ioram, filium suum, ad Regem David, ut salutaret eum congratulans et gratias ageret eo quod expugnasset Adadezer et percussisset eum, hostis quippe erat Thou Adadezer, et in manu eius erant vasa argentea et vasa aurea et vasa aerea, 11 quae et ipsa sanctificavit Rex David Domino, cum argento et auro quae sanctificaverat de universis gentibus quas subegerat, 12 de Syria et Moab et filiis Ammon et Philisthim et Amalech et de manubiis Adadezer, filii Roob, regis Soba. 13 Fecit quoque sibi David nomen cum reverteretur capta Syria in valle Salinarum, caesis decem et octo milibus. 14 Et posuit in Idumea custodes statuitque praesidium, et facta est universa Idumea serviens David, et servavit Dominus David in omnibus ad quaecumque profectus est.

15 Et regnavit David super omnem Israhel, faciebat quoque David iudicium et iustitiam omni populo suo. 16 Ioab autem, filius Sarviae, erat super exercitum, porro Iosaphat, filius Ahilud, erat a commentariis, 17 et Sadoc, filius Achitob, et Ahimelech, filius Abiathar, sacerdotes erant, et Saraias scriba, 18 Banaias autem, filius Ioiada, super Cherethi et Felethi, filii autem David sacerdotes erant.

9 And Toi, the king of Hamath, heard that David had defeated all the forces of Hadadezer, 10 and Toi sent Joram, his son, to King David, to salute him and to congratulate with him and to *return* him thanks because he had fought against Hadadezer and had defeated him, for Toi was an enemy to Hadadezer, and in his hand were vessels of gold and vessels of silver and vessels of brass, 11 and King David dedicated them to the Lord, together with the silver and gold that he had dedicated of all the nations which he had subdued, 12 of Syria and *of* Moab and *of* the children of Ammon and *of* the Philistines and *of* Amalek and of the spoils of Hadadezer, the son of Rehob, king of Zobah. 13 David also made himself a name when he returned after taking Syria in the valley of the saltpits, killing eighteen thousand. 14 And he put guards in Edom and placed there a garrison, and all Edom was made to serve David, and the Lord preserved David in all *enterprises* he went about.

15 And David reigned over all Israel, and David did judgment and justice to all his people. 16 And Joab, the son of Zeruiah, was over the army, and Jehoshaphat, the son of Ahilud, was *recorder,* 17 and Zadok, the son of Ahitub, and Ahimelech, the son of Abiathar, were the priests, and Seraiah was the scribe, 18 and Benaiah, the son of Jehoiada, was over the Cherethites and Pelethites, and the sons of David were the *princes.*

Caput 9

Et dixit David, "Putasne est aliquis qui remanserit de domo Saul ut faciam cum eo misericordiam propter Ionathan?" 2 Erat autem de domo Saul servus nomine Siba, quem cum vocasset rex ad se, dixit ei, "Tune es Siba?"

Et ille respondit, "Ego sum servus tuus."

3 Et ait rex, "Num superest aliquis de domo Saul ut faciam cum eo misericordiam Dei?"

Dixitque Siba regi, "Superest filius Ionathan, debilis pedibus."

4 "Ubi," inquit, "est?"

Et Siba ad regem, "Ecce," ait, "in domo est Machir, filii Amihel, in Lodabar."

5 Misit ergo Rex David et tulit eum de domo Machir, filii Amihel, de Lodabar. 6 Cum autem venisset Mifiboseth, filius Ionathan, filii Saul, ad David, corruit in faciem suam et adoravit. Dixitque David, "Mifiboseth?"

Qui respondit, "Adsum, servus tuus."

Chapter 9

David's kindness to Mephibosheth for the sake of his father Jonathan.

And David said, "Is there any one, think you, *left* of the house of Saul that I may shew kindness to him for Jonathan's sake?" 2 Now there was of the house of Saul a servant named Ziba, and when the king had called him to him, he said to him, "Art thou Ziba?"

And he answered, "I am *Ziba,* thy servant."

3 And the king said, "Is there any one left of the house of Saul that I may shew the mercy of God unto him?"

And Ziba said to the king, "There is a son of Jonathan left, *who is* lame of his feet."

4 "Where is he?" said he.

And Ziba said to the king, "Behold: he is in the house of Machir, the son of Ammiel, in Lo-debar."

5 Then King David sent and brought him out of the house of Machir, the son of Ammiel, of Lo-debar. 6 And when Mephibosheth, the son of Jonathan, the son of Saul, was come to David, he fell on his face and worshipped. And David said, "Mephibosheth?"

And he answered, "*Behold* thy servant."

7 Et ait ei David, "Ne timeas, quia faciens faciam in te misericordiam, propter Ionathan, patrem tuum, et restituam tibi omnes agros Saul, patris tui, et tu comedes panem in mensa mea semper."

8 Qui adorans eum dixit, "Quis ego sum, servus tuus, quoniam respexisti super canem mortuum similem mei?"

9 Vocavit itaque rex Sibam, puerum Saul, et dixit ei, "Omnia quaecumque fuerunt Saul et universam domum eius dedi filio domini tui. 10 Operare, igitur, ei terram, tu et filii tui et servi tui, et inferes filio domini tui cibos ut alatur, Mifiboseth autem, filius domini tui, comedet semper panem super mensam meam." Erant autem Sibae quindecim filii et viginti servi.

11 Dixitque Siba ad regem, "Sicut iussisti, domine mi, rex, servo tuo, sic faciet servus tuus, et Mifiboseth comedet super mensam tuam quasi unus de filiis regis."

12 Habebat autem Mifiboseth filium parvulum nomine Micha, omnis vero cognatio domus Siba serviebat Mifiboseth. 13 Porro Mifiboseth habitabat in Hierusalem, quia de mensa regis iugiter vescebatur. Et erat claudus utroque pede.

7 And David said to him, "Fear not, for I will *surely shew* thee mercy for Jonathan, thy father's, sake, and I will restore *the* lands of Saul, thy father, and thou shalt eat bread at my table always."

8 He bowed down to him and said, "Who am I, thy servant, that thou shouldst look upon such a dead dog as I am?"

9 Then the king called Ziba, the servant of Saul, and said to him, "All that belonged to Saul and all his house I have given to thy master's son. 10 Thou, therefore, and thy sons and thy servants shall till the land for him, and thou shalt bring in food for thy master's son that he may be maintained, and Mephibosheth, the son of thy master, shall always eat bread at my table." And Ziba had fifteen sons and twenty servants.

11 And Ziba said to the king, "As thou, my lord, the king, hast commanded thy servant, so will thy servant do, and Mephibosheth shall eat at my table as one of the sons of the king."

12 And Mephibosheth had a young son whose name was Mica, and all the kindred of the house of Ziba served Mephibosheth. 13 But Mephibosheth dwelt in Jerusalem, because he ate always of the king's table. And he was lame of both feet.

Caput 10

Factum est autem post haec ut moreretur rex filiorum Ammon et regnaret Anon, filius eius, pro eo. 2 Dixitque David, "Faciam misericordiam cum Anon, filio Naas, sicut fecit pater eius mecum misericordiam." Misit ergo David consolans eum per servos suos super patris interitu. Cum autem venissent servi David in terram filiorum Ammon, 3 dixerunt principes filiorum Ammon ad Anon, dominum suum, "Putas quod propter honorem patris tui David miserit ad te consolatores? Et non ideo ut investigaret et exploraret civitatem et everteret eam misit David servos suos ad te?" 4 Tulit itaque Anon servos David rasitque dimidiam partem barbae eorum et praecidit vestes eorum medias usque ad nates et dimisit eos.

5 Quod cum nuntiatum esset David, misit in occursum eorum, erant enim viri confusi turpiter valde, et mandavit eis David, "Manete Hiericho donec crescat barba vestra, et tunc revertimini." 6 Videntes autem filii Ammon quod iniuriam fecissent David miserunt et conduxerunt mercede Syrum Roob et Syrum Soba, viginti milia peditum, et a rege Maacha mille viros et ab Histob duodecim milia virorum.

Chapter 10

The Ammonites shamefully abuse the ambassadors of David. They hire the Syrians to their assistance but are overthrown with their allies.

And it came to pass after *this* that the king of the children of Ammon died and Hanun, his son, reigned in his stead. 2 And David said, "I will shew kindness to Hanun, the son of Nahash, as his father shewed kindness to me." So David sent *his servants to comfort* him for the death of his father. But when the servants of David were come into the land of the children of Ammon, 3 the princes of the children of Ammon said to Hanun, their lord, "Thinkest thou that for the honour of thy father David hath sent comforters to thee? And hath not David rather sent his servants to thee to search and spy into the city and overthrow it?" 4 Wherefore Hanun took the servants of David and shaved off the one half of their *beards* and cut away half of their garments even to the buttocks and sent them away.

5 When this was told David, he sent to meet them, for the men were *sadly put to confusion,* and David commanded them, *saying,* "Stay at Jericho till your *beards* be grown, and then return." 6 And the children of Ammon seeing that they had done an injury to David sent and hired the *Syrians* of Rehob and the *Syrians* of Zobah, twenty thousand footmen, and of the king of Maacah a thousand men and of Tob

7 Quod cum audisset David, misit Ioab et omnem exercitum bellatorum. 8 Egressi sunt ergo filii Ammon et direxerunt aciem ante ipsum introitum portae, Syrus autem Soba et Roob et Histob et Maacha seorsum erant in campo. 9 Videns igitur Ioab quod praeparatum esset adversum se proelium et ex adverso et post tergum elegit ex omnibus electis Israhel et instruxit aciem contra Syrum, 10 reliquam autem partem populi tradidit Abisai, fratri suo, qui direxit aciem adversum filios Ammon.

11 Et ait Ioab, "Si praevaluerint adversum me Syri, eris mihi in adiutorium, si autem filii Ammon praevaluerint adversum te, auxiliabor tibi. 12 Viriliter age, et pugnemus pro populo nostro et civitate Dei nostri, Dominus autem faciet quod bonum est in conspectu suo."

13 Iniit itaque Ioab et populus qui erat cum eo certamen contra Syros, qui statim fugerunt a facie eius. 14 Filii autem Ammon videntes quod fugissent Syri, fugerunt et ipsi a facie Abisai et ingressi sunt civitatem, reversusque est Ioab a filiis Ammon et venit Hierusalem. 15 Videntes igitur Syri quoniam corruissent coram Israhel congregati sunt pariter. 16 Misitque Adadezer et eduxit Syros qui erant trans fluvium et adduxit exercitum eorum, Sobach autem, magister militiae Adadezer, erat princeps eorum.

17 Quod cum nuntiatum esset David, contraxit omnem Israhelem et transivit Iordanem venitque in Helema. Et direxerunt aciem Syri ex adverso David et pugnaverunt contra eum. 18 Fugeruntque Syri a facie Israhel, et occidit David de Syris septingentos currus et quadraginta milia equitum et Sobach, principem militiae, percussit, qui statim mortuus

twelve thousand men. 7 And when David heard this, he sent Joab and the whole army of warriors. 8 And the children of Ammon came out and set their men in array at the entering in of the gate, but the *Syrians* of Zobah and of Rehob and of Tob and of Maacah were by themselves in the field. 9 Then Joab seeing that the battle was prepared against him both before and behind chose of all the choice men of Israel and put them in array against the *Syrians,* 10 and the rest of the people he delivered to Abishai, his brother, who set them in array against the children of Ammon.

11 And Joab said, "If the *Syrians are too strong for me,* then thou shalt help me, but if the children of Ammon *are too strong for thee,* then I will help thee. 12 *Be of good courage,* and let us fight for our people and for the city of our God, and the Lord will do what is good in his sight."

13 And Joab and the people that were with him began to fight against the Syrians, and they immediately fled *before him.* 14 And the children of Ammon seeing that the Syrians were fled, they fled also *before* Abishai and entered into the city, and Joab returned from the children of Ammon and came to Jerusalem. 15 Then the Syrians seeing that they had fallen before Israel gathered themselves together. 16 And Hadadezer sent and fetched the Syrians that were beyond the river and brought over their army, and Shobach, the captain of the host of Hadadezer, was their general.

17 And when this was told David, he gathered all Israel together and passed over the Jordan and came to Helam. And the Syrians set themselves in array against David and fought against him. 18 And the Syrians fled *before* Israel, and David slew of the Syrians the men of seven hundred chariots and forty thousand horsemen and smote Shobach, the captain

est. 19 Videntes autem universi reges qui erant in praesidio Adadezer victos se ab Israhel expaverunt et fugerunt, quinquaginta et octo milia coram Israhel. Et fecerunt pacem cum Israhel et servierunt eis, timueruntque Syri auxilium praebere ultra filiis Ammon.

Caput 11

Factum est autem vertente anno, eo tempore quo solent reges ad bella procedere, misit David Ioab et servos suos cum eo et universum Israhel, et vastaverunt filios Ammon et obsederunt Rabba, David autem remansit in Hierusalem. 2 Dum haec agerentur, accidit ut surgeret David de strato suo post meridiem et deambularet in solario domus regiae, viditque mulierem se lavantem ex adverso super solarium suum, erat autem mulier pulchra valde. 3 Misit ergo rex et requisivit quae esset mulier, nuntiatumque ei est quod ipsa esset Bethsabee, filia Heliam, uxor Uriae, Hetthei. 4 Missis itaque David nuntiis tulit eam, quae cum ingressa esset ad illum, dormivit cum ea, statimque sanctificata est ab inmun-

of the army, who presently died. 19 And all the kings that were *auxiliaries of* Hadadezer seeing themselves overcome by Israel were afraid and fled away, eight and fifty thousand men before Israel. And they made peace with Israel and served them, and *all* the Syrians were afraid to help the children of Ammon any more.

Chapter 11

David falleth into the crime of adultery with Bathsheba and
not finding other means to conceal it causeth her husband,
Uriah, to be slain, then marrieth her, who beareth him a son.

And it came to pass at the return of the year, at the time when kings *go* forth to war, that David sent Joab and his servants with him and all Israel, and they spoiled the children of Ammon and besieged Rabbah, but David remained in Jerusalem. 2 In the mean time, it happened that David arose from his bed after noon and walked upon the roof of the king's house, and he saw upon the roof of his house a woman washing herself over against him, and the woman was very beautiful, 3 and the king sent and inquired who the woman was. And it was told him that she was Bathsheba, the daughter of Eliam, the wife of Uriah, the Hittite. 4 And David sent messengers and took her, *and* she came in to him, *and* he slept with her, and presently she was purified from her un-

ditia sua, 5 et reversa est in domum suam concepto fetu. Mittensque nuntiavit David et ait, "Concepi."

6 Misit autem David ad Ioab, dicens, "Mitte ad me Uriam, Hettheum." Misitque Ioab Uriam ad David. 7 Et venit Urias ad David, quaesivitque David quam recte ageret Ioab et populus et quomodo administraretur bellum. 8 Et dixit David ad Uriam, "Vade in domum tuam, et lava pedes tuos." Et egressus est Urias de domo regis, secutusque est eum cibus regius. 9 Dormivit autem Urias ante portam domus regiae cum aliis servis domini sui et non descendit ad domum suam.

10 Nuntiatumque est David a dicentibus, "Non ivit Urias in domum suam."

Et ait David ad Uriam, "Numquid non de via venisti? Quare non descendisti in domum tuam?"

11 Et ait Urias ad David, "Arca Dei et Israhel et Iuda habitant in papilionibus, et dominus meus Ioab et servi domini mei super faciem terrae manent, et ego ingrediar domum meam ut comedam et bibam et dormiam cum uxore mea? Per salutem tuam et per salutem animae tuae non faciam rem hanc."

12 Ait ergo David ad Uriam, "Mane hic etiam hodie, et cras dimittam te." Mansit Urias in Hierusalem die illa et altera. 13 Et vocavit eum David ut comederet coram se et biberet, et inebriavit eum, qui egressus vespere dormivit in stratu suo cum servis domini sui et in domum suam non descendit. 14 Factum est ergo mane, et scripsit David epistulam ad Ioab, misitque per manum Uriae, 15 scribens in epistula, "Ponite Uriam ex adverso belli ubi fortissimum proelium est, et derelinquite eum ut percussus intereat." 16 Igitur cum

cleanness, 5 and she returned to her house having conceived. And she sent and told David and said, "I have conceived."

6 And David sent to Joab, saying, "Send me Uriah, the Hittite." And Joab sent Uriah to David. 7 And Uriah came to David, and David asked *how* Joab did and the people and how the war was carried on. 8 And David said to Uriah, "Go into thy house, and wash thy feet." And Uriah went out from the king's house, and there went out after him a mess of meat from the king. 9 But Uriah slept before the gate of the king's house with the other servants of his lord and went not down to his own house.

10 And it was told David by *some* that said, "Uriah went not to his house."

And David said to Uriah, "Didst thou not come from thy journey? Why didst thou not go down to thy house?"

11 And Uriah said to David, "The ark of God and Israel and Judah dwell in tents, and my lord Joab and the servants of my lord abide upon the face of the earth, and shall I go into my house to eat and to drink and to sleep with my wife? By thy welfare and by the welfare of thy soul I will not do this thing."

12 Then David said to Uriah, "Tarry here today also, and tomorrow I will send thee away." Uriah tarried in Jerusalem that day and the next. 13 And David called him to eat and to drink before him, and he made him drunk, and he went out in the evening and slept on his couch with the servants of his lord and went not down into his house. 14 *And when* the morning was come, *David* wrote a letter to Joab and sent it by the hand of Uriah, 15 writing in the letter, "Set ye Uriah in the front of the battle where the fight is strongest, and leave ye him that he may be wounded and die." 16 Wherefore as

Ioab obsideret urbem, posuit Uriam in loco quo sciebat viros esse fortissimos. 17 Egressique viri de civitate bellabant adversum Ioab, et ceciderunt de populo servorum David, et mortuus est etiam Urias, Hettheus.

18 Misit itaque Ioab, et nuntiavit David omnia verba proelii. 19 Praecepitque nuntio, dicens, "Cum conpleveris universos sermones belli ad regem, 20 si eum videris indignari et dixerit, 'Quare accessistis ad murum ut proeliaremini? An ignorabatis quod multa desuper ex muro tela mittantur? 21 Quis percussit Abimelech, filium Hierobaal? Nonne mulier misit super eum fragmen molae de muro et interfecit eum in Thebes? Quare iuxta murum accessistis?' dices, 'Etiam servus tuus Urias, Hettheus, occubuit.'"

22 Abiit ergo nuntius et venit et narravit David omnia quae ei praeceperat Ioab. 23 Et dixit nuntius ad David, "Praevaluerunt adversum nos viri, et egressi sunt ad nos in agrum, nos autem facto impetu persecuti eos sumus usque ad portam civitatis. 24 Et direxerunt iacula sagittarii ad servos tuos ex muro desuper, mortuique sunt de servis regis, quin etiam servus tuus Urias, Hettheus, mortuus est."

25 Et dixit David ad nuntium, "Haec dices Ioab: 'Non te frangat ista res, varius enim eventus est belli, et nunc hunc, nunc illum consumit gladius. Conforta bellatores tuos adversum urbem ut destruas eam, et exhortare eos.'"

26 Audivit autem uxor Uriae quod mortuus esset Urias, vir suus, et planxit eum. 27 Transactoque luctu, misit David et

Joab was besieging the city, he put Uriah in the place where he knew the bravest men were. 17 And the men coming out of the city fought against Joab, and there fell *some* of the people of the servants of David, and Uriah, the Hittite, was killed also.

18 Then Joab sent, and told David all things concerning the battle. 19 And he charged the messenger, saying, "When thou hast told all the words of the battle to the king, 20 if thou see him to be angry and he shall say, 'Why did you approach *so near* to the wall to fight? Knew you not that many darts are thrown from above off the wall? 21 Who killed Abimelech, the son of Jerubbaal? Did not a woman cast a piece of a millstone upon him from the wall and slew him in Thebez? Why did you go near the wall?' thou shalt say, 'Thy servant Uriah, the Hittite, is also slain.'"

22 So the messenger departed and came and told David all that Joab had commanded him. 23 And the messenger said to David, "The men prevailed against us, and they came out to us into the field, and we *vigorously charged and* pursued them even to the gate of the city. 24 And the archers shot their arrows at thy servants from off the wall above, and *some* of the king's servants are slain, *and* thy servant Uriah, the Hittite, is also dead."

25 And David said to the messenger, "Thus shalt thou say to Joab: 'Let not this thing discourage thee, for various is the event of war *and sometimes one, sometimes another is consumed by the sword.* Encourage thy warriors against the city, and exhort them that thou mayest overthrow it.'"

26 And the wife of Uriah heard that Uriah, her husband, was dead, and she mourned for him. 27 And the mourning

introduxit eam in domum suam, et facta est ei uxor, peperitque ei filium.

Et displicuit verbum hoc quod fecerat David coram Domino.

Caput 12

Misit ergo Dominus Nathan ad David, qui cum venisset ad eum dixit ei, "Duo viri erant in civitate una, unus dives, et alter pauper. 2 Dives habebat oves et boves plurimos valde, 3 pauper autem nihil habebat omnino praeter ovem unam parvulam quam emerat et nutrierat et quae creverat apud eum cum filiis eius simul, de pane illius comedens et de calice eius bibens et in sinu illius dormiens, eratque illi sicut filia. 4 Cum autem peregrinus quidam venisset ad divitem, parcens ille sumere de ovibus et de bubus suis ut exhiberet convivium peregrino illi qui venerat ad se tulit ovem viri pauperis et praeparavit cibos homini qui venerat ad se."

5 Iratus autem indignatione David adversus hominem il-

being over, David sent and brought her into his house, and she became his wife, and she bore him a son.

And this thing which David had done was displeasing to the Lord.

Chapter 12

Nathan's parable. David confesseth his sin and is forgiven, yet so as to be sentenced to most severe temporal punishments. The death of the child. The birth of Solomon. The taking of Rabbah.

And the Lord sent Nathan to David, and when he was come to him he said to him, "There were two men in one city, the one rich, and the other poor. 2 The rich man had exceeding many sheep and oxen, 3 but the poor man had nothing at all but one little ewe lamb which he had bought and nourished up and which had grown up in his house together with his children, eating of his bread and drinking of his cup and sleeping in his bosom, and it was unto him as a daughter. 4 And when a certain stranger was come to the rich man, he spared to take of his own sheep and oxen to make a feast for that stranger who was come to him but took the poor man's ewe and *dressed it* for the man that was come to him."

5 And *David's anger being* exceedingly *kindled* against that

lum nimis, dixit ad Nathan, "Vivit Dominus, quoniam filius mortis est vir qui fecit hoc. 6 Ovem reddet in quadruplum eo quod fecerit verbum istud et non pepercerit."

7 Dixit autem Nathan ad David, "Tu es ille vir. Haec dicit Dominus, Deus Israhel, 'Ego unxi te in regem super Israhel, et ego erui te de manu Saul 8 et dedi tibi domum domini tui et uxores domini tui in sinu tuo dedique tibi domum Israhel et Iuda, et si parva sunt ista, adiciam tibi multo maiora. 9 Quare ergo contempsisti verbum Domini ut faceres malum in conspectu meo? Uriam, Hettheum, percussisti gladio et uxorem illius accepisti in uxorem tibi et interfecisti eum gladio filiorum Ammon. 10 Quam ob rem non recedet gladius de domo tua usque in sempiternum, eo quod despexeris me et tuleris uxorem Uriae, Hetthei, ut esset uxor tua.'

11 "Itaque haec dicit Dominus, 'Ecce: ego suscitabo super te malum de domo tua, et tollam uxores tuas in oculis tuis et dabo proximo tuo, et dormiet cum uxoribus tuis in oculis solis huius, 12 tu enim fecisti abscondite, ego vero faciam verbum istud in conspectu omnis Israhel et in conspectu solis.'"

13 Et dixit David ad Nathan, "Peccavi Domino."

Dixitque Nathan ad David, "Dominus quoque transtulit peccatum tuum; non morieris. 14 Verumtamen, quoniam blasphemare fecisti inimicos Domini, propter verbum hoc filius qui natus est tibi morte morietur." 15 Et reversus est Nathan in domum suam. Percussit quoque Dominus parvulum quem pepererat uxor Uriae David, et desperatus est.

man, he said to Nathan, "As the Lord liveth, the man that hath done this is a child of death. 6 He shall restore the ewe fourfold because he did this thing and had no pity."

7 And Nathan said to David, "Thou art *the* man. Thus saith the Lord, the God of Israel, 'I anointed thee king over Israel, and I delivered thee from the hand of Saul 8 and gave thee thy master's house and thy master's wives into thy bosom and gave thee the house of Israel and Judah, and if these things be little, I shall add far greater things unto thee. 9 Why therefore hast thou despised the word of the Lord to do evil in my sight? Thou hast killed Uriah, the Hittite, with the sword and hast taken his wife to be thy wife and hast slain him with the sword of the children of Ammon. 10 Therefore the sword shall never depart from thy house, because thou hast despised me and hast taken the wife of Uriah, the Hittite, to be thy wife.'

11 "*Thus* saith the Lord, 'Behold: I will raise up evil against thee out of thy own house, and I will take thy wives before thy eyes and give them to thy neighbour, and he shall lie with thy wives in the sight of this sun, 12 for thou didst it secretly, but I will do this thing in the sight of all Israel and in the sight of the sun.'"

13 And David said to Nathan, "I have sinned against the Lord."

And Nathan said to David, "The Lord also hath taken away thy sin; thou shalt not die. 14 Nevertheless, because thou hast given occasion to the enemies of the Lord to blaspheme, for this thing the child that is born to thee shall *surely* die." 15 And Nathan returned to his house. The Lord also struck the child which the wife of Uriah had borne to David, and *his life* was despaired of.

16 Deprecatusque est David Dominum pro parvulo, et ieiunavit David ieiunio et ingressus seorsum iacuit super terram. 17 Venerunt autem seniores domus eius cogentes eum ut surgeret de terra, qui noluit, neque comedit cum eis cibum. 18 Accidit autem die septima ut moreretur infans, timueruntque servi David nuntiare ei quod mortuus esset parvulus, dixerunt enim, "Ecce: cum parvulus adhuc vive-ret, loquebamur ad eum, et non audiebat vocem nostram. Quanto magis si dixerimus mortuus est puer se adfliget?"

19 Cum ergo vidisset David servos suos musitantes, intel-lexit quod mortuus esset infantulus, dixitque ad servos suos, "Num mortuus est puer?"

Qui responderunt ei, "Mortuus est."

20 Surrexit igitur David de terra et lotus unctusque est, cumque mutasset vestem ingressus est domum Domini et adoravit, et venit in domum suam petivitque ut ponerent ei panem et comedit. 21 Dixerunt autem ei servi sui, "Quis est sermo quem fecisti? Propter infantem cum adhuc viveret ieiunasti et flebas, mortuo autem puero surrexisti et come-disti panem."

22 Qui ait, "Propter infantem dum adhuc viveret, ieiunavi et flevi, dicebam enim, 'Quis scit si forte donet eum mihi Dominus, et vivat infans?' 23 Nunc autem quia mortuus est, quare ieiuno? Numquid potero revocare eum amplius? Ego vadam magis ad eum, ille vero non revertetur ad me."

16 And David besought the Lord for the child, and David *kept* a fast and going in by himself lay upon the ground. 17 And the ancients of his house came *to make him rise* from the ground, but he would not, neither did he eat meat with them. 18 And it came to pass on the seventh day that the child died, and the servants of David feared to tell him that the child was dead, for they said, "Behold: when the child was yet alive, we spoke to him, and he would not hearken to our voice. How much more will he afflict himself if we tell him that the child is dead?"

19 But when David saw his servants whispering, he understood that the child was dead, and he said to his servants, "Is the child dead?"

They answered him, "He is dead."

20 Then David arose from the ground and washed and anointed himself, and when he had changed his apparel he went into the house of the Lord and worshipped, and *then* he came into his own house, and *he called for* bread and ate. 21 And his servants said to him, "What thing is this that thou hast done? Thou didst fast and weep for the child while it was alive, but when the child was dead, thou didst rise up and eat bread."

22 And he said, *"While the child* was yet alive, I fasted and wept for him, for I said, 'Who knoweth *whether* the Lord may not give him to me, and the child may live?' 23 But now that he is dead, why *should* I fast? Shall I be able to bring him back any more? I shall go to him rather, but he shall not return to me."

24 Et consolatus est David Bethsabee, uxorem suam, ingressusque ad eam dormivit cum ea, quae genuit filium, et vocavit nomen eius Salomon, et Dominus dilexit eum. 25 Misitque in manu Nathan, prophetae, et vocavit nomen eius Amabilis Domino, eo quod diligeret eum Dominus.

26 Igitur pugnabat Ioab contra Rabbath filiorum Ammon et expugnabat urbem regiam. 27 Misitque Ioab nuntios ad David, dicens, "Dimicavi adversum Rabbath et capienda est urbs Aquarum. 28 Nunc, igitur, congrega reliquam partem populi, et obside civitatem, et cape eam, ne cum a me vastata fuerit urbs nomini meo adscribatur victoria." 29 Congregavit itaque David omnem populum et profectus est adversum Rabbath, cumque dimicasset cepit eam. 30 Et tulit diadema regis eorum de capite eius, pondo auri talentum, habens gemmas pretiosissimas, et inpositum est super caput David, sed et praedam civitatis asportavit multam valde. 31 Populum quoque eius adducens serravit et circumegit super eos ferrata carpenta divisitque cultris et transduxit in typo laterum. Sic fecit universis civitatibus filiorum Ammon. Et reversus est David et omnis exercitus in Hierusalem.

24 And David comforted Bathsheba, his wife, and went in unto her and slept with her, and she bore a son, and he called his name Solomon, and the Lord loved him. 25 And he sent by the hand of Nathan, the prophet, and called his name Amiable to the Lord, because the Lord loved him.

26 And Joab fought against Rabbah of the children of Ammon and *laid close siege to* the royal city. 27 And Joab sent messengers to David, saying, "I have fought against Rabbah and the city of Waters is about to be taken. 28 Now, therefore, gather thou the rest of the people together, and besiege the city, and take it, lest when the city shall be wasted by me the victory be ascribed to my name." 29 Then David gathered all the people together and went out against Rabbah, and after fighting he took it. 30 And he took the crown of their king from his head, *the weight of which was* a talent of gold, *set with* most precious stones, and it was put upon David's head, and the spoils of the city, *which were* very great, he carried away. 31 And bringing forth the people thereof he sawed them and drove over them chariots armed with iron and divided them with knives and made them pass through brickkilns. So did he to all the cities of the children of Ammon. And David returned *with* all the army to Jerusalem.

Caput 13

Factum est autem post haec ut Absalom, filii David, sororem speciosissimam vocabulo Thamar adamaret Amnon, filius David. 2 Et deperiret eam valde ita ut aegrotaret propter amorem eius, quia cum esset virgo, difficile ei videbatur ut quippiam inhoneste ageret cum ea. 3 Erat autem Amnonis amicus nomine Ionadab, filius Semaa, fratris David, vir prudens valde, 4 qui dixit ad eum, "Quare sic adtenuaris macie, fili regis, per singulos dies? Cur non indicas mihi?"

Dixitque ei Amnon, "Thamar, sororem Absalom fratris mei, amo."

5 Cui respondit Ionadab, "Cuba super lectulum tuum, et languorem simula, cumque venerit pater tuus ut visitet te, dic ei, 'Veniat, oro, Thamar soror mea, ut det mihi cibum et faciat mihi pulmentum ut comedam de manu eius.'"

6 Accubuit itaque Amnon et quasi aegrotare coepit, cumque venisset rex ad visitandum eum, ait Amnon ad regem, "Veniat, obsecro, Thamar soror mea ut faciat in oculis meis duas sorbitiunculas et cibum capiam de manu eius."

Chapter 13

Amnon ravisheth Tamar, for which Absalom killeth him and flieth to Geshur.

And it came to pass after *this* that Amnon, the son of David, loved the sister of Absalom, the son of David, *who was* very beautiful, *and her name was* Tamar. 2 And he was exceedingly fond of her so that he fell sick for the love of her, for as she was a virgin, *he thought it* hard to do any thing dishonestly with her. 3 Now Amnon had a friend named Jonadab, the son of Shimeah, the brother of David, a very wise man, 4 and he said to him, "Why *dost thou grow so lean* from day to day, O son of the king? Why dost thou not tell me *the reason of it?*"

And Amnon said to him, "I am in love with Tamar, the sister of my brother Absalom."

5 And Jonadab said to him, "Lie down upon thy bed, and feign thyself sick, and when thy father shall come to visit thee, say to him, 'Let my sister Tamar, I pray thee, come to me to give me *to eat* and to make me a mess that I may eat it at her hand.'"

6 So Amnon lay down and *made as if he were* sick, and when the king came to visit him, Amnon said to the king, "I pray thee, let my sister Tamar come and make in my sight two little messes *that* I may eat at her hand."

7 Misit ergo David ad Thamar domum, dicens, "Veni in domum Amnon fratris tui, et fac ei pulmentum."

8 Venitque Thamar in domum Amnon, fratris sui, ille autem iacebat. Quae tollens farinam commiscuit, et liquefaciens in oculis eius coxit sorbitiunculas. 9 Tollensque quod coxerat effudit et posuit coram eo, et noluit comedere. Dixitque Amnon, "Eicite universos a me." Cumque eiecissent omnes, 10 dixit Amnon ad Thamar, "Infer cibum in conclave ut vescar de manu tua." Tulit ergo Thamar sorbitiunculas quas fecerat et intulit ad Amnon fratrem suum in conclave. 11 Cumque obtulisset ei cibum adprehendit eam et ait, "Veni; cuba mecum, soror mea."

12 Quae respondit ei, "Noli, frater mi; noli opprimere me, neque enim hoc fas est in Israhel. Noli facere stultitiam hanc, 13 ego enim ferre non potero obprobrium meum, et tu eris quasi unus de insipientibus in Israhel, quin potius loquere ad regem, et non negabit me tibi." 14 Noluit autem adquiescere precibus eius sed praevalens viribus oppressit eam et cubavit cum illa. 15 Et exosam eam habuit Amnon magno odio nimis ita ut maius esset odium quo oderat eam amore quo ante dilexerat. Dixitque ei Amnon, "Surge, et vade!"

16 Quae respondit ei, "Maius est hoc malum quod nunc agis adversum me quam quod ante fecisti expellens me."

Et noluit audire eam, 17 sed vocato puero qui ministrabat ei dixit, "Eice hanc a me foras, et claude ostium post eam." 18 Quae induta erat talari tunica, huiuscemodi enim filiae re-

7 Then David sent home to Tamar, saying, "Come to the house of thy brother Amnon, and make him a mess."

8 And Tamar came to the house of Amnon, her brother, but he *was laid down*. And she took meal and tempered it, and dissolving it in his sight she made little messes. 9 And taking what she had boiled she poured it out and set it before him, *but* he would not eat. And Amnon said, "Put out all persons from me." And when they had put all persons out, 10 Amnon said to Tamar, "Bring the mess into the chamber that I may eat at thy hand." And Tamar took the little messes which she had made and brought them in to her brother Amnon in the chamber. 11 And when she had presented him the meat he took hold of her and said, "Come; lie with me, my sister."

12 She answered him, "Do not so, my brother; do not force me, for *no such thing must be done* in Israel. Do not thou this folly, 13 for I shall not be able to bear my shame, and thou shalt be as one of the fools in Israel, but rather speak to the king, and he will not deny me to thee." 14 But he would not hearken to her prayers but *being stronger* overpowered her and lay with her. 15 Then Amnon hated her with an exceeding great hatred so that the hatred wherewith he hated her was greater than the love with which he had loved her before. And Amnon said to her, "Arise, and *get thee gone!*"

16 She answered him, "This evil which now thou dost against me in driving me away is greater than that which thou didst before."

And he would not hearken to her, 17 but calling the servant that ministered to him he said, "Thrust this woman out from me, and shut the door after her." 18 And she was clothed with a long robe, for the king's daughters that were virgins

gis virgines vestibus utebantur. Eiecit itaque eam minister illius foras clausitque fores post eam.

19 Quae aspergens cinerem capiti suo scissa talari tunica inpositisque manibus super caput suum ibat ingrediens et clamans. 20 Dixit autem ei Absalom, frater suus, "Num Amnon frater tuus concubuit tecum? Sed nunc, soror, tace— frater tuus est—neque adfligas cor tuum pro re hac." Mansit itaque Thamar contabescens in domo Absalom, fratris sui.

21 Cum autem audisset Rex David verba haec contristatus est valde. 22 Porro non est locutus Absalom ad Amnon nec malum nec bonum, oderat enim Absalom Amnon eo quod violasset Thamar sororem suam. 23 Factum est autem post tempus biennii ut tonderentur oves Absalom in Baalasor, quae est iuxta Ephraim, et vocavit Absalom omnes filios regis. 24 Venitque ad regem et ait ad eum, "Ecce: tondentur oves servi tui. Veniat, oro, rex cum servis suis ad servum suum."

25 Dixitque rex ad Absalom, "Noli, fili mi, noli rogare ut veniamus omnes et gravemus te." Cum autem cogeret eum et noluisset ire, benedixit ei.

26 Et ait Absalom, "Si non vis venire, veniat, obsecro, nobiscum saltem Amnon frater meus."

Dixitque ad eum rex, "Non est necesse ut vadat tecum." 27 Coegit itaque eum Absalom et dimisit cum eo Amnon et universos filios regis. Feceratque Absalom convivium quasi convivium regis. 28 Praeceperat autem Absalom pueris suis, dicens, "Observate cum temulentus fuerit Amnon vino et dixero vobis, 'Percutite eum, et interficite.' Nolite timere, ego enim sum qui praecipio vobis. Roboramini, et estote viri

used such kind of garments. Then his servant thrust her out and shut the door after her.

19 And she put ashes on her head and rent her long robe and laid her hands upon her head and *went on* crying. 20 And Absalom, her brother, said to her, "Hath thy brother Amnon lain with thee? But now, sister, hold thy peace—he is thy brother—and afflict not thy heart for this thing." So Tamar remained pining away in the house of Absalom, her brother.

21 And when King David heard of these things he was exceedingly grieved, *and he would not afflict the spirit of his son Amnon, for he loved him because he was his firstborn.* 22 But Absalom spoke not to Amnon neither good nor evil, for Absalom hated Amnon because he had ravished his sister Tamar. 23 And it came to pass after *two* years that the sheep of Absalom were shorn in Baal-hazor, which is near Ephraim, and Absalom *invited* all the king's sons. 24 And he came to the king and said to him, "Behold: thy servant's sheep are shorn. Let the king, I pray, with his servants come to his servant."

25 And the king said to Absalom, "Nay, my son, do not ask that we should all come and *be chargeable to* thee." And when he pressed him and he would not go, he blessed him.

26 And Absalom said, "If thou wilt not come, at least let my brother Amnon, I beseech thee, come with us."

And the king said to him, "It is not necessary that he should go with thee." 27 But Absalom pressed him *so that* he let Amnon and all the king's sons go with him. And Absalom made a feast as it were the feast of a king. 28 And Absalom had commanded his servants, saying, "Take notice when Amnon shall be drunk with wine and *when* I shall say to you, 'Strike him, and kill him.' Fear not, for it is I that

fortes." 29 Fecerunt ergo pueri Absalom adversum Amnon sicut praeceperat eis Absalom.

Surgentesque omnes filii regis ascenderunt singuli mulas suas et fugerunt. 30 Cumque adhuc pergerent in itinere, fama praevenit ad David, dicens, "Percussit Absalom omnes filios regis, et non remansit ex eis saltem unus." 31 Surrexit itaque rex et scidit vestimenta sua et cecidit super terram et omnes servi illius qui adsistebant ei sciderunt vestimenta sua. 32 Respondens autem Ionadab, filius Samaa, fratris David, dixit, "Ne aestimet dominus meus, rex, quod omnes pueri filii regis occisi sint. Amnon solus mortuus est, quoniam in ore Absalom erat positus ex die qua oppressit Thamar sororem eius. 33 Nunc, ergo, ne ponat dominus meus, rex, super cor suum verbum istud, dicens, 'Omnes filii regis occisi sunt,' quoniam Amnon solus mortuus est."

34 Fugit autem Absalom, et levavit puer speculator oculos suos et aspexit, et ecce: populus multus veniebat per iter devium ex latere montis. 35 Dixit autem Ionadab ad regem, "Ecce: filii regis adsunt. Iuxta verbum servi tui, sic factum est."

36 Cumque cessasset loqui, apparuerunt et filii regis, et intrantes levaverunt vocem suam et fleverunt, sed et rex et omnes servi eius fleverunt ploratu magno nimis. 37 Porro Absalom fugiens abiit ad Tholomai, filium Amiur, regem Gessur. Luxit ergo David filium suum cunctis diebus. 38 Absalom autem cum fugisset et venisset in Gessur fuit ibi tribus annis. 39 Cessavitque David Rex persequi Absalom eo quod consolatus esset super Amnon interitu.

command you. Take courage, and be valiant men." 29 And the servants of Absalom did to Amnon as Absalom had commanded them.

And all the king's sons arose and got up every man upon his mule and fled. 30 And while they were yet in the way, a rumour came to David, saying, "Absalom hath slain all the king's sons, and there is not *one* of them left." 31 Then the king rose up and rent his garments and fell upon the ground and all his servants that stood about him rent their garments. 32 But Jonadab, the son of Shimeah, David's brother, answering, said, "Let not my lord, the king, think that all the king's sons are slain. Amnon only is dead, for he was appointed by the mouth of Absalom from the day that he ravished his sister Tamar. 33 Now, therefore, let not my lord, the king, take this thing into his heart, saying, 'All the king's sons are slain,' for Amnon only is dead."

34 But Absalom fled away, and the young man that kept the watch lifted up his eyes and looked, and behold: there came much people by a by-way on the side of the mountain. 35 And Jonadab said to the king, "Behold: the king's sons are come. *As thy servant said, so it is.*"

36 And when he made an end of speaking, the king's sons also appeared, and coming in they lifted up their voice and wept, *and* the king also and all his servants wept *very much*. 37 *But* Absalom fled and went to Talmai, the son of Ammihud, the king of Geshur. *And* David mourned for his son every day. 38 And Absalom after he was fled and come into Geshur was there three years. 39 And King David ceased to pursue after Absalom because he was comforted concerning the death of Amnon.

Caput 14

Intellegens autem Ioab, filius Sarviae, quod cor regis versum esset ad Absalom 2 misit Thecuam et tulit inde mulierem sapientem dixitque ad eam, "Lugere te simula, et induere veste lugubri, et ne unguaris oleo, ut sis quasi mulier plurimo iam tempore lugens mortuum. 3 Et ingredieris ad regem et loqueris ad eum sermones huiuscemodi." Posuit autem Ioab verba in ore eius.

4 Itaque cum ingressa fuisset mulier Thecuites ad regem cecidit coram eo super terram et adoravit et dixit, "Serva me, rex."

5 Et ait ad eam rex, "Quid causae habes?"

Quae respondit, "Heu! Mulier vidua ego sum, mortuus est enim vir meus. 6 Et ancillae tuae erant duo filii, qui rixati sunt adversum se in agro, nullusque erat qui eos prohibere posset, et percussit alter alterum et interfecit eum. 7 Et ecce: consurgens universa cognatio adversum ancillam tuam dicit, 'Trade eum qui percussit fratrem suum ut occidamus eum pro anima fratris sui quem interfecit et deleamus heredem.' Et quaerunt extinguere scintillam meam quae relipenzeys spicta est ut non supersit viro meo nomen et reliquiae super terram."

Chapter 14

Joab procureth Absalom's return and his admittance to the king's presence.

And Joab, the son of Zeruiah, understanding that the king's heart was turned to Absalom 2 sent to Tekoa and fetched from thence a wise woman and said to her, "Feign *thyself to be a mourner,* and put on mourning apparel, and be not anointed with oil, that thou mayest be as a woman that had a long time been mourning for one dead. 3 And thou shalt go in to the king and shalt speak to him *in this manner.*" And Joab put the words in her mouth.

4 And when the woman of Tekoa was come in to the king she fell before him upon the ground and worshipped and said, "Save me, O king."

5 And the king said to her, "What *is the matter with thee?*"

She answered, "Alas! I am a widow woman, for my husband is dead. 6 And thy handmaid had two sons, and they quarrelled with each other in the field, and there was none *to* part them, and the one struck the other and slew him. 7 And behold: the whole kindred rising against thy handmaid saith, 'Deliver him that hath slain his brother that we may kill him for the life of his brother whom he slew and that we may destroy the heir.' And they seek to quench my spark which is left and will leave my husband no name nor remainder upon the earth."

8 Et ait rex ad mulierem, "Vade in domum tuam, et ego iubebo pro te."

9 Dixitque mulier Thecuites ad regem, "In me, domine mi, sit iniquitas et in domum patris mei, rex autem et thronus eius sit innocens."

10 Et ait rex, "Qui contradixerit tibi, adduc eum ad me, et ultra non addet ut tangat te."

11 Quae ait, "Recordetur rex Domini, Dei sui, ut non multiplicentur proximi sanguinis ad ulciscendum et nequaquam interficiant filium meum."

Qui ait, "Vivit Dominus, quia non cadet de capillis filii tui super terram."

12 Dixit ergo mulier, "Loquatur ancilla tua ad dominum meum, regem, verbum."

Et ait, "Loquere."

13 Dixitque mulier, "Quare cogitasti istiusmodi rem contra populum Dei, et locutus est rex verbum istud ut peccet et non reducat eiectum suum? 14 Omnes morimur, et quasi aquae delabimur in terram quae non revertuntur, nec vult perire Deus animam sed retractat, cogitans ne penitus pereat qui abiectus est. 15 Nunc, igitur, veni ut loquar ad regem, dominum meum, verbum hoc praesente populo. Et dixit ancilla tua, 'Loquar ad regem, si quo modo faciat rex verbum ancillae suae.' 16 Et audivit rex ut liberaret ancillam suam de manu omnium qui volebant delere me et filium meum simul de hereditate Dei. 17 Dicat ergo ancilla tua ut fiat verbum domini mei, regis, sicut sacrificium, sicut enim angelus Dei, sic est dominus meus, rex, ut nec benedictione

8 And the king said to the woman, "Go to thy house, and I will give charge concerning thee."

9 And the woman of Tekoa said to the king, "Upon me, my lord, be the iniquity and upon the house of my father, but may the king and his throne be guiltless."

10 And the king said, *"If any one shall say ought against* thee, bring him to me, and he shall not touch thee any more."

11 And she said, "Let the king remember the Lord, his God, that the next of kin be not multiplied to take revenge and that they may not kill my son."

And he said, "As the Lord liveth, there shall not one hair of thy son fall to the earth."

12 Then the woman said, "Let thy handmaid speak one word to my lord, the king."

And he said, "Speak."

13 And the woman said, "Why hast thou thought such a thing against the people of God, and why hath the king spoken this word to sin and not bring *home* again his own exile? 14 We all die, and like waters that return no more we fall down into the earth, neither will God have a soul to perish but recalleth, meaning that he that is cast off should not altogether perish. 15 Now, therefore, I am come to speak this word to my lord, the king, before the people. And thy handmaid said, 'I will speak to the king; *it may be* the king will perform the request of his handmaid.' 16 And the king hath hearkened *to me* to deliver his handmaid out of the hand of all that would destroy me and my son together out of the inheritance of God. 17 Then let thy handmaid say that the word of my lord, the king, be made as a sacrifice, for even as an angel of God, so is my lord, the king, that he is neither

nec maledictione moveatur, unde et Dominus, Deus tuus, est tecum.

18 Et respondens rex dixit ad mulierem, "Ne abscondas a me verbum quod te interrogo."

Dixitque ei mulier, "Loquere, domine mi, rex."

19 Et ait rex, "Numquid manus Ioab tecum est in omnibus istis?"

Respondit mulier et ait, "Per salutem animae tuae domine mi, rex, nec ad dextram nec ad sinistram est ex omnibus his quae locutus est dominus meus, rex, servus enim tuus Ioab, ipse praecepit mihi et ipse posuit in os ancillae tuae omnia verba haec 20 ut verterem figuram sermonis huius. Servus tuus Ioab praecepit istud, tu autem, domine mi, rex, sapiens es sicut habet sapientiam angelus Dei ut intellegas omnia super terram."

21 Et ait rex ad Ioab, "Ecce: placatus feci verbum tuum. Vade, igitur, et revoca puerum Absalom."

22 Cadensque Ioab super faciem suam in terram adoravit et benedixit regi, et dixit Ioab, "Hodie intellexit servus tuus quia inveni gratiam in oculis tuis, domine mi, rex, fecisti enim sermonem servi tui." 23 Surrexit ergo Ioab et abiit in Gessur et adduxit Absalom in Hierusalem.

24 Dixit autem rex, "Revertatur in domum suam, et faciem meam non videat." Reversus est itaque Absalom in domum suam et faciem regis non vidit, 25 porro sicut Absalom vir non erat pulcher in omni Israhel et decorus nimis. A vestigio pedis usque ad verticem non erat in eo ulla macula. 26 Et quando tondebat capillum (semel autem in anno ton-

moved with blessing nor cursing, wherefore the Lord, thy God, is also with thee."

18 And the king answering said to the woman, "Hide not from me the thing that I ask thee."

And the woman said to him, "Speak, my lord, the king."

19 And the king said, "Is not the hand of Joab with thee in all *this?*"

The woman answered and said, "By the health of thy soul, my lord, O king, it is neither on the left hand nor on the right in all these things which my lord, the king, hath spoken, for thy servant Joab, he commanded me and he put all these words into the mouth of thy handmaid 20 that I should *come about with this form of speech.* Thy servant Joab commanded this, but thou, my lord, O king, art wise *according to the wisdom of* an angel of God to understand all things upon earth."

21 And the king said to Joab, "Behold: I am appeased and have granted thy request. Go, therefore, and fetch back the boy Absalom."

22 And Joab falling down to the ground upon his face adored and blessed the king, and Joab said, "This day thy servant hath understood that I have found grace in thy sight, my lord, O king, for thou hast fulfilled the request of thy servant." 23 Then Joab arose and went to Geshur and brought Absalom to Jerusalem.

24 But the king said, "Let him return into his house, and let him not see my face." So Absalom returned into his house and saw not the king's face, 25 but in all Israel there was not a man so comely and so exceedingly beautiful as Absalom. From the sole of the foot to the crown *of his head* there was no blemish in him. 26 And when he polled his hair *(now he*

debatur, quia gravabat eum caesaries) ponderabat capillos capitis sui ducentis siclis, pondere publico. 27 Nati sunt autem Absalom filii tres et filia una, nomine Thamar, elegantis formae.

28 Mansitque Absalom Hierusalem duobus annis et faciem regis non vidit. 29 Misit itaque ad Ioab ut mitteret eum ad regem, qui noluit venire ad eum. Cumque secundo misisset et ille noluisset venire ad eum, 30 dixit servis suis, "Scitis agrum Ioab iuxta agrum meum habentem messem hordei; ite, igitur, et succendite eum igni." Succenderunt ergo servi Absalom segetem igni.

Et venientes servi Ioab scissis vestibus suis dixerunt, "Succenderunt servi Absalom partem agri igni."

31 Surrexitque Ioab et venit ad Absalom, in domum eius, et dixit, "Quare succenderunt servi tui segetem meam igni?"

32 Et respondit Absalom ad Ioab, "Misi ad te obsecrans ut venires ad me et mitterem te ad regem et diceres ei, 'Quare veni de Gessur? Melius mihi erat ibi esse.' Obsecro ergo ut videam faciem regis, quod si memor est iniquitatis meae, interficiat me."

33 Ingressus itaque Ioab ad regem nuntiavit ei omnia, vocatusque est Absalom, et intravit ad regem et adoravit super faciem terrae coram eo, osculatusque est rex Absalom.

was polled once a year, because his hair was burdensome to him) he weighed the hair of his head at two hundred sicles, according to the common weight. 27 And there were born to Absalom three sons and one daughter, *whose name was* Tamar, *and she was very beautiful.*

28 And Absalom dwelt two years in Jerusalem and saw not the king's face. 29 He sent therefore to Joab to send him to the king, but he would not come to him. And when he had sent the second time and he would not come to him, 30 he said to his servants, "You know the field of Joab near my field that hath a crop of barley; go now, and set it on fire." So the servants of Absalom set the corn on fire.

And Joab's servants coming with their garments rent said, "The servants of Absalom have set part of the field on fire."

31 Then Joab arose and came to Absalom, to his house, and said, "Why have thy servants set my corn on fire?"

32 And Absalom answered Joab, "I sent to thee beseeching thee to come to me *that* I might send thee to the king *to* say to him, 'Wherefore am I come from Geshur? It had been better for me to be there.' I beseech thee therefore that I may see the face of the king, *and* if he be mindful of my iniquity, let him kill me."

33 So Joab going in to the king told him all, and Absalom was called for, and he went in to the king and *prostrated himself* on the *ground* before him and the king kissed Absalom.

Caput 15

Igitur post haec, fecit sibi Absalom currus et equites et quinquaginta viros qui praecederent eum. 2 Et mane consurgens Absalom stabat iuxta introitum portae, et omnem virum qui habebat negotium ut veniret ad regis iudicium, vocabat Absalom ad se et dicebat, "De qua civitate es tu?"

Qui respondens aiebat, "Ex una tribu Israhel ego sum, servus tuus."

3 Respondebatque ei Absalom, "Videntur mihi sermones tui boni et iusti, sed non est qui te audiat constitutus a rege." Dicebatque Absalom, 4 "Quis me constituat iudicem super terram ut ad me veniant omnes qui habent negotium et iuste iudicem?" 5 Sed et cum accederet ad eum homo ut salutaret illum, extendebat manum suam et adprehendens osculabatur eum. 6 Faciebatque hoc omni Israhel venienti ad iudicium ut audiretur a rege, et sollicitabat corda virorum Israhel. 7 Post quardraginta autem annos, dixit Absalom ad Regem David, "Vadam et reddam vota mea quae vovi Domino in Hebron, 8 vovens enim vovit servus tuus cum esset in Gessur Syriae, dicens, 'Si reduxerit me Dominus in Hierusalem, sacrificabo Domino.'"

Chapter 15

Absalom's policy and conspiracy. David is obliged to flee.

Now after these things, Absalom made himself chariots and horsemen and fifty men to run before him. 2 And Absalom rising up early stood by the entrance of the gate, and *when any* man *had* business to come to the king's judgment, Absalom called *him* to him and said, "Of what city art thou?"

He answered and said, *"Thy servant is* of such a tribe of Israel."

3 And Absalom answered him, "Thy words seem to me good and just, but there is no man appointed by the king to hear thee." And Absalom said, 4 *"O that they* would make me judge over the land that all that have business might come to me that I might *do them justice!"* 5 Moreover when *any* man came to him to salute him, he put forth his hand and took him and kissed him. 6 And this he did to all Israel that came for judgment to be heard by the king, and he enticed the hearts of the men of Israel. 7 And after forty years, Absalom said to King David, "Let me go and pay my vows which I have vowed to the Lord in Hebron, 8 for thy servant *made a vow* when he was in Geshur of Syria, saying, 'If the Lord shall bring me again into Jerusalem, I will offer sacrifice to the Lord.'"

9 Dixitque ei Rex David, "Vade in pace." Et surrexit et abiit in Hebron.

10 Misit autem Absalom exploratores in universas tribus Israhel, dicens, "Statim ut audieritis clangorem bucinae, dicite, 'Regnavit Absalom in Hebron.'" 11 Porro cum Absalom ierunt ducenti viri de Hierusalem vocati euntes simplici corde et causam penitus ignorantes. 12 Accersivit quoque Absalom Ahitofel, Gilonitem, consiliarium David, de civitate sua Gilo.

Cumque immolaret victimas facta est coniuratio valida, populusque concurrens augebatur cum Absalom. 13 Venit igitur nuntius ad David, dicens, "Toto corde universus Israhel sequitur Absalom."

14 Et ait David servis suis qui erant cum eo in Hierusalem, "Surgite; fugiamus, neque enim erit nobis effugium a facie Absalom. Festinate egredi ne forte veniens occupet nos et inpellat super nos ruinam et percutiat civitatem in ore gladii."

15 Dixeruntque servi regis ad eum, "Omnia quaecumque praeceperit dominus noster, rex, libenter exsequemur servi tui." 16 Egressus est ergo rex et universa domus eius pedibus suis, et dereliquit rex decem mulieres, concubinas, ad custodiendam domum. 17 Egressusque rex et omnis Israhel pedibus suis stetit procul a domo, 18 et universi servi eius ambulabant iuxta eum et legiones Cherethi et Felethi et omnes Getthei, pugnatores validi, sescenti viri qui secuti eum fuerant de Geth pedites, praecedebant regem.

9 And King David said to him, "Go in peace." And he arose and went to Hebron.

10 And Absalom sent spies into all the tribes of Israel, saying, "As soon as you shall hear the sound of the trumpet, say ye, 'Absalom reigneth in Hebron.'" 11 Now there went with Absalom two hundred men out of Jerusalem that were called going with simplicity of heart and *knowing nothing* of the design. 12 Absalom also sent for Ahithophel, the Gilonite, David's counsellor, from his city Giloh.

And while he was offering sacrifices there was a strong conspiracy, and the people running together increased with Absalom. 13 And there came a messenger to David, saying, "All Israel with their whole heart followeth Absalom."

14 And David said to his servants that were with him in Jerusalem, "Arise, *and* let us flee, for *we shall not escape else* from the face of Absalom. Make haste to go out *lest* he come and overtake us and bring ruin upon us and smite the city with the edge of the sword."

15 And the king's servants said to him, "Whatsoever our lord, the king, shall command, we, thy servants, will willingly execute." 16 And the king went forth and all his household on foot, and the king left ten women, his concubines, to keep the house. 17 And the king going forth and all Israel on foot stood afar off from the house, 18 and all his servants walked by him and the bands of the Cherethites and the Pelethites and all the Gittites, valiant warriors, six hundred men who had followed him from Gath *on foot,* went before the king.

19 Dixit autem rex ad Ethai, Gettheum, "Cur venis nobiscum? Revertere, et habita cum rege, quia peregrinus es et egressus de loco tuo. 20 Heri venisti, et hodie inpelleris nobiscum egredi? Ego autem vadam quo iturus sum. Revertere, et reduc tecum fratres tuos, et Dominus faciet tecum misericordiam et veritatem, quia ostendisti gratiam et fidem."

21 Et respondit Ethai regi, dicens, "Vivit Dominus, et vivit dominus meus, rex, quoniam in quocumque loco fueris domine mi, rex, sive in morte sive in vita, ibi erit servus tuus."

22 Et ait David Ethai, "Veni, et transi." Et transivit Ethai, Gettheus, et omnes viri qui cum eo erant et reliqua multitudo. 23 Omnesque flebant voce magna, et universus populus transiebat, rex quoque transgrediebatur torrentem Cedron, et cunctus populus incedebat contra viam quae respicit ad desertum. 24 Venit autem et Sadoc, sacerdos, et universi Levitae cum eo portantes Arcam Foederis Dei, et deposuerunt arcam Dei, et ascendit Abiathar donec expletus transiret omnis populus qui egressus fuerat de civitate. 25 Et dixit rex ad Sadoc, "Reporta arcam Dei in urbem. Si invenero gratiam in oculis Domini, reducet me, et ostendet mihi eam et tabernaculum suum. 26 Si autem dixerit mihi, 'Non places,' praesto sum: faciat quod bonum est coram se." 27 Et dixit rex ad Sadoc, sacerdotem, "O videns, revertere in civitatem in pace, et Achimaas, filius tuus, et Ionathan, filius Abiathar, duo filii vestri, sint vobiscum. 28 Ecce: ego abscon-

19 And the king said to Ittai, the Gittite, "Why comest thou with us? Return, and dwell with the king, for thou art a stranger and art come out of thy own place. 20 Yesterday thou camest, and today shalt thou be forced to go forth with us? But I shall go whither I am going. Return thou, and take back thy brethren with thee, and the Lord will shew thee mercy and truth because thou hast shewn grace and fidelity."

21 And Ittai answered the king, saying, "As the Lord liveth, and as my lord, the king, liveth, in what place soever thou shalt be, my lord, O king, either in death or in life, there will thy servant be."

22 And David said to Ittai, "Come, and pass over." And Ittai, the Gittite, passed and all the men that were with him and the rest of the people. 23 And they all wept with a loud voice, and all the people passed over, the king also *himself* went over the brook Kidron, and all the people marched towards the way that looketh to the desert. 24 And Zadok, the priest, also came and all the Levites with him carrying the Ark of the Covenant of God, and they set down the ark of God, and Abiathar went up till all the people that was come out of the city had done passing. 25 And the king said to Zadok, "Carry back the ark of God into the city. If I shall find grace in the sight of the Lord, he will bring me again, and he will shew me it and his tabernacle. 26 But if he shall say to me, 'Thou pleasest me not,' I am ready: let him do that which is good before him." 27 And the king said to Zadok, the priest, "O seer, return into the city in peace, and let Ahimaaz, thy son, and Jonathan, the son of Abiathar, your two sons, be with you. 28 Behold: I will lie hid in the

dar in campestribus deserti donec veniat sermo a vobis indicans mihi." 29 Reportaverunt igitur Sadoc et Abiathar arcam Dei Hierusalem, et manserunt ibi.

30 Porro David ascendebat Clivum Olivarum, scandens et flens, operto capite et nudis pedibus incedens, sed et omnis populus qui erat cum eo operto capite ascendebat, plorans. 31 Nuntiatum est autem David quod et Ahitofel esset in coniuratione cum Absalom, dixitque David, "Infatua, quaeso, consilium Ahitofel, Domine."

32 Cumque ascenderet David summitatem montis in quo adoraturus erat Dominum, ecce: occurrit ei Husai, Arachites, scissa veste et terra pleno capite. 33 Et dixit ei David, "Si veneris mecum, eris mihi oneri, 34 si autem in civitatem revertaris et dixeris Absalom, 'Servus tuus sum, rex. Sicut fui servus patris tui, sic ero servus tuus,' dissipabis consilium Ahitofel. 35 Habes autem tecum Sadoc et Abiathar, sacerdotes, et omne verbum quodcumque audieris de domo regis, indicabis Sadoc et Abiathar, sacerdotibus. 36 Sunt autem cum eis duo filii eorum, Achimaas, filius Sadoc, et Ionathan, filius Abiathar, et mittetis per eos ad me omne verbum quod audieritis." 37 Veniente ergo Husai, amico David, in civitatem, Absalom quoque ingressus est Hierusalem.

plains of the wilderness till there come word from you *to certify* me." 29 So Zadok and Abiathar carried back the ark of God into Jerusalem, and they tarried there.

30 But David went up by the ascent of Mount Olivet, going up and weeping, walking barefoot and with his head covered, and all the people that were with them went up with their heads covered, weeping. 31 And it was told David that Ahithophel also was in the conspiracy with Absalom, and David said, "Infatuate, O Lord, I beseech thee, the counsel of Ahithophel."

32 And when David was come to the top of the mountain where he was about to adore the Lord, behold: Hushai, the Archite, *came to meet* him with his garment rent and his head covered with earth. 33 And David said to him, "If thou come with me, thou wilt be a burden to me, 34 but if thou return into the city and wilt say to Absalom, 'I am thy servant, O king. As I have been thy father's servant, so I will be thy servant,' thou shalt defeat the counsel of Ahithophel. 35 And thou hast with thee Zadok and Abiathar, the priests, and what thing soever thou shalt hear out of the king's house, thou shalt tell *it* to Zadok and Abiathar, the priests. 36 And there are with them their two sons, Ahimaaz, the son of Zadok, and Jonathan, the son of Abiathar, and you shall send by them to me every thing that you shall hear." 37 Then Hushai, the friend of David, went into the city, and Absalom came into Jerusalem.

Caput 16

Cumque David transisset paululum montis verticem, apparuit Siba, puer Mifiboseth, in occursum eius cum duobus asinis qui onerati erant ducentis panibus et centum alligaturis uvae passae et centum massis palatarum et utre vini. 2 Et dixit rex Sibae, "Quid sibi volunt haec?"

Responditque Siba, "Asini domesticis regis ut sedeant, et panes et palatae ad vescendum pueris tuis, vinum autem ut bibat si quis defecerit in deserto."

3 Et ait rex, "Ubi est filius domini tui?"

Responditque Siba regi, "Remansit in Hierusalem, dicens, 'Hodie restituet mihi domus Israhel regnum patris mei.'"

4 Et ait rex Sibae, "Tua sint omnia quae fuerunt Mifiboseth."

Dixitque Siba, "Adoro: inveniam gratiam coram te, domine mi, rex."

5 Venit ergo Rex David usque Baurim, et ecce: egrediebatur inde vir de cognatione domus Saul nomine Semei, filius Gera, procedebatque egrediens et maledicebat, 6 mittebatque lapides contra David et contra universos servos Regis David, omnis autem populus et universi bellatores a dextro

Chapter 16

Ziba bringeth provisions to David. Shimei curseth him.
Absalom defileth his father's wives.

And when David was a little past the top of the hill, *behold:* Ziba, the servant of Mephibosheth, *came* to meet him with two asses laden with two hundred loaves of bread and a hundred bunches of raisins, a hundred cakes of figs and a vessel of wine. 2 And the king said to Ziba, "What mean these things?"

And Ziba answered, "The asses are for the king's household to sit on, and the loaves and the figs for thy servants to eat, and the wine to drink if any man be faint in the desert."

3 And the king said, "Where is thy master's son?"

And Ziba answered the king, "He remained in Jerusalem, saying, 'Today will the house of Israel restore me the kingdom of my father.'"

4 And the king said to Ziba, "*I give thee* all that belonged to Mephibosheth."

And Ziba said, "I beseech thee: let me find grace before thee, my lord, O king."

5 And King David came as far as Bahurim, and behold: there came out from thence a man of the kindred of the house of Saul named Shimei, the son of Gera, and coming out he cursed as he went on, 6 and he threw stones at David and at all the servants of King David, and all the people and

et sinistro latere regis incedebant. 7 Ita autem loquebatur Semei cum malediceret regi, "Egredere! Egredere, vir sanguinum et vir Belial. 8 Reddidit tibi Dominus universum sanguinem domus Saul quoniam invasisti regnum pro eo, et dedit Dominus regnum in manu Absalom, filii tui, et ecce: premunt te mala tua quoniam vir sanguinum es."

9 Dixit autem Abisai, filius Sarviae, regi, "Quare maledicit canis hic mortuus domino meo, regi? Vadam et amputabo caput eius."

10 Et ait rex, "Quid mihi et vobis est, filii Sarviae? Dimittite eum ut maledicat, Dominus enim praecepit ei ut malediceret David. Et quis est qui audeat dicere, 'Quare sic fecerit?'" 11 Et ait rex Abisai et universis servis suis, "Ecce: filius meus, qui egressus est de utero meo, quaerit animam meam. Quanto magis nunc filius Iemini? Dimittite eum ut maledicat iuxta praeceptum Domini, 12 si forte respiciat Dominus adflictionem meam et reddat mihi Dominus bonum pro maledictione hac hodierna." 13 Ambulabat itaque David et socii eius per viam cum eo. Semei autem per iugum montis ex latere contra illum gradiebatur, maledicens et mittens lapides adversum eum terramque spargens. 14 Venit itaque rex et universus populus cum eo lassus et refocilati sunt ibi.

15 Absalom autem et omnis populus eius ingressi sunt Hierusalem, sed et Ahitofel cum eo. 16 Cum autem venisset Husai, Arachites, amicus David, ad Absalom, locutus est ad eum, "Salve, rex! Salve, rex!"

17 Ad quem Absalom, "Haec est," inquit, "gratia tua ad amicum tuum? Quare non isti cum amico tuo?"

all the warriors walked on the right and on the left side of the king. 7 And thus said Shimei when he cursed the king, "Come out! Come out, thou man of blood and thou man of Belial. 8 The Lord hath repaid thee *for* all the blood of the house of Saul because thou hast usurped the kingdom in his stead, and the Lord hath given the kingdom into the hand of Absalom, thy son, and behold: thy evils press upon thee because thou art a man of blood."

9 And Abishai, the son of Zeruiah, said to the king, "Why should this dead dog curse my lord, the king? I will go and cut off his head."

10 And the king said, *"What have I to do with you,* ye sons of Zeruiah? Let him alone, *and let him* curse, for the Lord hath bid him curse David. And who is he that shall dare say, 'Why hath he done so?'" 11 And the king said to Abishai and to all his servants, "Behold: my son, who came forth from my womb, seeketh my life. How much more now a son of Jemini? Let him alone that he may curse *as the Lord hath bidden him.* 12 *Perhaps* the Lord may look upon my affliction, and the Lord may render me good for the cursing of this day." 13 And David and his men with him went by the way. And Shimei *by the hill's side* went over against him, cursing and casting stones at him and scattering earth. 14 And the king and all the people with him came weary and refreshed themselves there.

15 But Absalom and all his people came into Jerusalem, *and* Ahithophel was with him. 16 And when Hushai, the Archite, David's friend, was come to Absalom, he said to him, "God save thee, O king! God save thee, O king!"

17 And Absalom said to him, "Is this thy kindness to thy friend? Why wentest thou not with thy friend?"

18 Responditque Husai ad Absalom, "Nequaquam, quia illius ero quem elegit Dominus et omnis hic populus et universus Israhel, et cum eo manebo. 19 Sed, ut et hoc inferam, cui ego serviturus sum? Nonne filio regis? Sicut parui patri tuo, sic parebo et tibi."

20 Dixit autem Absalom ad Ahitofel, "Inite consilium quid agere debeamus."

21 Et ait Ahitofel ad Absalom, "Ingredere ad concubinas patris tui, quas dimisit ad custodiendam domum, ut cum audierit omnis Israhel quod foedaveris patrem tuum roborentur manus eorum tecum." 22 Tetenderunt igitur Absalom tabernaculum in solario, ingressusque est ad concubinas patris sui coram universo Israhel.

23 Consilium autem Ahitofel quod dabat in diebus illis quasi si quis consuleret Deum. Sic erat omne consilium Ahitofel, et cum esset cum David et cum esset cum Absalom.

Caput 17

Dixit igitur Ahitofel ad Absalom, "Eligam mihi duodecim milia virorum, et consurgens persequar David hac nocte. 2 Et inruens super eum (quippe qui lassus est et solu-

18 And Hushai answered Absalom, "Nay, for I will be his whom the Lord hath chosen and all this people and all Israel, and with him will I abide. 19 *Besides* this, whom shall I serve? Is it not the king's son? As I have served thy father, so will I serve thee also."

20 And Absalom said to Ahithophel, "Consult what we are to do."

21 And Ahithophel said to Absalom, "Go in to the concubines of thy father, whom he hath left to keep the house, that when all Israel shall hear that thou hast disgraced thy father their hands may be strengthened with thee." 22 So they spread a tent for Absalom on the top of the house, and he went in to his father's concubines before all Israel.

23 Now the counsel of Ahithophel which he gave in those days was as if a man should consult God. So was all the counsel of Ahithophel, both when he was with David and when he was with Absalom.

Chapter 17

Ahithophel's counsel is defeated by Hushai, who sendeth intelligence to David. Ahithophel hangeth himself.

And Ahithophel said to Absalom, "I will choose me twelve thousand men, and I will arise and pursue after David this night. 2 And coming upon him (for he is now weary

tis manibus) percutiam eum. Cumque fugerit omnis populus qui cum eo est, percutiam regem desolatum. 3 Et reducam universum populum quomodo unus homo reverti solet, unum enim virum tu quaeris, et omnis populus erit in pace." 4 Placuitque sermo eius Absalom et cunctis maioribus natu Israhel.

5 Ait autem Absalom, "Vocate Husai, Arachiten, et audiamus quid etiam ipse dicat."

6 Cumque venisset Husai ad Absalom, ait Absalom ad eum, "Huiuscemodi sermonem locutus est Ahitofel; facere debemus an non? Quod das consilium?"

7 Et dixit Husai ad Absalom, "Non bonum consilium quod dedit Ahitofel hac vice." 8 Et rursum intulit Husai, "Tu nosti patrem tuum et viros qui cum eo sunt esse fortissimos et amaro animo veluti si ursa raptis catulis in saltu saeviat, sed et pater tuus vir bellator est nec morabitur cum populo. 9 Forsitan nunc latitat in foveis aut in uno quo voluerit loco, et cum ceciderit unus quilibet in principio, audiet quicumque audierit et dicet, 'Facta est plaga in populo qui sequebatur Absalom.' 10 Et fortissimus quisque cuius cor est quasi leonis pavore solvetur, scit enim omnis populus Israhel fortem esse patrem tuum, et robustos omnes qui cum eo sunt. 11 Sed hoc mihi videtur rectum esse consilium: congregetur ad te universus Israhel, a Dan usque Bersabee quasi harena maris innumerabilis, et tu eris in medio eorum. 12 Et inruemus super eum in quocumque loco fuerit inventus, et operiemus eum sicut cadere solet ros super terram, et non relin-

and weak handed) I will *defeat* him. And when all the people is *put to flight* that is with him, I will kill the king who will be left alone. 3 And I will bring back all the people *as if they were but one man,* for thou seekest *but* one man, and all the people shall be in peace." 4 And his saying pleased Absalom and all the ancients of Israel.

5 But Absalom said, "Call Hushai, the Archite, and let us hear what he also saith."

6 And when Hushai was come to Absalom, Absalom said to him, "Ahithophel hath spoken *after this manner; shall we do it or not? What counsel dost thou give?"

7 And Hushai said to Absalom, "The counsel that Ahithophel hath given this time is not good." 8 And again Hushai said, "Thou knowest thy father and the men that are with him, that they are very valiant and bitter in their mind as a bear raging in the wood when her whelps are taken away, *and* thy father is a warrior and will not lodge with the people. 9 Perhaps he now lieth hid in pits or in some *other* place where he list, and when any one shall fall at the first, *every one that heareth it* shall say, 'There is a slaughter among the people that followed Absalom.' 10 And *the most valiant man* whose heart is as *the heart* of a lion shall melt for fear, for all the people of Israel know thy father to be a valiant man, and that all who are with him are valiant. 11 But this seemeth to me to be good counsel: let all Israel be gathered to thee, from Dan to Beer-sheba as the sand of the sea which cannot be numbered, and thou shalt be in the midst of them. 12 And we shall come upon him in what place soever he shall be found, and we shall cover him as the dew *falleth* upon the ground, and we shall not leave of the men that are with him,

quemus de viris qui cum eo sunt, ne unum quidem. 13 Si autem urbem aliquam fuerit ingressus, circumdabit omnis Israhel civitati illi funes, et trahemus eam in torrentem ut non repperiatur nec calculus quidem ex ea."

14 Dixitque Absalom et omnes viri Israhel, "Melius consilium Husai, Arachitae, consilio Ahitofel." Domini autem nutu dissipatum est consilium Ahitofel utile ut induceret Dominus super Absalom malum.

15 Et ait Husai Sadoc et Abiathar, sacerdotibus, "Hoc et hoc modo consilium dedit Ahitofel Absalom et senibus Israhel, et ego tale et tale dedi consilium. 16 Nunc, ergo, mittite cito, et nuntiate David, dicentes, 'Ne moremini nocte hac in campestribus deserti, sed absque dilatione transgredere ne forte absorbeatur rex et omnis populus qui cum eo est.'"

17 Ionathan autem et Achimaas stabant iuxta fontem Rogel; abiit ancilla et nuntiavit eis, et illi profecti sunt ut referrent ad Regem David nuntium, non enim poterant videri aut introire civitatem. 18 Vidit autem eos quidam puer et indicavit Absalom, illi vero concito gradu ingressi sunt domum cuiusdam viri in Baurim qui habebat puteum in vestibulo suo, et descenderunt in eum. 19 Tulit autem mulier et expandit velamen super os putei quasi siccans ptisanas, et sic res latuit. 20 Cumque venissent servi Absalom in domum, ad mulierem dixerunt, "Ubi est Achimaas et Ionathan?"

Et respondit eis mulier, "Transierunt festinanter gustata paululum aqua." At hii qui quaerebant, cum non repperissent, reversi sunt in Hierusalem.

not so much as one. 13 And if he shall enter into any city, all Israel shall cast ropes round about that city, and we will draw it into the river so that there shall not be found so much as one small stone thereof."

14 And Absalom and all the men of Israel said, "The counsel of Hushai, the Archite, is better than the counsel of Ahithophel." And by the will of the Lord the profitable counsel of Ahithophel was defeated that the Lord might bring evil upon Absalom.

15 And Hushai said to Zadok and Abiathar, the priests, "Thus and thus did Ahithophel counsel Absalom and the ancients of Israel, and thus and thus did I counsel them. 16 Now, therefore, send quickly, and tell David, saying, 'Tarry not this night in the plains of the wilderness, but without delay pass over lest the king be swallowed up and all the people that is with him.'"

17 And Jonathan and Ahimaaz stayed by the fountain Rogel, *and* there went a maid and told them, and they went forward to carry the message to King David, for they *might* not be seen nor enter into the city. 18 But a certain boy saw them and told Absalom, but they making haste went into the house of a certain man in Bahurim who had a well in his court, and they went down into it. 19 And a woman took and spread a covering over the mouth of the well as it were to dry sodden barley, and so the thing was not known. 20 And when Absalom's servants were come into the house, they said to the woman, "Where is Ahimaaz and Jonathan?"

And the woman answered them, "They passed on in haste after they had tasted a little water." But they that sought them, when they found them not, returned into Jerusalem.

21 Cumque abissent, ascenderunt illi de puteo et pergentes nuntiaverunt Regi David atque dixerunt, "Surgite, et transite cito fluvium, quoniam huiuscemodi dedit consilium contra vos Ahitofel." 22 Surrexit ergo David et omnis populus qui erat cum eo, et transierunt Iordanem donec dilucesceret, et ne unus quidem residuus fuit qui non transisset fluvium. 23 Porro Ahitofel videns quod non fuisset factum consilium suum stravit asinum suum et surrexit et abiit in domum suam et in civitatem suam et disposita domo sua suspendio interiit et sepultus est in sepulchro patris sui. 24 David autem venit in Castra, et Absalom transivit Iordanem, ipse et omnes viri Israhel cum eo.

25 Amasam vero constituit Absalom pro Ioab super exercitum, Amasa autem erat filius viri qui vocabatur Iethra de Hiesreli, qui ingressus est ad Abigail, filiam Naas, sororem Sarviae, quae fuit mater Ioab. 26 Et castrametatus est Israhel cum Absalom in terra Galaad. 27 Cumque venisset David in Castra, Sobi, filius Naas de Rabbath, filiorum Ammon, et Machir, filius Ammihel de Lodabar, et Berzellai, Galaadites de Rogelim, 28 obtulerunt ei stratoria et tappetia et vasa fictilia, frumentum et hordeum et farinam et pulentam et fabam et lentem et frixum cicer 29 et mel et butyrum, oves et pingues vitulos, dederuntque David et populo qui cum eo erat ad vescendum, suspicati enim sunt populum fame et siti fatigari in deserto.

21 And when they were gone, they came up out of the well and going on told King David and said, "Arise, and pass quickly over the river, for this manner of counsel has Ahithophel given against you." 22 So David arose and all the people that were with him, and they passed over the Jordan until it grew light, and not one of them was left that was not gone over the river. 23 But Ahithophel seeing that his counsel was not *followed* saddled his ass and arose and went *home* to his house and to his city and putting his house in order hanged himself and was buried in the sepulchre of his father. 24 But David came to the Camp, and Absalom passed over the Jordan, he and all the men of Israel with him.

25 Now Absalom appointed Amasa in Joab's stead over the army, and Amasa was the son of a man who was called Ithra of Jezrael, who went in to Abigail, the daughter of Nahash, the sister of Zeruiah, who was the mother of Joab. 26 And Israel camped with Absalom in the land of Gilead. 27 And when David was come to the Camp, Shobi, the son of Nahash of Rabbah, of the children of Ammon, and Machir, the son of Ammiel of Lo-debar, and Barzillai, the Gileadite of Rogelim, 28 brought him beds and tapestry and earthen vessels *and* wheat and barley and meal and parched corn and beans and lentils and fried pulse 29 and honey and butter *and* sheep and fat calves, and they gave to David and the people that were with him to eat, for they suspected that the people were faint with hunger and thirst in the wilderness.

Caput 18

Igitur considerato David populo suo constituit super eos tribunos et centuriones 2 et dedit populi tertiam partem sub manu Ioab et tertiam partem sub manu Abisai, filii Sarviae, fratris Ioab, et tertiam partem sub manu Ethai, qui erat de Geth, dixitque rex ad populum, "Egrediar et ego vobiscum."

3 Et respondit populus, "Non exibis, sive enim fugerimus, non magnopere ad eos de nobis pertinebit, sive media pars ceciderit e nobis, non satis curabunt, quia tu unus pro decem milibus conputaris. Melius est, igitur, ut sis nobis in urbe praesidio."

4 Ad quos rex ait, "Quod vobis rectum videtur, hoc faciam." Stetit ergo rex iuxta portam, egrediebaturque omnis populus per turmas suas, centeni et milleni. 5 Et praecepit rex Ioab et Abisai et Ethai, dicens, "Servate mihi puerum Absalom." Et omnis populus audiebat praecipientem regem cunctis principibus pro Absalom.

6 Itaque egressus est populus in campum contra Israhel, et factum est proelium in saltu Ephraim. 7 Et caesus est ibi populus Israhel ab exercitu David, factaque est plaga magna

Chapter 18

Absalom is defeated and slain by Joab. David mourneth
for him.

And David having reviewed his people appointed over
them captains of thousands and of hundreds 2 and *sent forth*
a third part of the people under the hand of Joab and a third
part under the hand of Abishai, the son of Zeruiah, Joab's
brother, and a third part under the hand of Ittai, who was of
Gath, and the king said to the people, "I also will go forth
with you."

3 And the people answered, "Thou shalt not go forth, for
if we flee away, they will not much mind us, or if half of us
should fall, they will not greatly care, for thou alone art ac-
counted for ten thousand. It is better, therefore, that thou
shouldst be in the city to succour us."

4 And the king said to them, "What seemeth good to you,
that will I do." And the king stood by the gate, and all the
people went forth by their troops, by hundreds and by thousands. 5 And the king commanded Joab and Abishai and Ittai, saying, "Save me the boy Absalom." And all the people
heard the king giving charge to all the princes concerning
Absalom.

6 So the people went out into the field against Israel, and
the battle was fought in the forest of Ephraim. 7 And the
people of Israel were *defeated* there by David's army, and a

in die illa viginti milium. 8 Fuit autem ibi proelium disper-
sum super faciem omnis terrae, et multo plures erant quos
saltus consumpserat de populo quam hii quos voraverat gladius in die illa. 9 Accidit autem ut occurreret Absalom servis
David sedens mulo, cumque ingressus fuisset mulus subter
condensam quercum et magnam, adhesit caput eius quercui,
et, illo suspenso inter caelum et terram, mulus cui sederat
pertransivit. 10 Vidit autem hoc quispiam et nuntiavit Ioab,
dicens, "Vidi Absalom pendere de quercu."

11 Et ait Ioab viro qui nuntiaverat ei, "Si vidisti, quare non
confodisti eum cum terra? Et ego dedissem tibi decem argenti siclos et unum balteum."

12 Qui dixit ad Ioab, "Si adpenderes in manibus meis mille
argenteos, nequaquam mitterem manum meam in filium regis, audientibus enim nobis praecepit rex tibi et Abisai et
Ethai, dicens, 'Custodite mihi puerum Absalom.' 13 Sed et
si fecissem contra animam meam audacter, nequaquam hoc
regem latere potuisset—et tu stares ex adverso?"

14 Et ait Ioab, "Non sicut tu vis, sed adgrediar eum coram
te." Tulit ergo tres lanceas in manu sua et infixit eas in corde
Absalom, cumque adhuc palpitaret, herens in quercu, 15 cucurrerunt decem iuvenes, armigeri Ioab, et percutientes interfecerunt eum. 16 Cecinit autem Ioab bucina et retinuit
populum ne persequeretur fugientem Israhel, volens par-
cere multitudini. 17 Et tulerunt Absalom et proiecerunt eum
in saltu in foveam grandem, et conportaverunt super eum
acervum lapidum magnum nimis, omnis autem Israhel fugit
in tabernacula sua.

great slaughter was made that day of twenty thousand men. 8 And the battle there was scattered over the face of all the country, and there were many more of the people whom the forest consumed than whom the sword devoured that day. 9 And it happened that Absalom met the servants of David riding on a mule, and, as the mule went under a thick and large oak, his head stuck in the oak, and while he hung between the heaven and the earth, the mule on which he rode passed on. 10 And one saw this and told Joab, saying, "I saw Absalom hanging upon an oak."

11 And Joab said to the man that told him, "If thou sawest him, why didst thou not stab him to the ground? And I would have given thee ten sicles of silver and a belt."

12 And he said to Joab, "If thou wouldst have paid down in my hands a thousand pieces of silver, I would not lay my *hands* upon the king's son, for in our hearing he king charged thee and Abishai and Ittai, saying, 'Save me the boy Absalom.' 13 Yea and if I should have acted boldly against my own life, this could not have been hid from the king—and wouldst thou have stood *by me?*"

14 And Joab said, "Not as thou wilt, but I will set upon him *in thy sight.*" So he took three lances in his hand and thrust them into the heart of Absalom, and whilst he yet panted for life, sticking on the oak, 15 ten young men, armourbearers of Joab, ran up and striking him slew him. 16 And Joab sounded the trumpet and kept back the people from pursuing after Israel in their flight, being willing to spare the multitude. 17 And they took Absalom and cast him into a great pit in the forest, and they laid an exceeding great heap of stones upon him, but all Israel fled to their own dwellings.

18 Porro Absalom erexerat sibi cum adhuc viveret titulum, qui est in Valle Regis, dixerat enim, "Non habeo filium, et hoc erit monumentum nominis mei." Vocavitque titulum nomine suo, et appellatur Manus Absalom usque ad hanc diem.

19 Achimaas autem, filius Sadoc, ait, "Curram et nuntiabo regi quia iudicium fecerit ei Dominus de manu inimicorum eius."

20 Ad quem Ioab dixit, "Non eris nuntius in hac die sed nuntiabis in alia. Hodie nolo te nuntiare, filius enim regis est mortuus." 21 Et ait Ioab Chusi, "Vade, et nuntia regi quae vidisti." Adoravit Chusi Ioab et cucurrit.

22 Rursum autem Achimaas, filius Sadoc, dixit ad Ioab, "Quid inpedit si etiam ego curram post Chusi?"

Dixitque ei Ioab, "Quid vis currere, fili mi? Non eris boni nuntii baiulus."

23 Qui respondit, "Quid enim si cucurrero?"

Et ait ei, "Curre."

Currens ergo Achimaas per viam conpendii transivit Chusi. 24 David autem sedebat inter duas portas, speculator vero qui erat in fastigio portae super murum elevans oculos vidit hominem currentem solum, 25 et exclamans indicavit regi, dixitque rex, "Si solus est, bonus est nuntius in ore eius."

Properante autem illo et accedente propius, 26 vidit speculator hominem alterum currentem, et vociferans in culmine ait, "Apparet mihi alter homo currens solus."

Dixitque rex, "Et iste bonus est nuntius."

18 Now Absalom had reared up for himself *in his lifetime* a pillar, which is in the King's Valley, for he said, "I have no son, and this shall be the monument of my name." And he called the pillar by is own name, and it is called the Hand of Absalom to this day.

19 And Ahimaaz, the son of Zadok said, "I will run and tell the king that the Lord hath done judgment for him from the hand of his enemies."

20 And Joab said to him, "Thou shalt not be the messenger this day but shalt bear tidings another day. This day I will not have thee bear tidings because the king's son is dead."

21 And Joab said to Hushai, "Go, and tell the king what thou hast seen." Hushai bowed down to Joab and ran.

22 Then Ahimaaz, the son of Zadok, said to Joab again, *"Why might not I* also run after Hushai?"

And Joab said to him, "Why wilt thou run, my son? Thou wilt not be the bearer of good tidings."

23 He answered, "But what if I run?"

And he said to him, "Run."

Then Ahimaaz running by a nearer way passed Hushai. 24 And David sat between the two gates, and the watchman that was on the top of the gate upon the wall lifting up his eyes saw a man running alone, 25 and crying out he told the king, and the king said, "If he be alone, there are good tidings in his mouth."

And as he was coming apace and drawing nearer, 26 the watchman saw another man running, and crying aloud *from above* he said, *"I see* another man running alone."

And the king said, "He also is a good messenger."

27 Speculator autem, "Contemplor," ait, "cursum prioris quasi cursum Achimaas, filii Sadoc."

Et ait rex, "Vir bonus est et nuntium portans bonum venit."

28 Clamans autem Achimaas dixit ad regem, "Salve, rex!" Et adorans regem coram eo pronus in terram ait, "Benedictus Dominus, Deus tuus, qui conclusit homines qui levaverunt manus suas contra dominum, meum regem."

29 Et ait rex, "Estne pax puero Absalom?"

Dixitque Achimaas, "Vidi tumultum magnum cum mitteret Ioab, servus tuus, o rex, me, servum tuum; nescio aliud."

30 Ad quem rex, "Transi," ait, "et sta hic."

Cumque ille transisset et staret, 31 apparuit Chusi, et veniens ait, "Bonum adporto nuntium, domine mi, rex, iudicavit enim pro te Dominus hodie de manu omnium qui surrexerunt contra te."

32 Dixit autem rex ad Chusi, "Estne pax puero Absalom?"

Cui respondens Chusi, "Fiant," inquit, "sicut puer inimici domini mei, regis, et universi qui consurgunt adversum eum in malum."

33 Contristatus itaque rex ascendit cenaculum portae et flevit, et sic loquebatur vadens, "Fili mi Absalom, fili mi Absalom, quis mihi tribuat ut ego moriar pro te, Absalom, fili mi, fili mi Absalom?"

27 And the watchman said, *"The running of the foremost seemeth to me* like the running of Ahimaaz, the son of Zadok."

And the king said, "He is a good man and cometh *with* good news."

28 And Ahimaaz crying out said to the king, "God save thee, O king!" And *falling down before* the king with his face to the ground he said, "Blessed be the Lord, thy God, who hath shut up the men that have lifted up their hands against the lord, my king."

29 And the king said, "Is the young man Absalom safe?"

And Ahimaaz said, "I saw a great tumult, O king, when thy servant Joab sent me, thy servant; I know nothing else."

30 And the king said to him, "Pass, and stand here."

31 And when he had passed and stood still, Hushai appeared, and coming up he said, "I bring good tidings, my lord, the king, for the Lord hath judged for thee this day from the hand of all that have risen up against thee."

32 And the king said to Hushai, "Is the young man Absalom safe?"

And Hushai answering him said, "Let the enemies of my lord, the king, and all that rise against him unto evil be as the young man is."

33 The king therefore being *much moved* went up to the high chamber over the gate and wept, and as he went he spoke in this manner, "My son Absalom, Absalom, my son, *would God* that I might die for thee, Absalom, my son, my son Absalom."

Caput 19

Nuntiatum est autem Ioab quod rex fleret et lugeret filium suum, 2 et versa est victoria in die illa in luctum omni populo, audivit enim populus in die illa dici, "Dolet rex super filio suo." 3 Et declinabat populus in die illa ingredi civitatem quomodo declinare solet populus versus et fugiens de proelio. 4 Porro rex operuit caput suum et clamabat voce magna, "Fili mi Absalom, Absalom, fili mi, fili mi."

5 Ingressus ergo Ioab ad regem in domum dixit, "Confudisti hodie vultus omnium servorum tuorum qui salvam fecerunt animam tuam et animam filiorum tuorum et filiarum tuarum et animam uxorum tuarum et animam concubinarum tuarum. 6 Diligis odientes te, et odio habes diligentes te, et ostendisti hodie quia non curas de ducibus tuis et de servis tuis, et vere cognovi modo quia si Absalom viveret et nos omnes occubuissemus, tunc placeret tibi. 7 Nunc igitur surge, et procede, et adloquens satisfac servis tuis, iuro enim tibi per Dominum quod si non exieris, ne unus quidem remansurus sit tecum nocte hac, et peius erit hoc tibi quam omnia mala quae venerunt super te ab adulescentia tua usque in praesens."

Chapter 19

David at the remonstrances of Joab ceaseth his mourning.
He is invited back and met by Shimei and Mephibosheth.
A strife between the men of Judah and the men of Israel.

And it was told Joab that the king wept and mourned for his son, 2 and the victory that day was turned into mourning unto all the people, for the people heard say that day, "The king grieveth for his son." 3 And the people shunned the going into the city that day as a people would do *that hath turned their backs* and fled away from the battle. 4 And the king covered his head and cried with a loud voice, "O my son Absalom, O Absalom, my son, O my son."

5 Then Joab going into the house, to the king, said, "Thou hast shamed this day the faces of all thy servants that have saved thy life and the *lives* of thy sons and of thy daughters and the *lives* of thy wives and the *lives* of thy concubines. 6 Thou lovest them that hate thee, and thou hatest them that love thee, and thou hast shewn this day that thou carest not for thy nobles nor for thy servants, and I now *plainly perceive* that if Absalom had lived and all we had been slain, then it would have pleased thee. 7 Now therefore arise, and go out, and *speak to the satisfaction of* thy servants, for I swear to thee by the Lord that if thou wilt not go forth, there will not tarry with thee so much as one this night, and that will be worse to thee than all the evils that have befallen thee from thy youth until now."

8 Surrexit ergo rex et sedit in porta, et omni populo nuntiatum est quod rex sederet in porta, venitque universa multitudo coram rege, Israhel autem fugit in tabernacula sua. 9 Omnis quoque populus certabat in cunctis tribubus Israhel, dicens, "Rex liberavit nos de manu inimicorum nostrorum; ipse salvavit nos de manu Philisthinorum, et nunc fugit de terra propter Absalom. 10 Absalom autem, quem unximus super nos, mortuus est in bello. Usquequo siletis et non reducitis regem?"

11 Rex vero David misit ad Sadoc et Abiathar, sacerdotes, dicens, "Loquimini ad maiores natu Iuda, dicentes, 'Cur venitis novissimi ad reducendum regem in domum suam?' (sermo autem omnis Israhel pervenerat ad regem in domo eius), 12 'Fratres mei vos; os meum et caro mea vos. Quare novissimi reducitis regem?' 13 Et Amasae dicite, 'Nonne os meum es et caro mea? Haec faciat mihi Deus et haec addat, si non magister militiae fueris coram me omni tempore pro Ioab.'"

14 Et inclinavit cor omnium virorum Iuda quasi viri unius, miseruntque ad regem, dicentes, "Revertere, tu et omnes servi tui." 15 Et reversus est rex et venit usque ad Iordanem, et omnis Iuda venit usque in Galgala ut occurreret regi et transduceret eum Iordanem.

16 Festinavit autem Semei, filius Gera, filii Iemini de Baurim, et descendit cum viris Iuda in occursum Regis David 17 cum mille viris de Beniamin, et Siba, puer de domo Saul, et quindecim filii eius ac viginti servi erant cum eo. Et inrumpentes Iordanem, ante regem 18 transierunt vada ut

8 Then the king arose and sat in the gate, and it was told to all the people that the king sat in the gate, and all the *people* came before the king, but Israel fled to their own dwellings. 9 And all the people were at strife in all the tribes of Israel, saying, "The king delivered us out of the hand of our enemies, *and* he saved us out of the hand of the Philistines, and now he is fled out of the land for Absalom. 10 But Absalom, whom we anointed over us, is dead in the battle. How long are you silent and bring not back the king?"

11 And King David sent to Zadok and Abiathar, the priests, saying, "Speak to the ancients of Judah, saying, 'Why *are* you the last to bring the king back to his house?' (for the talk of all Israel was come to the king in his house), 12 'You are my brethren; you are my bone and my flesh. Why are you the last to bring back the king?' 13 And say ye to Amasa, 'Art not thou my bone and my flesh? So do God to me and add more, if thou be not the chief captain of the army before me always in the place of Joab.'"

14 And he inclined the heart of all the men of Judah as it were of one man, and they sent to the king, saying, "Return, thou and all thy servants." 15 And the king returned and came as far as the Jordan, and all Judah came as far as Gilgal to meet the king and to bring him over the Jordan.

16 And Shimei, the son of Gera, the son of Jemini of Bahurim, made haste and went down with the men of Judah to meet King David 17 with a thousand men of Benjamin, and Ziba, the servant of the house of Saul, and his fifteen sons and twenty servants were with him. And going over the Jordan 18 they passed the fords before the king that they might

transducerent domum regis et facerent iuxta iussionem eius. Semei autem, filius Gera, prostratus coram rege cum iam transisset Iordanem, 19 dixit ad eum, "Ne reputes mihi, domine mi, iniquitatem, neque memineris iniuriarum servi tui in die qua egressus es, domine mi, rex, de Hierusalem, neque ponas, rex, in corde tuo, 20 agnosco enim servus tuus peccatum meum, et idcirco hodie primus veni de omni domo Ioseph descendique in occursum domini mei, regis."

21 Respondens vero Abisai, filius Sarviae, dixit, "Numquid pro his verbis non occidetur Semei quia maledixit christo Domini?"

22 Et ait David, "Quid mihi et vobis, filii Sarviae? Cur efficimini mihi hodie in satan? Ergone hodie interficietur vir in Israhel? An ignoro hodie me factum regem super Israhel?"

23 Et ait rex Semei, "Non morieris." Iuravitque ei.

24 Mifiboseth quoque, filius Saul, descendit in occursum regis, inlotis pedibus et intonsa barba vestesque suas non laverat a die qua egressus fuerat rex usque ad diem reversionis eius in pace. 25 Cumque Hierusalem occurrisset regi, dixit ei rex, "Quare non venisti mecum, Mifiboseth?"

26 Et respondens ait, "Domine mi, rex, servus meus contempsit me, dixique ei ego, famulus tuus, ut sterneret mihi asinum et ascendens abirem cum rege, claudus enim sum, servus tuus. 27 Insuper, et accusavit me, servum tuum, ad te, dominum meum, regem, tu autem, domine mi, rex, sicut angelus Dei: fac quod placitum est tibi, 28 neque enim

help over the king's household and do according to his commandment. And Shimei, the son of Gera, falling down before the king when he was come over the Jordan, 19 said to him, "Impute not to me, my lord, the iniquity, nor remember the injuries of thy servant on the day that thou, my lord, the king, wentest out of Jerusalem, nor lay it up in thy heart, O king, 20 for I, thy servant, acknowledge my sin, and therefore I am come this day, the first of all the house of Joseph, and am come down to meet my lord, the king."

21 But Abishai, the son of Zeruiah, answering said, "Shall Shimei for these words not be put to death because he cursed the Lord's anointed?"

22 And David said, "What have I to do with you, ye sons of Zeruiah? Why *are* you a satan this day to me? Shall there *any* man be killed this day in Israel? Do not I know that this day I am made king over Israel?"

23 And the king said to Shimei, "Thou shalt not die." And he swore unto him.

24 And Mephibosheth, the son of Saul, came down to meet the king, and *he had neither washed* his feet *nor* trimmed his beard nor washed his garments from the day that the king went out until the day of his return in peace. 25 And when he met the king at Jerusalem, the king said to him, "Why camest thou not with me, Mephibosheth?"

26 And he answering said, "My lord, O king, my servant despised me, *for* I, thy servant, spoke to him to saddle me an ass *that* I might get on and go with the king, for I, thy servant, am lame. 27 Moreover, he hath also accused me, thy servant, to thee, my lord, the king, but thou, my lord, the king, art as an angel of God: do what pleaseth thee, 28 for all

fuit domus patris mei nisi morti obnoxia domino meo, regi, tu autem posuisti me, servum tuum, inter convivas mensae tuae. Quid igitur habeo iustae querellae? Aut quid possum ultra vociferari ad regem?"

29 Ait ergo ei rex, "Quid ultra loqueris? Fixum est quod locutus sum: tu et Siba, dividite possessiones."

30 Responditque Mifiboseth regi, "Etiam cuncta accipiat, postquam reversus est dominus meus, rex, pacifice in domum suam."

31 Berzellai quoque, Galaadites, descendens de Rogelim transduxit regem Iordanem paratus etiam ultra fluvium prosequi eum. 32 Erat autem Berzellai, Galaadites, senex valde, id est octogenarius, et ipse praebuit alimenta regi cum moraretur in Castris, fuit quippe vir dives nimis. 33 Dixit itaque rex ad Berzellai, "Veni mecum ut requiescas securus mecum in Hierusalem."

34 Et ait Berzellai ad regem, "Quot sunt dies annorum vitae meae ut ascendam cum rege in Hierusalem? 35 Octogenarius sum hodie; numquid vigent sensus mei ad discernendum suave aut amarum? Aut delectare potest servum tuum cibus et potus? Vel audire ultra possum vocem cantorum atque cantricum? Quare servus tuus sit oneri domino meo, regi? 36 Paululum procedam famulus tuus ab Iordane tecum; non indigeo hac vicissitudine. 37 Sed, obsecro ut revertar servus tuus et moriar in civitate mea et sepeliar iuxta sepulchrum patris mei et matris meae. Est autem servus tuus Chamaam; ipse vadat tecum, domine mi, rex, et fac ei quidquid tibi bonum videtur."

of my father's house were *no better than worthy* of death before my lord, the king, and thou hast set me, thy servant, among the guests of thy table. What just complaint therefore have I? Or what right to cry any more to the king?"

29 Then the king said to him, "Why speakest thou any more? What I have said is determined: thou and Ziba, divide the possessions."

30 And Mephibosheth answered the king, "Yea, let him take all, for as much as my lord, the king, is returned peaceably into his house."

31 Barzillai also, the Gileadite, coming down from Rogelim brought the king over the Jordan being ready also to wait on him beyond the river. 32 Now Barzillai, the Gileadite, was *of a great age,* that is to say fourscore years old, and he provided the king with sustenance when he abode in the Camp, for he was a man exceeding rich. 33 And the king said to Barzillai, "Come with me that thou mayest rest secure with me in Jerusalem."

34 And Barzillai said to the king, "How many are the days of the years of my life that I should go up with the king to Jerusalem? 35 I am this day fourscore years old; are my senses quick to discern sweet *and* bitter? Or can meat *or* drink delight thy servant? Or can I hear any more the voice of singing men and singing women? Why should thy servant be a burden to my lord, the king? 36 I, thy servant, will go on a little way from the Jordan with thee; I need not this recompense. 37 But, I beseech thee, *let* thy servant return and die in my own city and be buried by the sepulchre of my father and of my mother. But there is thy servant Chimham; let him go with thee, my lord, the king, and do to him whatsoever seemeth good to thee."

Caput 20

Accidit quoque ut ibi esset vir Belial nomine Seba, filius Bochri, vir Iemineus, et cecinit bucina et ait, "Non est nobis pars in David neque hereditas in filio Isai. Revertere in tabernacula tua, Israhel." 2 Et separatus est omnis Israhel a David secutusque est Seba, filium Bochri, viri autem Iuda adheserunt regi suo a Iordane usque Hierusalem.

3 Cumque venisset rex in domum suam in Hierusalem, tulit decem mulieres, concubinas, quas dereliquerat ad custodiendam domum, et tradidit eas in custodiam, alimenta eis praebens, et non est ingressus ad eas, sed erant clausae usque ad diem mortis suae in viduitate viventes. 4 Dixit autem rex Amasae, "Convoca mihi omnes viros Iuda in diem tertium, et tu adesto praesens." 5 Abiit ergo Amasa ut convocaret Iudam, et moratus est extra placitum quod ei constituerat rex. 6 Ait autem David ad Abisai, "Nunc magis adflicturus est nos Seba, filius Bochri, quam Absalom. Tolle igitur servos domini tui, et persequere eum ne forte inveniat civitates munitas et effugiat nos."

7 Egressi sunt ergo cum eo viri Ioab Cherethi quoque et

Chapter 20

Sheba's rebellion. Amasa is slain by Joab. Abel is besieged, but upon the citizens casting over the wall the head of Sheba, Joab departeth with all his army.

And there happened to be there a man of Belial *whose name was* Sheba, the son of Bichri, a man of Jemini, and he sounded the trumpet and said, "We have no part in David nor inheritance in the son of Jesse. Return to thy dwellings, O Israel." 2 And all Israel departed from David and followed Sheba, the son of Bichri, but the men of Judah stuck to their king from the Jordan unto Jerusalem.

3 And when the king was come into his house at Jerusalem, he took the ten women, his concubines whom he had left to keep the house, and put them in ward, allowing them provisions, and he went not in unto them, but they were shut up unto the day of their death living in widowhood. 4 And the king said to Amasa, "Assemble to me all the men of Judah against the third day, and be thou here present." 5 So Amasa went to assemble *the men of* Judah, *but* he tarried beyond the set time which the king had appointed him. 6 And David said to Abishai, "Now will Sheba, the son of Bichri, do us more harm than did Absalom. Take thou therefore the servants of thy lord, and pursue after him *lest* he find fenced cities and escape us."

7 So Joab's men went out with him and the Cherethites

Felethi, et omnes robusti exierunt de Hierusalem ad persequendum Seba, filium Bochri. 8 Cumque illi essent iuxta lapidem grandem qui est in Gabaon, Amasa veniens occurrit
eis. Porro Ioab vestitus erat tunica stricta ad mensuram habitus sui, et desuper accinctus gladio dependente usque ad
ilia in vagina, qui fabrefactus levi motu egredi poterat et percutere. 9 Dixit itaque Ioab ad Amasa, "Salve, mi frater." Et
tenuit manu dextra mentum Amasae quasi osculans eum,
10 porro Amasa non observavit gladium quem habebat Ioab,
qui percussit eum in latere et effudit intestina eius in terram
nec secundum vulnus adposuit, et mortuus est. Ioab autem
et Abisai, frater eius, persecuti sunt Seba, filium Bochri.

11 Interea, quidam viri cum stetissent iuxta cadaver Amasae de sociis Ioab dixerunt, "Ecce: qui esse voluit pro Ioab
comes David." 12 Amasa autem conspersus sanguine iacebat
in media via. Vidit hoc quidam vir, quod subsisteret omnis
populus ad videndum eum, et amovit Amasam de via in
agrum operuitque eum vestimento, ne subsisterent transeuntes propter eum. 13 Amoto igitur illo de via, transiebat
omnis vir sequens Ioab ad persequendum Seba, filium Bochri.

14 Porro ille transierat per omnes tribus Israhel in Abelam
et Bethmacha, omnesque viri electi congregati fuerant ad
eum. 15 Venerunt itaque et obpugnabant eum in Abela et in
Bethmacha, et circumdederunt munitionibus civitatem, et
obsessa est urbs, omnis autem turba quae erat cum Ioab mo-
liebatur destruere muros. 16 Et exclamavit mulier sapiens de
civitate, "Audite; audite; dicite Ioab, 'Adpropinqua huc, et

and the Pelethites, and all the valiant men went out of Jerusalem to pursue after Sheba, the son of Bichri. 8 And when they were at the great stone which is in Gibeon, Amasa coming met them. And Joab had on a close coat of equal length with his habit, and over it was girded with a sword hanging down to his flank in a scabbard, *made in such manner as to come out with the least* motion and strike. 9 And Joab said to Amasa, "God save thee, my brother." And he took Amasa by the chin with his right hand *to kiss* him, 10 but Amasa did not take notice of the sword which Joab had, and he struck him in the side and shed out his bowels to the ground and gave him not a second wound, and he died. And Joab and Abishai, his brother, pursued after Sheba, the son of Bichri.

11 In the mean time, some men of Joab's company *stopping* at the dead body of Amasa said, "Behold: he that would have been in Joab's stead the companion of David." 12 And Amasa imbrued with blood lay in the midst of the way. A certain man saw this, that all the people stood still to look upon him, *so* he removed Amasa out of the highway into the field and covered him with a garment, that they who passed might not stop on his account. 13 And when he was removed out of the way, all the people went on following Joab to pursue after Sheba, the son of Bichri.

14 Now he had passed through all the tribes of Israel unto Abel and Beth-maacah, and all the chosen men were gathered together unto him. 15 And they came and besieged him in Abel and in Beth-maacah, and they *cast up works round the city,* and the city was besieged, and all the people that were with Joab laboured to throw down the walls. 16 And a wise woman cried out from the city, "Hear; hear, *and* say to Joab,

loquar tecum.'" 17 Qui cum accessisset ad eam, ait illi, "Tu es Ioab?"

Et ille respondit. "Ego."

Ad quem sic locuta est: "Audi sermones ancillae tuae."

Qui respondit, "Audio."

18 Rursumque illa, "Sermo," inquit, "dicebatur in veteri proverbio: 'Qui interrogant, interrogent in Abela,' et sic perficiebant. 19 Nonne ego sum quae respondeo veritatem in Israhel, et tu quaeris subvertere civitatem et evertere matrem in Israhel? Quare praecipitas hereditatem Domini?"

20 Respondensque Ioab ait, "Absit, absit hoc a me; non praecipito neque demolior. 21 Non se sic habet res, sed homo de Monte Ephraim, Seba, filius Bochri, cognomine, levavit manum contra Regem David. Tradite illum solum, et recedemus a civitate."

Et ait mulier ad Ioab, "Ecce: caput eius mittetur ad te per murum." 22 Ingressa est ergo ad omnem populum et locuta est eis sapienter, qui abscisum caput Seba, filii Bochri, proiecerunt ad Ioab. Et ille cecinit tuba, et recesserunt ab urbe, unusquisque in tabernacula sua, Ioab autem reversus est Hierusalem, ad regem. 23 Fuit ergo Ioab super omnem exercitum Israhel, Banaias autem, filius Ioiadae, super Cheretheos et Feletheos, 24 Aduram vero super tributa, porro Iosaphat, filius Ahilud, a commentariis, 25 Sia autem scriba, Sadoc vero et Abiathar, sacerdotes, 26 Hira autem, Hiaiarites, erat sacerdos David.

'Come near hither, and I will speak with thee.'" 17 And when he was come near to her, she said to him, "Art thou Joab?"

And he answered, "I am."

And she spoke thus to him: "Hear the words of thy hand-maid."

He answered, "I do hear."

18 And she again said, "A saying was used in the old prov-erb: 'They that inquire, let them inquire in Abel,' and so they made an end. 19 Am not I she that answer truth in Israel, and thou seekest to destroy the city and to overthrow a mother in Israel? Why wilt thou throw down the inheritance of the Lord?"

20 And Joab answering said, "God forbid, God forbid that I should; I do not throw down nor destroy. 21 The matter is not so, but a man of Mount Ephraim, Sheba, the son of Bichri, by name, hath lifted up his hand against King David. Deliver him only, and we will depart from the city."

And the woman said to Joab, "Behold: his head shall be thrown to thee from the wall." 22 So she went to all the peo-ple and spoke to them wisely, *and they cut off* the head of Sheba, the son of Bichri, *and* cast it out to Joab. And he sounded the trumpet, and they departed from the city, ev-ery one to their *home,* and Joab returned to Jerusalem, to the king. 23 So Joab was over all the army of Israel, and Benaiah, the son of Jehoiada, was over the Cerethites and Phelethites, 24 but Adoram over the tributes, and Jehoshaphat, the son of Ahilud, was *recorder,* 25 and Sheva was scribe, and Zadok and Abiathar, priests, 26 and Ira the, Jairite, was the priest of David.

Caput 21

Facta est quoque fames in diebus David tribus annis iugiter, et consuluit David oraculum Domini. Dixitque Dominus, "Propter Saul et domum eius sanguinum, quia occidit Gabaonitas."

2 Vocatis ergo Gabaonitis rex dixit ad eos (porro Gabaonitae non erant de filiis Israhel sed reliquiae Amorreorum, filii quippe Israhel iuraverant eis et voluit Saul percutere eos zelo, quasi pro filiis Israhel et Iuda), 3 dixit ergo David ad Gabaonitas, "Quid faciam vobis? Et quod erit vestri piaculum ut benedicatis hereditati Domini?"

4 Dixeruntque ei Gabaonitae, "Non est nobis super argento et auro quaestio, sed contra Saul et contra domum eius, neque volumus ut interficiatur homo de Israhel."

Ad quos rex ait, "Quid ergo vultis ut faciam vobis?"

5 Qui dixerunt regi? "Virum qui adtrivit nos et oppressit inique ita delere debemus ut ne unus quidem residuus sit de stirpe eius in cunctis finibus Israhel. 6 Dentur nobis septem

Chapter 21

A famine of three years for the sin of Saul against the
Gibeonites at whose desire seven of Saul's race are crucified.
War again with the Philistines.

And there was a famine in the days of David for three
years successively, and David consulted the oracle of the
Lord. And the Lord said, "It is for Saul and his bloody house,
because he slew the Gibeonites."

2 Then the king calling for the Gibeonites said to them
(now the Gibeonites were not of the children of Israel but
the remains of the Amorites, and the children of Israel had
sworn to them and Saul *sought* to slay them out of zeal, as it
were for the children of Israel and Judah), 3 David therefore
said to the Gibeonites, "What shall I do for you? And what
shall be the atonement for you that you may bless the inheritance of the Lord?"

4 And the Gibeonites said to him, "We have no contest
about silver and gold, but against Saul and against his house,
neither do we desire that any man be slain of Israel."

And the king said to them, "What will you then that I
should do for you?"

5 And they said to the *king,* "The man that crushed us and
oppressed us unjustly we must destroy in such manner that
there be not so much as one left of his stock in all the coasts
of Israel. 6 Let seven men of his children be delivered unto

viri de filiis eius ut crucifigamus eos Domino in Gabaath Saul, quondam electi Domini."

Et ait rex, "Ego dabo."

7 Pepercitque rex Mifiboseth, filio Ionathan, filii Saul, propter iusiurandum Domini quod fuerat inter David et inter Ionathan, filium Saul. 8 Tulit itaque rex duos filios Respha, filiae Ahia, quos peperit Saul, Armoni et Mifiboseth, et quinque filios Michol, filiae Saul, quos genuerat Hadriheli, filio Berzellai qui fuit de Molathi, 9 et dedit eos in manus Gabaonitarum, qui crucifixerunt illos in monte coram Domino, et ceciderunt hii septem simul occisi in diebus messis primis incipiente messione hordei. 10 Tollens autem Respha, filia Ahia, cilicium substravit sibi super petram ab initio messis donec stillaret aqua super eos de caelo et non dimisit aves lacerare eos per diem neque bestias per noctem.

11 Et nuntiata sunt David quae fecerat Respha, filia Ahia, concubina Saul. 12 Et abiit David et tulit ossa Saul et ossa Ionathan, filii eius, a viris Iabes Galaad qui furati fuerant ea de platea Bethsan in qua suspenderant eos Philisthim cum interfecissent Saul in Gelboe. 13 Et asportavit inde ossa Saul et ossa Ionathan, filii eius, et colligentes ossa eorum qui adfixi fuerant, 14 sepelierunt ea cum ossibus Saul et Ionathan, filii eius, in terra Beniamin in latere, in sepulchro Cis, patris eius, feceruntque omnia quae praeceperat rex, et repropitiatus est Deus terrae post haec.

us that we may crucify them to the Lord in Gibeah of Saul, once the chosen of the Lord."

And the king said, "I will give them."

7 And the king spared Mephibosheth, the son of Jonathan, the son of Saul, because of the oath of the Lord that had been between David and Jonathan, the son of Saul. 8 So the king took the two sons of Rizpah, the daughter of Aiah, whom she bore to Saul, Armoni, and Mephibosheth, and the five sons of Michal, the daughter of Saul, whom she bore to Adriel, the son of Barzillai that was of Meholath, 9 and gave them into the hands of the Gibeonites, and they crucified them on a hill before the Lord, and these seven died together in the first days of the harvest when the barley began to be reaped. 10 And Rizpah, the daughter of Aiah, took haircloth and spread it under her upon the rock from the beginning of the harvest till water dropped upon them out of heaven and suffered neither the birds to tear them by day nor the beasts by night.

11 And it was told David what Rizpah, the daughter of Aiah, the concubine of Saul, had done. 12 And David went and took the bones of Saul and the bones of Jonathan, his son, from the men of Jabesh Gilead who had stolen them from the street of Beth-shan where the Philistines had hanged them when they had slain Saul in Gilboa. 13 And he brought from thence the bones of Saul and the bones of Jonathan, his son, and they gathered up the bones of them that were crucified, 14 and they buried them with the bones of Saul and of Jonathan, his son, in the land of Benjamin in the side, in the sepulchre of Kish, his father, and they did all that the king had commanded, and God shewed mercy again to the land after these things.

15 Factum est autem rursum proelium Philisthinorum adversum Israhel, et descendit David et servi eius cum eo et pugnabant contra Philisthim. Deficiente autem David, 16 Iesbidenob, qui fuit de genere Arafa, cuius ferrum hastae trecentas uncias adpendebat et accinctus erat ense novo, nisus est percutere David. 17 Praesidioque ei fuit Abisai, filius Sarviae, et percussum Philistheum interfecit. Tunc iuraverunt viri David dicentes, "Iam non egredieris nobiscum in bellum ne extinguas lucernam Israhel."

18 Secundum quoque fuit bellum in Gob contra Philistheos. Tunc percussit Sobbochai de Usathi Seph de stirpe Arafa de genere gigantum. 19 Tertium quoque fuit bellum in Gob contra Philistheos in quo percussit Adeodatus, filius Saltus, polymitarius Bethleemites, Goliath, Gettheum, cuius hastile hastae erat quasi liciatorium texentium. 20 Quartum bellum fuit in Geth, in quo vir fuit excelsus qui senos in manibus pedibusque habebat digitos, id est, viginti et quattuor, et erat de origine Arafa. 21 Et blasphemavit Israhel, percussit autem eum Ionathan, filius Sammaa, fratris David. 22 Hii quattuor nati sunt de Arafa in Geth, et ceciderunt in manu David et servorum eius.

15 And the Philistines made war again against Israel, and David went down and his servants with him and fought against the Philistines. And David growing faint, 16 Ishbi-benob, who was of the race of Arapha, the iron of whose spear weighed three hundred ounces, being girded with a new sword attempted to kill David. 17 And Abishai, the son of Zeruiah, rescued him and striking the Philistine killed him. Then David's men swore *unto him,* saying, "Thou shalt go no more out with us to battle lest thou put out the lamp of Israel."

18 There was also a second battle in Gob against the Philistines. Then Sibbecai of Hushath slew Saph of the race of Arapha, of the family of the giants. 19 And there was a third battle in Gob against the Philistines in which Adeodatus, the son of the Forrest, an embroiderer of Bethlehem, slew Goliath, the Gittite, the shaft of whose spear was like a weaver's beam. 20 A fourth battle was in Gath, where there was a man of great stature that had *six fingers on each hand and six toes on each foot,* four and twenty *in all,* and he was of the race of Arapha. 21 And he reproached Israel, and Jonathan, the son of Shimei, the brother of David, slew him. 22 These four were born of Arapha in Gath, and they fell by the hand of David and of his servants.

Caput 22

Locutus est autem David Domino verba carminis huius in die qua liberavit eum Dominus de manu omnium inimicorum suorum et de manu Saul, 2 et ait, "Dominus petra mea et robur meum et salvator meus. 3 Deus fortis meus; sperabo in eum. Scutum meum et cornu salutis meae, elevator meus et refugium meum. Salvator meus, de iniquitate liberabis me.

4 "Laudabilem invocabo Dominum, et ab inimicis meis salvus ero, 5 quia circumdederunt me contritiones mortis; torrentes Belial terruerunt me. 6 Funes inferi circumdederunt me; praevenerunt me laquei mortis. 7 In tribulatione mea invocabo Dominum, et ad Deum meum clamabo, et exaudiet de templo suo vocem meam, et clamor meus veniet ad aures eius.

8 "Commota est et contremuit terra; fundamenta montium concussa sunt et conquassata quoniam iratus est eis. 9 Ascendit fumus de naribus eius, et ignis de ore eius vorabit. Carbones incensi sunt ab eo. 10 Inclinavit caelos et descendit, et caligo sub pedibus eius. 11 Et ascendit super cherubin et volavit et lapsus est super pinnas venti. 12 Posuit tenebras in circuitu suo latibulum cribrans aquas de nubibus caelo-

Chapter 22

King David's psalm of thanksgiving for his deliverance from all his enemies.

And David spoke to the Lord the words of this canticle in the day that the Lord delivered him out of the hand of all his enemies and out of the hand of Saul, 2 and he said, "The Lord is my rock and my strength and my saviour. 3 God is my strong one; in him will I trust. My shield and the horn of my salvation, *he lifteth me up* and is my refuge. My saviour, thou wilt deliver me from iniquity.

4 "I will call on the Lord *who is* worthy to be praised, and I shall be saved from my enemies, 5 for the pangs of death have surrounded me; the floods of Belial have made me afraid. 6 The cords of hell compassed me; the snares of death prevented me. 7 In my distress I will call upon the Lord, and I will cry to my God, and he will hear my voice out of his temple, and my cry shall come to his ears.

8 "The earth shook and trembled; the foundations of the mountains were moved and shaken because he was angry with them. 9 A smoke went up from his nostrils, and a *devouring* fire out of his mouth. Coals were kindled by it. 10 He bowed the heavens and came down, and darkness was under his feet. 11 And he rode upon the cherubims and flew and slid upon the wings of the wind. 12 He made darkness a covering round about him dropping waters out of the clouds of

rum. 13 Prae fulgore in conspectu eius succensi sunt carbones ignis.

14 "Tonabit de caelis Dominus, et excelsus dabit vocem suam.

15 "Misit sagittas et dissipavit eos, fulgur et consumpsit eos. 16 Et apparuerunt effusiones maris, et revelata sunt fundamenta orbis ab increpatione Domini, ab inspiratione spiritus furoris eius.

17 "Misit de excelso et adsumpsit me et extraxit me de aquis multis. 18 Liberavit me ab inimico meo potentissimo et ab his qui oderant me, quoniam robustiores me erant. 19 Praevenit me in die adflictionis meae, et factus est Dominus firmamentum meum. 20 Et eduxit me in latitudinem; liberavit me quia complacui ei.

21 "Retribuet mihi Dominus secundum iustitiam meam et secundum munditiam manuum mearum reddet mihi 22 quia custodivi vias Domini et non egi impie a Deo meo, 23 omnia enim iudicia eius in conspectu meo, et praecepta eius non amovi a me. 24 Et ero perfectus cum eo et custodiam me ab iniquitate mea. 25 Et restituet Dominus mihi secundum iustitiam meam et secundum munditiam manuum mearum in conspectu oculorum suorum.

26 "Cum sancto sanctus eris et cum robusto, perfectus. 27 Cum electo electus eris, et cum perverso, perverteris. 28 Et populum pauperem salvum facies, oculisque tuis excelsos humiliabis. 29 Quia tu lucerna mea, Domine, et inluminabis tenebras meas, 30 in te enim curram accinctus; in Deo meo transiliam murum.

the heavens. 13 By the brightness *before* him the coals of fire were kindled.

14 "The Lord shall thunder from heaven, and the most high shall give forth his voice.

15 "He shot arrows and scattered them, lightning and consumed them. 16 And the overflowings of the sea appeared, and the foundations of the world were laid open at the rebuke of the Lord, at the blast of the spirit of his wrath.

17 "He sent from on high and took me and drew me out of many waters. 18 He delivered me from my most mighty enemy and from them that hated me, for they were *too strong for* me. 19 He prevented me in the day of my affliction, and the Lord became my stay. 20 And he brought me forth into a large place; he delivered me because I pleased him.

21 "The Lord will reward me according to my justice and according to the cleanness of my hands he will render to me 22 because I have kept the ways of the Lord and have not wickedly *departed* from my God, 23 for all his judgments are in my sight, and his precepts I have not removed from me. 24 And I shall be perfect with him and shall keep myself from my iniquity. 25 And the Lord will recompense me according to my justice and according to the cleanness of my hands in the sight of his eyes.

26 "With the holy one thou wilt be holy and with the valiant, perfect. 27 With the elect thou wilt be elect, and with the perverse thou wilt be perverted. 28 And the poor people thou wilt save, and with thy eyes thou wilt humble the haughty. 29 For thou art my lamp, O Lord, and thou wilt enlighten my darkness, 30 for in thee I will run girded; in my God I will leap over the wall.

31 "Deus, inmaculata via eius; eloquium Domini igne examinatum. Scutum est omnium sperantium in se. 32 Quis est Deus praeter Dominum, et quis fortis praeter Deum nostrum, 33 Deus qui accinxit me fortitudine et conplanavit perfectam viam meam, 34 coaequans pedes meos cervis et super excelsa mea statuens me, 35 docens manus meas ad proelium et conponens quasi arcum aereum brachia mea?

36 "Dedisti mihi clypeum salutis tuae, et mansuetudo tua multiplicavit me. 37 Dilatabis gressus meos subtus me, et non deficient tali mei. 38 Persequar inimicos meos et conteram et non revertar donec consumam eos. 39 Consumam eos et confringam ut non consurgant. Cadent sub pedibus meis.

40 "Accinxisti me fortitudine ad proelium; incurvasti resistentes mihi sub me. 41 Inimicos meos dedisti mihi dorsum, odientes me, et disperdam eos. 42 Clamabunt—et non erit qui salvet—ad Dominum, et non exaudiet eos. 43 Delebo eos ut pulverem terrae; quasi lutum platearum comminuam eos atque confringam.

44 "Salvabis me a contradictionibus populi mei; custodies in caput Gentium. Populus quem ignoro serviet mihi. 45 Filii alieni resistent mihi; auditu auris oboedient mihi. 46 Filii alieni defluxerunt et contrahentur in angustiis suis.

47 "Vivit Dominus, et benedictus Deus meus, et exaltabitur Deus fortis salutis meae. 48 Deus qui das vindictas mihi et deicis populos sub me, 49 qui educis me ab inimicis meis

31 "God, his way is immaculate; the word of the Lord is tried by fire. He is the shield of all that trust in him. 32 Who is God but the Lord, and who is strong but our God, 33 God who hath girded me with strength and made even my perfect way, 34 making my feet like the feet of harts and setting me upon my high places? 35 He teacheth my hands to war and maketh my arms like a bow of brass.

36 "Thou hast given me the shield of thy salvation, and thy mildness hath multiplied me. 37 Thou shalt enlarge my steps under me, and my ankles shall not fail. 38 I will pursue after my enemies and crush them and will not return again till I consume them. 39 I will consume them and break them in pieces so that they shall not rise. They shall fall under my feet.

40 "Thou hast girded me with strength to battle; thou hast made them that resisted me to bow under me. 41 My enemies thou hast made to turn their back to me, them that hated me, and I shall destroy them. 42 They shall cry—and there shall be none to save—to the Lord, and he shall not hear them. 43 I shall *beat them as small as* the dust of the earth; I shall crush them and *spread* them *abroad* like the mire of the streets.

44 "Thou wilt save me from the contradictions of my people; thou wilt keep me to be the head of the Gentiles. The people which I know not shall serve me. 45 The sons of the stranger will resist me; at the hearing of the ear they will obey me. 46 The *strangers* are melted away and shall be straitened in their distresses.

47 "The Lord liveth, and my God is blessed, and the strong God of my salvation shall be exalted. 48 God who giveth me revenge and bringest down people under me, 49 who bringest

et a resistentibus mihi elevas me, a viro iniquo liberabis me.

50 "Propterea confitebor tibi, Domine, in Gentibus et nomini tuo cantabo, 51 magnificanti salutes regis sui et facienti misericordiam christo suo David et semini eius in sempiternum."

Caput 23

Haec autem sunt verba novissima David. Dixit David filius Isai; dixit vir cui constitutum est de Christo Dei Iacob, egregius psalta Israhel, 2 "Spiritus Domini locutus est per me et sermo eius per linguam meam. 3 Dixit Deus Israhel mihi, locutus est; Fortis Israhel, 'Dominator hominum, iustus dominator in timore Dei, 4 sicut lux aurorae oriente sole, mane absque nubibus rutilat et sicut pluviis germinat herba de terra.' 5 Nec tanta est domus mea apud Deum ut pactum aeternum iniret mecum, firmum in omnibus atque munitum, cuncta enim salus mea et omnis voluntas, nec est quicquam ex ea quod non germinet.

6 "Praevaricatores autem quasi spinae evellentur universi quae non tolluntur manibus. 7 Et si quis tangere voluerit eas,

me forth from my enemies and liftest me up from them that resist me, from the wicked man thou shalt deliver me.

50 "Therefore will I give thanks to thee, O Lord, among the Gentiles and will sing to thy name, 51 *giving great salvation* to his king and shewing mercy to David, his anointed, and to his seed for ever."

Chapter 23

The last words of David. A catalogue of his valiant men.

Now these are David's last words: David, the son of Jesse, said; the man to whom it was appointed concerning the Christ of the God of Jacob, the excellent psalmist of Israel, *said,* 2 "The spirit of the Lord hath spoken by me and his word by my tongue. 3 The God of Israel said to me; the strong one of Israel spoke, 'The ruler of men, the just ruler in the fear of God, 4 as the light of the morning when the sun riseth, shineth in the morning without clouds and as the grass springeth out of the earth by rain.' 5 Neither is my house so great with God that he should make with me an eternal covenant, firm in all things and assured, for he is all my salvation and all my will, neither is there ought thereof that springeth not up.

6 "But transgressors shall all of them be plucked up as thorns which are not taken away with hands. 7 And if a man

armabitur ferro et ligno lanceato, igneque succensae conburentur usque ad nihilum."

8 Haec nomina fortium David. Sedens in cathedra sapientissimus princeps inter tres; ipse est quasi tenerrimus ligni vermiculus qui octingentos interfecit impetu uno. 9 Post hunc Eleazar, filius patrui eius Ahohites, inter tres fortes qui erant cum David quando exprobraverunt Philisthim, et congregati sunt illuc in proelium. 10 Cumque ascendissent viri Israhel, ipse stetit et percussit Philistheos donec deficeret manus eius et obrigesceret cum gladio, fecitque Dominus salutem magnam in die illa, et populus qui fugerat reversus est ad caesorum spolia detrahenda. 11 Et post hunc Semma, filius Age de Arari. Et congregati sunt Philisthim in statione, erat quippe ibi ager plenus lente. Cumque fugisset populus a facie Philisthim, 12 stetit ille in medio agri et tuitus est eum percussitque Philistheos, et fecit Dominus salutem magnam.

13 Nec non et ante descenderant tres qui erant principes inter triginta et venerant tempore messis ad David in speluncam Odollam, castra autem Philisthim erant posita in valle Gigantum. 14 Et David erat in praesidio, porro statio Philisthinorum tunc erat in Bethleem. 15 Desideravit igitur David et ait, "O si quis mihi daret potum aquae de cisterna quae est in Bethleem, iuxta portam." 16 Inruperunt ergo tres fortes castra Philisthinorum et hauserunt aquam de cisterna Bethleem quae erat iuxta portam et adtulerunt ad David, at

will touch them, he *must* be armed with iron and with the staff of a lance, *but* they shall be set on fire and burnt to nothing."

8 These are the names of the valiant men of David: *Jesbaham* sitting in the chair was the wisest chief among the three; he was like the most tender little worm of the wood who killed eight hundred men at one onset. 9 After him was Eleazar, the son of *Dodo,* the Ahohite, *one of the* three valiant men that were with David when they defied the Philistines, and they were there gathered together to battle. 10 And when the men of Israel were gone *away,* he stood and smote the Philistines till his hand was weary and grew stiff with the sword, and the Lord wrought a great *victory* that day, and the people that were fled away returned to take spoils of them that were slain. 11 And after him was Shammah, the son of Agee of Harar. And the Philistines were gathered together in a troop, for there was a field full of lentils. And when the people were fled from the face of the Philistines, 12 he stood in the midst of the field and defended it and defeated the Philistines, and the Lord gave a great *victory.*

13 Moreover also before this the three who were princes among the thirty went down and came to David in the harvest time into the cave of Adullam, and the camp of the Philistines *was* in the valley of the giants. 14 And David was then in a hold, and there was a garrison of the Philistines then in Bethlehem. 15 And David longed and said, "O that some man would get me a drink of the water out of the cistern that is in Bethlehem, by the gate." 16 And the three valiant men broke through the camp of the Philistines and drew water out of the cistern of Bethlehem that was by the gate and brought it to David, but he would not drink but offered

ille noluit bibere sed libavit illam Domino, 17 dicens, "Propitius mihi sit Dominus ne faciam hoc. Num sanguinem hominum istorum qui profecti sunt et animarum periculum bibam?" Noluit ergo bibere. Haec fecerunt tres robustissimi.

18 Abisai quoque, frater Ioab, filius Sarviae, princeps erat de tribus; ipse est qui elevavit hastam suam contra trecentos quos interfecit, nominatus in tribus 19 et inter tres nobilior eratque eorum princeps, sed usque ad tres primos non pervenerat.

20 Et Banaias, filius Ioiada, viri fortissimi magnorum operum, de Capsehel, ipse percussit duos leones Moab, et ipse descendit et percussit leonem in media cisterna in diebus nivis. 21 Ipse quoque interfecit Aegyptium, virum dignum spectaculo, habentem in manu hastam, itaque cum descendisset ad eum in virga vi extorsit hastam de manu Aegyptii, et interfecit eum hasta sua. 22 Haec fecit Banaias, filius Ioiadae. 23 Et ipse nominatus inter tres robustos qui erant inter triginta nobiliores, verumtamen usque ad tres non pervenerat, fecitque eum David sibi auricularium a secreto.

24 Asahel, frater Ioab, inter triginta; Eleanan, filius patrui eius de Bethleem; 25 Semma de Harodi; Helica de Arori; 26 Helas de Felthi; Hira, filius Aces de Thecua; 27 Abiezer de Anathoth; Mobonnai de Usathi; 28 Selmon, Aohites; Maharai, Netophathites; 29 Heled, filius Banaa, et ipse Netophathites; Hithai, filius Ribai de Gebeeth filiorum Beniamin; 30 Banahi, Aufrathonites; Heddai de torrente Gaas; 31 Abialbon, Arbathites; Azmaveth de Beromi; 32 Eliaba de Salboni; filii Iasen: Ionathan, 33 Semma de Horodi; Haiam, filius Sarar, Arorites; 34 Elifeleth, filius Aasbai, filii Maachathi; He-

it to the Lord, 17 saying, "The Lord be merciful to me that I may not do this. Shall I drink the blood of these men that went and the peril of their lives?" Therefore he would not drink. These things did these three *mighty men*.

18 Abishai also, the brother of Joab, the son of Zeruiah, was chief among three, *and he* lifted up his spear against three hundred whom he slew, *and* he was renowned among the three 19 and the noblest of three and was their chief, but to the three first he attained not.

20 And Benaiah, the son of Jehoiada, a most valiant man of great deeds, of Kabzeel, he slew the two lions of Moab, and he went down and slew a lion in the midst of a pit in the time of snow. 21 He also slew an Egyptian, a man worthy to be a sight, having a spear in his hand, *but* he went down to him with a rod *and* forced the spear out of the hand of the Egyptian, and slew him with his own spear. 22 These things did Benaiah, the son of Jehoiada. 23 And he was renowned among the three valiant men who were the most honourable among the thirty, but he attained not to the first three, and David made him of his privy council.

24 Asahel, the brother of Joab, *was one of* the thirty; El-hanan, the son of *Dodo* of Bethlehem; 25 Shammah of Harod; Elika of *Harod;* 26 Helez of Palti; Ira, the son of Ikkesh of Tekoa; 27 Abiezer of Anathoth; Mebunnai of Hushah; 28 Zal-mon, the Ahohite; Maharai, the Netophahite; 29 Heleb, the son of Baanah, also a Netophatite; Ittai, the son of Ribai of Gibeah of the children of Benjamin; 30 Banaiah the Pira-thonite; Hiddai of the torrent Gaash; 31 Abi-albon, the Ar-bathite; Azmaveth of Bahurim; 32 Eliahba of Shaalbon; the sons of Jashen: Jonathan, 33 Shammah of Harar; Ahiam, the son of Sharar, the Hararite; 34 Eliphelet, the son of Ahasbai,

liam, filius Ahitofel, Gelonites; 35 Esrai de Carmelo; Farai de Arbi; 36 Igaal, filius Nathan de Soba; Bonni de Gaddi; 37 Selech de Ammoni; Naharai, Berothites, armiger Ioab, filii Sarviae; 38 Hira, Hiethrites; Gareb, et ipse Hiethrites; 39 Urias Hettheus—omnes triginta septem.

Caput 24

Et addidit furor Domini irasci contra Israhel commovitque David in eis, dicentem, "Vade; numera Israhel et Iudam."

2 Dixitque rex ad Ioab, principem exercitus sui, "Perambula omnes tribus Israhel a Dan usque Bersabee, et numerate populum, ut sciam numerum eius."

3 Dixitque Ioab regi, "Adaugeat Dominus, Deus tuus, ad populum tuum quantus nunc est iterumque centuplicet in conspectu domini mei, regis. Sed quid sibi dominus meus, rex, vult in re huiuscemodi?" 4 Obtinuit autem sermo regis verba Ioab et principum exercitus, egressusque est Ioab

the son of Maacah; Eliam, the son of Ahithophel, the Gilonite; 35 Hezrai of Carmel; Paarai of Aarb; 36 Igal, the son of Nathan of Zobah; Bani of Gadi; 37 Zelek of Ammon; Naharai, the Beerothite, armourbearer of Joab, the son of Zeruiah; 38 Ira, the Ithrite; Gareb, also an Ithrite; 39 Uriah the Hittite — thirty *and* seven in all.

Chapter 24

David numbereth the people. God sendeth a pestilence
which is stopt by David's prayer and sacrifice.

And the anger of the Lord was again kindled against Israel and stirred up David among them, saying, "Go; number Israel and Judah."

2 And the king said to Joab, the general of his army, "Go through all the tribes of Israel from Dan to Beer-sheba, and number ye the people, that I may know the number of them."

3 And Joab said to the king, "The Lord, thy God, increase thy people and make them as many more as they are now and again multiply them a hundredfold in the sight of my lord, the king. But what meaneth my lord, the king, by this kind of thing?" 4 But the king's words prevailed over the words of Joab and of the captains of the army, and Joab and

et principes militum a facie regis ut numerarent populum Israhel.

5 Cumque pertransissent Iordanem, venerunt in Aroer, ad dextram urbis, quae est in valle Gad. 6 Et per Iazer transierunt in Galaad et in terram inferiorem Hodsi, et venerunt in Dan silvestria. Circumeuntesque iuxta Sidonem 7 transierunt propter moenia Tyri et omnem terram Hevei et Chananei, veneruntque ad meridiem Iuda in Bersabee. 8 Et lustrata universa terra adfuerunt post novem menses et viginti dies in Hierusalem. 9 Dedit ergo Ioab numerum descriptionis populi regi, et inventa sunt de Israhel octingenta milia virorum fortium qui educerent gladium et de Iuda quingenta milia pugnatorum.

10 Percussit autem cor David eum postquam numeratus est populus, et dixit David ad Dominum, "Peccavi valde in hoc facto, sed precor, Domine, ut transferas iniquitatem servi tui, quia stulte egi nimis."

11 Surrexit itaque David mane, et sermo Domini factus est ad Gad, propheten et videntem David, dicens, 12 "Vade, et loquere ad David, 'Haec dicit Dominus: "Trium tibi datur optio; elige unum quod volueris ex his ut faciam tibi."'" 13 Cumque venisset Gad ad David, nuntiavit ei, dicens, "Aut septem annis veniet tibi fames in terra tua, aut tribus mensibus fugies adversarios tuos, et illi te persequentur, aut certe tribus diebus erit pestilentia in terra tua. Nunc, ergo, delibera, et vide quem respondeam ei qui me misit sermonem."

the captains of the soldiers went out from the presence of the king to number the people of Israel.

5 And when they had passed the Jordan, they came to Aroer, to the right side of the city, which is in the vale of Gad. 6 And by Jazer they passed into Gilead and to the lower land of Hodshi, and they came into the woodlands of Dan. And going about by Sidon 7 they passed near the walls of Tyre and all the land of the Hivite and the Canaanite, and they came to the south of Judah into Beer-sheba. 8 And having gone through the whole land after nine months and twenty days they came to Jerusalem. 9 And Joab gave up the sum of the number of the people to the king, and there were found of Israel eight hundred thousand valiant men that drew the sword and of Judah five hundred thousand fighting men.

10 But David's heart struck him after the people were numbered, and David said to the Lord, "I have sinned very much in *what I have done,* but I pray thee, O Lord, to take away the iniquity of thy servant, because I have done exceeding foolishly."

11 And David arose in the morning, and the word of the Lord came to Gad, the prophet and the seer of David, saying, 12 "Go, and say to David, 'Thus saith the Lord: *I give thee thy choice* of three things; choose one of them which thou wilt that I may do it to thee.'" 13 And when Gad was come to David, he told him, saying, "Either *seven years of famine* shall come to thee in thy land, or thou shalt flee three months before thy adversaries, and they shall pursue thee, *or* for three days there shall be a pestilence in thy land. Now, therefore, deliberate, and see what *answer* I shall *return* to him that sent me."

14 Dixit autem David ad Gad, "Artor nimis, sed melius est ut incidam in manus Domini, multae enim misericordiae eius sunt, quam in manus hominum." 15 Inmisitque Dominus pestilentiam in Israhel de mane usque ad tempus constitutum, et mortui sunt ex populo a Dan usque Bersabee septuaginta milia virorum.

16 Cumque extendisset manum angelus Domini super Hierusalem ut disperderet eam, misertus est Dominus super adflictione et ait angelo percutienti populum, "Sufficit. Nunc contine manum tuam." Erat autem angelus Domini iuxta aream Areuna, Iebusei.

17 Dixitque David ad Dominum cum vidisset angelum caedentem populum, "Ego sum qui peccavi; ego inique egi. Isti qui oves sunt, quid fecerunt? Vertatur, obsecro, manus tua contra me et contra domum patris mei."

18 Venit autem Gad ad David in die illa et dixit ei, "Ascende, et constitue Domino altare in area Areuna, Iebusei." 19 Et ascendit David iuxta sermonem Gad quem praeceperat ei Dominus.

20 Conspiciensque Areuna animadvertit regem et servos eius transire ad se, 21 et egressus adoravit regem, prono vultu in terram, et ait, "Quid causae est ut veniat dominus meus, rex, ad servum suum?"

Cui David ait, "Ut emam a te aream et aedificem altare Domino et cesset interfectio quae grassatur in populo."

22 Et ait Areuna ad David, "Accipiat et offerat dominus meus, rex, sicut ei placet. Habes boves in holocaustum et plaustrum et iuga boum in usum lignorum." 23 Omnia dedit

14 And David said to Gad, "I am in a great strait, but it is better that I should fall into the hands of the Lord, for his mercies are many, than into the hands of men." 15 And the Lord sent a pestilence upon Israel from the morning unto the time appointed, and there died of the people from Dan to Beer-sheba seventy thousand men.

16 And when the angel of the Lord had stretched out his hand over Jerusalem to destroy it, the Lord had pity on the affliction and said to the angel that slew the people, "It is enough. Now hold thy hand." And the angel of the Lord was by the threshingfloor of Araunah, the Jebusite.

17 And David said to the Lord when he saw the angel striking the people, *"It is I; I am he that have sinned; I have done wickedly. These that are the sheep, what have they done? Let thy hand, I beseech thee, be turned against me and against my father's house."

18 And Gad came to David that day and *said,* "Go up, and build an altar to the Lord in the threshingfloor of Araunah, the Jebusite." 19 And David went up according to the word of Gad which the Lord had commanded him.

20 And Araunah looked and saw the king and his servants coming towards him, 21 and going out he worshipped the king, *bowing with his face* to the earth, and said, "Wherefore is my lord, the king, come to his servant?"

And David said to him, "To buy the threshingfloor of thee and build an altar to the Lord *that* the plague which rageth among the people may cease."

22 And Araunah said to David, "Let my lord, the king, take and offer as it seemeth good to him. Thou hast *here* oxen for a holocaust and the wain and the yokes of the oxen for wood." 23 All these things Araunah as a king gave to the

Areuna rex regi, dixitque Areuna ad regem, "Dominus, Deus tuus, suscipiat votum tuum."

24 Cui respondens rex ait, "Nequaquam ut vis, sed emam pretio a te, et non offeram Domino, Deo meo, holocausta gratuita." Emit ergo David aream et boves argenti siclis quinquaginta, 25 et aedificavit ibi David altare Domino et obtulit holocausta et pacifica, et propitiatus est Dominus terrae, et cohibita est plaga ab Israhel.

king, and Araunah said to the king, "The Lord, thy God, receive thy vow."

24 And the king answered him and said, *"Nay* but I will buy it of thee at a price, and I will not offer to the Lord, my God, holocausts free cost." So David bought the floor and the oxen for fifty sicles of silver, 25 and David built there an altar to the Lord and offered holocausts and peace offerings, and the Lord became merciful to the land, and the plague was stayed from Israel.

3 KINGS

Caput 1

Et Rex David senuerat habebatque aetatis plurimos dies, cumque operiretur vestibus non calefiebat. 2 Dixerunt ergo ei servi sui, "Quaeramus domino nostro, regi, adulescentulam virginem, et stet coram rege et foveat eum dormiatque in sinu suo et calefaciat dominum nostrum, regem." 3 Quaesierunt igitur adulescentulam speciosam in omnibus finibus Israhel, et invenerunt Abisag, Sunamitin, et adduxerunt eam ad regem. 4 Erat autem puella pulchra nimis, dormiebatque cum rege et ministrabat ei, rex vero non cognovit eam.

5 Adonias autem, filius Aggith, elevabatur, dicens, "Ego regnabo." Fecitque sibi currus et equites et quinquaginta viros qui ante eum currerent. 6 Nec corripuit eum pater suus aliquando, dicens, "Quare hoc fecisti?" Erat autem et ipse pulcher valde, secundus natu post Absalom. 7 Et sermo ei cum Ioab, filio Sarviae, et cum Abiathar, sacerdote, qui adiuvabant partes Adoniae. 8 Sadoc vero, sacerdos, et Banaias, filius Ioiadae, et Nathan, propheta, et Semei et Rhei et ro-

Chapter 1

King David growing old, Abishag, a Shunammitess, is brought to him. Adonijah pretending to reign, Nathan and Bathsheba obtain that Solomon should be declared and anointed king.

Now King David was old and *advanced in years,* and when he was covered with clothes he was not warm. 2 His servants therefore said to him, "Let us seek for our lord, the king, a young virgin, and let her stand before the king and cherish him and sleep in his bosom and warm our lord, the king." 3 So they sought a beautiful young woman in all the coasts of Israel, and they found Abishag, a Shunammitess, and brought her to the king. 4 And the damsel was exceeding beautiful, and she slept with the king and served him, but the king did not know her.

5 And Adonijah, the son of Haggith, exalted himself, saying, "I will be king." And he made himself chariots and horsemen and fifty men to run before him. 6 Neither did his father rebuke him at any time, saying, "Why hast thou done this?" And he also was very beautiful, the next in birth after Absalom. 7 And he conferred with Joab, the son of Zeruiah, and with Abiathar, the priest, who furthered Adonijah's side. 8 But Zadok, the priest, and Benaiah, the son of Jehoiada,

bur exercitus David non erat cum Adonia. 9 Immolatis ergo
Adonias arietibus et vitulis et universis pinguibus iuxta lapidem Zoheleth, qui erat vicinus fonti Rogel, vocavit universos fratres suos, filios regis, et omnes viros Iuda, servos regis,
10 Nathan autem, prophetam, et Banaiam et robustos quosque et Salomonem, fratrem suum, non vocavit.

11 Dixit itaque Nathan ad Bethsabee, matrem Salomonis,
"Num audisti quod regnaverit Adonias, filius Aggith, et dominus noster David hoc ignorat? 12 Nunc ergo veni, accipe a
me consilium, et salva animam tuam filiique tui Salomonis.
13 Vade, et ingredere ad Regem David, et dic ei, 'Nonne tu,
domine mi, rex, iurasti mihi, ancillae tuae, dicens, "Salomon,
filius tuus, regnabit post me et ipse sedebit in solio meo"?
Quare ergo regnat Adonias?' 14 Et adhuc ibi te loquente cum
rege ego veniam post te et conplebo sermones tuos."

15 Ingressa est itaque Bethsabee ad regem in cubiculo.
Rex autem senuerat nimis, et Abisag, Sunamitis, ministrabat
ei. 16 Inclinavit se Bethsabee et adoravit regem. Ad quam
rex, "Quid tibi," inquit, "vis?"

17 Quae respondens ait, "Domine mi, tu iurasti per Dominum, Deum tuum, ancillae tuae, 'Salomon, filius tuus, regnabit post me, et ipse sedebit in solio meo.' 18 Et ecce: nunc
Adonias regnat, te, domine mi, rex, ignorante. 19 Mactavit
boves et pinguia quaeque et arietes plurimos et vocavit omnes filios regis, Abiathar quoque, sacerdotem, et Ioab, principem militiae, Salomonem autem, servum tuum, non vocavit. 20 Verumtamen, domine mi, rex, in te oculi respiciunt

and Nathan, the prophet, and Shimei and Rei and the strength of David's army was not with Adonijah. 9 And Adonijah having slain rams and calves and all fat cattle by the stone of Zoheleth, which was near the fountain Rogel, invited all his brethren, the king's sons, and all the men of Judah, the king's servants, 10 but Nathan, the prophet, and Benaiah and all the valiant men and Solomon, his brother, he invited not.

11 And Nathan said to Bathsheba, the mother of Solomon, "Hast thou not heard that Adonijah, the son of Haggith, reigneth, and our lord David knoweth it not? 12 Now then come, take my counsel, and save thy life and the life of thy son Solomon. 13 Go, and get thee in to King David, and say to him, 'Didst not thou, my lord, O king, swear to me, thy handmaid, saying, "Solomon, thy son, shall reign after me, and he shall sit on my throne"? Why then doth Adonijah reign?' 14 And while thou art yet speaking there with the king I will come in after thee and will fill up thy words."

15 So Bathsheba went in to the king into the chamber. Now the king was very old, and Abishag, the Shunammitess, ministered to him. 16 Bathsheba bowed herself and worshipped the king. And the king said to her, "What is thy will?"

17 She answered and said, "My lord, thou didst swear to thy handmaid by the Lord, thy God, *saying,* 'Solomon, thy son, shall reign after me, and he shall sit on my throne.' 18 And behold: now Adonijah reigneth, and thou, my lord, the king, knowest nothing of it. 19 He hath killed oxen and all fat cattle and many rams and invited all the king's sons and Abiathar, the priest, and Joab, the general of the army, but Solomon, thy servant, he invited not. 20 And now, my

totius Israhel ut indices eis qui sedere debeat in solio tuo, domine mi, rex, post te. 21 Eritque cum dormierit dominus meus, rex, cum patribus suis erimus ego et filius meus Salomon peccatores."

22 Adhuc illa loquente cum rege, Nathan, prophetes, venit, 23 et nuntiaverunt regi, dicentes, "Adest Nathan, propheta."

Cumque introisset ante conspectum regis et adorasset eum pronus in terram, 24 dixit Nathan, "Domine mi, rex, tu dixisti, 'Adonias regnet post me, et ipse sedeat super thronum meum'? 25 Quia descendit hodie et immolavit boves et pinguia et arietes plurimos et vocavit universos filios regis et principes exercitus Abiathar quoque, sacerdotem, illisque vescentibus et bibentibus coram eo et dicentibus, 'Vivat rex Adonias!' 26 Me, servum tuum, et Sadoc, sacerdotem, et Banaiam, filium Ioiadae, et Salomonem, famulum tuum, non vocavit. 27 Numquid a domino meo, rege, exivit hoc verbum, et mihi non indicasti, servo tuo, qui sessurus esset super thronum domini mei, regis, post eum?"

28 Et respondit Rex David, dicens, "Vocate ad me Bethsabee." Quae cum fuisset ingressa coram rege et stetisset ante eum, 29 iuravit rex et ait, "Vivit Dominus, qui eruit animam meam de omni angustia, 30 quia sicut iuravi tibi per Dominum, Deum Israhel, dicens, 'Salomon, filius tuus, regnabit post me, et ipse sedebit super solium meum pro me,' sic faciam hodie."

31 Submissoque Bethsabee in terram vultu adoravit regem, dicens, "Vivat dominus meus David in aeternum."

32 Dixit quoque Rex David, "Vocate mihi Sadoc, sacerdo-

lord, O king, the eyes of all Israel *are* upon thee that thou shouldst tell them who shall sit on thy throne, my lord, the king, after thee. 21 *Otherwise, it shall come to pass* when my lord, the king, sleepeth with his fathers that I and my son Solomon shall be *counted* offenders."

22 As she was yet speaking with the king, Nathan, the prophet, came, 23 and they told the king, saying, "Nathan, the prophet, is here."

And when he was come in *before* the king and had worshipped bowing down to the ground, 24 Nathan said, "My lord, O king, hast thou said, 'Let Adonijah reign after me, and let him sit upon my throne'? 25 Because he is gone down today and hath killed oxen and fatlings and many rams and invited all the king's sons and the captains of the army and Abiathar, the priest, and they are eating and drinking before him and saying, 'God save King Adonijah!' 26 But me, thy servant, and Zadok, the priest, and Benaiah, the son of Jehoiada, and Solomon, thy servant, he hath not invited. 27 Is this word come out from my lord, the king, and hast thou not told me, thy servant, who should sit on the throne of my lord, the king, after him?"

28 And King David answered and said, "Call to me Bathsheba." And when she was come in to the king and stood before him, 29 the king swore and said, "As the Lord liveth, who hath delivered my soul out of all distress, 30 even as I swore to thee by the Lord, the God of Israel, saying, 'Solomon, thy son, shall reign after me, and he shall sit upon my throne in my stead,' so will I do this day."

31 And Bathsheba bowing with her face to the earth worshipped the king, saying, "May my lord *David* live for ever."

32 King David also said, "Call me Zadok, the priest, and

tem, et Nathan, propheten, et Banaiam, filium Ioiadae." Qui cum ingressi fuissent coram rege, 33 dixit ad eos, "Tollite vobiscum servos domini vestri, et inponite Salomonem filium meum super mulam meam, et ducite eum in Gion. 34 Et unguat eum ibi Sadoc, sacerdos, et Nathan, propheta, in regem super Israhel, et canetis bucina atque dicetis, 'Vivat Rex Salomon.' 35 Et ascendetis post eum, et veniet et sedebit super solium meum, et ipse regnabit pro me, illique praecipiam ut sit dux super Israhel et super Iudam."

36 Et respondit Banaias, filius Ioiadae, regi, dicens, "Amen. Sic loquatur Dominus, Deus domini mei, regis. 37 Quomodo fuit Dominus cum domino meo, rege, sic sit cum Salomone, et sublimius faciat solium eius a solio domini mei, Regis David."

38 Descendit ergo Sadoc, sacerdos, et Nathan, propheta, et Banaias, filius Ioiadae, et Cherethi et Felethi et inposuerunt Salomonem super mulam Regis David et adduxerunt eum in Gion. 39 Sumpsitque Sadoc, sacerdos, cornu olei de tabernaculo et unxit Salomonem, et cecinerunt bucina, et dixit omnis populus, "Vivat Rex Salomon!" 40 Et ascendit universa multitudo post eum, et populus canentium tibiis et laetantium gaudio magno, et insonuit terra a clamore eorum.

41 Audivit autem Adonias et omnes qui invitati fuerant ab eo, iamque convivium finitum erat. Sed et Ioab audita voce tubae ait, "Quid sibi vult clamor civitatis tumultuantis?"

42 Adhuc illo loquente Ionathan, filius Abiathar, sacerdotis, venit, cui dixit Adonias, "Ingredere, quia vir fortis es et bona nuntians."

Nathan, the prophet, and Benaiah, the son of Jehoiada." And when they were come in before the king, 33 he said to them, "Take with you the servants of your lord, and set my son Solomon upon my mule, and bring him to Gihon. 34 And let Zadok, the priest, and Nathan, the prophet, anoint him there king over Israel, and you shall sound the trumpet and shall say, 'God save King Solomon.' 35 And you shall come up after him, and he shall come and shall sit upon my throne, and he shall reign in my stead, and I will appoint him to be ruler over Israel and over Judah."

36 And Benaiah, the son of Jehoiada, answered the king, saying, "Amen. So say the Lord, the God of my lord, the king. 37 As the Lord hath been with my lord, the king, so be he with Solomon, and make his throne higher than the throne of my lord, King David."

38 So Zadok, the priest, and Nathan, the prophet, went down, and Benaiah, the son of Jehoiada, and the Cherethites and Pelethites, and they set Solomon upon the mule of King David and brought him to Gihon. 39 And Zadok, the priest, took a horn of oil out of the tabernacle and anointed Solomon, and they sounded the trumpet, and all the people said, "God save King Solomon!" 40 And all the multitude went up after him, and the people played with pipes and rejoiced with a great joy, and the earth rang *with the noise* of their cry.

41 And Adonijah and all that were invited by him heard it, and now the feast was at an end. Joab also hearing the sound of the trumpet said, "What meaneth this noise of the city in an uproar?"

42 While he yet spoke Jonathan, the son of Abiathar, the priest, came, and Adonijah said to him, "Come in, because thou art a valiant man and bringest good news."

43 Responditque Ionathan Adoniae, "Nequaquam, dominus enim noster, Rex David, regem constituit Salomonem 44 misitque cum eo Sadoc, sacerdotem, et Nathan, prophetam, et Banaiam, filium Ioiadae, et Cherethi et Felethi, et inposuerunt eum super mulam regis. 45 Unxeruntque eum Sadoc, sacerdos, et Nathan, propheta, regem in Gion, et ascenderunt inde laetantes, et insonuit civitas. Haec est vox quam audistis. 46 Sed et Salomon sedet super solio regni, 47 et ingressi servi regis benedixerunt domino nostro, Regi David, dicentes, 'Amplificet Deus nomen Salomonis super nomen tuum et magnificet thronum eius super thronum tuum.' Et adoravit rex in lectulo suo, 48 et haec locutus est: 'Benedictus Dominus, Deus Israhel, qui dedit hodie sedentem in solio meo, videntibus oculis meis.'"

49 Territi sunt ergo, et surrexerunt omnes qui invitati fuerant ab Adonia, et ivit unusquisque in viam suam. 50 Adonias autem, timens Salomonem, surrexit et abiit tenuitque cornu altaris. 51 Et nuntiaverunt Salomoni, dicentes, "Ecce Adonias, timens Regem Salomonem, tenuit cornu altaris, dicens, 'Iuret mihi hodie rex Salomon quod non interficiat servum suum gladio.'"

52 Dixitque Salomon, "Si fuerit vir bonus, non cadet ne unus quidem capillus eius in terram, sin autem malum inventum fuerit in eo, morietur." 53 Misit ergo Rex Salomon et eduxit eum ab altari, et ingressus adoravit Regem Salomonem, dixitque ei Salomon, "Vade in domum tuam."

43 And Jonathan answered Adonijah, "Not so, for our lord, King David, hath appointed Solomon king 44 and hath sent with him Zadok, the priest, and Nathan, the prophet, and Benaiah, the son of Jehoiada, and the Cherethites and Pelethites, and they have set him upon the king's mule. 45 And Zadok, the priest, and Nathan, the prophet, have anointed him king in Gihon, and they are gone up from thence rejoicing *so that* the city rang again. This is the noise that you have heard. 46 Moreover, Solomon sitteth upon the throne of the kingdom, 47 and the king's servants going in have blessed our lord, King David, saying, 'May God make the name of Solomon greater than thy name and make his throne greater than thy throne.' And the king adored in his bed, 48 and he *said,* 'Blessed be the Lord, the God of Israel, who hath given this day one *to sit* on my throne, my eyes seeing it.'"

49 *Then all the guests of Adonijah were afraid, and they all arose,* and every man went his way. 50 And Adonijah, fearing Solomon, arose and went and took hold on the horn of the altar. 51 And they told Solomon, saying, "Behold Adonijah, fearing King Solomon, hath taken hold of the horn of the altar, saying, 'Let King Solomon swear to me this day that he will not kill his servant with the sword.'"

52 And Solomon said, "If he be a good man, there shall not so much as one hair of his *head* fall to the ground, but if evil be found in him, he shall die." 53 Then King Solomon sent and brought him out from the altar, and going in he worshipped King Solomon, and Solomon said to him, "Go to thy house."

Caput 2

Adpropinquaverunt autem dies David ut moreretur, praecepitque Salomoni filio suo, dicens, 2 "Ego ingredior viam universae terrae. Confortare, et esto vir, 3 et observa custodias Domini, Dei tui, ut ambules in viis eius et custodias caerimonias eius et praecepta eius et iudicia et testimonia sicut scriptum est in lege Mosi ut intellegas universa quae facis et quocumque te verteris 4 ut confirmet Dominus sermones suos quos locutus est de me, dicens, 'Si custodierint filii tui vias suas et ambulaverint coram me in veritate in omni corde suo et in omni anima sua, non auferetur tibi vir de solio Israhel.' 5 Tu quoque nosti quae fecerit mihi Ioab, filius Sarviae, quae fecerit duobus principibus exercitus Israhel, Abner, filio Ner, et Amasa, filio Iether, quos occidit et effudit sanguinem belli in pace et posuit cruorem proelii in balteo suo qui erat circa lumbos eius et in calciamento suo quod erat in pedibus eius. 6 Facies ergo iuxta sapientiam tuam, et non deduces canitiem eius pacifice ad inferos. 7 Sed et filiis Berzellai, Galaaditis, reddes gratiam, eruntque come-

Chapter 2

David, after giving his last charge to Solomon, dieth. Adonijah is put to death. Abiathar is banished. Joab and Shimei are slain.

And the days of David drew nigh that he should die, and he charged his son Solomon, saying, 2 "I am going the way of all *flesh*. Take thou courage, and shew thyself a man, 3 and *keep the charge* of the Lord, thy God, to walk in his ways and observe his ceremonies and his precepts and judgments and testimonies as it is written in the law of Moses that thou mayest understand all thou dost and whithersoever thou shalt turn thyself 4 that the Lord may confirm his words which he hath spoken of me, saying, 'If thy children shall take heed to their ways and shall walk before me in truth with all their heart and with all their soul, there shall not be taken away from thee a man on the throne of Israel.' 5 Thou knowest also what Joab, the son of Zeruiah, hath done to me, what he did to the two captains of the army of Israel, to Abner, the son of Ner, and to Amasa, the son of Jether, whom he slew and shed the blood of war in peace and put the blood of war on his girdle that was about his loins and in his shoes that were on his feet. 6 Do therefore according to thy wisdom, and *let* not his hoary head *go down* to hell in peace. 7 But *shew* kindness to the sons of Barzillai, the Gileadite, and *let them eat* at thy table, for they met me when

dentes in mensa tua, occurrerunt enim mihi quando fugiebam a facie Absalom, fratris tui. 8 Habes quoque apud te Semei, filium Gera, filii Iemini de Baurim, qui maledixit mihi maledictione pessima quando ibam ad Castra, sed quia descendit mihi in occursum cum transirem Iordanem et iuravi ei per Dominum, dicens, 'Non te interficiam gladio,' 9 tu noli pati esse eum innoxium. Vir autem sapiens es ut scias quae facies ei, deducesque canos eius cum sanguine ad infernum."

10 Dormivit igitur David cum patribus suis et sepultus est in civitate David. 11 Dies autem quibus regnavit David super Israhel quadraginta anni sunt: in Hebron regnavit septem annis, in Hierusalem triginta tribus. 12 Salomon autem sedit super thronum David patris sui, et firmatum est regnum eius nimis. 13 Et ingressus est Adonias, filius Aggith, ad Bethsabee, matrem Salomonis, quae dixit ei, "Pacificusne ingressus tuus?"

Qui respondit, "Pacificus." 14 Addiditque, "Sermo mihi est ad te."

Cui ait, "Loquere."

Et ille, 15 "Tu," inquit, "nosti quia meum erat regnum, et me proposuerat omnis Israhel sibi in regem, sed translatum est regnum et factum est fratris mei, a Domino enim constitutum est ei. 16 Nunc, ergo, petitionem unam deprecor a te; ne confundas faciem meam."

Quae dixit ad eum, "Loquere."

17 Et ille ait, "Precor ut dicas Salomoni Regi, neque enim negare tibi quicquam potest, ut det mihi Abisag, Sunamitin, uxorem."

18 Et ait Bethsabee, "Bene, ego loquar pro te regi." 19 Venit ergo Bethsabee ad Regem Salomonem ut loqueretur ei

I fled from the face of Absalom, thy brother. 8 Thou hast also with thee Shimei, the son of Gera, the son of Jemini of Bahurim, who cursed me with a grievous curse when I went to the Camp, but because he came down to meet me when I passed over the Jordan and I swore to him by the Lord, saying, 'I will not kill thee with a sword,' 9 do not thou hold him guiltless. But thou art a wise man *and knowest* what *to do* with him, and thou shalt bring down his grey hairs with blood to hell."

10 So David slept with his fathers and was buried in the city of David. 11 And the days that David reigned in Israel were forty years: in Hebron he reigned seven years, in Jerusalem thirty-three. 12 And Solomon sat upon the throne of his father David, and his kingdom was strengthened exceedingly. 13 And Adonijah, the son of Haggith, came to Bathsheba, the mother of Solomon, and she said to him, "Is thy coming peaceable?"

He answered, "Peaceable." 14 And he added, "I have a word to speak with thee."

She said to him, "Speak."

And he said, 15 "Thou knowest that the kingdom was mine, and all Israel had *preferred* me to be their king, but the kingdom is transferred and is become my brother's, for it was appointed him by the Lord. 16 Now, therefore, I ask one petition of thee; turn not away my face."

And she said to him, *"Say on."*

17 And he said, "I pray thee speak to King Solomon, for he cannot deny thee any thing, to give me Abishag, the Shunammitess, to wife."

18 And Bathsheba said, "Well, I will speak for thee to the king." 19 Then Bathsheba came to King Solomon to speak to

pro Adonia, et surrexit rex in occursum eius adoravitque eam et sedit super thronum suum, positusque est thronus matri regis, quae sedit ad dexteram eius. 20 Dixitque ei, "Petitionem unam parvulam ego deprecor a te; ne confundas faciem meam."

Et dixit ei rex, "Pete, mater mi, neque enim fas est ut avertam faciem tuam."

21 Quae ait, "Detur Abisag, Sunamitis, Adoniae, fratri tuo, uxor."

22 Responditque Rex Salomon et dixit matri suae, "Quare postulas Abisag, Sunamitin, Adoniae? Postula ei et regnum, ipse est enim frater meus maior me et habet Abiathar, sacerdotem, et Ioab, filium Sarviae." 23 Iuravit itaque Rex Salomon per Dominum, dicens, "Haec faciat mihi Deus et haec addat, quia contra animam suam locutus est Adonias verbum hoc. 24 Et nunc, vivit Dominus, qui firmavit me et conlocavit me super solium David, patris mei, et qui fecit mihi domum sicut locutus est, quia hodie occidetur Adonias." 25 Misitque Rex Salomon per manum Banaiae, filii Ioiadae, qui interfecit eum, et mortuus est.

26 Abiathar quoque, sacerdoti, dixit rex, "Vade in Anathot, ad agrum tuum; es quidem vir mortis, sed hodie te non interficiam, quia portasti arcam Domini Dei coram David, patre meo, et sustinuisti laborem in omnibus in quibus laboravit pater meus." 27 Eiecit ergo Salomon Abiathar ut non esset sacerdos Domini ut impleretur sermo Domini quem locutus est super domum Heli in Silo.

28 Venit autem nuntius ad Ioab quod Ioab declinasset post Adoniam et post Salomonem non declinasset, fugit ergo

him for Adonijah, and the king arose to meet her and bowed to her and sat down upon his throne, and a throne was set for the king's mother, and she sat on his right hand. 20 And she said to him, "I desire one small petition of thee; do not *put me to confusion."*

And the king said to her, "My mother, ask, for I must not turn away thy face."

21 And she said, "Let Abishag, the Shunammitess, be given to Adonijah, thy brother, to wife."

22 And King Solomon answered and said to his mother, "Why dost thou ask Abishag, the Shunammitess, for Adonijah? Ask for him also the kingdom, for he is my elder brother and hath Abiathar, the priest, and Joab, the son of Zeruiah." 23 Then King Solomon swore by the Lord, saying, "So and so may God do to me and add more, if Adonijah hath not spoken this word against his own life. 24 And now, as the Lord liveth, who hath established me and placed me upon the throne of David, my father, and who hath made me a house as he *promised,* Adonijah shall be put to death this day." 25 And King Solomon sent by the hand of Benaiah, the son of Jehoiada, who slew him, and he died.

26 And the king said also to Abiathar, the priest, "Go to Anathoth, to thy *lands,* for indeed thou art *worthy* of death, but I will not at this time put thee to death, because thou didst carry the ark of the Lord God before David, my father, and hast endured trouble in all the troubles my father endured." 27 So Solomon cast out Abiathar *from being* the priest of the Lord that the word of the Lord might be fulfilled which he spoke concerning the house of Eli in Shiloh.

28 And the news came to Joab because Joab had turned after Adonijah and had not turned after Solomon, and Joab

Ioab in tabernaculum Domini et adprehendit cornu altaris.
29 Nuntiatumque est Regi Salomoni quod fugisset Ioab in
tabernaculum Domini et esset iuxta altare, misitque Salomon Banaiam, filium Ioiadae, dicens, "Vade; interfice eum."

30 Et venit Banaias ad tabernaculum Domini et dixit ei,
"Haec dicit rex, 'Egredere.'"

Qui ait, "Non egrediar, sed hic moriar."

Renuntiavit Banaias regi sermonem, dicens, "Haec locutus est Ioab, et haec respondit mihi."

31 Dixitque ei rex, "Fac sicut locutus est, et interfice eum,
et sepeli, et amovebis sanguinem innocentem qui effusus est
a Ioab a me et a domo patris mei. 32 Et reddet Dominus sanguinem eius super caput eius quia interfecit duos viros ius-
tos melioresque se et occidit eos gladio, patre meo David
ignorante, Abner, filium Ner, principem militiae Israhel, et
Amasa, filium Iether, principem exercitus Iuda. 33 Et revertetur sanguis illorum in caput Ioab et in caput seminis eius
in sempiternum. David autem et semini eius et domui et
throno illius sit pax usque in aeternum a Domino."

34 Ascendit itaque Banaias, filius Ioiadae, et adgressus
eum interfecit, sepultusque est in domo sua in deserto. 35 Et
constituit rex Banaiam, filium Ioiadae, pro eo super exercitum, et Sadoc, sacerdotem, posuit pro Abiathar. 36 Misit
quoque rex et vocavit Semei dixitque ei, "Aedifica tibi domum in Hierusalem, et habita ibi, et non egredieris inde huc
atque illuc, 37 quacumque autem die egressus fueris et trans-

fled into the tabernacle of the Lord and laid hold on the horn of the altar. 29 And it was told King Solomon that Joab was fled into the tabernacle of the Lord and was by the altar, and Solomon sent Benaiah, the son of Jehoiada, saying, "Go; kill him."

30 And Benaiah came to the tabernacle of the Lord and said to him, "Thus saith the king, 'Come forth.'"

And he said, "I will not come forth, but here I will die."

Benaiah brought word back to the king, saying, "Thus saith Joab, and thus he answered me."

31 And the king said to him, "Do as he hath said, and kill him, and bury him, and thou shalt remove the innocent blood which hath been shed by Joab from me and from the house of my father. 32 And the Lord shall return his blood upon his own head because he murdered two men just and better than himself and slew them with the sword, my father David not knowing it, Abner, the son of Ner, general of the army of Israel, and Amasa, the son of Jether, general of the army of Judah. 33 And their blood shall return upon the head of Joab and upon the head of his seed for ever. But to David and his seed and his house and to his throne be peace for ever from the Lord."

34 So Benaiah, the son of Jehoiada, went up, and setting upon him slew him, and he was buried in his house in the desert. 35 And the king appointed Benaiah, the son of Jehoiada, *in his room* over the army, and Zadok, the priest, he put in the place of Abiathar. 36 The king also sent and called for Shimei and said to him, "Build thee a house in Jerusalem, and dwell there, and go not out from thence any whither, 37 for on what day soever thou shalt go out and shalt

ieris torrentem Cedron, scito te interficiendum. Sanguis tuus erit super caput tuum."

38 Dixitque Semei regi, "Bonus sermo. Sicut locutus est dominus meus, rex, sic faciet servus tuus." Habitavit itaque Semei in Hierusalem diebus multis.

39 Factum est autem post annos tres ut fugerent servi Semei ad Achis, filium Maacha, regem Geth, nuntiatumque est Semei quod servi eius issent in Geth. 40 Et surrexit Semei et stravit asinum suum ivitque in Geth ad Achis ad requirendos servos suos, et adduxit eos de Geth. 41 Nuntiatum est autem Salomoni quod isset Semei in Geth de Hierusalem et redisset. 42 Et mittens vocavit eum dixitque illi, "Nonne testificatus sum tibi per Dominum et praedixi tibi, 'Quacumque die egressus ieris huc et illuc, scito te esse morituru,' et respondisti mihi, 'Bonus sermo quem audivi'? 43 Quare ergo non custodisti iusiurandum Domini et praeceptum quod praeceperam tibi?" 44 Dixitque rex ad Semei, "Tu nosti omne malum cuius tibi conscium est cor tuum quod fecisti David, patri meo; reddidit Dominus malitiam tuam in caput tuum, 45 et Rex Salomon benedictus et thronus David erit stabilis coram Domino usque in sempiternum."

46 Iussit itaque rex Banaiae, filio Ioiadae, qui egressus percussit eum, et mortuus est.

pass over the brook Kidron, know that thou shalt be put to death. Thy blood shall be upon thy own head.

38 And Shimei said to the king, "The saying is good. As my lord, the king, hath said, so will thy servant do." And Shimei dwelt in Jerusalem many days.

39 And it came to pass after three years that the servants of Shimei ran away to Achish, the son of Maacah, the king of Gath, and it was told Shimei that his servants were gone to Gath. 40 And Shimei arose and saddled his ass and went to Achish to Gath to seek his servants, and he brought them out of Gath. 41 And it was told Solomon that Shimei had gone from Jerusalem to Gath and was come back. 42 And sending he called for him and said to him, "Did I not *protest* to thee by the Lord and tell thee before, 'On what day soever thou shalt go out and walk abroad any whither, know that thou shalt die,' and thou answeredst me, 'The word that I have heard is good'? 43 Why then hast thou not kept the oath of the Lord and the commandment that I laid upon thee?" 44 And the king said to Shimei, "Thou knowest all the evil of which thy heart is conscious which thou didst to David, my father; the Lord hath returned thy wickedness upon thy own head, 45 and King Solomon shall be blessed and the throne of David shall be *established* before the Lord for ever."

46 So the king commanded Benaiah, the son of Jehoiada, and he went out and struck him, and he died.

Caput 3

Confirmatum est igitur regnum in manu Salomonis, et adfinitate coniunctus est Pharaoni, regi Aegypti, accepit namque filiam eius et adduxit in civitatem David donec conpleret aedificans domum suam et domum Domini et murum Hierusalem per circuitum, 2 attamen populus immolabat in excelsis, non enim aedificatum erat templum nomini Domini usque in die illo. 3 Dilexit autem Salomon Dominum, ambulans in praeceptis David, patris sui; excepto quod in excelsis immolabat et accendebat thymiama. 4 Abiit itaque in Gabaon ut immolaret ibi, illud quippe erat excelsum maximum. Mille hostias in holocaustum obtulit Salomon super altare illud in Gabaon. 5 Apparuit autem Dominus Salomoni per somnium nocte, dicens, "Postula quod vis ut dem tibi."

6 Et ait Salomon, "Tu fecisti cum servo tuo David, patre meo, misericordiam magnam, sicut ambulavit in conspectu tuo in veritate et iustitia et recto corde tecum; custodisti ei misericordiam tuam grandem et dedisti ei filium sedentem super thronum eius, sicut est hodie. 7 Et nunc, Domine Deus, tu regnare fecisti servum tuum pro David, patre meo, ego autem sum puer parvus et ignorans egressum et introi-

Chapter 3

Solomon marrieth Pharaoh's daughter. He sacrificeth in Gibeon. In the choice which God gave him, he preferreth wisdom. His wise judgment between the two harlots.

And the kingdom was established in the hand of Solomon, and he made affinity with Pharaoh, the king of Egypt, for he took his daughter and brought her into the city of David until he had made an end of building his own house and the house of the Lord and the wall of Jerusalem round about, 2 but yet the people sacrificed in the high places, for there was no temple built to the name of the Lord until that day. 3 And Solomon loved the Lord, walking in the precepts of David, his father; only he sacrificed in the high places and burnt incense. 4 He went therefore to Gibeon to sacrifice there, for that was the great high place. A thousand victims for *holocausts* did Solomon offer upon that altar in Gibeon. 5 And the Lord appeared to Solomon in a dream by night, saying, "Ask what thou wilt that I should give thee."

6 And Solomon said, "Thou hast *shewn* great mercy *to* thy servant David, my father, even as he walked before thee in truth and justice and an upright heart with thee, and thou hast kept thy great mercy for him and hast given him a son to sit on his throne, as it is this day. 7 And now, O Lord God, thou hast made thy servant king instead of David, my father, and I am *but* a child and know not *how to go out and come in.*

tum meum. 8 Et servus tuus in medio est populi quem elegisti, populi infiniti qui numerari et supputari non potest
prae multitudine. 9 Dabis ergo servo tuo cor docile ut iudicare possit populum tuum et discernere inter malum et bonum. Quis enim poterit iudicare populum istum, populum
tuum hunc multum.?"

10 Placuit ergo sermo coram Domino quod Salomon rem
huiuscemodi postulasset. 11 Et dixit Dominus Salomoni,
"Quia postulasti verbum hoc et non petisti tibi dies multos
nec divitias aut animas inimicorum tuorum, sed postulasti
tibi sapientiam ad discernendum iudicium, 12 ecce: feci tibi
secundum sermones tuos et dedi tibi cor sapiens et intellegens, in tantum ut nullus ante te similis tui fuerit nec post
te surrecturus sit. 13 Sed et haec quae non postulasti dedi
tibi, divitias, scilicet, et gloriam ut nemo fuerit similis tui in
regibus cunctis retro diebus. 14 Si autem ambulaveris in viis
meis et custodieris praecepta mea et mandata mea sicut ambulavit pater tuus, longos faciam dies tuos."

15 Igitur evigilavit Salomon et intellexit quod esset somnium, cumque venisset Hierusalem, stetit coram Arca Foederis Domini et obtulit holocausta et fecit victimas pacificas
et grande convivium universis famulis suis.

16 Tunc venerunt duae mulieres meretrices ad regem steteruntque coram eo, 17 quarum una ait, "Obsecro, mi domine, ego et mulier haec habitabamus in domo una, et peperi apud eam in cubiculo, 18 tertia autem die postquam ego
peperi peperit et haec, et eramus simul, nullusque alius in

8 And thy servant is in the midst of the people which thou hast chosen, an immense people which cannot be numbered nor counted for multitude. 9 *Give* therefore to thy servant an *understanding* heart to judge thy people and discern between good and evil. For who shall be able to judge this people, thy people *which is so numerous?*"

10 And the word was pleasing to the Lord that Solomon had asked such a thing. 11 And the Lord said to Solomon, "Because thou hast asked this thing and hast not asked for thyself *long life* or riches nor the lives of thy enemies, but hast asked for thyself wisdom to discern judgment, 12 behold: I have done for thee according to thy words and have given thee a wise and understanding heart, insomuch that there hath been no one like thee before thee nor shall arise after thee. 13 Yea, and the things also which thou didst not ask I have given thee, to wit, riches and glory as that no one hath been like thee among the kings in all days heretofore. 14 And if thou wilt walk in my ways and keep my precepts and my commandments as thy father walked, I will lengthen thy days."

15 And Solomon awaked and perceived that it was a dream, and when he was come to Jerusalem, he stood before the Ark of the Covenant of the Lord and offered holocausts and sacrificed victims of peace offerings and made a great feast for all his servants.

16 Then there came two women *that were* harlots to the king and stood before him, 17 and one of them said, "I beseech thee, my lord, I and this woman dwelt in one house, and I was delivered of a child with her in the chamber, 18 and the third day after that I was delivered she also was delivered, and we were together, and no other person with us

domo nobiscum, exceptis nobis duabus. 19 Mortuus est autem filius mulieris huius nocte, dormiens quippe oppressit eum. 20 Et consurgens intempesta nocte, tulit filium meum de latere meo, ancillae tuae, dormientis, et conlocavit in sinu suo suum autem filium qui erat mortuus posuit in sinu meo. 21 Cumque surrexissem mane ut darem lac filio meo, apparuit mortuus, quem diligentius intuens clara luce, deprehendi non esse meum quem genueram."

22 Responditque altera mulier, "Non est ita ut dicis, sed filius tuus mortuus est, meus autem vivit."

E contrario illa dicebat, "Mentiris, filius quippe meus vivit, et filius tuus mortuus est."

Atque in hunc modum contendebant coram rege.

23 Tunc rex ait, "Haec dicit, 'Filius meus vivit, et filius tuus mortuus est.' Et ista respondit, 'Non, sed filius tuus mortuus est, meus autem vivit.'" 24 Dixit ergo rex, "Adferte mihi gladium." Cumque adtulissent gladium coram rege, 25 "Dividite," inquit, "infantem vivum in duas partes, et date dimidiam partem uni et dimidiam partem alteri."

26 Dixit autem mulier cuius filius erat vivus ad regem (commota sunt quippe viscera eius super filio suo), "Obsecro, domine, date illi infantem vivum, et nolite interficere eum."

E contrario illa dicebat, "Nec mihi nec tibi sit, sed dividatur."

27 Respondit rex et ait, "Date huic infantem vivum, et non occidatur, haec est enim mater eius."

28 Audivit itaque omnis Israhel iudicium quod iudicasset rex, et timuerunt regem, videntes sapientiam Dei esse in eo ad faciendum iudicium.

in the house, only we two. 19 And this woman's child died in the night, for in her sleep she overlaid him. 20 And rising in the dead time of the night, she took my child from my side while I, thy handmaid, was asleep, and laid it in her bosom and laid her *dead child* in my bosom. 21 And when I rose in the morning to give my child suck—*behold*—it *was* dead, but considering him more diligently when it was clear day, I found that it was not mine which I bore."

22 And the other woman answered, "It is not so as thou sayest, but thy child is dead, and mine is alive."

On the contrary she said, "Thou liest, for my child liveth, and thy child is dead."

And in this manner they strove before the king.

23 Then said the king, "The one saith, 'My child is alive, and thy child is dead.' And the other answereth, 'Nay, but thy child is dead, and mine liveth.'" 24 The king therefore said, "Bring me a sword." And when they had brought a sword before the king, 25 "Divide," said he, "the living child in two, and give half to the one and half to the other."

26 But the woman whose child was alive said to the king (for her bowels were moved upon her child), "I beseech thee, my lord, give her the child alive, and do not kill it."

But the other said, "Let it be neither mine nor thine, but divide it."

27 The king answered and said, "Give the living child to this woman, and let it not be killed, for she is the mother thereof."

28 And all Israel heard the judgment which the king had judged, and they feared the king, seeing that the wisdom of God was in him to do judgment.

Caput 4

Erat autem rex Salomon regnans super omnem Israhel, 2 et hii principes quos habebat: Azarias, filius Sadoc, sacerdos; 3 Helioreph et Ahia, filii Sesa, scribae; Iosaphat, filius Ahilud, a commentariis; 4 Banaias, filius Ioiadae, super exercitum; Sadoc autem et Abiathar, sacerdotes; 5 Azarias, filius Nathan, super eos qui adsistebant regi; Zabud, filius Nathan, sacerdos, amicus regis; 6 et Ahisar, praepositus domus; et Adoniram, filius Abda, super tributa. 7 Habebat autem Salomon duodecim praefectos super omnem Israhel qui praebebant annonam regi et domui eius, per singulos enim menses in anno singuli necessaria ministrabant, 8 et haec nomina eorum: Benhur in Monte Ephraim; 9 Bendecar in Macces et in Salebbim et in Bethsemes et in Helon et in Bethanan; 10 Benesed in Araboth: ipsius erat Soccho et omnis terra Epher; 11 Benabinadab, cuius omnis Nepthad Dor: Tapheth, filiam Salomonis, habebat uxorem; 12 Bana, filius Ahilud, regebat Thanac et Mageddo et universam Bethsan, quae est iuxta Sarthana subter Hiezrahel, a Bethsan usque Abelmeula e regione Iecmaan; 13 Bengaber in Ramoth Galaad: habebat Avothiair, filii Manasse, in Galaad; ipse praeerat in omni regione Argob, quae est in Basan, sexaginta civitatibus magnis

Chapter 4

Solomon's chief officers, his riches and wisdom.

And king Solomon reigned over all Israel, 2 and these were the princes which he had: Azariah, the son of Zadok, the priest; 3 Elihoreph and Ahijah, the sons of Shisha, scribes; Jehoshaphat, the son of Ahilud, recorder; 4 Benaiah, the son of Jehoiada, over the army; and Zadok and Abiathar, priests; 5 Azariah, the son of Nathan, over them that were about the king; Zabud, the son of Nathan, the priest, the king's friend; 6 and Ahishar, governor of the house; and Adoniram, the son of Abda, over the tribute. 7 And Solomon had twelve governors over all Israel who provided victuals for the king and for his household, for every one provided necessaries, each man his month in the year, 8 and these are their names: Ben-hur in Mount Ephraim; 9 Ben-deker in Makaz and in Shaalbim and in Beth-shemesh and in Elon and in Beth-hanan; 10 Ben-hesed in Arubboth: his was So-coh and all the land of Hepher; 11 Ben-abinadab, to whom belonged all Naphath-dor: he had Taphath, the daughter of Solomon, to wife; 12 Baana, the son of Ahilud, *who* governed Taanach and Megiddo and all Beth-shean, which is by Zare-than beneath Jezreel, from Beth-shean unto Abel-meholah over against Jokmeam; 13 Ben-geber in Ramoth Gilead: he had *the towns of Jair*, the son of Manasseh, in Gilead; he was chief in all the country of Argob, which is in Bashan, three-

atque muratis quae habebant seras aereas; 14 Ahinadab, filius Addo, praeerat in Manaim; 15 Ahimaas in Nepthali: sed et ipse habebat Basmath, filiam Salomonis, in coniugio; 16 Baana, filius Usi, in Aser et in Balod; 17 Iosaphat, filius Pharue, in Isachar; 18 Semei, filius Hela, in Beniamin; 19 Gaber, filius Uri, in terra Galaad in terra Seon, regis Amorrei, et Og, regis Basan, super omnia quae erant in illa terra.

20 Iuda et Israhel innumerabiles, sicut harena maris in multitudine, comedentes et bibentes atque laetantes, 21 Salomon autem erat in dicione sua habens omnia regna a flumine terrae Philisthim usque ad terminum Aegypti, offerentium sibi munera et servientium ei cunctis diebus vitae eius. 22 Erat autem cibus Salomonis per dies singulos triginta chori similae et sexaginta chori farinae, 23 decem boves pingues et viginti boves pascuales et centum arietes excepta venatione cervorum, caprearum atque bubalorum et avium altilium, 24 ipse enim obtinebat omnem regionem quae erat trans flumen a Thapsa usque Gazam et cunctos reges illarum regionum, et habebat pacem ex omni parte in circuitu. 25 Habitabatque Iudas et Israhel absque timore ullo, unusquisque sub vite sua et sub ficu sua, a Dan usque Bersabee cunctis diebus Salomonis. 26 Et habebat Salomon quadraginta milia praesepia equorum currulium et duodecim milia equestrium. 27 Nutriebantque eos supradicti regis praefecti, sed et necessaria mensae Regis Salomonis cum ingenti cura praebebant in tempore suo. 28 Hordeum quoque et paleas equorum et iumentorum deferebant in locum ubi erat rex iuxta constitutum sibi. 29 Dedit quoque Deus sapientiam Salomoni et prudentiam multam nimis et latitudinem cordis quasi harenam quae est in litore maris. 30 Et praecedebat

score great cities *with walls and* brazen bolts; 14 Ahinadab, the son of Iddo, was chief in Mahanaim; 15 Ahimaaz in Naphtali: he also had Basemath, the daughter of Solomon, to wife; 16 Baana, the son of Hushai, in Asher and in Bealoth; 17 Jehoshaphat, the son of Paruah, in Issachar; 18 Shimei, the son of Ela, in Benjamin; 19 Geber, the son of Uri, in the land of Gilead in the land of Sihon, the king of the Amorites, and of Og, the king of Bashan, over all that were in that land.

20 Judah and Israel were innumerable, as the sand of the sea in multitude, eating and drinking and rejoicing, 21 and Solomon had under him all the kingdoms from the river to the land of the Philistines even to the border of Egypt, and they brought him presents and served him all the days of his life. 22 And the provision of Solomon for each day was thirty measures of fine flour and threescore measures of meal, 23 ten fat oxen and twenty out of the pastures and a hundred rams besides venison of harts, roes and buffles and fatted fowls, 24 for he had all the country which was beyond the river from Tiphsah to Gaza and all the kings of those countries, and he had peace on every side round about. 25 And Judah and Israel dwelt without any fear, every one under his vine and under his fig tree, from Dan to Beer-sheba all the days of Solomon. 26 And Solomon had forty thousand stalls of chariot horses and twelve thousand for the saddle. 27 And the foresaid governors of the king fed them, and they furnished the necessaries also for King Solomon's table with great care in their time. 28 They brought barley also and straw for the horses and beasts to the place where the king was according as it was appointed them. 29 And God gave to Solomon wisdom and understanding exceeding much and largeness of heart as the sand that is on the sea shore. 30 And

sapientia Salomonis sapientiam omnium Orientalium et Aegyptiorum, 31 et erat sapientior cunctis hominibus, sapientior Aethan, Ezraita, et Heman et Chalcal et Dorda, filiis Maol, et erat nominatus in universis gentibus per circuitum. 32 Locutus est quoque Salomon tria milia parabolas, et fuerunt carmina eius quinque et mille. 33 Et disputavit super lignis a cedro quae est in Libano usque ad hysopum quae egreditur de pariete, et disseruit de iumentis et volucribus et reptilibus et piscibus. 34 Et veniebant de cunctis populis ad audiendam sapientiam Salomonis et ab universis regibus terrae qui audiebant sapientiam eius.

Caput 5

Misit quoque Hiram, rex Tyri, servos suos ad Salomonem, audivit enim quod ipsum unxissent regem pro patre eius, quia amicus fuerat Hiram David omni tempore. 2 Misit autem Salomon ad Hiram, dicens, 3 "Tu scis voluntatem David, patris mei, et quia non potuerit aedificare domum nomini Domini, Dei sui, propter bella inminentia per circuitum donec daret Dominus eos sub vestigio pedum

the wisdom of Solomon surpassed the wisdom of all the Orientals and of the Egyptians, 31 and he was wiser than all men, wiser than Ethan, the Ezrahite, and Heman and Calcol and Darda, the sons of Mahol, and he was renowned in all nations round about. 32 Solomon also spoke three thousand parables, and his poems were a thousand and five. 33 And he treated about trees from the cedar that is in Libanus unto the hyssop that cometh out of the wall, and he discoursed of beasts and of fowls and of creeping things and of fishes. 34 And they came from all nations to hear the wisdom of Solomon and from all the kings of the earth who heard of his wisdom.

Chapter 5

Hiram, king of Tyre agreeth to furnish timber and workmen for building the temple. The number of workmen and overseers.

And Hiram, king of Tyre, sent his servants to Solomon, for he heard that they had anointed him king *in the room of* his father, for Hiram had always been David's friend. 2 And Solomon sent to Hiram, saying, 3 "Thou knowest the will of David, my father, and that he could not build a house to the name of the Lord, his God, because of the wars *that were* round about him until the Lord put them under the soles of

eius. 4 Nunc autem requiem dedit Dominus, Deus meus, mihi per circuitum, et non est satan neque occursus malus. 5 Quam ob rem cogito aedificare templum nomini Domini, Dei mei, sicut locutus est Dominus David, patri meo, dicens, 'Filius tuus quem dabo pro te super solium tuum, ipse aedificabit domum nomini meo.' 6 Praecipe, igitur, ut praecidant mihi servi tui cedros de Libano, et servi mei sint cum servis tuis, mercedem autem servorum tuorum dabo tibi quamcumque petieris, scis enim quomodo non est in populo meo vir qui noverit ligna caedere sicut Sidonii."

7 Cum ergo audisset Hiram verba Salomonis, laetatus est valde et ait, "Benedictus Dominus Deus hodie qui dedit David filium sapientissimum super populum hunc plurimum." 8 Et misit Hiram ad Salomonem, dicens, "Audivi quaecumque mandasti mihi; ego faciam omnem voluntatem tuam in lignis cedrinis et abiegnis. 9 Servi mei deponent ea de Libano ad mare, et ego conponam ea in ratibus in mari usque ad locum quem significaveris mihi et adplicabo ea ibi, et tu tolles ea. Praebebisque necessaria mihi ut detur cibus domui meae." 10 Itaque Hiram dabat Salomoni ligna cedrina et ligna abiegna iuxta omnem voluntatem eius. 11 Salomon autem praebebat Hiram viginti milia chororum tritici in cibum domui eius et viginti choros purissimi olei; haec tribuebat Salomon Hiram per annos singulos. 12 Dedit quoque Dominus sapientiam Salomoni sicut locutus est ei, et erat pax inter Hiram et Salomonem, et percusserunt foedus ambo.

13 Legitque Rex Salomon operarios de omni Israhel, et erat indictio triginta milia virorum, 14 mittebatque eos in

his feet. 4 But now the Lord, my God, hath given me rest round about, and there is no adversary nor evil occurrence. 5 Wherefore I purpose to build a temple to the name of the Lord, my God, as the Lord spoke to David, my father, saying, 'My son whom I will set upon the throne in thy place, he shall build a house to my name.' 6 Give orders, therefore, that thy servants cut me down cedar trees out of Libanus, and let my servants be with thy servants, and I will give thee the hire of thy servants whatsoever thou wilt ask, for thou knowest how there is not among my people a man that has skill to hew wood like to the Sidonians."

7 Now when Hiram had heard the words of Solomon, he rejoiced exceedingly and said, "Blessed be the Lord God this day who hath given to David a very wise son over this numerous people." 8 And Hiram sent to Solomon, saying, "I have heard all thou hast desired of me, *and* I will do all thy desire concerning cedar trees and fir trees. 9 My servants shall bring them down from Libanus to the sea, and I will put them together in floats in the sea *and convey them* to the place which thou shalt signify to me and will land them there, and thou shalt receive them. And thou shalt allow me necessaries *to furnish* food for my household." 10 So Hiram gave Solomon cedar trees and fir trees according to all his desire. 11 And Solomon allowed Hiram twenty thousand measures of wheat for provision for his house and twenty measures of the purest oil; thus gave Solomon to Hiram every year. 12 And the Lord gave wisdom to Solomon as he promised him, and there was peace between Hiram and Solomon, and they two made a league *together.*

13 And King Solomon chose workmen out of all Israel, and the levy was of thirty thousand men, 14 and he sent them

Libanum, decem milia per menses singulos vicissim, ita ut duobus mensibus essent in domibus suis, et Adoniram erat super huiuscemodi indictione. 15 Fueruntque Salomoni septuaginta milia eorum qui onera portabant et octoginta milia latomorum in monte 16 absque praepositis qui praeerant singulis operibus, numero trium milium, et trecentorum praecipientium populo et his qui faciebant opus. 17 Praecepitque rex ut tollerent lapides grandes, lapides pretiosos, in fundamentum templi et quadrarent eos, 18 quos dolaverunt cementarii Salomonis et cementarii Hiram, porro Giblii praeparaverunt ligna et lapides ad aedificandam domum.

Caput 6

Factum est autem quadringentesimo et octogesimo anno egressionis filiorum Israhel de terra Aegypti, in anno quarto, mense Zio (ipse est mensis secundus), regni Salomonis super Israhel, aedificare coepit domum Domino. 2 Domus autem quam aedificabat Rex Salomon Domino habebat sexaginta cubitos in longitudine et viginti cubitos in latitudine et triginta cubitos in altitudine. 3 Et porticus erat ante templum

to Libanus, ten thousand every month by turns, so that two months they were at home, and Adoniram was over this levy. 15 And Solomon had seventy thousand to carry burdens and eighty thousand *to hew* stones in the mountain 16 besides the overseers who were over every work, in number three thousand, and three hundred that ruled over the people and them that did the work. 17 And the king commanded that they should bring great stones, costly stones, for the foundation of the temple and should square them, 18 and the masons of Solomon and the masons of Hiram hewed them, and the Giblites prepared timber and stones to build the house.

Chapter 6

The building of Solomon's temple.

And it came to pass in the four hundred and eightieth year after the children of Israel came out of the land of Egypt, in the fourth year of the reign of Solomon over Israel, in the month Ziv (the same is the second month), he began to build a house to the Lord. 2 And the house which King Solomon built to the Lord was threescore cubits in length and twenty cubits in breadth and thirty cubits in height. 3 And there was a porch before the temple of twenty

viginti cubitorum longitudinis iuxta mensuram latitudinis templi, et habebat decem cubitos latitudinis ante faciem templi. 4 Fecitque in templo fenestras obliquas. 5 Et aedificavit super parietem templi tabulata per gyrum in parietibus domus per circuitum templi et oraculi, et fecit latera in circuitu. 6 Tabulatum quod subter erat quinque cubitos habebat latitudinis, et medium tabulatum sex cubitorum latitudinis, et tertium tabulatum septem habens cubitos latitudinis. Trabes autem posuit in domo per circuitum forinsecus ut non hererent muris templi. 7 Domus autem cum aedificaretur lapidibus dedolatis atque perfectis aedificata est, et malleus et securis et omne ferramentum non sunt audita in domo cum aedificaretur. 8 Ostium lateris medii in parte erat domus dexterae, et per cocleam ascendebant in medium cenaculum, et a medio in tertium. 9 Et aedificavit domum et consummavit eam, texit quoque domum laquearibus cedrinis. 10 Et aedificavit tabulatum super omnem domum quinque cubitis altitudinis, et operuit domum lignis cedrinis. 11 Et factus est sermo Domini ad Salomonem, dicens, 12 "Domus haec quam aedificas, si ambulaveris in praeceptis meis et iudicia mea feceris et custodieris omnia mandata mea, gradiens per ea, firmabo sermonem meum tibi quem locutus sum ad David, patrem tuum, 13 et habitabo in medio filiorum Israhel et non derelinquam populum meum Israhel."

14 Igitur aedificavit Salomon domum et consummavit eam. 15 Et aedificavit parietes domus intrinsecus tabulatis

cubits in length according to the measure of the breadth of the temple, and it was ten cubits in breadth before the face of the temple. 4 And he made in the temple oblique windows. 5 And upon the wall of the temple he built floors round about in the walls of the house round about the temple and the oracle, and he made sides round about. 6 The floor that was underneath was five cubits in breadth, and the middle floor was six cubits in breadth, and the third door was seven cubits in breadth. And he put beams in the house round about on the outside that they might not be fastened in the walls of the temple. 7 And the house when it was in building was built of stones hewed and made ready *so that there was neither* hammer nor axe nor any tool of iron heard in the house when it was in building. 8 The door for the middle side was on the right hand of the house, and by winding stairs they went up to the middle room, and from the middle to the third. 9 So he built the house and finished it, and he covered the house with roofs of cedar. 10 And he built a floor over all the house five cubits in height, and he covered the house with timber of cedar. 11 And the word of the Lord came to Solomon, saying, 12 "This house which thou buildest, if thou wilt walk in my statutes and execute my judgments and keep all my commandments, walking in them, I will fulfill my word to thee which I spoke to David, thy father, 13 and I will dwell in the midst of the children of Israel and will not forsake my people Israel."

14 So Solomon built the house and finished it. 15 And he built the walls of the house on the inside with boards of ce-

cedrinis, a pavimento domus usque ad summitatem parietum, et usque ad laquearia operuit lignis cedrinis intrinsecus, et texit pavimentum domus tabulis abiegnis. 16 Aedificavitque viginti cubitorum ad posteriorem partem templi tabulata cedrina, a pavimento usque ad superiora, et fecit interiorem domum oraculi in sanctum sanctorum. 17 Porro quadraginta cubitorum erat ipsum templum pro foribus oraculi. 18 Et cedro omnis domus intrinsecus vestiebatur habens tornaturas et iuncturas suas fabrefactas et celaturas eminentes. Omnia cedrinis tabulis vestiebantur, nec omnino lapis apparere poterat in pariete. 19 Oraculum autem in medio domus in interiori parte fecerat ut poneret ibi Arcam Foederis Domini. 20 Porro oraculum habebat viginti cubitos longitudinis et viginti cubitos latitudinis et viginti cubitos altitudinis, et operuit illud atque vestivit auro purissimo. Sed et altare vestivit cedro. 21 Domum quoque ante oraculum operuit auro purissimo et adfixit lamminas clavis aureis. 22 Nihilque erat in templo quod non auro tegeretur; sed et totum altare oraculi texit auro. 23 Et fecit in oraculo duo cherubin de lignis olivarum decem cubitorum altitudinis. 24 Quinque cubitorum ala cherub una, et quinque cubitorum ala cherub altera, id est, decem cubitos habentes a summitate alae unius usque ad alae alterius summitatem. 25 Decem quoque cubitorum erat cherub secundus, mensura pari et opus unum erat in duobus cherubin, 26 id est, altitudinem habebat unus cherub decem cubitorum, et similiter cherub secundus. 27 Posuitque cherubin in medio templi interioris, extendebant autem alas suas cherubin, et tangebat ala una

dar, from the floor of the house to the top of the walls, and to the roofs he covered it with boards of cedar on the inside, and he covered the floor of the house with planks of fir. 16 And he built up *twenty cubits with boards of cedar* at the hinder part of the temple, from the floor to the top, and made the inner house of the oracle to be the holy of holies. 17 And the temple itself before the doors of the oracle was forty cubits long. 18 And all the house was covered within with cedar having the turnings and the joints thereof artfully wrought and carvings projecting out. All was covered with boards of cedar, and no stone could be seen in the wall at all. 19 And he made the oracle in the midst of the house in the inner part to set there the Ark of the Covenant of the Lord. 20 Now the oracle was twenty cubits in length and twenty cubits in breadth and twenty cubits in height, and he covered and overlaid it with most pure gold. And the altar also he covered with cedar. 21 And the house before the oracle he overlaid with most pure gold and fastened on the plates with nails of gold. 22 And there was nothing in the temple that was not covered with gold; the whole altar of the oracle he covered also with gold. 23 And he made in the oracle two cherubims of olive tree of ten cubits in height. 24 One wing of the cherub was five cubits, and the other wing of the cherub was five cubits, that is, *in all* ten cubits from the extremity of one wing to the extremity of the other wing. 25 The second cherub also was ten cubits, *and the measure* and the work was the same in both the cherubims, 26 that is to say, one cherub was ten cubits high, and in like manner the other cherub. 27 And he set the cherubims in the midst of the inner temple, and the cherubims stretched forth their wings, and the wing of the one touched one wall, and the

parietem, et ala cherub secundi tangebat parietem alterum, alae autem alterae in media parte templi se invicem contingebant. 28 Texit quoque cherubin auro. 29 Et omnes parietes templi per circuitum scalpsit variis celaturis et torno, et fecit in eis cherubin et palmas et picturas varias, quasi prominentes de pariete et egredientes. 30 Sed et pavimentum domus texit auro intrinsecus et extrinsecus. 31 Et in ingressu oraculi fecit ostiola de lignis olivarum postesque angulorum quinque 32 et duo ostia de lignis olivarum, et scalpsit in eis picturas cherubin et palmarum species et anaglyfa valde prominentia, et texit ea auro, et operuit tam cherubin quam palmas et cetera auro. 33 Fecitque in introitu templi postes de lignis olivarum quadrangulatos 34 et duo ostia de lignis abiegnis, altrinsecus, et utrumque ostium duplex erat et se invicem tenens aperiebatur. 35 Et scalpsit cherubin et palmas et celaturas valde eminentes, operuitque omnia lamminis aureis opere quadro ad regulam. 36 Et aedificavit atrium interius tribus ordinibus lapidum politorum et uno ordine lignorum cedri.

37 Anno quarto fundata est domus Domini in mense Zio, 38 et in anno undecimo mense Bul (ipse est mensis octavus) perfecta est domus in omni opere suo et in universis utensilibus suis, aedificavitque eam annis septem.

wing of the other cherub touched the other wall, and the other wings in the midst of the temple touched one another. 28 And he overlaid the cherubims with gold. 29 And all the walls of the temple round about he carved with divers *figures* and *carvings,* and he made in them cherubims and palm trees and divers representations, as it were standing out and coming forth from the wall. 30 And the floor of the house he also overlaid with gold within and without. 31 And in the entrance of the oracle he made little doors of olive tree and posts of five corners 32 and two doors of olive tree, and he carved upon them figures of cherubims and figures of palm trees and carvings very much projecting, and he overlaid them with gold, and he covered both the cherubims and the palm trees and the other things with gold. 33 And he made in the entrance of the temple posts of olive tree foursquare 34 and two doors of fir tree, one of each side, and each door was double and *so opened with folding leaves.* 35 And he carved cherubims and palm trees and carved work standing very much out, and he overlaid all with golden plates in square work by rule. 36 And he built the inner court with three rows of polished stones and one row of beams of cedar.

37 In the fourth year was the house of the Lord founded in the month Ziv, 38 and in the eleventh year in the month Bul *(which* is the eighth month) the house was finished in all the *works* thereof and in all the appurtenances thereof, and *he was seven years in building it.*

Caput 7

Domum autem suam aedificavit Salomon tredecim annis et ad perfectum usque perduxit. 2 Aedificavit quoque domum saltus Libani; centum cubitorum longitudinis et quinquaginta cubitorum latitudinis et triginta cubitorum altitudinis et quattuor deambulacra inter columnas cedrinas, ligna quippe cedrina exciderat in columnas. 3 Et tabulatis cedrinis vestivit totam cameram, quae quadraginta et quinque columnis sustentabatur, unus autem ordo habebat columnas quindecim 4 contra se invicem positas 5 et e regione se respicientes aequali spatio inter columnas, et super columnas quadrangulata ligna in cunctis aequalia. 6 Et porticum columnarum fecit quinquaginta cubitorum longitudinis et triginta cubitorum latitudinis et alteram porticum in facie maioris porticus et columnas et epistylia super columnas. 7 Porticum quoque solii in qua tribunal est fecit et texit lignis cedrinis a pavimento usque ad summitatem. 8 Et domuncula in qua sedebatur ad iudicandum erat in media porticu, simili opere. Domum quoque fecit filiae Pharaonis (quam uxorem duxerat Salomon) tali opere quali et hanc porticum, 9 omnia lapidibus pretiosis qui ad normam quandam atque mensuram tam intrinsecus quam extrinsecus ser-

Chapter 7

Solomon's palace, his house in the forest and the queen's house, the work of the two pillars, the sea (or laver) and other vessels.

And Solomon built his own house in thirteen years and brought it to perfection. 2 He built also the house of the forest of Libanus; the length of it was a hundred cubits and the breadth fifty cubits and the height thirty cubits and four galleries between pillars of cedar, for he had cut cedar trees into pillars. 3 And he covered the whole vault with boards of cedar, and it was held up with five and forty pillars, and one row had fifteen pillars 4 set one against another 5 and looking one *upon* another with equal space between the pillars, and over the pillars were square beams in all things equal. 6 And he made a porch of pillars of fifty cubits in length and thirty cubits in breadth and another porch before the greater porch and pillars and chapiters upon the pillars. 7 He made also the porch of the throne wherein is the seat of judgment and covered it with cedar wood from the floor to the top. 8 And in the midst of the porch was a small house where *he* sat in judgment, of the like work. He made also a house for the daughter of Pharaoh (whom Solomon had taken to wife) of the same work as this porch, 9 all of costly stones which were sawed by a certain rule and measure both within and without from the foundation to the top of the

mitate columnarum desuper iuxta mensuram columnae contra retiacula, malogranatorum autem ducenti ordines erant in circuitu capitelli secundi. 21 Et statuit duas columnas in porticum templi, cumque statuisset columnam dexteram, vocavit eam nomine Iachin; similiter erexit columnam secundam et vocavit nomen eius Booz. 22 Et super capita columnarum opus in modum lilii posuit perfectumque est opus columnarum. 23 Fecit quoque mare fusile decem cubitorum a labio usque ad labium rotundum in circuitu; quinque cubitorum altitudo eius, et resticula triginta cubitorum cingebat illud per circuitum.

24 Et sculptura subter labium circumibat illud decem cubitis ambiens mare. Duo ordines sculpturarum histriatarum erant fusiles, 25 et stabat super duodecim boves, e quibus tres respiciebant ad aquilonem et tres ad occidentem et tres ad meridiem et tres ad orientem, et mare super eos desuper erat, quorum posteriora universa intrinsecus latitabant.

26 Grossitudo autem luteris trium unciarum erat, labiumque eius quasi labium calicis et folium repandi lilii: duo milia batos capiebat. 27 Et fecit bases decem aereas. Quattuor cubitorum longitudinis bases singulas, et quattuor cubitorum latitudinis et trium cubitorum altitudinis. 28 Et ipsum opus basium interrasile erat, et sculpturae inter iuncturas. 29 Et inter coronulas et plectas leones et boves et cherubin, et in iuncturis similiter desuper, et subter leones et boves quasi lora ex aere dependentia. 30 Et quattuor rotae per bases singulas et axes aerei, et per quattuor partes quasi umeruli subter luterem fusiles, contra se invicem respectantes. 31 Os

measure of the pillar over against the net-work, and of pomegranates there were two hundred *in* rows round about the other chapter. 21 And he set up the two pillars in the porch of the temple, and when he had set up the pillar on the right hand, he called the name thereof Jachin; in like manner he set up the second pillar and called the name thereof Boaz. 22 And upon the tops of the pillars he made lily work *so* the work of the pillars was finished. 23 He made also a molten sea of ten cubits from brim to brim round all about; the height of it was five cubits, and a line of thirty cubits compassed it round about.

24 And a graven work under the brim *of it* compassed it for ten cubits going about the sea. There were two rows cast of chamfered *sculptures,* 25 and it stood upon twelve oxen, of which three looked towards the north and three towards the west and three towards the south and three towards the east, and the sea was above upon them, and their hinder parts were all hid within.

26 And the laver was *a handbreadth* thick, and the brim thereof was like the brim of a cup *or* the leaf of a crisped lily: it contained two thousand bates. 27 And he made ten bases of brass. Every base was four cubits in length and four cubits in breadth and three cubits high. 28 And the work itself of the bases was intergraven, and there were gravings between the joinings. 29 And between the little crowns and the ledges were lions and oxen and cherubims, and in the joinings likewise above, and under the lions and oxen as it were bands of brass hanging down. 30 And every base had four wheels and axletrees of brass, and at the four sides were undersetters under the laver molten, looking one against another. 31 The

quoque luteris intrinsecus erat in capitis summitate, et quod forinsecus apparebat unius cubiti erat totum rotundum, pariterque habebat unum cubitum et dimidium, in angulis autem columnarum variae celaturae erant, et media intercolumnia quadrata, non rotunda. 32 Quattuor quoque rotae quae per quattuor angulos basis erant coherebant sibi subter basi; una rota habebat altitudinis cubitum et semis. 33 Tales autem rotae erant quales solent in curru fieri, et axes earum et radii et canti et modioli omnia fusilia. 34 Nam et umeruli illi quattuor per singulos angulos basis unius ex ipsa basi fusiles et coniuncti erant. 35 In summitate autem basis erat quaedam rotunditas dimidii cubiti, ita fabrefacta ut luter desuper possit inponi habens celaturas suas et sculpturas varias ex semet ipso. 36 Scalpsit quoque in tabulatis illis, quae erant ex aere, et in angulis cherubin et leones et palmas quasi in similitudinem stantis hominis ut non celata sed adposita per circuitum viderentur. 37 In hunc modum fecit decem bases fusura una et mensura sculpturaque consimili. 38 Fecit quoque decem luteres aereos: quadraginta batos capiebat luter unus eratque quattuor cubitorum, singulos quoque luteres per singulas, id est decem, bases posuit. 39 Et constituit decem bases, quinque ad dexteram partem templi et quinque ad sinistram, mare autem posuit ad dexteram partem templi contra orientem ad meridiem.

40 Fecit ergo Hiram lebetas et scutras et amulas et perfecit omne opus Regis Salomonis in templo Domini, 41 columnas duas et funiculos capitulorum super capitella columnarum duos et retiacula duo ut operirent duos funiculos qui

mouth also of the laver within was in the top of the chapiter, and that which appeared without was of one cubit all round, and together it was one cubit and a half, and in the corners of the pillars were divers engravings, and the spaces between the pillars were square, not round. 32 And the four wheels which were at the four corners of the base were joined one to another under the base; the height of a wheel was a cubit and a half. 33 And they were such wheels as are used to be made in a chariot, and their axletrees and spokes and strakes and naves were all cast. 34 *And* the four undersetters that were at every corner of each base were of the base itself cast and joined together. 35 And in the top of the base there was a *round compass* of half a cubit, so wrought that the laver might be set thereon having its gravings and divers sculptures of itself. 36 He engraved also in those plates, which were of brass, and in the corners cherubims and lions and palm *trees* in likeness of a man standing so that they seemed not to be engraven but added round about. 37 After this manner he made ten bases of one casting and measure and the like graving. 38 He made also ten lavers of brass: one laver contained four bates and was of four cubits, *and* upon every base, *in all* ten, he put as many lavers. 39 And he set the ten bases, five on the right side of the temple and five on the left, and the sea he put on the right side of the temple over against the east southward.

40 And Hiram made caldrons and shovels and basins and finished all the work of King Solomon in the temple of the Lord, 41 the two pillars and the two cords of the chapiters upon the chapiters of the pillars and the two net-works to cover the two cords that were upon the top of the pil-

erant super capita columnarum 42 et malogranata quadringenta in duobus retiaculis, duos versus malogranatorum in retiaculis singulis ad operiendos funiculos capitellorum qui erant super capita columnarum 43 et bases decem et luteres decem super bases 44 et mare unum et boves duodecim subter mare 45 et lebetas et scutras et amulas. Omnia vasa quae fecit Hiram Regi Salomoni in domo Domini de aurichalco erant. 46 In campestri regione Iordanis fudit ea rex in argillosa terra inter Socchoth et Sarthan, 47 et posuit Salomon omnia vasa, propter multitudinem autem nimiam non erat pondus aeris.

48 Fecitque Salomon omnia vasa in domo Domini, altare aureum et mensam super quam ponerentur panes propositionis auream, 49 et candelabra aurea, quinque ad dexteram et quinque ad sinistram contra oraculum, ex auro puro et quasi lilii flores et lucernas desuper aureas et forcipes aureos 50 et hydrias et fuscinulas et fialas et mortariola et turibula de auro purissimo, et cardines ostiorum domus interioris sancti sanctorum et ostiorum domus templi ex auro erant. 51 Et perfecit omne opus quod faciebat Salomon in domo Domini et intulit quae sanctificaverat David, pater suus, argentum et aurum et vasa reposuitque in thesauris domus Domini.

lars 42 and four hundred pomegranates for the two net-works, two rows of pomegranates for each net-work to cover the cords of the chapiters which were upon the tops of the pillars 43 and the ten bases and the ten lavers on the bases 44 and one sea and twelve oxen under the sea 45 and the caldrons and the shovels and the basins. All the vessels that Hiram made for King Solomon for the house of the Lord were of *fine* brass. 46 In the plains of the Jordan did the king cast them in a clay ground between Succoth and Zarethan, 47 and Solomon placed all the vessels, but for exceeding great multitude the brass could not be weighed.

48 And Solomon made all the vessels for the house of the Lord, the altar of gold and the table of gold upon which the loaves of proposition should be set, 49 and the golden candlesticks, five on the right hand and five on the left over against the oracle, of pure gold and the flowers like lilies and the lamps over them of gold and golden snuffers 50 and pots and fleshhooks and bowls and mortars and censers of most pure gold, and the hinges for the doors of the inner house of the holy of holies and for the doors of the house of the temple were of gold. 51 And Solomon finished all the work that he made in the house of the Lord and brought in the things that David, his father, had dedicated, the silver and the gold and the vessels, and laid them up in the treasures of the house of the Lord.

Caput 8

Tunc congregati sunt omnes maiores natu Israhel cum principibus tribuum et duces familiarum filiorum Israhel ad Regem Salomonem in Hierusalem ut deferrent Arcam Foederis Domini de civitate David, id est, de Sion. 2 Convenitque ad Regem Salomonem universus Israhel in mense Hethanim in sollemni die (ipse est mensis septimus). 3 Veneruntque cuncti senes de Israhel, et tulerunt sacerdotes arcam 4 et portaverunt arcam Domini et tabernaculum foederis et omnia vasa sanctuarii quae erant in tabernaculo, et ferebant ea sacerdotes et Levitae. 5 Rex autem Salomon et omnis multitudo Israhel quae convenerat ad eum gradiebatur cum illo ante arcam, et immolabant oves et boves absque aestimatione et numero. 6 Et intulerunt sacerdotes Arcam Foederis Domini in locum suum, in oraculum templi, in sanctum sanctorum subter alas cherubin, 7 siquidem cherubin expandebant alas super locum arcae et protegebant arcam et vectes eius desuper. 8 Cumque eminerent vectes, et apparerent summitates eorum foris sanctuarium ante oraculum; non apparebant ultra extrinsecus, qui et fuerunt ibi usque in praesentem diem.

Chapter 8

The dedication of the temple, Solomon's prayer and sacrifices.

Then all the ancients of Israel with the princes of the tribes and the heads of the families of the children of Israel were assembled to King Solomon in Jerusalem that they might carry the Ark of the Covenant of the Lord out of the city of David, that is, out of Zion. 2 And all Israel assembled themselves to King Solomon on the festival day in the month of Ethanim (the same is the seventh month). 3 And all the ancients of Israel came, and the priests took up the ark 4 and carried the ark of the Lord and the tabernacle of the covenant and all the vessels of the sanctuary that were in the tabernacle, and the priests and the Levites carried them. 5 And King Solomon and all the multitude of Israel that were assembled unto him went with him before the ark, and they sacrificed sheep and oxen *that could not be counted or numbered.* 6 And the priests brought in the Ark of the Covenant of the Lord into its place, into the oracle of the temple, into the holy of holies under the wings of the cherubims, 7 for the cherubims spread forth their wings over the place of the ark and covered the ark and the staves thereof above. 8 And whereas the staves stood out, *the* ends of them were seen without *in the* sanctuary before the oracle *but* were not seen farther out, and there they have been unto this day.

9 In arca autem non erat aliud nisi duae tabulae lapideae quas posuerat in ea Moses in Horeb quando pepigit foedus Dominus cum filiis Israhel cum egrederentur de terra Aegypti. 10 Factum est autem cum exissent sacerdotes de sanctuario nebula implevit domum Domini, 11 et non poterant sacerdotes stare et ministrare propter nebulam, impleverat enim gloria Domini domum Domini. 12 Tunc ait Salomon, "Dominus dixit ut habitaret in nebula. 13 Aedificans aedificavi domum in habitaculum tuum, firmissimum solium tuum in sempiternum." 14 Convertitque rex faciem suam et benedixit omni ecclesiae Israhel, omnis enim ecclesia Israhel stabat. 15 Et ait Salomon, "Benedictus Dominus, Deus Israhel, qui locutus est ore suo ad David, patrem meum, et in manibus eius perfecit, dicens, 16 'A die qua eduxi populum meum Israhel de Aegypto, non elegi civitatem de universis tribubus Israhel ut aedificaretur domus et esset nomen meum ibi, sed elegi David ut esset super populum meum Israhel.' 17 Voluitque David, pater meus, aedificare domum nomini Domini, Dei Israhel, 18 et ait Dominus ad David, patrem meum, 'Quod cogitasti in corde tuo aedificare domum nomini meo, bene fecisti hoc ipsum mente tractans. 19 Verumtamen tu non aedificabis mihi domum, sed filius tuus qui egredietur de renibus tuis, ipse aedificabit domum nomini meo.' 20 Confirmavit Dominus sermonem suum quem locutus est, stetique pro David, patre meo, et sedi super thronum Israhel sicut locutus est Dominus et aedificavi domum nomini Domini, Dei Israhel. 21 Et constitui ibi locum arcae in qua foedus est Domini quod percussit cum patribus nostris quando egressi sunt de terra Aegypti."

9 Now in the ark there was nothing else but the two tables of stone which Moses put there at Horeb when the Lord made a covenant with the children of Israel when they came out of the land of Egypt. 10 And it came to pass when the priests were come out of the sanctuary that a cloud filled the house of the Lord, 11 and the priests could not stand *to* minister because of the cloud, for the glory of the Lord had filled the house of the Lord. 12 Then Solomon said, "The Lord said that he would dwell in a cloud. 13 Building I have built a house for thy dwelling, *to be* thy most firm throne for ever." 14 And the king turned his face and blessed all the assembly of Israel, for all the assembly of Israel stood. 15 And Solomon said, "Blessed be the Lord, the God of Israel, who spoke with his mouth to David, my father, and with his own hands hath accomplished it, saying, 16 'Since the day that I brought my people Israel out of Egypt, I chose no city out of all the tribes of Israel for a house to be built *that* my name might be there, but I chose David to be over my people Israel.' 17 And David, my father, would have built a house to the name of the Lord, the God of Israel, 18 and the Lord said to David, my father, 'Whereas thou hast thought in thy heart to build a house to my name, thou hast done well *in having* this same thing in thy mind. 19 Nevertheless thou shalt not build me a house, but thy son that shall come forth out of thy loins, he shall build a house to my name.' 20 The Lord hath performed his word which he spoke, and I stand *in the room of* David, my father, and sit upon the throne of Israel as the Lord promised and have built a house to the name of the Lord, the God of Israel. 21 And I have set there a place for the ark wherein is the covenant of the Lord which he made with our fathers when they came out of the land of Egypt."

22 Stetit autem Salomon ante altare Domini in conspectu ecclesiae Israhel et expandit manus suas in caelum 23 et ait, "Domine Deus Israhel, non est similis tui Deus in caelo desuper et super terra deorsum qui custodis pactum et misericordiam servis tuis qui ambulant coram te in toto corde suo, 24 qui custodisti servo tuo David, patri meo, quae locutus es ei. Ore locutus es, et manibus perfecisti, ut haec dies probat. 25 Nunc, igitur, Domine Deus Israhel, conserva famulo tuo David, patri meo, quae locutus es ei, dicens, 'Non auferetur de te vir coram me qui sedeat super thronum Israhel ita tamen si custodierint filii tui viam suam ut ambulent coram me sicut tu ambulasti in conspectu meo.' 26 Et nunc, Domine Deus Israhel, firmentur verba tua quae locutus es servo tuo David, patri meo. 27 Ergone putandum est quod vere Deus habitet super Terram? Si enim caelum et caeli caelorum te capere non possunt, quanto magis domus haec quam aedificavi? 28 Sed respice ad orationem servi tui et ad preces eius Domine, Deus meus. Audi hymnum et orationem quam servus tuus orat coram te hodie 29 ut sint oculi tui aperti super domum hanc nocte et die, super domum de qua dixisti, 'Erit nomen meum ibi,' ut exaudias orationem quam orat ad te servus tuus in loco isto, 30 ut exaudias deprecationem servi tui et populi tui Israhel quodcumque oraverint in loco isto et exaudies in loco habitaculi tui in caelo, et cum exaudieris, propitius eris. 31 Si peccaverit homo in proximum suum et habuerit aliquod iuramentum quo teneatur adstric-

22 And Solomon stood before the altar of the Lord in the sight of the assembly of Israel and spread forth his hands towards heaven 23 and said, "Lord God of Israel, there is no God like thee in heaven above or on earth beneath who keepest covenant and mercy with thy servants that have walked before thee with all their heart, 24 who hast kept with thy servant David, my father, what thou hast promised him. With thy mouth thou didst speak, and with thy hands thou hast performed, as this day proveth. 25 Now, therefore, O Lord God of Israel, keep with thy servant David, my father, what thou hast spoken to him, saying, 'There shall not be taken away of thee a man *in my sight* to sit on the throne of Israel yet so *that* thy children take heed to their way that they walk before me as thou hast walked in my sight.' 26 And now, Lord God of Israel, let thy words be established which thou hast spoken to thy servant David, my father. 27 Is it then to be thought that God should indeed dwell upon Earth? For if heaven and the heavens of heavens cannot contain thee, how much *less* this house which I have built? 28 But have regard to the prayer of thy servant and to his supplications O Lord, my God. Hear the hymn and the prayer which thy servant prayeth before thee this day 29 that thy eyes may be open upon this house night and day, upon the house of which thou hast said, 'My name shall be there,' that thou mayest hearken to the prayer which thy servant prayeth in this place to thee, 30 that thou mayest hearken to the supplication of thy servant and of thy people Israel whatsoever they shall pray for in this place and hear them in the place of thy dwelling in heaven, and when thou hearest, shew them mercy. 31 If *any* man trespass against his neighbour and have *an* oath upon him wherewith he is bound and come because

tus et venerit propter iuramentum coram altari tuo in domum tuam, 32 tu exaudies in caelo, et facies, et iudicabis servos tuos condemnans impium et reddens viam suam super
caput eius iustificansque iustum et retribuens ei secundum
iustitiam suam. 33 Si fugerit populus tuus Israhel inimicos
suos (quia peccaturus est tibi) et agentes paenitentiam et
confitentes nomini tuo venerint et oraverint et deprecati
te fuerint in domo hac, 34 exaudi in caelo, et dimitte peccatum populi tui Israhel, et reduces eos in terram quam dedisti
patribus eorum. 35 Si clausum fuerit caelum et non pluerit
propter peccata eorum et orantes in loco isto paenitentiam
egerint nomini tuo et a peccatis suis conversi fuerint propter adflictionem suam, 36 exaudi eos in caelo, et dimitte peccata servorum tuorum et populi tui Israhel, et ostende eis
viam bonam per quam ambulent, et da pluviam super terram
tuam quam dedisti populo tuo in possessionem. 37 Fames si
oborta fuerit in terra aut pestilentia aut corruptus aer aut
aurugo aut lucusta vel rubigo, et adflixerit eum inimicus eius
portas obsidens, omnis plaga, universa infirmitas, 38 cuncta
devotatio et inprecatio quae acciderit omni homini de populo tuo Israhel, si quis cognoverit plagam cordis sui et ex-
panderit manus suas in domo hac, 39 tu audies in caelo in
loco habitationis tuae, et repropitiaberis, et facies ut des
unicuique secundum omnes vias suas sicut videris cor eius,
quia tu nosti solus cor omnium filiorum hominum, 40 ut ti-
meant te cunctis diebus quibus vivunt super faciem terrae
quam dedisti patribus nostris. 41 Insuper et alienigena qui
non est de populo tuo Israhel, cum venerit de terra longinqua propter nomen tuum, audietur enim nomen tuum mag-

of the oath before thy altar to thy house, 32 then *hear* thou in heaven, and *do,* and *judge* thy servants, condemning the wicked and bringing his way upon his own head and justifying the just and rewarding him according to his justice. 33 If thy people Israel shall fly before their enemies (because they will sin against thee) and doing penance and confessing to thy name shall come and pray and make supplications to thee in this house, 34 then hear thou in heaven, and forgive the sin of thy people Israel, and *bring* them back to the land which thou gavest to their fathers. 35 If heaven shall be shut up and there shall be no rain because of their sins and they praying in this place shall do penance to thy name and shall be converted from their sins by occasion of their affliction, 36 then hear thou them in heaven, and forgive the sins of thy servants and of thy people Israel, and shew them the good way wherein they should walk, and give rain upon thy land which thou hast given to thy people in possession. 37 If a famine arise in the land or a pestilence or corrupt air or blasting or locust or mildew, *if* their enemy afflict them besieging the gates, whatsoever plague, whatsoever infirmity, 38 whatsoever curse or imprecation shall happen to any man of thy people Israel, when a man shall know the wound of his own heart and shall spread forth his hands in this house, 39 then *hear thou* in heaven in the place of thy dwelling, and *forgive,* and *do* so as to give to every one according to his ways as thou shalt see his heart, for thou only knowest the heart of all the children of men, 40 that they may fear thee all the days that they live upon the face of the land which thou hast given to our fathers. 41 Moreover also the stranger who is not of thy people Israel, when he shall come out of a far country for thy name's sake, for they shall hear everywhere

num et manus tua fortis et brachium tuum 42 extentum ubi-
que, cum venerit ergo et oraverit in loco hoc, 43 tu exaudies
in caelo, in firmamento habitaculi tui, et facies omnia pro
quibus invocaverit te alienigena ut discant universi populi
terrarum nomen tuum timere sicut populus tuus Israhel et
probent quia nomen tuum invocatum est super domum
hanc quam aedificavi. 44 Si egressus fuerit populus tuus ad
bellum contra inimicos suos per viam quocumque miseris
eos, orabunt te contra viam civitatis quam elegisti et contra
domum quam aedificavi nomini tuo, 45 et exaudies in caelo
orationes eorum et preces eorum, et facies iudicium eorum.
46 Quod si peccaverint tibi, non est enim homo qui non
peccet, et iratus tradideris eos inimicis suis et captivi ducti
fuerint in terram inimicorum longe vel prope, 47 et egerint
paenitentiam in corde suo in loco captivitatis et conversi
deprecati te fuerint in captivitate sua, dicentes, 'Peccavimus; inique egimus; impie gessimus,' 48 et reversi fuerint ad
te in universo corde suo et tota anima sua in terra inimicorum suorum ad quam captivi ducti fuerint et oraverint te
contra viam terrae suae quam dedisti patribus eorum et civitatis quam elegisti et templi quod aedificavi nomini tuo,
49 exaudies in caelo, in firmamento solii tui, orationes eorum
et preces eorum, et facies iudicium eorum. 50 Et propitiabe-
ris populo tuo qui peccavit tibi et omnibus iniquitatibus eorum quibus praevaricati sunt in te, et dabis misericordiam
coram eis qui eos captivos habuerint ut misereantur eis,
51 populus enim tuus est et hereditas tua quos eduxisti de

of thy great name and thy mighty hand 42 and thy stretched out arm, so when he shall come and shall pray in this place, 43 then *hear thou* in heaven, in the firmament of thy dwelling place, and *do* all those things for which that stranger shall call upon thee that all the people of the earth may learn to fear thy name as do thy people Israel and may prove that thy name is called upon on this house which I have built. 44 If thy people go out to war against their enemies by what way soever thou shalt send them, they shall pray to thee towards the way of the city which thou hast chosen and towards the house which I have built to thy name, 45 and then *hear thou* in heaven their prayers and their supplications, and *do* judgment for them. 46 But if they sin against thee, for there is no man who sinneth not, and thou being angry deliver them up to their enemies *so that* they be led away captives into the land of their enemies far or near, 47 then if they do penance in their heart in the place of captivity and being converted make supplication to thee in their captivity, saying, 'We have sinned; we have done unjustly; we have committed wickedness,' 48 and return to thee with all their heart and all their soul in the land of their enemies to which they *have* been led captives and pray to thee towards the way of their land which thou gavest to their fathers and of the city which thou hast chosen and of the temple which I have built to thy name, 49 then *hear thou* in heaven, in the firmament of thy throne, their prayers and their supplications, and *do* judgment for them. 50 And *forgive* thy people that have sinned against thee and all their iniquities by which they have transgressed against thee, and give them mercy before them that have made them captives that they may have compassion on them, 51 for they are thy people and thy inheritance whom

terra Aegypti, de medio fornacis ferreae 52 ut sint oculi tui aperti ad deprecationem servi tui et populi tui Israhel et exaudias eos in universis pro quibus invocaverint te, 53 tu enim separasti eos tibi in hereditatem de universis populis terrae sicut locutus es per Mosen servum tuum quando eduxisti patres nostros de Aegypto, Domine Deus."

54 Factum est autem cum conplesset Salomon orans Dominum omnem orationem et deprecationem hanc surrexit de conspectu altaris Domini, utrumque enim genu in terram fixerat et manus expanderat ad caelum. 55 Stetit ergo et benedixit omni ecclesiae Israhel voce magna, dicens, 56 "Benedictus Dominus qui dedit requiem populo suo Israhel iuxta omnia quae locutus est. Non cecidit ne unus quidem sermo ex omnibus bonis quae locutus est per Mosen servum suum. 57 Sit Dominus, Deus noster, nobiscum sicut fuit cum patribus nostris non derelinquens nos neque proiciens, 58 sed inclinet corda nostra ad se ut ambulemus in universis viis eius et custodiamus mandata eius et caerimonias eius et iudicia quaecumque mandavit patribus nostris. 59 Et sint sermones mei isti quibus deprecatus sum coram Domino adpropinquantes Domino, Deo nostro, die et nocte ut faciat iudicium servo suo et populo suo Israhel per singulos dies, 60 ut sciant omnes populi terrae quia Dominus, ipse est Deus, et non est ultra absque eo. 61 Sit quoque cor nostrum perfectum cum Domino, Deo nostro, ut ambulemus in decretis eius et custodiamus mandata eius sicut et hodie."

62 Igitur rex et omnis Israhel cum eo immolabant victimas coram Domino. 63 Mactavitque Salomon hostias pa-

thou hast brought out of the land of Egypt, from the midst of the furnace of iron 52 that thy eyes may be open to the supplication of thy servant and of thy people Israel *to* hear them in all things for which they shall call upon thee, 53 for thou hast separated them to thyself for an inheritance from among all the people of the earth as thou hast spoken by Moses thy servant when thou broughtest our fathers out of Egypt, O Lord God."

54 And it came to pass when Solomon had made an end of praying all this prayer and supplication to the Lord that he rose from before the altar of the Lord, for he had fixed both knees on the ground and had spread his hands towards heaven. 55 And he stood and blessed all the assembly of Israel with a loud voice, saying, 56 "Blessed be the Lord who hath given rest to his people Israel according to all that he promised. There hath not failed so much as one word of all the good things that he promised by his servant Moses. 57 The Lord, our God, be with us as he was with our fathers and not leave us nor cast us off, 58 but may he incline our hearts to himself that we may walk in all his ways and keep his commandments and his ceremonies and all his judgments which he commanded our fathers. 59 And let these my words wherewith I have prayed before the Lord be nigh unto the Lord, our God, day and night that he may do judgment for his servant and for his people Israel day by day, 60 that all the people of the earth may know that the Lord, he is God, and there is no other besides him. 61 Let our heart also be perfect with the Lord, our God, that we may walk in his statutes and keep his commandments as at this day."

62 And the king and all Israel with him offered victims before the Lord. 63 And Solomon slew victims of peace offer-

cificas quas immolavit Domino, boum viginti duo milia et ovium centum viginti milia, et dedicaverunt templum Domini rex et filii Israhel. 64 In die illa sanctificavit rex medium atrii quod erat ante domum Domini; fecit quippe ibi holocaustum et sacrificium et adipem pacificorum quia altare aereum quod erat coram Domino minus erat et capere non poterat holocaustum et sacrificium et adipem pacificorum. 65 Fecit ergo Salomon in tempore illo festivitatem celebrem et omnis Israhel cum eo, multitudo magna ab introitu Emath usque ad rivum Aegypti, coram Domino, Deo nostro, septem diebus et septem diebus, id est, quattuordecim diebus. 66 et in die octava dimisit populos, qui benedicentes regi profecti sunt in tabernacula sua laetantes et alacri corde super omnibus bonis quae fecerat Dominus David, servo suo, et Israhel, populo suo.

Caput 9

Factum est autem cum perfecisset Salomon aedificium domus Domini et aedificium regis et omne quod optaverat et voluerat facere 2 apparuit Dominus ei secundo sicut ap-

ings which he sacrificed to the Lord, two and twenty thousand oxen and a hundred and twenty thousand sheep; so the king and the children of Israel dedicated the temple of the Lord. 64 In that day the king sanctified the middle of the court that was before the house of the Lord, for there he offered the holocaust and sacrifice and fat of the peace offerings because the brazen altar that was before the Lord was too little *to* receive the holocaust and sacrifice and fat of the peace offerings. 65 And Solomon made at the same time a solemn feast and all Israel with him, a great multitude from the entrance of Hamath to the river of Egypt, before the Lord, our God, seven days and seven days, that is, fourteen days. 66 And on the eighth day he sent away the people, and they blessed the king and went to their dwellings rejoicing and glad in heart for all the good things that the Lord had done for David, his servant, and for Israel, his people.

Chapter 9

The Lord appeareth again to Solomon. He buildeth cities.
He sendeth a fleet to Ophir.

And it came to pass when Solomon had finished the building of the house of the Lord and the king's house and all that he desired and *was pleased* to do 2 that the Lord appeared to him the second time as he had appeared to him

paruerat ei in Gabaon, 3 dixitque Dominus ad eum, "Exaudivi orationem tuam et deprecationem tuam quam deprecatus es coram me. Sanctificavi domum hanc quam aedificasti ut ponerem nomen meum ibi in sempiternum, et erunt oculi mei et cor meum ibi cunctis diebus. 4 Tu quoque si ambulaveris coram me sicut ambulavit pater tuus, in simplicitate cordis et in aequitate, et feceris omnia quae praecepi tibi et legitima mea et iudicia mea servaveris, 5 ponam thronum regni tui super Israhel in sempiternum sicut locutus sum David, patri tuo, dicens, 'Non auferetur de genere tuo vir de solio Israhel.' 6 Si autem aversione aversi fueritis vos et filii vestri non sequentes me nec custodientes mandata mea et caerimonias meas quas proposui vobis sed abieritis et colueritis deos alienos et adoraveritis eos, 7 auferam Israhel de superficie terrae quam dedi eis, et templum quod sanctificavi nomini meo proiciam a conspectu meo, eritque Israhel in proverbium et in fabulam cunctis populis, 8 et domus haec erit in exemplum: omnis qui transierit per eam stupebit et sibilabit et dicet, 'Quare fecit Dominus sic terrae huic et domui huic?' 9 Et respondebunt, 'Quia dereliquerunt Dominum, Deum suum, qui eduxit patres eorum de terra Aegypti et secuti sunt deos alienos et adoraverunt eos et coluerunt eos, idcirco induxit Dominus super eos omne malum hoc.'"

10 Expletis autem annis viginti postquam aedificaverat Salomon duas domos, id est, domum Domini et domum regis, 11 Hiram, rege Tyri, praebente Salomoni ligna cedrina et abiegna et aurum iuxta omne quod opus habuerat, tunc dedit Salomon Hiram viginti oppida in terra Galileae. 12 Egressusque est Hiram de Tyro ut videret oppida quae dederat

in Gibeon, 3 and the Lord said to him, "I have heard thy prayer and thy supplication which thou hast made before me. I have sanctified this house which thou hast built to put my name there for ever, and my eyes and my heart shall be there always. 4 And if thou wilt walk before me as thy father walked, in simplicity of heart and in uprightness, and wilt do all that I have commanded thee and wilt keep my ordinances and my judgments, 5 I will establish the throne of thy kingdom over Israel for ever as I promised David, thy father, saying, 'There shall not *fail* a man of thy race *upon* the throne of Israel.' 6 But if you and your children revolting shall turn away from following me and will not keep my commandments and my ceremonies which I have set before you but will go and worship strange gods and adore them, 7 I will take away Israel from the face of the land which I have given them, and the temple which I have sanctified to my name I will cast out of my sight, and Israel shall be a proverb and a byword among all people, 8 and this house shall be made an example of: every one that shall pass by it shall be astonished and shall hiss and say, 'Why hath the Lord done thus to this land and to this house?' 9 And they shall answer, 'Because they forsook the Lord, their God, who brought their fathers out of the land of Egypt and followed strange gods and adored them and worshipped them, therefore hath the Lord brought upon them all this evil.'"

10 And when twenty years were ended after Solomon had built the two houses, that is, the house of the Lord and the house of the king, 11 Hiram, the king of Tyre, furnishing Solomon with cedar trees and fir trees and gold according to all he had need of, then Solomon gave Hiram twenty cities in the land of Galilee. 12 And Hiram came out of Tyre to see

ei Salomon, et non placuerunt ei, 13 et ait, "Haecine sunt civitates quas dedisti mihi, frater?" Et appellavit eas terram Chabul usque in diem hanc. 14 Misit quoque Hiram ad Regem Salomonem centum viginti talenta auri. 15 Haec est summa expensarum quam obtulit Rex Salomon ad aedificandam domum Domini et domum suam et Mello et murum Hierusalem et Eser et Mageddo et Gazer.

16 Pharao, rex Aegypti, ascendit et cepit Gazer succenditque eam igni et Chananeum qui habitabat in civitate interfecit et dedit eam in dote filiae suae, uxori Salomonis. 17 Aedificavit ergo Salomon Gazer et Bethoron Inferiorem 18 et Baalath et Palmyram in terra solitudinis. 19 Et omnes vicos qui ad se pertinebant et erant absque muro munivit, et civitates curruum et civitates equitum et quodcumque ei placuit ut aedificaret in Hierusalem et in Libano et in omni terra potestatis suae. 20 Universum populum qui remanserat de Amorreis et Hettheis et Ferezeis et Eveis et Iebuseis qui non sunt de filiis Israhel, 21 horum filios qui remanserant in terra quos, scilicet, non potuerant filii Israhel exterminare, fecit Salomon tributarios usque ad diem hanc. 22 De filiis autem Israhel non constituit Salomon servire quemquam, sed erant viri bellatores et ministri eius et principes et duces et praefecti curruum et equorum. 23 Erant autem principes super omnia opera Salomonis praepositi quingenti quinquaginta, qui habebant subiectum populum et statutis operibus imperabant. 24 Filia autem Pharaonis ascendit de civitate David in domum suam quam aedificaverat ei Salomon; tunc aedificavit Mello.

the towns which Solomon had given him, and they pleased him not, 13 and he said, "Are these the cities which thou hast given me, brother?" And he called them the land of Cabul unto this day. 14 And Hiram sent to King Solomon a hundred and twenty talents of gold. 15 This is the sum of the expenses which King Solomon offered to build the house of the Lord and his own house and Millo and the wall of Jerusalem and Hazor and Megiddo and Gezer.

16 Pharaoh, the king of Egypt, came up and took Gezer and burnt it with fire and slew the Canaanite that dwelt in the city and gave it for a dowry to his daughter, Solomon's wife. 17 So Solomon built Gezer and Beth-horon the Nether 18 and Baalath and Palmira in the land of the wilderness. 19 And all the towns that belonged to himself and were not walled he fortified, the cities also of the chariots and the cities of the horsemen and whatsoever he had a mind to build in Jerusalem and in Libanus and in all the land of his dominion. 20 All the people that were left of the Amorites and Hittites and Perizzites and Hivites and Jebusites that are not of the children of Israel, 21 their children that were left in the land, to wit, *such as* the children of Israel had not been able to destroy, Solomon made tributary unto this day. 22 But of the children of Israel Solomon made not any to be bondmen, but they were men of war and his servants and his princes and captains and overseers of the chariots and horses. 23 And there were five hundred and fifty chief officers set over all the works of Solomon, and they had people under them and had charge over the appointed works. 24 And the daughter of Pharaoh came up out of the city of David to her house which Solomon had built for her; then did he build Millo.

25 Offerebat quoque Salomon tribus vicibus per annos singulos holocausta et pacificas victimas super altare quod aedificaverat Domino, et adolebat thymiama coram Domino, perfectumque est templum. 26 Classem quoque fecit Rex Salomon in Asiongaber, quae est iuxta Ailath in litore Maris Rubri in terra Idumea. 27 Misitque Hiram in classe illa servos suos, viros nauticos et gnaros maris, cum servis Salomonis. 28 Qui cum venissent in Ophir, sumptum inde aurum quadringentorum viginti talentorum detulerunt ad Regem Salomonem.

Caput 10

Sed et regina Saba, audita fama Salomonis in nomine Domini, venit temptare eum in enigmatibus. 2 Et ingressa Hierusalem multo comitatu et divitiis et camelis portantibus aromata et aurum infinitum nimis et gemmas pretiosas, venit ad Regem Salomonem et locuta est ei universa quae habebat in corde suo. 3 Et docuit eam Salomon omnia verba quae proposuerat; non fuit sermo qui regem posset latere et non responderet ei. 4 Videns autem regina Saba omnem sapientiam Salomonis et domum quam aedificave-

25 Solomon also offered three times every year holocausts and victims of peace offerings upon the altar which he had built to the Lord, and he burnt incense before the Lord, and the temple was finished. 26 And King Solomon made a fleet in Ezion-geber, which is by Eloth on the shore of the Red Sea in the land of Edom. 27 And Hiram sent his servants in the fleet, sailors *that had knowledge* of the sea, with the servants of Solomon. 28 *And they* came to Ophir, *and* they brought from thence to King Solomon four hundred and twenty talents of gold.

Chapter 10

The queen of Sheba cometh to King Solomon. His riches and glory.

And the queen of Sheba, having heard of the fame of Solomon in the name of the Lord, came to try him with hard questions. 2 And entering into Jerusalem with a great train and riches and camels that carried spices and an immense quantity of gold and precious stones, she came to King Solomon and spoke to him all that she had in her heart. 3 And Solomon informed her of all the things she proposed *to him;* there was not any word the king *was* ignorant of and which he could not answer her. 4 And when the queen of Sheba saw all the wisdom of Solomon and the house which he had

rat 5 et cibos mensae eius et habitacula servorum et ordines ministrantium vestesque eorum et pincernas et holocausta quae offerebat in domo Domini, non habebat ultra spiritum, 6 dixitque ad regem, "Verus est sermo quem audivi in terra mea 7 super sermonibus tuis et super sapientia tua. Et non credebam narrantibus mihi donec ipsa veni et vidi oculis meis et probavi quod media pars mihi nuntiata non fuerit: maior est sapientia et opera tua quam rumor quem audivi. 8 Beati viri tui, et beati servi tui qui stant coram te semper et audiunt sapientiam tuam. 9 Sit Dominus, Deus tuus, benedictus cui placuisti, et posuit te super thronum Israhel eo quod dilexerit Dominus Israhel in sempiternum et constituit te regem ut faceres iudicium et iustitiam." 10 Dedit ergo regi centum viginti talenta auri et aromata multa nimis et gemmas pretiosas; non sunt adlata ultra aromata tam multa quam ea quae dedit regina Saba Regi Salomoni. 11 Sed et classis Hiram quae portabat aurum de Ophir adtulit ex Ophir ligna thyina multa nimis et gemmas pretiosas. 12 Fecitque rex de lignis thyinis fulchra domus Domini et domus regiae et citharas lyrasque cantoribus. Non sunt adlata huiuscemodi ligna thyina neque visa usque in praesentem diem. 13 Rex autem Salomon dedit reginae Saba omnia quae voluit et petivit ab eo exceptis his quae ultro obtulerat ei munere regio. Quae reversa est et abiit in terram suam cum servis suis.

14 Erat autem pondus auri quod adferebatur Salomoni per annos singulos sescentorum sexaginta sex talentorum auri 15 excepto eo quod afferebant viri qui super vectigalia erant

built 5 and the meat of his table and the apartments of his servants and the *order* of his ministers and their apparel and the cupbearers and the holocausts which he offered in the house of the Lord, she had no longer any spirit *in her,* 6 and she said to the king, "The report is true which I heard in my own country 7 concerning thy words and concerning thy wisdom. And I did not believe them that told me till I came myself and saw with my own eyes and have found that the half hath not been told me: thy wisdom and thy works *exceed* the fame which I heard. 8 Blessed are thy men, and blessed are thy servants who stand before thee always and hear thy wisdom. 9 Blessed be the Lord, thy God, whom thou hast pleased, and who hath set thee upon the throne of Israel, because the Lord hath loved Israel for ever and hath appointed thee king to do judgment and justice." 10 And she gave the king a hundred and twenty talents of gold and *of spices a very great store* and precious stones; there was brought no more such *abundance of spices* as these which the queen of Sheba gave to King Solomon. 11 The navy also of Hiram which brought gold from Ophir brought from Ophir great plenty of thyine trees and precious stones. 12 And the king made of the thyine trees the rails of the house of the Lord and of the king's house and citterns and harps for singers. There were no such thyine trees as these brought nor seen unto this day. 13 And King Solomon gave the queen of Sheba all that she desired and asked of him besides what he offered he himself of his royal bounty. And she returned and went to her own country with her servants.

14 And the weight of the gold that was brought to Solomon every year was six hundred and sixty-six talents of gold 15 besides that which the men brought him that were over

et negotiatores universique scruta vendentes et omnes reges Arabiae ducesque terrae. 16 Fecit quoque Salomon ducenta scuta de auro purissimo (sescentos auri siclos dedit in lamminas scuti unius) 17 et trecentas peltas ex auro probato (trecentae minae auri unam peltam vestiebant), posuitque ea rex in domo silvae Libani. 18 Fecit etiam Rex Salomon thronum de ebore grandem et vestivit eum auro fulvo nimis. 19 Qui habebat sex gradus, et summitas throni rotunda erat in parte posteriori, et duae manus hinc atque inde tenentes sedile, et duo leones stabant, iuxta manus singulas. 20 Et duodecim leunculi stantes super sex gradus hinc atque inde; non est factum tale opus in universis regnis. 21 Sed et omnia vasa de quibus potabat Rex Salomon erant aurea et universa supellex domus saltus Libani de auro purissimo. Non erat argentum, nec alicuius pretii putabatur in diebus Salomonis, 22 quia classis regis per mare cum classe Hiram semel per tres annos ibat in Tharsis deferens inde aurum et argentum et dentes elefantorum et simias et pavos.

23 Magnificatus est ergo Rex Salomon super omnes reges terrae divitiis et sapientia. 24 Et universa terra desiderabat vultum Salomonis, ut audiret sapientiam eius quam dederat Deus in corde eius. 25 Et singuli deferebant ei munera, vasa argentea et aurea, vestes et arma bellica aromata quoque et equos et mulos per annos singulos. 26 Congregavitque Salomon currus et equites, et facti sunt ei mille quadringenti currus et duodecim milia equitum, et disposuit eos per civitates munitas et cum rege in Hierusalem. 27 Fecitque ut tanta esset abundantia argenti in Hierusalem quanta lapidum, et cedrorum praebuit multitudinem quasi sycomoros

the tributes and the merchants and *they that sold by retail* and all the kings of Arabia and the governors of the country. 16 And Solomon made two hundred shields of the purest gold (he allowed six hundred sicles of gold for the plates of one shield) 17 and three hundred targets of *fine* gold (three hundred pounds of gold covered one target), and the king put them in the house of the forest of Libanus. 18 King Solomon also made a great throne of ivory and overlaid it with the *finest* gold. 19 It had six steps, and the top of the throne was round behind, and there were two hands on either side holding the seat, and two lions stood, one at each hand. 20 And twelve little lions stood upon the six steps on the one side and on the other; there was no such work made in any kingdom. 21 Moreover all the vessels out of which King Solomon drank were of gold, and all the furniture of the house of the forest of Libanus was of most pure gold. There was no silver, nor *was any account made of it* in the days of Solomon, 22 for the king's navy once in three years went with the navy of Hiram by sea to Tarshish and brought from thence gold and silver and elephants' teeth and apes and peacocks.

23 And King Solomon *exceeded* all the kings of the earth in riches and wisdom. 24 And all the earth desired to see Solomon's face, to hear his wisdom which God had given in his heart. 25 And every one brought him presents, vessels of silver and of gold, garments and *armour and* spices and horses and mules every year. 26 And Solomon gathered together chariots and horsemen, and he had a thousand four hundred chariots and twelve thousand horseman, and he bestowed them in fenced cities and with the king in Jerusalem. 27 And he made silver to be as plentiful in Jerusalem as stones and *cedars to be as common as* sycamores which grow in the plains.

5 sed colebat Salomon Astharthen, deam Sidoniorum, et
Moloch, idolum Ammanitarum. 6 Fecitque Salomon quod
non placuerat coram Domino et non adimplevit ut sequeretur Dominum sicut David pater eius. 7 Tunc aedificavit Salomon fanum Chamos, idolo Moab, in monte qui est contra
Hierusalem et Moloch, idolo filiorum Ammon. 8 Atque in
hunc modum fecit universis uxoribus suis alienigenis, quae
adolebant tura et immolabant diis suis. 9 Igitur iratus est
Dominus Salomoni quod aversa esset mens eius a Domino,
Deo Israhel, qui apparuerat ei secundo 10 et praeceperat ei
de verbo hoc ne sequeretur deos alienos, et non custodivit
quae mandavit ei Dominus. 11 Dixit itaque Dominus Salomoni, "Quia habuisti hoc apud te et non custodisti pactum
meum et praecepta mea quae mandavi tibi, disrumpens
scindam regnum tuum et dabo illud servo tuo. 12 Verumtamen in diebus tuis non faciam propter David patrem tuum;
de manu filii tui scindam illud. 13 Nec totum regnum auferam, sed tribum unam dabo filio tuo propter David, servum
meum, et Hierusalem, quam elegi."

14 Suscitavit autem Dominus adversarium Salomoni,
Adad, Idumeum de semine regio, qui erat in Edom, 15 cum
enim esset David in Idumea et ascendisset Ioab, princeps
militiae, ad sepeliendos eos qui fuerant interfecti et occidisset omne masculinum in Idumea, 16 sex enim mensibus ibi
moratus est Ioab et omnis Israhel donec interimeret omne
masculinum in Idumea, 17 fugit Adad, ipse et viri Idumei
de servis patris eius cum eo ut ingrederetur Aegyptum, erat
autem Adad puer parvulus. 18 Cumque surrexissent de Madian, venerunt in Pharan, tuleruntque secum viros de Pha-

5 but Solomon worshipped Astarte, the goddess of the Sidonians, and Molech, the idol of the Ammonites. 6 And Solomon did that which was not pleasing before the Lord and *did not fully follow* the Lord as David, his father. 7 Then Solomon built a temple for Chemosh, the idol of Moab, on the hill that is over against Jerusalem and for Molech, the idol of the children of Ammon. 8 And he did in this manner for all his wives that were strangers, who burnt incense and offered sacrifice to their gods. 9 And the Lord was angry with Solomon because his mind was turned away from the Lord, the God of Israel, who had appeared to him twice 10 and had commanded him concerning this thing that he should not follow strange gods, *but* he kept not the things which the Lord commanded him. 11 The Lord therefore said to Solomon, "Because *thou hast done this* and hast not kept my covenant and my precepts which I have commanded thee, I will divide and rend thy kingdom and will give it to thy servant. 12 Nevertheless in thy days I will not do it for David thy father's sake, *but* I will rend it out of the hand of thy son. 13 Neither will I take away the whole kingdom, but I will give one tribe to thy son for the sake of David, my servant, and Jerusalem, which I have chosen."

14 And the Lord raised up an adversary to Solomon, Hadad, the Edomite of the king's seed, *in* Edom, 15 for when David was in Edom and Joab, the general of the army, was gone up to bury them that were slain and had killed every male in Edom, 16 for Joab remained there six months *with* all Israel till he had slain every male in Edom, 17 *then* Hadad fled, he and *certain* Edomites of his father's servants with him to go into Egypt, and Hadad was *then* a little boy. 18 And *they* arose out of Midian *and* came into Paran, and they took

ran et introierunt Aegyptum ad Pharaonem, regem Aegypti, qui dedit ei domum et cibos constituit et terram delegavit. 19 Et invenit Adad gratiam coram Pharao valde in tantum ut daret ei uxorem sororem uxoris suae germanam Tafnes, reginae. 20 Genuitque ei soror Tafnes Genebath filium, et nutrivit eum Tafnes in domo Pharaonis, eratque Genebath habitans apud Pharaonem cum filiis eius. 21 Cumque audisset Adad in Aegypto dormisse David cum patribus suis et mortuum esse Ioab, principem militiae, dixit Pharaoni, "Dimitte me ut vadam in terram meam."

22 Dixitque ei Pharao, "Qua, enim, re apud me indiges te ut quaeras ire ad terram tuam?"

At ille respondit, "Nulla, sed obsecro ut dimittas me."

23 Suscitavit quoque ei Deus adversarium, Razon, filium Heliada, qui fugerat Adadezer, regem Soba, dominum suum. 24 Et congregavit contra eum viros, et factus est princeps latronum cum interficeret eos David, abieruntque Damascum et habitaverunt ibi, et constituerunt eum regem in Damasco. 25 Eratque adversarius Israhel cunctis diebus Salomonis, et hoc est malum Adad et odium contra Israhel, regnavitque in Syria.

26 Hieroboam quoque, filius Nabath, Ephratheus de Sareda, cuius mater erat nomine Sarva, mulier vidua, servus Salomonis, levavit manum contra regem. 27 Et haec causa rebellionis adversus eum, quia Salomon aedificavit Mello et coaequavit voraginem civitatis David, patris sui. 28 Erat autem Hieroboam vir fortis et potens, vidensque Salomon adulescentem bonae indolis et industrium constituerat eum

men with them from Paran and went into Egypt to Pharaoh, the king of Egypt, who gave him a house and appointed him victuals and assigned him land. 19 And Hadad found great favour before Pharaoh insomuch that he gave him to wife the own sister of his wife Tahpenes, the queen. 20 And the sister of Tahpenes bore him his son Genubath, and Tahpenes brought him up in the house of Pharaoh, and Genubath dwelt with Pharaoh among his children. 21 And when Hadad heard in Egypt that David slept with his fathers and that Joab, the general of the army, was dead, he said to Pharaoh, "Let me depart that I may go to my own country."

22 And Pharaoh said to him, "*Why*, what is wanting to thee with me that thou seekest to go to thy own country?"

But he answered, "Nothing, yet I beseech thee to let me go."

23 God also raised up against him an adversary, Rezon, the son of Eliada, who had fled from his master Hadadezer, the king of Zobah. 24 And he gathered men against him, and he became a captain of robbers when David slew them *of Zobah*, and they went to Damascus and dwelt there, and they made him king in Damascus. 25 And he was an adversary to Israel all the days of Solomon, and this is the evil of Hadad and his hatred against Israel, and he reigned in Syria.

26 Jeroboam also, the son of Nebat, an Ephraimite of Zeredah, a servant of Solomon, whose mother was named Zeruah, a widow woman, lifted up his hand against the king. 27 And this is the cause of his rebellion against him, for Solomon built Millo and filled up the breach of the city of David, his father. 28 And Jeroboam was a valiant and mighty man, and Solomon seeing him a young man ingenious and industrious made him chief over the tributes of all the house

praefectum super tributa universae domus Ioseph. 29 Factum est igitur in tempore illo ut Hieroboam egrederetur de Hierusalem, et inveniret eum Ahias, Silonites, propheta in via opertus pallio novo, erant autem duo tantum in agro. 30 Adprehendensque Ahia pallium suum novum quo opertus erat scidit in duodecim partes, 31 et ait ad Hieroboam, "Tolle tibi decem scissuras, haec enim dicit Dominus, Deus Israhel, 'Ecce: ego scindam regnum de manu Salomonis et dabo tibi decem tribus, 32 porro una tribus remanebit ei propter servum meum David et Hierusalem, civitatem quam elegi ex omnibus tribubus Israhel, 33 eo quod dereliquerit me et adoraverit Astarthen, deam Sidoniorum, et Chamos, deum Moab, et Moloch, deum filiorum Ammon, et non ambulaverit in viis meis ut faceret iustitiam coram me et praecepta mea et iudicia sicut David, pater eius. 34 Nec auferam omne regnum de manu eius, sed ducem ponam eum cunctis diebus vitae suae propter David servum meum quem elegi, qui custodivit mandata mea et praecepta mea. 35 Auferam autem regnum de manu filii eius et dabo tibi decem tribus, 36 filio autem eius dabo tribum unam ut remaneat lucerna David servo meo cunctis diebus coram me in Hierusalem, civitatem quam elegi ut esset nomen meum ibi. 37 Te autem adsumam, et regnabis super omnia quae desiderat anima tua, erisque rex super Israhel. 38 Si igitur audieris omnia quae praecepero tibi, et ambulaveris in viis meis et feceris quod rectum est coram me custodiens mandata mea et praecepta mea sicut fecit David, servus meus, ero tecum et aedificabo tibi domum fidelem quomodo aedificavi David domum, et

of Joseph. 29 So it came to pass at that time that Jeroboam went out of Jerusalem, and the prophet Ahijah, the Shilonite, clad with a new garment found him in the way, and they two were alone in the field. 30 And Ahijah taking his new garment wherewith he was clad divided it into twelve parts, 31 and he said to Jeroboam, "Take to thee ten pieces, for thus saith the Lord, the God of Israel, 'Behold: I will rend the kingdom out of the hand of Solomon and will give thee ten tribes, 32 but one tribe shall remain to him for the sake of my servant David and Jerusalem, the city which I have chosen out of all the tribes of Israel, 33 because he hath forsaken me and hath adored Astarte, the goddess of the Sidonians, and Chemosh, the god of Moab, and Molech, the god of the children of Ammon, and hath not walked in my ways to do justice before me and *to keep* my precepts and judgments as did David, his father. 34 Yet I will not take away all the kingdom out of his hand, but I will make him prince all the days of his life for David my servant's sake whom I chose, who kept my commandments and my precepts. 35 But I will take away the kingdom out of his son's hand and will give thee ten tribes, 36 and to his son I will give one tribe that there may remain a lamp for my servant David before me always in Jerusalem, the city which I have chosen that my name might be there. 37 And I will take thee, and thou shalt reign over all that thy soul desireth, and thou shalt be king over Israel. 38 If then thou wilt hearken to all that I shall command thee and wilt walk in my ways and do what is right before me, keeping my commandments and my precepts as David, my servant, did, I will be with thee and will build thee up a faithful house as I built a house for David, and I

tradam tibi Israhel, 39 et adfligam semen David super hoc, verumtamen non cunctis diebus.'"

40 Voluit ergo Salomon interficere Hieroboam, qui surrexit et aufugit in Aegyptum ad Susac, regem Aegypti, et fuit in Aegypto usque ad mortem Salomonis. 41 Reliquum autem verborum Salomonis et omnia quae fecit et sapientia eius, ecce: universa scripta sunt in Libro Verborum Dierum Salomonis. 42 Dies autem quos regnavit Salomon in Hierusalem super omnem Israhel quadraginta anni sunt. 43 Dormivitque Salomon cum patribus suis et sepultus est in civitate David, patris sui, regnavitque Roboam, filius eius, pro eo.

Caput 12

Venit autem Roboam in Sychem, illuc enim congregatus erat omnis Israhel ad constituendum eum regem. 2 At Hieroboam, filius Nabath, cum adhuc esset in Aegypto, profugus a facie Regis Salomonis, audita morte eius reversus est de Aegypto. 3 Miseruntque et vocaverunt eum; venit ergo Hieroboam et omnis multitudo Israhel et locuti sunt ad Roboam, dicentes, 4 "Pater tuus durissimum iugum inposuit nobis; tu, itaque, nunc inminue paululum de imperio

will deliver Israel to thee, 39 and I will for this afflict the seed of David, but yet not for ever.'"

40 Solomon therefore sought to kill Jeroboam, but he arose and fled into Egypt to Shishak, the king of Egypt, and was in Egypt till the death of Solomon. 41 And the rest of the words of Solomon and all that he did and his wisdom, behold: they are all written in the Book of the Words of the Days of Solomon. 42 And the days that Solomon reigned in Jerusalem over all Israel were forty years. 43 And Solomon slept with his fathers and was buried in the city of David, his father, and Rehoboam, his son, reigned in his stead.

Chapter 12

Rehoboam, following the counsel of young men, alienateth
from him the minds of the people. They make Jeroboam
king over ten tribes. He setteth up idolatry.

And Rehoboam went to Shechem, for thither were all Israel come together to make him king. 2 But Jeroboam, the son of Nebat, who was yet in Egypt, a fugitive from the face of King Solomon, hearing of his death returned out of Egypt. 3 And they sent and called him, and Jeroboam came and all the multitude of Israel and they spoke to Rehoboam, saying, 4 "Thy father laid a grievous yoke upon us; now, therefore, do thou take off a little of the grievous service of

patris tui durissimo et de iugo gravissimo quod inposuit nobis, et serviemus tibi."

5 Qui ait eis, "Ite usque ad tertium diem, et revertimini ad me." Cumque abisset populus, 6 iniit consilium Rex Roboam cum senibus qui adsistebant coram Salomone, patre eius, dum adhuc viveret, et ait, "Quod mihi datis consilium ut respondeam populo huic?"

7 Qui dixerunt ei, "Si hodie oboedieris populo huic et servieris et petitioni eorum cesseris locutusque fueris ad eos verba lenia, erunt tibi servi cunctis diebus."

8 Qui dereliquit consilium senum quod dederant ei et adhibuit adulescentes qui nutriti fuerant cum eo et adsistebant illi. 9 Dixitque ad eos, "Quod mihi datis consilium ut respondeam populo huic qui dixerunt mihi, 'Levius fac iugum quod inposuit pater tuus super nos?'"

10 Et dixerunt ei iuvenes qui nutriti fuerant cum eo, "Sic loquere populo huic qui locuti sunt ad te, dicentes, 'Pater tuus adgravavit iugum nostrum; tu releva nos.' Sic loqueris ad eos: 'Minimus digitus meus grossior est dorso patris mei. 11 Et nunc pater meus posuit super vos iugum grave, ego autem addam super iugum vestrum; pater meus cecidit vos flagellis, ego autem caedam vos scorpionibus.'"

12 Venit ergo Hieroboam et omnis populus ad Roboam die tertia sicut locutus fuerat rex, dicens, "Revertimini ad me die tertia." 13 Responditque rex populo dura, derelicto consilio seniorum quod ei dederant, 14 et locutus est eis secundum consilium iuvenum, dicens, "Pater meus adgravavit iugum vestrum, ego autem addam iugo vestro; pater meus

thy father and of his most heavy yoke which he put upon us, and we will serve thee."

5 And he said to them, "Go till the third day, and come to me again." And when the people was gone, 6 King Rehoboam took counsel with the old men that stood before Solomon, his father, while he yet lived, and he said, "What counsel do you give me that I may answer this people?"

7 They said to him, "If thou wilt yield to this people today and condescend to them and grant their petition and wilt speak gentle words to them, they will be thy servants always."

8 But he left the counsel of the old men which they had given him and consulted with the young men that had been brought up with him and stood before him. 9 And he said to them, "What counsel do you give me that I may answer this people who have said to me, 'Make the yoke which thy father put upon us lighter?'"

10 And the young men that had been brought up with him said, "Thus *shalt thou speak* to this people who have spoken to thee, saying, 'Thy father made our yoke heavy; do thou ease us.' *Thou* shalt say to them, 'My little finger is thicker than the back of my father. 11 And now my father put a heavy yoke upon you, but I will add to your yoke; my father beat you with whips, but I will beat you with scorpions.'"

12 So Jeroboam and all the people came to Rehoboam the third day as the king had appointed, saying, "Come to me again the third day." 13 And the king answered the people roughly, leaving the counsel of the old men which they had given him, 14 and he spoke to them according to the counsel of the young men, saying, "My father made your yoke heavy, but I will add to your yoke; my father beat you with whips,

cecidit vos flagellis, ego autem caedam vos scorpionibus."
15 Et non adquievit rex populo, quoniam aversatus eum fuerat Dominus ut suscitaret verbum suum quod locutus fuerat
in manu Ahiae, Silonitae, ad Hieroboam, filium Nabath.

16 Videns itaque populus quod noluisset eos audire rex
respondit ei, dicens, "Quae nobis pars in David? Vel quae
hereditas in filio Isai? Vade in tabernacula tua, Israhel; nunc,
vide domum tuam, David." Et abiit Israhel in tabernacula
sua. 17 Super filios autem Israhel quicumque habitabant in
civitatibus Iuda, regnavit Roboam. 18 Misit igitur Rex Roboam Aduram qui erat super tributa, et lapidavit eum omnis
Israhel, et mortuus est. Porro rex Roboam festinus ascendit
currum, et fugit in Hierusalem.

19 Recessitque Israhel a domo David usque in praesentem diem. 20 Factum est autem cum audisset omnis Israhel
quod reversus esset Hieroboam miserunt et vocaverunt eum
congregato coetu et constituerunt regem super omnem Israhel, nec secutus est quisquam domum David praeter tribum Iuda solam. 21 Venit autem Roboam Hierusalem et
congregavit universam domum Iuda et tribum Beniamin,
centum octoginta milia electorum virorum bellatorum, ut
pugnaret contra domum Israhel et reduceret regnum Roboam, filio Salomonis. 22 Factus est vero sermo Domini ad
Semeiam, virum Dei, dicens, 23 "Loquere ad Roboam, filium
Salomonis, regem Iuda, et ad omnem domum Iuda et Beniamin et reliquos de populo, dicens, 24 'Haec dicit Dominus:
"Non ascendetis nec bellabitis contra fratres vestros, filios
Israhel. Revertatur vir in domum suam, a me enim factum

but I will beat you with scorpions." 15 And the king conde-
scended not to the people, for the Lord was turned away
from him to make good his word which he had spoken in
the hand of Ahijah, the Shilonite, to Jeroboam, the son of
Nebat.

16 Then the people seeing that the king would not hearken to them answered him, saying, "What portion have we
in David? Or what inheritance in the son of Jesse? Go home
to thy dwellings, O Israel; now, David, look to thy own
house." So Israel departed to their dwellings. 17 But as for
all the children of Israel that dwelt in the cities of Judah, Rehoboam reigned over them. 18 Then King Rehoboam sent
Adoram who was over the tribute, and all Israel stoned him,
and he died. Wherefore King Rehoboam made haste to get
him up into his chariot, and he fled to Jerusalem.

19 And Israel revolted from the house of David unto this
day. 20 And it came to pass when all Israel heard that Jeroboam was come again that they gathered an assembly and
sent and called him and made him king over all Israel, and
there was none that followed the house of David but the
tribe of Judah only. 21 And Rehoboam came to Jerusalem and
gathered together all the house of Judah and the tribe of
Benjamin, a hundred four-score thousand chosen men for
war, to fight against the house of Israel and to bring the
kingdom again under Rehoboam, the son of Solomon. 22 But
the word of the Lord came to Shimeias, the man of God,
saying, 23 "Speak to Rehoboam, the son of Solomon, the
king of Judah, and to all the house of Judah and Benjamin
and the rest of the people, saying, 24 'Thus saith the Lord:
"You shall not go up nor fight against your brethren, the
children of Israel. Let every man return to his house, for this

est verbum hoc.""" Audierunt sermonem Domini et reversi sunt de itinere sicut eis praeceperat Dominus.

25 Aedificavit autem Hieroboam Sychem in Monte Ephraim et habitavit ibi, et egressus inde aedificavit Phanuhel. 26 Dixitque Hieroboam in corde suo, "Nunc revertetur regnum ad domum David, 27 si ascenderit populus iste ut faciat sacrificia in domo Domini in Hierusalem, et convertetur cor populi huius ad dominum suum Roboam, regem Iuda, interficientque me et revertentur ad eum." 28 Et excogitato consilio fecit duos vitulos aureos et dixit eis, "Nolite ultra ascendere in Hierusalem. Ecce dii tui, Israhel, qui eduxerunt te de terra Aegypti." 29 Posuitque unum in Bethel et alterum in Dan. 30 Et factum est verbum hoc in peccatum, ibat enim populus ad adorandum vitulum usque in Dan. 31 Et fecit fana in excelsis et sacerdotes de extremis populi qui non erant de filiis Levi. 32 Constituitque diem sollemnem in mense octavo quintadecima die mensis in similitudinem sollemnitatis quae celebrabatur in Iuda. Et ascendens altare, similiter fecit in Bethel ut immolaret vitulis quos fabricatus fuerat, constituitque in Bethel sacerdotes excelsorum quae fecerat. 33 Et ascendit super altare quod extruxerat in Bethel quintadecima die mensis octavi quem finxerat de corde suo, et fecit sollemnitatem filiis Israhel et ascendit super altare ut adoleret incensum.

thing is from me."'" They hearkened to the word of the Lord and returned from their journey as the Lord had commanded them.

25 And Jeroboam built Shechem in Mount Ephraim and dwelt there, and going out from thence he built Penuel. 26 And Jeroboam said in his heart, "Now shall the kingdom return to the house of David, 27 if this people go up to offer sacrifices in the house of the Lord at Jerusalem, and the heart of this people will turn to their lord Rehoboam, the king of Judah, and they will kill me and return to him." 28 And finding out a device he made two golden calves and said to them, "Go ye up no more to Jerusalem. Behold thy gods, O Israel, who brought thee out of the land of Egypt." 29 And he set the one in Bethel and the other in Dan. 30 And this thing became an occasion of sin, for the people went to adore the calf as far as Dan. 31 And he made temples in the high places and priests of the lowest of the people who were not of the sons of Levi. 32 And he appointed a *feast* in the eighth month on the fifteenth day of the month after the manner of the feast that was celebrated in Judah. And going up to the altar, he did in like manner in Bethel to sacrifice to the calves which he had made, and he placed in Bethel priests of the high places which he had made. 33 And he went *up to* the altar which he had built in Bethel on the fifteenth day of the eighth month which he had devised of his own heart, and he ordained a feast to the children of Israel and went upon the altar to burn incense.

Caput 13

Et ecce: vir Dei venit de Iuda in sermone Domini in Bethel Hieroboam stante super altare et tus iaciente. 2 Et exclamavit contra altare in sermone Domini et ait, "Altare, altare, haec dicit Dominus: 'Ecce: filius nascetur domui David, Iosias nomine, et immolabit super te sacerdotes excelsorum qui nunc in te tura succendunt, et ossa hominum incendet super te.'" 3 Deditque in die illa signum, dicens, "Hoc erit signum quod locutus est Dominus: 'Ecce: altare scindetur, et effundetur cinis qui in eo est.'"

4 Cumque audisset rex sermonem hominis Dei quem inclamaverat contra altare in Bethel, extendit manum suam de altari, dicens, "Adprehendite eum." Et exaruit manus eius quam extenderat contra eum, nec valuit retrahere eam ad se. 5 Altare quoque scissum est, et effusus cinis de altari iuxta signum quod praedixerat vir Dei in sermone Domini. 6 Et

Chapter 13

A prophet sent from Judah to Bethel foretelleth the birth of
Josiah and the destruction of Jeroboam's altar. Jeroboam's
hand offering violence to the prophet withereth but is
restored by the prophet's prayer. The same prophet is
deceived by another prophet and slain by a lion.

And behold: there came a man of God out of Judah by
the word of the Lord to Bethel when Jeroboam was standing upon the altar and burning incense. 2 And he cried out
against the altar in the word of the Lord and said, "O altar,
altar, thus saith the Lord: 'Behold: a child shall be born to
the house of David, Josiah by name, and he shall immolate
upon thee the priests of the high places who now burn incense upon thee, and he shall burn men's bones upon thee.'"
3 And he gave a sign the same day, saying, "This shall be the
sign that the Lord hath spoken: 'Behold: the altar shall be
rent, and the ashes that are upon it shall be poured out.'"

4 And when the king had heard the word of the man of
God which he had cried out against the altar in Bethel, he
stretched forth his hand from the altar, saying, "Lay hold
on him." And his hand which he stretched forth against
him withered, and he was not able to draw it back again to
him. 5 The altar also was rent, and the ashes were poured out
from the altar according to the sign which the man of God
had *given* before in the word of the Lord. 6 And the king said

ait rex ad virum Dei, "Deprecare faciem Domini, Dei tui, et ora pro me ut restituatur manus mea mihi." Oravitque vir Dei faciem Domini, et reversa est manus regis ad eum, et facta est sicut prius fuerat. 7 Locutus est autem rex ad virum Dei, "Veni mecum domum ut prandeas, et dabo tibi munera."

8 Responditque vir Dei ad regem, "Si dederis mihi mediam partem domus tuae, non veniam tecum nec comedam panem neque bibam aquam in loco isto, 9 sic enim mandatum est mihi in sermone Domini praecipientis, 'Non comedes panem neque bibes aquam nec reverteris per viam qua venisti.'" 10 Abiit ergo per aliam viam et non est reversus per iter quo venerat in Bethel.

11 Prophetes autem quidam senex habitabat in Bethel, ad quem venerunt filii sui et narraverunt ei omnia opera quae fecerat vir Dei illa die in Bethel, et verba quae locutus fuerat ad regem narraverunt patri suo. 12 Et dixit eis pater eorum, "Per quam viam abiit?" Ostenderunt ei filii sui viam per quam abierat vir Dei qui venerat de Iuda. 13 Et ait filiis suis, "Sternite mihi asinum." Qui cum stravissent, ascendit 14 et abiit post virum Dei et invenit eum sedentem subtus terebinthum, et ait illi, "Tune es vir Dei qui venisti de Iuda?"

Respondit ille, "Ego sum."

15 Dixitque ad eum, "Veni mecum domum ut comedas panem."

to the man of God, "Entreat the face of the Lord, thy God, and pray for me that my hand may be restored to me." And the man of God besought the face of the Lord, and the king's hand was restored to him, and it became as it was before. 7 And the king said to the man of God, "Come home with me to dine, and I will *make* thee presents."

8 And the man of God answered the king, "If thou wouldst give me half thy house, I will not go with thee nor eat bread nor drink water in this place, 9 for so it was enjoined me by the word of the Lord commanding *me,* 'Thou shalt not eat bread nor drink water nor return by the *same* way that thou camest.'" 10 So he departed by another way and returned not by the way that he came into Bethel.

11 Now a certain old prophet dwelt in Bethel, and his sons came to him and told him all the works that the man of God had done that day in Bethel, and they told their father the words which he had spoken to the king. 12 And their father said to them, "What way went he?" His sons shewed him the way by which the man of God went who came out of Judah. 13 And he said to his sons, "Saddle me the ass." And when they had saddled him, he got up 14 and went after the man of God and found him sitting under a turpentine tree, and he said to him, "Art thou the man of God that camest from Judah?"

He answered, "I am."

15 And he said to him, "Come home with me to eat bread."

16 Qui ait, "Non possum reverti neque venire tecum, nec comedam panem nec bibam aquam in loco isto 17 quia locutus est Dominus ad me in sermone Domini, dicens, 'Non comedes panem, et non bibes ibi aquam nec reverteris per viam qua ieris.'"

18 Qui ait illi, "Et ego propheta sum similis tui, et angelus locutus est mihi in sermone Domini, dicens, 'Reduc eum tecum in domum tuam ut comedat panem et bibat aquam.'" Fefellit eum 19 et reduxit secum, comedit ergo panem in domo eius et bibit aquam. 20 Cumque sederent ad mensam factus est sermo Domini ad prophetam qui reduxerat eum, 21 et exclamavit ad virum Dei qui venerat de Iuda, dicens, "Haec dicit Dominus: 'Quia non oboediens fuisti ori Domini et non custodisti mandatum quod praecepit tibi Dominus, Deus tuus, 22 et reversus es et comedisti panem et bibisti aquam in loco in quo praecepit tibi ne comederes panem neque biberes aquam, non inferetur cadaver tuum in sepulchrum patrum tuorum.'" 23 Cumque comedisset et bibisset, stravit asinum suum prophetae quem reduxerat.

24 Qui cum abisset, invenit eum leo in via et occidit, et erat cadaver eius proiectum in itinere, asinus autem stabat iuxta illum, et leo stabat iuxta cadaver. 25 Et ecce: viri transeuntes viderunt cadaver proiectum in via et leonem stantem iuxta cadaver. Et venerunt et divulgaverunt in civitate in qua prophetes senex ille habitabat. 26 Quod cum audisset

16 But he said, "I *must* not return nor go with thee, neither will I eat bread nor drink water in this place 17 because the Lord spoke to me in the word of the Lord, saying, 'Thou shalt not eat bread, and thou shalt not drink water there nor return by the way thou wentest.'"

18 He said to him, "I also am a prophet like unto thee, and an angel spoke to me in the word of the Lord, saying, 'Bring him back with thee into thy house that he may eat bread and drink water.'" He deceived him 19 and brought him back with him, so he ate bread and drank water in his house.

20 And as they sat at table the word of the Lord came to the prophet that brought him back, 21 and he cried out to the man of God who came out of Judah, saying, "Thus saith the Lord: 'Because thou hast not been obedient *to* the Lord and hast not kept the commandment which the Lord, thy God, commanded thee 22 and hast returned and eaten bread and drunk water in the place wherein he commanded thee that thou shouldst not eat bread nor drink water, thy dead body shall not be brought into the sepulchre of thy fathers.'" 23 And when he had eaten and drunk, he saddled his ass for the prophet whom he had brought back.

24 And when he was gone, a lion found him in the way and killed him, and his body was cast in the way, and the ass stood by him, and the lion stood by the dead body. 25 And behold: men passing by saw the dead body cast in the way and the lion standing by the body. And they came and told it in the city wherein that old prophet dwelt. 26 And when that

propheta ille qui reduxerat eum de via, ait, "Vir Dei est qui inoboediens fuit ori Domini, et tradidit eum Dominus leoni, et confregit eum et occidit iuxta verbum Domini quod locutus est ei." 27 Dixitque ad filios suos, "Sternite mihi asinum." Qui cum stravissent 28 et ille abisset, invenit cadaver eius proiectum in via et asinum et leonem stantes iuxta cadaver. Non comedit leo de cadavere nec laesit asinum.

29 Tulit ergo prophetes cadaver viri Dei et posuit illud super asinum et reversus intulit in civitatem prophetae senis ut plangerent eum. 30 Et posuit cadaver eius in sepulchro suo, et planxerunt eum, "Heu! Heu, mi frater!"

31 Cumque planxissent eum, dixit ad filios suos, "Cum mortuus fuero, sepelite me in sepulchro in quo vir Dei sepultus est. Iuxta ossa eius ponite ossa mea, 32 profecto enim veniet sermo quem praedixit in sermone Domini contra altare quod est in Bethel et contra omnia fana excelsorum quae sunt in urbibus Samariae." 33 Post verba haec non est reversus Hieroboam de via sua pessima, sed e contrario fecit de novissimis populi sacerdotes excelsorum. Quicumque volebat, implebat manum suam, et fiebat sacerdos excelsorum. 34 Et propter hanc causam peccavit domus Hieroboam et eversa est et deleta de superficie terrae.

prophet who had brought him back out of the way heard of it, he said, "It is the man of God that was disobedient to the mouth of the Lord, and the Lord hath delivered him to the lion, and he hath torn him and killed him according to the word of the Lord which he spoke to him." 27 And he said to his sons, "Saddle me an ass." And when they had saddled it 28 and he was gone, he found *the* dead body cast in the way and the ass and the lion standing by the carcass. The lion had not eaten of the dead body nor hurt the ass.

29 And the prophet took up the body of the man of God and laid it upon the ass and going back brought it into the city of the old prophet *to* mourn for him. 30 And he laid his dead body in his own sepulchre, and they mourned over him, *saying,* "Alas! Alas, my brother!"

31 And when they had mourned over him, he said to his sons, "When I am dead, bury me in the sepulchre wherein the man of God is buried. Lay my bones beside his bones, 32 for assuredly the word shall come to pass which he hath foretold in the word of the Lord against the altar that is in Bethel and against all the temples of the high places that are in the cities of Samaria." 33 After these words Jeroboam came not back from his wicked way, but on the contrary he made of the meanest of the people priests of the high places. Whosoever would, he filled his hand, and he was made a priest of the high places. 34 And for this cause did the house of Jeroboam sin and was cut off and destroyed from the face of the earth.

Caput 14

In tempore illo aegrotavit Abia, filius Hieroboam, 2 dixit-que Hieroboam uxori suae, "Surge, et commuta habitum ne cognoscaris quod sis uxor Hieroboam, et vade in Silo ubi est Ahia, propheta, qui locutus est mihi quod regnaturus essem super populum hunc. 3 Tolle quoque in manu tua decem pa-nes et crustula et vas mellis, et vade ad illum, ipse enim indi-cabit tibi quid eventurum sit huic puero."

4 Fecit ut dixerat uxor Hieroboam et consurgens abiit in Silo et venit in domum Ahia, at ille non poterat videre, quia caligaverant oculi eius prae senectute. 5 Dixit autem Domi-nus ad Ahiam, "Ecce: uxor Hieroboam ingreditur ut consu-lat te super filio suo qui aegrotat; haec et haec loqueris ei."

Cum ergo illa intraret et dissimularet se esse quae erat, 6 audivit Ahias sonitum pedum eius introeuntis per ostium et ait, "Ingredere, uxor Hieroboam. Quare aliam esse te si-mulas? Ego autem missus sum ad te durus nuntius. 7 Vade, et dic Hieroboam, 'Haec dicit Dominus, Deus Israhel: "Quia exaltavi te de medio populi et dedi te principem super po-

Chapter 14

Ahijah prophesieth the destruction of the family of Jeroboam. He dieth and is succeeded by his son Nadab. The king of Egypt taketh and pillageth Jerusalem. Rehoboam dieth, and his son Abijam succeedeth.

At that time Abijah, the son of Jeroboam, fell sick, 2 and Jeroboam said to his wife, "Arise, and change thy dress that thou be not known to be the wife of Jeroboam, and go to Shiloh where Ahijah, the prophet, is who told me that I should reign over this people. 3 Take also *with thee* ten loaves and cracknels and a pot of honey, and go to him, for he will tell thee what shall become of this child."

4 Jeroboam's wife did as he told her and rising up went to Shiloh and came to the house of Ahijah, but he could not see, for his eyes were dim by reason of his age. 5 And the Lord said to Ahijah, "Behold: the wife of Jeroboam cometh in to consult thee concerning her son that is sick; thus and thus shalt thou speak to her."

So when she was coming in and made as if she were another woman, 6 Ahijah heard the sound of her feet coming in at the door and said, "Come in, thou wife of Jeroboam. Why dost thou feign thyself to be another? But I am sent to thee with heavy tidings. 7 Go, and tell Jeroboam, 'Thus saith the Lord, the God of Israel: "Forasmuch as I exalted thee from among the people and made thee prince over my peo-

pulum meum Israhel 8 et scidi regnum domus David et dedi illud tibi, et non fuisti sicut servus meus David qui custodivit mandata mea et secutus est me in toto corde suo, faciens quod placitum esset in conspectu meo, 9 sed operatus es malum super omnes qui fuerunt ante te et fecisti tibi deos alienos et conflatiles ut me ad iracundiam provocares me autem proiecisti post corpus tuum, 10 idcirco ecce: ego inducam mala super domum Hieroboam et percutiam de Hieroboam mingentem ad parietem et clausum et novissimum in Israhel, et mundabo reliquias domus Hieroboam sicut mundari solet fimus usque ad purum. 11 Qui mortui fuerint de Hieroboam in civitate comedent eos canes, qui autem mortui fuerint in agro vorabunt eos aves caeli, quia Dominus locutus est. 12 Tu igitur surge, et vade in domum tuam, et in ipso introitu pedum tuorum in urbem, morietur puer, 13 et planget eum omnis Israhel et sepeliet, iste enim solus inferetur de Hieroboam in sepulchrum, quia inventus est super eo sermo bonus a Domino, Deo Israhel, in domo Hieroboam. 14 Constituet autem sibi Dominus regem super Israhel qui percutiet domum Hieroboam in hac die et in hoc tempore, 15 et percutiet Dominus Deus Israhel sicut moveri solet harundo in aqua, et evellet Israhel de terra bona hac quam dedit patribus eorum et ventilabit eos trans Flumen quia fecerunt sibi lucos ut inritarent Dominum. 16 Et tradet Dominus Israhel propter peccata Hieroboam qui peccavit et peccare fecit Israhel."

17 Surrexit itaque uxor Hieroboam et abiit et venit in Thersa, cumque illa ingrederetur limen domus, puer mortuus est, 18 et sepelierunt eum. Et planxit illum omnis Isra-

ple Israel 8 and rent the kingdom *away from* the house of David and gave it to thee, and thou hast not been as my servant David who kept my commandments and followed me with all his heart, doing that which was well pleasing in my sight, 9 but hast done evil above all that were before thee and hast made thee strange gods and molten gods to provoke me to anger and hast cast me behind thy back, 10 therefore behold: I will bring evils upon the house of Jeroboam and will cut off from Jeroboam him that pisseth against the wall and him that is shut up and the last in Israel, and I will sweep away the remnant of the house of Jeroboam as dung is swept away till *all be* clean. 11 Them that shall die of Jeroboam in the city the dogs shall eat, and them that shall die in the field the birds of the air shall devour, for the Lord hath spoken it. 12 Arise thou therefore, and go to thy house, and when thy feet shall be entering into the city, the child shall die, 13 and all Israel shall mourn for him and shall bury him, for he only of Jeroboam shall be laid in a sepulchre, because in his regard there is found a good word from the Lord, the God of Israel, in the house of Jeroboam. 14 And the Lord hath appointed himself a king over Israel who shall cut off the house of Jeroboam in this day and in this time, 15 and the Lord God shall strike Israel as a reed is shaken in the water, and he shall root up Israel out of this good land which he gave to their fathers and shall scatter them beyond the *river* because they have made to themselves groves to provoke the Lord. 16 And the Lord shall give up Israel for the sins of Jeroboam who hath sinned and made Israel to sin."

17 And the wife of Jeroboam arose and departed and came to Tirzah, and when she was coming in to the threshold of the house, the child died, 18 and they buried him. And all Is-

hel iuxta sermonem Domini quem locutus est in manu servi sui Ahiae, prophetae. 19 Reliqua autem verborum Hieroboam, quomodo pugnaverit et quomodo regnaverit, ecce: scripta sunt in Libro Verborum Dierum Regum Israhel. 20 Dies autem quibus regnavit Hieroboam viginti duo anni sunt, et dormivit cum patribus suis, regnavitque Nadab, filius eius, pro eo. 21 Porro Roboam, filius Salomonis, regnavit in Iuda. Quadraginta et unius anni erat Roboam cum regnare coepisset; decem et septem annis regnavit in Hierusalem, civitatem quam elegit Dominus ut poneret nomen suum ibi ex omnibus tribubus Israhel. Nomen autem matris eius Naama, Ammanites.

22 Et fecit Iudas malum coram Domino et inritaverunt eum super omnibus quae fecerant patres eorum in peccatis suis quae peccaverunt, 23 aedificaverunt enim et ipsi sibi aras et statuas et lucos super omnem collem excelsum et subter omnem arborem frondosam. 24 Sed et effeminati fuerunt in terra, feceruntque omnes abominationes gentium quas adtrivit Dominus ante faciem filiorum Israhel.

25 In quinto autem anno regni Roboam, ascendit Sesac, rex Aegypti, in Hierusalem. 26 Et tulit thesauros domus Domini et thesauros regios et universa diripuit, scuta quoque aurea quae fecerat Salomon. 27 Pro quibus fecit rex Roboam scuta aerea et tradidit ea in manum ducum scutariorum et eorum qui excubabant ante ostium domus regis. 28 Cumque ingrederetur rex in domum Domini, portabant ea qui praeeundi habebant officium, et postea reportabant ad ar-

rael mourned for him according to the word of the Lord which he spoke by the hand of his servant Ahijah, the prophet. 19 And the rest of the acts of Jeroboam, how he fought and how he reigned, behold: they are written in the Book of the Words of the Days of the Kings of Israel. 20 And the days that Jeroboam reigned were two and twenty years, and he slept with his fathers, and Nadab, his son, reigned in his stead. 21 And Rehoboam, the son of Solomon, reigned in Judah. Rehoboam was one and forty years old when he began to reign, *and* he reigned seventeen years in Jerusalem, the city which the Lord chose out of all the tribes of Israel to put his name there. And his mother's name was Naamah, an Ammonitess.

22 And Judah did evil in the sight of the Lord and provoked him above all that their fathers had done in their sins which they committed, 23 for they also built them altars and statues and groves upon every high hill and under every green tree. 24 There were also the effeminate in the land, and they did *according to* all the abominations of the people whom the Lord had destroyed before the face of the children of Israel.

25 And in the fifth year of the reign of Rehoboam, Shishak, king of Egypt, came up against Jerusalem. 26 And he took away the treasures of the house of the Lord and the king's treasures and carried all off, *as* also the shields of gold which Solomon had made. 27 And Rehoboam made shields of brass instead of them and delivered them into the hand of the captains of the shieldbearers and of them that kept watch before the gate of the king's house. 28 And when the king went into the house of the Lord, they whose office it was to go before him carried them, and afterwards they brought

6 Attamen bellum fuit inter Roboam et Hieroboam omni tempore vitae eius, 7 reliqua autem sermonum Abiam et omnia quae fecit, nonne haec scripta sunt in Libro Verborum Dierum Regum Iuda? Fuitque proelium inter Abiam et Hieroboam. 8 Et dormivit Abiam cum patribus suis, et sepelierunt eum in civitate David, regnavitque Asa, filius eius, pro eo. 9 In anno ergo vicesimo Hieroboam, regis Israhel, regnavit Asa, rex Iuda, 10 et quadraginta et uno anno regnavit in Hierusalem. Nomen matris eius Maacha, filia Abessalom. 11 Et fecit Asa rectum ante conspectum Domini, sicut David, pater eius, 12 et abstulit effeminatos de terra, purgavitque universas sordes idolorum quae fecerant patres eius. 13 Insuper et Maacham, matrem suam, amovit ne esset princeps in sacris Priapi et in luco quem consecraverat, subvertitque specum eius et confregit simulacrum turpissimum et conbusit in torrente Cedron, 14 excelsa autem non abstulit. Verumtamen cor Asa perfectum erat cum Domino cunctis diebus suis, 15 et intulit ea quae sanctificaverat pater suus et voverat in domum Domini, argentum et aurum et vasa.

16 Bellum autem erat inter Asa et Baasa, regem Israhel, cunctis diebus eorum. 17 Ascendit quoque Baasa, rex Israhel, in Iudam et aedificavit Rama ut non posset quispiam egredi vel ingredi de parte Asa, regis Iudae. 18 Tollens itaque Asa omne argentum et aurum quod remanserat in thesauris domus Domini et in thesauris domus regiae dedit illud in manus servorum suorum et misit ad Benadad, filium Tabremmon, filii Ezion, regem Syriae, qui habitabat in Damasco, dicens, 19 "Foedus est inter me et te et inter patrem meum

6 But there was war between Rehoboam and Jeroboam all the time of his life, 7 and the rest of the words of Abijam and all that he did, are they not written in the Book of the Words of the Days of the Kings of Judah? And there was war between Abijam and Jeroboam. 8 And Abijam slept with his fathers, and they buried him in the city of David, and Asa, his son, reigned in his stead. 9 So in the twentieth year of Jeroboam, king of Israel, reigned Asa, king of Judah, 10 and he reigned one and forty years in Jerusalem. His mother's name was Maacah, the daughter of Abishalom. 11 And Asa did that which was right in the sight of the Lord, as did David, his father, 12 and he took away the effeminate out of the land, and he removed all the filth of the idols which his fathers had made. 13 Moreover he also removed his mother, Maacah, from being the princess in the sacrifices of Priapus and in the grove which she had consecrated *to him,* and he destroyed her den and broke in pieces the filthy idol and burnt it *by* the torrent Kidron, 14 but the high places he did not take away. Nevertheless the heart of Asa was perfect with the Lord all his days, 15 and he brought in the things which his father had dedicated and he had vowed into the house of the Lord, silver and gold and vessels.

16 And there was war between Asa and Baasha, king of Israel, all their days. 17 And Baasha, king of Israel, went up against Judah and built Ramah that no man might go out or come in of the side of Asa, king of Judah. 18 Then Asa took all the silver and gold that remained in the treasures of the house of the Lord and in the treasures of the king's house and delivered it into the hands of his servants and sent them to Ben-hadad, son of Tabrimmon, the son of Hezion, king of Syria, who dwelt in Damascus, saying, 19 "There is a league

et patrem tuum, ideo misi tibi munera argentum et aurum, et peto ut venias et irritum facias foedus quod habes cum Baasa, rege Israhel, et recedat a me."

20 Adquiescens Benadad Regi Asa misit principes exercitus sui in civitates Israhel, et percusserunt Ahion et Dan et Abel domum Maacha et universam Cenneroth, omnem, scilicet, terram Nepthalim. 21 Quod cum audisset Baasa, intermisit aedificare Rama et reversus est in Thersa. 22 Rex autem Asa nuntium misit in omnem Iudam, dicens, "Nemo sit excusatus." Et tulerunt lapides de Rama et ligna eius quibus aedificaverat Baasa, et extruxit de eis rex Asa Gaba Beniamin et Maspha. 23 Reliqua autem omnium sermonum Asa et universae fortitudines eius et cuncta quae fecit et civitates quas extruxit, nonne haec scripta sunt in Libro Verborum Dierum Regum Iuda? Verumtamen in tempore senectutis suae doluit pedes, 24 et dormivit cum patribus suis et sepultus est cum eis in civitate David, patris sui. Regnavitque Iosaphat, filius eius, pro eo.

25 Nadab vero, filius Hieroboam, regnavit super Israhel anno secundo Asa, regis Iuda, regnavitque super Israhel duobus annis, 26 et fecit quod malum est in conspectu Domini et ambulavit in viis patris sui et in peccatis eius quibus peccare fecit Israhel. 27 Insidiatus est autem ei Baasa, filius Ahia de domo Isachar, et percussit eum in Gebbethon, quae est urbs Philisthinorum, siquidem Nadab et omnis Israhel obsidebant Gebbethon. 28 Interfecit igitur illum Baasa in anno tertio Asa, regis Iuda, et regnavit pro eo. 29 Cumque regnasset, percussit omnem domum Hieroboam; non dimisit ne unam quidem animam de semine eius donec deleret eum

between me and thee and between my father and thy father, therefore I have sent thee presents of silver and gold, and I desire thee to come and break *thy* league with Baasha, king of Israel, *that* he may depart from me."

20 Ben-hadad hearkening to King Asa sent the captains of his army against the cities of Israel, and they smote Ijon and Dan and *Abel-beth-maacah* and all Chinneroth, that is, all the land of Naphtali. 21 And when Baasha had heard this, he left off building Ramah and returned into Tirzah. 22 But King Asa sent word into all Judah, saying, "Let no man be excused." And they took away the stones from Ramah and the timber thereof wherewith Baasha had been building, and with them Asa built Geba of Benjamin and Mizpah. 23 But the rest of all the acts of Asa and all his strength and all that he did and the cities that he built, are they not written in the Book of the Words of the Days of the Kings of Judah? But in the time of his old age he was diseased in his feet, 24 and he slept with his fathers and was buried with them in the city of David, his father. And Jehoshaphat, his son, reigned in his place.

25 But Nadab, the son of Jeroboam, reigned over Israel the second year of Asa, king of Judah, and he reigned over Israel two years, 26 and he did evil in the sight of the Lord and walked in the ways of his father and in his sins wherewith he made Israel to sin. 27 And Baasha, the son of Ahijah of the house of Issachar, conspired against him and slew him in Gibbethon, which is a city of the Philistines, for Nadab and all Israel besieged Gibbethon. 28 So Baasha slew him in the third year of Asa, king of Judah, and reigned in his place. 29 And when he was king, he cut off all the house of Jeroboam; he left not so much as one soul of his seed till he had

iuxta verbum Domini quod locutus fuerat in manu servi sui Ahiae, Silonitis, 30 propter peccata Hieroboam quae peccaverat et quibus peccare fecerat Israhel et propter delictum quo inritaverat Dominum, Deum Israhel. 31 Reliqua autem sermonum Nadab et omnia quae operatus est, nonne haec scripta sunt in Libro Verborum Dierum Regum Israhel? 32 Fuitque bellum inter Asa et Baasa, regem Israhel, cunctis diebus eorum. 33 Anno tertio Asa, regis Iuda, regnavit Baasa, filius Ahia, super omnem Israhel in Thersa, viginti quattuor annis. 34 Et fecit malum coram Domino ambulavitque in viis Hieroboam et in peccatis eius quibus peccare fecit Israhel.

Caput 16

Factus est autem sermo Domini ad Hieu, filium Anani, contra Baasa, dicens, 2 "Pro eo quod exaltavi te de pulvere et posui te ducem super populum meum Israhel tu autem ambulasti in via Hieroboam et peccare fecisti populum meum Israhel ut me inritares in peccatis eorum, 3 ecce: ego demetam posteriora Baasa et posteriora domus eius, et faciam

utterly destroyed him according to the word of the Lord which he had spoken in the hand of *Ahijah,* the Shilonite, 30 because of the sin of Jeroboam which he had sinned and wherewith he had made Israel to sin and for the offence wherewith he provoked the Lord, the God of Israel. 31 But the rest of the acts of Nadab and all that he did, are they not written in the Book of the Words of the Days of the Kings of Israel? 32 And there was war between Asa and Baasha, the king of Israel, all their days. 33 In the third year of Asa, king of Judah, Baasha, the son of Ahijah, reigned over all Israel in Tirzah, four and twenty years. 34 And he did evil before the Lord and walked in the ways of Jeroboam and in his sins wherewith he made Israel to sin.

Chapter 16

Jehu prophesieth against Baasha. His son Elah is slain and all his family destroyed by Zimri. Of the reign of Omri, father of Ahab.

Then the word of the Lord came to Jehu, the son of Hanani, against Baasha, saying, 2 "Forasmuch as I have exalted thee out of the dust and made thee *prince* over my people Israel and thou hast walked in the way of Jeroboam and hast made my people Israel to sin to *provoke me to anger* with their sins, 3 behold: I will cut down the posterity of Baasha and

domum tuam sicut domum Hieroboam, filii Nabath. 4 Qui mortuus fuerit de Baasa in civitate comedent eum canes, et qui mortuus fuerit ex eo in regione comedent eum volucres caeli." 5 Reliqua autem sermonum Baasa et quaecumque fecit et proelia eius, nonne haec scripta sunt in Libro Verborum Dierum Regum Israhel? 6 Dormivit ergo Baasa cum patribus suis sepultusque est in Thersa, et regnavit Hela, filius eius, pro eo. 7 Cum autem in manu Hieu, filii Anani, prophetae, verbum Domini factum esset contra Baasa et contra domum eius et contra omne malum quod fecerat coram Domino ad inritandum eum in operibus manuum suarum, ut fieret sicut domus Hieroboam, ob hanc causam occidit eum, hoc est, Hieu, filium Anani, prophetam.

8 Anno vicesimo sexto Asa, regis Iuda, regnavit Hela, filius Baasa, super Israhel in Thersa duobus annis. 9 Et rebellavit contra eum servus suus Zamri, dux mediae partis equitum. Erat autem Hela in Thersa bibens et temulentus in domo Arsa, praefecti Thersa, 10 inruens ergo Zamri percussit et occidit eum anno vicesimo septimo Asa, regis Iuda, et regnavit pro eo. 11 Cumque regnasset et sedisset super solium eius, percussit omnem domum Baasa, et non dereliquit ex eo mingentem ad parietem et propinquos et amicos eius. 12 Delevitque Zamri omnem domum Baasa iuxta verbum Domini quod locutus fuerat ad Baasa in manu Hieu, prophetae, 13 propter universa peccata Baasa et peccata Hela, filii eius, qui peccaverunt et peccare fecerunt Israhel provocantes Dominum, Deum Israhel, in vanitatibus suis. 14 Reliqua autem sermonum Hela et omnia quae fecit, nonne haec scripta sunt in Libro Verborum Dierum Regum Israhel?

the posterity of his house, and I will make thy house as the house of Jeroboam, the son of Nebat. 4 Him that dieth of Baasha in the city the dogs shall eat, and him that dieth of his in the country the fowls of the air shall devour." 5 But the rest of the acts of Baasha and all that he did and his battles, are they not written in the Book of the Words of the Days of the Kings of Israel? 6 So Baasha slept with his fathers and was buried in Tirzah, and Elah, his son, reigned in his stead. 7 And when the word of the Lord came in the hand of Jehu, the son of Hanani, the prophet, against Baasha and against his house and against all the evil that he had done before the Lord to *provoke him to anger* by the works of his hands, to become as the house of Jeroboam, for this cause he slew him, that is to say, Jehu, the son of Hanani, the prophet.

8 In the six and twentieth year of Asa, king of Judah, Elah, the son of Baasha, reigned over Israel in Tirzah two years. 9 And his servant Zimri, who was captain of half the horsemen, rebelled against him. Now Ela was drinking in Tirzah and drunk in the house of Arza, the governor of Tirzah, 10 and Zimri rushing in struck him and slew him in the seven and twentieth year of Asa, king of Judah, and he reigned in his stead. 11 And when he was king and sat upon his throne, he slew all the house of Baasha, and he left not *one* thereof *to piss* against a wall and *all* his kinsfolks and friends. 12 And Zimri destroyed all the house of Baasha according to the word of the Lord that he had spoken to Baasha in the hand of Jehu, the prophet, 13 for all the sins of Baasha and the sins of Elah, his son, who sinned and made Israel to sin provoking the Lord, the God of Israel, with their vanities. 14 But the rest of the acts of Elah and all that he did, are they not written in the Book of the Words of the Days of the Kings of Israel?

15 Anno vicesimo et septimo Asa, regis Iuda, regnavit Zamri septem diebus in Thersa: porro exercitus obsidebat Gebbethon, urbem Philisthinorum. 16 Cumque audisset rebellasse Zamri et occidisse regem, fecit sibi regem omnis Israhel Amri qui erat princeps militiae super Israhel in die illa in castris. 17 Ascendit ergo Amri et omnis Israhel cum eo de Gebbethon, et obsidebant Thersa. 18 Videns autem Zamri quod expugnanda esset civitas ingressus est palatium et succendit se cum domo regia, et mortuus est 19 in peccatis suis quae peccaverat faciens malum coram Domino et ambulans in via Hieroboam et in peccato eius quo fecit peccare Israhel. 20 Reliqua autem sermonum Zamri et insidiarum eius et tyrannidis, nonne haec scripta sunt in Libro Verborum Dierum Regum Israhel?

21 Tunc divisus est populus Israhel in duas partes: media pars populi sequebatur Thebni, filium Gineth, ut constitueret eum regem, et media pars Amri. 22 Praevaluit autem populus qui erat cum Amri populo qui sequebatur Thebni, filium Gineth, mortuusque est Thebni, et regnavit Amri. 23 Anno tricesimo primo Asa, regis Iuda, regnavit Amri super Israhel duodecim annis; in Thersa regnavit sex annis. 24 Emitque montem Samariae a Somer duobus talentis argenti, et aedificavit eum, et vocavit nomen civitatis quam extruxerat nomine Somer, domini montis Samariae. 25 Fecit autem Amri malum in conspectu Domini et operatus est nequiter super omnes qui fuerunt ante eum. 26 Ambulavitque in omni via Hieroboam, filii Nabath, et in peccatis eius quibus peccare fecerat Israhel ut inritaret Dominum, Deum

15 In the seven and twentieth year of Asa, king of Judah, Zimri reigned seven days in Tirzah: now the army was besieging Gibbethon, a city of the Philistines. 16 And when they heard that Zimri had rebelled and slain the king, all Israel made Omri their king who was general over Israel in the camp that day. 17 And Omri went up and all Israel with him from Gibbethon, and they besieged Tirzah. 18 And Zimri seeing that the city was about to be taken went into the palace and burnt himself with the king's house, and he died 19 in his sins which he had sinned doing evil before the Lord and walking in the way of Jeroboam and in his sin wherewith he made Israel to sin. 20 But the rest of the acts of Zimri and of his conspiracy and tyranny, are they not written in the Book of the Words of the Days of the Kings of Israel?

21 Then were the people of Israel divided into two parts: one half of the people followed Tibni, the son of Ginath, to make him king, and one half followed Omri. 22 But the people that were with Omri prevailed over the people that followed Tibni, the son of Ginath, and Tibni died, and Omri reigned. 23 In the one and thirtieth year of Asa, king of Judah, Omri reigned over Israel twelve years; in Tirzah he reigned six years. 24 And he bought the hill of Samaria of Shemer for two talents of silver, and he built upon it, and he called the city which he built *Samaria,* after the name of Shemer, the owner of the hill. 25 And Omri did evil in the sight of the Lord and acted wickedly above all that were before him. 26 And he walked in all the way of Jeroboam, the son of Nebat, and in his sins wherewith he made Israel to sin to *provoke* the Lord, the God of Israel, *to anger* with their

Israhel, in vanitatibus suis. 27 Reliqua autem sermonum Amri et proelia quae fecit, nonne haec scripta sunt in Libro Verborum Dierum Regum Israhel? 28 Et dormivit Amri cum patribus suis et sepultus est in Samaria, regnavitque Ahab, filius eius, pro eo.

29 Ahab vero, filius Amri, regnavit super Israhel anno tricesimo octavo Asa, regis Iuda. Et regnavit Ahab, filius Amri, super Israhel in Samaria viginti et duobus annis. 30 Et fecit Ahab, filius Amri, malum in conspectu Domini super omnes qui fuerunt ante eum, 31 nec suffecit ei ut ambularet in peccatis Hieroboam, filii Nabath, insuper duxit uxorem Hiezabel, filiam Ethbaal, regis Sidoniorum. Et abiit et servivit Baal et adoravit eum, 32 et posuit aram Baal in templo Baal quod aedificaverat in Samaria, 33 et plantavit lucum, et addidit Ahab in opere suo inritans Dominum, Deum Israhel, super omnes reges Israhel qui fuerunt ante eum.

34 In diebus eius aedificavit Ahiel de Bethel Hiericho; in Abiram, primitivo suo, fundavit eam, et in Segub, novissimo suo, posuit portas eius iuxta verbum Domini quod locutus fuerat in manu Iosue, filii Nun.

vanities. 27 Now the rest of the acts of Omri and the battles he *fought,* are they not written in the Book of the Words of the Days of the Kings of Israel? 28 And Omri slept with his fathers and was buried in Samaria, and Ahab, his son, reigned in his stead.

29 Now Ahab, the son of Omri, reigned over Israel in the eight and thirtieth year of Asa, king of Judah. And Ahab, the son of Omri, reigned over Israel in Samaria two and twenty years. 30 And Ahab, the son of Omri, did evil in the sight of the Lord above all that were before him, 31 nor was it enough for him to walk in the sins of Jeroboam, the son of Nebat, but he also took to wife Jezebel, daughter of Ethbaal, king of the Sidonians. And he went and served Baal and adored him, 32 and he set up an altar for Baal in the temple of Baal which he had built in Samaria, 33 and he planted a grove, and Ahab *did more to provoke* the Lord, the God of Israel, than all the kings of Israel that were before him.

34 In his days Hiel of Bethel built Jericho; in Abiram, his firstborn, he laid its foundations, and in his youngest son, Segub, he set up the gates thereof according to the word of the Lord which he spoke in the hand of Joshua, the son of Nun.

Caput 17

Et dixit Helias, Thesbites de habitatoribus Galaad, ad Ahab, "Vivit Dominus, Deus Israhel in cuius conspectu sto, si erit annis his ros et pluvia nisi iuxta oris mei verba."

2 Et factum est verbum Domini ad eum, dicens, 3 "Recede hinc, et vade contra orientem, et abscondere in torrente Charith, qui est contra Iordanem, 4 et ibi de torrente bibes, corvisque praecepi ut pascant te ibi."

5 Abiit ergo et fecit iuxta verbum Domini, cumque abisset sedit in torrente Charith, qui est contra Iordanem. 6 Corvi quoque deferebant ei panem et carnes mane, similiter panem et carnes vesperi, et bibebat de torrente. 7 Post dies autem aliquantos siccatus est torrens, non enim pluerat super terram. 8 Factus est igitur sermo Domini ad eum, dicens, 9 "Surge, et vade in Sareptha Sidoniorum, et manebis ibi, praecepi enim ibi mulieri viduae ut pascat te."

10 Surrexit et abiit in Sareptham, cumque venisset ad portam civitatis, apparuit ei mulier vidua colligens ligna, et vocavit eam dixitque ei, "Da mihi paululum aquae in vase ut

Chapter 17

Elijah shutteth up the heaven from raining. He is fed by ravens and afterwards by a widow of Zarephath. He raiseth the widow's son to life.

And Elijah, the Tishbite of the inhabitants of Gilead, said to Ahab, "As the Lord liveth, the God of Israel in whose sight I stand, there shall not be dew nor rain these years but according to the words of my mouth."

2 And the word of the Lord came to him, saying, 3 "Get thee hence, and go towards the east, and hide thyself *by* the torrent of Cherith, which is over against the Jordan, 4 and there thou shalt drink of the torrent, and I have commanded the ravens to feed thee there."

5 So he went and did according to the word of the Lord, and going he *dwelt by* the torrent Cherith, which is over against the Jordan. 6 And the ravens brought him bread and flesh in the morning *and* bread and flesh in the evening, and he drank of the torrent. 7 But after *some time* the torrent was dried up, for it had not rained upon the earth. 8 Then the word of the Lord came to him, saying, 9 "Arise, and go to Zarephath of the Sidonians, and *dwell* there, for I have commanded a widow woman there to feed thee."

10 He arose and went to Zarephath, and when he was come to the gate of the city, he saw the widow woman gathering sticks, and he called her and said to her, "Give me a

bibam." 11 Cumque illa pergeret ut adferret, clamavit post tergum eius, dicens, "Adfer mihi, obsecro, et buccellam panis in manu tua."

12 Quae respondit, "Vivit Dominus, Deus tuus, quia non habeo panem nisi quantum pugillus capere potest farinae in hydria et paululum olei in lecytho. En: colligo duo ligna ut ingrediar et faciam illud mihi et filio meo ut comedamus et moriamur."

13 Ad quam Helias ait, "Noli timere, sed vade, et fac sicut dixisti, verumtamen mihi primum fac de ipsa farinula subcinericium panem parvulum, et adfer ad me, tibi autem et filio tuo facies postea, 14 haec enim dicit Dominus, Deus Israhel: 'Hydria farinae non deficiet nec lecythus olei minuetur usque ad diem in qua daturus est Dominus pluviam super faciem terrae.'" 15 Quae abiit et fecit iuxta verbum Heliae, et comedit ipse et illa et domus eius, et ex illa die 16 hydria farinae non defecit, et lecythus olei non est inminutus iuxta verbum Domini quod locutus fuerat in manu Heliae.

17 Factum est autem post haec aegrotavit filius mulieris, matris familiae, et erat languor fortis nimis ita ut non remaneret in eo halitus. 18 Dixit ergo ad Heliam, "Quid mihi et tibi, vir Dei? Ingressus es ad me ut rememorarentur iniquitates meae et interficeres filium meum?"

19 Et ait ad eam Helias, "Da mihi filium tuum." Tulitque eum de sinu illius et portavit in cenaculum ubi ipse manebat et posuit super lectulum suum. 20 Et clamavit ad Dominum et dixit, "Domine, Deus meus, etiamne viduam apud quam ego utcumque sustentor adflixisti ut interficeres filium eius?" 21 Et expandit se atque mensus est super pue-

little water in a vessel that I may drink." 11 And when she was going to fetch it, he called after her, saying, "Bring me also, I beseech thee, a morsel of bread in thy hand."

12 And she answered, "As the Lord, thy God, liveth, I have no bread but only a *handful* of meal in a pot and a little oil in a cruse. Behold: I am gathering two sticks that I may go in and dress it for me and my son that we may eat it and die."

13 And Elijah said to her, "Fear not, but go, and do as thou hast said, but first make for me of the same meal a little hearth cake, and bring it to me, and after make for thyself and thy son, 14 for thus saith the Lord, the God of Israel: 'The pot of meal shall not waste nor the cruse of oil be diminished until the day wherein the Lord will give rain upon the face of the earth.'" 15 She went and did according to the word of Elijah, and he ate and she and her house, and from that day 16 the pot of meal wasted not, and the cruse of oil was not diminished according to the word of the Lord which he spoke in the hand of Elijah.

17 And it came to pass after this that the son of the woman, the mistress of the house, fell sick, and the sickness was very grievous so that there was no breath left in him. 18 And she said to Elijah, "What have I to do with thee, thou man of God? Art thou come to me that my iniquities should be remembered and that thou shouldst kill my son?"

19 And Elijah said to her, "Give me thy son." And he took him out of her bosom and carried him into the upper chamber where he abode and laid him upon his own bed. 20 And he cried to the Lord and said, "O Lord, my God, hast thou afflicted also the widow with whom I am after a sort maintained so as to kill her son?" 21 And he stretched and measured himself upon the child three times and cried to the

rum tribus vicibus clamavitque ad Dominum et ait, "Domine, Deus meus, revertatur, oro, anima pueri huius in viscera eius." 22 Et exaudivit Dominus vocem Heliae, et reversa est anima pueri intra eum, et revixit. 23 Tulitque Helias puerum et deposuit eum de cenaculo in inferiorem domum et tradidit matri suae et ait illi, "En: vivit filius tuus."

24 Dixitque mulier ad Heliam, "Nunc in isto cognovi quoniam vir Dei es tu, et verbum Domini in ore tuo verum est."

Caput 18

Post dies multos verbum Domini factum est ad Heliam in anno tertio, dicens, "Vade, et ostende te Ahab ut dem pluviam super faciem terrae." 2 Ivit ergo Helias ut ostenderet se Ahab, erat autem fames vehemens in Samaria.

3 Vocavitque Ahab Abdiam, dispensatorem domus suae. Abdias autem timebat Dominum valde, 4 nam cum interficeret Hiezabel prophetas Domini, tulit ille centum prophetas et abscondit eos quinquagenos et quinquagenos in

Lord and said, "O Lord, my God, let the soul of this child, I beseech thee, return into his body." 22 And the Lord heard the voice of Elijah, and the soul of the child returned into him, and he revived. 23 And Elijah took the child and brought him down from the upper chamber to the house below and delivered him to his mother and said to her, "Behold: thy son liveth."

24 And the woman said to Elijah, "Now by this I know that thou art a man of God, and the word of the Lord in thy mouth is true."

Chapter 18

Elijah cometh before Ahab. He convinceth the false prophets by bringing fire from heaven. He obtaineth rain by his prayer.

After many days the word of the Lord came to Elijah in the third year, saying, "Go, and shew thyself to Ahab that I may give rain upon the face of the earth." 2 And Elijah went to shew himself to Ahab, and there was a grievous famine in Samaria.

3 And Ahab called Obadiah, the governor of his house. Now Obadiah feared the Lord very much, 4 for when Jezebel killed the prophets of the Lord, he took a hundred prophets and hid them by fifty and fifty in caves and fed them with

speluncis et pavit eos pane et aqua. 5 Dixit ergo Ahab ad Abdiam, "Vade in terram ad universos fontes aquarum et in cunctas valles si forte invenire possimus herbam et salvare equos et mulos et non penitus iumenta intereant." 6 Diviseruntque sibi regiones ut circuirent eas; Ahab ibat per viam unam et Abdias per viam alteram seorsum. 7 Cumque esset Abdias in via Helias occurrit ei, qui cum cognovisset eum cecidit super faciem suam et ait, "Num tu es domine mi Helias?"

8 Cui ille respondit, "Ego. Vade, et dic domino tuo, 'Adest Helias.'"

9 Et ille, "Quid peccavi," inquit, "quoniam tradis me, servum tuum, in manu Ahab ut interficiat me? 10 Vivit Dominus, Deus tuus, non est gens aut regnum quo non miserit dominus meus te requirens, et respondentibus cunctis, 'Non est hic,' adiuravit regna singula et gentes eo quod minime repperireris. 11 Et nunc dicis mihi, 'Vade, et dic domino tuo, "Adest Helias."' 12 Cumque recessero a te, spiritus Domini asportabit te in locum quem ego ignoro, et ingressus nuntiabo Ahab, et non inveniens te interficiet me. Servus autem tuus timet Dominum ab infantia sua. 13 Numquid non indicatum est tibi, domino meo, quid fecerim cum interficeret Hiezabel prophetas Domini, quod absconderim de prophetis Domini centum viros quinquagenos et quinquagenos in speluncis et paverim eos pane et aqua? 14 Et nunc tu dicis, 'Vade, et dic domino tuo, "Adest Helias,"' ut interficiat me."

15 Et dixit Helias, "Vivit Dominus exercituum ante cuius vultum sto, quia hodie apparebo ei." 16 Abiit ergo Abdias in occursum Ahab et indicavit ei, venitque Ahab in occursum Heliae.

bread and water. 5 And Ahab said to Obadiah, "Go into the land unto all fountains of waters and into all valleys *to see if* we can find grass and save the horses and mules *that* the beasts may not utterly perish." 6 And they divided the countries between them that they might go round about them; Ahab went one way and Obadiah another way by himself. 7 And as Obadiah was in the way Elijah met him, and he knew him and fell on his face and said, "Art thou my lord Elijah?"

8 And he answered, "I am. Go, and tell thy master, 'Elijah is here.'"

9 And he said, "What have I sinned that thou *wouldst deliver* me, thy servant, into the hand of Ahab that he should kill me? 10 As the Lord, thy God, liveth, there is no nation or kingdom whither my lord hath not sent to seek thee, and when all answered, 'He is not here,' he took an oath of every kingdom and nation because thou wast not found. 11 And now thou sayest to me, 'Go, and tell thy master, "Elijah is here."' 12 And when I am gone from thee, the spirit of the Lord will carry thee into a place that I know not, and I shall go in and tell Ahab, and he not finding thee will kill me. But thy servant feareth the Lord from his infancy. 13 Hath it not been told thee, my lord, what I did when Jezebel killed the prophets of the Lord, *how* I hid a hundred men of the prophets of the Lord by fifty and fifty in caves and fed them with bread and water? 14 And now thou sayest, 'Go, and tell thy master, "Elijah is here,"' that he may kill me."

15 And Elijah said, "As the Lord of hosts liveth before whose face I stand, this day I will shew myself unto him." 16 Obadiah therefore went to meet Ahab and told him, and Ahab came to meet Elijah.

17 Et cum vidisset eum, ait, "Tune es ille qui conturbas Israhel?"

18 Et ille ait, "Non ego turbavi Israhel, sed tu et domus patris tui qui dereliquistis mandata Domini et secuti estis Baalim. 19 Verumtamen nunc mitte, et congrega ad me universum Israhel in Monte Carmeli et prophetas Baal, quadringentos quinquaginta, prophetasque lucorum, quadringentos, qui comedunt de mensa Hiezabel." 20 Misit Ahab ad omnes filios Israhel et congregavit prophetas in Monte Carmeli.

21 Accedens autem Helias ad omnem populum ait, "Usquequo claudicatis in duas partes? Si Dominus est Deus, sequimini eum, si autem Baal, sequimini illum." Et non respondit ei populus verbum. 22 Et ait rursum Helias ad populum, "Ego remansi propheta Domini solus, prophetae autem Baal quadringenti et quinquaginta viri sunt. 23 Dentur nobis duo boves, et illi eligant sibi bovem unum et in frusta caedentes ponant super ligna ignem autem non subponant, et ego faciam bovem alterum, et inponam super ligna ignemque non subponam. 24 Invocate nomina deorum vestrorum, et ego invocabo nomen Domini mei, et Deus qui exaudierit per ignem, ipse sit Deus."

Respondens omnis populus ait, "Optima propositio."

25 Dixit ergo Helias prophetis Baal, "Eligite vobis bovem unum, et facite primi, quia vos plures estis, et invocate nomina deorum vestrorum, ignemque non subponatis."

26 Qui cum tulissent bovem quem dederat eis, fecerunt, et invocabant nomen Baal de mane usque ad meridiem, di-

17 And when he had seen him, he said, "Art thou he that troublest Israel?"

18 And he said, "I have not troubled Israel, but thou and thy father's house who have forsaken the commandments of the Lord and have followed Baalim. 19 Nevertheless send now, and gather unto me all Israel *unto* Mount Carmel and the prophets of Baal, four hundred and fifty, and the prophets of the groves, four hundred, who eat at Jezebel's table." 20 Ahab sent to all the children of Israel and gathered together the prophets *unto* Mount Carmel.

21 And Elijah coming to all the people said, "How long do you halt between two sides? If the Lord be God, follow him, but if Baal, then follow him." And the people did not answer him a word. 22 And Elijah said again to the people, "I only remain a prophet of the Lord, but the prophets of Baal are four hundred and fifty men. 23 Let two bullocks be given us, and let them choose one bullock for themselves and cut it in pieces and lay it upon wood but put no fire under, and I will dress the other bullock and lay it on wood and put no fire under it. 24 Call ye on the names of your gods, and I will call on the name of my Lord, and the God that shall answer by fire, let him be God."

And all the people answering said, "A very good proposal."

25 Then Elijah said to the prophets of Baal, "Choose you one bullock, and dress it first, because you are many, and call on the names of your gods, but put no fire under."

26 *And* they took the bullock which he gave them *and* dressed it, and they called on the name of Baal from morning even till noon, saying, "O Baal, hear us." *But* there was no

centes, "Baal, exaudi nos." Et non erat vox nec qui responderet, transiliebantque altare quod fecerant.

27 Cumque esset iam meridies, inludebat eis Helias, dicens, "Clamate voce maiore, Deus enim est, et forsitan loquitur aut in diversorio est aut in itinere, aut certe dormit ut excitetur." 28 Clamabant ergo voce magna et incidebant se iuxta ritum suum cultris et lanceolis donec perfunderentur sanguine. 29 Postquam autem transiit meridies et illis prophetantibus, venerat tempus quo sacrificium offerri solet, nec audiebatur vox, neque aliquis respondebat nec adtendebat orantes.

30 Dixit Helias omni populo, "Venite ad me." Et accedente ad se populo, curavit altare Domini quod destructum fuerat, 31 et tulit duodecim lapides iuxta numerum tribuum filiorum Iacob ad quem factus est sermo Domini, dicens, "Israhel erit nomen tuum." 32 Et aedificavit lapidibus altare in nomine Domini, fecitque aquaeductum quasi per duas aratiunculas in circuitu altaris. 33 Et conposuit ligna divisitque per membra bovem et posuit super ligna. 34 Et ait, "Implete quattuor hydrias aqua, et fundite super holocaustum et super ligna." Rursumque dixit, "Etiam secundo hoc facite." Qui cum fecissent secundo ait, "Etiam tertio id ipsum facite." Feceruntque tertio. 35 Et currebant aquae circa altare, et fossa aquaeductus repleta est.

36 Cumque iam tempus esset ut offerretur holocaustum, accedens Helias, propheta, ait, "Domine, Deus Abraham et Isaac et Israhel, hodie ostende quia tu es Deus Israhel et ego servus tuus et iuxta praeceptum tuum feci omnia verba haec. 37 Exaudi me, Domine. Exaudi me ut discat populus iste

voice nor any that answered, and they leaped over the altar that they had made.

27 And when it was now noon, Elijah jested at them, saying, "Cry with a louder voice, for he is *a god,* and perhaps he is talking or is in an inn or on a journey, or *perhaps* he is asleep *and* must be awaked." 28 So they cried with a loud voice and cut themselves after their manner with knives and lancets till they were all covered with blood. 29 And after midday was past and while they were prophesying, the time was come *of offering* sacrifice, and there was no voice heard, nor did any one answer nor *regard* them as they prayed.

30 Elijah said to all the people, "Come ye unto me." And the people coming near unto him, he repaired the altar of the Lord that was broken down, 31 and he took twelve stones according to the number of the tribes of the sons of Jacob to whom the word of the Lord came, saying, "Israel shall be thy name." 32 And he built with the stones an altar to the name of the Lord, and he made a trench for water *of the breadth of* two furrows round about the altar. 33 And he laid the wood in order and cut the bullock in pieces and laid it upon the wood. 34 And he said, "Fill four buckets with water, and pour it upon the burnt offering and upon the wood." And again he said, "Do the same the second time." And when they had done it the second time, he said, "Do the same also the third time." And they did so the third time. 35 And the water run round about the altar, and the trench was filled with water.

36 And when it was now time to offer the holocaust, Elijah, the prophet, came near and said, "O Lord, God of Abraham and Isaac and Israel, shew this day that thou art the God of Israel and I thy servant and that according to thy commandment I have done all these things. 37 Hear me, O

quia tu es Dominus Deus et tu convertisti cor eorum iterum."

38 Cecidit autem ignis Domini et voravit holocaustum et ligna et lapides pulverem quoque et aquam quae erat in aquaeductu lambens. 39 Quod cum vidisset omnis populus, cecidit in faciem suam, et ait, "Dominus, ipse est Deus; Dominus, ipse est Deus."

40 Dixitque Helias ad eos, "Adprehendite prophetas Baal, et ne unus quidem fugiat ex eis." Quos cum conprehendissent, duxit eos Helias ad torrentem Cison et interfecit eos ibi. 41 Et ait Helias ad Ahab, "Ascende; comede, et bibe, quia sonus multae pluviae est." 42 Ascendit Ahab ut comederet et biberet, Helias autem ascendit in verticem Carmeli et pronus in terram posuit faciem inter genua sua, 43 et dixit ad puerum suum, "Ascende, et prospice contra mare."

Qui cum ascendisset et contemplatus esset, ait, "Non est quicquam."

Et rursum ait illi, "Revertere septem vicibus." 44 In septima autem vice, ecce: nubicula parva quasi vestigium hominis ascendebat de mari. Qui ait, "Ascende, et dic Ahab, 'Iunge currum tuum, et descende, ne occupet te pluvia.'" 45 Cumque se verteret huc atque illuc, ecce: caeli contenebrati sunt et nubes et ventus, et facta est pluvia grandis. Ascendens itaque Ahab abiit in Hiezrahel, 46 et manus Domini facta est super Heliam, accinctisque lumbis currebat ante Ahab donec veniret in Hiezrahel.

Lord. Hear me that this people may learn that thou art the Lord God and that thou hast turned their heart again."

38 Then the fire of the Lord fell and consumed the holocaust and the wood and the stones and the dust and licked up the water that was in the trench. 39 And when all the people saw this, they fell on their faces, and they said, "The Lord, he is God; the Lord, he is God."

40 And Elijah said to them, "Take the prophets of Baal, and let not one of them escape." And when they had taken them, Elijah brought them *down* to the torrent Cison and killed them there. 41 And Elijah said to Ahab, "Go up; eat, and drink, for there is a sound of abundance of rain." 42 Ahab went up to eat and drink, and Elijah went up to the top of Carmel and casting himself down upon the earth put his face between his knees, 43 and he said to his servant, "Go up, and look toward the sea."

And he went up and looked *and* said, "There is nothing."

And again he said to him, "Return seven times." 44 And at the seventh time, behold: a little cloud arose out of the sea like a man's foot. And he said, "Go up, and say to Ahab, 'Prepare thy chariot, and go down, lest the rain prevent thee.'"

45 And while he turned himself this way and that way, behold: the heavens grew dark *with* clouds and wind, and there fell a great rain. And Ahab getting up went away to Jezreel, 46 and the hand of the Lord was upon Elijah, and he girded up his loins and ran before Ahab till he came to Jezreel.

tudine cibi illius quadraginta diebus et quadraginta noctibus usque ad montem Dei, Horeb.

9 Cumque venisset illuc, mansit in spelunca, et ecce: sermo Domini ad eum, dixitque illi, "Quid hic agis, Helia?"

10 At ille respondit, "Zelo zelatus sum pro Domino, Deo exercituum, quia dereliquerunt pactum tuum filii Israhel; altaria tua destruxerunt, et prophetas tuos occiderunt gladio, et derelictus sum ego solus, et quaerunt animam meam ut auferant eam."

11 Et ait ei, "Egredere, et sta in monte coram Domino, et ecce: Dominus transit, et spiritus grandis et fortis subvertens montes et conterens petras ante Dominum (non in spiritu Dominus) et post spiritum commotio (non in commotione Dominus) 12 et post commotionem ignis (non in igne Dominus) et post ignem sibilus aurae tenuis."

13 Quod cum audisset Helias, operuit vultum suum pallio et egressus stetit in ostio speluncae, et ecce vox ad eum, dicens, "Quid agis hic, Helia?"

14 Et ille respondit, "Zelo zelatus sum pro Domino, Deo exercituum, quia dereliquerunt pactum tuum filii Israhel. Altaria tua destruxerunt, et prophetas tuos occiderunt gladio, et derelictus sum ego solus, et quaerunt animam meam ut auferant eam."

drank and walked in the strength of that food forty days and forty nights unto the mount of God, Horeb.

9 And when he was come thither, he abode in a cave, and behold: the word of the Lord *came* unto him, and he said to him, "What dost thou here, Elijah?"

10 And he answered, "With zeal have I been zealous for the Lord, God of hosts, for the children of Israel have forsaken thy covenant; they have thrown down thy altars; *they* have slain thy prophets with the sword, and I alone am left, and they seek my life to take it away."

11 And he said to him, "Go forth, and stand upon the mount before the Lord, and behold: the Lord passeth, and a great and strong wind before the Lord overthrowing the mountains and breaking the rocks in pieces (the Lord is not in the wind) and after the wind an earthquake (the Lord is not in the earthquake) 12 and after the earthquake a fire (the Lord is not in the fire) and after the fire a whistling of a gentle air."

13 And when Elijah heard it, he covered his face with his mantle and coming forth stood in the entering in of the cave, and behold a voice unto him, saying, "What dost thou here, Elijah?"

And he answered, 14 "With zeal have I been zealous for the Lord, God of hosts, because the children of Israel have forsaken thy covenant. They have destroyed thy altars; *they* have slain thy prophets with the sword, and I alone am left, and they seek my life to take it away."

15 Et ait Dominus ad eum, "Vade, et revertere in viam tuam per desertum in Damascum, cumque perveneris illuc, ungues Azahel regem super Syriam. 16 Et Hieu, filium Namsi, ungues regem super Israhel, Heliseum autem, filium Saphat qui est de Abelmaula, ungues prophetam pro te. 17 Et erit quicumque fugerit gladium Azahel occidet eum Hieu, et quicumque fugerit gladium Hieu interficiet eum Heliseus. 18 Et derelinquam mihi in Israhel septem milia virorum quorum genua non sunt incurvata ante Baal et omne os quod non adoravit eum osculans manus."

19 Profectus ergo inde Helias repperit Heliseum, filium Saphat, arantem duodecim iugis boum, et ipse in duodecim iugis boum arantibus unus erat, cumque venisset Helias ad eum, misit pallium suum super illum. 20 Qui statim relictis bubus cucurrit post Heliam et ait, "Osculer, oro te, patrem meum et matrem meam, et sic sequar te."

Dixitque ei, "Vade, et revertere, quod enim meum erat feci tibi."

21 Reversus autem ab eo, tulit par boum et mactavit illud et in aratro boum coxit carnes et dedit populo, et comederunt, consurgensque abiit et secutus est Heliam et ministrabat ei.

15 And the Lord said to him, "Go, and return on thy way through the desert to Damascus, and when thou art come thither, thou shalt anoint Hazael to be king over Syria. 16 And thou shalt anoint Jehu, the son of Nimshi, to be king over Israel, and Elisha, the son of Shaphat *of* Abel-meholah, thou shalt anoint *to be* prophet *in thy room.* 17 And it shall come to pass that whosoever shall escape the sword of Hazael *shall be slain by Jehu,* and whosoever shall escape the sword of Jehu *shall be slain by Elisha.* 18 And I will leave me seven thousand men in Israel whose knees have not been bowed before Baal and every mouth that hath not worshipped him kissing the hands."

19 And Elijah departing from thence found Elisha, the son of Shaphat, ploughing with twelve yoke of oxen, and he was one of them that were ploughing with twelve yoke of oxen, and when Elijah came *up* to him, he cast his mantle upon him. 20 And he forthwith left the oxen and ran after Elijah and said, "Let me, I pray thee, kiss my father and my mother, and then I will follow thee."

And he said to him, "Go, and return back, for that which was my part I have done to thee."

21 And returning back from him, he took a yoke of oxen and killed them and boiled the flesh with the plough of the oxen and gave to the people, and they ate, and rising up he went away and followed Elijah and ministered to him.

Caput 20

Porro Benadad, rex Syriae, congregavit omnem exercitum suum, et triginta et duos reges secum et equos et currus, et ascendens pugnabat contra Samariam et obsidebat eam. 2 Mittensque nuntios ad Ahab, regem Israhel, in civitatem 3 ait, "Haec dicit Benadad: 'Argentum tuum et aurum tuum meum est, et uxores tuae et filii tui optimi mei sunt.'"

4 Responditque rex Israhel, "Iuxta verbum tuum, domine mi, rex, tuus sum ego et omnia mea."

5 Revertentesque nuntii dixerunt, "Haec dicit Benadad qui misit nos ad te: 'Argentum tuum et aurum tuum et uxores tuas et filios tuos dabis mihi. 6 Cras, igitur, hac eadem hora mittam servos meos ad te, et scrutabuntur domum tuam et domum servorum tuorum, et omne quod eis placuerit ponent in manibus suis et auferent.'"

7 Vocavit autem rex Israhel omnes seniores terrae et ait, "Animadvertite, et videte quoniam insidietur nobis, misit enim ad me pro uxoribus meis et filiis et pro argento et auro, et non abnui."

8 Dixeruntque omnes maiores natu et universus populus ad eum, "Non audias, neque adquiescas illi."

Chapter 20

The Syrians besiege Samaria. They are twice defeated by Ahab who is reprehended by a prophet for letting Ben-hadad go.

And Ben-hadad, king of Syria, gathered together all his host, and there were two and thirty kings with him and horses and chariots, and going up he fought against Samaria and besieged it. 2 And sending messengers to Ahab, king of Israel, into the city 3 he said, "Thus saith Ben-hadad: 'Thy silver and thy gold is mine, and thy wives and thy goodliest children are mine.'"

4 And the king of Israel answered, "According to thy word, my lord, O king, I am thine and all that I have."

5 And the messengers came again and said, "Thus saith Ben-hadad who sent us unto thee: 'Thy silver and thy gold and thy wives and thy children thou shalt deliver up to me. 6 Tomorrow, therefore, at this same hour I will send my servants to thee, and they shall search thy house and the *houses* of thy servants, and all that pleaseth them they shall put in their hands and take away.'"

7 And the king of Israel called all the ancients of the land and said, "Mark, and see that he layeth snares for us, for he sent to me for my wives and for my children and for my silver and gold, and I said not nay."

8 And all the ancients and all the people said to him, "Hearken not to him, nor consent to him."

18 Et ille, "Sive," ait, "pro pace veniunt, adprehendite eos vivos, sive ut proelientur, vivos eos capite." 19 Egressi sunt ergo pueri principum provinciarum, ac reliquus exercitus sequebatur, 20 et percussit unusquisque virum qui contra se venerat, fugeruntque Syri, et persecutus est eos Israhel, fugit quoque Benadad, rex Syriae, in equo cum equitibus suis. 21 Nec non egressus rex Israhel percussit equos et currus et percussit Syriam plaga magna.

22 Accedens autem propheta ad regem Israhel dixit ei, "Vade, et confortare, et scito et vide quid facias, sequenti enim anno rex Syriae ascendet contra te."

23 Servi vero regis Syriae dixerunt ei, "Dii montium sunt dii eorum, ideo superaverunt nos, sed melius est ut pugnemus contra eos in campestribus, et obtinebimus eos. 24 Tu ergo verbum hoc fac: amove reges singulos ab exercitu tuo, et pone principes pro eis, 25 et instaura numerum militum qui ceciderunt de tuis et equos secundum equos pristinos et currus secundum currus quos ante habuisti, et pugnabimus contra eos in campestribus, et videbis quod obtinebimus eos." Credidit consilio eorum et fecit ita. 26 Igitur postquam annus transierat, recensuit Benadad Syros et ascendit in Afec ut pugnaret contra Israhel. 27 Porro filii Israhel recensiti sunt et acceptis cibariis profecti sunt ex adverso castraque metati sunt contra eos quasi duo parvi greges caprarum, Syri autem repleverunt terram.

28 Et accedens unus vir Dei dixit ad regem Israhel, "Haec dicit Dominus: 'Quia dixerunt Syri, "Deus montium est

18 And he said, "Whether they come for peace, take them alive, or whether they come to fight, take them alive." 19 So the servants of the princes of the provinces went out, and the rest of the army followed, 20 and every one slew the man that came against him, and the Syrians fled, and Israel pursued after them, and Ben-hadad, king of Syria, fled away on horseback with his horsemen. 21 But the king of Israel going out overthrew the horses and chariots and slew the Syrians with a great slaughter.

22 And a prophet coming to the king of Israel said to him, "Go, and strengthen thyself, and know and see what thou dost, for the next year the king of Syria will come up against thee."

23 But the servants of the king of Syria said to him, "Their gods are gods of the hills, therefore they have overcome us, but it is better that we should fight against them in the plains, and we shall overcome them. 24 Do thou therefore this thing: remove all the kings from thy army, and put captains in their stead, 25 and make up the number of soldiers that have been slain of thine and horses according to the former horses and chariots according to the chariots which thou hadst before, and we will fight against them in the plains, and thou shalt see that we shall overcome them." He believed their counsel and did so. 26 *Wherefore at the return of the year,* Ben-hadad mustered the Syrians and went up to Aphek to fight against Israel. 27 And the children of Israel were mustered and taking victuals went out on the other side and camped over against them like two little flocks of goats, but the Syrians filled the land.

28 And a man of God coming said to the king of Israel, "Thus saith the Lord: 'Because the Syrians have said, "The

Dominus et non est Deus vallium," dabo omnem multitudinem grandem hanc in manu tua, et scietis quia ego Dominus.'"

29 Dirigebantque septem diebus ex adverso hii atque illi acies, septima autem die commissum est bellum, percusseruntque filii Israhel de Syris centum milia peditum in die una. 30 Fugerunt autem qui remanserant in Afec in civitatem, et cecidit murus super viginti septem milia hominum qui remanserant. Porro Benadad fugiens ingressus est civitatem, in cubiculum quod erat intra cubiculum. 31 Dixeruntque ei servi sui, "Ecce: audivimus quod reges domus Israhel clementes sint, ponamus itaque saccos in lumbis nostris et funiculos in capitibus nostris et egrediamur ad regem Israhel. Forsitan salvabit animas nostras."

32 Accinxerunt saccis lumbos suos et posuerunt funes in capitibus veneruntque ad regem Israhel et dixerunt ei, "Servus tuus Benadad dicit, 'Vivat, oro te, anima mea.'"

Et ille ait, "Si adhuc vivit, frater meus est."

33 Quod acceperunt viri pro omine et festinantes rapuerunt verbum ex ore eius atque dixerunt, "Frater tuus Benadad."

Et dixit eis, "Ite, et adducite eum ad me."

Egressus est ergo ad eum Benadad, et levavit eum in currum suum, 34 qui dixit ei, "Civitates quas tulit pater meus a patre tuo reddam, et plateas fac tibi in Damasco sicut fecit pater meus in Samaria, et ego foederatus recedam a te." Pepigit ergo foedus et dimisit eum.

35 Tunc vir quidam de filiis prophetarum dixit ad socium suum in sermone Domini, "Percute me." At ille noluit per-

Lord is God of the hills but is not God of the valleys," I will deliver all this great multitude into thy hand, and you shall know that I am the Lord.'"

29 And *both* sides set their armies in array one against the other seven days, and on the seventh day the battle was fought, and the children of Israel slew of the Syrians a hundred thousand footmen in one day. 30 And they that remained fled to Aphek into the city, and the wall fell upon seven and twenty thousand men that were left. And Ben-hadad fleeing went into the city, into a chamber that was within a chamber. 31 And his servants said to him, "Behold: we have heard that the kings of the house of Israel are merciful, so let us put sackcloth on our loins and ropes on our heads and go out to the king of Israel. Perhaps he will save our lives."

32 So they girded sackcloth on their loins and put ropes on their heads and came to the king of Israel and said to him, "Thy servant Ben-hadad saith, 'I beseech thee, *let me have my life.*'"

And he said, "If he be yet alive, he is my brother."

33 The men took this for a sign and in haste caught the word out of his mouth and said, "Thy brother Ben-hadad."

And he said to them, "Go, and bring him to me."

Then Ben-hadad came out to him, and he lifted him up into his chariot, 34 and he said to him, "The cities which my father took from thy father I will restore, and do thou make thee streets in Damascus as my father made in Samaria, and having made a league I will depart from thee." So he made a league with him and let him go.

35 Then a certain man of the sons of the prophets said to his companion in the word of the Lord, "Strike me." But

cutere. 36 Cui ait, "Quia noluisti audire vocem Domini, ecce: recedes a me, et percutiet te leo." Cumque paululum recessisset ab eo, invenit eum leo atque percussit.

37 Sed et alterum inveniens virum dixit ad eum, "Percute me." Qui percussit eum et vulneravit. 38 Abiit ergo propheta et occurrit regi in via et mutavit aspersione pulveris os et oculos suos. 39 Cumque rex transiret, clamavit ad regem et ait, "Servus tuus egressus est ad proeliandum comminus, cumque fugisset vir unus, adduxit eum quidam ad me et ait, "Custodi virum istum, qui si lapsus fuerit, erit anima tua pro anima eius, aut talentum argenti adpendes. 40 Dum autem ego turbatus huc illucque me verterem, subito non conparuit."

Et ait rex Israhel ad eum, "Hoc est iudicium tuum quod ipse decrevisti."

41 At ille statim abstersit pulverem de facie sua, et cognovit eum rex Israhel quod esset de prophetis. 42 Qui ait ad eum, "Haec dicit Dominus: 'Quia dimisisti virum dignum morte de manu tua, erit anima tua pro anima eius et populus tuus pro populo eius.'" 43 Reversus est igitur rex Israhel in domum suam audire contemnens et furibundus venit in Samariam.

he would not strike. 36 Then he said to him, "Because thou wouldst not hearken to the word of the Lord, behold: thou shalt depart from me, and a lion shall slay thee." And when he was gone a little from him, a lion found him and slew him.

37 Then he found another man and said to him, "Strike me." And he struck him and wounded him. 38 So the prophet went and met the king in the way and *disguised himself by sprinkling dust on his face and his eyes.* 39 And as the king passed by, he cried to the king and said, "Thy servant went out to fight hand to hand, and when a certain man was run away, one brought him to me and said, "Keep this man, and if he shall slip away, thy life shall be for his life, or thou shalt pay a talent of silver. 40 And whilst I in a hurry turned this way and that, on a sudden he was not to be seen."

And the king of Israel said to him, "This is thy judgment which thyself hast decreed."

41 But he forthwith wiped off the dust from his face, and the king of Israel knew him that he was one of the prophets. 42 And he said to him, "Thus saith the Lord: 'Because thou hast let go out of thy hand a man worthy of death, thy life shall be for his life and thy people for his people.'" 43 And the king of Israel returned to his house slighting to hear and raging came into Samaria.

Caput 21

Post verba autem haec, tempore illo vinea erat Naboth, Hiezrahelitae, qui erat in Hiezrahel, iuxta palatium Ahab, regis Samariae. 2 Locutus est ergo Ahab ad Naboth, dicens, "Da mihi vineam tuam ut faciam mihi hortum holerum quia vicina est et prope domum meam, daboque tibi pro ea vineam meliorem, aut, si tibi commodius putas, argenti pretium quanto digna est."

3 Cui respondit Naboth, "Propitius mihi sit Dominus ne dem hereditatem patrum meorum tibi."

4 Venit ergo Ahab in domum suam indignans et frendens super verbo quod locutus fuerat ad eum Naboth, Hiezrahelites, dicens, "Non dabo tibi hereditatem patrum meorum." Et proiciens se in lectulum suum, avertit faciem ad parietem et non comedit panem. 5 Ingressa est autem ad eum Hiezabel, uxor sua, dixitque ei, "Quid est hoc unde anima tua contristata est? Et quare non comedis panem?"

6 Qui respondit ei, "Locutus sum Naboth, Hiezrahelitae, et dixi ei, 'Da mihi vineam tuam, accepta pecunia, aut, si tibi placet, dabo tibi vineam meliorem pro ea.' Et ille ait, 'Non dabo tibi vineam meam.'"

Chapter 21

Naboth for denying his vineyard to King Ahab is by Jezebel's commandment falsely accused and stoned to death, for
which crime Elijah denounceth to Ahab the judgments of
God. Upon his humbling himself the sentence is mitigated.

And after these things, Naboth, the Jezreelite, who was
in Jezreel, had at that time a vineyard near the palace of
Ahab, king of Samaria. 2 And Ahab spoke to Naboth, saying,
"Give me thy vineyard that I may make me a garden of herbs
because it is nigh and adjoining to my house, and I will give
thee for it a better vineyard, or, if thou think it more convenient for thee, I will give thee the worth of it in money."

3 Naboth answered him, "The Lord be merciful to me and
not let me give thee the inheritance of my fathers."

4 And Ahab came into his house angry and fretting because of the word that Naboth, the Jezreelite, had spoken to
him, saying, "I will not give thee the inheritance of my fathers." And casting himself upon his bed, he turned away his
face to the wall and *would eat no* bread. 5 And Jezebel, his
wife, went in to him, and said to him, "What is the matter
that thy soul is so grieved? And why eatest thou no bread?"

6 And he answered her, "I spoke to Naboth, the Jezreelite,
and said to him, 'Give me thy vineyard, and take money for
it, or, if it please thee, I will give thee a better vineyard for
it.' And he said, 'I will not give thee my vineyard.'"

7 Dixit ergo ad eum Hiezabel, uxor eius, "Grandis auctoritatis es et bene regis regnum Israhel. Surge, et comede panem, et aequo esto animo. Ego dabo tibi vineam Naboth, Hiezrahelitae." 8 Scripsit itaque litteras ex nomine Ahab et signavit eas anulo eius et misit ad maiores natu et optimates qui erant in civitate eius et habitabant cum Naboth. 9 Litterarum autem erat ista sententia: "Praedicate ieiunium, et sedere facite Naboth inter primos populi, 10 et submittite duos viros, filios Belial, contra eum, et falsum testimonium dicant quod benedixit Deum et regem, et educite eum, et lapidate, sicque moriatur."

11 Fecerunt ergo cives eius, maiores natu et optimates qui habitabant cum eo in urbe, sicut praeceperat eis Hiezabel, et, sicut scriptum erat in litteris quas miserat ad eos, 12 praedicaverunt ieiunium et sedere fecerunt Naboth inter primos populi 13 et adductis duobus viris, filiis diaboli, fecerunt eos sedere contra eum, at illi, scilicet ut viri diabolici, dixerunt contra eum testimonium coram multitudine, "Benedixit Naboth Deo et regi," quam ob rem eduxerunt eum extra civitatem et lapidibus interfecerunt. 14 Miseruntque ad Hiezabel, dicentes, "Lapidatus est Naboth et mortuus est."

15 Factum est autem cum audisset Hiezabel lapidatum Naboth et mortuum locuta est ad Ahab, "Surge, et posside vineam Naboth, Hiezrahelitae, qui noluit tibi adquiescere et dare eam accepta pecunia, non enim vivit Naboth sed mortuus est." 16 Quod cum audisset Ahab mortuum, videlicet, Naboth, surrexit et descendebat in vineam Naboth, Hiezrahelitae, ut possideret eam.

7 Then Jezebel, his wife, said to him, "Thou art of great authority indeed and governest well the kingdom of Israel. Arise, and eat bread, and be of *good cheer.* I will give thee the vineyard of Naboth, the Jezreelite." 8 So she wrote letters in Ahab's name and sealed them with his ring and sent them to the ancients and the chief men that were in his city and that dwelt with Naboth. 9 And this was the tenor of the letters: "Proclaim a fast, and make Naboth sit among the chief of the people, 10 and suborn two men, sons of Belial, against him, and let them bear false witness that he hath *blasphemed* God and the king, and *then* carry him out, and stone him, and so let him die."

11 And the men of his city, the ancients and nobles that dwelt with him in the city, did as Jezebel had commanded them, and, as it was written in the letters which she had sent to them, 12 they proclaimed a fast and made Naboth sit among the chief of the people, 13 and bringing two men, sons of the devil, they made them sit against him, and they, like men of the devil, bore witness against him before the people, *saying,* "Naboth hath *blasphemed* God and the king," wherefore they brought him forth without the city and stoned him to death. 14 And they sent to Jezebel, saying, "Naboth is stoned and is dead."

15 And it came to pass when Jezebel heard that Naboth was stoned and dead that she said to Ahab, "Arise, and take possession of the vineyard of Naboth, the Jezreelite, who would not agree with thee and give it thee *for* money, for Naboth is not alive but dead." 16 And when Ahab heard this, to wit, that Naboth was dead, he arose and went down to the vineyard of Naboth, the Jezreelite, to take possession of it.

17 Factus est igitur sermo Domini ad Heliam, Thesbiten, dicens, 18 "Surge, et descende in occursum Ahab, regis Israhel, qui est in Samaria. Ecce: ad vineam Naboth descendit ut possideat eam, 19 et loqueris ad eum, dicens, 'Haec dicit Dominus: "Occidisti; insuper et possedisti."' Et post haec addes, 'Haec dicit Dominus: "In loco hoc in quo linxerunt canes sanguinem Naboth, lambent tuum quoque sanguinem."'"

20 Et ait Ahab ad Heliam, "Num invenisti me inimicum tibi?"

Qui dixit, "Inveni eo quod venundatus sis ut faceres malum in conspectu Domini. 21 Ecce: ego inducam super te malum, et demetam posteriora tua, et interficiam de Ahab mingentem ad parietem et clausum et ultimum in Israhel. 22 Et dabo domum tuam sicut domum Hieroboam, filii Nabath, et sicut domum Baasa, filii Ahia, quia egisti ut me ad iracundiam provocares et peccare fecisti Israhel."

23 Sed et de Hiezabel locutus est Dominus, dicens, "Canes comedent Hiezabel in agro Hiezrahel. 24 Si mortuus fuerit Ahab in civitate, comedent eum canes, si autem mortuus fuerit in agro, comedent eum volucres caeli." 25 Igitur non fuit alter talis ut Ahab qui venundatus est ut faceret malum in conspectu Domini, concitavit enim eum Hiezabel uxor sua, 26 et abominabilis effectus est in tantum ut sequeretur idola quae fecerant Amorrei quos consumpsit Dominus a facie filiorum Israhel. 27 Itaque cum audisset Ahab sermones istos, scidit vestimenta sua et operuit cilicio carnem suam ieiunavitque et dormivit in sacco et ambulabat dimisso capite.

28 Factus est autem sermo Domini ad Heliam, Thesbiten,

17 And the word of the Lord came to Elijah, the Tishbite, saying, 18 "Arise, and go down to meet Ahab, king of Israel, who is in Samaria. Behold: he is going down to the vineyard of Naboth to take possession of it, 19 and thou shalt speak to him, saying, 'Thus saith the Lord: "Thou hast slain; moreover also thou hast taken possession."' And after these words thou shalt add, 'Thus saith the Lord, "In this place wherein the dogs have licked the blood of Naboth, they shall lick thy blood also."'"

20 And Ahab said to Elijah, "Hast thou found me thy enemy?"

He said, "I have found thee because thou art sold to do evil in the sight of the Lord. 21 Behold: I will bring evil upon thee, and I will cut down thy posterity, and I will kill of Ahab him that pisseth against the wall and him that is shut up and the last in Israel. 22 And I will make thy house like the house of Jeroboam, the son of Nebat, and like the house of Baasha, the son of Ahijah, for what thou hast done to provoke me to anger and for making Israel to sin."

23 And of Jezebel also the Lord spoke, saying, "The dogs shall eat Jezebel in the field of Jezreel. 24 If Ahab die in the city, the dogs shall eat him, but if he die in the field, the birds of the air shall eat him." 25 Now there was not such another as Ahab who was sold to do evil in the sight of the Lord, for his wife Jezebel set him on, 26 and he became abominable insomuch that he followed the idols which the Amorites had made whom the Lord destroyed before the face of the children of Israel. 27 And when Ahab had heard these words, he rent his garments and put haircloth upon his flesh and fasted and slept in sackcloth and walked with his head cast down.

28 And the word of the Lord came to Elijah, the Tishbite,

dicens, 29 "Nonne vidisti humiliatum Ahab coram me? Quia, igitur, humiliatus est mei causa, non inducam malum in diebus eius, sed in diebus filii sui inferam malum domui eius."

Caput 22

Transierunt igitur tres anni absque bello inter Syriam et Israhel. 2 In anno autem tertio, descendit Iosaphat, rex Iuda, ad regem Israhel. 3 Dixitque rex Israhel ad servos suos, "Ignoratis quod nostra sit Ramoth Galaad, et neglegimus tollere eam de manu regis Syriae?" 4 Et ait ad Iosaphat, "Veniesne mecum ad proeliandum in Ramoth Galaad?"

5 Dixitque Iosaphat ad regem Israhel, "Sicut ego sum, ita et tu. Populus meus et populus tuus unum sunt, et equites mei, equites tui." Dixitque Iosaphat ad regem Israhel, "Quaere, oro te, hodie sermonem Domini."

6 Congregavit ergo rex Israhel prophetas, quadringentos

saying, 29 "Hast thou not seen Ahab humbled before me? Therefore, because he hath humbled himself for my sake, I will not bring the evil in his days, but in his son's days will I bring the evil upon his house."

Chapter 22

Ahab believing his false prophets rather than Micaiah is slain in Ramoth Gilead. Ahaziah succeedeth him. Good King Jehoshaphat dieth, and his son Jehoram succeedeth him.

And there passed three years without war between Syria and Israel. 2 And in the third year, Jehoshaphat, king of Judah, came down to the king of Israel. 3 And the king of Israel said to his servants, "Know ye not that Ramoth Gilead is ours, and we neglect to take it out of the hand of the king of Syria?" 4 And he said to Jehoshaphat, "Wilt thou come with me to battle to Ramoth Gilead?"

5 And Jehoshaphat said to the king of Israel, "As I am, so art thou. My people and thy people are one, and my horsemen, thy horsemen." And Jehoshaphat said to the king of Israel, "Inquire, I beseech thee, this day the word of the Lord."

6 Then the king of Israel assembled the prophets, about

circiter viros, et ait ad eos, "Ire debeo in Ramoth Galaad ad bellandum, an quiescere?"

Qui responderunt, "Ascende, et dabit Dominus in manu regis."

7 Dixit autem Iosaphat, "Non est hic propheta Domini quispiam ut interrogemus per eum?"

8 Et ait rex Israhel ad Iosaphat, "Remansit vir unus per quem possimus interrogare Dominum, sed ego odi eum, quia non prophetat mihi bonum sed malum, Micheas, filius Hiemla."

Cui Iosaphat ait, "Ne loquaris ita, rex."

9 Vocavit ergo rex Israhel eunuchum quendam et dixit ei, "Festina adducere Micheam, filium Hiemla."

10 Rex autem Israhel et Iosaphat, rex Iuda, sedebat unusquisque in solio suo vestiti cultu regio in area iuxta ostium portae Samariae, et universi prophetae prophetabant in conspectu eorum. 11 Fecit quoque sibi Sedecias, filius Chanaan, cornua ferrea et ait, "Haec dicit Dominus: 'His ventilabis Syriam donec deleas eam.'" 12 Omnesque prophetae similiter prophetabant, dicentes, "Ascende in Ramoth Galaad, et vade prospere, et tradet Dominus in manus regis."

13 Nuntius vero qui ierat ut vocaret Micheam locutus est ad eum, dicens, "Ecce: sermones prophetarum ore uno bona regi praedicant. Sit ergo sermo tuus similis eorum, et loquere bona."

14 Cui Micheas ait, "Vivit Dominus, quia quodcumque dixerit mihi Dominus, hoc loquar."

15 Venit itaque ad regem, et ait illi rex, "Michea, ire debemus in Ramoth Galaad ad proeliandum an cessare?"

four hundred men, and he said to them, "Shall I go to Ramoth Gilead to fight, or shall I forbear?"

They answered, "Go up, and the Lord will deliver it into the hand of the king."

7 And Jehoshaphat said, "Is there not here some prophet of the Lord that we may inquire by him?"

8 And the king of Israel said to Jehoshaphat, "There is one man left by whom we may inquire of the Lord, Micaiah, the son of Imlah, but I hate him, for he doth not prophesy good to me but evil."

And Jehoshaphat said, "Speak not so, O king."

9 Then the king of Israel called an eunuch and said to him, "Make haste, *and* bring hither Micaiah, the son of Imlah."

10 And the king of Israel and Jehoshaphat, king of Judah, sat each on his throne clothed with royal robes in a court by the entrance of the gate of Samaria, and all the prophets prophesied before them. 11 And Zedekiah, the son of Chenaanah, made himself horns of iron and said, "Thus saith the Lord: 'With these shalt thou push Syria till thou destroy it.'" 12 And all the prophets prophesied in like manner, saying, "Go up to Ramoth Gilead, and *prosper, for* the Lord will deliver it into the king's hands."

13 And the messenger that went to call Micaiah spoke to him, saying, "Behold: the words of the prophets with one mouth declare good things to the king. Let thy word therefore be like to theirs, and speak that which is good."

14 But Micaiah said to him, "As the Lord liveth, whatsoever the Lord shall say to me, that will I speak."

15 So he came to the king, and the king said to him, "Micaiah, shall we go to Ramoth Gilead to battle, or shall we forbear?"

26 Et ait rex Israhel, "Tollite Micheam, et maneat apud Amon, principem civitatis, et apud Ioas, filium Ammelech, 27 et dicite eis, 'Haec dicit rex: "Mittite virum istum in carcerem, et sustentate eum pane tribulationis et aqua angustiae donec revertar in pace."'"

28 Dixitque Micheas, "Si reversus fueris in pace, non est locutus Dominus in me."

Et ait, "Audite, populi omnes."

29 Ascendit itaque rex Israhel et Iosaphat, rex Iuda, in Ramoth Galaad. 30 Dixit itaque rex Israhel ad Iosaphat, "Sume arma, et ingredere proelium, et induere vestibus tuis." Porro rex Israhel mutavit habitum suum et ingressus est bellum.

31 Rex autem Syriae praeceperat principibus curruum triginta duobus, dicens, "Non pugnabitis contra minorem aut maiorem quempiam nisi contra regem Israhel solum." 32 Cum ergo vidissent principes curruum Iosaphat, suspicati sunt quod ipse esset rex Israhel, et impetu facto pugnabant contra eum, et exclamavit Iosaphat. 33 Intellexeruntque principes curruum quod non esset rex Israhel, et cessaverunt ab eo.

34 Vir autem quidam tetendit arcum, in incertum sagittam dirigens, et casu percussit regem Israhel inter pulmonem et stomachum. At ille dixit aurigae suo, "Verte manum tuam, et eice me de exercitu, quia graviter vulneratus sum." 35 Commissum est ergo proelium in die illa, et rex Israhel stabat in curru suo contra Syros, et mortuus est vesperi, fluebat autem sanguis plagae in sinum currus.

36 Et praeco personuit in universo exercitu antequam sol

26 And the king of Israel said, "Take Micaiah, and let him abide with Ammon, the governor of the city, and with Joash, the son of Amalek, 27 and tell them, 'Thus saith the king: "Put this man in prison, and feed him with bread of affliction and water of distress till I return in peace.""'"

28 And Micaiah said, "If thou return in peace, the Lord hath not spoken by me."

And he said, "Hear, all ye people."

29 So the king of Israel and Jehoshaphat, king of Judah, went up to Ramoth Gilead. 30 And the king of Israel said to Jehoshaphat, "Take armour, and go into the battle, and put on thy own garments." But the king of Israel changed his dress and went into the battle.

31 And the king of Syria had commanded the two and thirty captains of the chariots, saying, "You shall not fight against any small or great but against the king of Israel only." 32 So when the captains of the chariots saw Jehoshaphat, they suspected that he was the king of Israel, and making a violent assault they fought against him, and Jehoshaphat cried out. 33 And the captains of the chariots perceived that he was not the king of Israel, and they turned away from him.

34 And a certain man bent his bow, shooting *at a venture,* and chanced to strike the king of Israel between the lungs and the stomach. But he said to the driver of his chariot, "Turn thy hand, and carry me out of the army, for I am grievously wounded." 35 And the battle was fought that day, and the king of Israel stood in his chariot against the Syrians, and he died in the evening, and the blood ran out *of the wound* into the midst of the chariot.

36 And the herald proclaimed through all the army before

occumberet, dicens, "Unusquisque revertatur in civitatem et in terram suam." 37 Mortuus est autem rex et perlatus est in Samariam, sepelieruntque regem in Samaria. 38 Et laverunt currum eius in piscina Samariae, et linxerunt canes sanguinem eius, et habenas laverunt iuxta verbum Domini quod locutus fuerat. 39 Reliqua vero sermonum Ahab et universa quae fecit et domus eburneae quam aedificavit cunctarumque urbium quas extruxit, nonne scripta sunt haec in Libro Verborum Dierum Regum Israhel? 40 Dormivit ergo Ahab cum patribus suis, et regnavit Ohozias, filius eius, pro eo.

41 Iosaphat vero filius Asa, regnare coeperat super Iudam anno quarto Ahab, regis Israhel. 42 Triginta quinque annorum erat cum regnare coepisset, et viginti et quinque annos regnavit in Hierusalem. Nomen matris eius Azuba, filia Salai. 43 Et ambulavit in omni via Asa, patris sui, et non declinavit ex ea, fecitque quod rectum erat in conspectu Domini. 44 Verumtamen excelsa non abstulit, adhuc enim populus sacrificabat et adolebat incensum in excelsis. 45 Pacemque habuit Iosaphat cum rege Israhel. 46 Reliqua autem verborum Iosaphat et opera eius quae gessit et proelia, nonne haec scripta sunt in Libro Verborum Dierum Regum Iuda? 47 Sed et reliquias effeminatorum qui remanserant in diebus Asa, patris eius, abstulit de terra. 48 Nec erat tunc rex constitutus in Edom, 49 rex vero Iosaphat fecerat classes in mari quae navigarent in Ophir propter aurum, et ire non potuerunt quia confractae sunt in Asiongaber. 50 Tunc ait Ohozias, filius Ahab, ad Iosaphat, "Vadant servi mei cum servis tuis in

the sun set, saying, "Let every man return to his own city and to his own country." 37 And the king died and was carried into Samaria, and they buried the king in Samaria. 38 And they washed his chariot in the pool of Samaria, and the dogs licked up his blood, and they washed the reins according to the word of the Lord which he had spoken. 39 But the rest of the acts of Ahab and all that he did and the house of ivory that he made and all the cities that he built, are they not written in the Book of the Words of the Days of the Kings of Israel? 40 So Ahab slept with his fathers, and Ahaziah, his son, reigned in his stead.

41 But Jehoshaphat, the son of Asa, began to reign over Judah in the fourth year of Ahab, king of Israel. 42 He was five and thirty years old when he began to reign, and he reigned five and twenty years in Jerusalem. The name of his mother was Azubah, the daughter of Shilhi. 43 And he walked in all the way of Asa, his father, and he declined not from it, and he did that which was right in the sight of the Lord. 44 Nevertheless he took not away the high places, for as yet the people offered sacrifices and burnt incense in the high places. 45 And Jehoshaphat had peace with the king of Israel. 46 But the rest of the acts of Jehoshaphat and his works which he did and his battles, are they not written in the Book of the Words of the Days of the Kings of Judah? 47 And the remnant also of the effeminate who remained in the days of Asa, his father, he took out of the land. 48 And there was then no king appointed in Edom, 49 but king Jehoshaphat made navies on the sea to sail into Ophir for gold, *but* they could not go, for the ships were broken in Eziongeber. 50 Then Ahaziah, the son of Ahab, said to Jehoshaphat, "Let my servants go with thy servants in the ships."

navibus." Et noluit Iosaphat. 51 Dormivitque Iosaphat cum patribus suis et sepultus est cum eis in civitate David, patris sui, regnavitque Ioram, filius eius, pro eo.

52 Ohozias autem, filius Ahab, regnare coeperat super Israhel in Samaria anno septimodecimo Iosaphat, regis Iuda, regnavitque super Israhel duobus annis, 53 et fecit malum in conspectu Domini et ambulavit in via patris sui et matris suae et in via Hieroboam, filii Nabath, qui peccare fecit Israhel. 54 Servivit quoque Baal et adoravit eum et inritavit Dominum, Deum Israhel, iuxta omnia quae fecerat pater eius.

And Jehoshaphat would not. 51 And Jehoshaphat slept with his fathers and was buried with them in the city of David, his father, and Jehoram, his son, reigned in his stead.

52 And Ahaziah, the son of Ahab, began to reign over Israel in Samaria in the seventeenth gear of Jehoshaphat, king of Judah, and he reigned over Israel two years, 53 and he did evil in the sight of the Lord and walked in the way of his father and his mother and in the way of Jeroboam, the son of Nebat, who made Israel to sin. 54 He served also Baal and worshipped him and provoked the Lord, the God of Israel, according to all that his father had done.

4 KINGS

Caput 1

Praevaricatus est autem Moab in Israhel postquam mortuus est Ahab. 2 Cceciditque Ohozias per cancellos cenaculi sui quod habebat in Samaria et aegrotavit, misitque nuntios, dicens ad eos, "Ite; consulite Beelzebub, deum Accaron, utrum vivere queam de infirmitate mea hac."

3 Angelus autem Domini locutus est ad Heliam, Thesbiten, dicens, "Surge, et ascende in occursum nuntiorum regis Samariae, et dices ad eos, 'Numquid non est Deus in Israhel ut eatis ad consulendum Beelzebub, deum Accaron? 4 Quam ob rem haec dicit Dominus: "De lectulo super quem ascendisti non descendes, sed morte morieris."'" Et abiit Helias.

5 Reversique sunt nuntii ad Ohoziam, qui dixit eis, "Quare reversi estis?"

6 At illi responderunt ei, "Vir occurrit nobis et dixit ad nos, 'Ite, et revertimini ad regem qui misit vos, et dicetis ei, "Haec dicit Dominus, 'Numquid quia non erat Deus in

Chapter 1

Ahaziah sendeth to consult Baal-zebub. Elijah foretelleth
his death and causeth fire to come down from heaven upon
two captains and their companies.

And Moab rebelled against Israel after *the death of* Ahab.
2 And Ahaziah fell through the lattices of his upper chamber which he had in Samaria and was sick, and he sent messengers, saying to them, "Go; consult Baal-zebub, the god of Ekron, whether I *shall* recover of this my illness."

3 And an angel of the Lord spoke to Elijah, the Tishbite, saying, "Arise, and go up to meet the messengers of the king of Samaria, and *say* to them, 'Is there not a God in Israel that ye go to consult Baal-zebub, the god of Ekron? 4 Wherefore thus saith the Lord: "From the bed on which thou art gone up thou shalt not come down, but thou shalt surely die."'" And Elijah went away.

5 And the messengers turned back to Ahaziah, and he said to them, "Why are you come back?"

6 But they answered him, "A man met us and said to us, 'Go, and return to the king that sent you, and you shall say to him, "Thus saith the Lord, 'Is it because there was no

Israhel mittis ut consulatur Beelzebub, deus Accaron? Idcirco de lectulo super quem ascendisti non descendes, sed morte morieris.'"'"

7 Qui dixit eis, "Cuius figurae et habitus est vir ille qui occurrit vobis et locutus est verba haec?"

8 At illi dixerunt, "Vir pilosus et zona pellicia accinctus renibus."

Qui ait, "Helias, Thesbites, est."

9 Misitque ad eum quinquagenarium principem et quinquaginta qui erant sub eo, qui ascendit ad eum sedentique in vertice montis ait, "Homo Dei, rex praecepit ut descendas."

10 Respondensque Helias dixit quinquagenario, "Si homo Dei sum, descendat ignis e caelo et devoret te et quinquaginta tuos." Descendit itaque ignis e caelo et devoravit eum et quinquaginta qui erant cum eo.

11 Rursumque misit ad eum principem quinquagenarium alterum et quinquaginta cum eo, qui locutus est illi, "Homo Dei, haec dicit rex: 'Festina; descende.'"

12 Respondens Helias ait, "Si homo Dei ego sum, descendat ignis e caelo et devoret te et quinquaginta tuos." Descendit ergo ignis e caelo et devoravit illum et quinquaginta eius.

13 Iterum misit principem quinquagenarium tertium et quinquaginta qui erant cum eo. Qui cum venisset, curvavit genua contra Heliam et precatus est eum et ait, "Homo Dei, noli despicere animam meam et animas servorum tuorum qui mecum sunt. 14 Ecce: descendit ignis de caelo et devoravit duos principes quinquagenarios primos et quinquagenos qui cum eis erant, sed nunc obsecro ut miserearis animae meae."

God in Israel that thou sendest *to* Baal-zebub, the god of Ekron? Therefore thou shalt not come down from the bed on which thou art gone up, but thou shalt surely die.'"'"

7 And he said to them, "What *manner of man was he* who met you and spoke these words?"

8 But they said, "A hairy man *with* a girdle of leather about his loins."

And he said, "It is Elijah, the Tishbite."

9 And he sent to him a captain of fifty and the fifty men that were under him, and he went up to him and as he was sitting on the top of a hill said to him, "Man of God, the king hath commanded that thou come down."

10 And Elijah answering said to the captain of fifty, "If I be a man of God, let fire come down from heaven and consume thee and thy fifty." And there came down fire from heaven and consumed him and the fifty that were with him.

11 And again he sent to him another captain of fifty men and his fifty with him, and he said to him, "Man of God, thus saith the king: 'Make haste, *and* come down.'"

12 Elijah answering said, "If I be a man of God, let fire come down from heaven and consume thee and thy fifty." And fire came down from heaven and consumed him and his fifty.

13 Again he sent a third captain of fifty men and the fifty that were with him. And when he was come, he *fell upon* his knees before Elijah and besought him and said, "Man of God, despise not my life and the lives of thy servants that are with me. 14 Behold: fire came down from heaven and consumed the two first captains of fifty men and the fifties that were with them, but now I beseech thee to *spare* my life."

15 Locutus est autem angelus Domini ad Heliam, dicens, "Descende cum eo; ne timeas."

Surrexit igitur et descendit cum eo ad regem 16 et locutus est ei, "Haec dicit Dominus: 'Quia misisti nuntios ad consulendum Beelzebub, deum Accaron, quasi non esset Deus in Israhel a quo possis interrogare sermonem, ideo de lectulo super quem ascendisti non descendes, sed morte morieris.'" 17 Mortuus est ergo iuxta sermonem Domini quem locutus est Helias, et regnavit Ioram, frater eius, pro eo anno secundo Ioram, filii Iosaphat, regis Iudae, non enim habebat filium. 18 Reliqua autem verborum Ohoziae quae operatus est, nonne haec scripta sunt in Libro Sermonum Dierum Regum Israhel?

Caput 2

Factum est autem cum levare vellet Dominus Heliam per turbinem in caelum ibant Helias et Heliseus de Galgalis. 2 Dixitque Helias ad Heliseum, "Sede hic quia Dominus misit me usque Bethel."

15 And the angel of the Lord spoke to Elijah, saying, "Go down with him; fear not."

He arose therefore and went down with him to the king 16 and said to him, "Thus saith the Lord: 'Because thou hast sent messengers to consult Baal-zebub, the god of Ekron, as though there were not a God in Israel of whom thou mightest inquire the word, therefore from the bed on which thou art gone up thou shalt not come down, but thou shalt surely die.'" 17 So he died according to the word of the Lord which Elijah spoke, and Jehoram, his brother, reigned in his stead in the second year of Jehoram, the son of Jehoshaphat, king of Judah, because he had no son. 18 But the rest of the acts of Ahaziah which he did, are they not written in the Book of the Words of the Days of the Kings of Israel?

Chapter 2

Elisha will not part from Elijah. The water of the Jordan is divided by Elijah's cloak. Elijah is taken up in a fiery chariot and his double spirit is given to Elisha. Elisha healeth the waters by casting in salt. Boys are torn by bears for mocking Elisha.

And it came to pass when the Lord would take up Elijah into heaven by a whirlwind that Elijah and Elisha were going from Gilgal. 2 And Elijah said to Elisha, "Stay thou here because the Lord hath sent me as far as Bethel."

Cui ait Heliseus, "Vivit Dominus, et vivit anima tua, quia non derelinquam te."

Cumque descendissent Bethel, 3 egressi sunt filii prophetarum qui erant in Bethel ad Heliseum et dixerunt ei, "Numquid nosti quia hodie Dominus tollet dominum tuum a te?"

Qui respondit, "Et ego novi. Silete."

4 Dixit autem Helias ad Heliseum, "Sede hic quia Dominus misit me in Hiericho."

Et ille ait, "Vivit Dominus, et vivit anima tua, quia non derelinquam te."

Cumque venissent Hierichum 5 accesserunt filii prophetarum qui erant in Hiericho ad Heliseum et dixerunt ei, "Numquid nosti quia hodie Dominus tollet dominum tuum a te?"

Et ait, "Et ego novi. Silete."

6 Dixit autem ei Helias, "Sede hic quia Dominus misit me usque ad Iordanem."

Qui ait, "Vivit Dominus, et vivit anima tua, quia non derelinquam te."

Ierunt igitur ambo pariter, 7 et quinquaginta viri de filiis prophetarum secuti sunt eos qui et steterunt e contra longe, illi autem ambo stabant super Iordanem. 8 Tulitque Helias pallium suum et involvit illud et percussit aquas, quae divisae sunt in utramque partem, et transierunt ambo per siccum. 9 Cumque transissent, Helias dixit ad Heliseum, "Postula quod vis ut faciam tibi antequam tollar a te."

And Elisha said to him, "As the Lord liveth and as thy soul liveth, I will not leave thee."

And when they were come down to Bethel, 3 the sons of the prophets that were at Bethel came forth to Elisha and said to him, "Dost thou know that this day the Lord will take away thy master from thee?"

And he answered, "I also know it. Hold your peace."

4 And Elijah said to Elisha, "Stay here because the Lord hath sent me to Jericho."

And he said, "As the Lord liveth, and as thy soul liveth, I will not leave thee."

And when they were come to Jericho 5 the sons of the prophets that were at Jericho came to Elisha and said to him, "Dost thou know that this day the Lord will take away thy master from thee?"

And he said, "I also know it. Hold your peace."

6 And Elijah said to him, "Stay here because the Lord hath sent me as far as the Jordan."

And he said, "As the Lord liveth, and as thy soul liveth, I will not leave thee."

And they two went on together, 7 and fifty men of the sons of the prophets followed them *and stood in sight* at a distance, but they two stood by the Jordan. 8 And Elijah took his mantle and folded it together and struck the waters, and they were divided hither and thither, and they both passed over on dry ground. 9 And when they were gone over, Elijah said to Elisha, "Ask what thou wilt have me to do for thee before I be taken away from thee."

Dixitque Heliseus, "Obsecro ut fiat duplex spiritus tuus in me."

10 Qui respondit, "Rem difficilem postulasti. Attamen, si videris me quando tollar a te, erit tibi quod petisti, si autem non videris, non erit."

11 Cumque pergerent et incedentes sermocinarentur, ecce: currus igneus et equi ignei diviserunt utrumque, et ascendit Helias per turbinem in caelum. 12 Heliseus autem videbat et clamabat, "Pater mi, pater mi! Currus Israhel et auriga eius!" Et non vidit eum amplius, adprehenditque vestimenta sua et scidit illa in duas partes. 13 Et levavit pallium Heliae quod ceciderat ei, reversusque stetit super ripam Iordanis, 14 et pallio Heliae quod ceciderat ei percussit aquas, et non sunt divisae. Et dixit, "Ubi est Deus Heliae etiam nunc?" Percussitque aquas, et divisae sunt huc atque illuc, et transiit Heliseus.

15 Videntes autem filii prophetarum qui erant in Hiericho de contra dixerunt, "Requievit spiritus Heliae super Heliseum." Et venientes in occursum eius adoraverunt eum proni in terram, 16 dixeruntque illi, "Ecce: cum servis tuis sunt quinquaginta viri fortes qui possint ire et quaerere dominum tuum, ne forte tulerit eum spiritus Domini et proiecerit eum in uno montium aut in unam vallium."

And Elisha said, "I beseech thee that in me may be thy double spirit."

10 And he answered, "Thou hast asked a hard thing. Nevertheless, if thou see me when I *am* taken from thee, thou shalt have what thou hast asked, but if thou see me not, thou shalt not have it."

11 And as they went on *walking and talking* together, behold: a fiery chariot and fiery horses parted them both asunder, and Elijah went up by a whirlwind into heaven. 12 And Elisha saw him and cried, "My father, my father! The chariot of Israel and the driver thereof!" And he saw him no more, and he took hold of his own garments and rent them in two pieces. 13 And he took up the mantle of Elijah that fell *from* him, and going back he stood upon the bank of the Jordan, 14 and he struck the waters with the mantle of Elijah that had fallen *from* him, and they were not divided. And he said, "Where is now the God of Elijah?" And he struck the waters, and they were divided hither and thither, and Elisha passed over.

15 And the sons of the prophets *at* Jericho who were over against him seeing it said, "The spirit of Elijah hath rested upon Elisha." And coming to meet him they worshipped him falling to the ground, 16 and they said to him, "Behold: there are with thy servants fifty strong men that can go and seek thy master, lest perhaps the spirit of the Lord hath taken him up and cast him upon *some* mountain or into *some* valley."

Qui ait, "Nolite mittere." 17 Coegeruntque eum donec adquiesceret et diceret, "Mittite." Et miserunt quinquaginta viros, qui cum quaesissent tribus diebus non invenerunt. 18 Et reversi sunt ad eum, at ille habitabat in Hiericho, dixitque eis, "Numquid non dixi vobis, 'Nolite mittere'?"

19 Dixerunt quoque viri civitatis ad Heliseum, "Ecce: habitatio civitatis huius optima est, sicut tu ipse, domine, perspicis, sed aquae pessimae sunt et terra sterilis."

20 At ille ait, "Adferte mihi vas novum, et mittite in illud sal." Quod cum adtulissent, 21 egressus ad fontem aquarum misit in eum sal et ait, "Haec dicit Dominus: 'Sanavi aquas has, et non erit ultra in eis mors neque sterilitas.'" 22 Sanatae sunt ergo aquae usque ad diem hanc iuxta verbum Helisei quod locutus est.

23 Ascendit autem inde in Bethel, cumque ascenderet per viam pueri parvi egressi sunt de civitate et inludebant ei, dicentes, "Ascende, calve! Ascende, calve!" 24 Qui cum respexisset vidit eos et maledixit eis in nomine Domini, egressique sunt duo ursi de saltu et laceraverunt ex eis quadraginta duos pueros. 25 Abiit autem inde in Montem Carmeli, et inde reversus est in Samariam.

And he said, "Do not send." 17 *But* they pressed him till he consented and said, "Send." And they sent fifty men, *and* they sought three days *but* found him not. 18 And they came back to him, *for* he abode at Jericho, and he said to them, "Did I not say to you, 'Do not send'?"

19 And the men of the city said to Elisha, "Behold: the situation of this city is very good, as thou, my lord, seest, but the waters are very bad and the ground barren."

20 And he said, "Bring me a new vessel, and put salt into it." And when they had brought it, 21 he went out to the spring of the waters and cast the salt into it and said, "Thus saith the Lord: 'I have healed these waters, and there shall be no more in them death or barrenness.'" 22 And the waters were healed unto this day according to the word of Elisha which he spoke.

23 And he went up from thence to Bethel, and as he was going up by the way little boys came out of the city and mocked him, saying, "Go up, thou bald-head! Go up, thou bald-head!" 24 And looking back he saw them and cursed them in the name of the Lord, and there came forth two bears out of the forest and tore of them two and forty boys. 25 And from thence he went to Mount Carmel, and from thence he returned to Samaria.

Caput 3

Ioram vero, filius Ahab, regnavit super Israhel in Samaria anno octavodecimo Iosaphat, regis Iudae, regnavitque duodecim annis. 2 Et fecit malum coram Domino, sed non sicut pater suus et mater, tulit enim statuas Baal quas fecerat pater eius. 3 Verumtamen in peccatis Hieroboam, filii Nabath, qui peccare fecit Israhel adhesit, nec recessit ab eis.

4 Porro Mesa, rex Moab, nutriebat pecora multa, et solvebat regi Israhel centum milia agnorum et centum milia arietum cum velleribus suis. 5 Cumque mortuus fuisset Ahab praevaricatus est foedus quod habebat cum rege Israhel. 6 Egressus est igitur Rex Ioram in die illa de Samaria et recensuit universum Israhel. 7 Misitque ad Iosaphat, regem Iuda, dicens, "Rex Moab recessit a me; veni mecum contra eum ad proelium."

Qui respondit, "Ascendam. Qui meus est tuus est, populus meus, populus tuus et equi mei, equi tui."

8 Dixitque, "Per quam viam ascendemus?"

At ille respondit, "Per desertum Idumeae."

Chapter 3

The kings of Israel, Judah and Edom fight against the king of Moab. They want water, which Elisha procureth without rain and prophesieth victory. The king of Moab is overthrown. His city is besieged. He sacrificeth his firstborn son, so the Israelites raise the siege.

And Jehoram, the son of Ahab, reigned over Israel in Samaria in the eighteenth year of Jehoshaphat, king of Judah, and he reigned twelve years. 2 And he did evil before the Lord, but not like his father and his mother, for he took away the statues of Baal which his father had made. 3 Nevertheless he stuck to the sins of Jeroboam, the son of Nebat, who made Israel to sin, nor did he depart from them.

4 Now Mesha, king of Moab, nourished many sheep, and he paid to the king of Israel a hundred thousand lambs and a hundred thousand rams with their fleeces. 5 And when Ahab was dead he broke the league which he had made with the king of Israel. 6 And King Jehoram went out that day from Samaria and mustered all Israel. 7 And he sent to Jehoshaphat, king of Judah, saying, "The king of Moab is revolted from me; come with me against him to battle."

And he answered, "I will come up. He that is mine is thine, my people, thy people and my horses, thy horses."

8 And he said, "Which way shall we go up?"

But he answered, "By the desert of Edom."

9 Perrexerunt igitur rex Israhel et rex Iuda et rex Edom, et circumierunt per viam septem dierum, nec erat aqua exercitui et iumentis quae sequebantur eos. 10 Dixitque rex Israhel, "Eheu! Eheu! Eheu, congregavit nos Dominus tres reges ut traderet in manus Moab!"

11 Et ait Iosaphat, "Estne hic propheta Domini, ut deprecemur Dominum per eum?"

Et respondit unus de servis regis Israhel, "Est hic Heliseus, filius Saphat, qui fundebat aquam super manus Heliae."

12 Et ait Iosaphat, "Est apud eum sermo Domini." Descenditque ad eum rex Israhel et Iosaphat, rex Iuda, et rex Edom.

13 Dixit autem Heliseus ad regem Israhel, "Quid mihi et tibi est? Vade ad prophetas patris tui et matris tuae."

Et ait illi rex Israhel, "Quare congregavit Dominus tres reges hos ut traderet eos in manus Moab?"

14 Dixit autem ad eum Heliseus, "Vivit Dominus exercituum in cuius conspectu sto, quod si non vultum Iosaphat, regis Iudae, erubescerem, ne adtendissem quidem te nec respexissem. 15 Nunc autem adducite mihi psalten." Cumque caneret psaltes, facta est super eum manus Domini, et ait, 16 "Haec dicit Dominus: 'Facite alveum torrentis huius fossas et fossas,' 17 haec enim dicit Dominus: 'Non videbitis ventum neque pluviam, et alveus iste replebitur aquis, et bibetis, vos et familiae vestrae et iumenta vestra.'18 Parumque hoc est in conspectu Domini. Insuper, tradet etiam Moab in

9 So the king of Israel and the king of Judah and the king of Edom went, and they fetched a compass of seven days' journey, and there was no water for the army and for the beasts that followed them. 10 And the king of Israel said, "Alas! Alas! Alas, the Lord hath gathered us three kings together to deliver us into the hands of Moab!"

11 And Jehoshaphat said, "Is there not here a prophet of the Lord, that we may beseech the Lord by him?"

And one of the servants of the king of Israel answered, "Here is Elisha, the son of Shaphat, who poured water on the hands of Elijah."

12 And Jehoshaphat said, "The word of the Lord is with him." And the king of Israel and Jehoshaphat, king of Judah, and the king of Edom went down to him.

13 And Elisha said to the king of Israel, "What have I to do with thee? Go to the prophets of thy father and thy mother."

And the king of Israel said to him, "Why hath the Lord gathered together these three kings to deliver them into the hands of Moab?"

14 And Elisha said to him, "As the Lord of hosts liveth in whose sight I stand, if I did not reverence the face of Jehoshaphat, king of Judah, I would not have hearkened to thee nor looked on thee. 15 But now bring me hither a minstrel." And when the minstrel played, the hand of the Lord came upon him, and he said, 16 "Thus saith the Lord: 'Make the channel of this torrent *full of ditches,*' 17 for thus saith the Lord: 'You shall not see wind nor rain, and *yet* this channel shall be filled with waters, and you shall drink, you and your families and your beasts.' 18 And this is a small thing in the sight of the Lord. Moreover, he will deliver also Moab into

manus vestras. 19 Et percutietis omnem civitatem munitam et omnem urbem electam et universum lignum fructiferum succidetis cunctosque fontes aquarum obturabitis, et omnem agrum egregium operietis lapidibus."

20 Factum est igitur mane, quando sacrificium offerri solet, et ecce: aquae veniebant per viam Edom, et repleta est terra aquis. 21 Universi autem Moabitae audientes quod ascendissent reges ut pugnarent adversum eos convocaverunt omnes qui accincti erant balteo desuper et steterunt in terminis. 22 Primoque mane surgentes, et orto iam sole ex adverso aquarum, viderunt Moabitae contra aquas rubras quasi sanguinem, 23 dixeruntque, "Sanguis est gladii. Pugnaverunt reges contra se, et caesi sunt mutuo. Nunc perge ad praedam, Moab." 24 Perrexeruntque in castra Israhel, porro consurgens Israhel percussit Moab, at illi fugerunt coram eis.

Venerunt igitur qui vicerant et percusserunt Moab. 25 Et civitates destruxerunt, et omnem agrum optimum, mittentes singuli lapides, repleverunt, et universos fontes aquarum obturaverunt et omnia ligna fructifera succiderunt, ita ut muri tantum fictiles remanerent, et circumdata est civitas a fundibalariis et magna ex parte percussa. 26 Quod cum vidisset rex Moab, praevaluisse, scilicet, hostes, tulit secum septingentos viros educentes gladium ut inrumperet ad regem Edom, et non potuerunt. 27 Arripiensque filium suum primogenitum qui regnaturus erat pro eo obtulit holocaustum super murum. Et facta est indignatio magna in Israhel, statimque recesserunt ab eo et reversi sunt in terram suam.

your hands. 19 And you shall destroy every fenced city and every choice city and shall cut down every fruitful tree and shall stop up all the springs of waters, and every goodly field you shall cover with stones."

20 And it came to pass in the morning, when the sacrifices used to be offered, *that,* behold: water came by the way of Edom, and the country was filled with water. 21 And all the Moabites hearing that the kings were come up to fight against them gathered together all that were girded with a belt upon them and stood in the borders. 22 And they rose early in the morning, and the sun being now up and shining upon the waters, the Moabites saw the waters over against them red like blood, 23 and they said, "It is the blood of the sword. The kings have fought among themselves, and they have killed one another. Go now, Moab, to the spoils." 24 And they went into the camp of Israel, but Israel rising up defeated Moab, *who* fled before them.

And they being conquerors went and smote Moab. 25 And they destroyed the cities, and they filled every goodly field, every man casting his stone, and they stopt up all the springs of waters and cut down all the trees that bore fruit, so that brick walls only remained, and the city was beset by the slingers and a great part thereof destroyed. 26 And when the king of Moab saw this, to wit, that the enemies had prevailed, he took with him seven hundred men that drew the sword to break in upon the king of Edom, *but* they could not. 27 Then he took his eldest son that should have reigned in his stead and offered him for a burnt offering upon the wall. And there was great indignation in Israel, and presently they departed from him and returned into their own country.

Caput 4

Mulier autem quaedam de uxoribus prophetarum clamabat ad Heliseum, dicens, "Servus tuus, vir meus, mortuus est, et tu nosti quia servus tuus fuit timens Dominum, et ecce: creditor venit ut tollat duos filios meos ad serviendum sibi."

2 Cui dixit Heliseus, "Quid vis ut faciam tibi? Dic mihi, quid habes in domo tua?"

At illa respondit, "Non habeo, ancilla tua, quicquam in domo mea nisi parum olei quo unguear."

3 Cui ait, "Vade; pete mutuo ab omnibus vicinis tuis vasa vacua non pauca, 4 et ingredere, et claude ostium tuum cum intrinsecus fueris tu et filii tui, et mitte inde in omnia vasa haec, et cum plena fuerint, tolles."

5 Ivit itaque mulier et clusit ostium super se et super filios suos. Illi offerebant vasa, et illa infundebat. 6 Cumque plena fuissent vasa, dixit ad filium suum, "Adfer mihi adhuc vas."

Et ille respondit, "Non habeo." Stetitque oleum.

7 Venit autem illa et indicavit homini Dei. Et ille, "Vade," inquit, "vende oleum, et redde creditori tuo, tu autem et filii tui vivite de reliquo."

8 Facta est autem quaedam dies et transiebat Heliseus per Sunam. Erat autem ibi mulier magna quae tenuit eum ut

Chapter 4

Miracles of Elisha. He raiseth a dead child to life.

Now a certain woman of the wives of the prophets cried to Elisha, saying, "Thy servant, my husband, is dead, and thou knowest that thy servant was one that feared God, and behold: the creditor is come to take away my two sons to serve him."

2 And Elisha said to her, "What wilt thou have me to do for thee? Tell me, what hast thou in thy house?"

And she answered, "I, thy handmaid, have nothing in my house but a little oil to anoint me."

3 And he said to her, "Go; borrow of all thy neighbours empty vessels not a few, 4 and go in, and shut thy door when thou art within and thy sons, and pour out thereof into all those vessels, and when they are full, take them away."

5 So the woman went and shut the door upon her and upon her sons. They brought her the vessels, and she poured in. 6 And when the vessels were full, she said to her son, "Bring me yet a vessel."

And he answered, "I have *no more.*" And the oil stood.

7 And she came and told the man of God. And he said, "Go; sell the oil, and pay thy creditor, and thou and thy sons live of the rest."

8 And *there was a day when* Elisha passed by Shunem. Now there was a great woman there who detained him to eat

comederet panem, cumque frequenter inde transiret devertebat ad eam ut comederet panem. 9 Quae dixit ad virum suum, "Animadverto quod vir Dei sanctus est iste qui transit per nos frequenter. 10 Faciamus ergo ei cenaculum parvum et ponamus ei in eo lectulum et mensam et sellam et candelabrum ut cum venerit ad nos maneat ibi."

11 Facta est igitur dies quaedam et veniens devertit in cenaculum et requievit ibi. 12 Dixitque ad Giezi, puerum suum, "Voca Sunamitin istam." Qui cum vocasset eam et illa stetisset coram eo 13 dixit ad puerum suum, "Loquere ad eam, 'Ecce: sedule in omnibus ministrasti nobis; quid vis ut faciam tibi? Numquid habes negotium, et vis ut loquar regi sive principi militiae?'"

Quae respondit, "In medio populi mei habito."

14 Et ait, "Quid ergo vult ut faciam ei?"

Dixitque Giezi, "Ne quaeras, filium enim non habet, et vir eius senex est."

15 Praecepit itaque ut vocaret eam, quae cum vocata fuisset et stetisset ante ostium 16 dixit ad eam, "In tempore isto et in hac eadem hora si vita comes fuerit, habebis in utero filium."

At illa respondit, "Noli, quaeso, domine mi, vir Dei, noli mentiri ancillae tuae." 17 Et concepit mulier et peperit filium in tempore et in hora eadem quam dixerat Heliseus.

18 Crevit autem puer, et cum esset quaedam dies et egressus isset ad patrem suum ad messores 19 ait patri suo, "Caput meum doleo; caput meum doleo!"

bread, and as he passed often that way he turned into *her house* to eat bread. 9 And she said to her husband, "I perceive that this is a holy man of God who often passeth by us. 10 Let us therefore make him a little chamber and put a little bed in it for him and a table and a stool and a candlestick that when he cometh to us he may abide there."

11 Now *there was* a certain day *when* he came and turned in to the chamber and rested there. 12 And he said to Gehazi, his servant, "Call this Shunammitess." And when he had called her and she stood before him 13 he said to his servant, "Say to her, 'Behold: thou hast diligently served us in all things; what wilt thou have me to do for thee? Hast thou any business, and wilt thou that I speak to the king or to the general of the army?'"

And she answered, "I dwell in the midst of my own people."

14 And he said, "What will she then that I do for her?"

And Gehazi said, "Do not ask, for she hath no son, and her husband is old."

15 Then he bid him call her, and when she was called and stood before the door 16 he said to her, "At this time and this same hour if life accompany, thou shalt have a son in thy womb."

But she answered, "Do not, I beseech thee, my lord, thou man of God, do not lie to thy handmaid." 17 And the woman conceived and brought forth a son in the time and at the same hour that Elisha had said.

18 And the child grew, and *on a certain day when* he went out to his father to the reapers 19 he said to his father, "My head acheth; my head acheth!"

At ille dixit puero, "Tolle, et duc eum ad matrem suam." 20 Qui cum tulisset et adduxisset eum ad matrem suam posuit eum illa super genua sua usque ad meridiem, et mortuus est.

21 Ascendit autem et conlocavit eum super lectulum hominis Dei et clusit ostium, et egressa 22 vocavit virum suum et ait, "Mitte mecum, obsecro, unum de pueris et asinam ut excurram usque ad hominem Dei et revertar."

23 Qui ait illi, "Quam ob causam vadis ad eum? Hodie non sunt kalendae neque sabbatum."

Quae respondit, "Vadam." 24 Stravitque asinam et praecepit puero, "Mina, et propera; ne mihi moram facias in eundo, et hoc age quod praecipio tibi."

25 Profecta est igitur et venit ad virum Dei in Montem Carmeli, cumque vidisset eam vir Dei de contra ait ad Giezi, puerum suum, "Ecce Sunamitis illa. 26 Vade ergo in occursum eius, et dic ei, 'Rectene agitur circa te et circa virum tuum et circa filium tuum?'"

Quae respondit, "Recte."

27 Cumque venisset ad virum Dei in montem adprehendit pedes eius, et accessit Giezi ut amoveret eam. Et ait homo Dei, "Dimitte illam, anima enim eius in amaritudine est, et Dominus celavit a me et non indicavit mihi."

28 Quae dixit illi, "Numquid petivi filium a domino meo? Numquid non dixi tibi, 'Ne inludas me'?"

29 Et ille ait ad Giezi, "Accinge lumbos tuos, et tolle baculum meum in manu tua, et vade. Si occurrerit tibi homo, non salutes eum, et si salutaverit te quispiam, non respondeas illi, et pones baculum meum super faciem pueri."

But he said to his servant, "Take him, and carry him to his mother." 20 And when he had taken him and brought him to his mother she set him on her knees until noon, and *then* he died.

21 And she went up and laid him upon the bed of the man of God and shut the door, and going out 22 she called her husband and said, "Send with me, I beseech thee, one of thy servants and an ass that I may run to the man of God and come again."

23 And he said to her, "Why dost thou go to him? Today is neither new moon nor sabbath."

She answered, "I will go." 24 And she saddled an ass and commanded her servant, "Drive, and make haste; *make* no stay in going, and do that which I bid thee."

25 So she went forward and came to the man of God to Mount Carmel, and when the man of God saw her *coming towards* he said to Gehazi, his servant, "Behold that Shunammitess. 26 Go therefore to meet her, and say to her, 'Is all well with thee and with thy husband and with thy son?'"

And she answered, "Well."

27 And when she came to the man of God to the mount she caught hold on his feet, and Gehazi came to remove her. And the man of God said, "Let her alone, for her soul is in anguish, and the Lord hath hid it from me and hath not told me."

28 And she said to him, "Did I ask a son of my lord? Did I not say to thee, 'Do not deceive me'?"

29 Then he said to Gehazi, "Gird up thy loins, and take my staff in thy hand, and go. If *any* man meet thee, salute him not, and if any man salute thee, answer him not, and *lay* my staff upon the face of the child."

30 Porro mater pueri ait, "Vivit Dominus, et vivit anima tua; non dimittam te." Surrexit ergo et secutus est eam.

31 Giezi autem praecesserat eos et posuerat baculum super faciem pueri, et non erat vox neque sensus, reversusque est in occursum eius et nuntiavit ei, dicens, "Non surrexit puer."

32 Ingressus est ergo Heliseus domum, et ecce: puer mortuus iacebat in lectulo eius. 33 Ingressusque clusit ostium super se et super puerum et oravit ad Dominum. 34 Et ascendit et incubuit super puerum, posuitque os suum super os eius et oculos suos super oculos eius et manus suas super manus eius, et incurvavit se super eum, et calefacta est caro pueri. 35 At ille reversus deambulavit in domo, semel huc et illuc, et ascendit et incubuit super eum, et oscitavit puer septies aperuitque oculos. 36 At ille vocavit Giezi et dixit ei, "Voca Sunamitin hanc." Quae vocata ingressa est ad eum, qui ait, "Tolle filium tuum." 37 Venit illa et corruit ad pedes eius et adoravit super terram tulitque filium suum et egressa est.

38 Et Heliseus reversus est in Galgala, erat autem fames in terra, et filii prophetarum habitabant coram eo. Dixitque uni de pueris suis, "Pone ollam grandem, et coque pulmentum filiis prophetarum." 39 Et egressus est unus in agrum ut colligeret herbas agrestes, invenitque quasi vitem silvestrem et collegit ex ea colocyntidas agri et implevit pallium suum, et reversus concidit in ollam pulmenti, nesciebat enim quid esset.

40 Infuderunt ergo sociis ut comederent, cumque gustassent de coctione exclamaverunt, dicentes, "Mors in olla, vir Dei!" Et non potuerunt comedere.

30 But the mother of the child said, "As the Lord liveth, and as thy soul liveth, I will not leave thee." He arose therefore and followed her.

31 But Gehazi was gone before them and laid the staff upon the face of the child, and there was no voice nor sense, and he returned to meet him and told him, saying, "The child is not risen."

32 Elisha therefore went into the house, and behold: the child lay dead on his bed. 33 And going in he shut the door upon him and upon the child and prayed to the Lord. 34 And he went up and lay upon the child, and he put his mouth upon his mouth and his eyes upon his eyes and his hands upon his hands, and he bowed himself upon him, and the child's flesh grew warm. 35 Then he returned and walked in the house, once to and fro, and he went up and lay upon him, and the child gaped seven times and opened his eyes. 36 And he called Gehazi and said to him, "Call this Shunammitess." And she being called went in to him, and he said, "Take up thy son." 37 She came and fell at his feet and worshipped upon the ground and took up her son and went out.

38 And Elisha returned to Gilgal, and there was a famine in the land, and the sons of the prophets dwelt before him. And he said to one of his servants, "Set on the great pot, and boil pottage for the sons of the prophets." 39 And one went out into the field to gather wild herbs, and he found something like a wild vine and gathered of it wild gourds of the field and filled his mantle, and coming back he shred them into the pot of pottage, for he knew not what it was.

40 And they poured it out for their companions to eat, and when they had tasted of the pottage they cried out, saying, "Death is in the pot, O man of God!" And they could not eat thereof.

41 At ille, "Adferte," inquit, "farinam." Cumque tulissent, misit in ollam et ait, "Infunde turbae ut comedant." Et non fuit amplius quicquam amaritudinis in olla.

42 Vir autem quidam venit de Balsalisa deferens viro Dei panes primitiarum et viginti panes hordiacios et frumentum novum in pera sua. At ille dixit, "Da populo ut comedat."

43 Responditque ei minister eius, "Quantum est hoc ut adponam coram centum viris?"

Rursum ille, "Da," ait, "populo ut comedat, haec enim dicit Dominus: 'Comedent, et supererit.'"

44 Posuit itaque coram eis, qui comederunt, et superfuit iuxta verbum Domini.

Caput 5

Naaman, princeps militiae regis Syriae, erat vir magnus apud dominum suum et honoratus, per illum enim dedit Dominus salutem Syriae, erat autem vir fortis et dives, sed leprosus. 2 Porro de Syria egressi fuerant latrunculi et captivam duxerant de terra Israhel puellam parvulam, quae erat

41 But he said, "Bring *some* meal." And when they had brought it, he cast it into the pot and said, "Pour out for the people that they may eat." And there was *now* no bitterness in the pot.

42 And a certain man came from Baal-shalishah bringing to the man of God bread of the firstfruits, twenty loaves of barley and new corn in his scrip. And he said, "Give to the people that they may eat."

43 And his servant answered him, "How much is this that I should set it before a hundred men?"

He said again, "Give to the people that they may eat, for thus saith the Lord: 'They shall eat, and there shall be left.'"

44 So he set it before them, and they ate, and there was left according to the word of the Lord.

Chapter 5

Naaman, the Syrian, is cleansed of his leprosy. He professeth his belief in one God, promising to serve him. Gehazi taketh gifts of Naaman and is struck with leprosy.

Naaman, general of the army of the king of Syria, was a great man with his master and honourable, for by him the Lord gave deliverance to Syria, and he was a valiant man and rich, but a leper. 2 Now there had gone out robbers from Syria and had led away captive out of the land of Israel a lit-

in obsequio uxoris Naaman. 3 Quae ait ad dominam suam, "Utinam fuisset dominus meus ad prophetam qui est in Samaria. Profecto curasset eum a lepra quam habet."

4 Ingressus est itaque Naaman ad dominum suum et nuntiavit ei, dicens, "Sic et sic locuta est puella de terra Israhel."

5 Dixitque ei rex Syriae, "Vade, et mittam litteras ad regem Israhel." Qui cum profectus esset et tulisset secum decem talenta argenti et sex milia aureos et decem mutatoria vestimentorum 6 detulit litteras ad regem Israhel in haec verba, "Cum acceperis epistulam hanc, scito quod miserim ad te Naaman, servum meum, ut cures eum a lepra sua."

7 Cumque legisset rex Israhel litteras scidit vestimenta sua et ait, "Numquid Deus sum, ut occidere possim et vivificare, quia iste misit ad me ut curem hominem a lepra sua? Animadvertite, et videte quod occasiones quaerat adversum me."

8 Quod cum audisset Heliseus, vir Dei, scidisse, videlicet, regem Israhel vestimenta sua, misit ad eum, dicens, "Quare scidisti vestimenta tua? Veniat ad me, et sciat esse prophetam in Israhel."

9 Venit ergo Naaman cum equis et curribus et stetit ad ostium domus Helisei, 10 misitque ad eum Heliseus nuntium, dicens, "Vade, et lavare septies in Iordane, et recipiet sanitatem caro tua, atque mundaberis."

11 Iratus Naaman recedebat, dicens, "Putabam quod egrederetur ad me et stans invocaret nomen Domini, Dei sui, et tangeret manu sua locum leprae et curaret me. 12 Numquid

tle maid, and she waited upon Naaman's wife. 3 And she said to her mistress, "I wish my master had been with the prophet that is in Samaria. He would certainly have healed him of the leprosy which he hath."

4 Then Naaman went in to his lord and told him, saying, "Thus and thus said the girl from the land of Israel."

5 And the king of Syria sad to him, "Go, and I will send a letter to the king of Israel." *And* he departed and took with him ten talents of silver and six thousand pieces of gold and ten changes of raiment 6 *and* brought the letter to the king of Israel in these words, "When thou shalt receive this letter, know that I have sent to thee Naaman, my servant, that thou mayest heal him of his leprosy."

7 And when the king of Israel had read the letter he rent his garments and said, "Am I God, to be able to kill and give life, that this man hath sent to me to heal a man of his leprosy? Mark, and see *how* he seeketh occasions against me."

8 And when Elisha, the man of God, had heard this, to wit, that the king of Israel had rent his garments, he sent to him, saying, "Why hast thou rent thy garments? Let him come to me, and let him know that there is a prophet in Israel."

9 So Naaman came with his horses and chariots and stood at the door of the house of Elisha, 10 and Elisha sent a messenger to him, saying, "Go, and wash seven times in the Jordan, and thy flesh shall recover health, and thou shalt be clean."

11 Naaman was angry and went away, saying, "I thought he would have come out to me and standing would have invoked the name of the Lord, his God, and touched with his hand the place of the leprosy and healed me. 12 Are not the

non meliores sunt Abana et Pharphar, fluvii Damasci, omnibus aquis Israhel ut laver in eis et munder?"

Cum ergo vertisset se et abiret indignans, 13 accesserunt ad eum servi sui et locuti sunt ei, "Pater, et si rem grandem dixisset tibi propheta, certe facere debueras. Quanto magis quia nunc dixit tibi, 'Lavare, et mundaberis'?" 14 Descendit et lavit in Iordane septies iuxta sermonem viri Dei, et restituta est caro eius sicut caro pueri parvuli, et mundatus est.

15 Reversusque ad virum Dei cum universo comitatu suo, venit et stetit coram eo et ait, "Vere scio quod non sit alius Deus in universa terra nisi tantum in Israhel. Obsecro itaque ut accipias benedictionem a servo tuo."

16 At ille respondit, "Vivit Dominus ante quem sto, quia non accipiam." Cumque vim faceret penitus non adquievit.

17 Dixitque Naaman, "Ut vis, sed, obsecro, concede mihi, servo tuo, ut tollam onus duorum burdonum de terra, non enim faciet ultra servus tuus holocaustum aut victimam diis alienis, nisi Domino. 18 Hoc autem solum est de quo depreceris Dominum pro servo tuo, quando ingredietur dominus meus templum Remmon ut adoret et illo innitente super manum meam, si adoravero in templo Remmon adorante eo in eodem loco: ut ignoscat mihi Dominus, servo tuo, pro hac re."

19 Qui dixit ei, "Vade in pace." Abiit ergo ab eo electo terrae tempore.

Abana and the Pharpar, rivers of Damascus, better than all the waters of Israel that I may wash in them and be made clean?"

So as he turned and was going away with indignation, 13 his servants came to him and said to him, "Father, *if* the prophet had bid thee do some great thing, surely thou shouldst have done it. How much rather *what* he now hath said to thee, 'Wash, and thou shalt he clean'?" 14 *Then* he went down and washed in the Jordan seven times according to the word of the man of God, and his flesh was restored like the flesh of a little child, and he was made clean.

15 And returning to the man of God with all his train, he came and stood before him and said, "In truth I know there is no other God in all the earth but only in Israel. I beseech thee therefore, *take* a blessing of thy servant."

16 But he answered, "As the Lord liveth before whom I stand, I will receive none." And when he *pressed him he still refused.*

17 And Naaman said, "As thou wilt, but, I beseech thee, grant to me, thy servant, to take *from hence* two mules' burden of earth, for thy servant will not henceforth offer holocaust or victim to other gods, but to the Lord. 18 But there is only this for which thou shalt entreat the Lord for thy servant, when my master *goeth* into the temple of Rimmon to worship and he leaneth upon my hand, if I bow down in the temple of Rimmon when he boweth down in the same place: that the Lord pardon me, thy servant, for this thing."

19 And he said to him, "Go in peace." So he departed from him in the *spring* time of the earth.

20 Dixitque Giezi, puer viri Dei, "Pepercit dominus meus Naaman, Syro isti, ut non acciperet ab eo quae adtulit. Vivit Dominus, quia curram post eum et accipiam ab eo aliquid."

21 Et secutus est Giezi post tergum Naaman, quem cum vidisset ille currentem ad se desilivit de curru in occursum eius et ait, "Rectene sunt omnia?"

22 Et ille ait, "Recte. Dominus meus misit me ad te, dicens, 'Modo venerunt ad me duo adulescentes de Monte Ephraim ex filiis prophetarum. Da eis talentum argenti et vestes mutatorias duplices.'"

23 Dixitque Naaman, "Melius est ut accipias duo talenta." Et coegit eum ligavitque duo talenta argenti in duobus saccis et duplicia vestimenta et inposuit duobus pueris suis, qui et portaverunt coram eo.

24 Cumque venisset (iam vesperi) tulit de manu eorum et reposuit in domo dimisitque viros, et abierunt. 25 Ipse autem ingressus stetit coram domino suo. Et dixit Heliseus, "Unde venis, Giezi?"

Qui respondit, "Non ivit servus tuus quoquam."

26 At ille, "Nonne," ait, "cor meum in praesenti erat quando reversus est homo de curru suo in occursum tui? Nunc igitur accepisti argentum et accepisti vestes ut emas oliveta et vineta et oves et boves et servos et ancillas, 27 sed et lepra Naaman adherebit tibi et semini tuo in sempiternum." Et egressus est ab eo leprosus quasi nix.

20 *But* Gehazi, the servant of the man of God, said, "My master hath spared Naaman, this Syrian, *in not receiving* of him that which he brought. As the Lord liveth, I will run after him and take some thing of him."

21 And Gehazi followed after Naaman, and when he saw him running after him he leapt down from his chariot to meet him and said, "Is all well?"

22 And he said, "Well. My master hath sent me to thee, saying, 'Just now there are come to me from Mount Ephraim two young men of the sons of the prophets. Give them a talent of silver and two changes of garments.'"

23 And Naaman said, "It is better that thou take two talents." And he forced him and bound two talents of silver in two bags and *two changes of* garments and laid them upon two of his servants, and they carried them before him.

24 And when he was come *(and* now it was the evening) he took them from their *hands* and laid them up in the house and sent the men away, and they departed. 25 But he went in and stood before his master. And Elisha said, "Whence comest thou, Gehazi?"

He answered, "Thy servant went no whither."

26 But he said, "Was not my heart present when the man turned back from his chariot to meet thee? So now thou hast received money and received garments to buy oliveyards and vineyards and sheep and oxen and menservants and maidservants, 27 but the leprosy of Naaman shall also stick to thee and to thy seed for ever." And he went out from him a leper *as white as* snow.

Caput 6

Dixerunt autem filii prophetarum ad Heliseum, "Ecce: locus in quo habitamus coram te angustus est nobis. 2 Eamus usque ad Iordanem, et tollant singuli de silva materias singulas ut aedificemus nobis ibi locum ad habitandum."

Qui dixit, "Ite."

3 Et ait unus ex illis, "Veni ergo et tu cum servis tuis."

Respondit, "Ego veniam."

4 Et abiit cum eis, cumque venissent ad Iordanem caedebant ligna, 5 accidit autem ut cum unus materiem succidisset caderet ferrum securis in aquam, exclamavitque ille et ait, "Eheu! Eheu! Eheu, domine mi, et hoc ipsum mutuo acceperam!"

6 Dixit autem homo Dei, "Ubi cecidit?" At ille monstravit ei locum. Praecidit ergo lignum et misit illuc, natavitque ferrum. 7 Et ait, "Tolle." Qui extendit manum et tulit illud.

Chapter 6

Elisha maketh iron to swim upon the water. He leadeth the
Syrians that were sent to apprehend him into Samaria
where, their eyes being opened, they are courteously entertained. The Syrians besiege Samaria. The famine there
causeth a woman to eat her own child. Upon this the king
commandeth Elisha to be put to death.

And the sons of the prophets said to Elisha, "Behold:
the place where we dwell *with thee is too* strait for us. 2 Let
us go as far as the Jordan, and take out of the wood every
man a piece of timber that we may build us there a place to
dwell in."

And he said, "Go."

3 And one of them said, "But come thou also with thy servants."

He answered, "I will come."

4 So he went with them, and when they were come to the
Jordan they cut down wood, 5 and it happened as one was
felling *some* timber that the head of the axe fell into the water, and he cried out and said, "Alas! Alas! Alas, my lord, *for*
this same *was borrowed!*"

6 And the man of God said, "Where did it fall?" And he
shewed him the place. Then he cut off a piece of wood and
cast it in thither, and the iron swam. 7 And he said, "Take it
up." And he put out his hand and took it.

8 Rex autem Syriae pugnabat contra Israhel consiliumque iniit cum servis suis, dicens, "In loco illo et illo ponamus insidias."

9 Misit itaque vir Dei ad regem Israhel, dicens, "Cave ne transeas in locum illum, quia ibi Syri in insidiis sunt." 10 Misit itaque rex Israhel ad locum quem dixerat ei vir Dei et praeoccupavit eum et observavit se ibi non semel neque bis.

11 Conturbatumque est cor regis Syriae pro hac re, et convocatis servis suis, ait, "Quare non indicatis mihi quis proditor mei sit apud regem Israhel?"

12 Dixitque unus servorum eius, "Nequaquam, domine mi, rex, sed Heliseus, propheta qui est in Israhel, indicat regi Israhel omnia verba quaecumque locutus fueris in conclavi tuo."

13 Dixitque eis, "Ite, et videte ubi sit ut mittam et capiam eum."

Adnuntiaveruntque ei, dicentes, "Ecce: in Dothan."

14 Misit ergo illuc equos et currus et robur exercitus, qui cum venissent nocte circumdederunt civitatem. 15 Consurgens autem diluculo minister viri Dei egressus est viditque exercitum in circuitu civitatis et equos et currus, nuntiavitque ei, dicens, "Eheu! Eheu! Eheu, domine mi, quid faciemus?"

16 At ille respondit, "Noli timere, plures enim nobiscum sunt quam cum illis." 17 Cumque orasset Heliseus ait, "Domine, aperi oculos huius ut videat." Et aperuit Dominus oculos pueri, et vidit. Et ecce: mons plenus equorum et curruum igneorum in circuitu Helisei. 18 Hostes vero descende-

8 And the king of Syria warred against Israel and took counsel with his servants, saying, "In such and such a place let us lay ambushes."

9 And the man of God sent to the king of Israel, saying, "Beware that thou pass not to such a place, for the Syrians are there in ambush." 10 And the king of Israel sent to the place which the man of God had told him and prevented him and looked well to himself there not once nor twice.

11 And the heart of the king of Syria was troubled for this thing, and calling together his servants, he said, "Why do you not tell me who it is that betrays me to the king of Israel?"

12 And one of his servants said, "No one, my lord, O king, but Elisha, the prophet that is in Israel, telleth the king of Israel all the words that thou speakest in thy privy chamber."

13 And he said to them, "Go, and see where he is that I may send and take him."

And they told him, saying, "Behold: he is in Dothan."

14 Therefore he sent thither horses and chariots and the strength of an army, *and* they came by night *and* beset the city. 15 And the servant of the man of God rising early went out and saw an army round about the city and horses and chariots, and he told him, saying, "Alas! Alas! Alas, my lord, what shall we do?"

16 But he answered, "Fear not, for there are more with us than with them." 17 *And* Elisha prayed *and* said, "Lord, open his eyes that he may see." And the Lord opened the eyes of the servant, and he saw. And behold: the mountain was full of horses and chariots of fire round about Elisha. 18 And the

runt ad eum, porro Heliseus oravit ad Dominum, dicens, "Percute, obsecro, gentem hanc caecitate." Percussitque eos Dominus ne viderent iuxta verbum Helisei. 19 Dixit autem ad eos Heliseus, "Non est haec via, nec ista est civitas. Sequimini me, et ostendam vobis virum quem quaeritis." Duxit ergo eos in Samariam. 20 Cumque ingressi fuissent in Samariam, dixit Heliseus, "Domine, aperi oculos istorum ut videant." Aperuitque Dominus oculos eorum, et viderunt esse se in medio Samariae.

21 Dixitque rex Israhel ad Heliseum cum vidisset eos, "Numquid percutiam eos, pater mi?"

22 At ille ait, "Non percuties, neque enim cepisti eos gladio et arcu tuo ut percutias, sed pone panem et aquam coram eis ut comedant et bibant et vadant ad dominum suum." 23 Adpositaque est eis ciborum magna praeparatio, et comederunt et biberunt, et dimisit eos, abieruntque ad dominum suum, et ultra non venerunt latrones Syriae in terram Israhel.

24 Factum est autem post haec congregavit Benadad, rex Syriae, universum exercitum suum et ascendit et obsidebat Samariam. 25 Factaque est fames magna in Samaria, et tamdiu obsessa est donec venundaretur caput asini octoginta argenteis et quarta pars cabi stercoris columbarum quinque argenteis. 26 Cumque rex Israhel transiret per murum mulier quaedam exclamavit ad eum, dicens, "Salva me, domine mi, rex."

enemies came down to him, but Elisha prayed to the Lord, saying, "Strike, I beseech thee, this people with blindness." And the Lord struck them *with blindness* according to the word of Elisha. 19 And Elisha said to them, "This is not the way, neither is this the city. Follow me, and I will shew you the man whom you seek." So he led them into Samaria. 20 And when they were come into Samaria, Elisha said, "Lord, open the eyes of these men that they may see." And the Lord opened their eyes, and they saw themselves to be in the midst of Samaria.

21 And the king of Israel said to Elisha when he saw them, "My father, shall I kill them?"

22 And he said, "Thou shalt not kill them, for thou didst not take them with thy sword or thy bow that thou mayst kill them, but set bread and water before them that they may eat and drink and go to their master." 23 And a great provision of meats was set before them, and they ate and drank, and he let them go, and they went away to their master, and the robbers of Syria came no more into the land of Israel.

24 And it came to pass after these things that Ben-hadad, king of Syria, gathered together all his army and went up and besieged Samaria. 25 And there was a great famine in Samaria, and so long *did the siege continue* till the head of an ass was sold for fourscore pieces of silver and the fourth part of a cabe of pigeon's dung for five pieces of silver. 26 And as the king of Israel was passing by the wall a certain woman cried out to him, saying, "Save me, my lord, O king."

27 Qui ait, "Non, te salvet Dominus; unde salvare te possum? De area, an de torculari?" Dixitque ad eam rex, "Quid tibi vis?"

Quae respondit, 28 "Mulier ista dixit mihi, 'Da filium tuum ut comedamus eum hodie, et filium meum comedemus cras.' 29 Coximus ergo filium meum et comedimus. Dixique ei die altera, 'Da filium tuum ut comedamus eum.' Quae abscondit filium suum."

30 Quod cum audisset rex scidit vestimenta sua et transiebat per murum. Viditque omnis populus cilicium quo vestitus erat ad carnem intrinsecus. 31 Et ait rex, "Haec mihi faciat Deus, et haec addat, si steterit caput Helisei, filii Saphat, super eum hodie."

32 Heliseus autem sedebat in domo sua, et senes sedebant cum eo, praemisit itaque virum, et antequam veniret nuntius ille dixit ad senes, "Numquid scitis quod miserit filius homicidae hic ut praecidatur caput meum? Videte ergo: cum venerit nuntius, cludite ostium, et non sinatis eum introire, ecce enim, sonitus pedum domini eius post eum est."

33 Adhuc illo loquente eis, apparuit nuntius qui veniebat ad eum, et ait, "Ecce: tantum malum a Domino est. Quid amplius expectabo a Domino?"

27 And he said, "*If* the Lord *doth not save* thee, how can I save thee? Out of the barnfloor, or out of the winepress?" And the king said to her, "*What aileth thee?*"

And she answered, 28 "This woman said to me, 'Give thy son that we may eat him today, and we will eat my son tomorrow.' 29 So we boiled my son and ate him. And I said to her on the next day, 'Give thy son that we may eat him.' And she hath hid her son."

30 When the king heard this he rent his garments and passed by *upon* the wall. And all the people saw the haircloth which he wore within next to his flesh. 31 And the king said, "May God do so and so to me, and may he add more, if the head of Elisha, the son of Shaphat, shall stand on him this day."

32 But Elisha sat in his house, and the ancients sat with him, so he sent a man before, and before that messenger came he said to the ancients, "Do you know that this son of a murderer hath sent to cut off my head? Look then: when the messenger shall come, shut the door, and suffer him not to come in, for behold, the sound of his master's feet is behind him."

33 While he was yet speaking to them, the messenger appeared who was coming to him, and he said, "Behold: so great an evil is from the Lord. What shall I look for more from the Lord?"

Caput 7

Dixit autem Heliseus, "Audite verbum Domini. Haec dicit Dominus: 'In tempore hoc cras modius similae uno statere erit et duo modii hordei statere uno in porta Samariae.'"

2 Respondens unus de ducibus super cuius manum rex incumbebat homini Dei, ait, "Si Dominus fecerit etiam cataractas in caelo, numquid poterit esse quod loqueris?"

Qui ait, "Videbis oculis tuis et inde non comedes."

3 Quattuor ergo viri erant leprosi iuxta introitum portae, qui dixerunt ad invicem, "Quid hic esse volumus donec moriamur? 4 Sive ingredi voluerimus civitatem, fame moriemur, sive manserimus hic, moriendum nobis est. Venite, igitur, et transfugiamus ad castra Syriae. Si pepercerint nobis, vivemus, si autem occidere voluerint, nihilominus moriemur." 5 Surrexerunt igitur vesperi ut venirent ad castra Syriae, cumque venissent ad principium castrorum Syriae nullum

Chapter 7

Elisha prophesieth a great plenty, which presently ensueth upon the sudden flight of the Syrians, of which four lepers bring the news to the city. The incredulous nobleman is trod to death.

And Elisha said, "Hear ye the word of the Lord. Thus saith the Lord: 'Tomorrow *about* this time a bushel of fine hour shall be sold for a stater and two bushels of barley for a stater in the gate of Samaria.'"

2 Then one of the lords upon whose hand the king leaned, answering the man of God, said, "If the Lord should make flood-gates in heaven, can that possibly be which thou sayest?"

And he said, "Thou shalt see it with thy eyes but shalt not eat thereof."

3 Now there were four lepers at the entering in of the gate, and they said one to another, "What mean we to stay here till we die? 4 If we will enter into the city, we shall die with the famine, and if we will remain here, we must also die. Come, therefore, and let us run over to the camp of the Syrians. If they spare us, we shall live, but if they kill us, we shall but die." 5 So they arose in the evening to go to the Syrian camp, and when they were come to the first part of the

ibidem reppererunt, 6 siquidem Dominus sonitum audiri fecerat in castris Syriae curruum et equorum et exercitus plurimi, dixeruntque ad invicem, "Ecce: mercede conduxit adversum nos rex Israhel reges Hettheorum et Aegyptiorum, et venerunt super nos." 7 Surrexerunt ergo et fugerunt in tenebris et dereliquerunt tentoria sua et equos et asinos in castris fugeruntque animas tantum suas salvare cupientes. 8 Igitur cum venissent leprosi illi ad principium castrorum ingressi sunt unum tabernaculum et comederunt et biberunt, tuleruntque inde argentum et aurum et vestes et abierunt et absconderunt, et rursum reversi sunt ad aliud tabernaculum et inde similiter auferentes absconderunt. 9 Dixeruntque ad invicem, "Non recte facimus, haec enim dies boni nuntii est. Si tacuerimus et noluerimus nuntiare usque mane, sceleris arguemur. Venite; eamus et nuntiemus in aula regis." 10 Cumque venissent ad portam civitatis narraverunt eis, dicentes, "Ivimus ad castra Syriae, et nullum ibidem repperimus hominem nisi equos et asinos alligatos et fixa tentoria." 11 Ierunt ergo portarii et nuntiaverunt in palatio regis intrinsecus.

12 Qui surrexit nocte et ait ad servos suos, "Dico vobis quid fecerint nobis Syri: sciunt quia fame laboramus, et idcirco egressi sunt de castris et latitant in agris, dicentes, 'Cum egressi fuerint de civitate capiemus eos viventes, et tunc civitatem ingredi poterimus.'"

13 Respondit autem unus servorum eius, "Tollamus quin-

camp of the Syrians they found no man there, 6 for the Lord had made them hear in the camp of Syria the noise of chariots and of horses and of a very great army, and they said one to another, "Behold: the king of Israel hath hired against us the kings of the Hittites and of the Egyptians, and they are come upon us." 7 *Wherefore* they arose and fled away in the dark and left their tents and their horses and asses in the camp and fled *desiring* to save their lives. 8 So when these lepers were come to the beginning of the camp they went into one tent and ate and drank, and they took from thence silver and gold and raiment and went and hid it, and they came again and went into another tent and carried from thence in like manner and hid it. 9 Then they said one to another, "We do not well, for this is a day of good tidings. If we hold our peace and do not tell it till the morning, we shall be charged with a crime. Come; let us go and tell it in the king's court." 10 *So* they came to the gate of the city *and* told them, saying, "We went to the camp of the Syrians, and we found no man there but horses and asses tied and the tents standing." 11 Then the guards of the gate went and told it within the king's palace.

12 And he arose in the night and said to his servants, "I tell you what the Syrians have done to us: they know that we suffer *great* famine, and therefore they are gone out of the camp and lie hid in the fields, saying, 'When they come out of the city we shall take them alive, and then we may get into the city.'"

13 And one of his servants answered, "Let us take the five

que equos qui remanserunt in urbe, quia ipsi tantum sunt in universa multitudine Israhel, alii enim consumpti sunt, et mittentes explorare poterimus."

14 Adduxerunt ergo duos equos, misitque rex in castra Syrorum, dicens, "Ite, et videte." 15 Qui abierunt post eos usque ad Iordanem, ecce autem: omnis via plena erat vestibus et vasis quae proiecerant Syri cum turbarentur, reversique nuntii indicaverunt regi. 16 Et egressus populus diripuit castra Syriae, factusque est modius similae statere uno et duo modii hordei statere uno iuxta verbum Domini.

17 Porro rex ducem illum in cuius manu incubuerat constituit ad portam, quem conculcavit turba in introitu portae, et mortuus est iuxta quod locutus fuerat vir Dei quando descenderat rex ad eum. 18 Factumque est secundum sermonem viri Dei quem dixerat regi quando ait, "Duo modii hordei statere uno erunt et modius similae statere uno hoc eodem tempore cras in porta Samariae," 19 quando responderat dux ille viro Dei et dixerat, "Etiam si Dominus fecerit cataractas in caelo, numquid fieri poterit quod loqueris?" et dixit ei, "Videbis oculis tuis et inde non comedes."

20 Evenit ergo ei sicut praedictum erat, et conculcavit eum populus in porta, et mortuus est.

horses that are remaining in the city, because there are no more in the whole multitude of Israel, for the rest are consumed, and *let us send and see."*

14 They brought therefore two horses, and the king sent into the camp of the Syrians, saying, "Go, and see." 15 And they went after them as far as the Jordan, and behold: all the way was full of garments and vessels which the Syrians had cast away *in their fright,* and the messengers returned and told the king. 16 And the people going out pillaged the camp of the Syrians, and a bushel of fine flour *was sold for* a stater and two bushels of barley for a stater according to the word of the Lord.

17 And the king appointed that lord on whose hand he leaned to stand at the gate, and the people trod upon him in the entrance of the gate, and he died as the man of God had said when the king came down to him. 18 And it came to pass according to the word of the man of God which he spoke to the king when he said, "Two bushels of barley shall be for a stater and a bushel of fine flour for a stater at this very time tomorrow in the gate of Samaria," 19 when that lord answered the man of God and said, "Although the Lord should make flood-gates in heaven, could this come to pass which thou sayest?" and he said to him, "Thou shalt see with thy eyes and shalt not eat thereof."

20 And so it fell out to him as it was foretold, and the people trod upon him in the gate, and he died.

Caput 8

Heliseus autem locutus est ad mulierem cuius vivere fecerat filium, dicens, "Surge; vade tu et domus tua, et peregrinare ubicumque reppereris, vocavit enim Dominus famem, et veniet super terram septem annis."

2 Quae surrexit et fecit iuxta verbum hominis Dei, et vadens cum domo sua peregrinata est in terra Philisthim diebus multis. 3 Cumque finiti essent anni septem reversa est mulier de terra Philisthim, et egressa est ut interpellaret regem pro domo sua et pro agris suis. 4 Rex autem loquebatur cum Giezi, puero viri Dei, dicens, "Narra mihi omnia magnalia quae fecit Heliseus." 5 Cumque ille narraret regi quomodo mortuum suscitasset apparuit mulier cuius vivificaverat filium, clamans ad regem pro domo sua et pro agris suis.

Dixitque Giezi, "Domine mi, rex, haec est mulier, et hic filius eius quem suscitavit Heliseus!"

6 Et interrogavit rex mulierem, quae narravit ei, deditque ei rex eunuchum unum, dicens, "Restitue ei omnia quae sua

Chapter 8

After seven years' famine foretold by Elisha, the Shunammitess returning home recovereth her lands and revenues. Elisha foresheweth the death of Ben-hadad, king of Syria, and the reign of Hazael. Jehoram's wicked reign in Judah. He dieth, and his son Ahaziah succeedeth.

And Elisha spoke to the woman whose son he had restored to life, saying, "Arise, *and* go thou and thy household, and sojourn wheresoever thou canst find, for the Lord hath called a famine, and it shall come upon the land seven years."

2 And she arose and did according to the word of the man of God, and going with her household she sojourned in the land of the Philistines many days. 3 And when the seven years were ended the woman returned out of the land of the Philistines, and she went forth to speak to the king for her house and for her lands. 4 And the king talked with Gehazi, the servant of the man of God, saying, "Tell me all the great things that Elisha hath done." 5 And when he was telling the king how he had raised one dead to life the woman appeared whose son he had restored to life, crying to the king for her house and her lands.

And Gehazi said, "My lord, O king, this is the woman, and this is her son whom Elisha raised to life!"

6 And the king asked the woman, and she told him, and the king appointed her an eunuch, saying, "Restore her all

sunt et universos reditus agrorum a die qua reliquit terram usque ad praesens."

7 Venit quoque Heliseus Damascum, et Benadad, rex Syriae, aegrotabat, nuntiaveruntque ei, dicentes, "Venit vir Dei huc."

8 Et ait rex ad Azahel, "Tolle tecum munera, et vade in occursum viri Dei, et consule Dominum per eum, dicens, 'Si evadere potero de infirmitate mea hac?'"

9 Ivit igitur Azahel in occursum eius habens secum munera et omnia bona Damasci, onera quadraginta camelorum. Cumque stetisset coram eo, ait, "Filius tuus Benadad, rex Syriae, misit me ad te, dicens, 'Si sanari potero de infirmitate mea hac?'"

10 Dixitque ei Heliseus, "Vade; dic ei, 'Sanaberis, porro ostendit mihi Dominus quia morte morietur.'"

11 Stetitque cum eo et conturbatus est usque ad suffusionem vultus, flevitque vir Dei. 12 Cui Azahel ait, "Quare dominus meus flet?"

At ille dixit, "Quia scio quae facturus sis filiis Israhel mala. Civitates eorum munitas igne succendes, et iuvenes eorum interficies gladio, et parvulos eorum elides et praegnantes divides."

13 Dixitque Azahel, "Quid enim sum, servus tuus, canis, ut faciam rem istam magnam?"

Et ait Heliseus, "Ostendit mihi Dominus te regem Syriae fore."

14 Qui cum recessisset ab Heliseo venit ad dominum suum, qui ait ei, "Quid tibi dixit Heliseus?"

At ille respondit, "Dixit mihi, 'Recipies sanitatem.'"

that is hers and all the revenues of the lands from the day that she left the land to this present."

7 Elisha also came to Damascus, and Ben-hadad, king of Syria, was sick, and they told him, saying, "The man of God is come hither."

8 And the king said to Hazael, "Take with thee presents, and go to meet the man of God, and consult the Lord by him, saying, 'Can I *recover* of this my illness?'"

9 And Hazael went to meet him *taking* with him presents and all the good things of Damascus, the burdens of forty camels. And when he stood before him, he said, "Thy son Ben-hadad, the king of Syria, hath sent me to thee, saying, 'Can I recover of this my illness?'"

10 And Elisha said to him, "Go; tell him, 'Thou shalt recover, but the Lord hath shewn me that he shall surely die.'"

11 And he stood with him and was troubled so far as to blush, and the man of God wept. 12 And Hazael said to him, "Why doth my lord weep?"

And he said, "Because I know the evil that thou wilt do to the children of Israel. Their strong cities thou wilt burn with fire, and their young men thou wilt kill with the sword, and thou wilt dash their children and rip up their pregnant women."

13 And Hazael said, "But what am I, thy servant, a dog, that I should do this great thing?"

And Elisha said, "The Lord hath shewn me that thou shalt be king of Syria."

14 And when he was departed from Elisha he came to his master, who said to him, "What saith Elisha to thee?"

And he answered, "He told me, 'Thou shalt recover.'"

enim domus Ahab fuit. 28 Abiit quoque cum Ioram, filio Ahab, ad proeliandum contra Azahel, regem Syriae, in Ramoth Galaad, et vulneraverunt Syri Ioram, 29 qui reversus est ut curaretur in Hiezrahel quia vulneraverant eum Syri in Rama proeliantem contra Azahel, regem Syriae. Porro Ahazias, filius Ioram, rex Iuda, descendit invisere Ioram, filium Ahab, in Hiezrahel quia aegrotabat ibi.

Caput 9

Heliseus autem, prophetes, vocavit unum de filiis prophetarum et ait illi, "Accinge lumbos tuos, et tolle lenticulam olei hanc in manu tua, et vade in Ramoth Galaad. 2 Cumque veneris illuc videbis Hieu, filium Iosaphat, filii Namsi, et ingressus suscitabis eum de medio fratrum suorum et introduces in interius cubiculum. 3 Tenensque lenticulam olei fundes super caput eius et dices, 'Haec dicit Dominus: "Unxi te regem super Israhel."' Aperiesque ostium et fugies et non ibi subsistes."

in-law of the house of Ahab. 28 He went also with Joram, son of Ahab, to fight against Hazael, king of Syria, in Ramoth Gilead, and the Syrians wounded Joram, 29 and he went back to be healed in Jezreel because the Syrians had wounded him in Ramah when he fought against Hazael, king of Syria. And Ahaziah, the son of Jehoram, king of Judah, went down to visit Joram, the son of Ahab, in Jezreel because he was sick there.

Chapter 9

Jehu is anointed king of Israel to destroy the house of Ahab
and Jezebel. He killeth Joram, king of Israel, and Ahaziah,
king of Judah. Jezebel is eaten by dogs.

And Elisha, the prophet, called one of the sons of the prophets and said to him, "Gird up thy loins, and take this little bottle of oil in thy hand, and go to Ramoth Gilead. 2 And when thou art come thither thou shalt see Jehu, the son of Jehoshaphat, the son of Nimshi, and going in thou shalt make him rise up from amongst his brethren and carry him into an inner chamber. 3 Then taking the little bottle of oil thou shalt pour it on his head and shalt say, 'Thus saith the Lord: "I have anointed thee king over Israel."' And thou shalt open the door and flee and shalt not stay there."

4 Abiit ergo adulescens, puer prophetae, in Ramoth Galaad 5 et ingressus est illuc, ecce autem: principes exercitus sedebant, et ait, "Verbum mihi ad te, O princeps."

Dixitque Hieu, "Ad quem ex omnibus nobis?"

At ille dixit, "Ad te, O princeps."

6 Et surrexit et ingressus est cubiculum, at ille fudit oleum super caput eius et ait, "Haec dicit Dominus, Deus Israhel, 'Unxi te regem super populum Domini, Israhel. 7 Et percuties domum Ahab, domini tui, et ulciscar sanguinem servorum meorum, prophetarum, et sanguinem omnium servorum Domini de manu Hiezabel. 8 Perdamque omnem domum Ahab, et interficiam de Ahab mingentem ad parietem et clausum et novissimum in Israhel. 9 Et dabo domum Ahab sicut domum Hieroboam, filii Nabath, et sicut domum Baasa, filii Ahia. 10 Hiezabel quoque comedent canes in agro Hiezrahel, nec erit qui sepeliat eam.'" Aperuitque ostium et fugit.

11 Hieu autem egressus est ad servos domini sui, qui dixerunt ei, "Rectene sunt omnia? Quid venit insanus iste ad te?"

Qui ait eis, "Nostis hominem et quid locutus sit."

12 At illi responderunt, "Falsum est, sed magis narra nobis."

Qui ait eis, "Haec et haec locutus est mihi, et ait, 'Haec dicit Dominus: "Unxi te regem super Israhel."'"

13 Festinaverunt itaque et unusquisque tollens pallium

4 So the young man, the servant of the prophet, went away to Ramoth Gilead 5 and went in thither, and behold: the captains of the army were sitting, and he said, "I have a word to thee, O prince."

And Jehu said, "Unto whom of us all?"

And he said, "To thee, O prince."

6 And he arose and went into the chamber, and he poured the oil upon his head and said, "Thus saith the Lord, God of Israel, 'I have anointed thee king over Israel, the people of the Lord. 7 And thou shalt cut off the house of Ahab, thy master, and I will revenge the blood of my servants, the prophets, and the blood of all the servants of the Lord at the hand of Jezebel. 8 And I will destroy all the house of Ahab, and I will cut off from Ahab him that pisseth against the wall and him that is shut up and the meanest in Israel. 9 And I will make the house of Ahab like the house of Jeroboam, the son of Nebat, and like the house of Baasha, the son of Ahijah. 10 And the dogs shall eat Jezebel in the field of Jezreel, and there shall be no one to bury her.'" And he opened the door and fled.

11 Then Jehu went forth to the servants of his lord, and they said to him, "Are all things well? Why came this mad man to thee?"

And he said to them, "You know the man and what he said."

12 But they answered, "It is false, but rather do thou tell us."

And he said to them, "Thus and thus did he speak to me, and he said, 'Thus saith the Lord: "I have anointed thee king over Israel."'"

13 Then they made haste and taking every man his gar-

suum posuerunt sub pedibus eius in similitudinem tribunalis, et cecinerunt tuba atque dixerunt, "Regnavit Hieu."

14 Coniuravit ergo Hieu, filius Iosaphat, filii Namsi, contra Ioram. Porro Ioram obsederat Ramoth Galaad, ipse et omnis Israhel contra Azahel, regem Syriae, 15 et reversus fuerat ut curaretur in Hiezrahel propter vulnera, quia percusserant eum Syri proeliantem contra Azahel, regem Syriae. Dixitque Hieu, "Si placet vobis, nemo egrediatur profugus de civitate ne vadat et nuntiet in Hiezrahel."

16 Et ascendit et profectus est in Hiezrahel, Ioram enim aegrotabat ibi, et Ahazia, rex Iuda, descenderat ad visitandum Ioram. 17 Igitur speculator qui stabat super turrem Hiezrahel vidit globum Hieu venientis et ait, "Video ego globum."

Dixitque Ioram, "Tolle currum, et mitte in occursum eorum, et dicat vadens, 'Rectene sunt omnia?'"

18 Abiit igitur qui ascenderat currum in occursum eius et ait, "Haec dicit rex: 'Pacatane sunt omnia?'"

Dixitque Hieu, "Quid tibi et paci? Transi, et sequere me."

Nuntiavit quoque speculator, dicens, "Venit nuntius ad eos, et non revertitur."

19 Misit etiam currum equorum secundum, venitque ad eos et ait, "Haec dicit rex: 'Num pax est?'"

Et ait Hieu, "Quid tibi et paci? Transi, et sequere me."

20 Nuntiavit autem speculator, dicens, "Venit usque ad eos et non revertitur, est autem incessus quasi incessus Hieu, filii Namsi, praeceps enim graditur."

ment laid it under his feet after the manner of a judgment seat, and they sounded the trumpet and said, "Jehu is king."

14 So Jehu, the son of Jehoshaphat, the son of Nimshi, conspired against Joram. Now Joram had besieged Ramoth Gilead, he and all Israel fighting with Hazael, king of Syria, 15 and was returned to be healed in Jezreel of his wounds, for the Syrians had wounded him when he fought with Hazael, king of Syria. And Jehu said, "If it please you, let no man go forth *or flee* out of the city lest he go and tell in Jezreel."

16 And he got up and went into Jezreel, for Joram was sick there, and Ahaziah, king of Judah, was come down to visit Joram. 17 The watchmen therefore that stood upon the tower of Jezreel saw the troop of Jehu coming and said, "I see a troop."

And Joram said, "Take a chariot, and send to meet them, and let him that goeth say, 'Is all well?'"

18 So there went one *in* a chariot to meet him and said, "Thus saith the king: 'Are all things peaceable?'"

And Jehu said, "What hast thou to do with peace? Go *behind,* and follow me."

And the watchman told, saying, "The messenger came to them, *but* he returneth not."

19 And he sent a second chariot of horses, and he came to them and said, "Thus saith the king: 'Is there peace?'"

And Jehu said, "What hast thou to do with peace? Pass, and follow me."

20 And the watchman told, saying, "He came even to them *but* returneth not, and the driving is like the driving of Jehu, the son of Nimshi, for he *drives furiously.*"

21 Et ait Ioram, "Iunge currum." Iunxeruntque currum eius, et egressus est Ioram, rex Israhel, et Ahazias, rex Iuda, singuli in curribus suis, egressique sunt in occursum Hieu et invenerunt eum in agro Naboth, Hiezrahelitis. 22 Cumque vidisset Ioram Hieu dixit, "Pax est, Hieu?"

At ille respondit, "Quae pax adhuc fornicationes Hiezabel, matris tuae, et veneficia eius multa vigent?"

23 Convertit autem Ioram manum suam et fugiens ait ad Ahaziam, "Insidiae, Ahazia!"

24 Porro Hieu tetendit arcum manu et percussit Ioram inter scapulas, et egressa est sagitta per cor eius, statimque corruit in curru suo. 25 Dixitque Hieu ad Baddacer, ducem, "Tolle; proice eum in agro Naboth, Hiezrahelitae, memini enim quando ego et tu sedentes in curru sequebamur Ahab, patrem huius, quod Dominus onus hoc levaverit super eum, dicens, 26 'Si non pro sanguine Naboth et pro sanguine filiorum eius quem vidi heri, ait Dominus, reddam tibi in agro isto, dicit Dominus.' Nunc igitur tolle, et proice eum in agrum iuxta verbum Domini."

27 Ahazias autem, rex Iuda, videns hoc fugit per viam domus horti, persecutusque est eum Hieu et ait, "Etiam hunc percutite in curru suo." Et percusserunt eum in ascensu Gaber, qui est iuxta Ieblaam, qui fugit in Mageddo et mortuus est ibi. 28 Et inposuerunt eum servi eius super currum suum et tulerunt in Hierusalem, sepelieruntque in sepulchro cum patribus suis in civitate David.

21 And Joram said, "Make ready the chariot." And they made ready his chariot, and Joram, king of Israel, and Ahaziah, king of Judah, went out, each in his chariot, and they went out to meet Jehu and *met* him in the field of Naboth, the Jezreelite. 22 And when Joram saw Jehu he said, "Is there peace, Jehu?"

And he answered, "What peace so long as the fornications of Jezebel, thy mother, and her many sorceries are in their vigour?"

23 And Joram turned his hand and fleeing said to Ahaziah, "There is treachery, Ahaziah!"

24 But Jehu bent his bow with his hand and shot Joram between the shoulders, and the arrow went out through his heart, and immediately he fell in his chariot. 25 And Jehu said to Bidkar, *his* captain, "Take him, *and* cast him into the field of Naboth, the Jezreelite, for I remember when I and thou sitting in a chariot followed Ahab, this man's father, that the Lord laid this burden upon him, saying, 26 'If I do not requite thee in this field, saith the Lord, for the blood of Naboth and for the blood of his children which I saw yesterday, saith the Lord.' So now take him, and cast him into the field according to the word of the Lord."

27 But Ahaziah, king of Judah, seeing this fled by the way of the garden house, and Jehu pursued him and said, "Strike him also in his chariot." And they struck him in the going up to Gur, which is by Ibleam, and he fled into Megiddo and died there. 28 And his servants laid him upon his chariot and carried him to Jerusalem, and they buried him in his sepulchre with his fathers in the city of David.

29 Anno undecimo Ioram, filii Ahab, regnavit Ahazia super Iudam, 30 venitque Hieu in Hiezrahel. Porro Hiezabel introitu eius audito depinxit oculos suos stibio et ornavit caput suum et respexit per fenestram 31 ingredientem Hieu per portam et ait, "Numquid pax esse potest Zamri qui interfecit dominum suum?"

32 Levavitque Hieu faciem suam ad fenestram et ait, "Quae est ista?" Et inclinaverunt se ad eum duo vel tres eunuchi. 33 At ille dixit eis, "Praecipitate eam deorsum." Et praecipitaverunt eam, aspersusque est sanguine paries, et equorum ungulae conculcaverunt eam. 34 Cumque ingressus esset ut comederet biberetque ait, "Ite, et videte maledictam illam, et sepelite eam quia filia regis est." 35 Cumque issent ut sepelirent eam non invenerunt nisi calvariam et pedes et summas manus. 36 Reversique nuntiaverunt ei, et ait Hieu, "Sermo Domini est quem locutus est per servum suum Heliam, Thesbiten, dicens, 'In agro Hiezrahel comedent canes carnes Hiezabel, 37 et erunt carnes Hiezabel sicut stercus super faciem terrae in agro Hiezrahel ita ut praetereuntes dicant, "Haecine est illa Hiezabel?"'"

29 In the eleventh year of Joram, the son of Ahab, Ahaziah reigned over Judah, 30 and Jehu came into Jezreel. But Jezebel hearing of his coming in painted her face with stibic stone and adorned her head and looked out of a window 31 at Jehu coming in at the gate and said, "Can there be peace for Zimri that hath killed his master?"

32 And Jehu lifted up his face to the window and said, "Who is this?" And two or three eunuchs bowed down to him. 33 And he said to them, "Throw her down headlong." And they threw her down, and the wall was sprinkled with her blood, and the hoofs of the horses trod upon her. 34 And when he was come in to eat and to drink he said, "Go, and see *after* that cursed woman, and bury her because she is a king's daughter." 35 And when they went to bury her they found nothing but the skull and the feet and the extremities of her hands. 36 And coming back they told him, and Jehu said, "It is the word of the Lord which he spoke by his servant Elijah, the Tishbite, saying, 'In the field of Jezreel the dogs shall eat the flesh of Jezebel, 37 and the flesh of Jezebel shall be as dung upon the face of the earth in the field of Jezreel so that they who pass by shall say, "Is this that *same* Jezebel?"'"

Caput 10

Erant autem Ahab septuaginta filii in Samaria, scripsit ergo Hieu litteras et misit in Samariam ad optimates civitatis et ad maiores natu et ad nutricios Ahab, dicens, 2 "Statim ut acceperitis litteras has, qui habetis filios domini vestri et currus et equos et civitates firmas et arma, 3 eligite meliorem et eum qui vobis placuerit de filiis domini vestri, et ponite eum super solium patris sui, et pugnate pro domo domini vestri."

4 Timuerunt illi vehementer et dixerunt, "Ecce: duo reges non potuerunt stare coram eo, et quomodo nos valebimus resistere?"

5 Miserunt ergo praepositi domus et praefecti civitatis et maiores natu et nutricii ad Hieu, dicentes, "Servi tui sumus; quaecumque iusseris faciemus, nec constituemus nobis regem. Quodcumque tibi placet fac."

6 Rescripsit autem eis litteras secundo, dicens, "Si mei estis et oboeditis mihi, tollite capita filiorum domini vestri, et venite ad me hac eadem hora cras in Hiezrahel."

Porro filii regis, septuaginta viri, apud optimates civitatis nutriebantur, 7 cumque venissent litterae ad eos tulerunt fi-

Chapter 10

Jehu destroyeth the house of Ahab, abolisheth the worship
of Baal and killeth the worshippers but sticketh to the
calves of Jeroboam. Israel is afflicted by the Syrians.

And Ahab had seventy sons in Samaria, so Jehu wrote letters and sent to Samaria to the chief men of the city and to
the ancients and to *them that brought up Ahab's children,* saying, 2 "As soon as you receive these letters, ye that have your
master's sons and chariots and horses and fenced cities and
armour, 3 choose the best and him that shall please you *most*
of your master's sons, and set him on his father's throne, and
fight for the house of your master."

4 But they were exceedingly afraid and said, "Behold: two
kings could not stand before him, and how shall we be able
to resist?"

5 Therefore the overseers of the house and the rulers of
the city and the ancients and the tutors sent to Jehu, saying,
"We are thy servants; whatsoever thou shalt command us
we will do, neither will we make us a king. Do thou all that
pleaseth thee."

6 And he wrote letters the second time to them, saying,
"If you be mine and will obey me, take the heads of the sons
of your master, and come to me to Jezreel *by* tomorrow this
time."

Now the king's sons being seventy men were brought up
with the chief men of the city, 7 and when the letters came

lios regis et occiderunt septuaginta viros et posuerunt capita eorum in cofinis et miserunt ad eum in Hiezrahel. 8 Venit autem nuntius et indicavit ei, dicens, "Adtulerunt capita filiorum regis."

Qui respondit, "Ponite ea in duos acervos iuxta introitum portae usque mane." 9 Cumque diluxisset egressus est et stans dixit ad omnem populum, "Iusti estis. Si ego coniuravi contra dominum meum et interfeci eum, quis percussit omnes hos? 10 Videte ergo nunc quoniam non cecidit de sermonibus Domini in terram quos locutus est Dominus super domum Ahab, et Dominus fecit quod locutus est in manu servi sui Heliae."

11 Percussit igitur Hieu omnes qui reliqui erant de domo Ahab in Hiezrahel et universos optimates eius et notos et sacerdotes donec non remanerent ex eo reliquiae. 12 Et surrexit et venit in Samariam, cumque venisset ad camaram pastorum in via 13 invenit fratres Ahaziae, regis Iuda, dixitque ad eos, "Quinam estis vos?"

Qui responderunt, "Fratres Ahaziae sumus et descendimus ad salutandos filios regis et filios reginae."

14 Qui ait, "Conprehendite eos vivos." Quos cum conprehendissent vivos iugulaverunt eos in cisterna iuxta camaram, quadraginta duos viros, et non reliquit ex eis quemquam. 15 Cumque abisset inde invenit Ionadab, filium Rechab, in occursum sibi, et benedixit ei, et ait ad eum, "Numquid est cor tuum rectum sicut cor meum cum corde tuo?"

Et ait Ionadab, "Est."

"Si est," inquit, "da mihi manum tuam."

Qui dedit ei manum suam. At ille levavit eum ad se in currum, 16 dixitque ad eum, "Veni mecum, et vide zelum meum

to them they took the king's sons and slew seventy persons and put their heads in baskets and sent them to him to Jezreel. 8 And a messenger came and told him, saying, "They have brought the heads of the king's sons."

And he *said,* "Lay ye them in two heaps by the entering in of the gate until the morning." 9 And when it was light he went out and standing said to all the people, "You are just. If I conspired against my master and slew him, who hath slain all these? 10 See therefore now that there hath not fallen to the ground *any* of the words of the Lord which the Lord spoke concerning the house of Ahab, and the Lord hath done that which he spoke in the hand of his servant Elijah."

11 So Jehu slew all that were left of the house of Ahab in Jezreel and all his chief men and his friends and his priests till there were no remains left of him. 12 And he arose and went to Samaria, and when he was come to the shepherds' cabin in the way 13 he *met with* the brethren of Ahaziah, king of Judah, and he said to them, "Who are you?"

And they answered, "We are the brethren of Ahaziah and are come down to salute the sons of the king and the sons of the queen."

14 And he said, "Take them alive." *And they* took them alive *and* killed them at the pit by the cabin, two and forty men, and he left not any of them. 15 And when he was departed thence he found Jehonadab, the son of Rechab, coming to meet him, and he blessed him, and he said to him, "Is thy heart right as my heart is with thy heart?"

And Jehonadab said, "It is."

"If it be," said he, "give me thy hand."

He gave him his hand. And he lifted him up to him into the chariot, 16 and he said to him, "Come with me, and see

pro Domino." Et inpositum in curru suo 17 duxit in Samariam. Et percussit omnes qui reliqui fuerant de Ahab in Samaria usque ad unum iuxta verbum Domini quod locutus est per Heliam.

18 Congregavit ergo Hieu omnem populum et dixit ad eos, "Ahab coluit Baal parum, ego autem colam eum amplius. 19 Nunc, igitur, omnes prophetas Baal et universos servos eius et cunctos sacerdotes ipsius vocate ad me—nullus sit qui non veniat—sacrificium enim grande est mihi Baal. Quicumque defuerit non vivet." Porro Hieu faciebat hoc insidiose, ut disperderet cultores Baal. 20 Et dixit, "Sanctificate diem sollemnem Baal." Vocavitque, 21 et misit in universos terminos Israhel, et venerunt cuncti servi Baal. Non fuit residuus ne unus quidem qui non veniret. Et ingressi sunt templum Baal, et repleta est domus Baal a summo usque ad summum. 22 Dixitque his qui erant super vestes, "Proferte vestimenta universis servis Baal." Et protulerunt eis vestes. 23 Ingressusque Hieu et Ionadab, filius Rechab, templum Baal ait cultoribus Baal, "Perquirite, et videte ne quis forte vobiscum sit de servis Domini, sed ut sint soli servi Baal." 24 Ingressi sunt igitur ut facerent victimas et holocausta, Hieu autem praeparaverat sibi foris octoginta viros et dixerat eis, "Quicumque fugerit de hominibus his quos ego adduxero in manus vestras, anima eius erit pro anima illius." 25 Factum est autem cum conpletum esset holocaustum praecepit Hieu militibus et ducibus suis, "Ingredimini, et percutite eos; nullus evadat." Percusseruntque eos in ore gladii et proiecerunt milites et duces, et ierunt in civitatem

my zeal for the Lord." *So he made him ride* in his chariot 17 and brought him into Samaria. And he slew all that were left of Ahab in Samaria to a man according to the word of the Lord which he spoke by Elijah.

18 And Jehu gathered together all the people and said to them, "Ahab worshipped Baal a little, but I will worship him more. 19 Now, therefore, call to me all the prophets of Baal and all his servants and all his priests — let none be *wanting* — for I have a great sacrifice *to offer* to Baal. Whosoever shall be wanting shall not live." Now Jehu did this craftily, that he might destroy the worshippers of Baal. 20 And he said, *"Proclaim* a festival for Baal." And he called, 21 and he sent into all the borders of Israel, and all the servants of Baal came. There was not one left that did not come. And they went into the temple of Baal, and the house of Baal was filled from one end to the other. 22 And he said to them that were over the wardrobe, "Bring forth garments for all the servants of Baal." And they brought them forth garments. 23 And Jehu and Jehonadab, the son of Rechab, went to the temple of Baal and said to the worshippers of Baal, "Search, and see *that* there be not any with you of the servants of the Lord, but that there be the servants of Baal only." 24 And they went in to offer sacrifices and burnt offerings, but Jehu had prepared him fourscore men without and said to them, *"If any* of the men escape whom I have brought into your hands, *he that letteth him go shall answer life for life."* 25 And it came to pass when the burnt offering was ended that Jehu commanded his soldiers and captains, *saying,* "Go in, and kill them; let none escape." And the soldiers and captains slew them with the edge of the sword and cast them out, and

templi Baal 26 et protulerunt statuam de fano Baal et conbuserunt 27 et comminuerunt eam. Destruxerunt quoque aedem Baal et fecerunt pro ea latrinas usque ad diem hanc.

28 Delevit itaque Hieu Baal de Israhel, 29 verumtamen a peccatis Hieroboam, filii Nabath, qui peccare fecerat Israhel non recessit, nec dereliquit vitulos aureos qui erant in Bethel et in Dan. 30 Dixit autem Dominus ad Hieu, "Quia studiose fecisti quod rectum erat et placebat in oculis meis et omnia quae erant in corde meo fecisti contra domum Ahab, filii tui usque ad quartam generationem sedebunt super thronum Israhel." 31 Porro Hieu non custodivit ut ambularet in lege Domini, Dei Israhel, in toto corde suo, non enim recessit a peccatis Hieroboam qui peccare fecerat Israhel.

32 In diebus illis coepit Dominus taedere super Israhel, percussitque eos Azahel in universis finibus Israhel 33 a Iordane contra orientalem plagam, omnem terram Galaad et Gad et Ruben et Manasse, ab Aroer, quae est super torrentem Arnon, et Galaad et Basan. 34 Reliqua autem verborum Hieu et universa quae fecit et fortitudo eius, nonne haec scripta sunt in Libro Verborum Dierum Regum Israhel? 35 Et dormivit Hieu cum patribus suis, sepelieruntque eum in Samaria, et regnavit Ioachaz, filius eius, pro eo. 36 Dies autem quos regnavit Hieu super Israhel viginti et octo anni sunt in Samaria.

they went into the city of the temple of Baal 26 and brought the statue out of Baal's temple and burnt it 27 and broke it in pieces. They destroyed also the temple of Baal and made a jakes in its place unto this day.

28 So Jehu destroyed Baal out of Israel, 29 but yet he departed not from the sins of Jeroboam, the son of Nebat, who made Israel to sin, nor did he forsake the golden calves that were in Bethel and Dan. 30 And the Lord said to Jehu, "Because thou hast diligently executed that which was right and pleasing in my eyes and hast done to the house of Ahab *according to* all that was in my heart, thy children shall sit upon the throne of Israel to the fourth generation." 31 But Jehu took no heed to walk in the law of the Lord, the God of Israel, with all his heart, for he departed not from the sins of Jeroboam who had made Israel to sin.

32 In those days the Lord began to be weary of Israel, and Hazael ravaged them in all the coasts of Israel 33 from the Jordan eastward, all the land of Gilead and Gad and Reuben and Manasseh, from Aroer, which is upon the torrent Arnon, and Gilead and Bashan. 34 But the rest of the acts of Jehu and all that he did and his strength, are they not written in the Book of the Words of the Days of the Kings of Israel? 35 And Jehu slept with his fathers, and they buried him in Samaria, and Jehoahaz, his son, reigned in his stead. 36 And the *time* that Jehu reigned over Israel in Samaria *was* eight and twenty years.

Caput 11

Athalia vero, mater Ahaziae, videns mortuum filium suum, surrexit et interfecit omne semen regium. 2 Tollens autem Iosaba, filia Regis Ioram, soror Ahaziae, Ioas, filium Ahaziae, furata est eum de medio filiorum regis qui interficiebantur et nutricem eius de triclinio et abscondit eum a facie Athaliae ut non interficeretur. 3 Eratque cum ea in domo Domini clam sex annis. Porro Athalia regnavit super terram. 4 Anno autem septimo misit Ioiada et adsumens centuriones et milites introduxit ad se in templum Domini pepigitque cum eis foedus et adiurans eos in domo Domini ostendit eis filium regis, 5 et praecepit illis, dicens, "Iste sermo quem facere debetis: 6 tertia pars vestrum introeat sabbato et observet excubitum domus regis, tertia autem pars sit ad portam Sir, et tertia pars ad portam quae est post habitaculum scutariorum, et custodietis excubitum domus Messa. 7 Duae vero partes e vobis, omnes egredientes sabbato, custodiant excubias domus Domini circum regem. 8 Et vallabitis eum habentes arma in manibus vestris, si quis autem ingressus fuerit septum templi, interficiatur, eritisque cum rege introeunte et egrediente." 9 Et fecerunt centu-

Chapter 11

Athaliah's usurpation and tyranny. Jehoash is made king.
Athaliah is slain.

And Athaliah, the mother of Ahaziah, seeing that her son was dead, arose and slew all the royal seed. 2 But Jehosheba, the daughter of King Joram, sister of Ahaziah, took Joash, the son of Ahaziah, and stole him from among the king's sons that were slain out of the *bedchamber* with his nurse and hid him from the face of Athaliah so that he was not slain. 3 And he was with her six years hid in the house of the Lord. And Athaliah reigned over the land. 4 And in the seventh year Jehoiada sent and taking the centurions and the soldiers brought them in to him into the temple of the Lord and made a covenant with them and taking an oath of them in the house of the Lord shewed them the king's son, 5 and he commanded them, saying, "This is the thing that you must do: 6 let a third part of you go in on the sabbath and keep the watch of the king's house, and let a third part be at the gate of Sur, and let a third part be at the gate behind the dwelling of the shieldbearers, and you shall keep the watch of the house of Messa. 7 But let two parts of you, all that go forth on the sabbath, keep the watch of the house of the Lord about the king. 8 And you shall compass him round about having weapons in your hands, and if any man shall enter the precinct of the temple, let him be slain, and you shall be with the king coming in and going out." 9 And the

riones iuxta omnia quae praeceperat eis Ioiada, sacerdos, et adsumentes singuli viros suos qui ingrediebantur sabbatum cum his qui egrediebantur e sabbato venerunt ad Ioiada, sacerdotem. 10 Qui dedit eis hastas et arma Regis David quae erant in domo Domini. 11 Et steterunt singuli habentes arma in manu sua a parte templi dextra usque ad partem sinistram altaris et aedis circum regem. 12 Produxitque filium regis et posuit super eum diadema et testimonium, feceruntque eum regem et unxerunt, et plaudentes manu dixerunt, "Vivat rex!"

13 Audivit autem Athalia vocem currentis populi, et ingressa ad turbas in templum Domini 14 vidit regem stantem super tribunal, iuxta morem, et cantores et tubas propter eum omnemque populum terrae laetantem et canentem tubis, et scidit vestimenta sua clamavitque, "Coniuratio! Coniuratio!"

15 Praecepit autem Ioiada centurionibus qui erant super exercitum et ait eis, "Educite eam extra consepta templi, et quicumque secutus eam fuerit feriatur gladio, dixerat enim sacerdos, 'Non occidatur in templo Domini.'" 16 Inposueruntque ei manus et inpegerunt eam per viam introitus equorum iuxta palatium, et interfecta est ibi. 17 Pepigit igitur Ioiada foedus inter Dominum et inter regem et inter populum ut esset populus Domini et inter regem et populum. 18 Ingressusque est omnis populus terrae templum Baal et destruxerunt aras eius, et imagines contriverunt valide. Matthan quoque, sacerdotem Baal, occiderunt coram altari.

centurions did according to all things that Jehoiada, the priest, had commanded them and taking every one their men that went in on the sabbath with them that went out on the sabbath came to Jehoiada, the priest. 10 And he gave them the spears and the arms of King David which were in the house of the Lord. 11 And they stood having every one their weapons in their *hands* from the right side of the temple unto the left side of the altar and of the temple about the king. 12 And he brought forth the king's son and put the diadem upon him and the testimony, and they made him king and anointed him, and clapping *their hands* they said, "God save the king!"

13 And Athaliah heard the noise of the people running, and going in to the people into the temple of the Lord 14 she saw the king standing upon a tribunal, as the manner was, and the singers and the trumpets near him and all the people of the land rejoicing and sounding the trumpets, and she rent her garments and cried, "A conspiracy! A conspiracy!"

15 But Jehoiada commended the centurions that were over the army and said to them, "Have her forth without the precinct of the temple, and whosoever shall follow her let him be slain with the sword, for the priest had said, 'Let her not be slain in the temple of the Lord.'" 16 And they laid hands on her and thrust her out by the way by which the horses go in by the palace, and she was slain there. 17 And Jehoiada made a covenant between the Lord and the king and the people that they should be the people of the Lord and between the king and the people. 18 And all the people of the land went into the temple of Baal and broke down his altars, and his images they broke in pieces thoroughly. They slew also Mattan, the priest of Baal, before the altar. And

Et posuit sacerdos custodias in domo Domini, 19 tulitque centuriones et Cherethi et Felethi legiones et omnem populum terrae, deduxeruntque regem de domo Domini, et venerunt per viam portae scutariorum in palatium, et sedit super thronum regum. 20 Laetatusque est omnis populus terrae, et civitas conquievit, Athalia autem occisa est gladio in domo regis. 21 Septemque annorum erat Ioas cum regnare coepisset.

Caput 12

Anno septimo Hieu, regnavit Ioas, et quadraginta annis regnavit in Hierusalem. Nomen matris eius Sebia de Bersabee. 2 Fecitque Ioas rectum coram Domino cunctis diebus quibus docuit eum Ioiada, sacerdos. 3 Verumtamen excelsa non abstulit, adhuc enim populus immolabat et adolebat in excelsis incensum. 4 Dixitque Ioas ad sacerdotes, "Omnem pecuniam sanctorum, quae inlata fuerit in templum Domini a praetereuntibus, quae offertur pro pretio animae

the priest set guards in the house of the Lord, 19 and he took the centurions and the bands of the Cherethites and the Pelethites and all the people of the land, and they brought the king from the house of the Lord, and they came by the way of the gate of the shieldbearers into the palace, and he sat on the throne of the kings. 20 And all the people of the land rejoiced, and the city was quiet, but Athaliah was slain with the sword in the king's house. 21 Now Jehoash was seven years old when he began to reign.

Chapter 12

The temple is repaired. Hazael is bought off from attacking Jerusalem. Joash is slain.

In the seventh year of Jehu, Jehoash began to reign, and he reigned forty years in Jerusalem. The name of his mother was Zibiah of Beer-sheba. 2 And Jehoash did that which was right before the Lord all the days that Jehoiada, the priest, taught him. 3 But yet he took not away the high places, for the people still sacrificed and burnt incense in the high places. 4 And Jehoash said to the priests, "All the money of the sanctified things, which is brought into the temple of the Lord by those that pass, which is offered for the price

et quam sponte et arbitrio cordis sui inferunt in templum Domini, 5 accipiant illam sacerdotes iuxta ordinem suum et instaurent sarta tecta domus si quid necessarium viderint instauratione."

6 Igitur usque ad vicesimum tertium annum Regis Ioas non instauraverunt sacerdotes sarta tecta templi, 7 vocavitque Rex Ioas Ioiada, pontificem, et sacerdotes, dicens eis, "Quare sarta tecta non instauratis templi? Nolite ergo amplius accipere pecuniam iuxta ordinem vestrum, sed ad instaurationem templi reddite eam." 8 Prohibitique sunt sacerdotes ultra accipere pecuniam a populo et instaurare sarta tecta domus. 9 Et tulit Ioiada, pontifex, gazofilacium unum aperuitque foramen desuper et posuit illud iuxta altare ad dexteram ingredientium domum Domini, mittebantque in eo sacerdotes qui custodiebant ostia omnem pecuniam quae deferebatur ad templum Domini. 10 Cumque viderent nimiam pecuniam esse in gazofilacio, ascendebat scriba regis et pontifex effundebantque et numerabant pecuniam quae inveniebatur in domo Domini, 11 et dabant eam iuxta numerum atque mensuram in manu eorum qui praeerant cementariis domus Domini, qui inpendebant eam in fabris lignorum et in cementariis his qui operabantur in domo Domini 12 et sarta tecta faciebant et in his qui caedebant saxa et ut emerent ligna et lapides qui excidebantur ita ut impleretur instauratio domus Domini in universis quae indigebant expensa ad muniendam domum. 13 Verumtamen non fiebant

of a soul and which of their own accord and *of their own free heart* they bring into the temple of the Lord, 5 let the priests take it according to their order and repair the house wheresoever they shall see any thing that wanteth repairing."

6 Now till the three and twentieth year of King Jehoash the priests did not make the repairs of the temple, 7 and King Jehoash called Jehoiada, the high priest, and the priests, saying to them, "Why do you not repair the temple? Take you therefore money no more according to your order, but restore it for the repairing of the temple." 8 And the priests were forbidden to take any more money of the people and to make the repairs of the house. 9 And Jehoiada, the high priest, took a chest and *bored* a hole in the top and set it by the altar at the right hand of them that came into the house of the Lord, and the priests that kept the doors put therein all the money that was brought to the temple of the Lord. 10 And when they saw that there was very much money in the chest, the king's scribe and the high priest came up and poured it out and counted the money that was found in the house of the Lord, 11 and they gave it out by number and measure into the *hands* of them that were over the builders of the house of the Lord, and they laid it out to the carpenters and the masons that wrought in the house of the Lord 12 and made the repairs and to them that cut stones and to buy timber and stones to be hewed that the repairs of the house of the Lord might be completely finished *and wheresoever* there was need of expenses to uphold the house. 13 But

ex eadem pecunia hydriae templi Domini et fuscinulae et turibula et tubae et omne vas aureum et argenteum de pecunia quae inferebatur in templum Domini, 14 his enim qui faciebant opus dabatur ut instauraretur templum Domini. 15 Et non fiebat ratio his hominibus qui accipiebant pecuniam ut distribuerent eam artificibus, sed in fide tractabant eam. 16 Pecuniam vero pro delicto et pecuniam pro peccatis non inferebant in templum Domini, quia sacerdotum erat.

17 Tunc ascendit Azahel, rex Syriae, et pugnabat contra Geth cepitque eam et direxit faciem suam ut ascenderet in Hierusalem. 18 Quam ob rem tulit Ioas, rex Iuda, omnia sanctificata quae consecraverant Iosaphat et Ioram et Ahazia, patres eius, reges Iuda, et quae ipse obtulerat et universum argentum quod inveniri potuit in thesauris templi Domini et in palatio regis misitque Azaheli, regi Syriae, et recessit ab Hierusalem.

19 Reliqua autem sermonum Ioas et universa quae fecit, nonne haec scripta sunt in Libro Verborum Dierum Regum Iuda? 20 Surrexerunt autem servi eius et coniuraverunt inter se percusseruntque Ioas in domo Mello in descensu Sela, 21 Iozachar namque, filius Semath, et Iozabad, filius Somer, servi eius, percusserunt eum, et mortuus est, et sepelierunt eum cum patribus suis in civitate David, regnavitque Amasias, filius eius, pro eo.

there were not made of the same money for the temple of the Lord bowls *or* fleshhooks *or* censers *or* trumpets *or any* vessel of gold and silver of the money that was brought into the temple of the Lord, 14 for it was given to them that did the work that the temple of the Lord might be repaired. 15 And *they reckoned not* with the men that received the money to distribute it to the workmen, but they bestowed it faithfully. 16 But the money for trespass and the money for sins they brought not into the temple of the Lord, because it was for the priests.

17 Then Hazael, king of Syria, went up and fought against Gath and took it and set his face to go up to Jerusalem. 18 Wherefore Jehoash, king of Judah, took all the sanctified things which Jehoshaphat and Jehoram and Ahaziah, his fathers, the kings of Judah, had *dedicated to holy uses* and which he himself had offered and all the silver that could be found in the treasures of the temple of the Lord and in the king's palace and sent it to Hazael, king of Syria, and he went off from Jerusalem.

19 And the rest of the acts of Joash and all that he did, are they not written in the Book of the Words of the Days of the Kings of Judah? 20 And his servants arose and conspired among themselves and slew Joash in the house of Millo in the descent of Silla, 21 for Jozacar, the son of Shimeath, and Jehozabad, the son of Shomer, his servants, struck him, and he died, and they buried him with his fathers in the city of David, and Amaziah, his son, reigned in his stead.

Caput 13

Anno vicesimo tertio Ioas, filii Ahaziae, regis Iudae, regnavit Ioachaz, filius Hieu, super Israhel in Samaria decem et septem annis. 2 Et fecit malum coram Domino secutusque est peccata Hieroboam, filii Nabath, qui peccare fecit Israhel, et non declinavit ab eis. 3 Iratusque est furor Domini contra Israhel, et tradidit eos in manu Azahelis, regis Syriae, et in manu Benadad, filii Azahel, cunctis diebus. 4 Deprecatus est autem Ioachaz faciem Domini, et audivit eum Dominus, vidit enim angustiam Israhel, quia adtriverat eos rex Syriae. 5 Et dedit Dominus Israheli salvatorem, et liberatus est de manu regis Syriae, habitaveruntque filii Israhel in tabernaculis suis sicut heri et nudius tertius, 6 verumtamen non recesserunt a peccatis domus Hieroboam, qui peccare fecit Israhel, sed in ipsis ambulaverunt, siquidem et lucus permansit in Samaria. 7 Et non sunt derelicti Ioachaz de populo nisi quinquaginta equites et decem currus et decem milia peditum, interfecerat enim eos rex Syriae et redegerat quasi pulverem in tritura areae. 8 Reliqua autem sermonum Ioachaz et universa quae fecit et fortitudo eius, nonne haec scripta sunt in Libro Sermonum Dierum Regum Israhel? 9 Dormivitque Ioachaz cum patribus suis, et

Chapter 13

The reign of Jehoahaz and of Jehoash, kings of Israel. The last acts and death of Elisha, the prophet. A dead man is raised to life by the touch of his bones.

In the three and twentieth year of Joash, son of Ahaziah, king of Judah, Jehoahaz, the son of Jehu, reigned over Israel in Samaria seventeen years. 2 And he did evil before the Lord and followed the sins of Jeroboam, the son of Nebat, who made Israel to sin, and he departed not from them. 3 And the wrath of the Lord was kindled against Israel, and he delivered them into the hand of Hazael, the king of Syria, and into the hand of Ben-hadad, the son of Hazael, all days. 4 But Jehoahaz besought the face of the Lord, and the Lord heard him, for he saw the distress of Israel, because the king of Syria had oppressed them. 5 And the Lord gave Israel a saviour, and they were delivered out of the hand of the king of Syria, and the children of Israel dwelt in their pavilions as yesterday and the day before, 6 but yet they departed not from the sins of Jeroboam, who made Israel to sin, but walked in them, and there still remained a grove also in Samaria. 7 And Jehoahaz had no more left of the people than fifty horsemen and ten chariots and ten thousand footmen, for the king of Syria had slain them and had brought them low as dust by thrashing in the barnfloor. 8 But the rest of the acts of Jehoahaz and all that he did and his valour, are they not written in the Book of the Words of the Days of the Kings of Israel? 9 And Jehoahaz slept with his fathers,

sepelierunt eum in Samaria, regnavitque Ioas, filius eius, pro eo.

10 Anno tricesimo septimo Ioas, regis Iuda, regnavit Ioas, filius Ioachaz, super Israhel in Samaria sedecim annis. 11 Et fecit quod malum est in conspectu Domini. Non declinavit ab omnibus peccatis Hieroboam, filii Nabath, qui peccare fecit Israhel, sed in ipsis ambulavit. 12 Reliqua autem sermonum Ioas et universa quae fecit et fortitudo eius, quomodo pugnaverit contra Amasiam, regem Iuda, nonne haec scripta sunt in Libro Sermonum Dierum Regum Israhel? 13 Et dormivit Ioas cum patribus suis, Hieroboam autem sedit super solium eius. Porro Ioas sepultus est in Samaria cum regibus Israhel.

14 Heliseus autem aegrotabat infirmitate qua et mortuus est, descenditque ad eum Ioas, rex Israhel, et flebat coram eo dicebatque, "Pater mi, pater mi, currus Israhel et auriga eius!"

15 Et ait illi Heliseus, "Adfer arcum et sagittas." Cumque adtulisset ad eum arcum et sagittas 16 dixit ad regem Israhel, "Pone manum tuam super arcum." Et cum posuisset ille manum suam superposuit Heliseus manus suas manibus regis 17 et ait, "Aperi fenestram orientalem." Cumque aperuisset dixit Heliseus, "Iace sagittam." Et iecit, et ait Heliseus, "Sagitta salutis Domini et sagitta salutis contra Syriam. Percutiesque Syriam in Afec donec consumas eam." 18 Et ait, "Tolle sagittas." Qui cum tulisset rursum dixit ei, "Percute iaculo terram." Et cum percussisset tribus vicibus et stetisset, 19 iratus est contra eum vir Dei et ait, "Si percussisses quinquies aut sexies sive septies, percussisses Syriam usque ad consumptionem, nunc autem tribus vicibus percuties

and they buried him in Samaria, and Joash, his son, reigned in his stead.

10 In the seven and thirtieth year of Joash, king of Judah, Jehoash, the son of Jehoahaz, reigned over Israel in Samaria sixteen years. 11 And he did that which is evil in the sight of the Lord. He departed not from all the sins of Jeroboam, the son of Nebat, who made Israel to sin, but he walked in them. 12 But the rest of the acts of Joash and all that he did and his valour *wherewith* he fought against Amaziah, king of Judah, are they not written in the Book of the Words of the Days of the Kings of Israel? 13 And Joash slept with his fathers, and Jeroboam sat upon his throne. But Joash was buried in Samaria with the kings of Israel.

14 Now Elisha was sick of the illness *whereof* he died, and Joash, king of Israel, went down to him and wept before him and said, "O my father, my father, the chariot of Israel and the guider thereof!"

15 And Elisha said to him, "Bring a bow and arrows." And when he had brought him a bow and arrows 16 he said to the king of Israel, "Put thy hand upon the bow." And when he had put his hand Elisha put his hands over the king's hands 17 and said, "Open the window to the east." And when he had opened it Elisha said, "Shoot an arrow." And he shot, and Elisha said, "The arrow of the Lord's deliverance and the arrow of the deliverance from Syria. And thou shalt strike the Syrians in Aphek till thou consume them." 18 And he said, "Take the arrows." And when he had taken *them* he said to him, "Strike with an arrow *upon* the ground." *And* he struck three times and stood still. 19 *And* the man of God was angry with him and said, "If thou hadst smitten five or six or seven times, thou hadst smitten Syria even to utter destruction, but now three times shalt thou smite

eam." 20 Mortuus est ergo Heliseus, et sepelierunt eum. Latrunculi autem de Moab venerunt in terram in ipso anno. 21 Quidam autem sepelientes hominem viderunt latrunculos et proiecerunt cadaver in sepulchro Helisei. Quod cum tetigisset ossa Helisei revixit homo et stetit super pedes suos.

22 Igitur Azahel, rex Syriae, adflixit Israhel cunctis diebus Ioachaz, 23 et misertus est Dominus eorum et reversus est ad eos propter pactum suum quod habebat cum Abraham et Isaac et Iacob, et noluit disperdere eos neque proicere penitus usque in praesens tempus. 24 Mortuus est autem Azahel, rex Syriae, et regnavit Benadad, filius eius, pro eo. 25 Porro Ioas, filius Ioachaz, tulit urbes de manu Benadad, filii Azahel, quas tulerat de manu Ioachaz, patris sui, iure proelii. Tribus vicibus percussit eum Ioas, et reddidit civitates Israheli.

Caput 14

Anno secundo Ioas, filii Ioachaz, regis Israhel, regnavit Amasias, filius Ioas, regis Iuda. 2 Viginti quinque annorum erat cum regnare coepisset, viginti autem et novem annis reg-

it." 20 And Elisha died, and they buried him. And the rovers from Moab came into the land the same year. 21 And some that were burying a man saw the rovers and cast the body into the sepulchre of Elisha. And when it had touched the bones of Elisha the man came to life and stood upon his feet.

22 Now Hazael, king of Syria, afflicted Israel all the days of Jehoahaz, 23 and the Lord had mercy on them and returned to them because of his covenant which he had *made* with Abraham and Isaac and Jacob, and he would not destroy them nor utterly cast them away unto this present time. 24 And Hazael, king of Syria, died, and Ben-hadad, his son, reigned in his stead. 25 Now Jehoash, the son of Jehoahaz, took the cities out of the hand of Ben-hadad, the son of Hazael, which he had taken out of the hand of Jehoahaz, his father, by *war.* Three times did Joash beat him, and he restored the cities to Israel.

Chapter 14

Amaziah reigneth in Judah. He overcometh the Edomites
but is overcome by Jehoash, king of Israel. Jeroboam the
Second reigneth in Israel.

In the second year of Joash, son of Jehoahaz, king of Israel, reigned Amaziah, son of Joash, king of Judah. 2 He was five and twenty years old when he began to reign, and nine and

navit in Hierusalem. Nomen matris eius Ioaden de Hierusalem. 3 Et fecit rectum coram Domino verumtamen non ut David, pater eius. Iuxta omnia quae fecit Ioas, pater suus, fecit, 4 nisi hoc tantum: quod excelsa non abstulit, adhuc enim populus immolabat et adolebat incensum in excelsis. 5 Cumque obtinuisset regnum percussit servos suos qui interfecerant regem, patrem suum, 6 filios autem eorum qui occiderant non occidit iuxta quod scriptum est in libro legis Mosi sicut praecepit Dominus, dicens, "Non morientur patres pro filiis, neque filii morientur pro patribus, sed unusquisque in peccato suo morietur."

7 Ipse percussit Edom in Valle Salinarum decem milia et adprehendit Petram in proelio vocavitque nomen eius Iecethel usque in praesentem diem. 8 Tunc misit Amasias nuntios ad Ioas, filium Ioachaz, filii Hieu, regis Israhel, dicens, "Veni; videamus nos."

9 Remisitque Ioas, rex Israhel, ad Amasiam, regem Iuda, dicens, "Carduus Libani misit ad cedrum quae est in Libano, dicens, 'Da filiam tuam filio meo uxorem.' Transieruntque bestiae saltus quae sunt in Libano et conculcaverunt carduum. 10 Percutiens invaluisti super Edom, et sublevavit te cor tuum. Contentus esto gloria, et sede in domo tua. Quare provocas malum ut cadas tu et Iuda tecum?"

11 Et non adquievit Amasias. Ascenditque Ioas, rex Israhel, et viderunt se ipse et Amasias, rex Iuda, in Bethsames, oppido Iudae. 12 Percussusque est Iuda coram Israhel, et fu-

twenty years he reigned in Jerusalem. The name of his mother was Jehoaddin of Jerusalem. 3 And he did that which was right before the Lord but yet not like David, his father. He did according to all things that Joash, his father, did, 4 but this only: that he took not away the high places, for yet the people sacrificed and burnt incense in the high places. 5 And when he had possession of the kingdom he put his servants to death that had slain the king, his father, 6 but the children of *the murderers* he did not put to death according to that which is written in the book of the law of Moses *wherein* the Lord commanded, saying, "The fathers shall not be put to death for the children, neither shall the children be put to death for the fathers, but every man shall die *for* his own *sins.*"

7 He slew of Edom in the Valley of the Saltpits ten thousand men and took The Rock by war and called the name thereof Jokte-el unto this day. 8 Then Amaziah sent messengers to Jehoash, son of Jehoahaz, son of Jehu, king of Israel, saying, "Come; let us see one another."

9 And Jehoash, king of Israel, sent again to Amaziah, king of Judah, saying, "A thistle of Libanus sent to a cedar tree which is in Libanus, saying, 'Give thy daughter to my son to wife.' And the beasts of the forest that are in Libanus passed and trod down the thistle. 10 Thou hast beaten and prevailed over Edom, and thy heart hath lifted thee up. Be content with the glory, and sit at home. Why provokest thou evil that thou shouldst fall and Judah with thee?"

11 *But* Amaziah did not *rest satisfied.* So Jehoash, king of Israel, went up, and he and Amaziah, king of Judah, saw one another in Beth-shemesh, a town in Judah. 12 And Judah was *put to the worse* before Israel, and they fled every man to their

gerunt unusquisque in tabernacula sua. 13 Amasiam vero, regem Iuda, filium Ioas, filii Ahaziae, cepit Ioas, rex Israhel, in Bethsames et adduxit eum in Hierusalem, et interrupit murum Hierusalem a Porta Ephraim usque ad Portam Anguli, quadringentis cubitis. 14 Tulitque omne aurum et argentum et universa vasa quae inventa sunt in domo Domini et in thesauris regis et obsides et reversus est in Samariam. 15 Reliqua autem verborum Ioas quae fecit et fortitudo eius qua pugnavit contra Amasiam, regem Iuda, nonne haec scripta sunt in Libro Sermonum Dierum Regum Israhel? 16 Dormivitque Ioas cum patribus suis et sepultus est in Samaria cum regibus Israhel, et regnavit Hieroboam, filius eius, pro eo.

17 Vixit autem Amasias, filius Ioas, rex Iuda, postquam mortuus est Ioas, filius Ioachaz, regis Israhel, quindecim annis. 18 Reliqua autem sermonum Amasiae, nonne haec scripta sunt in Libro Sermonum Dierum Regum Iuda? 19 Factaque est contra eum coniuratio in Hierusalem, at ille fugit in Lachis. Miseruntque post eum in Lachis et interfecerunt eum ibi. 20 Et asportaverunt in equis, sepultusque est in Hierusalem cum patribus suis in civitate David. 21 Tulit autem universus populus Iudae Azariam, annos natum sedecim, et constituerunt eum regem pro patre eius Amasia.

22 Ipse aedificavit Ahilam et restituit eam Iudae; postquam dormivit rex cum patribus suis. 23 Anno quintodecimo Amasiae, filii Ioas, regis Iuda, regnavit Hieroboam, filius Ioas, regis Israhel, in Samaria quadraginta et uno anno. 24 Et fecit quod malum est coram Domino. Non recessit ab omnibus peccatis Hieroboam, filii Nabath, qui peccare fecit

dwellings. 13 But Jehoash, king of Israel, took Amaziah, king of Judah, the son of Jehoash, the son of Ahaziah, in Beth-shemesh and brought him into Jerusalem, and he broke down the wall of Jerusalem from the Gate of Ephraim to the Gate of the Corner, four hundred cubits. 14 And he took all the gold and silver and all the vessels that were found in the house of the Lord and in the king's treasures and hostages and returned to Samaria. 15 But the rest of the acts of Jehoash which he did and his valour wherewith he fought against Amaziah, king of Judah, are they not written in the Book of the Words of the Days of the Kings of Israel? 16 And Jehoash slept with his fathers and was buried in Samaria with the kings of Israel, and Jeroboam, his son, reigned in his stead.

17 And Amaziah, the son of Joash, king of Judah, lived after the death of Jehoash, son of Jehoahaz, king of Israel, fifteen years. 18 And the rest of the acts of Amaziah, are they not written in the Book of the Words of the Days of the Kings of Judah? 19 Now they made a conspiracy against him in Jerusalem, and he fled to Lachish. And they sent after him to Lachish and killed him there. 20 And they brought him away upon horses, and he was buried in Jerusalem with his fathers in the city of David. 21 And all the people of Judah took Azariah, *who was* sixteen years old, and made him king instead of his father Amaziah.

22 He built Elath and restored it to Judah; after that the king slept with his fathers. 23 In the fifteenth year of Amaziah, son of Joash, king of Judah, reigned Jeroboam, the son of Joash, king of Israel, in Samaria one and forty years. 24 And he did that which was evil before the Lord. He departed not from all the sins of Jeroboam, the son of Nebat, who made

Israhel. 25 Ipse restituit terminos Israhel ab introitu Emath usque ad Mare Solitudinis iuxta sermonem Domini, Dei Israhel, quem locutus est per servum suum Ionam, filium Amathi, prophetam, qui erat de Geth, quae est in Opher, 26 vidit enim Dominus adflictionem Israhel amaram nimis et quod consumpti essent usque ad clausos carcere et extremos et non esset qui auxiliaretur Israhel. 27 Nec locutus est Dominus ut deleret nomen Israhel de sub caelo, sed salvavit eos in manu Hieroboam, filii Ioas. 28 Reliqua autem sermonum Hieroboam et universa quae fecit et fortitudo eius qua proeliatus est et quomodo restituit Damascum et Emath Iudae in Israhel, nonne haec scripta sunt in Libro Sermonum Dierum Regum Israhel? 29 Dormivitque Hieroboam cum patribus suis, regibus Israhel, et regnavit Zaccharias, filius eius, pro eo.

Caput 15

Anno vicesimo septimo Hieroboam, regis Israhel, regnavit Azarias, filius Amasiae, regis Iudae. 2 Sedecim annorum erat cum regnare coepisset, et quinquaginta duobus annis

Israel to sin. 25 He restored the borders of Israel from the entrance of Hamath unto the Sea of the Wilderness according to the word of the Lord, the God of Israel, which he spoke by his servant Jonah, the son of Amittai, the prophet, who was of Gath, which is in Hepher, 26 for the Lord saw the affliction of Israel *that it was* exceeding bitter and that they were consumed even to them that were shut up in prison and the lowest persons and that there was no one to help Israel. 27 And the Lord did not say that he would blot out the name of Israel from under heaven, but he saved them by the hand of Jeroboam, the son of Joash. 28 But the rest of the acts of Jeroboam and all that he did and his valour wherewith he fought and how he restored Damascus and Hamath to Judah in Israel, are they not written in the Book of the Words of the Days of the Kings of Israel? 29 And Jeroboam slept with his fathers, the kings of Israel, and Zechariah, his son, reigned in his stead.

Chapter 15

The reign of Azariah and Jotham in Judah and of Zechariah, Shallum, Menahem, Pekahiah and Pekah in Israel.

In the seven and twentieth year of Jeroboam, king of Israel, reigned Azariah, son of Amaziah, king of Judah. 2 He was sixteen years old when he began to reign, and he reigned

regnavit in Hierusalem. Nomen matris eius Iecelia de Hierusalem. 3 Fecitque quod erat placitum coram Domino iuxta omnia quae fecit Amasias pater eius. 4 Verumtamen excelsa non est demolitus, adhuc populus sacrificabat et adolebat incensum in excelsis. 5 Percussit autem Dominus regem, et fuit leprosus usque in diem mortis suae, et habitabat in domo libera seorsum, Ioatham vero, filius regis, gubernabat palatium et iudicabat populum terrae. 6 Reliqua autem sermonum Azariae et universa quae fecit, nonne haec scripta sunt in Libro Verborum Dierum Regum Iuda? 7 Et dormivit Azarias cum patribus suis, sepelieruntque eum cum maioribus suis in civitate David, et regnavit Ioatham, filius eius, pro eo.

8 Anno tricesimo octavo Azariae, regis Iudae, regnavit Zaccharias, filius Hieroboam, super Israhel in Samaria sex mensibus, 9 et fecit quod malum est coram Domino sicut fecerant patres eius. Non recessit a peccatis Hieroboam, filii Nabath, qui peccare fecit Israhel. 10 Coniuravit autem contra eum Sellum, filius Iabes, percussitque eum palam et interfecit regnavitque pro eo. 11 Reliqua autem verborum Zacchariae, nonne haec scripta sunt in Libro Sermonum Dierum Regum Israhel?

12 Iste est sermo Domini quem locutus est ad Hieu, dicens, "Filii tui usque ad quartam generationem sedebunt super thronum Israhel." Factumque est ita. 13 Sellum, filius Iabes, regnavit tricesimo nono anno Azariae, regis Iudae, regnavit autem uno mense in Samaria. 14 Et ascendit Manahem, filius Gaddi, de Thersa, venitque in Samariam et percussit Sellum, filium Iabes, in Samaria et interfecit eum regnavitque pro eo. 15 Reliqua autem verborum Sellum et

two and fifty years in Jerusalem. The name of his mother was Jecoliah of Jerusalem. 3 And he did that which was pleasing before the Lord according to all that his father Amaziah had done. 4 But the high places he did not destroy, for the people sacrificed and burnt incense in the high places. 5 And the Lord struck the king *so that* he was a leper unto the day of his death, and he dwelt in a free house apart, but Jotham, the king's son, governed the palace and judged the people of the land. 6 And the rest of the acts of Azariah and all that he did, are they not written in the Book of the Words of the Days of the Kings of Judah? 7 And Azariah slept with his fathers, and they buried him with his ancestors in the city of David, and Jotham, his son, reigned in his stead.

8 In the eight and thirtieth year of Azariah, king of Judah, reigned Zechariah, son of Jeroboam, over Israel in Samaria six months, 9 and he did that which is evil before the Lord as his fathers had done. He departed not from the sins of Jeroboam, the son of Nebat, who made Israel to sin. 10 And Shallum, the son of Jabesh, conspired against him and struck him publicly and killed him and reigned in his place. 11 Now the rest of the acts of Zechariah, are they not written in the Book of the Words of the Days of the Kings of Israel?

12 This *was* the word of the Lord which he spoke to Jehu, saying, "Thy children to the fourth generation shall sit upon the throne of Israel." And so it came to pass. 13 Shallum, the son of Jabesh, *began to reign* in the nine and thirtieth year of Azariah, king of Judah, and reigned one month in Samaria. 14 And Menahem, the son of Gadi, went up from Tirzah, and he came into Samaria and struck Shallum, the son of Jabesh, in Samaria and slew him and reigned in his stead. 15 And the rest of the acts of Shallum and his conspiracy *which he made,*

coniuratio eius per quam tetendit insidias, nonne haec scripta sunt in Libro Sermonum Dierum Regum Israhel?

16 Tunc percussit Manahem Thapsam et omnes qui erant in ea et terminos eius de Thersa noluerant enim aperire ei, et interfecit omnes praegnantes eius et scidit eas. 17 Anno tricesimo nono Azariae, regis Iuda, regnavit Manahem, filius Gaddi, super Israhel decem annis in Samaria. 18 Fecitque quod erat malum coram Domino. Non recessit a peccatis Hieroboam, filii Nabath, qui peccare fecit Israhel cunctis diebus eius. 19 Veniebat Phul, rex Assyriorum, in terram, et dabat Manahem Phul mille talenta argenti ut esset ei in auxilio et firmaret regnum eius. 20 Indixitque Manahem argentum super Israhel cunctis potentibus et divitibus ut daret regi Assyriorum quinquaginta siclos argenti per singulos, reversusque est rex Assyriorum et non est moratus in terra. 21 Reliqua autem sermonum Manahem et universa quae fecit, nonne haec scripta sunt in Libro Sermonum Dierum Regum Israhel? 22 Et dormivit Manahem cum patribus suis, regnavitque Phaceia, filius eius, pro eo.

23 Anno quinquagesimo Azariae, regis Iudae, regnavit Phaceia, filius Manahem, super Israhel in Samaria biennio. 24 Et fecit quod erat malum coram Domino. Non recessit a peccatis Hieroboam, filii Nabath, qui peccare fecit Israhel. 25 Coniuravit autem adversum eum Phacee, filius Romeliae, dux eius, et percussit eum in Samaria in turre domus regiae iuxta Argob et iuxta Ari et cum eo quinquaginta viros de filiis Galaaditarum, et interfecit eum regnavitque pro eo. 26 Reliqua autem sermonum Phaceia et universa quae fecit, nonne haec scripta sunt in Libro Sermonum Dierum Regum Israhel?

are they not written in the Book of the Words of the Days of the Kings of Israel?

16 Then Menahem destroyed Tiphsah and all that were in it and the borders thereof from Tirzah because they would not open to him, and he slew all the women thereof that were with child and ripped them up. 17 In the nine and thirtieth year of Azariah, king of Judah, reigned Menahem, son of Gadi, over Israel ten years in Samaria. 18 And he did that which was evil before the Lord. He departed not from the sins of Jeroboam, the son of Nebat, who made Israel to sin all his days. 19 And Pul, king of the Assyrians, came into the land, and Menahem gave Pul a thousand talents of silver to aid him and to establish *him in the* kingdom. 20 And Menahem laid a tax upon Israel on all that were mighty and rich to give the king of the Assyrians each man fifty sicles of silver, so the king of the Assyrians turned back and did not stay in the land. 21 And the rest of the acts of Menahem and all that he did, are they not written in the Book of the Words of the Days of the Kings of Israel? 22 And Menahem slept with his fathers, and Pekahiah, his son, reigned in his stead.

23 In the fiftieth year of Azariah, king of Judah, reigned Pekahiah, the son of Menahem, over Israel in Samaria two years. 24 And he did that which was evil before the Lord. He departed not from the sins of Jeroboam, the son of Nebat, who made Israel to sin. 25 And Pekah, the son of Remaliah, his captain, conspired against him and smote him in Samaria in the tower of the king's house near Argob and near Arieh and with him fifty men of the sons of the Galaadites, and he slew him and reigned in his stead. 26 And the rest of the acts of Pekahiah and all that he did, are they not written in the Book of the Words of the Days of the Kings of Israel?

27 Anno quinquagesimo secundo Azariae, regis Iudae, regnavit Phacee, filius Romeliae, super Israhel in Samaria viginti annis. 28 Et fecit quod malum erat coram Domino. Non recessit a peccatis Hieroboam, filii Nabath, qui peccare fecit Israhel. 29 In diebus Phacee, regis Israhel, venit Theglathfalassar, rex Assur, et cepit Aiom et Abel Domum Maacha et Ianoe et Cedes et Asor et Galaad et Galileam et universam terram Nepthalim et transtulit eos in Assyrios. 30 Coniuravit autem et tetendit insidias Osee, filius Hela, contra Phacee, filium Romeliae, et percussit eum et interfecit regnavitque pro eo vicesimo anno Ioatham, filii Oziae. 31 Reliqua autem sermonum Phacee et universa quae fecit, nonne haec scripta sunt in Libro Sermonum Dierum Regum Israhel?

32 Anno secundo Phacee, filii Romeliae, regis Israhel, regnavit Ioatham, filius Oziae, regis Iuda. 33 Viginti quinque annorum erat cum regnare coepisset, et sedecim annis regnavit in Hierusalem. Nomen matris eius Hierusa, filia Sadoc. 34 Fecitque quod erat placitum coram Domino. Iuxta omnia quae fecerat Ozias pater suus operatus est. 35 Verumtamen excelsa non abstulit. Adhuc populus immolabat et adolebat incensum in excelsis. Ipse aedificavit portam domus Domini sublimissimam. 36 Reliqua autem sermonum Ioatham et universa quae fecit, nonne haec scripta sunt in Libro Verborum Dierum Regum Iuda? 37 In diebus illis coepit Dominus mittere in Iudam Rasin, regem Syriae, et Phacee, filium Romeliae. 38 Et dormivit Ioatham cum patribus suis sepultusque est cum eis in civitate David, patris sui, et regnavit Ahaz, filius eius, pro eo.

27 In the two and fiftieth year of Azariah, king of Judah, reigned Pekah, the son of Remaliah, over Israel in Samaria twenty years. 28 And he did that which was evil before the Lord. He departed not from the sins of Jeroboam, the son of Nebat, who made Israel to sin. 29 In the days of Pekah, king of Israel, came Tiglath-pileser, king of Assyria, and took Ijon and Abel Domum Maacah and Janoah and Kedesh and Hazor and Gilead and Galilee and all the land of Naphtali and carried them *captives* into Assyria. 30 Now Hoshea, son of Elah, conspired and formed a plot against Pekah, the son of Remaliah, and struck him and slew him and reigned in his stead in the twentieth year of Jotham, the son of Uzziah. 31 But the rest of the acts of Pekah and all that he did, are they not written in the Book of the Words of the Days of the Kings of Israel?

32 In the second year of Pekah, the son of Remaliah, king of Israel, reigned Jotham, son of Uzziah, king of Judah. 33 He was five and twenty years old when he began to reign, and he reigned sixteen years in Jerusalem. The name of his mother was Jerusha, the daughter of Zadok. 34 And he did that which was *right* before the Lord. According to all that his father Uzziah had done, *so* did he. 35 But the high places he took not away. The people still sacrificed and burnt incense in the high places. He built the highest gate of the house of the Lord. 36 But the rest of the acts of Jotham and all that he did, are they not written in the Book of the Words of the Days of the Kings of Judah? 37 In those days the Lord began to send into Judah Rezin, king of Syria, and Pekah, the son of Remaliah. 38 And Jotham slept with his fathers and was buried with them in the city of David, his father, and Ahaz, his son, reigned in his stead.

Caput 16

Anno septimodecimo Phacee, filii Romeliae, regnavit Ahaz, filius Ioatham, regis Iuda. 2 Viginti annorum erat Ahaz cum regnare coepisset, et sedecim annis regnavit in Hierusalem. Non fecit quod erat placitum in conspectu Domini, Dei sui, sicut David, pater eius, 3 sed ambulavit in via regum Israhel. Insuper et filium suum consecravit, transferens per ignem secundum idola gentium quae dissipavit Dominus coram filiis Israhel. 4 Immolabat quoque victimas et adolebat incensum in excelsis et in collibus et sub omni ligno frondoso.

5 Tunc ascendit Rasin, rex Syriae, et Phacee, filius Romeliae, rex Israhel, in Hierusalem ad proeliandum, cumque obsiderent Ahaz non valuerunt superare eum. 6 In tempore illo restituit Rasin, rex Syriae, Ahilam Syriae et eiecit Iudaeos de Ahilam, et Idumei venerunt in Ahilam et habitaverunt ibi usque in diem hanc. 7 Misit autem Ahaz nuntios ad Theglathfalassar, regem Assyriorum, dicens, "Servus tuus et filius tuus ego sum. Ascende, et salvum me fac de manu regis Syriae et de manu regis Israhel, qui consurrexerunt adversum me." 8 Et cum collegisset argentum et aurum quod inveniri

Chapter 16

The wicked reign of Ahaz. The kings of Syria and Israel war against him. He hireth the king of the Assyrians to assist him. He causeth an altar to be made after the pattern of that of Damascus.

In the seventeenth year of Pekah, the son of Remaliah, reigned Ahaz, the son of Jotham, king of Judah. 2 Ahaz was twenty years old when he began to reign, and he reigned sixteen years in Jerusalem. He did not that which was pleasing in the sight of the Lord, his God, as David, his father, 3 but he walked in the way of the kings of Israel. Moreover he consecrated also his son, making him pass through the fire according to the idols of the nations which the Lord destroyed before the children of Israel. 4 He sacrificed also *and* burnt incense in the high places and on the hills and under every *green* tree.

5 Then Rezin, king of Syria, and Pekah, son of Remaliah, king of Israel, came up to Jerusalem to fight, *and* they besieged Ahaz *but* were not able to overcome him. 6 At that time Rezin, king of Syria, restored Elath to Syria and drove the men of Judah out of Elath, and the Edomites came into Elath and dwelt there unto this day. 7 And Ahaz sent messengers to Tiglath-pileser, king of the Assyrians, saying, "I am thy servant and thy son. Come up, and save me out of the hand of the king of Syria and out of the hand of the king of Israel, who are risen up together against me." 8 And when

potuit in domo Domini et in thesauris regis, misit regi Assyriorum munera. 9 Qui et adquievit voluntati eius, ascendit enim rex Assyriorum in Damascum et vastavit eam, et transtulit habitatores eius Cyrenen, Rasin autem interfecit.

10 Perrexitque Rex Ahaz in occursum Theglathfalassar, regis Assyriorum, in Damascum cumque vidisset altare Damasci misit Rex Ahaz ad Uriam, sacerdotem, exemplar eius et similitudinem iuxta omne opus eius. 11 Extruxitque Urias, sacerdos, altare iuxta omnia quae praeceperat Rex Ahaz de Damasco. Ita fecit Urias, sacerdos, donec veniret Rex Ahaz de Damasco. 12 Cumque venisset rex de Damasco, vidit altare et veneratus est illud ascenditque et immolavit holocausta et sacrificium suum 13 et libavit libamina et fudit sanguinem pacificorum quae obtulerat super altare. 14 Porro altare aeneum quod erat coram Domino transtulit de facie templi et de loco altaris et de loco templi Domini, posuitque illud ex latere altaris ad aquilonem. 15 Praecepit quoque Rex Ahaz Uriae, sacerdoti, dicens, "Super altare maius offer holocaustum matutinum et sacrificium vespertinum et holocaustum regis et sacrificium eius et holocaustum universi populi terrae et sacrificia eorum et libamina eorum et omnem sanguinem holocausti, et universum sanguinem victimae super illud effundes, altare vero aeneum erit paratum ad voluntatem meam." 16 Fecit igitur Urias, sacerdos, iuxta omnia quae praeceperat rex Ahaz. 17 Tulit autem Rex Ahaz celatas bases et luterem qui erat desuper, et mare deposuit

he had gathered together the silver and gold that could be found in the house of the Lord and in the king's treasures, he sent *it for a present* to the king of the Assyrians. 9 And he agreed to his desire, for the king of the Assyrians went up against Damascus and laid it waste, and he carried away the inhabitants thereof to Cyrene, but Rezin he slew.

10 And King Ahaz went to Damascus to meet Tiglath-pileser, king of the Assyrians, and when he had seen the altar of Damascus King Ahaz sent to Uriah, the priest, a pattern of it and its likeness according to all the work thereof. 11 And Uriah, the priest, built an altar according to all that King Ahaz had commanded from Damascus. So did Uriah, the priest, until King Ahaz came from Damascus. 12 And when the king was come from Damascus, he saw the altar and worshipped it and went up and offered holocausts and his own sacrifice 13 and offered libations and poured the blood of the peace offerings which he had offered upon the altar. 14 But the altar of brass that was before the Lord he removed from the face of the temple and from the place of the altar and from the place of the temple of the Lord, and he set it at the side of the altar toward the north. 15 And King Ahaz commanded Uriah, the priest, saying, "Upon the great altar offer the morning holocaust and the evening sacrifice and the king's holocaust and his sacrifice and the holocaust of the whole people of the land and their sacrifices and their libations and all the blood of the holocaust, and all the blood of the victim thou shalt pour out upon it, but the altar of brass shall be ready at my pleasure." 16 So Uriah, the priest, did according to all that King Ahaz had commanded him. 17 And King Ahaz took away the graven bases and the laver that was upon them, and he took down the sea from the bra-

de bubus aeneis qui sustentabant illud et posuit super pavimentum stratum lapide. 18 Musach quoque sabbati quod aedificaverat in templo et ingressum regis exterius convertit in templum Domini propter regem Assyriorum. 19 Reliqua autem verborum Ahaz quae fecit, nonne haec scripta sunt in Libro Sermonum Dierum Regum Iuda? 20 Dormivitque Ahaz cum patribus suis et sepultus est cum eis in civitate David et regnavit Ezechias, filius eius, pro eo.

Caput 17

Anno duodecimo Ahaz, regis Iuda, regnavit Osee, filius Hela, in Samaria super Israhel novem annis. 2 Fecitque malum coram Domino, sed non sicut reges Israhel qui ante eum fuerant. 3 Contra hunc ascendit Salmanassar, rex Assyriorum, et factus est ei Osee servus reddebatque illi tributa. 4 Cumque deprehendisset rex Assyriorum Osee quod rebellare nitens misisset nuntios ad Sua, regem Aegypti, ne praestaret tributa regi Assyriorum sicut singulis annis solitus erat, obsedit eum, et vinctum misit in carcerem, 5 pervaga-

zen oxen that held it up and put it upon a pavement *of* stone. 18 The Musach also for the sabbath which he had built in the temple and the king's entry from without he turned into the temple of the Lord because of the king of the Assyrians. 19 Now the rest of the acts of Ahaz which he did, are they not written in the Book of the Words of the Days of the Kings of Judah? 20 And Ahaz slept with his fathers and was buried with them in the city of David, and Hezekiah, his son, reigned in his stead.

Chapter 17

The reign of Hoshea. The Israelites for their sins are carried into captivity. Other inhabitants are sent to Samaria, who make a mixture of religion.

In the twelfth year of Ahaz, king of Judah, Hoshea, the son of Elah, reigned in Samaria over Israel nine years. 2 And he did evil before the Lord, but not as the kings of Israel that had been before him. 3 Against him came up Shalmaneser, king of the Assyrians, and Hoshea became his servant and paid him tribute. 4 And when the king of the Assyrians found that Hoshea endeavouring to rebel had sent messengers to So, the king of Egypt, that he might not pay tribute to the king of the Assyrians as he *had done* every year, he besieged him, bound him and cast him into prison, 5 and he went

tusque est omnem terram, et ascendens Samariam obsedit eam tribus annis. 6 Anno autem nono Osee, cepit rex Assyriorum Samariam et transtulit Israhel in Assyrios, posuitque eos in Ala et in Habor iuxta fluvium Gozan in civitatibus Medorum. 7 Factum est enim cum peccassent filii Israhel Domino, Deo suo, qui eduxerat eos de terra Aegypti de manu Pharaonis, regis Aegypti, coluerunt deos alienos. 8 Et ambulaverunt iuxta ritum gentium quas consumpserat Dominus in conspectu filiorum Israhel et regum Israhel quia similiter fecerant. 9 Et offenderunt filii Israhel verbis non rectis Dominum, Deum suum, et aedificaverunt sibi excelsa in cunctis urbibus suis a turre custodum usque ad civitatem munitam. 10 Feceruntque sibi statuas et lucos in omni colle sublimi et subter omne lignum nemorosum. 11 Et adolebant ibi incensum super aras in more gentium quas transtulerat Dominus a facie eorum, feceruntque verba pessima, inritantes Dominum. 12 Et coluerunt inmunditias de quibus praecepit Dominus eis ne facerent verbum hoc. 13 Et testificatus est Dominus in Israhel et in Iuda per manum omnium prophetarum et videntum, dicens, "Revertimini a viis vestris pessimis, et custodite praecepta mea et caerimonias iuxta omnem legem quam praecepi patribus vestris et sicut misi ad vos in manu servorum meorum prophetarum." 14 Qui non audierunt sed induraverunt cervicem suam iuxta cervicem patrum suorum qui noluerunt oboedire Domino, Deo suo. 15 Et abiecerunt legitima eius et pactum quod pepigit cum patribus eorum et testificationes quibus contestatus est eos, secutique sunt vanitates et vane egerunt, et secuti sunt gentes quae erant per circuitum eorum super quibus

through all the land, and going up to Samaria he besieged it three years. 6 And in the ninth year of Hoshea, the king of the Assyrians took Samaria and carried Israel away to Assyria, and he placed them in Halah and Habor by the river of Gozan in the cities of the Medes. 7 For *so it was that* the children of Israel had sinned against the Lord, their God, who brought them out of the land of Egypt from under the hand of Pharaoh, king of Egypt, *and* they worshipped strange gods. 8 And they walked according to the way of the nations which the Lord had destroyed in the sight of the children of Israel and of the kings of Israel because they had done in like manner. 9 And the children of Israel offended the Lord, their God, with things that were not right and built them high places in all their cities from the tower of the watchmen to the fenced city. 10 And they made them statues and groves on every high hill and under every shady tree. 11 And they burnt incense there upon altars after the manner of the nations which the Lord had removed from their face, and they did wicked things, provoking the Lord. 12 And they worshipped abominations concerning which the Lord had commanded them that they should not do this thing. 13 And the Lord testified to them in Israel and in Judah by the hand of all the prophets and seers, saying, "Return from your wicked ways, and keep my precepts and ceremonies according to all the law which I commanded your fathers and as I have sent to you in the hand of my servants the prophets." 14 And they hearkened not but hardened their *necks* like to the neck of their fathers who would not obey the Lord, their God. 15 And they rejected his ordinances and the covenant that he made with their fathers and the testimonies which he testified against them, and they followed vanities and acted

praeceperat Dominus eis ut non facerent sicut et illae faciebant. 16 Et dereliquerunt omnia praecepta Domini, Dei sui,
feceruntque sibi conflatiles duos vitulos et lucos et adoraverunt universam militiam caeli, servieruntque Baal 17 et
consecrabant filios suos et filias suas per ignem, et divinatio-
nibus inserviebant et auguriis, et tradiderunt se ut facerent
malum coram Domino, ut inritarent eum. 18 Iratusque est
Dominus vehementer Israhel et abstulit eos de conspectu
suo, et non remansit nisi tribus Iuda tantummodo. 19 Sed
nec ipse Iuda custodivit mandata Domini, Dei sui, verum
ambulavit in erroribus Israhel quos operatus fuerat. 20 Proie-
citque Dominus omne semen Israhel et adflixit eos et tradidit in manu diripientium donec proiceret eos a facie sua
21 ex eo iam tempore quo scissus est Israhel a domo David et
constituerunt sibi regem Hieroboam, filium Nabath, separavit enim Hieroboam Israhel a Domino et peccare eos fecit
peccatum magnum. 22 Et ambulaverunt filii Israhel in universis peccatis Hieroboam quae fecerat, et non recesserunt
ab eis 23 usquequo auferret Dominus Israhel a facie sua sicut
locutus fuerat in manu omnium servorum suorum prophetarum, translatusque est Israhel de terra sua in Assyrios usque in diem hanc.

24 Adduxit autem rex Assyriorum de Babylone et de
Chutha et de Haiath et de Emath et de Sepharvaim et conlocavit eos in civitatibus Samariae pro filiis Israhel, qui
possederunt Samariam et habitaverunt in urbibus eius.
25 Cumque ibi habitare coepissent non timebant Dominum,

vainly, and they followed the nations that were round about them concerning which the Lord had commanded them that they should not do as they did. 16 And they forsook all the precepts of the Lord, their God, and made to themselves two molten calves and groves and adored all the host of heaven, and they served Baal 17 and consecrated their sons and their daughters through fire, and they gave themselves to divinations and soothsayings, and they delivered themselves up to do evil before the Lord, to provoke him. 18 And the Lord was very angry with Israel and removed them from his sight, and there remained only the tribe of Judah. 19 But neither did Judah itself keep the commandments of the Lord, their God, but they walked in the errors of Israel which they had wrought. 20 And the Lord cast off all the seed of Israel and afflicted them and delivered them into the hand of spoilers till he cast them away from his face 21 even from that time when Israel was rent from the house of David and made Jeroboam, son of Nebat, their king, for Jeroboam separated Israel from the Lord and made them commit a great sin. 22 And the children of Israel walked in all the sins of Jeroboam which he had done, and they departed not from them 23 till the Lord removed Israel from his face as he had spoken in the hand of all his servants the prophets, and Israel was carried away out of their land to Assyria unto this day.

24 And the king of the Assyrians brought people from Babylon and from Cuthah and from Avva and from Hamath and from Sepharvaim and placed them in the cities of Samaria instead of the children of Israel, and they possessed Samaria and dwelt in the cities thereof. 25 And when they began to dwell there they feared not the Lord, and the Lord

et inmisit eis Dominus leones qui interficiebant eos. 26 Nuntiatumque est regi Assyriorum, et dictum, "Gentes quas transtulisti et habitare fecisti in civitatibus Samariae ignorant legitima Dei terrae, et inmisit in eos Dominus leones, et ecce: interficiunt eos eo quod ignorent ritum Dei terrae."

27 Praecepit autem rex Assyriorum, dicens, "Ducite illuc unum de sacerdotibus quos inde captivos adduxistis, et vadat et habitet cum eis, et doceat eos legitima Dei terrae." 28 Igitur cum venisset unus de sacerdotibus his qui captivi ducti fuerant de Samaria habitavit in Bethel et docebat eos quomodo colerent Dominum. 29 Et unaquaeque gens fabricata est deum suum posueruntque eos in fanis excelsis quae fecerant Samaritae, gens et gens in urbibus suis in quibus habitabant, 30 viri enim Babylonii fecerunt Socchothbenoth, viri autem chutheni fecerunt Nergel, et viri de Emath fecerunt Asima, 31 porro Evei fecerunt Nebaaz et Tharthac, hii autem qui erant de Sepharvaim conburebant filios suos igni Adramelech et Anamelech, diis Sepharvaim. 32 Et nihilominus colebant Dominum. Fecerunt autem sibi de novissimis sacerdotes excelsorum, et ponebant eos in fanis sublimibus. 33 Et cum Dominum colerent, diis quoque suis serviebant iuxta consuetudinem gentium de quibus translati fuerant Samariam.

34 Usque in praesentem diem morem sequuntur antiquum. Non timent Dominum, neque custodiunt caerimonias eius et iudicia et legem et mandatum quod praeceperat Dominus filiis Iacob, quem cognominavit Israhel,

sent lions among them which killed them. 26 And it was told the king of the Assyrians, and it was said, "The nations which thou hast removed and made to dwell in the cities of Samaria know not the ordinances of the God of the land, and the Lord hath sent lions among them, and behold: they kill them because they know not the manner of the God of the land."

27 And the king of the Assyrians commanded, saying, "Carry thither one of the priests whom you brought from thence captive, and let him go and dwell with them, and let him teach them the ordinances of the God of the land." 28 So *one* of the priests who had been carried away captive from Samaria came *and* dwelt in Bethel and taught them how they should worship the Lord. 29 And every nation made *gods of their own* and put them in the temples *of the high places* which the Samaritans had made, *every nation* in their cities where they dwelt, 30 for the men of Babylon made Succoth-benoth, and the Cuthites made Nergal, and the men of Hamath made Ashima, 31 and the Avvites made Nibhaz and Tartak, and they that were of Sepharvaim burnt their children in fire to Adrammelech and Anammelech, the gods of Sepharvaim. 32 And nevertheless they worshipped the Lord. And they made to themselves of the lowest of the people priests of the high places, and they placed them in the temples *of the high places.* 33 And when they worshipped the Lord, they served also their own gods according to the custom of the nations out of which they were brought to Samaria.

34 Unto this day they follow the old manner. They fear not the Lord, neither do they keep his ceremonies and judgments and law and the commandment which the Lord commanded the children of Jacob, whom he surnamed Israel,

35 et percusserat cum eis pactum et mandaverat eis, dicens, "Nolite timere deos alienos, et non adoretis eos neque colatis et non immoletis eis. 36 Sed Dominum, Deum vestrum, qui eduxit vos de terra Aegypti in fortitudine magna et in brachio extento, ipsum timete, et illum adorate, et ipsi immolate. 37 Caerimonias quoque et iudicia et legem et mandatum quod scripsit vobis, custodite ut faciatis cunctis diebus, et non timeatis deos alienos. 38 Et pactum quod percussit vobiscum nolite oblivisci, nec colatis deos alienos. 39 Sed Dominum, Deum vestrum, timete, et ipse eruet vos de manu omnium inimicorum vestrorum." 40 Illi vero non audierunt sed iuxta consuetudinem suam pristinam perpetrabant. 41 Fuerunt igitur gentes istae timentes quidem Dominum sed nihilominus et idolis suis servientes. Nam et filii eorum et nepotes, sicut fecerunt patres sui, ita faciunt usque in praesentem diem.

Caput 18

Anno tertio Osee, filii Hela, regis Israhel, regnavit Ezechias, filius Ahaz, regis Iuda. 2 Viginti quinque annorum erat cum regnare coepisset, et viginti et novem annis regna-

35 *with whom* he made a covenant and charged them, saying, "You shall not fear strange gods, nor shall you adore them nor worship them nor sacrifice to them. 36 But the Lord, your God, who brought you out of the land of Egypt with great power and a stretched out arm, him shall you fear, and him shall you adore, and to him shall you sacrifice. 37 And the ceremonies and judgments and law and the commandment which he wrote for you, you shall observe to do them always, and you shall not fear strange gods. 38 And the covenant that he made with you you shall not forget, neither shall ye worship strange gods. 39 But fear the Lord, your God, and he shall deliver you out of the hand of all your enemies." 40 But they did not hearken but did according to their old custom. 41 So these nations feared the Lord but nevertheless served also their idols. *Their* children also and grandchildren, as their fathers did, so do they unto this day.

Chapter 18

The reign of Hezekiah. He abolisheth idolatry and prospereth. Sennacherib cometh up against him. Rabshakeh soliciteth the people to revolt and blasphemeth the Lord.

In the third year of Hoshea, the son of Elah, king of Israel, reigned Hezekiah, the son of Ahaz, king of Judah. 2 He was five and twenty years old when he began to reign, and he

vit in Hierusalem. Nomen matris eius Abi, filia Zacchariae. 3 Fecitque quod erat bonum coram Domino iuxta omnia quae fecerat David, pater suus. 4 Ipse dissipavit excelsa et contrivit statuas et succidit lucos confregitque serpentem aeneum quem fecerat Moses, siquidem usque ad illud tempus filii Israhel adolebant ei incensum, vocavitque nomen eius Naasthan. 5 In Domino, Deo Israhel, speravit itaque post eum non fuit similis ei de cunctis regibus Iuda sed neque in his qui ante eum fuerunt. 6 Et adhesit Domino et non recessit a vestigiis eius fecitque mandata eius quae praeceperat Dominus Mosi. 7 Unde et erat Dominus cum eo et in cunctis ad quae procedebat sapienter se agebat. Rebellavit quoque contra regem Assyriorum et non servivit ei. 8 Ipse percussit Philistheos usque Gazam et omnes terminos eorum a turre custodum usque ad civitatem muratam. 9 Anno quarto Regis Ezechiae, qui erat annus septimus Osee, filii Hela, regis Israhel, ascendit Salmanassar, rex Assyriorum, in Samariam et obpugnavit eam 10 et cepit, nam post annos tres, anno sexto Ezechiae, id est, nono anno Osee, regis Israhel, capta est Samaria, 11 et transtulit rex Assyriorum Israhel in Assyrios conlocavitque eos in Ala et in Habor fluviis Gozan in civitatibus Medorum 12 quia non audierunt vocem Domini, Dei sui, sed praetergressi sunt pactum eius. Omnia quae praeceperat Moses, servus Domini, non audierunt neque fecerunt.

reigned nine and twenty years in Jerusalem. The name of his mother was Abi, the daughter of Zechariah. 3 And he did that which was good before the Lord according to all that David, his father, had done. 4 He destroyed the high places and broke the statues in pieces and cut down the groves and broke the brazen serpent which Moses had made, for till that time the children of Israel burnt incense to it, and he called its name Nehushtan. 5 He trusted in the Lord, the God of Israel, so that after him there was none like him among all the kings of Judah *nor any* of them that were before him. 6 And he stuck to the Lord and departed not from his steps *but kept* his commandments which the Lord commanded Moses. 7 Wherefore the Lord also was with him and in all things to which he went forth he behaved himself wisely. And he rebelled against the king of the Assyrians and served him not. 8 He smote the Philistines as far as Gaza and all their borders from the tower of the watchmen to the fenced city. 9 In the fourth year of King Hezekiah, which was the seventh year of Hoshea, the son of Elah, king of Israel, Shalmaneser, king of the Assyrians, came up to Samaria and besieged it 10 and took it, for after three years, in the sixth year of Hezekiah, that is, in the ninth year of Hoshea, king of Israel, Samaria was taken, 11 and the king of the Assyrians carried away Israel into Assyria and placed them in Halah and in Habor by the rivers of Gozan in the cities of the Medes 12 because they hearkened not to the voice of the Lord, their God, but transgressed his covenant. All that Moses, the servant of the Lord, commanded they would not hear nor do.

13 Anno quartodecimo Regis Ezechiae, ascendit Sennacherib, rex Assyriorum, ad universas civitates Iuda munitas
et cepit eas. 14 Tunc misit Ezechias, rex Iuda, nuntios ad regem Assyriorum in Lachis, dicens, "Peccavi. Recede a me,
et omne quod inposueris mihi feram." Indixit itaque rex Assyriorum Ezechiae, regi Iudae, trecenta talenta argenti et
triginta talenta auri. 15 Deditque Ezechias omne argentum
quod reppertum fuerat in domo Domini et in thesauris regis. 16 In tempore illo confregit Ezechias valvas templi Domini et lamminas auri quas ipse adfixerat et dedit eas regi
Assyriorum.

17 Misit autem rex Assyriorum Tharthan et Rabsaris et
Rabsacen de Lachis ad Regem Ezechiam cum manu valida
Hierusalem, qui cum ascendissent venerunt Hierusalem, et
steterunt iuxta aquaeductum piscinae superioris quae est in
via agri fullonis. 18 Vocaveruntque regem, egressus est autem
ad eos Eliachim, filius Helciae, praepositus domus, et Sobna, scriba, et Ioahe, filius Asaph, a commentariis. 19 Dixitque ad eos Rabsaces, "Loquimini Ezechiae, 'Haec dicit rex
magnus, rex Assyriorum: "Quae est ista fiducia qua niteris?
20 Forsitan inisti consilium ut praepares te ad proelium. In
quo confidis ut audeas rebellare? 21 An speras in baculo harundineo atque confracto, Aegypto, super quem si incubuerit homo, comminutus ingredietur manum eius et perforabit
eam? Sic est Pharao, rex Aegypti, omnibus qui confidunt in
se. 22 Quod si dixeritis mihi, 'In Domino, Deo nostro, habe-

13 In the fourteenth year of King Hezekiah, Sennacherib, king of the Assyrians, came up against *the* fenced cities of Judah and took them. 14 Then Hezekiah, king of Judah, sent messengers to the king of the Assyrians to Lachish, saying, "I have offended. Depart from me, and all that thou shalt put upon me I will bear." And the king of the Assyrians put a tax upon Hezekiah, king of Judah, of three hundred talents of silver and thirty talents of gold. 15 And Hezekiah gave all the silver that was found in the house of the Lord and in the king's treasures. 16 At that time Hezekiah broke the doors of the temple of the Lord and the plates of gold which he had fastened on them and gave them to the king of the Assyrians.

17 And the king of the Assyrians sent Tartan and Rab-saris and Rabshakeh from Lachish to King Hezekiah with a strong army to Jerusalem, and *they* went up *and* came to Jerusalem, and they stood by the conduit of the upper pool which is in the way of the fuller's field. 18 And they called for the king, and there went out to them Eliakim, the son of Hilkiah, who was over the house, and Shebnah, the scribe, and Joah, the son of Asaph, the recorder. 19 And Rabshakeh said to them, "Speak to Hezekiah, 'Thus saith the great king, the king of the Assyrians: "What is this confidence wherein thou trustest? 20 Perhaps thou hast taken counsel to prepare thyself for battle. On whom dost thou trust that thou darest to rebel? 21 Dost thou trust in Egypt, a staff of a broken reed, upon which if a man lean, it will break and go into his hand and pierce it? So is Pharaoh, king of Egypt, to all that trust in him. 22 But if you say to me, 'We trust in the Lord, our

mus fiduciam,' nonne iste est cuius abstulit Ezechias excelsa et altaria et praecepit Iudae et Hierusalem, 'Ante altare hoc adorabitis in Hierusalem?' 23 Nunc igitur transite ad dominum meum, regem Assyriorum, et dabo vobis duo milia equorum, et videte an habere valeatis ascensores eorum. 24 Et quomodo potestis resistere ante unum satrapam de servis domini mei minimis? An fiduciam habes in Aegypto propter currus et equites? 25 Numquid sine Domini voluntate ascendi ad locum istum ut demolirer eum? Dominus dixit mihi, 'Ascende ad terram hanc, et demolire eam.'"'"

26 Dixerunt autem Eliachim, filius Helciae, et Sobna et Ioahe Rabsaci, "Precamur ut loquaris nobis, servis tuis, Syriace, siquidem intellegimus hanc linguam, et non loquaris nobis Iudaice audiente populo qui est super murum."

27 Responditque eis Rabsaces, dicens, "Numquid ad dominum tuum et ad te misit me dominus meus ut loquerer sermones hos et non potius ad viros qui sedent super murum ut comedant stercora sua et bibant urinam suam vobiscum?"

28 Stetit itaque Rabsaces et clamavit voce magna Iudaice et ait, "Audite verba regis magni, regis Assyriorum. 29 Haec dicit rex: 'Non vos seducat Ezechias, non enim poterit eruere vos de manu mea, 30 neque fiduciam vobis tribuat super Domino, dicens, "Eruens liberabit nos Dominus, et non tradetur civitas haec in manu regis Assyriorum." 31 Nolite audire Ezechiam, haec enim dicit rex Assyriorum: "Facite mecum quod vobis est utile, et egredimini ad me, et comedet unusquisque de vinea sua et de ficu sua, et bibetis aquas

God,' is it not he whose high places and altars Hezekiah hath taken away and hath commanded Judah and Jerusalem, 'You shall worship before this altar in Jerusalem?' 23 Now therefore come over to my master, the king of the Assyrians, and I will give you two thousand horses, and see whether you be able to have riders for them. 24 And how can you stand against one lord of the least of my master's servants? Dost thou trust in Egypt for chariots and for horsemen? 25 Is it without the will of the Lord that I am come up to this place to destroy it? The Lord said to me, 'Go up to this land, and destroy it.'"'"

26 Then Eliakim, the son of Hilkiah, and Shebnah and Joah said to Rabshakeh, "We pray thee, *speak* to us, thy servants, in Syriac, for we understand that tongue, and speak not to us in the Jews' language in the hearing of the people that are upon the wall."

27 And Rabshakeh answered them, saying, "Hath my master sent me to thy master and to thee to speak these words and not rather to the men that sit upon the wall that they may eat their own dung and drink their urine with you?"

28 Then Rabshakeh stood and cried out with a loud voice in the Jews' language and said, "Hear the words of the great king, the king of the Assyrians. 29 Thus saith the king: 'Let not Hezekiah deceive you, for he shall not be able to deliver you out of my hand, 30 neither let him make you trust in the Lord, saying, "The Lord will *surely* deliver us, and this city shall not be given into the hand of the king of the Assyrians." 31 Do not hearken to Hezekiah, for thus saith the king of the Assyrians: "Do with me that which is for your advantage, and come out to me, and every man of you shall eat of his own vineyard and of his own fig tree, and you shall drink wa-

de cisternis vestris 32 donec veniam et transferam vos in terram quae similis terrae vestrae est, in terram fructiferam et fertilem vini, terram panis et vinearum, terram olivarum et olei ac mellis, et vivetis et non moriemini. Nolite audire Ezechiam, qui vos decipit, dicens, 'Dominus liberabit nos.' 33 Numquid liberaverunt dii gentium terram suam de manu regis Assyriorum? 34 Ubi est deus Emath et Arfad? Ubi est deus Sepharvaim, Ana et Ava? Numquid liberaverunt Samariam de manu mea? 35 Quinam illi sunt in universis diis terrarum qui eruerunt regionem suam de manu mea ut possit eruere Dominus Hierusalem de manu mea?'" "

36 Tacuit itaque populus et non respondit ei quicquam, siquidem praeceptum regis acceperant ut non responderent ei. 37 Venitque Eliachim, filius Helciae, praepositus domus, et Sobna, scriba, et Ioahe, filius Asaph, a commentariis, ad Ezechiam scissis vestibus et nuntiaverunt ei verba Rabsacis.

ter of your own cisterns 32 till I come and take you away to a land like to your own land, a fruitful land and plentiful in wine, a land of bread and vineyards, a land of olives and oil and honey, and you shall live and not die. Hearken not to Hezekiah, who deceiveth you, saying, 'The Lord will deliver us.' 33 Have *any of* the gods of the nations delivered their land from the hand of the king of Assyria? 34 Where is the god of Hamath and of Arpad? Where is the god of Sephar-vaim, of Hena and of Ivvah? Have they delivered Samaria out of my hand? 35 Who are they among all the gods of the nations that have delivered their country out of my hand that the Lord may deliver Jerusalem out of my hand?" ' "

36 But the people held their peace and answered him not a word, for they had received commandment from the king that they should not answer him. 37 And Eliakim, the son of Hilkiah, who was over the house, and Shebnah, the scribe, and Joah, the son of Asaph, the recorder, came to Hezekiah with their garments rent and told him the words of Rab-shakeh.

Caput 19

Quae cum audisset Rex Ezechias scidit vestimenta sua et opertus est sacco ingressusque est domum Domini. 2 Et misit Eliachim, praepositum domus, et Sobnam, scribam, et senes de sacerdotibus opertos saccis ad Esaiam, prophetam, filium Amos, 3 qui dixerunt ei, "Haec dicit Ezechias: 'Dies tribulationis et increpationis et blasphemiae dies iste. Venerunt filii usque ad partum, et vires non habet parturiens, 4 si forte audiat Dominus, Deus tuus, universa verba Rabsacis quem misit rex Assyriorum, dominus suus, ut exprobraret Deum viventem et argueret verbis quae audivit Dominus, Deus tuus, et fac orationem pro reliquiis quae reppertae sunt.'"

5 Venerunt ergo servi Regis Ezechiae ad Esaiam, 6 dixitque eis Esaias, "Haec dicetis domino vestro: 'Haec dicit Dominus: "Noli timere a facie sermonum quos audisti quibus

Chapter 19

Hezekiah is assured of God's help by Isaiah, the prophet. The king of the Assyrians still threateneth and blasphemeth. Hezekiah prayeth, and God promiseth to protect Jerusalem. An angel destroyeth the army of the Assyrians. Their king returneth to Nineveh and is slain by his two sons.

And when King Hezekiah heard these words he rent his garments and covered himself with sackcloth and went into the house of the Lord. 2 And he sent Eliakim, who was over the house, and Shebnah, the scribe, and the ancients of the priests covered with sackcloths to Isaiah, the prophet, the son of Amoz, 3 and they said to him, "Thus saith Hezekiah: 'This day is a day of tribulation and of rebuke and of blasphemy. The children are come to the birth, and the woman in travail hath not strength. 4 *It may be* the Lord, thy God, will hear all the words of Rabshakeh whom the king of the Assyrians, his master, hath sent to reproach the living God and to reprove with words which the Lord, thy God, hath heard, and do thou offer prayer for the remnants that are found.'"

5 So the servants of King Hezekiah came to Isaiah, 6 and Isaiah said to them, "Thus shall you say to your master: 'Thus saith the Lord: "Be not afraid for the words which thou hast heard with which the servants of the king of the

blasphemaverunt pueri regis Assyriorum me. 7 Ecce: ego in-
mittam ei spiritum, et audiet nuntium et revertetur in terram suam, et deiciam eum gladio in terra sua.'"''

8 Reversus est igitur Rabsaces et invenit regem Assyriorum expugnantem Lobnam, audierat enim quod recessisset
de Lachis. 9 Cumque audisset de Tharaca, rege Aethiopiae,
dicentes, "Ecce: egressus est ut pugnet adversum te," et iret
contra eum, misit nuntios ad Ezechiam, dicens, 10 "Haec dicite Ezechiae, regi Iudae: 'Non te seducat Deus tuus in quo
habes fiduciam, neque dicas, "Non tradetur Hierusalem in
manus regis Assyriorum," 11 tu enim ipse audisti quae fecerint reges Assyriorum universis terris, quomodo vastaverint
eas, num ergo solus poteris liberari? 12 Numquid liberaverunt dii gentium singulos quos vastaverunt patres mei, Gozan, videlicet, et Aran et Reseph et filios Eden qui erant in
Thelassar? 13 Ubi est rex Emath et rex Arfad et rex civitatis
Sepharvaim, Ana et Ava?'"

14 Itaque cum accepisset Ezechias litteras de manu nuntiorum et legisset eas ascendit in domum Domini et expandit eas coram Domino, 15 et oravit in conspectu eius, dicens,
"Domine, Deus Israhel, qui sedes super cherubin, tu es Deus
solus regum omnium terrae. Tu fecisti caelum et terram.
16 Inclina aurem tuam, et audi; aperi, Domine, oculos tuos,
et vide. Et audi omnia verba Sennacherib qui misit ut exprobraret nobis Deum viventem. 17 Vere, Domine, dissipave-
runt reges Assyriorum gentes et terras omnium, 18 et miserunt deos eorum in ignem, non enim erant dii sed opera

Assyrians have blasphemed me. 7 Behold: I will send a spirit upon him, and he shall hear a message and shall return into his own country, and I will make him fall by the sword in his own country."'"

8 And Rabshakeh returned and found the king of the Assyrians besieging Libnah, for he had heard that he was departed from Lachish. 9 And when he heard *say* of Tirhakah, king of Ethiopia, "Behold: he is come out to fight with thee," and was going against him, he sent messengers to Hezekiah, saying, 10 "Thus shall you say to Hezekiah, king of Judah: 'Let not thy God deceive thee in whom thou trustest, and do not say, "Jerusalem shall not be delivered into the hands of the king of the Assyrians." 11 *Behold:* thou hast heard what the kings of the Assyrians have done to all countries, how they have laid them waste, and canst thou alone be delivered? 12 Have the gods of the nations delivered *any of* them whom my fathers have destroyed, to wit, Gozan and Haran and Rezeph and the children of Eden that were in Telassar? 13 Where is the king of Hamath and the king of Arpad and the king of the city of Sepharvaim, of Hena and of Ivvah?'"

14 And when Hezekiah had received the letter of the hand of the messengers and had read it he went up to the house of the Lord and spread it before the Lord, 15 and he prayed in his sight, saying, "O Lord, God of Israel, who sitteth upon the cherubims, thou alone art the God of all the kings of the earth. Thou madest heaven and earth. 16 Incline thy ear, and hear; open, O Lord, thy eyes, and see. And hear all the words of Sennacherib who hath sent to upbraid unto us the living God. 17 Of a truth, O Lord, the kings of the Assyrians have destroyed nations and the lands of them all, 18 and they have cast their gods into the fire, for they were not gods but the

manuum hominum e ligno et lapide, et perdiderunt eos. 19 Nunc igitur Domine, Deus noster, salvos nos fac de manu eius ut sciant omnia regna terrae quia tu es Dominus, Deus solus."

20 Misit autem Esaias, filius Amos, ad Ezechiam, dicens, "Haec dicit Dominus, Deus Israhel: 'Quae deprecatus es me super Sennacherib, rege Assyriorum, audivi. 21 Iste est sermo quem locutus est Dominus de eo: "Sprevit te et subsannavit te virgo, filia Sion. Post tergum tuum caput movit filia Hierusalem.

22 ""Cui exprobrasti, et quem blasphemasti? Contra quem exaltasti vocem et elevasti in excelsum oculos tuos? Contra Sanctum Israhel. 23 Per manum servorum tuorum exprobrasti Domino et dixisti, 'In multitudine curruum meorum ascendi excelsa montium, in summitate Libani et succidi sublimes cedros eius et electas abietes eius. Et ingressus sum usque ad terminos eius et saltum Carmeli eius. 24 Ego succidi, et bibi aquas alienas et siccavi vestigiis pedum meorum omnes aquas clausas.'

25 ""Numquid non audisti quid ab initio fecerim? Ex diebus antiquis plasmavi illud, et nunc adduxi eruntque in ruinam collium pugnantium civitates munitae. 26 Et qui sedent in eis humiles manu. Contremuerunt et confusi sunt. Facti sunt quasi faenum agri et virens herba tectorum quae arefacta est antequam veniret ad maturitatem.

27 ""Habitaculum tuum et egressum tuum et introitum

works of men's hands of wood and stone, and they destroyed them. 19 Now therefore O Lord, our God, save us from his hand that all the kingdoms of the earth may know that thou art the Lord, the only God."

20 And Isaiah, the son of Amoz, sent to Hezekiah, saying, "Thus saith the Lord, the God of Israel: 'I have heard *the prayer thou hast made to* me concerning Sennacherib, king of the Assyrians. 21 This is the word that the Lord hath spoken of him: "The virgin, the daughter of Zion, hath despised thee and *laughed* thee *to scorn*. The daughter of Jerusalem hath wagged her head behind thy back.

22 """Whom hast thou reproached, and whom hast thou blasphemed? Against whom hast thou exalted thy voice and lifted up thy eyes on high? Against the Holy One of Israel. 23 By the hand of thy servants thou hast reproached the Lord and hast said, 'With the multitude of my chariots I have gone up to the height of the mountains, to the top of Libanus and have cut down its tall cedars and its choice fir trees. And I have entered into the furthest parts thereof and the forest of its Carmel. 24 I have cut down, and I have drunk strange waters and have dried up with the soles of my feet all the shut up waters.'

25 """Hast thou not heard what I have done from the beginning? From the days of old I have formed it, and now I have brought it to effect *that* fenced cities of fighting men *should* be *turned* to heaps of ruin. 26 And the inhabitants of them were weak of hand. They trembled and were confounded. They became like the grass of the field and the green herb on the tops of houses which withered before it came to maturity.

27 """Thy dwelling and thy going out and thy coming in

tuum et viam tuam ego praescivi et furorem tuum contra me. 28 Insanisti in me, et superbia tua ascendit in aures meas. Ponam itaque circulum in naribus tuis et camum in labris tuis, et reducam te in viam per quam venisti.

29 ""Tibi autem, Ezechia, hoc erit signum: comede hoc anno quod reppereris, in secundo autem anno quae sponte nascuntur, porro in anno tertio seminate et metite. Plantate vineas, et comedite fructum earum. 30 Et quodcumque reliquum fuerit de domo Iuda mittet radicem deorsum et faciet fructum sursum, 31 de Hierusalem quippe egredientur reliquiae et quod salvetur de Monte Sion. Zelus Domini exercituum faciet hoc.

32 ""Quam ob rem haec dicit Dominus de rege Assyriorum: 'Non ingredietur urbem hanc nec mittet in eam sagittam, nec occupabit eam clypeus, nec circumdabit eam munitio. 33 Per viam qua venit revertetur, et civitatem hanc non ingredietur, dicit Dominus. 34 Protegamque urbem hanc et salvabo eam propter me et propter David, servum meum.'"""

35 Factum est igitur in nocte illa venit angelus Domini et percussit in castris Assyriorum centum octoginta quinque milia. Cumque diluculo surrexisset vidit omnia corpora mortuorum. Et recedens abiit, 36 et reversus est Sennacherib, rex Assyriorum, et mansit in Nineve. 37 Cumque adoraret in templo Neserach, deum suum, Adramelech et Sarasar, filii eius, percusserunt eum gladio, fugeruntque in terram Armeniorum, et regnavit Eseraddon, filius eius, pro eo.

and thy way I knew before and thy rage against me. 28 Thou hast been mad against me, and thy pride hath come up to my ears. Therefore I will put a ring in thy nose and a bit between thy lips, and I will turn thee back by the way by which thou camest.

29 ""And to thee, O Hezekiah, this shall be a sign: eat this year what thou shalt find, and in the second year such things as spring of themselves, but in the third year sow and reap. Plant vineyards, and eat the fruit of them. 30 And whatsoever shall be left of the house of Judah shall take root downward and bear fruit upward, 31 for out of Jerusalem shall go forth a remnant and that which shall be saved out of Mount Zion. The zeal of the Lord of hosts shall do this.

32 ""Wherefore thus saith the Lord concerning the king of the Assyrians: 'He shall not come into this city nor shoot an arrow into it nor *come before it with shield* nor *cast a trench about* it. 33 By the way that he came he shall return, and into this city he shall not come, saith the Lord. 34 And I will protect this city and will save it for my own sake and for David my servant's sake.'"""

35 And it came to pass that night that an angel of the Lord came and slew in the camp of the Assyrians a hundred and eighty-five thousand. And when he arose early in the morning he saw all the bodies of the dead. 36 And Sennacherib, king of the Assyrians, departing went away, and he returned and abode in Nineveh. 37 And as he was worshipping in the temple of Nisroch, his god, Adrammelech and Sharezer, his sons, slew him with the sword, and they fled into the land of the Armenians, and Esar-haddon, his son, reigned in his stead.

7 Dixitque Esaias, "Adferte massam ficorum." Quam cum adtulissent et posuissent super ulcus eius curatus est.

8 Dixerat autem Ezechias ad Esaiam, "Quod erit signum quia Dominus me sanabit et quia ascensurus sum die tertio templum Domini?"

9 Cui ait Esaias, "Hoc erit signum a Domino quod facturus sit Dominus sermonem quem locutus est. Vis ut accedat umbra decem lineis an ut revertatur totidem gradibus?"

10 Et ait Ezechias, "Facile est umbram crescere decem lineis, nec hoc volo ut fiat, sed ut revertatur retrorsum decem gradibus." 11 Invocavit itaque Esaias, propheta, Dominum, et reduxit umbram per lineas quibus iam descenderat in horologio Ahaz retrorsum decem gradibus.

12 In tempore illo misit Berodach Baladan, filius Baladan, rex Babyloniorum, litteras et munera ad Ezechiam, audierat enim quod aegrotasset Ezechias. 13 Laetatus est autem in adventum eorum Ezechias, et ostendit eis domum aromatum et aurum et argentum et pigmenta varia unguenta quoque et domum vasorum suorum et omnia quae possidebat in thesauris suis. Non fuit quod non monstraret eis Ezechias in domo sua et in omni potestate sua. 14 Venit autem Esaias, propheta, ad Regem Ezechiam dixitque ei, "Quid dixerunt viri isti? Aut unde venerunt ad te?"

Cui ait Ezechias, "De terra longinqua venerunt ad me, de Babylone."

15 At ille respondit, "Quid viderunt in domo tua?"

Ait Ezechias, "Omnia quaecumque sunt in domo mea vi-

7 And Isaiah said, "Bring me a lump of figs." And when they had brought it and laid it upon his boil he was healed.

8 And Hezekiah had said to Isaiah, "What shall be the sign that the Lord will heal me and that I shall go up to the temple of the Lord the third day?"

9 And Isaiah said to him, "This shall be the sign from the Lord that the Lord will do the word which he hath spoken. Wilt thou that the shadow go forward ten lines or that it go back so many degrees?"

10 And Hezekiah said, "It is an easy matter for the shadow to go forward ten lines, and I do not desire that this be done, but *let* it return back ten degrees." 11 And Isaiah, the prophet, called upon the Lord, and he brought the shadow ten degrees backwards by the lines by which it had already gone down in the dial of Ahaz.

12 At that time Merodach Baladan, the son of Baladan, king of the Babylonians, sent letters and presents to Hezekiah, for he had heard that Hezekiah had been sick. 13 And Hezekiah rejoiced at their coming, and he shewed them the house of his aromatical spices and the gold and the silver and divers *precious odours* and ointments and the house of his vessels and all that he had in his treasures. There was nothing in his house nor in all his dominions that Hezekiah shewed them not. 14 And Isaiah, the prophet, came to King Hezekiah and said to him, "What said these men? Or from whence came they to thee?"

And Hezekiah said to him, "From a far country they came to me, out of Babylon."

15 And he *said,* "What did they see in thy house?"

Hezekiah said, "They saw all the things *that* are in my

derunt. Nihil est quod non monstraverim eis in thesauris meis."

16 Dixit itaque Esaias Ezechiae, "Audi sermonem Domini: 17 'Ecce: dies venient et auferentur omnia quae sunt in domo tua et quae condiderunt patres tui usque in diem hanc in Babylonem. Non remanebit quicquam,' ait Dominus, 18 'Sed et de filiis tuis qui egredientur ex te quos generabis tollentur, et erunt eunuchi in palatio regis Babylonis.'"

19 Dixit Ezechias ad Esaiam, "Bonus sermo Domini quem locutus es. Sit pax et veritas in diebus meis." 20 Reliqua autem sermonum Ezechiae et omnis fortitudo eius et quomodo fecerit piscinam et aquaeductum et introduxerit aquas in civitatem, nonne haec scripta sunt in Libro Sermonum Dierum Regum Iuda? 21 Dormivitque Ezechias cum patribus suis, et regnavit Manasses, filius eius, pro eo.

Caput 21

Duodecim annorum erat Manasses cum regnare coepisset, et quinquaginta quinque annis regnavit in Hierusalem. Nomen matris eius Aphsiba. 2 Fecitque malum in conspectu

house. There is nothing among my treasures that I have not shewn them."

16 And Isaiah said to Hezekiah, "Hear the word of the Lord: 17 'Behold: the days shall come *that* all that is in thy house and that thy fathers have laid up in store unto this day shall be carried into Babylon. Nothing shall be left,' saith the Lord, 18 'And of thy sons also that shall issue from thee whom thou shalt beget they shall take away, and they shall be eunuchs in the palace of the king of Babylon.'"

19 Hezekiah said to Isaiah, "The word of the Lord which thou hast spoken is good. Let peace and truth be in my days." 20 And the rest of the acts of Hezekiah and all his might and how he made a pool and a conduit and brought waters into the city, are they not written in the Book of the Words of the Days of the Kings of Judah? 21 And Hezekiah slept with his fathers, and Manasseh, his son, reigned in his stead.

Chapter 21

The wickedness of Manasseh. God's threats by his prophets. His wicked son Amon succeedeth him and is slain by his servants.

M anasseh was twelve years old when he began to reign, and he reigned five and fifty years in Jerusalem. The name of his mother was Hephzibah. 2 And he did evil in the sight of

Domini iuxta idola gentium quas delevit Dominus a facie filiorum Israhel. 3 Conversusque est et aedificavit excelsa quae dissipaverat Ezechias, pater eius, et erexit aras Baal et fecit lucos sicut fecerat Ahab, rex Israhel, et adoravit omnem militiam caeli et coluit eam. 4 Extruxitque aras in domo Domini de qua dixit Dominus, "In Hierusalem ponam nomen meum." 5 Et extruxit altaria universae militiae caeli in duobus atriis templi Domini. 6 Et transduxit filium suum per ignem, et ariolatus est et observavit auguria et fecit pythones et aruspices multiplicavit ut faceret malum coram Domino et inritaret eum. 7 Posuit quoque idolum luci quem fecerat in templo Domini super quo locutus est Dominus ad David et ad Salomonem, filium eius, "In templo hoc et in Hierusalem quam elegi de cunctis tribubus Israhel ponam nomen meum in sempiternum. 8 Et ultra non faciam commoveri pedem Israhel de terra quam dedi patribus eorum, sic tamen si custodierint opere omnia quae praecepi eis, universam legem quam mandavit eis servus meus Moses." 9 Illi vero non audierunt sed seducti sunt a Manasse ut facerent malum super gentes quas contrivit Dominus a facie filiorum Israhel.

10 Locutusque est Dominus in manu servorum suorum, prophetarum, dicens, 11 "Quia fecit Manasses, rex Iuda, abominationes istas pessimas super omnia quae fecerunt Amorrei ante eum et peccare fecit etiam Iudam in inmunditiis suis, 12 propterea haec dicit Dominus, Deus Israhel, 'Ecce: ego inducam mala super Hierusalem et Iudam ut quicum-

the Lord according to the idols of the nations which the Lord destroyed from before the face of the children of Israel. 3 And he turned and built up the high places which Hezekiah, his father, had destroyed, and he set up altars to Baal and made groves as Ahab, the king of Israel, had done, and he adored all the host of heaven and served them. 4 And he built altars in the house of the Lord of which the Lord said, "In Jerusalem I will put my name." 5 And he built altars for all the host of heaven in the two courts of the temple of the Lord. 6 And he made his son pass through fire, and he used divination and observed omens and appointed pythons and multiplied soothsayers to do evil before the Lord and to provoke him. 7 He set also an idol of the grove which he had made in the temple of the Lord concerning which the Lord said to David and to Solomon, his son, "In this temple and in Jerusalem which I have chosen out of all the tribes of Israel I will put my name for ever. 8 And I will no more make the *feet* of Israel to be moved out of the land which I gave to their fathers, *only* if they will observe to do all that I have commanded them *according to* the law which my servant Moses commanded them." 9 But they hearkened not but were seduced by Manasseh to do evil more than the nations which the Lord destroyed before the children of Israel.

10 And the Lord spoke in the hand of his servants, the prophets, saying, 11 "Because Manasseh, king of Judah, hath done these most wicked abominations beyond all that the Amorites did before him and hath made Judah also to sin with his filthy doings, 12 therefore thus saith the Lord, the God of Israel, 'Behold: I will bring on evils upon Jerusalem and Judah that whosoever shall hear *of them* both his ears

que audierit tinniant ambae aures eius. 13 Et extendam super Hierusalem funiculum Samariae et pondus domus Ahab, et delebo Hierusalem sicut deleri solent tabulae, et delens vertam et ducam crebrius stilum super faciem eius. 14 Dimittam vero reliquias hereditatis meae et tradam eas in manus inimicorum eius, eruntque in vastitatem et in rapinam cunctis adversariis suis 15 eo quod fecerint malum coram me et perseveraverint inritantes me ex die qua egressi sunt patres eorum ex Aegypto usque ad diem hanc.'"

16 Insuper et sanguinem innoxium fudit Manasses multum nimis donec impleret Hierusalem usque ad os absque peccatis suis quibus peccare fecit Iudam, ut faceret malum coram Domino. 17 Reliqua autem sermonum Manasse et universa quae fecit et peccatum eius quod peccavit, nonne haec scripta sunt in Libro Sermonum Dierum Regum Iuda? 18 Dormivitque Manasses cum patribus suis et sepultus est in horto domus suae in horto Aza, et regnavit Amon, filius eius, pro eo.

19 Viginti et duo annorum erat Amon cum regnare coepisset, duobus quoque annis regnavit in Hierusalem. Nomen matris eius Mesallemeth, filia Arus de Iethba. 20 Fecitque malum in conspectu Domini sicut fecerat Manasses, pater eius. 21 Et ambulavit in omni via per quam ambulaverat pater eius, servivitque inmunditiis quibus servierat pater suus, et adoravit eas 22 et dereliquit Dominum, Deum patrum suorum, et non ambulavit in via Domini. 23 Tetenderuntque ei insidias servi sui et interfecerunt regem in domo sua, 24 percussit autem populus terrae omnes qui coniuraverant contra Regem Amon et constituerunt sibi regem Iosiam, filium

shall tingle. 13 And I will stretch over Jerusalem the line of Samaria and the weight of the house of Ahab, and I will efface Jerusalem as tables are wont to be effaced, and I will erase and turn it and draw the pencil often over the face thereof. 14 And I will leave the remnants of my inheritance and will deliver them into the hands of their enemies, and they shall become a *prey* and a spoil to all their enemies 15 because they have done evil before me and have continued to provoke me from the day that their fathers came out of Egypt even unto this day.'"

16 Moreover Manasseh shed also very much innocent blood till he filled Jerusalem up to the mouth besides his sins wherewith he made Judah to sin, to do evil before the Lord. 17 Now the rest of the acts of Manasseh and all that he did and his sin which he sinned, are they not written in the Book of the Words of the Days of the Kings of Judah? 18 And Manasseh slept with his fathers and was buried in the garden of his own house in the garden of Uzza, and Amon, his son, reigned in his stead.

19 Two and twenty years old was Amon when he began to reign, and he reigned two years in Jerusalem. The name of his mother was Meshullemeth, the daughter of Haruz of Jotbah. 20 And he did evil in the sight of the Lord as Manasseh, his father, had done. 21 And he walked in all the way in which his father had walked, and he served the abominations which his father had served, and he adored them 22 and forsook the Lord, the God of his fathers, and walked not in the way of the Lord. 23 And his servants *plotted* against him and slew the king in his own house, 24 but the people of the land slew all them that had conspired against King Amon

eius, pro eo. 25 Reliqua autem sermonum Amon quae fecit, nonne haec scripta sunt in Libro Sermonum Dierum Regum Iuda? 26 Sepelieruntque eum in sepulchro suo in horto Aza, et regnavit Iosias filius eius pro eo.

Caput 22

Octo annorum erat Iosias cum regnare coepisset. Triginta et uno anno regnavit in Hierusalem. Nomen matris eius Idida, filia Phadaia de Besecath. 2 Fecitque quod placitum erat coram Domino et ambulavit per omnes vias David, patris sui. Non declinavit ad dextram sive ad sinistram. 3 Anno autem octavodecimo Regis Iosiae, misit rex Saphan, filium Aslia, filii Mesullam, scribam templi Domini, dicens ei, 4 "Vade ad Helciam, sacerdotem magnum, ut confletur pecunia quae inlata est in templum Domini quam college-

and made Josiah, his son, their king in his stead. 25 But the rest of the acts of Amon which he did, are they not written in the Book of the Words of the Days of the Kings of Judah? 26 And they buried him in his sepulchre in the garden of Uzza, and his son Josiah reigned in his stead.

Chapter 22

Josiah repaireth the temple. The Book of the Law is found, upon which they consult the Lord and are told that great evils shall fall upon them but not in the time of Josiah.

J osiah was eight years old when he began to reign. He reigned one and thirty years in Jerusalem. The name of his mother was Jedidah, the daughter of Adaiah of Bozkath. 2 And he did that which was right in the sight of the Lord and walked in all the ways of David, his father. He turned not aside to the right hand or to the left. 3 And in the eighteenth year of King Josiah, the king sent Shaphan, the son of Azaliah, the son of Meshullam, the scribe of the temple of the Lord, saying to him, 4 "Go to Hilkiah, the high priest, that the money may be put together which is brought into the temple of the Lord which the doorkeepers of the tem-

runt ianitores templi a populo. 5 Deturque fabris per prae-
positos domus Domini, qui et distribuent eam his qui ope-
rantur in templo Domini ad instauranda sarta tecta templi,
6 tignariis, videlicet, et cementariis et his qui interrupta
conponunt, et ut emantur ligna et lapides de lapidicinis ad
instaurandum templum Domini. 7 Verumtamen non suppu-
tetur eis argentum quod accipiunt, sed in potestate habeant
et in fide."

8 Dixit autem Helcias, pontifex, ad Saphan, scribam,
"Librum Legis repperi in domo Domini." Deditque Helcias
volumen Saphan, qui et legit illud.

9 Venit quoque Saphan, scriba, ad regem et renuntiavit ei
quod praeceperat et ait, "Conflaverunt servi tui pecuniam
quae repperta est in domo Domini, et dederunt ut distri-
bueretur fabris a praefectis operum templi Domini." 10 Narravit quoque Saphan, scriba, regi, dicens, "Librum dedit
mihi Helcias, sacerdos."

Quem cum legisset Saphan coram rege 11 et audisset rex
verba legis Domini, scidit vestimenta sua. 12 Et praecepit
Helciae, sacerdoti, et Ahicham, filio Saphan, et Achobor, filio Micha, et Saphan, scribae, et Asaiae, servo regis, dicens,
13 "Ite, et consulite Dominum super me et super populo et
super omni Iuda de verbis voluminis istius quod inventum
est, magna enim ira Domini succensa est contra nos quia
non audierunt patres nostri verba libri huius ut facerent
omne quod scriptum est nobis."

ple have gathered of the people. 5 And let it be given to the workmen by the overseers of the house of the Lord, *and let them* distribute it to those that work in the temple of the Lord to repair the temple, 6 that is, to carpenters and masons and to such as mend breaches, and that timber may be bought and stones out of the quarries to repair the temple of the Lord. 7 But let there be no reckoning made with them of the money which they receive, but let them have it in their power and in their trust."

8 And Hilkiah, the high priest, said to Shaphan, the scribe, "I have found the Book of the Law in the house of the Lord." And Hilkiah gave the book to Shaphan, and he read it.

9 And Shaphan, the scribe, came to the king and brought him word again concerning that which he had commanded and said, "Thy servants have gathered together the money that was found in the house of the Lord, and they have given it to be distributed to the workmen by the overseers of the works of the temple of the Lord." 10 And Shaphan, the scribe, told the king, saying, "Hilkiah, the priest, hath delivered to me a book."

And when Shaphan had read it before the king 11 and the king had heard the words of the law of the Lord, he rent his garments. 12 And he commanded Hilkiah, the priest, and Ahikam, the son of Shaphan, and Achbor, the son of Mikaiah, and Shaphan, the scribe, and Asaiah, the king's servant, saying, 13 "Go, and consult the Lord for me and for the people and for all Judah concerning the words of this book which is found, for the great wrath of the Lord is kindled against us because our fathers have not hearkened to the words of this book to do all that is written for us."

14 Ierunt itaque Helcias, sacerdos, et Ahicham et Achobor et Saphan et Asaia ad Oldam, propheten, uxorem Sellum, filii Thecue, filii Araas, custodis vestium, quae habitabat in Hierusalem in Secunda, locutique sunt ad eam. 15 Et illa respondit eis, "Haec dicit Dominus, Deus Israhel: 'Dicite viro qui misit vos ad me, 16 "Haec dicit Dominus: 'Ecce: ego adducam mala super locum hunc et super habitatores eius, omnia verba legis quae legit rex Iuda, 17 quia dereliquerunt me et sacrificaverunt diis alienis, inritantes me in cunctis operibus manuum suarum. Et succendetur indignatio mea in loco hoc et non extinguetur.'" 18 Regi autem Iuda qui misit vos ut consuleretis Dominum sic dicetis: "Haec dicit Dominus, Deus Israhel: 'Pro eo quod audisti verba voluminis 19 et perterritum est cor tuum et humiliatus es coram Domino auditis sermonibus contra locum istum et habitatores eius, quod, videlicet, fierent in stuporem et in maledictum, et scidisti vestimenta tua et flevisti coram me, et ego audivi, ait Dominus. 20 Idcirco colligam te ad patres tuos, et colligeris ad sepulchrum tuum in pace ut non videant oculi tui omnia mala quae inducturus sum super locum istum.'"""

14 So Hilkiah, the priest, and Ahikam and Achbor and Shaphan and Asaiah went to Huldah, the prophetess, the wife of Shallum, the son of Tikvah, the son of Harhas, keeper of the wardrobe, who dwelt in Jerusalem in the Second, and they spoke to her. 15 And she said to them, "Thus saith the Lord, the God of Israel: 'Tell the man that sent you to me, 16 "Thus saith the Lord: 'Behold: I will bring evils upon this place and upon the inhabitants thereof, all the words of the law which the king of Judah hath read, 17 because they have forsaken me and have sacrificed to strange gods, provoking me by all the works of their hands. Therefore my indignation shall be kindled against this place and shall not be quenched.'" 18 But to the king of Judah who sent you to consult the Lord thus shall you say: "Thus saith the Lord, the God of Israel: 'Forasmuch as thou hast heard the words of the book 19 and thy heart hath been moved to fear and thou hast humbled thyself before the Lord hearing the words against this place and the inhabitants thereof, to wit, that they should become a wonder and a curse, and thou hast rent thy garments and wept before me, I also have heard thee, saith the Lord. 20 Therefore I will gather thee to thy fathers, and thou shalt be gathered to thy sepulchre in peace that thy eyes may not see all the evils which I will bring upon this place.'"'"

Caput 23

Et renuntiaverunt regi quod dixerat. Qui misit, et congregati sunt ad eum omnes senes Iuda et Hierusalem. 2 Ascenditque rex templum Domini et omnes viri Iuda universique qui habitabant in Hierusalem cum eo, sacerdotes et prophetae et omnis populus a parvo usque ad magnum, legitque cunctis audientibus omnia verba Libri Foederis, qui inventus est in domo Domini. 3 Stetitque rex super gradum et percussit foedus coram Domino ut ambularent post Dominum et custodirent praecepta eius et testimonia et caerimonias in omni corde et in tota anima et suscitarent verba foederis huius quae scripta erant in libro illo, adquievitque populus pacto.

4 Et praecepit rex Helciae, pontifici, et sacerdotibus secundi ordinis et ianitoribus ut proicerent de templo Domini omnia vasa quae facta fuerant Baal et in luco et universae militiae caeli, et conbusit ea foris Hierusalem in convalle Cedron, et tulit pulverem eorum in Bethel. 5 Et delevit aru-

Chapter 23

Josiah readeth the law before all the people. They promise to observe it. He abolisheth all idolatry, celebrateth the phase, is slain in battle by the king of Egypt. The short reign of Jehoahaz, in whose place Jehoiakim is made king.

And they brought the king word again what she had said. And he sent, and all the ancients of Judah and Jerusalem were assembled to him. 2 And the king went up to the temple of the Lord and all the men of Judah and all *the inhabitants* of Jerusalem with him, the priests and the prophets and all the people *both* little *and* great, and in the hearing of them all he read all the words of the Book of the Covenant, which was found in the house of the Lord. 3 And the king stood upon the step and made a covenant with the Lord to walk after the Lord and to keep his commandments and his testimonies and his ceremonies with all their heart and with all their soul and to perform the words of this covenant which were written in that book, and the people agreed to the covenant.

4 And the king commanded Hilkiah, the high priest, and the priests of the second order and the doorkeepers to cast out of the temple of the Lord all the vessels that had been made for Baal and *for* the grove and for all the host of heaven, and he burnt them without Jerusalem in the valley of Kidron, and he carried the ashes of them to Bethel. 5 And he

spices quos posuerant reges Iuda ad sacrificandum in excelsis per civitates Iuda et in circuitu Hierusalem, et eos qui adolebant incensum Baal et soli et lunae et duodecim signis et omni militiae caeli. 6 Et efferri fecit lucum de domo Domini foras Hierusalem in convalle Cedron, et conbusit eum ibi et redegit in pulverem et proiecit super sepulchra vulgi. 7 Destruxit quoque aediculas effeminatorum quae erant in domo Domini pro quibus mulieres texebant quasi domunculas luci. 8 Congregavitque omnes sacerdotes de civitatibus Iuda, et contaminavit excelsa ubi sacrificabant sacerdotes de Gabaa usque Bersabee, et destruxit aras portarum in introitu ostii Iosue, principis civitatis, quod erat ad sinistram portae civitatis. 9 Verumtamen, non ascendebant sacerdotes excelsorum ad altare Domini in Hierusalem sed tantum comedebant azyma in medio fratrum suorum. 10 Contaminavit quoque Thafeth, quod est in convalle filii Ennom, ut nemo consecraret filium suum aut filiam per ignem Moloch. 11 Abstulit quoque equos quos dederant reges Iudae soli in introitu templi Domini iuxta exedram Nathanmelech, eunuchi qui erat in Farurim, currus autem solis conbusit igni. 12 Altaria quoque quae erant super tecta cenaculi Ahaz quae fecerant reges Iuda et altaria quae fecerat Manasses in duobus atriis templi Domini destruxit rex, et cucurrit inde et dispersit cinerem eorum in torrentem Cedron. 13 Excelsa

destroyed the soothsayers whom the kings of Judah had appointed to sacrifice in the high places in the cities of Judah and round about Jerusalem, them also that burnt incense to Baal and to the sun and to the moon and to the twelve signs and to all the host of heaven. 6 And he caused the grove to be carried out from the house of the Lord without Jerusalem to the valley of Kidron, and he burnt it there and reduced it to dust and cast the dust upon the graves of the common people. 7 He destroyed also the pavilions of the effeminate which were in the house of the Lord for which the women wove as it were little dwellings for the grove. 8 And he gathered together all the priests out of the cities of Judah, and he defiled the high places where the priests offered sacrifice from Geba to Beer-sheba, and he broke down the altars of the gates that were in the entering in of the gate of Joshua, governor of the city, which was on the left hand of the gate of the city. 9 However, the priests of the high places came not up to the altar of the Lord in Jerusalem but only ate of the unleavened bread among their brethren. 10 And he defiled Topheth, which is in the valley of the son of Hinnom, that no man should consecrate *there* his son or his daughter through fire to Molech. 11 And he took away the horses which the kings of Judah had given to the sun at the entering in of the temple of the Lord near the chamber of Nathan-melech, the eunuch who was in Pharurim, and he burnt the chariots of the sun with fire. 12 And the altars that were upon the top of the upper chamber of Ahaz which the kings of Judah had made and the altars which Manasseh had made in the two courts of the temple of the Lord the king broke down, and he ran from thence and cast the ashes of them into the torrent Kidron. 13 The high places also that

quoque quae erant in Hierusalem ad dexteram partem Montis Offensionis quae aedificaverat Salomon, rex Israhel, Astharoth, idolo Sidoniorum, et Chamos, offensioni Moab, et Melchom, abominationi filiorum Ammon, polluit rex. 14 Et contrivit statuas et succidit lucos, replevitque loca eorum ossibus mortuorum. 15 Insuper et altare quod erat in Bethel et excelsum quod fecerat Hieroboam, filius Nabath, qui peccare fecit Israhel, et altare illud et excelsum destruxit atque conbusit et comminuit in pulverem succenditque etiam lucum. 16 Et conversus Iosias vidit ibi sepulchra quae erant in monte, misitque et tulit ossa de sepulchris et conbusit ea super altare et polluit illud iuxta verbum Domini quod locutus est vir Dei qui praedixerat verba haec. 17 Et ait, "Quis est titulus ille quem video?"

Responderuntque ei cives illius urbis, "Sepulchrum est hominis Dei qui venit de Iuda et praedixit verba haec quae fecisti super altare Bethel."

18 Et ait, "Dimittite eum. Nemo commoveat ossa eius." Et intacta manserunt ossa illius cum ossibus prophetae qui venerat de Samaria. 19 Insuper et omnia fana excelsorum quae erant in civitatibus Samariae, quae fecerant reges Israhel ad inritandum Dominum, abstulit Iosias, et fecit eis secundum omnia opera quae fecerat in Bethel. 20 Et occidit universos sacerdotes excelsorum qui erant ibi super altaria, et conbusit ossa humana super ea reversusque est Hierusalem.

21 Et praecepit omni populo, dicens, "Facite phase Domino, Deo vestro, secundum quod scriptum est in libro foederis huius." 22 Nec enim factum est phase tale a diebus iudi-

were at Jerusalem on the right side of the Mount of Offence which Solomon, king of Israel, had built to Astarte, the idol of the Sidonians, and to Chemosh, the scandal of Moab, and to Milcom, the abomination of the children of Ammon, the king defiled. 14 And he broke in pieces the statues and cut down the groves, and he filled their places with the bones of dead men. 15 Moreover the altar also that was at Bethel and the high place which Jeroboam, the son of Nebat, who made Israel to sin, had made, both the altar and the high place he broke down and burnt and reduced to powder and burnt the *grove.* 16 And as Josiah turned himself he saw there the sepulchres that were in the mount, and he sent and took the bones out of the sepulchres and burnt them upon the altar and defiled it according to the word of the Lord which the man of God spoke who had foretold these things. 17 And he said, "What is that monument which I see?"

And the men of that city answered, "It is the sepulchre of the man of God who came from Judah and foretold these things which thou hast done upon the altar of Bethel."

18 And he said, "Let him alone. Let no man move his bones." So his bones were left untouched with the bones of the prophet that came out of Samaria. 19 Moreover all the temples of the high places which were in the cities of Samaria, which the kings of Israel had made to provoke the Lord, Josiah took away, and he did to them according to all the acts that he had done in Bethel. 20 And he slew all the priests of the high places that were there upon the altars, and he burnt men's bones upon them and returned to Jerusalem.

21 And he commanded all the people, saying, "Keep the phase to the Lord, your God, according as it is written in the book of this covenant." 22 Now there was no such a phase

cum qui iudicaverunt Israhel et omnium dierum regum Israhel et regum Iuda 23 sicut in octavodecimo anno regis Iosiae factum est phase istud Domino in Hierusalem. 24 Sed et pythones et ariolos et figuras idolorum et inmunditias abominationesque quae fuerant in terra Iuda et Hierusalem abstulit Iosias ut statueret verba legis quae scripta sunt in libro quem invenit Helcias, sacerdos, in templo Domini.

25 Similis illi non fuit ante eum rex qui reverteretur ad Dominum in omni corde suo et in tota anima sua et in universa virtute sua iuxta omnem legem Mosi, neque post eum surrexit similis illi. 26 Verumtamen non est aversus Dominus ab ira furoris sui magni quo iratus est furor eius contra Iudam propter inritationes quibus provocaverat eum Manasses. 27 Dixit itaque Dominus, "Etiam Iudam auferam a facie mea sicut abstuli Israhel, et proiciam civitatem hanc quam elegi Hierusalem et domum de qua dixi, 'Erit nomen meum ibi.'"

28 Reliqua autem verba Iosiae et universa quae fecit, nonne haec scripta sunt in Libro Verborum Dierum Regum Iuda? 29 In diebus eius ascendit Pharao Necho, rex Aegypti, contra regem Assyriorum ad flumen Eufraten, et abiit Iosias Rex in occursum eius et occisus est in Mageddo cum vidisset eum. 30 Et portaverunt eum servi sui mortuum de Mageddo, et pertulerunt in Hierusalem et sepelierunt eum in sepulchro suo. Tulitque populus terrae Ioahaz, filium Iosiae, et unxerunt eum et constituerunt eum regem pro patre suo.

kept from the days of the judges who judged Israel nor in all the days of the kings of Israel and of the kings of Judah 23 as *was* this phase *that was* kept to the Lord in Jerusalem in the eighteenth year of king Josiah. 24 Moreover the diviners by spirits and soothsayers and the figures of idols and the uncleannesses and the abominations that had been in the land of Judah and Jerusalem Josiah took away that he might perform the words of the law that were written in the book which Hilkiah, the priest, had found in the temple of the Lord.

25 There was no king before him like unto him that returned to the Lord with all his heart and with all his soul and with all his strength according to all the law of Moses, neither after him did there arise *any* like him. 26 But yet the Lord turned not away from the wrath of his great indignation wherewith his anger was kindled against Judah because of the provocations wherewith Manasseh had provoked him. 27 And the Lord said, "I will remove Judah also from before my face as I have removed Israel, and I will cast off this city Jerusalem which I chose and the house of which I said, 'My name shall be there.'"

28 Now the rest of the acts of Josiah and all that he did, are they not written in the Book of the Words of the Days of the Kings of Judah? 29 In his days Pharaoh Neco, king of Egypt, went up against the king of Assyria to the river Euphrates, and King Josiah went to meet him and was slain at Megiddo when he had seen him. 30 And his servants carried him dead from Megiddo, and they brought him to Jerusalem and buried him in his own sepulchre. And the people of the land took Jehoahaz, the son of Josiah, and they anointed him and made him king in his father's stead.

31 Viginti trium annorum erat Ioahaz cum regnare coepisset, et tribus mensibus regnavit in Hierusalem. Nomen matris eius Amithal, filia Hieremiae de Lobna. 32 Et fecit malum coram Domino iuxta omnia quae fecerant patres eius. 33 Vinxitque eum Pharao Necho in Rebla, quae est in terra Emath, ne regnaret in Hierusalem, et inposuit multam terrae centum talentis argenti et talento auri. 34 Regemque constituit Pharao Necho Eliachim, filium Iosiae, pro Iosia, patre eius, vertitque nomen eius Ioiachim. Porro Ioahaz tulit et duxit in Aegyptum, et mortuus est ibi. 35 Argentum autem et aurum dedit Ioiachim Pharaoni cum indixisset terrae per singulos ut conferretur iuxta praeceptum Pharaonis, et, unumquemque secundum vires suas, exegit tam argentum quam aurum de populo terrae ut daret Pharaoni Necho. 36 Viginti quinque annorum erat Ioiachim cum regnare coepisset, et undecim annis regnavit in Hierusalem. Nomen matris eius Zebida, filia Phadaia de Ruma. 37 Et fecit malum coram Domino iuxta omnia quae fecerant patres eius.

31 Jehoahaz was three and twenty years old when he began to reign, and he reigned three months in Jerusalem. The name of his mother was Hamutal, the daughter of Jeremiah of Libnah. 32 And he did evil before the Lord according to all that his fathers had done. 33 And Pharaoh Neco bound him at Riblah, which is in the land of Hamath, that he should not reign in Jerusalem, and he set a fine upon the land of a hundred talents of silver and a talent of gold. 34 And Pharaoh Neco made Eliakim, the son of Josiah, king in the room of Josiah, his father, and turned his name to Jehoiakim. And he took Jehoahaz away and carried him into Egypt, and he died there. 35 And Jehoiakim gave the silver and the gold to Pharaoh after he had taxed the land for every man to contribute according to the commandment of Pharaoh, and he exacted both the silver and the gold of the people of the land, of every man according to his ability, to give to Pharaoh Neco. 36 Jehoiakim was five and twenty years old when he began to reign, and he reigned eleven years in Jerusalem. The name of his mother was Zebidah, the daughter of Pedaiah of Rumah. 37 And he did evil before the Lord according to all that his fathers had done.

Caput 24

In diebus eius ascendit Nabuchodonosor, rex Babylonis, et factus est ei Ioiachim servus tribus annis. Et rursum rebellavit contra eum. 2 Inmisitque ei Dominus latrunculos Chaldeorum et latrunculos Syriae et latrunculos Moab et latrunculos filiorum Ammon, et inmisit eos in Iudam ut disperderent eum iuxta verbum Domini quod locutus erat per servos suos, prophetas. 3 Factum est autem hoc per verbum Domini contra Iudam ut auferret eum coram se propter peccata Manasse universa quae fecit 4 et propter sanguinem innoxium quem effudit, et implevit Hierusalem cruore innocentium, et ob hanc rem noluit Dominus propitiari. 5 Reliqua autem sermonum Ioiachim et universa quae fecit, nonne haec scripta sunt in Libro Sermonum Dierum Regum Iuda? Et dormivit Ioiachim cum patribus suis, 6 regnavitque Ioiachin, filius eius, pro eo. 7 Et ultra non addidit rex Aegypti ut egrederetur de terra sua, tulerat enim rex Babylonis a rivo Aegypti usque ad fluvium Eufraten omnia quae fuerant regis Aegypti.

8 Decem et octo annorum erat Ioiachin cum regnare coepisset, et tribus mensibus regnavit in Hierusalem. Nomen matris eius Naestha, filia Helnathan de Hierusalem. 9 Et fecit malum coram Domino iuxta omnia quae fecerat pater

Chapter 24

The reign of Jehoiakim, Jehoiachin and Zedekiah.

In his days Nebuchadnezzar, king of Babylon, came up, and Jehoiakim became his servant three years. Then again he rebelled against him. 2 And the Lord sent against him the rovers of the Chaldeans and the rovers of Syria and the rovers of Moab and the rovers of the children of Ammon, and he sent them against Judah to destroy it according to the word of the Lord which he had spoken by his servants, the prophets. 3 And this came by the word of the Lord against Judah to remove *them from* before him for all the sins of Manasseh which he did 4 and for the innocent blood that he shed, *filling* Jerusalem with innocent blood, and therefore the Lord would not be appeased. 5 But the rest of the acts of Jehoiakim and all that he did, are they not written in the Book of the Words of the Days of the Kings of Judah? And Jehoiakim slept with his fathers, 6 and Jehoiachin, his son, reigned in his stead. 7 And the king of Egypt came not again any more out of his own country, for the king of Babylon had taken all that had belonged to the king of Egypt from the river of Egypt unto the river Euphrates.

8 Jehoiachin was eighteen years old when he began to reign, and he reigned three months in Jerusalem. The name of his mother was Nehushta, the daughter of Elnathan of Jerusalem. 9 And he did evil before the Lord according to

Caput 25

Factum est autem anno nono regni eius, mense decimo, decima die mensis, venit Nabuchodonosor, rex Babylonis, ipse et omnis exercitus eius, in Hierusalem, et circumdederunt eam et extruxerunt in circuitu eius munitiones. 2 Et clausa est civitas atque vallata usque ad undecimum annum Regis Sedeciae, 3 nona die mensis, praevaluitque fames in civitate, nec erat panis populo terrae. 4 Et interrupta est civitas, et omnes viri bellatores nocte fugerunt per viam portae quae est inter duplicem murum ad hortum regis (porro Chaldei obsidebant in circuitu civitatem), fugit itaque Sedicias per viam quae ducit ad campestria solitudinis. 5 Et persecutus est exercitus Chaldeorum regem conprehenditque eum in planitie Hiericho, et omnes bellatores qui erant cum eo dispersi sunt et reliquerunt eum.

6 Adprehensum ergo regem duxerunt ad regem Babylonis in Reblatha, qui locutus est cum eo iudicium. 7 Filios autem Sedeciae occidit coram eo, et oculos eius effodit vinxitque eum catenis et adduxit in Babylonem. 8 Mense quinto, sep-

Chapter 25

Jerusalem is besieged and taken by Nebuchadnezzar.
Zedekiah is taken. The city and temple are destroyed.
Gedaliah, who is left governor, is slain. Jehoiachin is exalted
by Evil-merodach.

And it came to pass in the ninth year of his reign, in the tenth month, the tenth day of the month, that Nebuchadnezzar, king of Babylon, came, he and all his army, against Jerusalem, and they surrounded it and raised works round about it. 2 And the city was shut up and besieged till the eleventh year of King Zedekiah, 3 the ninth day of the month, and a famine prevailed in the city, and there was no bread for the people of the land. 4 And a breach was made into the city, and all the men of war fled in the night *between* the two walls by the king's garden (now the Chaldeans besieged the city round about), and Zedekiah fled by the way that leadeth to the plains of the wilderness. 5 And the army of the Chaldeans pursued after the king and overtook him in the plains of Jericho, and all the warriors that were with him were scattered and left him.

6 So they took the king and brought him to the king of Babylon to Riblah, and he gave judgment upon him. 7 And he slew the sons of Zedekiah before his face, and he put out his eyes and bound him with chains and brought him to Babylon. 8 In the fifth month, the seventh day of the month,

tima die mensis, ipse est annus nonusdecimus regis Babylonis, venit Nabuzardan, princeps exercitus, servus regis Babylonis, in Hierusalem. 9 Et succendit domum Domini et domum regis et domos Hierusalem, omnemque domum conbusit igni. 10 Et muros Hierusalem in circuitu destruxit omnis exercitus Chaldeorum qui erat cum principe militum. 11 Reliquam autem populi partem qui remanserat in civitate et perfugas qui transfugerant ad regem Babylonis et reliquum vulgus transtulit Nabuzardan, princeps militiae. 12 Et de pauperibus terrae reliquit vinitores et agricolas. 13 Columnas autem aereas quae erant in templo Domini et bases et mare aereum quod erat in domo Domini confregerunt Chaldei et transtulerunt aes omne in Babylonem. 14 Ollas quoque aereas et trullas et tridentes et scyphos et mortariola et omnia vasa aerea in quibus ministrabant tulerunt. 15 Nec non et turibula et fialas quae aurea et quae argentea tulit princeps militiae, 16 id est, columnas duas, mare unum et bases quas fecerat Salomon in templo Domini. Non erat pondus aeris omnium vasorum. 17 Decem et octo cubitos altitudinis habebat columna una, et capitellum aereum super se altitudinis trium cubitorum, et reticulum et malogranata super capitellum columnae omnia aerea, similem et columna secunda habebat ornatum.

18 Tulit quoque princeps militiae Seraian, sacerdotem primum, et Sophoniam, sacerdotem secundum, et tres ianitores 19 et de civitate eunuchum unum qui erat praefectus super viros bellatores et quinque viros de his qui steterant

that is the nineteenth year of the king of Babylon, came Nebuzaradan, commander of the army, a servant of the king of Babylon, into Jerusalem. 9 And he burnt the house of the Lord and the king's house and the houses of Jerusalem, and every house he burnt with fire. 10 And all the army of the Chaldeans which was with the commander of the troops broke down the walls of Jerusalem round about. 11 And Nebuzaradan, the commander of the army, carried away the rest of the people that remained in the city and the fugitives that had gone over to the king of Babylon and the remnant of the common people. 12 *But* of the poor of the land he left some dressers of vines and husbandmen. 13 And the pillars of brass that were in the temple of the Lord and the bases and the sea of brass which was in the house of the Lord the Chaldeans broke in pieces and carried all the brass *of them* to Babylon. 14 They took away also the pots of brass and the mazers and the forks and the cups and the mortars and all the vessels of brass with which they ministered. 15 Moreover also the censers and the bowls *such as* were of gold *in gold* and *such as* were of silver *in silver* the general of the army took away, 16 that is, two pillars, one sea and the bases which Solomon had made in the temple of the Lord. The brass of all these vessels was without weight. 17 One pillar was eighteen cubits high, and the chapiter of brass *which was* upon it was three cubits high, and the net-work and the pomegranates *that were* upon the chapiter of the pillar were all of brass, and the second pillar had the like adorning.

18 And the general of the army took Seraiah, the chief priest, and Zephaniah, the second priest, and three door-keepers 19 and out of the city one eunuch who was captain over the men of war and five men of them that had stood

coram rege quos repperit in civitate et Sopher, principem exercitus, qui probabat tirones de populo terrae, et sexaginta viros e vulgo qui inventi fuerant in civitate. 20 Quos tollens Nabuzardan, princeps militum, duxit ad regem Babylonis in Reblatha. 21 Percussitque eos rex Babylonis et interfecit in Reblatha in terra Emath. Et translatus est Iuda de terra sua.

22 Populo autem qui relictus erat in terra Iuda quem dimiserat Nabuchodonosor, rex Babylonis, praefecit Godoliam, filium Ahicham, filii Saphan. 23 Quod cum audissent omnes duces militum, ipsi et viri qui erant cum eis, videlicet, quod constituisset rex Babylonis Godoliam, venerunt ad Godoliam in Maspha, Ismahel, filius Nathaniae, et Iohanan, filius Caree, et Sareia, filius Thenaameth, Nethophathites, et Iezonias, filius Maachathi, ipsi et socii eorum. 24 Iuravitque eis Godolias et sociis eorum, dicens, "Nolite timere servire Chaldeis. Manete in terra, et servite regi Babylonis, et bene erit vobis." 25 Factum est autem in mense septimo venit Ismahel, filius Nathaniae, filii Elisama de semine regio, et decem viri cum eo percusseruntque Godoliam qui et mortuus est sed et Iudaeos et Chaldeos qui erant cum eo in Maspha. 26 Consurgens autem omnis populus a parvo usque ad magnum et principes militum venerunt in Aegyptum, timentes Chaldeos.

27 Factum est vero anno tricesimo septimo transmigrationis Ioiachin, regis Iudae, mense duodecimo, vicesima septima die mensis, sublevavit Evilmerodach, rex Babylonis,

before the king whom he found in the city and Sopher, the captain of the army, who exercised the young soldiers of the people of the land, and threescore men of the common people who were found in the city. 20 These Nebuzaradan, the general of the army, took away and carried them to the king of Babylon to Riblah. 21 And the king of Babylon smote them and slew them at Riblah in the land of Hamath. So Judah was carried away out of their land.

22 But over the people that remained in the land of Judah which Nebuchadnezzar, king of Babylon, had left he gave the government to Gedaliah, the son of Ahikam, the son of Shaphan. 23 And when all the captains of the soldiers had heard this, they and the men that were with them, to wit, that the king of Babylon had made Gedaliah governor, they came to Gedaliah to Mizpah, Ishmael, the son of Nethaniah, and Johanan, the son of Kareah, and Seraiah, the son of Tanhumeth, the Netophathite, and Jaazaniah, the son of Maachathi, they and their men. 24 And Gedaliah swore to them and to their men, saying, "Be not afraid to serve the Chaldeans. Stay in the land, and serve the king of Babylon, and it shall be well with you." 25 But it came to pass in the seventh month that Ishmael, the son of Nethaniah, the son of Elishama of the seed royal, came and ten men with him and smote Gedaliah *so that he* died and also the Jews and the Chaldeans that were with him in Mizpah. 26 And all the people *both* little *and* great and the captains of the soldiers rising up went to Egypt, fearing the Chaldeans.

27 And it came to pass in the seven and thirtieth year of the captivity of Jehoiachin, king of Judah, in the twelfth month, the seven and twentieth day of the month, Evil-merodach, king of Babylon, in the year that he began to

anno quo regnare coeperat caput Ioiachin, regis Iuda, de carcere. 28 Et locutus est ei benigne, et posuit thronum eius super thronum regum qui erant cum eo in Babylone. 29 Et mutavit vestes eius quas habuerat in carcere, et comedebat panem semper in conspectu eius cunctis diebus vitae suae. 30 Annonam quoque constituit ei absque intermissione quae et dabatur ei a rege per singulos dies omnibus diebus vitae.

reign lifted up the head of Jehoiachin, king of Judah, out of prison. 28 And he spoke kindly to him, and he set his throne above the throne of the kings that were with him in Babylon. 29 And he changed his garments which he had in prison, and he ate bread always *before him* all the days of his life. 30 And he appointed him a *continual* allowance which was also given him by the king day by day all the days of his life.

Note on the Text

This edition is meant to present a Latin text close to what the Douay-Rheims translators saw. Therefore the readings in this edition are not necessarily preferred in the sense that they are thought to be "original"; instead, they represent the Latin Bible as it was read by many from the eighth through the sixteenth century. Furthermore, in the service of economy, sources for the text are cited according to a hierarchy and consequently the lists of sources following the lemmas and alternate readings are not necessarily comprehensive. If a reading appears in Weber's text or apparatus, no other sources are cited; if it is not in Weber but is in Quentin, only the sources cited by Quentin are reproduced. The complete list of sources for the Latin text, in their hierarchical order, is Weber, the Sixto-Clementine edition, Weber's apparatus, Quentin, his apparatus, the Vetus Latina edition of Pierre Sabatier (1682–1742), the *Glossa Ordinaria* attributed (wrongly) to Walafrid Strabo in the Patrologia Latina, and the database of the Beuroner Vetus Latina-Institut.

When no source can be found for what seems to be the correct Latin, a reconstruction is proposed in the Notes to the Text but the Weber text is generally printed in the edition. Trivial differences between the Weber and Sixto-Clementine editions in word order and orthography, alternative spellings and inflections of proper names, and synco-

pation of verbs have not been noted, nor have many differences that do not affect translation, such as the omission or inclusion of forms of *esse*, variant forms of personal pronouns, conjunctions treated by the Douay-Rheims translators as synonymous, and the omission or inclusion of certain pronouns or possessive adjectives.

Whenever it has been necessary to stray from Weber's text (about one thousand times in the first volume), the departures are recorded in the Notes to the Text. These notes by no means constitute a true *apparatus criticus,* but they enable interested readers to see both the deviations from Weber (whose text is preferable for people wanting to get as close as possible to the earliest versions of the many Latin texts which, combined, form the Vulgate Bible) and significant differences among the Weber, Sixto-Clementine, and Douay-Rheims texts.

When the translation reflects a reading closer to Weber's than to the Sixto-Clementine edition, the Sixto-Clementine variation is printed in the Notes to the Text. Less frequently, there are two readings that would translate the same way but that differ sufficiently to warrant noting, as at Gen 19:6, where Weber reads "umbraculum tegminis" while the Sixto-Clementine version has "umbra culminis."

Often the punctuation of the Douay-Rheims edition reflects an understanding of the Latin different from that of the Weber, Sixto-Clementine, or both editions. The Weber edition has no punctuation marks in most books; rather, the editors inserted line breaks to mark new clauses or sentences, a punctuation style known as *per cola et commata,* which is meant to assist readers without inserting anachronistic markings. These line breaks have been represented in

the notes by slashes (/). In general, differences in punctuation among this edition, the Sixto-Clementine Bible, and Weber's edition have been cited only when they demonstrate considerably different understandings of the Latin. Often Weber's presentation is too equivocal to shed light on his understanding; in these cases, his edition is not cited.

While the Douay-Rheims translation belongs to a tradition of exceptionally literal renderings of the Latin Bible, Challoner's revision contains some divergences from the Latin. Any English that does not square with the text *en face* is italicized, and where possible, Challoner's source has been indicated in the Notes to the Text. When Challoner's source is given, it is not necessarily quoted word for word in the lemma; indeed, the Septuagint is cited as a source, yet almost no Greek is quoted in the notes. Whenever there can be doubt of a source based on a slight difference between its reading and Challoner's, the difference has been recorded following the lemma, either in parentheses or in brackets when containing explanatory material that is not a quotation from the source. Sources for the English text are cited in a hierarchical fashion similar to that of the Latin, in the following order: Douay-Rheims, Sixto-Clementine, King James, Septuagint, Hebrew text; this means that if an English reading is found in the King James Version that may also be in the Septuagint, only the King James Version is cited. Also, if Challoner's translation seems to approximate a source that is cited, the distance between source and translation is indicated by a question mark following the siglum.

Words cited from biblical sources are in italics in the notes, and the sigla and any comments are in roman type. Lemmas precede colons; other readings follow them. Occa-

sionally Challoner indicated that he was adding words to his revision that did not appear in the Latin text; he did this by italicizing the relevant words, much as the authors of the King James Version printed occasional words in roman as opposed to black-letter type to indicate an addition. Bracketed explanations or underlinings draw attention to these typographical variations in the Notes to the Text where necessary.

Notes to the Text

SIGLA

*D-R = Latin text that seems to give rise to the D-R translation but that is not represented in S-C, Weber, the manuscripts cited in those editions, or the Old Latin Bible.

D-R = The Holie Bible: Faithfully Translated into English out of the Authentical Latin (The English Colleges of Douay and Rheims, OT 1609–10, NT 1582)

D-R/C = The Holy Bible: Translated from the Latin Vulgat (Challoner's 1752 revision, Dublin?)

Heb = Hebrew sources for the text

KJV = The Holy Bible, Conteyning the Old Testament, and the New: Newly Translated out of the Originall tongues: & with the former Translations diligently compared and reuised: by his Maiesties speciall Comandement Appointed to be read in Churches (London, 1611, rpr. 1990)

KJVn = marginalia in KJV

PL = J.-P. Migne, ed., Patrologia Latina (Paris, 1844–1865)

Quentin = Biblia sacra: iuxta Latinam Vulgatam versionem (Typis Polyglottis Vaticanis, 1926–[1995])

S = A. Rahlfs, ed., Septuaginta, 2nd ed. (Stuttgart: Deutsche Bibelgesellschaft, 1979)

S-C = Biblia Sacra: Vulgatae Editionis Sixti V Pont. Max. iussu recognita et Clementis VIII auctoritate edita (Vatican City: Marietti, 1959)

Smyth = H. W. Smyth, ed., G. M. Messing, rev., *Greek Grammar* (Cambridge, MA: Harvard University Press, 1956)

Weber = R. Weber, ed., *Biblia Sacra Vulgata,* 5th ed. (Stuttgart, 2007)

The use of sigla from Rahlfs's, Weber's, and Quentin's critical apparatus is indicated in brackets following the sigla.

Other abbreviations follow those found in H. J. Frede, *Kirchenschriftsteller: Verzeichnis und Sigel* (Freiburg: Herder, 1995) and R. Gryson, *Altlateinische Handschriften,* 2 vols. (Freiburg: Herder, 1999), and those sigla are introduced by "Frede" or "Gryson" to indicate their source. Sigla without citations following them are to be understood to refer to the verse indicated by the lemma.

Joshua

1:1　*post*: *ut post* Weber; *ut loqueretur*: *loqueretur* Weber
<1:2　*thy* D-R/C: *al the* D-R>
1:5　*ero et*: *ero* S-C
1:8　*de*: *ab* S-C
1:13　*terram hanc* r [Quentin's siglum]: *terram* S-C, Weber
<1:14　*on this side of the* KJV: *beyond* D-R; *of you* D-R/C: omitted in D-R>
1:17　*Deus tuus*: *Deus* Weber
2:1　*ad explorandum* 100 E, HI loc 155.8 (*ad investigandam et noscendam*), HIL my 2.8.1 (*ad speculandam terram*): *exploratores* S-C, Weber; *in abscondito*: *abscondito* Weber
<2:5　*at the time of shutting the gate* KJV: *when the gate was a shutting* D-R; *after them* KJV: omitted in D-R>
<2:7　*fords* KJV: *ford* D-R>
<2:8　*when* D-R/C: *and* D-R>
<2:12　*also will shew mercy to* KJV (*will also shew kindnesse vnto*): *also doe with* D-R>
2:13　*ut*: *et* Weber; *de*: *a* S-C
<2:14　*show thee* D-R/C [by analogy to Jos 2:12]: *doe in thee* D-R>
2:15　*Demisit*: *dimisit* Weber

2:16   *latete*: *latitate* S-C

<2:22   *having sought them* D-R/C [KJV also has *sought them,* but syntax is different]: *seeking* D-R>

3:1   *per tres*: *tres* S-C

<3:4   *gone this way* KJV (*passed* for *gone*): *walked by it* D-R>

3:9   *verbum*: *verba* Weber

3:10   *disperdet*: *disperdat* Weber; *et Hettheum*: *Hettheum* Weber; *Iebuseum et Amorreum*: *Amorreum et Iebuseum* Weber

3:14   *transirent*: *transiret* S-C

3:15   *Iordanis*: *cum Iordanis* Weber; *impleverat*: *impleret* Weber

3:16   *instar*: *ad instar* S-C

<3:16   *were seen* D-R/C: *appeared* D-R>

3:17   *Hiericho*: *Iordanem* Weber

<4:3   *midst* KJV: *middes of the chanel* D-R>

4:5   *portate inde*: *portate* Weber

4:8   *medio Iordanis alveo*: *alveo Iordanis* *D-R

4:12   *dimidiae*: *dimidia* S-C

<4:12   *half the tribe* KJV: *the half tribe* D-R>

4:25   *ut et*: *et ut* Weber

<5:1   *Now* D-R/C *when* KJV: *Therfore after that* D-R; *failed them* D-R/C: *failed* D-R>

5:1   *Magno Mari*: *magni maris* S-C

5:4   *ex*: *de* S-C

<5:4   *that were males* KJV: *of the malekinde* D-R; *during the time of the long going about in the way* D-R/C: *by the long circuites of the way* D-R>

<5:6   *all* KJV: omitted in D-R>

5:6   *ut non*: *ut* Weber

<5:7   *uncircumsised* KJV: *in the prepuce* D-R>

5:9   *praesentem*: *hanc praesentem* *D-R

5:13   *se*: *se et* Weber

5:15   *Dominus*: *dominus* Weber

5:16   *calciamentum tuum*: *calciamentum* Weber

<5:16   *shoes* D-R/C *from off* KJV: *shoe from* D-R>

<6:1   *close shut up* KJV (*straightly* for *close*): *shut* D-R>

6:2   *manus tuas*: *manu tua* S-C

<6:5   *give a longer and broken tune* D-R/C: *sound in length and with a broken tune* D-R>

<6:6   *jubilee* D-R/C: *iubilees* D-R>

6:7   *Vadite*: *Ite* S-C

<6:9   *men* KJV: *hoste* D-R; *sound of the trumpets was heard on all sides* D-R/C: *al places sounded with the trumpettes* D-R>

6:13   *iobeleo*: *iobeleis* Weber

<6:13   *the trumpets* KJV: omitted in D-R>

6:19   *aut* FRYaels cum LXX [Quentin's sigla]: *et* S-C, Weber

<6:19   *or* D-R/C: *and* D-R>

<6:20   *when* KJV: *after that* D-R>

<6:21   *man and woman, young and old* KJV: *from man to woman, from the infant to the old man* D-R>

<6:22   *harlot's* KJV: *of the woman the harlotte* D-R>

6:23   *castra Israhel*: *castra* *D-R

6:24   *inventa sunt* Qunetin: *erant* S-C, *sunt* Weber; *auro et argento*: *argento et auro* Weber

<6:24   *were* S-C [KJV has *was*]: *were found* D-R>

<6:25   *saved* KJV: *caused to liue* D-R>

<7:2   *command* D-R/C: *commandmentes* D-R>

7:3   *vexabitur*: *vexatur* Weber

<7:3   *should* D-R/C: *shal* D-R>

7:4   *pugnatores*: *pugnatorum* S-C

7:5   *et sex*: *sex* S-C; *usque*: *usque ad* S-C

<7:5   *struck with fear* S: *much afrayd* D-R>

<7:12   *but* KJV: *and* D-R>

7:17   *domos*: *viros* Weber

<7:18   *bringing* D-R/C [KJV has *he brought*]: *diuiding* D-R>

7:19   *ait Iosue*: *ait* Weber

<7:21   *in* KJV: *against* D-R; *I dug* D-R/C: *digged* D-R>

<7:24   *and all Israel with him took* KJV: *taking* D-R; *the tent also* KJV (*and his tent*): *and the tabernacle itself* D-R>

7:24   *filios quoque et filias eius*: *filiosque eius et filias* Weber

7:26   *Congregaveruntque*: *congregaverunt quoque* Weber

<8:4   *be ye* KJV: *ye shal . . . be* D-R>

8:7   *persequentibus*: *sequentibus* Weber

8:8   *et sic*: *sic* Weber

<8:12   *to lie* KJV: omitted in D-R>

8:12   *Bethel*: *Bethaven* Weber

8:13   *multitudinis*: *illius mutitudinis* S-C

<8:13   *that* S-C: *the* D-R>

<8:15   *making as if they were afraid* KJV (*beaten* for *afraid*): *feyning feare* D-R>

8:17   *unus* PL 86 400A, Gryson 100 E (*nemo* for *ne unus*): *unus quidem* S-C, Weber

<8:22   *to meet* D-R/C: *against* D-R; *to cut off the enemies who were surrounded by them* D-R/C: *to strike the enemies in the middes of them* D-R; *so that* KJV: *When . . . therfore* D-R>

<8:25   *number of them . . . was* D-R/C: *there were* D-R; *that* KJV: *that same* D-R; *both of . . . and* KJV: *from . . . vnto* D-R>

8:25   *eodem*: *eo* Weber

8:29   *Praecepitque*: *Praecepitque Iosue* S-C

<8:29   *Then* D-R/C *Joshua* S-C: *And he* D-R>

8:31   *altare*: *altare vero* S-C

<8:33   *both . . . and* S [Jos 9:2^d]: *as wel . . . as also* D-R; *he that was born among them* KJV: *the man of the same countrie* D-R>

9:1   *campestribus*: *in campestribus* Weber; *Chananeus*: *et Chananeus* Weber

<9:1   *coasts* KJV: *shore* D-R>

9:2   *eademque*: *unaque* *D-R

9:4   *callide* W^M els [Quentin's sigla]: *et callide* S-C, Weber

<9:7   *Perhaps* D-R/C: *Lest perhaps* D-R; *falls to our lot; if so* D-R/C: *is dew to us by lotte, and* D-R>

9:7   *forsitan*: *forte* S-C

<9:8   *them* KJV: *whom* D-R>

9:8   *estis*: *estis vos* S-C

9:10   *qui fuerunt trans*: *trans* Weber

<9:11   *with you* KJV: *in your handes* D-R>

9:12   *panes*: *hii panes* *D-R

<9:12   *by being exceeding old* D-R/C: *for ouer much oldnesse* D-R>

<9:13   *These* [both times] KJV: *the* D-R; *when we filled them were* D-R/C: *we filled being* D-R; *by reason of the very long journey* KJV: *for the length of the long way* D-R>

9:13   *longioris*: *largioris* Weber

<9:17   *the names of which are* D-R/C: *whose names are these* D-R>

<9:20   *their lives be saved* D-R/C: *them be reserued in dede aliue* D-R, literally, *them indeed be saved that they may live*>

<9:21   *as to serve the whole multitude in hewing wood and bringing* D-R/C: *that for the vses of the whole multitude they hew wood, and carie* D-R>

<9:22   *impose upon us* D-R/C: *deceiue vs by fraude* D-R; *saying* KJV: *to say* D-R>

<9:23   *your race shall always be hewers of wood and carriers* D-R/C: *there shal not faile of your stocke a hewer of wood, and a carier* D-R>

9:24   *quod*: *quae* Weber

9:26   *manu*: *manibus* Weber

<10:1   *gone over* D-R/C [after S?]: *fled* D-R>

10:4   *et ad*: *et* Weber

<10:5   *they and* KJV: *together with* D-R>

10:10   *est eos*: *est* Weber

10:11   *usque*: *usque ad* S-C

<10:11   *were slain by the swords of the children of Israel* D-R/C: *they whom the children of Israel had strooken with the sword* D-R>

10:14   *ante*: *antea* S-C

10:17   *urbis Maceda*: *Maceda* Weber

10:18   *sociis et ait*: *eis dicens* *D-R

<10:18   *them that were with him, saying* S-C: *them saying* D-R>

10:19   *nec*: *ne* Weber

<10:19   *shelter themselves* D-R/C: *enter into the fortes* D-R>

<10:21   *without the loss of any one* D-R/C: *the ful number* D-R; *move his tongue* KJV: *once mutter* D-R>

10:23   *Feceruntque*: *fecerunt* Weber

<10:24   *put their feet upon the necks* KJV: *troden with their feete the neckes* D-R>

<10:27   *where* Heb: *wherin* D-R; *day* KJV (*very day*): *present* D-R>

10:28   *die, Macedam* Q^{H†} [without punctuation, Quentin's sigla]: *quoque die Macedam* S-C, *die Macedam quoque* Weber; *percussit eam*: *percussit* Weber

10:29   *autem cum*: *cum* Weber

10:30   *manus*: *manu* Weber

10:31   *Lachis cum omni Israhel*: *Lachis* Weber

<10:31 *investing it with his army* D-R/C: *placing the hoste round about* D-R>

10:32 *manus: manu* Weber

<10:32 *put it to the sword* D-R/C: *stroke it in the edge of the sword* D-R>

10:33 *Horam: Hiram* Weber

<10:33 *so as to leave none alive* D-R/C: *to vtter destruction* D-R>

<10:35 *put to the sword* D-R/C: *stroke in the edge of the sword* D-R>

10:37 *cepit eam: cepitque* Weber

<10:37 *putting to the sword* D-R/C: *consuming with the sword* D-R>

<10:40 *breathed* KJV: *could breath* D-R>

10:42 *universosque: universos* Weber; *pugnabat: pugnavit* S-C

11:3 *Chananeum quoque: Chananeumque* Weber

<11:3 *to* KJV *the Canaanites* S: *the Chananeite* D-R; *to the Hivite* KJV: *the Heueite* D-R>

<11:4 *a* S: *of* D-R>

<11:5 *together* KJV: *together in one* D-R>

11:8 *manus: manu* Weber

11:9 *Fecitque: fecit* Weber; *conbusit: conbusit igni* S-C

<11:10 *was the head of all these kingdoms* KJV: *among al these kingdomes held the principalitie* D-R>

<11:11 *cut off* D-R/C: *stroke* D-R; *utterly destroyed* KJV: *to vtter destruction he wasted* D-R; *burned* KJV: *destroyed* D-R>

11:11 *peremit: permisit* Weber

<11:12 *and put to the sword* D-R/C: *stroke* D-R>

11:12 *Dei* C [Quentin's siglum]: *Domini* S-C, Weber

<11:13 *only Hazor that was very strong* D-R/C: *one onlie Asor verie wel fensed* D-R>

11:15 *ne: nec* S-C

<11:15 *left not one thing undone* KJV (*nothing* for *not one thing*): *ommitted . . . not so much as one word* D-R>

11:17 *percussit et: percussit* Weber

11:19 *se: se non* Weber; *omnes enim: omnes* Weber

11:20 *sententia: sententiae* Weber

<12:2 *and* KJV [italicized in D-R/C and in roman type in KJV]: omitted in D-R>

12:2 *dimidiique: dimidiaeque* S-C

12:3   *subiacet*: *subiacent* Weber; *Asedoth usque Phasga* W^M gre [Quentin's sigla]: *Asedoth Phasga* S-C, *Asedothphasga* Weber

<12:3   *Asedoth, Pisgah* D-R/C: *Asedoth, as farre as Phasga* D-R>

12:8   *in solitudine ac in*: *solitudine ac* Weber

12:24   *triginta*: *triginta et* Weber

<12:24   *and* KJV: omitted in D-R>

<13:1   *far advanced* D-R/C: *striken* D-R; *years* KJV: *age* D-R>

<13:3   *lords* D-R/C: *fiue Lordes* D-R>

13:3   *Gazeos*: *Gazeos et* S-C

<13:5   *to the entering* KJV: *til thou enter* D-R>

<13:6   *mountains* D-R/C: *mountaine* D-R; *in as a part* D-R/C: *into a portion* D-R>

13:6   *partem*: *parte* Weber

<13:10   *Amorites* KJV: *Amorrheite* D-R>

13:11   *usque*: *usque ad* S-C

<13:14   *are* KJV: *that is* D-R>

13:18   *et Iessa*: *Iessa* Weber

13:19   *et Cariathaim*: *Cariathaim* Weber

13:20   *Asedoth, Phasga*: *Asedothphasga* Weber

13:21   *et omnes*: *omnes* Weber

<13:23   *was* KJV: *was made* D-R>

13:31   *et Ashtaroth*: *Ashtaroth* Weber

14:4   *successerunt*: *successerant* Weber

<14:4   *of* D-R/C: *in the* D-R>

14:5   *praeceperat*: *praecepit* Weber

<14:7   *brought him word again as* KJV: *reported to him that which* D-R>

14:9   *Terram*: *terra* S-C

<14:12   *so be, the Lord will* KJV: *perhaps our Lord* D-R>

14:13   *tradidit ei*: *tradidit* Weber

14:15   *antea*: *ante* S-C

15:1   *Edom usque* L^{L*}S^{TM}W^{SJ*M} g [Quentin's sigla]: *Edom* S-C, Weber

15:3   *ascendens ad*: *ascendens* Weber

<15:5   *towards* D-R/C: *those places that looke to* D-R; *Jordan* D-R/C: *of Iordan* D-R>

15:5   *respiciunt ad*: *respiciunt* Weber; *Iordanis fluvium*: *Iordanem fluvium* Weber

<15:7   *the border* KJV [italicized in D-R/C]: omitted in D-R>

<15:8   *the same* KJV: *this* D-R; *ascending* D-R/C: *rearing it self* D-R>

<15:9   *towards* S: *into* D-R>

<15:11   *northward to a part* D-R/C: *toward the North coast of a part* D-R; *is bounded westward with the Great Sea* D-R/C: *is shut vp with the end of the great sea toward the West* D-R>

<15:13   *which* KJV: *that* D-R>

15:15   *Cariathsepher*: *Cariath Sepher* S-C

15:16   *Cariathsepher*: *Cariath Sepher* S-C

15:18   *suasa est a viro suo*: *suasit viro* Weber

<15:19   *give me also* KJV *a land that is watered* D-R/C [*land* is italicized in D-R/C]: *ioyne also a waterie* D-R>

15:22   *et Adeda*: *Adeda* Weber

15:23   *et Iethnan*: *Iethnan* Weber

15:24   *et Baloth*: *Baloth* Weber

15:25   *Asor Nova*: *et Asor Nova* Weber; *Carioth, Hesrom*: *Carioth, Hesron* S-C, *Cariothesrom* Weber

15:27   *et Bethfeleth*: *Bethfeleth* Weber

15:29   *et Bala*: *Bala* Weber; *et Esem*: *Esem* Weber

15:30   *et Exiil*: *Exiil* Weber

15:31   *et Siceleg*: *Siceleg* Weber

15:32   *Aen et Remmon*: *Aenremmon* Weber

15:34   *et Thaffua*: *Thaffua* Weber

15:35   *et Adulam*: *Adulam* Weber

15:36   *et Adithaim*: *Adithaim* Weber

15:41   *et Bethdagon*: *Bethdagon* Weber

15:44   *et Ceila*: *Ceila* Weber

15:47   *et Mare*: *mare* Weber

<15:47   *that is* D-R/C: *is* D-R>

15:49   *et Cariathsenna*: *Cariathsenna* Weber

15:53   *et Ianum*: *Ianum* Weber

15:62   *et Anepsan*: *Anepsan* Weber

16:2   *Archi Atharoth*: *Archiahtaroth* Weber

<16:5   *was* KJV: *was made* D-R>

16:5   *Atharothaddar*: *Ataroth Addar* S-C

16:8   *pertransit*: *pertransitque* Weber; *Vallem*: *valle* Weber

17:1　　*sors*: *haec sors* *D-R

17:3　　*et Egla*: *Egla* Weber

<17:8　*the lot of Manasseh took in the land* D-R/C: *in the lotte of Manasses was fallen the Land* D-R; *and belongs to the children* KJV (*belonged* for *and belongs*): *the childrens* D-R>

<17:9　*the border goeth down to the Valley of the Reeds* S: *the border of the Reede valley went downe* D-R>

<17:10　*is the border of* KJV: *incloseth* D-R>

17:11　*villulis* [all three times]: *viculis* S-C

17:12　*sua*: *ista* Weber

<17:14　*but one lot and one portion to possess* KJV: *the possession of one lotte and corde* D-R>

<17:15　*too* KJV: omitted in D-R>

<17:16　*low lands* D-R/C: *champayne countrie* D-R; *in* S: *possessing* D-R; *have* KJV: *vse* D-R>

<17:18　*the wood* KJV: omitted in D-R>

<18:3　*indolent and slack* D-R/C: *slack with cowardenes* D-R>

18:6　*sortem* A m [Quentin's sigla]: *hic sortem* S-C, Weber

<18:6　*lots* KJV: *the lotte* D-R>

<18:7　*eastward* S: *at the East side* D-R>

<18:8　*that* D-R/C: *that here* D-R; *lots* KJV: *the lotte* D-R>

18:8　*Domino*: *Domino Deo* Weber

18:12　*ad solitudinem*: *in solitudinem* Weber

18:13　*Atharothaddar*: *Ataroth Addar* S-C

18:14　*ad meridiem*: *a meridie* Weber; *ad occidentem*: *et occidentem* Weber

18:16　*in Gehennom*: *Gehennom* Weber; *Vallis Ennom*: *Vallem Ennom* S-C

<18:19　*north of the Most Salt Sea at the south end of the Jordan* KJV (*North bay of the salt Sea at the South end of Iordane*): *brincke of the most salt sea on the North in the end of Iordan to the south quarter* D-R>

18:20　*suas*: *singulas* Weber

18:23　*et Avim*: *Avim* Weber

18:26　*et Cafera*: *Cafera* Weber

<19:1　*for* KJV: *of* D-R>

19:4　*et Arma*: *Arma* Weber

19:5　*et Asersusa*: *Asersusa* Weber

<19:8 *and* KJV: omitted in D-R>

19:8 *Balaath Ber Ramath*: *balaath beer ramath* c [Weber's siglum]; *Baalathbeer, Ramath* S-C; *Balaath Berrameth* Weber

19:10 *Ceciditque*: *cecidit quoque* Weber

<19:10 *to* D-R/C: *of* D-R; *was* KJV: *was made* D-R>

19:13 *ad*: *usque ad* S-C; *et Thacasin*: *Etthacasin* Weber

19:14 *Nathon*: *Hanathon* S-C; *et Nathon* Weber

19:19 *et Seon*: *Seon* Weber

19:22 *terminus eius*: *terminus* Weber; *erantque* W^{SJ} ar [Quentin's sigla]: *eruntque* S-C, Weber

<19:22 *shall be* S-C *at* KJV: *were* D-R>

19:24 *Ceciditque*: *cecidit* Weber

19:26 *et Elmelech*: *Elmelech* S-C; *Sior et Labanath*: *Siorlabanath* Weber

19:31 *urbesque*: *urbes* Weber

<19:32 *to* KJV: *Of* D-R>

19:32 *sors*: *pars* Weber

19:35 *et Chenereth*: *Chenereth* Weber

19:44 *Helthecen, Gebthon*: *Helthecen et Gebthon* Weber [S-C has no comma]

19:45 *et Iud et Bene et Barach*: *Iud et Benebarach* Weber

19:46 *et Meiarcon*: *aquae Hiercon* Weber

<19:47 *terminated there* D-R/C: *shut vp with the same end* D-R; *put it to the sword* D-R/C: *stroke it in the edge of the sword* D-R>

19:47 *percusserunt eam*: *percusserunt* Weber; *Lesem Dan*: *Lesemdan* Weber

19:50 *Thamnath Seraa*: *Thamnath Saraa* S-C, *Thamnathseraa* Weber

<20:2 *Appoint cities of refuge* KJV: *Separate the cities of the fugitiues* D-R>

<20:3 *person* KJV: *soule* D-R>

20:4 *stabit*: *stabitque* Weber

<20:4 *such things as* D-R/C: *those thinges, that* D-R>

<20:6 *to give an account* D-R/C: *rendring a cause* D-R; *the death of the high priest* KJV: *the high priest die* D-R>

20:9 *habitabant*: *habitant* Weber

<20:9 *whosoever* KJV: *he . . . which* D-R>

<21:1 *of* KJV: *in* D-R>

<21:4 *for* KJV: *vnto* D-R>

21:5 *superfuerant*: *superflui erant* Weber

<21:6 *thirteen cities* KJV: *cities in number thirtene* D-R>

<21:11 *the city of Arba* KJV: *Cariatharbe* D-R>

21:15 *et Dabir*: *Dabir* Weber

<21:21 *one of the* D-R/C: omitted in D-R>

21:21 *urbes*: *urbs* Weber

<21:26 *were ten with their suburbs* KJV *which* D-R/C: *ten, and their suburbes* D-R>

<21:27 *out* D-R/C: *he gave* D-R; *one of the* D-R/C [*one of* italicized]: omitted in D-R>

21:27 *confugii civitates*: *confugii civitatem* Weber

<21:32 *one of the* D-R/C [*one of* italicized]: omitted in D-R>

21:32 *civitates confugii*: *civitatem confugii* Weber

<21:34 *were* D-R/C: *was* D-R>

21:36 verse omitted in Weber but printed in appendix; this edition follows S-C with punctuation after D-R

<21:36 *one of the* D-R/C [*one of* italicized]: omitted in D-R>

<21:37 *one of the* D-R/C [*one of* italicized]: omitted in D-R>

<21:39 *within* KJV: *in the middes of* D-R>

21:41 *Dominus Deus*: *Dominus* Weber

<21:42 *from* D-R/C: *on* D-R; *under* D-R/C: *into* D-R>

21:42 *dicionem*: *ditionem* S-C

<21:43 *all came to pass* KJV: *al things were accomplished in deedes* D-R>

22:4 *possessionis vestrae*: *possessionis uestre* L^HW cum Lugd. [Quentin's sigla], *possessionis* S-C, Weber

22:5 *servus*: *famulus* S-C; *mandata*: *omnia mandata* *D-R

22:7 *Tribui autem Manasse mediae*: *Dimidiae autem tribui Manasse* S-C; *occidentem*: *occidentem eius* Weber

<22:7 *to the west* D-R/C: *at the West side* D-R>

<22:9 *So* D-R/C: *And* D-R>

22:10 *terram*: *terra* Weber

<22:10 *immensely great* D-R/C: *of an infinite greatnes* D-R>

<22:11 *brought them an account* D-R/C: *reported to them* D-R>

22:13 *sacerdotis*: *sacerdotem* Weber

<22:16 *meaneth* D-R/C: *is* D-R>

<22:19 *depart* D-R/C [KJV also has imperative]: *that you depart* D-R>

<22:22 *also* D-R/C: *together* D-R>

22:22 *puniat nos: puniat* Weber

<22:25 *best* D-R/C: *better* D-R>

<22:27 *yours* D-R/C: *your progenie* D-R>

22:27 *et holocausta: holocausta* Weber

<22:29 *any* D-R/C: *this* D-R; *leave off following* KJV (*turne . . . from follow-ing*): *leave* D-R>

22:32 *in terram* r cum Lugd. [Quentin's sigla]: *finium* S-C, Weber

<22:32 *brought them word again* KJV: *reported to them* D-R>

<23:1 *far advanced in years* D-R/C: *of a great age* D-R>

23:2 *iudices* Gryson 100 E: *duces* S-C, Weber

<23:2 *far advanced in years* D-R/C: *farre gone in age* D-R>

<23:4 *east* D-R/C: *East part* D-R>

<23:7 *among* KJV: *to* D-R; *remain* KJV: *be* D-R>

23:9 *Dominus Deus: Dominus* Weber

<23:13 *for a certainty* KJV: *euen now* D-R; *in your way* D-R/C: *for you* D-R>

23:14 *ingredior: ingrediar* Weber; *vobis: nobis* Weber

<23:14 *failed* KJV: *escaped without effect* D-R>

<23:15 *all the evils* KJV (*all euill things*): *what euils soeuer* D-R>

<23:16 *when* KJV: *because* D-R>

23:16 *de: ab* Weber

<24:2 *of old* KJV (*in old time*): *from the beginning* D-R>

<24:4 *And* KJV: *Of whom* D-R; *for his possession* D-R/C: *to possesse* D-R>

24:8 *in terram: ad terram* Weber

24:12 *et: nec in* S-C

<24:12 *not with thy sword nor with thy bow* KJV: *not in thy sword and bow* D-R>

<24:15 *you have your choice* D-R/C: *choise is geuen you* D-R; *whom you would rather* D-R/C: *whom you ought especially to* D-R; *as for me* KJV: *I* D-R>

<24:19 *mighty and jealous* D-R/C [KJV has *jealous*]: *a mightie æmulator* D-R>

<24:20 *turn* KJV: *turne him self* D-R; *all the good he hath done you* KJV (*with-out all the*): *he hath geuen you good thinges* D-R>

24:23 *vestrum: vestri* S-C

24:24 *et oboedientes erimus: oboedientes* Weber

24:26 *Scripsit quoque: scripsitque* Weber; *legis Domini: legis Dei* Weber

24:29 *et decem*: *decem* Weber

24:31 *noverant*: *noverunt* S-C

24:32 *in possessione*: *in possessionem* S-C

<24:32 *that belonged to* KJV (*pertained* for *belonged*): *of* D-R>

JUDGES

1:3 *sortem meam*: *sorte mea* Weber; *sortem tuam*: *sorte tua* Weber

<1:4 *of them* KJV [italicized in D-R/C]: omitted in D-R>

1:6 *persecuti*: *secuti* Weber

<1:8 *put it to* D-R/C: *stroke it in the edge of* D-R>

1:10 *cuius*: *cui* D-R

<1:13 *Othniel . . . having taken* D-R/C: *when Othoniel . . . had taken* D-R>

1:13 *Axam filiam*: *filiam* Weber

1:14 *asino*: *in asino* S-C

<1:17 *Canaanites* KJV: *Chananeite* D-R>

<1:21 *Jebusites that inhabited* KJV: *Iebuseite the inhabiter of* D-R>

<1:27 *nor* KJV: *and* D-R>

<1:30 *among them* KJV: *in the middes of him* D-R>

<1:32 *Canaanites, the inhabitants* KJV: *Chananeite the inhabiter* D-R>

<1:35 *upon him* D-R/C [italicized]: omitted in D-R>

1:36 *petra*: *Petra* Weber

<2:1 *made you go* KJV: *brought you* D-R>

2:2 *sed*: *et* Weber

2:4 *elevaverunt*: *elevaverunt ipsi* S-C

2:5 *Locus Flentium*: *Flentium* S-C

<2:7 *who* KJV: omitted in D-R>

2:12 *deosque*: *deos quoque* Weber

2:14 *manus*: *manibus* Weber

<2:15 *as he had* KJV (*as the Lord had*): omitted in D-R>

<2:18 *to* D-R/C: *with* D-R>

2:19 *peiora*: *maiora* Weber; *servientes*: *et servientes* Weber; *consueverunt*: *consueverant* Weber

<2:20 *Behold* D-R/C: *Because* D-R>

<2:21 *when* KJV: *and* D-R>

3:2 *ut*: *et* Weber

<3:2   *trained up* D-R/C: *accustomed* D-R>

<3:3   *all the Canaanites and the Sidonians and the Hivites* KJV: *the Chana-
         neite and Sidonian and Heueite* D-R

3:8   *Chusan Rasathaim*: *Chusanrasathaim* Weber

3:10   *manus*: *manu* Weber; *Chusan Rasathaim*: *Chusanrasathaim* Weber

<3:15   *the left hand as well as* D-R/C: *both handes for* D-R>

<3:22   *went in after* KJV: *folowed* D-R; *so that he did not* KJV (*could* for *did*):
         Neither did he D-R>

3:24   *posticam*: *posticum* S-C

<3:24   *is easing nature* D-R/C: *purgeth his bellie* D-R>

<3:25   *the door* KJV (*the doores*): omitted in D-R>

3:30   *die*: *in die* S-C

4:2   *manus*: *manu* Weber

4:7   *ducam*: *adducam* S-C

4:8   *venire mecum*: *venire* Weber

<4:18   *And* KJV: *therfore* D-R>

4:18   *Intra; ne timeas*: *intra ne timeas* S-C, Weber

<4:20   *and inquire of thee* KJV: *asking thee, and* D-R>

4:20   *dices* Frede AU loc 7.21 p. 461.79, Gryson 100 E: *respondebis* S-C,
         Weber

4:21   *pariter et*: *pariter* Weber; *consocians*: *socians* Weber

<4:21   *also* D-R/C: *withal . . . also* D-R; *and so passing from deep sleep to death*
         D-R/C: *who ioyning deepe sleepe and death together* D-R>

<4:22   *her tent* KJV [*tent* in roman type in KJV]: *her* D-R>

4:22   *tempora* VCΛLF [Weber's sigla]: *tempore* S-C, Weber

<5:1   *and said* S [Rahlfs' siglum A]: *saying* D-R>

<5:4   *heavens* D-R/C: *heuens and cloudes* D-R>

5:4   *distillaverunt*: *stillaverunt* Weber

<5:8   *A shield and spear was not seen* KJV (*was there a shield or speare seene*):
         shield and speare if there appeared D-R>

<5:15   *headlong and into a* D-R/C: *into a headlong and bottomeles* D-R>

<5:20   *courses* KJV: *course* D-R>

5:24   *et benedicatur*: *benedicatur* Weber

<5:25   *He asked her water, and* KJV: *To him that asked water* D-R>

<5:26   *temples* KJV: *temple* D-R>

5:28   *prospiciens*: *respiciens* S-C

<5:28   *out at* KJV: *through* D-R; *is his chariot so long in coming* KJV: *lingereth his chariote to come* D-R; *so* D-R/C: omitted in D-R>

<6:1   *again* D-R/C: omitted in D-R>

<6:4   *for sustenance of* D-R/C [*sustenance* is in KJV]: *that perteyned to mans* D-R; *nor* [three times] KJV (*neither* for first *nor*): *not* [three times] D-R>

6:4   *vitam*: *vitam humanam* *D-R

6:5   *tabernaculis suis*: *tabernaculis* Weber

6:9   *manu*: *manibus* *D-R

6:12   *ei angelus Domini*: *ei* Weber

6:13   *mi Domine*: *mi domine* S-C, *Domine* Weber; *omnia mala* CSL [Weber's sigla]: *omnia* S-C, Weber; *Dominus et*: *et* Weber; *manu*: *manibus* Weber

<6:13   *saying* KJV: *and said* D-R>

6:17   *loquaris*: *loqueris* S-C

6:18   *nec*: *ne* Weber

<6:19   *and the broth* D-R: literally, *and putting the broth*>

6:19   *quercum*: *quercu* S-C

6:21   *panes consumpsit*: *consumpsit* Weber

6:22   *mi*: *mihi* Weber

6:24   *Aedificavitque* X (*edificabitque*) [Quentin's siglum]: *Aedificavit ergo* S-C, Weber [without capitalization]; *Cumque*: *cum* Weber

6:27   *praeceperat ei*: *praeceperat* Weber; *id facere*: *facere* Weber

<6:29   *this* KJV: *these thinges* D-R>

6:30   *tuum huc*: *tuum* Weber

6:31   *ut pugnetis*: *et pugnatis* Weber

6:32   *altare*: *aram* S-C

6:34   *sequeretur se*: *sequeretur* Weber

<6:35   *came to meet* KJV: *mette* D-R>

6:36   *Deum*: *Dominum* Weber

<6:36   *wilt save* KJV: *saue* D-R>

<6:37   *it be dry* KJV: *there shal be . . . drienes* D-R>

<6:38   *was so* KJV: *came so to passe* D-R; *before day* [After S?]: *in the night* D-R>

6:38   *conplevit*: *implevit* Weber

6:39   *Deum*: *Dominum* Weber

6:40   *Deum*: *Dominum* Weber

<6:40   *it was dry* KJV: *there was drienes* D-R>

<7:1   *the same as* D-R/C: *also* D-R>

7:1   *collis excelsi*: *Collis Excelsi* S-C, *collis Excelsi* Weber

<7:3   *Whosoever* KJV: *He that* D-R; *home* D-R/C: omitted in D-R>

7:3   *reversa*: *reversi* S-C; *sunt* Gryson 100 E: *sunt de populo* S-C, *sunt ex populo* Weber

<7:4   *too many* KJV: *great* D-R; *This shall go with thee* KJV: *that he goe with thee* D-R>

7:4   *vadat ipse, pergat*: *vadat, ipse pergat* S-C

<7:6   *casting it with the hand* D-R/C: *their hand casting* D-R>

7:8   *trecentis* Frede PS-PHo 36.1, 212 (*CCC*), Frede AN s Et 4, 75 (*trecenti*): *trecentis viris* S-C, Weber

<7:8   *him* KJV: omitted in D-R>

7:12   *litore*: *litoribus* Weber

7:14   *Dominus in manus*: *Deus in manu* Weber

<7:14   *hand* KJV: *handes* D-R>

7:15   *reversus est*: *reversus* Weber; *et ait*: *ait* Weber

<7:17   *the same* D-R/C: *that* D-R; *do you as I shall do* KJV (*as I doe, so shall ye doe*): *that which I shal doe folow you* D-R>

<7:18   *on every side of the camp* KJV: *round about the campe* D-R; D-R/C omits to translate *et conclamite, 'Domino et Gedeoni!'* D-R renders the clause *crie together . . . To our Lord and to Gedeon.*>

7:19   *partem*: *parte* Weber

<7:20   *their trumpets* KJV: omitted in D-R; *with their right hands the trumpets which they blew* D-R/C: *with the right they sounded the trumpettes* D-R, more naturally, *with their right hands the sounding trumpets*>

7:23   *usque*: *usque ad* S-C

7:24   *praeoccupate* Gryson 100 E: *occupate* S-C, Weber

<7:25   *they* KJV: *he* D-R>

<8:1   *And they chid* KJV: *chyding* D-R>

8:2   *Quid enim*: *Quid* *D-R [not unlike Gryson 100 E]

<8:4   *who were so weary that* D-R/C: *and for wearines* D-R>

<8:5   *faint* KJV: *verie faint* D-R>

8:10   *et educentium*: *educentium* S-C

<8:10   *that* S-C [and KJV]: *and those that* D-R>

<8:11   *east* KJV: *East side* D-R>

<8:14   *unto him* KJV: omitted in D-R>

  8:19   *respondit*: *ait* Weber

<8:19   *As* KJV [italicized in D-R/C]: omitted in D-R; *if* KJV: *that if* D-R>

  8:23   *vobis Dominus*: *Dominus* Weber

<8:26   *that were about the camels' necks* KJV: *of the camels* D-R>

  8:34   *manibus*: *manu* Weber

<9:1   *kindred* D-R/C: *kinred of the house* D-R>

  9:2   *vobis unus*: *unus* S-C

  9:3   *cor*: *corda* *D-R

<9:4   *wherewith he* KJV: *Who* D-R>

  9:5   *in Ephra*: *Ephra* Weber

<9:5   *only* D-R/C [in italics]: omitted in D-R; *who* D-R/C: *and* D-R>

<9:9   *to* D-R/C: *and* D-R>

<9:10   *reign* KJV: *take the kingdome* D-R>

  9:11   *promovear*: *commovear* Weber

  9:12   *Locutaque sunt*: *locuta sunt quoque* Weber

  9:13   *respondit eis*: *respondit* Weber; *promoveri*: *commoveri* Weber

<9:15   *king* D-R/C: *your king* D-R>

  9:15   *sin*: *si* S-C

<9:16   *done . . . in appointing* D-R/C: *appointed* D-R>

  9:21   *ob metum*: *metu* Weber

  9:23   *Dominus*: *Deus* Weber

  9:24   *Sycimarum*: *Sichimorum* S-C

  9:25   *praestolabantur*: *praestolantur* Weber

<9:25   *all* KJV: *them* D-R>

<9:27   *singing and dancing* D-R/C: *gathering companies of musicions* D-R>

<9:28   *and Gaal, the son of Ebed, cried* KJV (*said* for *cried*): *Gaal the sonne of Obed crying* D-R>

  9:28   *serviemus*: *servimus* Weber

<9:35   *places* D-R/C: *place* D-R>

<9:36   *this is thy mistake* D-R/C: *with this errour thou art deceiued* D-R>

<9:40   *and put him to flight* D-R/C: *fleeing* D-R; *people* D-R/C: *part* D-R>

<9:42   *and it was* KJV (*and they*): *which being* D-R>

<9:43   *and* KJV: omitted in D-R>

<9:44   *whilst* D-R/C: *and* D-R>

  9:44   *persequebantur*: *sequebantur* Weber

<9:48   *he and all his people with him* KJV: *with al his people* D-R>

  9:48   *videtis*: *vidistis* Weber

<9:49   *every man as fast as he could* D-R: literally, *in competition*>

  9:49   *Qui . . . praesidium*: *Quos . . . praesidio* Weber; *hominum*: *homines* S-C

<9:51   *and having shut and strongly barred the gate* D-R/C: *the gate being shut
             very strongly* D-R>

  10:4   *Avoth Iair*: *Avothiair* Weber

  10:6   *colebant*: *coluerunt* S-C

  10:7   *quos Dominus*: *quos* Weber; *manus*: *manu* Weber

  10:8   *quae*: *qui* S-C

<10:8   *who* S-C: *which* D-R>

  10:10   *Dominum, Deum*: *Deum* Weber

<10:13   *deliver* KJV: *adde to deliuer* D-R>

  10:16   *Domino, Deo*: *Deo* Weber

<10:16   *their* D-R/C: omitted in D-R>

<10:18   *one to another* KJV: *euerie one to their neighbours* D-R; *Whosoever* S
             [Rahlfs' siglum B]: *Who* D-R>

<11:1   *and his father was Gilead* D-R/C: *who was borne of Galaad* D-R>

<11:2   *inherit* KJV: *be heyre* D-R>

  11:2   *generatus*: *natus* S-C

<11:8   *the inhabitants of* KJV: *that dwell in* D-R>

<11:9   *hand* D-R/C: *handes* D-R>

  11:9   *princeps vester?*: *vester princeps.* S-C

  11:10   *faciemus*: *faciamus* Weber

<11:12   *hast thou to do with me* KJV: *is betwen me and thee* D-R>

  11:17   *Dimitte me*: *dimitte* Weber; *quoque*: *quoque et* Weber

<11:17   *request* D-R/C: *requestes* D-R>

<11:18   *Moab.* D-R/C: D-R adds *for Arnon is the border of the Land of Moab*>

<11:20   *made strong opposition* D-R/C: *resisted strongly* D-R>

  11:21   *manus*: *manu* Weber

  11:24   *possedit*: *possidet* S-C

<11:24   *possesseth* S-C: *possessed* D-R; *by conquest shall be* D-R/C: *conquerour,
             shal come to* D-R>

<11:26 *and* KJV: *or* D-R>

<11:27 *and decide* D-R/C *this day* KJV: *the arbiter of this day* D-R>

<11:31 *the same* D-R/C: *him* D-R>

<11:33 *them* KJV: omitted in D-R>

11:34 *Revertente: revertenti* Weber; *occurrit ei: occurrit* Weber; *filia: filia sua* S-C

11:35 *Heu me: Heu* Weber; *mi: mea* S-C

<11:35 *Alas* KJV: *Wo is me* D-R>

11:39 *mos increbuit: mos increbruit* S-C, *mos* *D-R

<11:40 *from year to year* KJVn: *after the compasse of a yeare* D-R>

<12:1 *And* KJV: *For* D-R>

12:1 *incendemus: incendimus* Weber

<12:3 *to fight* KJV: *in battel* D-R>

12:5 *permittatis: permittas* Weber

12:7 *Iudicavavit itaque: iudicavitque* Weber

12:13 *Israhel: in Israhel* Weber

12:14 *Israhel: in Israhel* Weber

<13:2 *whose name was Manoah, and his wife was barren* KJV: *named Manue, hauing a wife barren* D-R>

<13:3 *said* D-R/C: *said to her* D-R>

<13:4 *and drink no wine nor* KJV: *that thou drinke not wine and* D-R>

13:4 *nec: ne* Weber

13:6 *maritum: maritum suum* S-C

<13:7 *thus* D-R/C: *this* D-R; *from* S-C: *and from* D-R>

13:7 *nec siceram: et siceram* Weber; *et ex: ex* S-C

13:8 *Dominum: Deum* Weber

13:9 *precantem: deprecantem* S-C; *Domini: Dei* S-C

<13:9 *the prayer of Manoah* KJV (*voyce* for *prayer*): *Manue praying* S-C>

<13:13–14 No Latin words indicate the gender of these pronouns, but they are most likely masculine (as D-R translates). KJV has feminine pronouns.>

<13:14 *neither let her* KJV: *let him not* D-R>

<13:15 *kid* KJV: *kid of goates* D-R>

13:16 *Sin: si* S-C; *Domini: Dei* Weber

13:20 *vidisset: vidissent* S-C

<13:22 *We shall certainly die* KJV (*surely* for *certainly*): *Dying we shal die* D-R>

14:2   *matri suae*: *matri* Weber

<14:2   *her* KJV: *which* (before *I*) D-R>

<14:5   *behold*: *a young lion* KJV: *a lions whelpe* D-R; *met him* D-R/C: *there appeared* (before *a lions*) D-R>

14:5   *saevus et*: *saevus* Weber

14:6   *concerperet*: *discerpens* S-C

<14:9   *went on eating* KJV: *did eate in the way* D-R; *of it* D-R/C: *part* D-R; *and they* KJV: *who also them selues* D-R>

14:11   *loci illius*: *loci* Weber; *qui*: *ut* S-C

14:15   *incendemus te*: *incendimus et te* Weber

<14:16   *So she wept* D-R/C: *Who shed teares* D-R; *how* D-R/C: omitted in D-R>

15:1   *aliquantum*: *aliquantulum* S-C

<15:1   *would not suffer* KJV: *prohibited* D-R>

<15:2   *take her* KJV *to wife* D-R/C: *let this be thy wife* D-R>

<15:3   *I shall be blameless* KJV: *there shal be no fault* D-R; *in what I do* D-R/C [italicized in D-R/C]: omitted in D-R>

<15:4   *between the tails* KJV (*two* for *the*): *in the middes* D-R>

<15:5   *the foxes* D-R/C: *them* D-R; *was yet standing* (without *was yet*) KJV: *yet stoode in the stalke* D-R>

<15:6   *And* KJV: *To whom* D-R; *answered* KJV: *said* D-R>

<15:7   *be revenged* KJV (*avenged* for *revenged*): *require reuenge* D-R>

15:9   *terram*: *terra* Weber; *sunt*: *sunt / et* Weber; *ubi eorum*: *eorum* Weber; *effusus*: *fusus* Weber

<15:10   *pay him for what* D-R/C: *repay him the thinges* D-R>

15:11   *sic feci*: *feci* Weber

15:12   *ait, "et spondete*: *respondit* Weber

15:13   *occidemus*: *occidimus* Weber; *trademus*: *tradimus* Weber; *tulerunt*: *tulerunt eum* S-C

15:18   *et en*: *en* S-C

16:3   *umeris*: *humeris suis* S-C

<16:5   *his great strength lieth* KJV [*lieth* in roman type]: *he hath so great strength* D-R; *to bind and afflict* D-R/C: *and being bound to afflict* D-R: *of us* KJV: omitted in D-R>

16:5   *et centum*: *centum* Weber

<16:6   *lieth* KJV [in roman type]: *is* D-R; *if thou wert* D-R/C: *being* D-R>

16:7   *nerviceis*: *nervicis* Weber

16:9 *sputamine* L^HBW̱ arels: *putamine* S-C, Weber

<16:9 *smelleth* KJV n: *taketh the odour of* D-R; *so* KJV: *and* D-R; *lay* D-R/C: *was* D-R>

16:10 *indica mihi*: *indica* Weber

16:13 *Cui Samson respondit, "Si*: *si inquit* Weber

16:15 *ames*: *amas* S-C

<16:15 *told me lies* D-R/C: *lies to me* D-R; *lieth* KJV [in roman type]: *is* D-R>

<16:16 *pressed him much* KJV (*daily* for *much*): *molested him* D-R>

16:17 *Nazareus, id est, consecratus Deo sum de utero matris meae* sense of Frede ORA Vis 1085 (350.24): *nazaraeus (id est consecratus) Deo sum de utero matris meae* S-C *ut*: *sicut* S-C

16:18 *Vidensque*: *videns* Weber

<16:18 *saying* KJV: *and willed them* D-R>

16:19 *abicere*: *abigere* S-C

<16:21 *Then . . . him* KJV (*But* for *Then*): *Whom when* D-R>

16:24 *adversarium nostrum*: *adversarium* Weber

<16:25 *good cheer* D-R: literally, *feasts*>

<16:26 *which support the whole house* D-R/C: *on which al the house stayeth* D-R>

16:26 *et recliner*: *ut recliner* Weber

16:27 *spectantes*: *spectabant* Weber

<16:28 *he called upon the Lord, saying* D-R/C: *he inuocating our Lord, said* D-R>

<16:30 *me* D-R: literally, *my soul*>

17:2 *Mille et*: *mille* Weber

<17:3 *so* D-R/C: *and* D-R>

<17:5 *god* D-R/C: *God* D-R>

17:7 *ex*: *et* Weber

17:8 *Montem*: *monte* Weber

17:9 *venisset*: *venis* Weber

<17:9 *a place* KJV [in roman type]: omitted in D-R>

17:10 *Dixitque Michas, "Mane*: *mane inquit* Weber

<17:10 *thy victuals* KJV: *the thinges that be necessarie for victual* D-R>

17:13 *benefaciet mihi*: *bene mihi faciat* Weber

<18:2 *they went into . . . and* D-R/C: *and had entered . . . they* D-R>

<18:3 *lodging with him* D-R/C: *vsing his lodging* D-R>

18:5   *ut scire: et scire* Weber

<18:5   *their journey* D-R/C *should be prosperous* KJV: *they should goe on a prosperous iourney* D-R>

18:6   *in: cum* Weber

18:7   *igitur: itaque* Weber; *eis: ei* S-C

<18:7   *how the people dwelt* KJV (*they* for *the people*): *the people dwelling* D-R; *living* D-R/C: omitted in D-R>

<18:8   *who asked them what they had done, to whom they answered* D-R/C: *and asking what they had done they answered them* D-R>

18:9   *et ascendamus: ascendamus* S-C

<18:10   *a people that is* KJV (without *that is*): *them being* D-R; *any thing* KJV: *those thinges* D-R>

<18:12   *is called* S: *tooke the name* D-R>

<18:16   *appointed with their arms* KJV (*weapons of warre* for *arms*): *so as they were armed* D-R>

<18:21   *put* KJV: *made . . . to goe* D-R>

<18:25   *lest* KJV: *and* D-R; *enraged* D-R/C: *prouoked in mind* D-R>

<18:27   *the city was burnt with fire* KJV (*burnt the citie with fire*): *the citie they deliuered to fyre* D-R>

<18:29   *who was the son of Israel* D-R/C: *whom Israel had begotten* D-R>

<18:30   *he* KJV [italicized in D-R/C]: omitted in D-R>

<19:1   *Levite* KJV *who dwelt* D-R/C: *man a Leuite dwelling* D-R>

19:2   *in Bethleem: Bethleem* Weber

<19:3   *with him* KJV: *in his companie* D-R; *with joy* D-R/C: *ioyful* D-R>

<19:7   *pressed* S: *stayed* D-R>

19:8   *Mane autem: mane* Weber; *iter: iter facere* *D-R

<19:9   *declining* D-R/C: *more declining to the west* D-R>

19:9   *propinquet: propinquat* S-C

19:10   *vocatur: vocabatur* Weber

19:11   *aderant: erant* S-C

<19:11   *was far spent* KJV: *changed into night* D-R>

<19:12   *who are* D-R/C: *which is* D-R>

<19:14   *journey* D-R/C [KJV also lacks an equivalent for *coeptum*]: *iourney begone* D-R; *when they were by* KJV [*when they were* in roman type]: *byside* D-R>

<19:15   *for* KJV: *and* D-R; *to lodge* D-R: literally, *with lodging*>

19:15 *volebat*: *voluit* S-C

<19:16 *they saw* D-R/C: *there appeared* D-R>

19:16 *vespere*: *vesperi* S-C

19:18 *in Bethleem*: *Bethleem* Weber

<19:23 *so wickedly* KJV: *this euil* D-R; *I pray you* KJV: omitted in D-R>

<19:24 *and* KJV: *that* D-R>

<19:25 *abandoned her to their wickedness* D-R/C: *deliuered her to them to be illuded* D-R>

<19:26 *at the dawning of the day* KJV: *when the darkenes departed* D-R>

<19:27 *in the morning* KJV: *Morning being come* D-R>

19:28 *et ambulemus*: *ut ambulemus* Weber; *erat mortua*: *erat* Weber

<19:29 *And when he was come home* KJV (*into his house* for *home*): *Which when he was entered vnto* D-R>

<20:1 *with* KJV: *and* D-R>

<20:2 *chiefs* KJV: *corners* D-R; *fit for war* D-R/C: *warriers* D-R>

<20:5 *was* D-R/C: *taried* D-R>

20:9 *faciemus*: *faciamus* S-C

<20:10 *we will take ten men* KJV: *Let ten men be chosen* D-R>

20:10 *pugnare*: *pungantes* Weber; *et reddere*: *reddere* Weber

20:11 *eadem*: *una* *D-R

<20:12 *to them* D-R/C: omitted in D-R>

<20:16 *not miss* KJV *by the stone's going on either side* D-R/C: *the stroke of the stone should not be carried awry on either part* D-R>

20:18 *Deum*: *eum* Weber

<20:18 *to go to the battle* KJV: *general of the battel* D-R>

20:21 *viginti et* L g [Quentin's sigla]: *viginti* S-C, Weber; *viros*: *virorum* S-C

20:22 *filii Israhel*: *Israhel* *D-R

20:23 *eos*: *eum* Weber

20:24 *filios Beniamin*: *Beniamin* Weber

<20:25 *made* D-R/C: *raged with* D-R>

20:27 *Domini* VCLFST [Weber's sigla]: *Dei* Weber, S-C

<20:31 *And* KJV: *But . . . also* D-R; *seeing their enemies flee pursued them* D-R/C: *pursewed . . . the aduersaries fleeing* D-R; *whilst they fled* D-R/C: *turning their backes* D-R>

20:31 *ferebat*: *ferebatur* S-C; *et altera*: *altera* Weber

<20:32 *to cut them off,* D-R/C *as they did before* S, Rahlfs' siglum A?: *to kil*

them *after their accustomed manner* D-R; *by their seeming to flee*
D-R/C: *as it were fleing* D-R>

<20:33 *the places where they were* D-R/C: *their seates* D-R>

<20:34 *And* KJV: *Yea and* D-R; *chosen* KJV: omitted in D-R; *attacked*
D-R/C: *prouoked . . . to skirmishes* D-R>

<20:37 *they that were in ambush* S: omitted in D-R>

20:38 *ut ascendente*: *et ascendente* Weber

<20:39 *in the battle* KJV: *being in the verie fight* D-R>

20:39 *persequebantur*: *sequebantur* Weber

20:40 *cum captam*: *captam* Weber

<20:40 *saw* D-R/C: *when he saw* D-R>

<20:41 *turned their backs* KJV: *were turned into flight* D-R>

<20:42 *And* KJV: *But* D-R; *came . . . out to meet* D-R/C: *mette* D-R>

<20:45 *that is called* D-R/C: *the name wherof is* D-R>

20:45 *viros*: *virorum* S-C; *alia*: *alios* Weber

<20:48 *both . . . and* D-R/C: *from . . . euen to* D-R; *were consumed with devour-
ing flames* D-R/C: *the deuouring flame did consume* D-R>

<21:1 *saying* KJV: *and said* D-R>

<21:2 *began to lament and weep* D-R/C: *with great wayling beganne to weepe*
D-R>

<21:3 *so great an* D-R/C: *this* D-R>

<21:5 *is there . . . that* KJV: [*is there* in roman type]: omitted in D-R; *whoso-
ever* D-R/C: *which* D-R>

21:8 *Iabis Galaad*: *Iabisgalaad* Weber

<21:10 *saying* KJV: omitted in D-R; *put . . . to the sword* D-R/C: *strike . . . in
the edge of the sword* D-R; *with . . . and* KJV: *as wel . . . as* D-R>

21:10 *Iabis Galaad*: *Iabisgalaad* Weber

21:11 *debebitis*: *debetis* Weber; *interficite, virgines autem reservate*: *interficite*
Weber

21:12 *Iabis Galaad*: *Iabisgalaad* Weber; *ad*: *in* Weber; *terram*: *terra* Weber

21:14 *Iabis Galaad*: *Iabisgalaad* Weber

21:15 *paenitudinem*: *paenitentiam* S-C

21:16 *omnes enim* $\Lambda^L\Sigma^{OM}$B [Quentin's sigla]: *Omnes* S-C, Weber [without
capitalization]

<21:17 *use all care and provide with great diligence* D-R/C: *very carefully, and
with great studie prouide* D-R>

21:18 *filias enim*: *filias* Weber

<21:18 *as to* D-R/C: omitted in D-R; *them* D-R/C: refers to Benjaminites>

21:20 *latete*: *latitate* S-C

21:21 *ex eis*: *eas* Weber

<21:22 *war or conquest* D-R/C: *warryers and conquerours* D-R>

RUTH

<1:1 *of the judges* D-R/C: *Iudge* D-R; *certain* KJV: omitted in D-R>

1:2 *et uxor*: *uxor* Weber; *et duo filli*: *e duobus filiis* Weber

1:4 *altera vero*: *altera* Weber

<1:5 *was left* KJV *alone* D-R/C: *remayned* D-R>

<1:8 *home to your mothers* D-R/C: *into your mothers house* D-R>

1:11 *mi*: *meae* S-C

<1:12 *again* KJV: omitted in D-R>

1:12 *et abite*: *abite* Weber

<1:13 *come to man's estate* D-R/C: *be of mans age* D-R, literally, *complete the years of youth*>

<1:16 *to desire* D-R/C: *to the end that* D-R>

1:16 *quocumque enim*: *quocumque* Weber; *et ubi*: *ubi* Weber

<1:17 *will I be buried* KJV: *wil I take a place for my burial* D-R; *Lord* S-C: *God* D-R; *aught but death* KJV [*ought* (for *aught*) in roman type]: *death onlie shal not* D-R>

1:17 *Deus*: *Dominus* S-C

<1:18 *steadfastly* KJV: *with a stidfast mind* D-R>

<1:19 *so* KJV: *and* D-R>

<1:22 *in the beginning of the barley harvest* KJV: *when barley was first reaped* D-R>

2:1 *viro*: *vir* Weber

<2:2 *wilt* D-R/C: *command* D-R>

<2:3 *after* KJV: *after the backes* D-R>

2:3 *dominum*: *dominum nomine* S-C

2:6 *Cui*: *qui* Weber

<2:7 *hath been* D-R/C: *stayeth* D-R>

2:8 *Audi*: *Audi me* *D-R

<2:8 *any* D-R/C: *an* D-R>

<2:9 *not to* S: *that no man* D-R; *and* KJV: *but* D-R; *drink* D-R/C: *also doe drinke* D-R>

<2:11   *how* KJV [in roman type]: *that* D-R>

2:11   *dereliqueris*: *reliqueris* S-C

2:13   *apud*: *ante* Weber

<2:14   *At mealtime* KJV: *When the houre shal come to eate* D-R>

<2:16   *let fall some of your handfuls* KJV [*some* in roman type]: *of your owne handfuls also cast forth* D-R; *leave them* KJV: *let them remaine* D-R>

2:19   *esset*: *fuisset* S-C

<2:21   *He* KJV: *This . . . he* D-R>

<2:22   *for thee . . . to go* D-R/C: *that thou goe* D-R>

<2:23   *continued to glean* D-R/C: *reaped* D-R>

<3:1   *Naomi said to her* KJV: *she heard of her* D-R>

<3:2   *behold* KJV: omitted in D-R; *barley in the threshingfloor* KJV: *the barne floore of the barley* D-R>

3:3   *Lava*: *Lavare* S-C

<3:4   *clothes* KJVn: *mantel* D-R; *lay thyself down* KJV (*thee* for *thyself*): *cast thy self downe and lie* D-R>

<3:7   *was merry, he* KJV: *was made pleasant, and* D-R; *and* KJV: omitted in D-R; *uncovering his feet* KJV (*vncouered* for *uncovering*): *discouering the mantel, at his feete* D-R>

<3:10   *thy latter kindness has surpassed the former* D-R/C: *the former mercie thou hast passed with the later* D-R>

3:10   *a Domino*: *Domino* Weber; *filia mi* θ^{H2} [Quentin's sigla]: *filia* S-C, Weber

<3:13   *all is well* D-R/C: *the thing is wel done* D-R; *as* KJV [italicized in D-R/C]: omitted in D-R>

3:14   *surrexit itaque*: *surrexitque* Weber

3:15   *palliolum*: *pallium* S-C

<3:17   *for* KJV: *and* D-R>

<4:1   *he had spoken* Heb: *the talke was had* D-R>

4:3   *residentibus*: *sedentibus* S-C; *vendet*: *vendit* Weber

<4:4   *here* D-R/C [italicized]: omitted in D-R; *so* D-R/C: *the same* D-R>

4:7   *ut si*: *et si* Weber

<4:7   *cession of right* D-R/C: *yelding* D-R>

4:8   *propinquo suo*: *propinquus* Weber; *calciamentum*: *calciamentum tuum* S-C

<4:9   *And* KJV: *But* D-R; *of the hand of Naomi* KJV: *Noemi deliuering them*
          D-R>

<4:10   *cut off* KJV: *abolished* D-R>

4:14   *ut vocaretur* T$^*\theta^{G^*}$ [Quentin's sigla]: *et vocaretur* S-C, Weber

<4:16   *she carried it and was a nurse unto it* D-R/C: *did the office of a nource
          and of one that should carie him* D-R>

1 Kings

1:1   *Ramathaimsophim*: *Ramathaim Sophim* S-C

1:7   *templum*: *ad templum* S-C

<1:7   *did not eat* KJV: *tooke not meat* D-R>

1:10   *esset Anna*: *esset* Weber; *oravit ad*: *oravit* Weber

<1:10   *shedding many tears* D-R/C: *weeping aboundantly* D-R>

<1:11   *wilt look down on* KJV (without *down*): *regarding thou wilt behold*
          D-R>

1:11   *omnes dies*: *omnibus diebus* S-C

1:12   *autem*: *ergo* Weber

<1:13   *but* KJV: *and* D-R>

<1:14   *of which thou hast taken too much* D-R/C: *wherewith thou art wette*
          D-R>

<1:15   *nor any strong drink* KJV: *and whatsoeuer may inebriate* D-R>

1:17   *petitionem tuam*: *petitionem* Weber

<1:18   *So* KJV: *And* D-R; *changed* D-R/C: *changed otherwise* D-R>

<1:20   *when the time was come about* KJV: *after a certaine compasse of dayes*
          D-R>

1:21   *vir eius*: *vir* Weber

<1:22   *but* KJV: *and* D-R>

1:22   *ut*: *et* Weber

1:26   *ait Anna*: *ait* Weber

1:28   *cunctis diebus quibus fuerit accommodatus*: *cunctis diebus quibus fue-
          rit commodatus* S-C, *cunctis diebus quibus vixerit ut applicatus sit*
          *D-R

<1:28   *of his life he shall be lent* KJV (*as he liueth* for *of his life*): *which he shal
          liue, that he may be applied* D-R>

2:1   *et exultatum*: *exultatum* Weber; *Deo meo*: *Domino* Weber

2:3   *scientiarum*: *omnis scientiae* *D-R

2:5   *Saturati*: *repleti* S-C; *pane*: *panibus* S-C

<2:5   so that KJV: *vntil* D-R>

2:6   *infernum*: *inferos* S-C

2:9   *fortitudine sua*: *fortitudine* Weber

2:10   *et super*: *super* Weber; *Christi*: *christi* S-C

<2:13   with KJV: *and had* D-R>

<2:16   then KJV: omitted in D-R; *but* KJV: *for* D-R>

2:17   *detrahebant homines sacrificio*: *retrahebant homines a sacrificio* S-C

2:20   *dixitque ei*: *dixitque* Weber

<2:25   one man . . . another KJV: *man . . . man* D-R>

2:25   *Domino*: *Dominum* S-C

2:26   *Domino*: *Deo* Weber

2:28   *altare*: *ad altare* S-C

<2:28   of all D-R/C: *al thinges of* D-R>

2:29   *abiecistis*: *abicitis* Weber

<2:29   kicked KJV *away my victims* D-R/C: *with your heele reiectied my victime* D-R>

<2:30   thus S: omitted in D-R: *I said indeed* KJV: *Speaking I speake* D-R; *despised* D-R/C: *base* D-R>

2:35   *faciet*: *faciat* Weber

2:36   *veniet* θ^{S2} cum Isid. in I Reg. 2.6 et Brev. goth. (PL 86.453) [Quentin's sigla]: *veniat* S-C, Weber; *dicatque*: *dicetque* *D-R

<2:36   somewhat KJVn *of the priestly office* KJV: *one priestly part* D-R>

<3:2   when KJV: omitted in D-R>

3:3   *Samuhel*: *Samuhel autem* Weber

3:4   *Dominus Samuhel*: *Dominus*: *Samuhel* S-C

<3:4   answered KJV: *answering said* D-R>

3:5   *et dormi*: *dormi* Weber

<3:10   the other times KJV: *twise* D-R>

3:10   *Domine, quia*: *quia* Weber

3:13   *corripuit*: *corripuerit* S-C

<3:16   answered KJV: *answering, said* D-R>

3:17   *est Dominus*: *est* Weber

<3:19   not one KJV (*none*): *not* D-R>

<3:21   revealed himself KJV: *had bene reueled* D-R>

4:1   *Et factum est in diebus illis convenerunt Philisthiim in pugnam, et egressus est: egressus est namque* Weber

4:4   *Dei*: *Domini* Weber

<4:5   *again* KJV: omitted in D-R>

4:7   *ingemuerunt, dicentes*: *ingemuerunt* Weber

4:8   *servabit*: *salvabit* S-C

<4:8   *all the plagues* KJV: *al plague* D-R>

<4:9   *behave like* KJV (*quit your selues* for *behave*): *be* D-R>

4:9   *sicut et*: *sicut* Weber

<4:10   *for* KJV: *and* D-R>

4:11   *duo quoque*: *duoque* Weber

4:13   *aspectans*: *spectans* S-C; *Dei*: *Domini* Weber

<4:13   *the man was come into the city, he told it* KJV: *And that man after he was entred in, told it to the citie* D-R>

<4:14   *meaneth the noise* KJV: *is this sound* D-R>

4:14   *adnuntiavit*: *nuntiavit* S-C

<4:16   *have fled* KJV (*I* for *have*): *I he that fled* D-R>

4:17   *qui*: *ille qui* S-C

<4:17   *that* S-C: omitted in D-R; *of* D-R/C: *in* D-R>

<4:19   *fell in labour* D-R/C: *was deliuered* D-R>

<4:20   *death* D-R/C: *her death* D-R>

5:2   *Tuleruntque*: *tulerunt* Weber

<5:3   *upon his face* KJV: *flatte* D-R>

5:3   *terram*: *terra* S-C; *locum suum*: *loco suo* Weber

5:4   *altera*: *alio* Weber

<5:5   *neither . . . nor any . . . tread* KJV: *and al . . . tread not* D-R; *the* D-R/C: *his* D-R>

5:6   *eius. Et ebullierunt villae et agri in medio regionis illius, et nati sunt mures, et facta est confusio mortis magnae in civitate*: *eius* Weber

<5:6   *with emerods* [that is, hemorrhoids] KJV: *in the secrete part of the fundament* D-R; *in the villages and fields* D-R/C: *the townes and fieldes bubbled forth* D-R; *there came forth a multitude of mice* D-R/C: *and there came forth mise* D-R>

<5:7   *The ark . . . shall not* KJV: *Let not the arke* D-R>

5:9   *Domini*: *Dei* Weber; *eorum. Inieruntque Gethaei consilium et fecerunt sibi sedes pelliceas*: *eorum* Weber

<5:9   *both . . . and* KJV: *from . . . vnto* D-R; *they had emerods in their secret*
          parts D-R: literally, *their hemorrhoids, sticking out, were rotting*>

<5:11   *and* KJV: *with* D-R>

<5:12   *with the emerods* KJV: *in the secrete part of the buttockes* D-R>

6:2   *Domini*: *Dei* Weber; *remittamus*: *remittemus* Weber

<6:5   *to see if* D-R/C: *if perhaps* D-R>

6:6   *gravatis*: *aggravatis* S-C

6:8   *capsellam*: *capsella* Weber

<6:9   *if* KJV: *if so be that* D-R>

6:11   *similitudines*: *similitudinem* Weber

<6:12   *along the* KJV: *one* D-R; *and* KJV: *but . . . also* D-R>

<6:13   *to see* KJV: *when they had seene* D-R>

<6:16   *the same* KJV: *that* D-R>

6:18   *Abel magnum*: *Abel-magnum* S-C

<6:18   *(the stone)* [italicized in D-R/C] KJV (*great stone of Abel* for *Abel (the*
          stone)): omitted in D-R>

<6:19   *people* KJV: *common people* D-R>

6:21   *reducite*: *ducite* Weber

<6:21   *up* KJV: *backe* D-R>

7:1   *reduxerunt*: *duxerunt* Weber

<7:1   *up* KJV: *backe* D-R>

7:2   *arca Domini*: *arca* Weber

7:3   *vestri, Baalim et*: *estrum et* Weber

<7:3   *with* KJV: *in* D-R; *from among* KJV: *out of the middes of* D-R>

<7:7   *of* KJV: *at the face of* D-R>

7:9   *lactentem*: *lactantem* Weber

7:10   *autem*: *ergo* Weber; *facie*: *filiis* Weber

<7:10   *overthrown* D-R/C: *slaine* D-R>

<7:11   *till they came* KJV: *vnto the place, that was* D-R>

7:12   *loci illius*: *eius* Weber

<7:12   *the* D-R/C: *the name of that* D-R>

7:14   *liberavitque*: *liberavit* Weber

8:5   *sicut et*: *sicut* Weber

<8:5   *as* KJV (*like*): *as also* D-R>

8:6   *Displicuitque*: *Displicuit* S-C; *ad Dominum*: *Dominum* Weber

<8:6   *that they should say* D-R/C: *because they had sayd* D-R>

<8:11   *to run* D-R/C: omitted in D-R>

<8:12   *of* D-R/C: omitted in D-R>

<8:13   *take to make him ointments and to be* D-R (without *him,* which is only in D-R/C): literally *make for himself perfumers and* literal translation.>

8:17   *Greges quoque*: *greges* Weber

8:18   *illa, quia petistis vobis regem*: *illa* Weber

<8:19   *and* KJV: *but* D-R; *but* KJV: *for* D-R>

<8:22   *make them a king* KJV: *appoynt a king ouer them* D-R>

<9:1   *and strong* D-R/C: *in strength* D-R>

<9:2   *his shoulders* KJV: *the shoulder* D-R>

<9:3   *arise* KJV: *rising* D-R>

<9:4   *and* KJV: *yea and* D-R>

9:5   *puerum*: *puerum suum* Weber; *Veni* 116 E, ed. Levin, f. iv (*ueni*): *Veni et* S-C, Weber (without capitalization)

<9:5   *forget* D-R/C: *hath let alone* D-R>

9:6   *absque*: *sine* S-C

<9:6   *perhaps* KJV (*peraduenture*): *if perhaps* D-R>

<9:7   *But* KJV: omitted in D-R>

9:7   *virum Dei*: *virum* Weber

9:8   *sicli* Gryson 93 E 218, Frede HI Ez 6 254.885, Frede HI Mi 1 464.254: *stateris* S-C, Weber

<9:9   *let* S: *and let* D-R>

<9:10   *where* KJV: *wherein* D-R>

<9:11   *to* KJV: *of* D-R>

<9:12   *He is* KJV: *Here he is* D-R>

9:12   *civitatem*: *civitate* Weber

<9:13   *As soon as you come* KJV: *Entring* Weber>

<9:14   *behold: Samuel was coming* KJV (*came* for *was coming*): *Samuel appeared coming* D-R>

<9:16   *Tomorrow about this same hour* KJV (*time* for *same hour*): *This very houre, that now is, to morrow* D-R>

9:17   *ait*: *dixit* S-C

9:25   *solario, stravitque Saul in solario, et dormivit*: *solario* Weber

9:26   *dilucesceret*: *elucesceret* S-C; *ut*: *et* S-C

10:1   *est eum et*: *eum* Weber; *principem, et liberabis populum suum de manibus*

inimicorum eius qui in circuitu eius sunt. Et hoc tibi signum quia unxit te Deus in principem: princeipem Weber

<10:2   for KJV: concerning D-R>

<10:4   they will salute thee and KJV: when they haue saluted thee, they D-R>

10:5   Dei: Domini Weber; obviam: obvium S-C

<10:5   that KJV: these thinges D-R; with KJV: and D-R>

<10:7   these KJV: al these D-R>

10:8   quae: quid S-C

10:9   omnia signa: omnia *D-R

10:10   insilivet: insiluit S-C; Domini: Dei Weber

<10:11   is this that KJV: thing D-R>

10:11   in prophetis: inter prophetas S-C

<10:13   when he had made an end of prophesying, he KJV: he ceased to prophecie, and D-R>

10:15   Samuhel: Samuel? S-C

10:20   super tribum $\Lambda^H\Omega$ agre cum Greg. M in I Reg 4, 5, 34 (col. 307 B) [Quentin's sigla]: tribus S-C, Weber

10:24   cunctus: omnis S-C

11:1   Et factum est quasi post mensem ascendit: ascendit autem Weber; Iabes Galaad: Iabesgalaad Weber

<11:1   this D-R/C: omitted in D-R>

11:3   ad universos: in universos Weber

11:4   verba haec: verba Weber

<11:9   of KJV: that are in D-R>

11:9   Iabes Galaad: Iabesgalaad Weber

<11:10   what S?: whatsoeuer D-R>

<11:11   two of them were not left together KJV: there were not left among them two together D-R>

11:12   num: non Weber; Date nobis Palimpsestus Vindobonensis: Antiquis- simae Veteris Testamenti, ed. Belsheim 1885, p. 17 (Trade for Date): Date S-C, Weber (without capitalization)

<11:12   Bring KJV: Geue vs D-R>

12:3   an: aut S-C

<12:7   shown to . . . to D-R/C: done with . . . with D-R>

12:8   ex: de S-C

<12:8   made them dwell KJV: placed D-R>

<12:9 *hands* S: *hand* D-R>

<12:10 *but now* KJV: *now therefore* D-R>

<12:12 *was your king* KJV: *did reigne among you* D-R>

  12:15 *sermones eius*: *sermonem Domini* Weber

<12:16 *Now then* KJV (*therefore* for *then*): *But now also* D-R>

<12:17 *send thunder* KJV: *geue noyses* D-R; *yourselves* D-R/C: *to your selues*
        D-R>

<12:18 *sent thunder* KJV: *gaue noyses* D-R>

  12:18 *pluviam*: *pluvias* S-C

<12:19 *this* KJV: omitted in D-R>

<12:20 *following* KJV: *the backe of* D-R>

  12:20 *sed*: *et* Weber

<12:21 *never* D-R/C: *not* D-R>

<12:25 *still do wickedly* KJV: *persuer in malice* D-R>

<13:3 *the trumpet* KJV *over* D-R/C: *with the trumpet in* D-R>

<13:4 *this report* D-R/C: *this manner of bruite* D-R; *And the people were
        called together* KJV: *The people therfore cried* D-R>

<13:5 *a multitude of people besides* D-R/C: *the rest of the common people* D-R;
        for number D-R/C: *very much* D-R>

  13:6 *arto sitos, (adflictus est enim*: *arcto positos (afflictus enim erat* S-C

<13:6 *that they were straitened* KJV (*in a strait* for *staitened*): *them selues put
        in a streict* D-R>

<13:7 *some of* KJV [*some of* italicized in D-R/C, *some* in roman type in
        KJV]: omitted in D-R>

  13:7 *in terram*: *terram* Weber

  13:10 *ut*: *et* *D-R

<13:13 *And . . . thus* D-R/C: *Which* D-R>

<13:14 *not continue* KJV: *no farder arise* D-R>

  13:15 *Beniamin. Et reliqui populi ascenderunt post Saul obviam populo qui ex-
        pugnabant eos, venientes de Galgala in Gabaa in colle Beniamin*: *Be-
        niamin* Weber

<13:16 *present* KJV: *found* D-R>

<13:18 *turned* KJV: *turned it self* D-R>

<13:19 *smith* KJV: *yron smith* D-R; *them swords or spears* KJV: *sword or speare*
        D-R>

<13:21 *their shares and their spades and their forks and their axes* D-R/C: *the*

edges of the shares, and spades, & forkes with three teeth, and axes D-R>

<13:22 *any of* KJV: *al* D-R>

13:22 *Saul et*: *Saul et cum* Weber

<14:1 *that bore his armour* D-R: *his armorbearer* literal translation>

<14:3 *the son* KJV: *which was borne* D-R; *And the people* KJV: *But the people also* D-R>

14:3 *quo*: *quod* Weber

14:4 *hinc*: *hinc et* S-C

<14:4 *the one side and on the other* KJV: *on either side* D-R>

<14:5 *stood* D-R/C: *standing* D-R>

14:5 *ad meridiem*: *a meridie* Weber

<14:6 *that bore his armour* D-R: literally, *his armorbearer; It may be* KJV: *if haply* D-R; *easy* D-R/C: *not hard* D-R>

14:6 *multis*: *multitudine* Weber

14:7 *et ero*: *ero* Weber

<14:8 *be seen by* D-R/C: *appeare to* D-R>

<14:9 *still* KJV: omitted in D-R>

14:12 *ostendemus*: *ostendimus* Weber; *manus*: *manu* Weber

14:14 *qua*: *quam* Weber

<14:14 *of land* KJV: omitted in D-R>

14:19 *resonabat*: *reboabat* Weber

<14:19 *was heard* D-R/C: *soanded* D-R>

<14:22 *countrymen* D-R/C: *fellowes* D-R>

14:22 *proelio. Et erant cum Saul quasi decem milia virorum*: *proelio* Weber

14:23 *usque*: *usque ad* Weber

14:24 *viri . . . sociati . . . sunt*: *vir . . . sociatus . . . est* Weber

<14:24 *So none of the people tasted any food* KJV: *And the whole people did eate no bread* D-R>

<14:25 *people* D-R/C: *people of the land* D-R; *ground* KJV: *face of the field* D-R>

<14:26 *And when . . . behold*: *the honey dropped, but* KJV: *therefore . . . and there appeared dropping honie, and* D-R>

14:27 *favum*: *favo* Weber

14:28 *vir qui*: *qui* Weber

<14:28 *any food* KJV: *bread* D-R>

<14:33 *that* D-R/C: *saying that* D-R>

<14:34 *stone* D-R/C: *same* D-R; *with him* KJV: *in his hand* D-R>

14:35 *Domino* [both times]: *Domini* Weber

<14:36 *the morning light* KJV: *it waxe light in the morning* D-R>

14:36 *de*: *ex* S-C

14:37 *Dominum*: *Deum* Weber; *manus*: *manu* Weber

<14:39 *who is* D-R/C: omitted in D-R; *surely* KJV: *without reuoking* D-R>

14:39 *de omni*: *de* *D-R

<14:40 *on* KJV: *seperated into* D-R>

14:40 *altera*: *una* Weber; *Responditque*: *respondit* Weber

14:41 *Domine, Deus* Λ Φ [without capitalization or punctuation, Weber's sigla]: *Deum Israhel* S-C (*Israel* for *Israhel*), Weber; *indicium*: *indicium: Quid est quod non responderis servo tuo hodie? Si in me aut in Ionatha filio meo est iniquitas haec, da Ostensionem; aut si haec iniquitas est in populo tuo, da Sanctitatem.* S-C

<14:41 *by which we may know what the meaning is that thou answerest not thy servant today. If this iniquity be in me or in my son Jonathan, give a proof, or if this iniquity be in thy people, give holiness* S-C [*which we may know* italicized in D-R/C]: omitted in D-R>

<14:42 *lots* KJV: *lotte* D-R>

<14:43 *I did but taste* KJV: *Tasting I tasted* D-R; *must* KJV [italicized in D-R/C]: omitted in D-R>

<14:45 *This must not be* D-R/C: *this is vnlawful* D-R; *one* KJV: *a* D-R>

14:47 *Et*: *at* Weber

14:49 *Et nomina*: *nomina* Weber

14:50 *nomen principis*: *nomina principum* Weber

14:51 *Porro Cis*: *Cis* Weber

<15:2 *all that* D-R/C: *whatsoeuer* D-R>

15:3 *ei, et non concupiscas ex rebus ipsius aliquid*: *ei* Weber; *lactentem*: *lactantem* Weber

<15:3 *utterly* KJV: omitted in D-R; *any thing that is his* D-R/C: *ought of his thinges* D-R; *both man and woman, child* KJV: *from man vnto woman, both childe* D-R>

<15:6 *I destroy* KJV: *perhaps I wrappe* D-R>

15:7 *Sur*: *ad Sur* S-C

<15:9 *of the* KJV: omitted in D-R; *good for nothing* S?: *refuse* D-R>

<15:10 *came* KJV: *was made* D-R>

<15:11 *executed my commandments* KJV (*performed* for *executed*): *fulfilled my wordes in worke* D-R>

15:12 *quod* Λ^{H}BΩ^{M} gw [Quentin's sigla]: *eo quod* S-C, Weber

<15:12 *choicest* D-R/C: *first* D-R>

15:12–13 *et Saul offerebat holocaustum Domino de initiis praedarum quae adtulerat ex Amalech. Et cum venisset Samuhel ad Saul: et* Weber

<15:14 *bleating . . . lowing* KJV: *voice* D-R>

<15:15 *best of the* KJV: *better* D-R>

15:16 *Dixit: Ait* S-C; *nocte: hac nocte* *D-R

15:17 *regem: in regem* S-C

15:18 *via: viam* S-C

<15:18 *thou hast utterly destroyed them* D-R/C: *the vtter destruction of them* D-R>

15:22 *et victimas: aut victimas* Weber

15:23 *idolatriae: idololatriae* S-C; *te Dominus: te* Weber

<15:27 *and it* KJV: *which also* D-R>

15:30 *senibus: senioribus* S-C

15:32 *pinguissimus, tremens* Σ [without punctuation, Weber's siglum]: *pinguissimus et tremens* S-C, *pinguissimus* Weber

<15:32 *and* S-C; omitted in D-R>

15:33 *eum Samuhel: Samuhel Agag* Weber

15:35 *eum regem: regem Saul* Weber

16:1 *cum ego proiecerim eum: quem ego proiecerim* *D-R

<16:2 *with thee* KJV: *in thy hand* D-R>

16:4 *Pacificus: Pacificusne est* S-C

<16:5 *to the sacrifice* KJV: *that I may immolate* D-R>

<16:11 *Are here all thy sons* KJV (*children* for *sons*): *Are al thy sonnes now fully come* D-R; *who* D-R/C: *and he* D-R>

16:11 *venerit: veniat* S-C

16:12 *et ungue* ΛB$\Pi^{Z^{*}}$EθP^{2}HI$\Gamma^{B}\Psi^{B^{*}D}\Psi^{JM}$d^{2}n agrels cum Greg. M. in I Reg. 6, 3, 17, 18 (col. 457 D) et 29 (col. 466 C) et Brev. goth. (P. L. 86.568) [Quentin's sigla]: *Surge, unge* S-C, *surge ungue* Weber

16:13 *deinceps: in reliquum* Weber

<16:13 *came* KJV: *was directed vpon* D-R>

<16:15 *Now* KJV: omitted in D-R>

16:16 *quaerent*: *quaerant* Weber; *Domini*: *Dei* Weber

<16:16 *is upon* KJV: *shal take* D-R>

16:17 *ergo mihi*: *mihi* Weber

<16:17 *can play* KJV: *playeth* D-R>

16:20 *Tulit itaque*: *tulitque* Weber

<16:21 *and* KJV: *but* D-R>

<16:22 *sight* KJV: *eies* D-R>

16:23 *Domini malus*: *Dei* Weber

<16:23 *was upon* KJV: *caught* D-R; *played* KJV: *strooke* D-R>

17:2 *filii*: *viri* Weber; *vallem*: *valle* Weber

<17:4 *whose height was* KJV: *in height* D-R>

17:4 *palmi*: *palmo* Weber

17:5 *hamata*: *squamata* S-C; *aeris*: *aeris erat* S-C

<17:5 *with scales* S-C: *linked* D-R>

17:8 *venistis*: *venitis* Weber

<17:8 *hand to hand* D-R: literally, *in single combat*>

<17:10 *hand to hand* D-R: literally, *in single combat*>

17:11 *omnes*: *omnes viri* Weber

<17:11 *these* KJV (*those*): *such* D-R>

<17:12 *that* KJV: *a man that was an* D-R; *before mentioned* D-R/C: *of whom there was mention before* D-R>

<17:13 *followed* KJV: *went after* D-R>

17:13 *perrexerunt*: *perrexerant* Weber

<17:16 *presented himself* KJV: *stoode* D-R>

<17:18 *carry* KJV: *thou shalt carie* D-R; *go see* D-R/C: *shalt visite* D-R>

17:18 *sint*: *sunt* S-C

<17:19 *were in the valley of Terebinth fighting* KJV: *fought in the Valley of terebinth* D-R>

<17:23 *showed himself* D-R/C: *appeared* D-R>

17:23 *ex*: *de* S-C

17:25 *vidistis*: *vidisti* Weber

<17:27 *words* D-R/C: *worde* D-R>

<17:28 *Now* D-R/C: omitted in D-R; *hither* KJV: omitted in D-R>

<17:29 *cause to speak* D-R: literally, *word*>

17:30 *sicut*: *sicut et* Weber

<17:31 *rehearsed before* KJV: *told in the sight of* D-R>

<17:33   *but* KJV [italicized in D-R/C and in KJV]: omitted in D-R>

17:35   *persequebar*: *sequebar* Weber

<17:35   *them by the throat* D-R/C: *their chinne* D-R>

17:36   *eis. Nunc vadam et auferam opprobrium populi, quoniam quis est iste Philisthaeus incircumcisus*: *eis* Weber; *qui*: *quia* Weber; *exercitum*: *exercitui* S-C

17:37   *eripuit*: *eruit* Weber

17:39   *veste sua*: *vestem suam* S-C; *nec*: *non* S-C

<17:40   *smooth* KJV: *most bright* D-R>

17:46   *cadavera*: *cadaver* Weber

<17:46   *army* Heb: *campe* D-R>

<17:48   *to meet* [both times] KJV: *against* D-R>

17:49   *et circumducens*: *et* Weber

17:50   *et*: *et in* Weber

17:51   *de*: *eum de* S-C

<17:51   *their champion* KJV: *the strongest of them* D-R>

<17:52   *many* D-R/C [italicized in D-R/C]: omitted in D-R>

17:52   *usque ad Geth et usque*: *et usque ad Geth et usque ad* S-C

<17:55   *Philistines* D-R/C: *Philistian* D-R>

<17:57   *with* KJV: *hauing* D-R>

18:1   *conligata*: *conglutinata* S-C

<18:2   *let* KJV: *grant vnto him to* D-R>

<18:4   *And* KJV: *For* D-R>

18:4   *tunicam*: *tunica* S-C; *vestitus*: *indutus* S-C

<18:5   *whatsoever business* D-R/C: *al thinges wherestosoeuer* D-R>

18:5   *quocumque* d [Quentin's siglum]: *quaecumque* S-C, Weber

<18:7   *his thousands . . . his ten thousands* KJV: *a thousand . . . ten thousand* D-R>

<18:8   *but* KJV [italicized in D-R/C and in roman type in KJV]: omitted in D-R; *can he have more but* KJV: *remayneth for him but only* D-R>

<18:9   *a good eye* D-R/C: *right eies* D-R>

18:9   *ex*: *a* S-C

<18:10   *at other times* KJV: *euery day* D-R; *in his hand* KJV: omitted in D-R>

<18:11   *to* D-R/C: *that he could* D-R; *stept aside* D-R/C *out of his presence twice* KJV: *declined from his face the second time* D-R>

<18:17 *Now Saul said within himself* D-R/C: *And Saul thought saying* D-R>
<18:19 *it came to pass at the time* D-R: literally, *the time came*>
  18:21 *Dixitque Saul ad: dixit ergo Saul ad* Weber
<18:22 *to speak* D-R/C: *Speake* D-R; *privately* D-R/C: *secretly out of my presence* D-R>
<18:24 *told him* KJV: *reported* D-R>
<18:25 *desireth* KJV: *needeth* D-R; *to be avenged* KJV: *that reuenge may be made* D-R>
  18:25 *manus: manibus* Weber
  18:26 *dixerat Saul: diximus* Weber
  18:27 *percussit ex Philisthim ducentos viros et adtulit: percussis Philisthim ducentis viris / adtulit* Weber
  18:28 *quia: quod* S-C
<18:29 *continually* KJV: *al daies* D-R>
<19:2 *in a secret place* KJV: *secretly* D-R>
  19:3 *fuerit* RCΣΛh [Weber's sigla]: *fueris* S-C, Weber
<19:3 *where thou art* KJV: *wheresoeuer he shal be* D-R>
<19:5 *wilt thou sin* KJV: *sinnest thou* D-R>
<19:6 *words* D-R/C: *voice* D-R>
<19:9 *in his hand* KJV: omitted in D-R>
  19:9 *manu: in manu* Weber
<19:10 *out of the presence* KJV: *from the face* D-R; *missed him and* D-R/C: *without making wound* D-R; *escaped* KJV: *was saued* D-R>
<19:11 *that* D-R/C: *& that* D-R; *David's wife, had told him* KJV: *his wife had told David* D-R>
<19:12 *escaped* KJV: *was saued* D-R>
<19:13 *goat's skin with the hair* D-R/C: *hearie skinne of goates* D-R>
<19:15 *sent* S: *sent messengers* D-R>
<19:16 *a goat's skin* D-R/C: *skinnes of goates* D-R>
<19:17 *and* S: *that he might* D-R>
<19:18 *escaped* KJV: *was saued* D-R>
  19:21 *misit: misi et* S-C [*misi* is probably a typo for *misit*]; *prophetaverunt. Et iratus iracundia Saul: prophetaverunt* Weber
<19:21 *messengers the third time* KJV: *the third messengers* D-R; *exceedingly angry* D-R/C: *wrath for anger* D-R>

19:22 *abiit*: *abiit autem* Weber

19:23 *Domini*: *Dei* Weber

<19:23 *went on* KJV: *walked going* D-R>

20:1 *est in*: *erat in* Weber

<20:3 *David* D-R: literally, *he; there is but one step . . . between me and death* KJV: *by one degree only . . . I and death are diuided* D-R; *may* D-R/C: *may so* D-R>

20:3 *conspectu tuo* θ^{MG} [Quentin's sigla]: *oculis tuis* S-C, Weber

<20:5 *tomorrow is the new moon* KJV: *the calendes are to morowe* D-R>

20:6 *Si respiciens*: *si* Weber

<20:7 *come to its height* D-R/C: *complete* D-R>

20:9 *certo*: *certe* S-C

<20:9 *I could do no otherwise than* D-R/C: *neither can it be, that* D-R>

20:10 *nuntiabit*: *renuntiabit* S-C; *dure de me*: *dure* Weber

20:11 *et egrediamur foras*: *egrediamur* Weber

<20:11 *out* KJV: *forth abroad* D-R>

20:13 *addat*: *augeat* Weber

<20:13 *it* KJV: omitted in D-R>

20:15 *auferes*: *auferas* Weber; *terra, auferat Ionathan de domo sua, et requirat Dominus de manu (manibus *D-R) inimicorum David*: *terra* Weber

20:16 *manu*: *manibus* *D-R

<20:18 *is the new moon* KJV: *are the calendes* D-R; *missed* KJV: *asked for* D-R>

<20:19 *empty* KJV: *inquired of* D-R; *remain* KJV: *sit* D-R>

<20:21 *And I will send* KJV: *I wil send also* D-R>

20:22 *vade in pace*: *vade* Weber

20:23 *sumus*: *fuimus* Weber

<20:24 *new moon* KJV: *calendes* D-R>

20:27 *inluxisset*: *venisset* *D-R

<20:27 *new moon* D-R/C: *calendes* D-R>

<20:30 *that* KJV: *which of her owne accord* D-R>

<20:31 *as long as* KJV: *al the dayes, that* D-R>

20:32 *morietur*: *moritur* Weber

20:33 *a patre*: *patri* Weber

<20:34 *great anger* KJV (*fierce* for *great*): *anger of furie* D-R; *after the new moon* D-R/C: *of the calendes* D-R>

20:38 *Clamavitque iterum*: *clamavitque* Weber; *pueri, dicens*: *pueri* Weber

20:40 *et defer*: *defer* Weber

20:41 *alterutrum*: *se alterutrum* S-C

<20:42 *and let all stand that* D-R/C: *whatsoeuer* D-R>

20:43 *David et*: *et* Weber

<20:43 *And* KJV: *but* D-R>

<21:1 *at David's coming* D-R/C: *because Dauid was come* D-R; *with* KJV: *is with* D-R>

<21:2 *and* KJV: *for . . . also* D-R>

21:4 *David*: *ad David* S-C; *ait* XΣ^T2 [Quentin's sigla]: *ait illi* S-C, *ait ei* Weber

<21:5 *as to what concerneth women* D-R/C: *if the matter be concerning wemen* D-R>

<21:6 *before* KJV: omitted in D-R>

21:7 *vir quidam*: *vir* Weber

21:9 *Ecce: hic gladius*: *gladius* Weber

21:11 *ei*: *ad eum* S-C; *Achis, cum vidissent David*: *Achis* Weber

<21:11 *his thousands . . . his ten thousands* KJV: *a thousand . . . ten thousand* D-R>

<22:2 *under affliction of* D-R/C: *of a pensiue* D-R>

<22:3 *of* KJV: *which is* D-R>

<22:4 *under the eyes* D-R/C: *before the face* D-R>

22:5 *est David et*: *David* Weber

22:6 *nemore*: *Nemore* S-C; *servi*: *socii* Weber

<22:6 *by* D-R/C: *in* D-R>

22:7 *Audite me nunc* Ω agrels [Quentin's sigla]: *Audite nunc* S-C; *audite* Weber

<22:8 *giveth . . . any information* D-R/C: *telleth* D-R>

22:9 *Achitob, sacerdotem*: *Achitob* Weber

<22:10 *and* KJV: *yea and* D-R>

22:12 *Saul ad Achimelech*: *Saul* Weber

22:13 *Dominum* RΛDΦ [Weber's sigla]: *Deum* S-C, Weber

<22:14 *who is* KJV (*which* for *who*): *and* D-R>

<22:15 *or any one* D-R/C [italicised in D-R/C]: omitted in D-R>

22:17 *et non: non* Weber; *manus suas: manum suam* Weber

22:18 *rex ad: rex* Weber

<22:19 *both* KJV: omitted in D-R>

22:19 *bovemque: bovem* Weber

<22:22 *have been the occasion of the death* KJV (*occasioned* for *have been the occasion of*): *am giltie* D-R>

<22:23 *for he that seeketh* KJV: *if any man shal seeke* D-R>

23:1 *nuntiaverunt: annuntiaverunt* S-C

23:5 *Abiit ergo: abiit* Weber

<23:5 *made a great slaughter of them* D-R/C: *stroke them with a great slaughter* D-R>

23:7 *serae: serae sunt* S-C

23:10 *in Ceila: ad Ceila* Weber

23:12 *manus: manu* D-R

<23:13 *who were* KJV: omitted in D-R; *where they should stay* D-R/C: omitted in D-R; *escaped* KJV: *was saued* D-R; *forbore* KJV: *dissembled* D-R>

23:13 *Ceila et salvatus esset: Celia* Weber

<23:14 *strong holds* KJV: *most strong places* D-R; *woody* D-R/C: *shadowed* D-R; *but* KJV: *and* D-R>

23:14 *Ziph, in monte opaco: Ziph* Weber

<23:15 *And* KJV: *Moreouer* D-R>

23:16 *silvam: silva* Weber

23:17 *pater* P*Z [Quentin's sigla]: *Saul pater* S-C, Weber

23:19 *Nonne, ecce: nonne* Weber

<23:19 *strong holds* KJV: *most safe places* D-R>

23:22 *Abite, ergo: abite* Weber; *vel: et* *D-R

<23:22 *use all diligence* D-R/C: *prepare diligently* D-R>

23:23 *terram: terra* Weber

<23:23 *go down . . . to hide himself* D-R/C: *stoppe vp himselfe* D-R>

<23:24 *plain* KJV: *champaine country* D-R>

23:25 *quaerendum eum: quaerendum* Weber

<23:26 *round about* KJV: *in maner of a ring* D-R>

<23:27 *to* D-R/C: *and* D-R>

<23:28 *of Division* KJVn: *diuiding* D-R>

<24:1 *strong holds* KJV: *the safest places* D-R>

<24:2   *from following* KJV: *after he pursued* D-R>

24:4   *caulas*: *caulas quoque* D-R

<24:4   *were in his way* D-R/C: *fel in his way as he went* D-R; *ease nature* D-R/C: *doe his easement* D-R, literally, *empty his stomach* literal translation>

<24:5   *secretly* S: *softly* D-R>

<24:6   *which* D-R/C: *this* D-R>

<24:8   *way* KJV: *iourney begunne* D-R>

<24:10   *thy hurt* KJV: *euil against thee* D-R>

24:12   *praeciderem*: *praescinderem* S-C

<24:13   *my hand shall not be* KJV: *be not my hand* D-R>

<24:14   *my hand shall not be* KJV: *be not . . . my hand* D-R>

<24:15   *After* [first two times] KJV: omitted in D-R; *come out* KJV: *persecute* D-R; *After a dead dog; after a flea* KJV: *thou persecutest a dead dog, and a flea* D-R>

24:15   *persequeris* [first and third times]: *sequeris* Weber

24:16   *diiudicet*: *iudicet* S-C

<24:17   *these* KJV: *such* D-R>

24:19   *manum tuam*: *manu tua* Weber

<24:20   *well away* KJV: *in a good way* D-R>

<25:2   *possessions were* KJV: *possession* D-R; *he was shearing his sheep* KJV: *his flocke was shorne* D-R>

<25:3   *prudent and very comely* S?: *very wise and beutiful* D-R>

<25:5   *go . . . salute* KJV (*greete* for *salute*): *you shal come . . . shal salute* D-R>

25:6   *dicetis, 'Sit*: *dicetis sic* Weber

25:8   *pueri tui*: *pueri* Weber

25:13   *pueris*: *viris* Weber; *gladio suo*: *gladiis suis* S-C

25:14   *pueris suis*: *pueris* Weber; *adversatus*: *aversus* Weber

<25:15   *very* KJV: *ynough* D-R; *gave us no trouble* D-R/C: *not trublesome* D-R>

25:15   *sumus*: *fuimus* S-C

<25:16   *were with them keeping the sheep* KJV: *fed the flockes with them* D-R>

25:18   *inposuit*: *posuit* S-C

<25:19   *after you* KJV: *you at your backe* D-R>

25:22   *eum*: *ipsum* Weber

<25:25   *regard* KJV: *set his hart vpon* D-R>

<25:26 *all* D-R/C: omitted in D-R>

<25:28 *will surely make* KJV (*certainely* for *surely*): *making wil make* D-R>

<25:29 *souls* KJV: *life* D-R>

<25:31 *grief* KJV: *sobbing* D-R>

25:34 *me ne malum facerem*: *me malum facere* Weber

25:36 *usque in*: *usque* S-C

<25:39 *treated with* D-R/C: *spake to* D-R>

26:4 *quod illuc*: *quod* Weber

26:5 *David clam*: *David* Weber; *et Saulem*: *Saulem* Weber

<26:8 *even to* KJV: *in* D-R>

26:9 *extendet*: *extendit* Weber

26:12 *videret et*: *videret aut* *D-R; *aut* Γ [Quentin's siglum]: *et* S-C, Weber; *vigilaret*: *evigilaret* S-C

26:15 *quis* Frede LUC Ath 1.15 (p. 93.5): *quis alius* S-C, Weber

<26:16 *where* D-R/C: *behold where* D-R; *the cup of water* KJV (*cruse* for *cup*): *where the cup of water is* D-R>

26:16 *sit scyphus*: *scyphus* Weber

26:17 *Num*: *Numquid* S-C; *Et ait*: *et* Weber

<26:19 *him accept* KJV: *there be odoure* D-R>

26:21 *male tibi faciam*: *tibi malefaciam* S-C; *tuis hodie; apparet enim*: *tuis: hodie apparet enim* S-C, *tuis hodie / apparet* Weber

26:22 *regis et*: *et* Weber

26:23 *in manum meam*: *in manu mea* Weber; *extendere*: *levare* Weber

26:24 *sicuti*: *sicut* S-C

<26:24 *much set by* [both times] KJV: *magnified* D-R>

27:1 *uno*: *in uno* Weber; *manus*: *manu* Weber

<27:1 *I shall one day or other fall* D-R/C: *at length I shal fal one day* D-R; *of me* KJV: omitted in D-R>

<27:2 *both* D-R/C: omitted in D-R>

<27:3 *with* [first time] KJV: *&* D-R; *and David* S-C: omitted in D-R; *with* [second time] KJV: *and* D-R>

27:3 *eius, et* Γ^B2 agesc* [without punctuation, Quentin's sigla]: *eius, et David et* S-C, *eius / David et* Weber

27:4 *ut quaereret*: *quaerere* S-C

<27:6 *belongeth to* KJV (*pertaineth vnto*): *became* D-R>

<27:7 *time* KJV: *number of the daies* D-R>

<27:8 *pillaged* D-R/C: *draue prayes* D-R; *countries* D-R/C: *land* D-R>

<27:9 *man nor woman alive* KJV: *anie man or woman* D-R>

27:9 *viventem virum et: virum aut* *D-R

27:10 *Respondebat: respondebatque* Weber

<27:11 *saved* KJV: *gaue life . . . to* D-R; *such was his proceeding* D-R/C: *this was decreed* D-R>

<27:12 *much harm* D-R/C: *Manie euils* D-R>

<28:1 *assuredly* KJV: *Knowing* D-R; *to the war* D-R/C: *in the campe* D-R>

<28:2 *to guard my life* D-R/C: *keper of my head* D-R>

<28:5 *army* Heb: *campe* D-R>

28:8 *et abiit: abiit* Weber; *ait illi: ait* Weber

<28:8 *disguised himself* KJV: *changed his habite* D-R; *thy divining* D-R/C: *the pythonical* D-R>

<28:9 *all that* D-R/C: *what great thinges* D-R>

28:10 *eveniet: veniet* Weber

28:14 *Et intellexit: intellexit* Weber

<28:14 *with . . . to* KJV: *upon . . . on* D-R>

<28:15 *my rest* D-R/C: *me* D-R>

<28:17 *by me* KJV: *in my hande* D-R>

28:17 *regnum tuum: regnum* Weber

28:19 *manus* [both times]: *manu* Weber

<28:19 *and* S: *yea* D-R; *army* Heb: *campe* D-R>

28:21 *mulier illa: mulier* Weber; *Saul: Saul et ait* Weber; *tuos quos: quos* *D-R

28:22 *et ponam: ut ponam* Weber; *ut comedens: et comedens* Weber; *et possis: ut possis* Weber; *agere: facere* Weber

<29:2 *lords* KJV: *princes in dede* D-R; *with their . . . their* D-R/C: *in* D-R; *rear* KJV (*rere-ward*): *last companie* D-R>

29:3 *Philisthim ad Achis: Philisthim* Weber

<29:3 *hath been* KJV: *is* D-R>

29:4 *vir iste: vir* Weber

29:5 *choris: choro* Weber

<29:6 *so* D-R/C: omitted in D-R; *army* D-R/C: *campe* D-R>

29:6 *ad diem: in diem* S-C

29:7 *offendas: offendes* Weber

<29:8 *But* KJV: *For* D-R>

29:9 *oculis meis: conspectu meo* *D-R

<29:11 *So David and his men arose* KJV: *Dauid therefore arose in the night, he and his men* D-R>

30:2 *a: et a* Weber; *in itinere: itinere* S-C

<30:2 *that were in it* KJV (*therein* for *in it*): *out of it* D-R; *both . . . and* D-R/C: *from . . . vnto* D-R>

30:3 *venissent: venisset* Weber

<30:6 *grieved* KJV: *affected* D-R>

<30:7 *Bring me hither* KJV: *Applie vnto me* D-R>

30:8 *latrunculos hos, et conprehendam eos, an non: an non latrunculos hos et conprehendam eos* Weber; *ei Dominus: ei* Weber; *Persequere: Persequere eos* *D-R

<30:8 *after* [first time] KJV: omitted in D-R; *after* [second time] D-R/C: omitted in D-R>

30:11 *ut biberet: biberet* S-C

<30:12 *as* D-R/C: *and* D-R, literally, *but*>

30:13 *Et quo: quo* Weber; *ait: ait ei* Weber

<30:13 *dost thou come* D-R/C: omitted in D-R>

30:14 *plagam: partem*

30:15 *manus: manu* Weber; *istum. Et iuravit ei David: istum* Weber

<30:19 *small or great, neither of their sons or their daughters* KJV: *from litle to great as wel of their sonnes as of their daughters* D-R>

<30:22 *all the . . . men* KJV?: *euerie . . . felow of the men* D-R; *let every man take his wife and his children and be contented with them and go his way* D-R/C: *let their wife and chlidren suffice euerie man, whom when they haue receiued, let them depart* D-R>

<30:23 *with* KJV: *of* D-R; *who* KJV: *and* D-R; *invaded* S: *were broken out against* D-R>

30:23 *manus nostras: manu nostra* Weber

<30:24 *but* KJV: *For* D-R>

<30:25 *forward* KJV *and since* D-R/C: *and euer after* D-R>

30:25 *Israhel usque ad diem hanc: Israel, usque in diem hanc* S-C, *Israhel* *D-R

<30:27 *to* KJV: omitted in D-R>

<30:28 *to* KJV: omitted in D-R>

30:31 *David* XDΦ^{RZGV}P*ZΩ ael [Quentin's sigla]: *David, ipse* S-C, Weber [without punctuation]

<30:31 *with* D-R/C: *and* D-R>

<31:1 *Philistines* KJV: *face of the Philistijms* D-R>

31:2 *et in*: *et* Weber

31:4 *timore*: *terrore* S-C

31:9 *expoliaverunt*: *spoliaverunt* S-C

<31:9 *to publish it* KJV: *that it should be declared* D-R>

31:11 *Iabes Galaad*: *Iabesgalaad* Weber

31:12 *Iabes Galaad*: *Iabes* Weber

2 KINGS

<1:1 *the Amalekites* KJV: *Amalec* D-R>

1:2 *aspersus*: *conspersus* S-C

1:4 *e proelio*: *ex proelio* S-C

1:5 *nuntiabat ei*: *nuntiabat* Weber

1:6 *Et ait*: *ait* Weber; *narrabat*: *nuntiabat* S-C [probable typographical error for *nunciabat*]

<1:7–8 *And I answered, 'Here am I.' And* KJV: *To whom when I had answered, here I am* D-R>

<1:9 *anguish is come upon* KJV: *anguishes hold* D-R>

1:9 *anima mea*: *anima* Weber

<1:10 *that was on* KJV: *from* D-R>

<1:11 *Then . . . likewise* KJV: *And . . . and* D-R>

1:12 *quod*: *eo quod* S-C

1:14 *Et ait*: *ait* *D-R

1:15 *pueris suis*: *pueris* Weber

<1:15 *so that* KJV (without *so*): *and* D-R>

1:18 *Iustorum.) ¶ Et ait, "Considera, Israel, pro his qui mortui sunt, super excelsa tua vulnerati*: *Iustorum* Weber

<1:20 *lest* KJV: *lest perhaps* D-R>

1:21 *pluvia*: *pluviae* Weber

<1:25 *How was Jonathan slain* D-R/C [*How was* italicized]: *Ionathas bene slayne* D-R>

1:25   *occisus* h; θ^G cum Ps. Hier. quaest. hebr *Hier. dicit quod hebr. non habet «est» sed subauditur* [Quentin's sigla]: *occisus est* S-C, Weber

<1:26   *to me* KJV [italicized in D-R/C]: omitted in D-R>

1:26   *mulierum. Sicut mater unicum amat filium suum, ita ego te diligebam*: *mulierum* Weber

<2:3   *And* KJV: *yea and* D-R>

2:4   *Iabes Galaad*: *Iabesgalaad* Weber

2:5   *Iabes Galaad*: *Iabesgalaad* Weber

<2:6   *and* KJV: *but* D-R; *for* D-R/C *this* KJV: *the* D-R>

2:6   *feceritis*: *fecistis* S-C

2:7   *viri* B [Quentin's siglum]: *filii* S-C, Weber; *regem*: *in regem* S-C

2:8   *castra*: *Castra* S-C, Weber

2:11   *mensuum*: *mensium* S-C

2:12   *castris*: *Castris* S-C, Weber

<2:13   *the one . . . the other* KJV: *these . . . they* D-C>

2:18   *ex*: *de* S-C

2:19   *sive*: *neque* S-C

<2:19   *from following* KJV: *omitting to pursue* D-R>

2:22   *Recede, et* arels [Quentin's sigla, without punctuation or capitalization]: *Recede, noli* S-C, Weber [the latter without punctuation or captialization]; *sequi, ne*: *sequi; ne* S-C

<2:23   *wherefore* KJV: *therefore* D-R>

2:23   *locum illum*: *locum* Weber

2:24   *aquaeductus*: *Aquaeductus* Weber; *vallis*: *vallis et* Weber

<2:24   *Abner* KJV: *Abner fleeing* D-R; *lieth* KJV [in roman type in KJV]: *is* D-R>

<2:26   *to drive people to despair* D-R/C: *desperation* D-R>

<2:27   *sooner, even* D-R/C [*even* italicized]: omitted in D-R>

2:27   *fratres suos* $\Lambda X \Sigma^M B \Psi^{B^*}$ [Qunetin's sigla]: *fratrem suum* S-C, Weber

<2:28   *fight any more* KJV: *enter into fight* D-R>

2:29   *castra*: *Castra* S-C, Weber

<2:31   *all* D-R/C: *also* D-R>

<2:32   *break of day* KJV: *the very twilight* D-R>

3:1   *proficiens*: *proficiscens* S-C

<3:1   *growing . . . stronger and stronger* KJV (*waxing* for *growing*): *stronger then himself* D-R>

3:2   *Natique*: *nati quoque* Weber

<3:3   *his second* KJV: *after him* D-R>

3:8   *proximos*: *proximos amicos* *D-R; *manus*: *manu* Weber

<3:8   *with a matter concerning* KJV (*fault* for *matter*): *for* D-R>

<3:11   *a word* KJV: *any thing* D-R>

3:12   *Et ut*: *et* Weber

<3:12   *a league* KJV: *amitie* D-R>

3:16   *Vade, et*: *vade* Weber

3:18   *manu Philisthim*: *manibus Philisthim* *D-R

3:23   *a narrantibus*: *quod* *D-R

3:25   *venit ad te*: *venit* Weber

3:27   *abduxit*: *adduxit* S-C

3:29   *et tenens*: *tenens* Weber

<3:29   *or* [four times] KJV: *and* D-R>

<3:31   *And King David himself* KJV: *Moreouer king Dauid* D-R>

3:32   *Rex David*: *rex* Weber

3:33   *rex et lugens*: *rex* Weber

3:34   *sic corruisti*: *corruisti* Weber

<3:36   *and they were pleased* KJV (*and it pleased them*): omitted in D-R>

4:1   *autem Isboseth*: *autem* Weber

4:3   *usque in*: *usque ad* S-C

<4:5   *And the doorkeeper of the house, who was cleansing wheat, was fallen asleep.* S-C: omitted in D-R>

4:5   *meridie*: *meridie, et ostiaria domus purgans triticum obdormivit* S-C

4:6   *domum latenter*: *domum* Weber

4:7   *lectulum*: *lectum* S-C

<4:7   *for* KJV: *And* D-R; *walking* [italicized in D-R/C] D-R/C: omitted in D-R>

4:8   *ultionem*: *ultiones* Weber

4:9   *Berothitae*: *Berothei* Weber

4:10   *eum in*: *in* Weber; *me dare*: *dare* S-C

<4:10   *brought good tidings* KJV: *told prosperous thinges* D-R; *who should have been rewarded* S-C: *to whom I should haue geuen a reward* D-R>

4:11   *interfecerint*: *interfecerunt* S-C; *lectulum*: *lectum* S-C

4:12   *pueris suis*: *pueris* Weber

5:3   *senes de*: *seniores* S-C

5:4   *Triginta* Frede AUX 35 p. 164.34: *Filius triginta* S-C, Weber (without capitalization)

<5:6   *Jebusites, the inhabitants* KJV: *Iebuseite the inhabiter* D-R>

5:6   *est ad*: *est* S-C

<5:7   *the same* KJV: *this* S-C>

5:8   *David in*: *in* Weber; *qui*: *cuiquam qui* *D-R; *et abstulisset*: *et* Weber; *ad templum*: *templum* Weber

<5:8   *Jebusites* KJV: *Iebuseite* D-R>

5:13   *David adhuc*: *adhuc* Weber

5:17   *ergo*: *vero* Weber; *regem*: *in regem* S-C

5:19   *manum meam* J. Belsheim, ed., *Palimpsestus Vindobonensis* (Christianae: 1885) 24: *manu mea* S-C, Weber

<5:19   *I will surely deliver* KJV (*doubtlesse* for *surely*): *deliuering I wil geue* D-R; *into* KJV: *in* D-R>

5:20   *Baal Pharasim* [both times]: *Baalpharasim* Weber

<5:22   *came up again* D-R/C: *added yet to go vp* D-R>

5:23   *Dominum, "Si ascendam contra Philistheos, et trades eos in manus meas*: *Dominum* Weber; *trades* $\Lambda^H\Pi\Sigma^M$KIΓΩ [Quentin's sigla]: *tradas* S-C; *ascendas contra eos*: *ascendas* Weber; *pirorum*: *Pyrorum* S-C

5:24   *pirorum*: *Pyrorum* S-C

<5:24   *tops* KJV: *toppe* D-R; *army* KJV (*host*): *campe* D-R>

6:2   *David et*: *et* Weber

<6:2   *with* KJV: *and* D-R>

6:3   *Dei*: *Domini* Weber

<6:5   *manner of instruments made of* KJV: *wrought* D-R; *on* D-R/C: *both on* D-R>

<6:6   *when* KJV: *after* D-R>

6:6   *boves et declinaverunt eam*: *boves* Weber

6:10   *devertere*: *divertere* S-C; *civitatem*: *civitate* Weber; *devertit*: *divertit* Weber; *domum*: *domo* Weber

<6:10   *brought in* D-R/C: *turne* D-R; *be carried* D-R/C: *turne* D-R>

6:12   *est*: *es* S-C [typographical error]; *quod benedixisset*: *benedixit* Weber; *gaudio*: *gaudio; et erant cum David septem chori et victima vituli* S-C

<6:12   *And there were with David seven choirs and calves for victims.* S-C: omitted in D-R>

<6:15   *with joyful shouting* KJV (without *joyful*): *in iubilation* D-R>

6:16   *in civitatem*: *civitatem* Weber

6:17   *posuerunt*: *imposuerunt* S-C

6:18   *holocausta*: *holocaustum* Weber

6:20   *est David*: *est et David* Weber

6:21   *in Israhel*: *Israhel* Weber

6:23   *ad*: *in* S-C

<7:4   *night* KJV: *night: and behold* D-R; *came* KJV: omitted in D-R>

<7:6   *Whereas* KJV: *For* D-R>

7:6   *die*: *die illa* S-C; *sed*: *sed ambulans* Weber

<7:7   *did ever I speak a word to any* KJV (*spake I* for *ever did I speak*): *speaking did I speak to* D-R>

<7:8   *from* KJV: omitted in D-R>

7:9   *ubicumque* ANT-M 272 r (215): *in omnibus ubicumque* S-C, Weber

<7:10   *therein* D-R/C: *vnder it* D-R>

<7:14   *a* [both times] D-R/C: *for a* D-R>

7:15   *tua*: *mea* S-C

<7:15   *my* S-C: *thy* D-R>

7:22   *Deus extra*: *deus extra* Weber

<7:23   *whom* KJV: *for the which* D-R>

7:23   *gentibus et diis* r *earum* θ^{G} [Quentin's sigla; *earum* is in the notes to the cited manuscript, which also reads *gentibus et diis*]: *gentem et deum eius* S-C, Weber

7:24   *Firmasti enim*: *et firmasti* Weber; *Domine Deus*: *Domine* Weber

7:26   *ut*: *et* Weber

<7:27   *in* KJV: omitted in D-R>

<7:29   *And now* S: *therefore* D-R; *endure* KJV (*continue*): *be* D-R>

<8:1   *this* D-R/C: *these thinges* D-R>

<8:3   *extend his* S?: *haue* D-R>

<8:4   *only* D-R/C *reserved of them for* KJV: *leift of them* D-R>

<8:5   *Syrians* [both times] KJV: *Syria* D-R>

<8:6   *garrisons* KJV: *a garrison* D-R; *served* D-R/C: *became seruing* D-R>

8:6   *servavitque*: *servavit* Weber

<8:10   *return* D-R/C: *geue* D-R>

<8:12   *of* [four times] KJV: omitted in D-R>

8:13   *decem et octo*: *duodecim* Weber

<8:14   *enterprises* D-R/C: *thinges to whatsoeuer* D-R>

<8:16 *recorder* D-R: literally, *among the registers*>

8:17 *sacerdotes erant: sacerdotes* Weber

<8:18 *princes* D-R: literally, *priests* [as noted both in D-R and in D-R/C]>

<9:1 *left* KJV: *that is remaining* D-R>

<9:2 *Ziba* D-R/C: *so* D-R>

9:3 *Num: Numquid* S-C

<9:3 *who is* KJV: omitted in D-R>

<9:6 *Behold* KJV: *Here I am* D-R>

<9:7 *I will surely shew* KJV: *doing I wil do* D-R>

9:7 *tibi omnes agros: agros* *D-R

<10:1 *this* KJV: *these thinges* D-R>

10:1 *regnaret: regnavit* S-C

<10:2 *his servants to comfort* D-R/C: *conforting him by his seruants* D-R>

<10:4 *beards* KJV: *breard* [sic] D-R>

10:4 *praecidit: praescidit* S-C

10:5 *Manete: Manete in* S-C

<10:5 *sadly put to confusion* D-R/C: *confounded very fowly* D-R; *saying*
        D-R/C [in italics]: omitted in D-R; *beards: beard* D-R>

<10:6 *Syrians* [both times] KJV: *Syrian* D-R>

<10:8 *Syrians* KJV: *Syrian* D-R>

<10:9 *Syrians* KJV: *Syrian* D-R>

10:11 *praevaluerint adversum me Syri: praevaluerit adversum me Syrus* *D-R

<10:11 *Syrians are too strong for me* KJV: *Syrian shal preuayle against me* D-R;
        are too strong for thee KJV: *shal prevayle agaynst thee* D-R>

10:12 *Viriliter age* Gryson 93 E, p. 364: *Esto vir fortis* S-C, Weber

<10:12 *Be of good courage* KJV: *Play the man* D-R>

<10:13 *before him* KJV: *from his face* D-R>

<10:14 *before* KJV: *from the face of* D-R>

10:16 *fluvium: Fluvium* Weber

<10:18 *before* KJV: *from the face of* D-R>

10:19 *ab Israhel expaverunt et fugerunt, quinquaginta et octo milia coram
        Israhel. Et: ab Israhel* Weber; *ultra filiis: filiis* Weber

<10:19 *auxiliaries of* D-R/C: *to aid* D-R; *all* D-R/C: omitted in D-R>

11:1 *est autem: est ergo* Weber

<11:1 *go* KJV: *are wont to procede* D-R>

11:2 *strato: stratu* Weber

<11:4   *and she* KJV: *who when* D-R; *and* KJV: omitted in D-R>

11:5   *est in*: *est* Weber

<11:7   *how* KJV: *how wel* D-R>

11:8   *Et egressus*: *egressus* Weber

<11:10   *some* D-R/C: *them* D-R>

11:10   *in* [both times]: *ad* Weber

11:11   *Arca Dei*: *arca* Weber; *non*: *quod non* Weber

11:12   *die*: *in die* S-C

<11:14   *And when the morning was come, David* D-R/C: *The morning therefore was come, and Dauid* D-R>

11:16   *quo*: *ubi* S-C

<11:17   *some* KJV: omitted in D-R>

<11:20   *so near* KJV (*nigh* for *near*): omitted in D-R>

11:21   *Hierobaal*: *Hieroboseth* Weber

<11:23   *vigorously charged and* D-R/C: *violently* D-R>

<11:24   *some* KJV: omitted in D-R; *and* KJV: *yea and* D-R>

11:25   *belli*: *proelii* Weber

<11:25   *and sometimes one, sometimes another is consumed by the sword* D-R/C: *now this man, and now that man the sword consumeth* D-R>

11:27   *in domum*: *domum* Weber

<12:4   *dressed it* KJV: *made meates therof* D-R>

<12:5   *David's anger being exceedingly kindled* KJV (*Dauids anger was greatly kindled*): *Dauid being exedingly wrath with indignation* D-R>

<12:7   *the* KJV: *that* D-R>

12:9   *in uxorem tibi*: *uxorem* Weber

<12:11   *Thus* KJV: *Therfore thus* D-R>

<12:14   *surely* KJV: *dying* D-R>

12:15   *in domum*: *domum* Weber; *Percussit quoque*: *percussitque* Weber

<12:15   *his life* D-R/C: *he* D-R>

<12:16   *kept* D-R/C: *fasted* D-R>

<12:17   *to make him rise* KJV (*to raise*): *being earnest with him, that he would rise* D-R>

12:20   *ut ponerent ei panem*: *panem* *D-R

<12:20   *then* KJV: omitted in D-R>

<12:22   *While the child* KJV: *for the infant, whiles he* D-R; *whether* KJV (in roman type): *if perhaps* D-R>

12:22 *vivat*: *vivet* Weber

12:23 *ieiuno*: *ieiunem* S-C

<12:23 *should* S-C: *do* D-R>

<12:26 *laid close seige to* D-R/C: *wonne* D-R>

<12:30 *the weight of which was* KJV: *in weight* D-R; *set with* KJV (without *set*): *hauing* D-R; *which were* D-R/C: omitted in D-R>

<12:31 *with* D-R/C: *and* D-R>

12:31 *exercitus in*: *exercitus* Weber

<13:1 *this* KJV: *these thinges* D-R; *who was* D-R/C: *being* D-R; *and her name was* KJV: *called* D-R>

<13:2 *he thought it* KJV (*Amnon* for *he*): *it semed vnto him* D-R>

<13:4 *dost thou grow so lean* D-R/C: *art thou so worne away with leanenes* D-R; *the reason of it* D-R/C: omitted in D-R>

13:5 *lectulum*: *lectum* S-C; *faciat mihi* Ω^M [Quentin's siglum; *michi* for *mihi*]: *faciat* S-C, Weber

<13:5 *to eat* D-R/C: *meate* D-R>

<13:6 *made as if he were* D-R/C: *began as it were to be* D-R; *that* KJV: *and* D-R>

<13:8 *was laid down* KJV: *lay* D-R>

<13:9 *but* KJV: *and* D-R>

<13:12 *no such thing must be done* KJV (*ought to* for *must*): *this is not lawful* D-R>

13:13 *ego*: *et ego* Weber

<13:14 *being stronger* KJV: *preuayling by force* D-R>

13:15 *et vade*: *vade* Weber

<13:15 *get thee gone* KJV (*be* for *get thee*): *goe* D-R>

<13:19 *went on* KJV: *went going on, and* D-R>

13:20 *Num*: *Numquid* S-C

13:21 *valde*: *valde; et noluit contristare spiritum Amnon filii sui quoniam diligebat eum, quia prmogenitus erat ei* S-C

<13:21 *and he would not afflict the spirit of his son Amnon, for he loved him because he was his firstborn* S-C: omitted in D-R>

<13:23 *two* KJV: *the space of two* D-R; *invited* KJV: *called* D-R>

<13:25 *be chargeable to* KJV: *charge* D-R>

<13:27 *so that* KJV: *and* D-R>

13:27 *regis. Feceratque Absalom convivium quasi convivium regis*: *regis* Weber

<13:28 *when* KJV: omitted in D-R>

13:28 *praecipio: praecepi* Weber

13:30 *praevenit: pervenit* S-C

<13:30 *one* KJV: *so much as one* D-R>

13:31 *illius: ipsius* Weber

13:32 *meus, rex: meus* Weber

13:34 *levavit: elevavit* S-C

13:35 *verbum: verba* *D-R

<13:35 *as thy servant said, so it is* KJV: *according to the wordes of thy seruant so is it done* D-R>

<13:36 *and* KJV: *yea* D-R; *very much* KJV (*sore* for *much*): *with an exceding great weeping* D-R>

<13:37 *But* KJV: *Moreouer* D-R; *And* KJV: *therefore* D-R>

<14:2 *thyself to be a mourner* KJV: *that thou mournest* D-R>

<14:3 *in this manner* KJV: *these maner of wordes* D-R>

<14:5 *is the matter with thee* D-R/C: *matter hast thou* D-R>

14:6 *prohibere posset: prohiberet* *D-R

14:9 *mi, sit* *D-R [not unlike PL 113, col. 0574B]: *mi rex, sit* S-C, *mi rex* Weber

<14:10 *If any one shall say ought against* D-R/C: *He that shal gaynesay* D-R>

14:11 *interficiant: interficient* Weber

14:13 *istiusmodi: huiuscemodi* S-C

<14:13 *home* KJV: omitted in D-R>

14:14 *delabimur: dilabimur* S-C

<14:15 *it may be* KJV: *if by any meanes* D-R>

<14:16 *to me* D-R/C: omitted in D-R>

14:17 *sicut sacrificium: quasi sacrificium* Weber

14:18 *ei mulier: mulier* Weber

<14:19 *this* KJV: *these thinges* D-R>

14:20 *mi, rex: mi* Weber

<14:20 *come about with this form of speech* KJV (*fetch* for *come*): *change the forme of this speach* D-R; *according to the wisdom of an angel of God* KJV: *as an Angel of God hath wisdom* D-R>

<14:25 *of his head* KJV: omitted in D-R>

14:26 *tondebat: tondebatur* Weber; *semel autem: semel* *D-R

<14:26 *now* D-R/C: omitted in D-R>

14:27 *elegantis formae*: *eleganti forma* Weber

<14:27 *whose name was* KJV: *named* D-R; *and she was very beautiful* D-R/C: *of a goodly beautie* D-R>

14:28 *Absalom*: *Absalom in* S-C

14:29 *venire ad eum*: *venire* Weber

14:30 *igni. ¶ Et venientes servi Ioab scissis vestibus suis dixerunt, "Succenderunt servi Absalom partem agri igni."*: *igni* Weber

14:32 *et diceres*: *ut diceres* Weber; *quod*: *et* *D-R

<14:32 *that . . . to* KJV: *and . . . and* D-R>

14:33 *Ingressus itaque Ioab ad regem nuntiavit ei omnia, vocatusque est Absalom, et*: *ingressus Ioab ad regem nuntiavit ei / vocatusque Absalom* Weber

<14:33 *prostrated himself on the ground* D-R/C: *adored vpon the face of the earth* D-R>

15:1 *currus*: *currum* Weber

<15:2 *when any* KJV: *euerie man* D-R; *had* KJV: *that had* D-R; *him* KJV: omitted in D-R; *Thy servant is* KJV: *am I thy seruant* D-R>

<15:4 *O that they* D-R/C: *Oh who* D-R; *do them justice* KJV (*him* for *them*): *iudge iustly* D-R>

<15:5 *any* KJV: *a* D-R>

15:6 *venienti*: *qui veniebat* Weber

15:7 *quadraginta*: *quattuor* Weber; *Regem David*: *regem* Weber

<15:8 *made a vow* D-R/C: *vowing did vow* D-R>

15:9 *Rex David*: *rex* Weber

<15:11 *knowing nothing* KJV (*they knew not any thing*): *vtterly ignorant* D-R>

15:12 *Cumque*: *cum* Weber: *et facta*: *facta* Weber

<15:14 *and* KJV: omitted in D-R; *we shall not escape else* KJV [*else* in roman type in KJV and in italics in D-R]: *there wil be no escape for vs* D-R; *lest he come* D-R/C: *lest coming perhaps* D-R>

15:15 *exsequemur*: *exsequimur* Weber

15:18 *Getthei, pugnatores validi*: *Getthei* Weber; *Geth pedites*: *Geth* Weber

<15:18 *on foot* S: *footemen* D-R>

15:20 *inpelleris*: *compelleris* S-C; *tuos, et Dominus faciet tecum misericordiam et veritatem, quia*: *tuos* Weber

<15:23 *himself* KJV: omitted in D-R>

15:24 *sacerdos, et*: *et* Weber; *transiret* I [Quentin's siglum]: *esset* S-C, *est*
Weber

15:26 *dixerit mihi*: *dixerit* Weber

<15:28 *to certify* KJV: *aduertising* D-R>

<15:32 *came to meet* KJV: *mette* D-R>

<15:35 *it* KJV [in roman type]: omitted in D-R>

15:36 *filius Sadoc, et Ionathan, filius*: *Sadoc et Ionathan* Weber

<16:1 *behold* KJV: omitted in D-R; *came* D-R/C: *appeared* D-R>

16:1 *utre*: *utribus* Weber

16:2 *domesticis*: *domestici* Weber: *et panes*: *panes* S-C

<16:4 *I give thee all* D-R/C: *Let al thinges be thine* D-R>

16:4 *Adoro*: *Oro ut* S-C

16:5 *procedebatque*: *procedebat* Weber

16:6 *et sinistro*: *et a sinistro* S-C

<16:8 *for* D-R/C: omitted in D-R>

16:9 *mortuus*: *moriturus* Weber

16:10 *vobis est*: *vobis* Weber; *eum ut*: *eum* Weber

<16:10 *What have I to do with you* KJV: *What is it to me and you* D-R; *and let
him* S: *that he may* D-R>

<16:11 *as the Lord hath bidden him* KJV (*for* for *as*): *according to the precept of
our Lord* D-R>

<16:12 *Perhaps* S: *if perhaps* D-R>

16:12 *mihi Dominus*: *mihi* Weber

<16:13 *by the hill's side* KJV: *by the banke on the hils side* D-R>

16:15 *eius*: *Israhel* Weber

<16:15 *and* KJV: *yea and* D-R>

16:17 *isti*: *ivisti* S-C

<16:19 *Besides this* D-R/C: *Yea that I may adde this also* D-R>

<17:2 *defeat* D-R/C: *strike* D-R; *put to flight* D-R/C: *fled* D-R>

17:3 *unus homo*: *omnis* Weber

<17:3 *as if they were but one man* D-R/C: *as one man is wont to returne* D-R;
but D-R/C [italicized]: omitted in D-R>

17:5 *Vocate*: *vocate et* Weber

<17:6 *after this manner* KJV: *This maner of speache* D-R>

<17:8 *and* KJV: *yea and* D-R>

<17:9 *other* KJV: *one* D-R; *every one that heareth it* KJV: *there shal one heare whosoeuer shal heare it* D-R>

17:10 *quisque*: *quoque* Weber

<17:10 *the most valiant man* D-R/C: *euerie one of the most valiant* D-R; *the heart* KJV: omitted in D-R>

<17:12 *falleth* KJV: *is wont to fal* D-R>

17:13 *Si autem* J. Belsheim, ed., *Codex Vindobonensis* (Leipzig, T. O. Weigel, 1885) p. 32: *Quod si* S-C, Weber [without capitalization]; *nec: ne* S-C

17:14 *omnes viri*: *omnies filii* *D-R, *omnis vir* Weber

17:15 *senibus*: *senioribus* S-C

17:16 *moremini*: *moreris* S-C

<17:17 *and* KJV: omitted in D-R; *might* KJV: *could* D-R>

17:20 *in domum, ad mulierem*: *ad mulierem in domum* Weber; *festinanter gustata*: *gustata* Weber; *sunt in*: *sunt* Weber

17:21 *et transite*: *transite* Weber

<17:23 *followed* KJV: *executed* D-R; *home* KJV: omitted in D-R>

17:24 *omnes viri*: *omnis vir* Weber

<17:28 *and* KJV: omitted in D-R>

17:28 *et pulentam*: *pulentam* Weber; *et frixum*: *frixum* Weber

<17:29 *and* KJV: omitted in D-R>

18:1 *eos*: *eum* Weber

<18:2 *sent forth* KJV: *gaue* D-R>

18:2 *partem sub manu Abisai*: *in manu Abisai* Weber; *partem sub manu Ethai*: *sub manu Ethai* Weber

18:4 *omnis populus* J. Belsheim, ed., *Codex Vindobonensis* (Leipzig, T. O. Weigel, 1885) p. 35: *populus* S-C, Weber

<18:7 *defeated* D-R/C: *slayne* D-R>

18:7 *plaga*: *ibi plaga* Weber

18:9 *sederat*: *insederat* S-C

18:12 *manum meam*: *manus meas* *D-R

<18:13 *by me* D-R/C: *agaynst it* D-R>

18:13 No question mark in S-C, Weber lacks all punctuation.

<18:14 *in thy sight* S?: *before thee* D-R>

<18:18 *in his lifetime* KJV: *whiles he yet liued* D-R>

<18:22 *Why might not I* D-R/C: *What letteth if I* D-R>

18:23   *ei Ioab*: *Ioab* Weber

<18:26   *from above* D-R/C: *in the toppe* D-R; *I see* D-R/C: *There appeareth vnto me* D-R>

18:26   *alter homo*: *homo* Weber

<18:27   *The running of the foremost seemeth to me* D-R/C: *I behold . . . the running of the former* D-R; *with* KJV: *bringing* D-R>

18:28   *Salve rex*: *salve* Weber

<18:28   *falling down before the king* KJV (*hee fell downe . . . before the King*): *adoring the king before him* D-R>

<18:33   *much moved* KJV: *made sorie* D-R; *would God* KJV: *who would graunt me that* D-R>

18:33   *fili mi Absalom* [third time]: *fili mi* Weber

19:3   *declinabat*: *declinavit* S-C

<19:3   *that hath turned their backs* D-R/C: *turned* D-R>

19:5   *domum*: *domo* Weber

<19:5   *lives* [three times] KJV: *life* D-R>

<19:6   *plainly* D-R/C *perceive* KJV: *in deede . . . knowe* D-R>

<19:7   *speak to the satisfaction of* KJVn (*heart* for *satisfaction*): *speaking vnto them satisfie* D-R>

<19:8   *people* KJV: *multitude* D-R>

<19:9   *and* KJV: omitted in D-R>

19:11   *et*: *et ad* Weber

<19:11   *are you the* KJV: *come you* D-R>

19:15   *et omnis*: *et* Weber; *usque in*: *in* Weber

19:17   *Iordanem, ante* R (line break for comma) [Quentin's siglum]: *Iordanem ante* S-C, Weber

19:19   *inuriarum*: *inuriam* Weber

19:22   *satan* *D-R: *Satan* S-C, Weber

<19:22   *are you* D-R/C: *are you made* D-R; *any* KJV: omitted in D-R>

<19:24   *he had neither washed his feet nor* KJV (*dressed* for *washed*): *his feete vnwashed, and* D-R>

19:26   *Et: qui* Weber; *dixique*: *dixi* Weber; *asinum et*: *asinum ut* *D-R

<19:26   *for* KJV: *and* D-R>

<19:28   *no better than worthy* D-R/C: *neither . . . ought els, but guiltie* D-R>

<19:32   *of a great age* D-R/C: *verie old* D-R>

19:33   *securus*: *secure* Weber

19:34   *rege in*: *rege* Weber
<19:35   *and* KJV: *or* D-R; *or* KJV: *and* D-R>
19:35   *cantricum*: *cantricarum* S-C; *sit*: *fit* Weber
19:36   *non*: *nec* Weber
<19:37   *let thy servant* KJV: *that I thy seruant may* D-R>
19:37   *mea et sepeliar*: *mea* Weber; *quidquid*: *quod* Weber
19:38   *Dixit itaque*: *dixitque* Weber
19:42   *responderunt omnes viri* B² [Quentin's siglum]: *respondit omnis vir*
        S-C, Weber
<19:42   *any* KJV: omitted in D-R>
<20:1   *whose name was* KJV: *named* D-R>
20:1   *Revertere*: *vir* Weber
20:3   *suam in*: *suam* Weber; *usque ad*: *usque in* S-C
<20:5   *the men of Judah, but* KJV: *Iuda, and* D-R>
20:5   *constituerat rex*: *constituerat* Weber
<20:6   *lest* KJV: *lest perhaps* D-R>
20:8   *lapidem grandem*: *Lapidem Grandem* S-C; *fabrefactus*: *fabricatus* S-C
<20:8   *made in such manner as to come out with the least* D-R/C: *which being*
        made for the purpose could with light D-R>
<20:9   *to kiss* KJV: *as it were kissing* D-R>
20:10   *adposuit, et mortuus est*: *adposuit* Weber
<20:11   *stopping* D-R/C: *when they stoode* D-R>
20:11   *David*: *David pro Ioab*
<20:12   *so* D-R/C: *and* D-R>
20:14   *et*: *et in* Weber; *viri electi*: *electi* Weber
<20:15   *cast up works round the city* KJV (*a banke against* for *works round*):
        compassed the citie with munitions D-R>
<20:16   *and* D-R/C: omitted in D-R>
20:19   *veritatem in*: *veritatem* Weber; *subvertere*: *subruere* Weber
20:22   *abscisum*: *abscissum* S-C
<20:22   *and they cut off the head of Sheba . . . and cast* KJV: *who threw the head*
        of Seba . . . being cut of D-R; *home* D-R/C: *tabernacles* D-R>
<20:24   *recorder* KJV: *register* D-R; literally, *among the registers*>
21:1   *sanginum*: *et sanguinem* Weber
21:2   *erant*: *sunt* Weber
<21:2   *sought to* KJV: *would* D-R>

21:4   *sed contra*: *contra* Weber; *rex ait*: *ait* Weber

21:5   *regi?* *D-R: *regi*: S-C

21:6   *ut*: *et* Weber

21:9   *manus*: *manu* Weber

21:10   *super*: *supra* S-C

21:12   *Iabes Galaad*: *Iabesgalaad* Weber

<21:17   unto him KJV: omitted in D-R>

21:17   *Iam non*: *non* Weber

21:18   *Arafa de genere gigantum*: *Arafa* Weber

21:20   *vir fuit*: *vir* Weber

<21:20   six fingers on each hand and six toes on each foot D-R: six digits on his
         hands and feet literal translation; in all D-R/C [KJV has in num-
         ber]: omitted in D-R>

21:21   *Et blasphemavit*: *blasphemavit* Weber

22:3   *Deus*: *Deus meus* Weber

<22:3   he lifteth me up D-R/C: my lifter vp D-R>

<22:4   who is KJV: omitted in D-R>

22:6   *inferi*: *inferni* S-C

22:8   *est eis*: *est* Weber

22:9   *vorabit*: *voravit* Weber; *incensi*: *succensi* S-C

<22:9   devouring fire D-R/C: fyre . . . shal deuoure D-R>

22:10   *Inclinavit*: *et inclinavit* Weber

<22:13   before KJV: in his presence D-R>

22:14   *excelsus*: *Excelsus* Weber

22:17   *me et*: *me* Weber

22:18   *et ab*: *ab* Weber

<22:18   too strong for me KJV: stronger then I D-R>

22:20   *complacui*: *placuit* Weber

<22:22   departed KJV: done D-R>

22:29   *et* Σ [Weber's siglum]: *et tu, Domine* S-C, *et Domine* Weber

22:32   *Deus*: *deus* Weber

22:33   *accinxit*: *accingit* Weber

22:36   *tua*: *mea* Weber

22:38   *revertar*: *convertar* S-C

22:40   *incurvasti*: *incurvabis* Weber; *sub*: *subtus* S-C

22:43   *confringam*: *conpingam* Weber

<22:43 *beat them as small as* KJV: *destroy them as* D-R; *spread them abroad* KJV: *breake them* D-R>

<22:46 *strangers* KJV: *children alienes* D-R>

22:51 *magnificanti . . . facienti: magnificans . . . faciens* S-C

<22:51 *giving great salvation* D-R/C: *Magnifyng the saluations* D-R>

23:1 *novissima David: novissima quae* Weber; *psalta: psaltes* S-C

<23:1 *said* KJV: omitted in D-R>

<23:7 *must* KJV: *shal* D-R; *but* D-R/C: *and* D-R>

<23:8 *Jesbaham* D-R/C: omitted in D-R>

23:9 *Ahohites: Ahoi* Weber

<23:9 *Dodo* KJV: *his vncle* D-R; *one of the* KJV: *among* D-R>

<23:10 *away* KJV: *vp* D-R; *victory* D-R: literally, *salvation*>

<23:12 *victory* D-R: literally, *salvation*>

23:13 *non et: non* Weber

<23:13 *was* S: *was placed* D-R>

23:15 *O si: si* Weber

<23:17 *mighty men* KJV: *strongest* D-R>

23:18 *elevavit: levavit* Weber

<23:18 *and he* KJV: *it is he that* D-R; *and* KJV: omitted in D-R>

23:20 *in diebus: diebus* Weber

23:21 *Aegyptium* Frede PS-AU mir 2.34 (2192), Frede PS-BREN (33; *Egyptium* for *Aegyptium*): *virum Aegyptium* S-C, Weber

<23:21 *but* KJV: *therfore when* D-R; *and* KJV: omitted in D-R>

<23:24 *was one of* KJV [*was* in roman type]: *among* D-R; *Dodo* KJV: *his vncle* D-R>

23:25 *Harodi: Arari* Weber; *Arori* S-C [1592 edition, according to Weber]: *Harodi* [1593 and 1598 edtions, according to Weber], *Arodi* Weber

<23:25 *Harod* S-C [1593 and 1598 edtions, according to Weber]: *Harori* D-R>

<23:39 *and* KJV: omitted in D-R>

24:3 *populum tuum: populum* Weber

24:6 *silvestria: Silvestria* S-C

24:7 *propter: prope* S-C

<24:10 *what I have done* KJV: *this fact* D-R>

24:11 *propheten: prophetam* S-C

<24:12 *I give thee thy choice* D-R/C: *Choyse is geuen thee* D-R>

24:13 *illi te*: *illi* Weber

<24:13 *seven years of famine shall come to thee* KJV: *famine shal come to thee seuen yeares* D-R; *or* KJV: *or certes* D-R; *answer I shall return* KJV: *word I shal answer* D-R>

24:14 *Artor*: *Coarctor* S-C; *manus Domini*: *manu Domini* Weber; *manus hominum*: *manu hominis* Weber

24:15 *usque*: *usque ad* S-C

24:16 *Domini super*: *Dei super* Weber; *Sufficit. Nunc contine*: *Sufficit nunc, contine* S-C

<24:17 *It is I* D-R/C: omitted in D-R>

<24:18 *said* D-R/C: *sayd to him* D-R>

24:18 *et constitue*: *constitue* Weber

24:21 *terram*: *terra* Weber

<24:21 *bowing with his face* D-R/C: *with his face bowing* D-R; *that* KJV: *and* D-R>

<24:22 *here* KJV [in roman type]: omitted in D-R>

<24:24 *Nay* KJV: *Not so as thou wilt* D-R>

24:25 *propitiatus*: *repropitiatus* Weber

3 KINGS

<1:1 *advanced in years* KJV [*stricken* for *advanced*]: *had manie daies* D-R>

1:2 *suo*: *tuo* Weber

1:5 *currus*: *currum* Weber

1:13 *dicens*: *dicens / quod* Weber; *regnat*: *regnavit* Weber

1:15 *cubiculo*: *cubiculum* S-C

1:17 *tuae*: *tuae quod* *D-R

<1:17 *saying* KJV [in roman type]: *that* D-R>

1:18 *regnat*: *regnavit* Weber

<1:20 *are* KJV [in roman type]: *look* D-R>

1:20: *qui*: *quis* S-C

<1:21 *Otherwise, it shall come to pass* KJV: *And it shal be* D-R; *counted* KJV: omitted in D-R>

1:22 *prophetes*: *propheta* S-C

1:23 *ante conspectum regis*: *in conspectu regis* S-C, *ad regem* *D-R

<1:23 *before* KJV: *to* D-R>

 1:27 *qui*: *quis* S-C

 1:31 *meus David*: *meus rex David* Weber, *meus* *D-R

 1:40 *a clamore*: *ad clamorem* Weber

<1:40 *with the noise* KJV [*sound* for *noise*]: omitted in D-R>

<1:45 *so that* KJV: *and* D-R>

 1:46 *sedet*: *sedit* Weber; *solio*: *solium* S-C

 1:48 *et*: *insuper et* Weber; *et haec*: *et* S-C

<1:48 *said* S-C: *hath thus spoken* D-R; *to sit* KJV: *sitting* D-R>

<1:49 *Then all the guests of Adonijah were afraid, and they all arose* KJV: *They therfore were terrified, and they al arose, that had beene inuited of Adonias* D-R>

<1:52 *head* D-R/C: omitted in D-R>

 2:1 *Adpropinquaverunt*: *adpropinquaverant* Weber

<2:2 *flesh* D-R: literally, *the earth*>

<2:3 *keep the charge* KJV: *obserue the watches* D-R>

 2:3 *et custodias*: *ut custodias* S-C

 2:4 *vias suas*: *viam suam* Weber

<2:6 *let . . . go down* KJV: *bring* D-R>

<2:7 *shew* KJV: *render* D-R; *let them eat* KJV [*be of those that eate* for *eat*]: *they shal eate* D-R>

 2:9 *ut scias quae facies*: *et scies quae facias* Weber; *infernum*: *inferos* S-C

<2:9 *and knowest what to do* KJV: *so that thou knowest what thou shalt doe* D-R>

 2:15 *proposuerat*: *praeposuerat* S-C

<2:15 *preferred* S-C: *purposed* D-R>

 2:16 *deprecor*: *precor* S-C

<2:16 *Say on* KJV: *Speake* D-R>

 2:19 *positusque*: *positus quoque* S-C

<2:20 *put me to confusion* D-R/C: *confound . . . my face* D-R>

 2:20 *Et dixit*: *dixit* Weber; *mi*: *mea* S-C

 2:24 *me super*: *super* Weber

<2:24 *promised* KJV: *spake* D-R>

 2:26 *quidem*: *equidem* S-C

<2:26 *lands* D-R/C [KJV is also plural]: *field* D-R; *worthy* KJV: *a man* D-R>

<2:27   *from being* KJV: *that he should not be* D-R>

2:28   *Salomonem*: *Absalom* Weber

2:30   *Et venit*: *venit* Weber

2:32   *reddet*: *reddat* Weber

<2:35   *in his room* KJV: *for him* D-R>

2:39   *issent*: *essent* Weber

2:40   *requirendos*: *requirendum* S-C

<2:42   *protest* KJV: *testifie* D-R>

2:42   *quem audivi*: *audivi* Weber

<2:45   *established* KJV: *stable* D-R>

3:2   *attamen*: *et tamen* Weber

<3:4   *holocausts* D-R/C: *holocaust* D-R>

3:5   *Apparuit autem*: *apparuit* Weber

<3:6   *shewn . . . to* KJV: *done . . . with* D-R>

3:6   *est*: *et* Weber

3:7   *parvus*: *parvulus* S-C

<3:7   *but a* KJV: *a litle* D-R; *how to go out and come in* KJV: *my going out and coming in* D-R>

3:9   *poterit*: *potest* Weber

<3:9   *Give* KJV: *Thou shalt . . . geue* D-R; *understanding* KJV: *docible* D-R; *which is so numerous* D-R/C: *great in number* D-R>

3:11   *Dominus*: *Deus* Weber; *animas*: *animam* Weber

<3:11   *long life* KJV: *manie dayes* D-R>

<3:16   *that were* KJV: omitted in D-R>

3:18   *autem*: *vero* Weber

3:20   *intempesta*: *intempestae* S-C *nocte* Frede AM off 2.44 115 A, AU s 10.1 153.12, HI ep 74.4 27.4: *noctis silento* S-C, *nocte silentio* Weber

<3:20   *dead child* KJV: *childe that was dead* D-R>

<3:21   *behold—it was* KJV: *he appeared* D-R>

3:22   *ita ut dicis*: *ita* Weber

3:23   *meus autem*: *et filius meus* Weber

3:26   *E contrario*: *contra* Weber; *sit, sed*: *sit* Weber

<3:26   *But the other* KJV: *On the contrarie part she* D-R>

3:27   *Respondit rex et*: *respondens rex* Weber; *est enim*: *est* Weber

4:2   *sacerdos*: *sacerdotis* S-C

4:9   *in Helon et in*: *Helon* Weber

<4:12   *who* D-R/C: omitted in D-R>
4:13   *Avothiair*: *Avoth Iair* S-C
<4:13   *the towns of Jair* KJV: *Auothiair* D-R; *with walls and* KJV: *and walled, which had* D-R>
4:21   *a*: *sicut a* Weber
4:24   *a*: *sicut a* Weber; *usque*: *usque ad* S-C
<5:1   *in the room of* KJV: *for* D-R>
5:2   *autem*: *autem et* Weber
<5:3   *that were* KJV: *imminent* D-R>
5:4   *dedit Dominus*: *dedit* Weber; *et non*: *non* Weber; *satan* *D-R: *Satan* S-C, Weber
5:6   *mihi servi tui*: *mihi* Weber; *petieris*: *praeceperis* Weber; *quomodo*: *quoniam* Weber
5:7   *Dominus Deus*: *Dominus* Weber
<5:8   *and* KJV [in roman type]: omitted in D-R>
<5:9   *and convey them to* KJV: *vnto* D-R; *to furnish food* D-R/C: *that there be meate geuen* D-R>
5:11   *chororum*: *coros* S-C
<5:12   *together* KJV: omitted in D-R>
5:13   *Legitque*: *Elegitque* S-C; *operarios*: *operas* S-C
5:15   *Fueruntque*: *fuerunt itaque* Weber
<5:15   *to hew* D-R/C: *hewers of* D-R>
5:18   *Giblii*: *Biblii* Weber
6:1   *autem* DΦ [Weber's sigla]: *ergo* S-C, *igitur* Weber; *regni*: *regis* Weber; *aedificare coepit domum*: *aedificari coepit domus* S-C
6:7   *lapidibus dedolatis*: *de lapidibus dolatis* S-C
<6:7   *so that there was neither* KJV: *and . . . were not* D-R>
6:15   *lignis cedrinis*: *lignis* Weber
<6:16   *twenty cubits with boards of cedar* KJV: *loftes of cedre timber of twentie cubites* D-R>
6:18   *et iuncturas suas*: *suas et iuncturas* Weber
6:23   *duo*: *duos* S-C
<6:24   *in all* D-R/C: *hauing* D-R>
6:24   *alae unius*: *alae* Weber
6:25   *mensura*: *in mensura* S-C
<6:25   *and the measure* D-R/C: *in like measure* D-R>

6:29   *scalpsit*: *sculpsit* S-C

<6:29   *figures* KJV: *engrauings* D-R; *carvings* D-R/C: *caruing* D-R>

6:32   *scalpsit*: *sculpsit* S-C; *picturas* Π^{G}P^{2}HI: *picturam* S-C, Weber

6:33   *introitu*: *introitum* Weber

<6:34   *so opened with folding leaves* D-R: literally, *holding itself by turns*>

6:35   *scalpsit*: *sculpsit* S-C

6:38   *utensilibus suis*: *utensilibus* Weber; *omni opere suo* S-C, Weber: *omnibus operibus suis* *D-R

<6:38   *which* KJV: *that* D-R; *he was seven years in building it* KJV *he was building it seuen yeares* D-R>

7:2   *saltus*: *Saltus* S-C

7:3   *et quinque* P^{2}H: *quinque* S-C, Weber

<7:5   *upon* D-R/C: *ouer against* D-R>

7:8   *sedebatur*: *sedetur* Weber

<7:8   *he* KJV: *they* D-R>

7:9   *et extrinsecus*: *et intrinsecus* Weber

<7:11   *planks* D-R/C [in italics]: omitted in D-R>

<7:12   *was made* D-R/C [in italics]: omitted in D-R; *planks of* KJV [*beames* for *planks*]: *planed* D-R>

7:16   *fusilia ex*: *fusili* Weber

<7:16   *of molten* KJV: *cast of* D-R>

<7:17   *and* KJV: omitted in D-R>

<7:20   *in* KJV: omitted in D-R>

7:21   *porticum*: *porticu* S-C

<7:22   *so* KJV: *and* D-R>

7:24   *scalptura*: *sculptura* S-C; *scalpturarum histriatarum*: *sculpturarum striatarum* S-C>

<7:24   *of it* KJV: omitted in D-R; *sculptures* S-C: *grauings* D-R>

<7:26   *a handbreadth* KJV: *three ounces* D-R; *or* D-R/C: *and* D-R>

7:27   *aereas*: *aeneas* S-C

7:28   *scalpturae*: *sculpturae* S-C

7:32   *sibi subter*: *subter* Weber; *basi*: *basim* S-C

<7:34   *And* KJV: *For . . . also* D-R>

<7:35   *round compass* KJV: *certayne roundnes* D-R>

7:35–36 *possit*: *posset* S-C; *et scalpturas varias ex semet ipso. Scalpsit*: *variasque sculpturas ex semetipsa. Sculpsit* S-C

<7:36   *trees* KJV: *trees as it were* D-R>

7:37   *scalpturaque*: *sculpturaque* S-C

7:38   *aereos*: *aeneos* S-C

<7:38   *and* KJV [in roman type]: *also* D-R; *in all* D-R/C: *that is* D-R>

7:41   *capitulorum*: *capitellorum* S-C

7:45   *lebetas*: *lebetes* S-C

<7:45   *fine* D-R/C: *bright* D-R>

7:49   *puro*: *primo* Weber

8:1   *congregati sunt*: *congregavit* Weber

8:3   *de*: *ex* Weber

<8:5   *that could not be counted or numbered* KJV [*told* for *counted*]: *without estimation & number* D-R>

8:8   *sanctuarium*: *in sanctuario* *D-R

<8:8   *the* KJV: *and the* D-R; *but* D-R/C: *and* D-R>

8:9   *erat*: *est* Weber

<8:11   *to* KJV: *and* D-R>

<8:13   *to be* D-R/C: omitted in D-R>

8:15   *ait Salomon*: *ait* Weber

<8:16   *that* KJV: *and* D-R>

<8:18   *in having* D-R/C: *casting* D-R>

8:19   *mihi domum*: *domum* Weber

<8:20   *in the room of* KJV: *for* D-R>

8:20   *Dominus*: *dominus* S-C

8:24   *ut*: *ut et* Weber

<8:25   *in my sight* KJV: *before me* D-R; *that* KJV: *if* D-R>

8:26   *Domine Deus*: *Deus* Weber

<8:27   *less* KJV: *more* D-R>

8:29   *quam orat ad*: *qua orat* Weber

<8:31   *any* KJV: *a* D-R; *an* KJV: *any* D-R>

<8:32   *hear thou . . . do, and judge* KJV: *thou shalt heare . . . shalt doe, and iudge* D-R>

<8:34   *bring them back* KJV: *thou shalt reduce* D-R>

8:37   *aut aurugo aut lucusta vel*: *aurugo lucusta* Weber; *inimicus*: *et inimicus* Weber

<8:37   *if* KJV: *and* D-R>

8:39   *audies*: *exaudies* S-C

<8:39   *hear thou . . . forgive . . . do so* KJV: *thou shalt heare . . . shalt be merciful . . . shalt so do* D-R>

<8:43   *hear thou . . . do* KJV: *thou shalt heare . . . shalt doe* D-R>

  8:45   *orationes*: *orationem* Weber

<8:45   *hear thou . . . do* KJV (*mainteine* for *do*): *thou shalt heare . . . shalt doe* D-R>

<8:46   *so that* KJV: *and* D-R>

  8:46   *captivi*: *capti* Weber

<8:48   *have* D-R/C [KJV also has past tense]: *shal be* D-R>

  8:48   *fuerint*: *sunt* Weber

  8:49   *orationes*: *orationem* Weber; *preces eorum*: *preces* Weber

<8:49–50 *hear thou . . . do . . . forgive* KJV (*mainteine* for *do*): *thou shalt heare . . . shalt doe . . . shalt be merciful* D-R>

<8:52   *to* KJV: *and thou* D-R>

  8:54   *ad*: *in* S-C

  8:58   *caerimonias eius*: *caerimonias* D-R

  8:59   *ut sciant*: *et sciant* S-C

  8:62   *Domino*: *domino* S-C

  8:63   *et ovium*: *ovium* Weber

  8:64   *poterat holocaustum*: *poterat holocausta* Weber

<8:64   *to* KJV: *and could not* D-R>

<9:1   *was pleased* KJV: *would* D-R>

  9:3   *quam*: *qua* S-C

<9:5   *fail . . . upon* KJV: *be taken away from* D-R>

  9:6   *meas quas*: *quas* Weber

  9:9   *coluerunt eos*: *coluerunt* Weber

  9:12   *Egressusque*: *Et egressus* S-C

  9:14   *Regem Salomonem*: *regem* Weber

  9:16   *dote*: *dotem* S-C

<9:21   *such as* D-R/C: *whom* D-R>

  9:21   *ad*: *in* S-C

  9:24   *ei Salomon*: *ei* Weber

  9:26   *Ailath*: *Ahilam* Weber

<9:27   *that had knowledge* KJV: *& skilful* D-R>

<9:28   *And they* KJV: *Who when* D-R; *and* KJV: omitted in D-R>

10:2 *multo*: *multo cum* S-C; *et camelis* Ω^M [Quntin's siglum]: *camelis* S-C,
Weber; *Regem Salomonem*: *Salomonem* Weber

<10:3 *to him* D-R/C: omitted in D-R; *was* D-R/C: *could be* D-R>

10:5 *ordines*: *ordinem* Weber; *Domini*: *domini* S-C

<10:5 *order* S?: *orders* D-R; *in her* KJV: omitted in D-R>

<10:7 *exceed* KJV: *greater is* D-R [before *thy wisdom*]>

10:8 *qui*: *hii qui* Weber

10:9 *placuisti*: *complacuisti* S-C

<10:10 *of spices a very great store* KJV: *spices exceeding much* D-R; *abundance of
spices* KJV: *so much spice* D-R>

10:15 *afferebant*: *offerebant* Weber

<10:15 *they that sold by retail* D-R/C: *al that sold light wares* D-R>

10:16 *Salomon* Gryson 93 E 500: *rex Salomon* S-C, Weber; *purissimo*: *puro*
Weber

<10:17 *fine* D-R/C: *tried* D-R>

10:17 *ea*: *eas* S-C; *silvae*: *saltus* S-C

<10:18 *finest* KJV (*best*): *exceeding yellow* D-R>

10:21 *vasa de*: *vasa* S-C

<10:21 *nor was any account made of it* KJV (*it was nothing accounted of*): *nei-
ther was it thought of any price* D-R>

10:22 *et dentes; dentes* Weber

<10:23 *exceeded* KJV: *was magnified aboue* D-R>

<10:25 *armour and spices* KJV: *instrumentes for warre, spices also* D-R>

10:27 *quanta*: *quanta et* S-C

<10:27 *cedars to be as common as* KJV (without *common as*); *of ceder trees he
caused such a multitude, as if it were* D-R>

11:1 *amavit*: *adamavit* S-C

<11:1 *besides the daughter* KJVn: *the daughter also* D-R>

<11:2 *and* D-R/C: omitted in D-R>

11:2 *certissimo*: *certissime* S-C

<11:6 *did not fully follow* KJV (*went not fully*): *accomplished not to folow* D-R>

11:6 *sicut David*: *sicut* Weber

11:10 *praeceperat ei* Ω^J* [Quentin's siglum]: *praeceperat* S-C, Weber

<11:10 *but* KJV: *&* D-R>

<11:11 *thou hast done this* D-R: literally, *you had this in you*>

<11:12 *but* KJV [in roman type in KJV]: omitted in D-R>

<11:14 *in* KJV: *who was in* D-R>

11:15 *sepeliendos*: *sepeliendum* S-C

<11:16 *with* KJV: *and* D-R>

11:16 *interimeret*: *interimerent* Weber

<11:17 *then* [first time] D-R/C: omitted in D-R; *certain* KJV: omitted in D-R; *then* [second time] KJV (*yet*): omitted in D-R>

<11:18 *And they . . . and* KJV: *And when they* D-R>

<11:22 *Why* D-R/C: *For* D-R>

11:22 *te ut*: *ut* Weber

<11:24 *of Zobah* KJV [in italics in D-R/C and roman type in KJV]: omitted in D-R>

11:30 *opertus*: *coopertus* S-C

11:33 *dereliquerit*: *dereliquerint* Weber; *adoraverit*: *adoraverint* Weber; *Astarthen*: *Astharoth* Weber; *Moloch*: *Melchom* Weber; *ambulaverit*: *ambulaverint* Weber; *faceret*: *facerent* Weber

<11:33 *to keep* KJV [in roman type in KJV and italics in D-R/C]: omitted in D-R>

11:38 *David domum*: *David* Weber

11:41 *Verborum Dierum*: *verborum* Weber

12:2 *At*: *At vero* S-C

12:6 *adhuc viveret*: *adviveret* Weber; *populo huic*: *populo* Weber

12:10 *loquere*: *loqueris* S-C; *locuti*: *locutis* S-C [typographical error]

<12:10 *shalt thou speak* S-C: *speake* D-R; *Thou shalt* D-R/C: *Thus shalt thou* D-R>

12:11 *caedam vos*: *caedam* Weber

12:14 *ego autem caedam vos*: *et ego caedam* Weber

12:16 *Vade in*: *in* Weber

12:18 *tributa*: *tributum* Weber

12:20 *regem*: *eum regem* S-C

12:21 *virorum*: *virorum et* Weber; *pugnaret*: *pugnarent* S-C; *reduceret*: *reducerent* S-C

<12:24 *thing is from me* KJV: *word is done by me* D-C>

12:28 *ascendere in*: *ascendere* Weber

<12:32 *feast* KJV: *solemne day* D-R>

12:32 *celebrabatur*: *celebratur* Weber; *fuerat*: *erat* Weber

<12:33 *up to* KJVn: *vpon* D-R>

13:3 *scindetur, et effundetur: scinditur et effunditur* Weber

13:5 *effusus: effusus est* S-C

<13:5 *given* KJV: *told* D-R>

13:6 *Oravitque: oravit* Weber

<13:7 *make* D-R/C: *geue* D-R>

<13:9 *me* D-R/C: omitted in D-R; *same* KJV: omitted in D-R>

13:11 *venerunt filii sui et narraverunt: venit filius suus / et narravit* Weber; *regem: regem / et* Weber

13:15 *Dixitque: dixit* Weber

<13:16 *must* KJV (*may*): *can* D-R>

13:18 *ut: et* Weber

13:21 *non oboediens: inoboediens* Weber

<13:21 *to* D-R/C: *to the mouth of* D-R>

13:23 *asinum suum: asinum* Weber

<13:28 *the* D-R/C: *his* D-R>

13:29 *plangerent: plangeret* S-C

<13:29 *to* S-C: *that they might* D-R>

<13:30 *saying* KJV [in roman type in KJV and in italics in D-R/C]: omitted in D-R>

13:30 *Heu! Heu, mi: heu* Weber

<14:3 *with thee* KJV: *in thy hand* D-R>

14:3 *crustula: crustulam* S-C; *ipse enim: ipse* Weber

14:7 *principem* PL 69 356B: *ducem* S-C, Weber

<14:8 *away from* KJV: *of* D-R>

14:9 *malum* Ω^S [Quentin's siglum]: *mala* S-C, *male* Weber

<14:10 *all be* D-R: literally would be omitted>

14:13 *inferetur: infertur* Weber; *a Domnio, Deo: ad Dominum Deum* Weber

14:14 *percutiet: percutiat* Weber

14:15 *Dominus Deus: Dominus* Weber; *Flumen: flumen* S-C

<14:15 *river* S-C: *River* D-R>

14:21 *decem: et decem* Weber; *annis: annos* S-C

<14:21 *and* KJV: omitted in D-R>

14:22 *peccaverunt: peccaverant* Weber

<14:24 *according to* KJV: omitted in D-R>

<14:26 *as* D-R/C: omitted in D-R>

14:27   *manum*: *manu* Weber

14:29   *omnia*: *omnium* Weber; *Verborum*: *sermonum* S-C

14:31   *Dormivitque*: *dormivit itaque* Weber

15:2   *Abessalom*: *Absalom* Weber

15:4   *statueret*: *staret* Weber

<15:5   *any thing*: *al thinges* D-R>

15:6   *et*: *et inter* Weber

15:7   *Hieroboam* R [Weber's siglum]: *inter Hieroboam* S-C, Weber

15:10   *et uno*: *uno* Weber; *Abessalom*: *Absalom* Weber

15:13   *luco* after Frede 6.1.13 (*cultura luci*): *luco eius* S-C, Weber

<15:13   *to him* S-C?: omitted in D-R; *by* KJV: *in* D-R>

15:14   *Domino*: *Deo* Weber

15:17   *posset*: *possit* Weber

15:18   *dedit*: *et dedit* S-C; *manus*: *manu* Weber

<15:19   *thy* S: *that thou hast* D-R; *that* KJV: *and* D-R>

<15:20   *Abel-beth-maacah* KJV: *Abeldomum of Maacha* D-R>

15:22   *Iudam, dicens*: *Iudam* Weber: *de Rama*: *Rama* Weber

15:29   *manu servi sui*: *manu* *D-R

15:34   *viis* R [Weber's siglum]: *via* S-C, Weber>

16:2   *te ducem*: *ducem* Weber

<16:2   *prince* KJV: *duke* D-R; *provoke me to anger* KJV: *anger* D-R>

<16:7   *provoke him to anger* KJV: *anger* D-R>

16:7   *eum, hoc est, Hieu, filium Anani, prophetam*: *eum* Weber

16:11   *eo*: *ea* S-C; *mingentem*: *unum qui mingat* *D-R

<16:11   *all* D-R/C: omitted in D-R>

16:15   *et septimo*: *septimo* S-C

16:18   *se cum domo regia*: *secum domum regiam* Weber

16:24   *eum*: *eam* Weber; *Samariae*: *Samariam* S-C

<16:24   *Samaria, after the name of Shemer, the owner of the hill* KJV: *by the name of Semer the lord of the mount of Samaria* D-R>

16:25   *fuerunt*: *fuerant* Weber

<16:26   *provoke . . . to anger* KJV: *anger* D-R>

16:27   *proelia* E* [Quentin's siglum]: *proelia eius* S-C, Weber; *fecit* C [Weber's siglum]: *gessit* S-C, Weber

<16:27   *fought* S-C: *made* D-R>

<16:33   *did more to provoke* KJV: *added in his worke, prouoking* D-R>

16:33   *fuerunt*: *fuerant* Weber

<17:3 *by* KJV: *in* D-R>

<17:5 *dwelt by* KJV: *sate in* D-R>

17:6 *ei panem*: *panem* Weber

<17:6 *and* KJV: *in like maner* D-R>

17:7 *autem aliquantos* Ω^{S}ae [Quentin's sigla]: *autem* S-C, Weber

<17:7 *some time* D-R/C: *certayne daies* D-R>

<17:9 *dwell* KJV: *thou shal tarie* D-R>

17:10 *abiit in*: *abiit* Weber: *Sareptham*: *Sarephta* S-C; *dixitque ei*: *dixitque* Weber

<17:12 *handful* KJV: *so much . . . as a hand can hold* D-R>

17:12 *illud*: *illum* S-C

17:14 *enim* θ^M [Quentin's siglum]: *autem* S-C, Weber

17:17 *haec*: *verba haec* Weber; *familiae*: *familias* S-C; *fortis nimis*: *fortissimus* S-C

17:19 *eam Helias*: *eam* Weber

17:21 *oro*: *obsecro* S-C

17:22 *Et exaudivit*: *exaudivit* Weber

18:4 *quinquagenos et quinquagenos*: *quinquagenos* Weber

<18:5 *to see if* D-R/C: *if perhaps* D-R; *that* KJV: *and* D-R>

18:8 *et dic*: *dic* Weber

18:9 *tradis*: *trades* Weber

<18:9 *wouldst deliver* KJV: *deliuerest* D-R>

18:10 *tuus, non*: *tuus, quia non* S-C

18:12 *et ingressus*: *ingressus* Weber; *inveniens te*: *inveniet te et* Weber

<18:13 *how* KJV: *that* D-R>

18:15 *Et dixit*: *dixit* Weber

18:18 *Non ego*: *non* Weber

<18:19 *unto* KJV: *in* D-R>

<18:20 *unto* KJV: *in* D-R>

18:23 *sibi bovem*: *bovem* Weber; *ignemque*: *ignem autem* S-C

18:24 *mei, et Deus*: *et deus* Weber

<18:26 *And . . . and* KJV: *when* D-R; *But* KJV: *And* D-R>

18:27 *Deus* *D-R: *deus* S-C, Weber

<18:27 *perhaps* KJV (*peraduenture*): *at the least* D-R; *and* KJV: *that he* D-R>

<18:29 *of offering* KJV: *when they vsed to offer* D-R; *regard* KJV: *attend* D-R>

18:32 *lapidibus*: *de lapidibus* S-C

<18:32 *of the breadth of* D-R/C: *as it were by* D-R>

18:34 *fecissent*: *fecissent et* Weber; *Feceruntque*: *feceruntque et* Weber

18:35 *circa*: *circum* S-C

18:36 *et Isaac*: *Isaac* Weber

18:40 *fugiat*: *effugiat* S-C; *conprehendissent*: *apprehendissent* S-C

<18:40 *down* KJV: omitted in D-R>

18:42 *verticem*: *vertice* Weber

<18:43 *And . . . and* KJV: *when . . . he* D-R>

18:44 *Iunge currum tuum*: *iunge* Weber

18:45 *verteret*: *verterent* Weber

<18:45 *with* KJV: *and* D-R>

<19:3 *he had a mind* D-R/C: *his wil caried him* D-R>

19:4 *viam*: *via* Weber

19:5 *angelus Domini*: *angelus* Weber; *et comede*: *comede* Weber

<19:9 *came* KJV [in roman type in KJV and italics in D-R/C]: omitted in D-R>

19:10 *tuum*: *Domini* Weber; *et prophetas*: *prophetas* S-C; *et derelictus*: *derelictus* S-C

<19:10 *they* S-C: *& . . . they* D-R>

19:14 *et prophetas*: *prophetas* S-C; *et derelictus*: *derelictus* S-C

<19:14 Verse begins here in S-C: verse begins before previous *And* in D-R; *they* S-C: *and . . . they* D-R>

19:15 *perveneris illuc*: *perveneris* Weber

<19:16 *of* KJV: *which is of* D-R; *to be prophet in thy room* KJV: *prophet for thee* D-R>

19:17 *et quicumque*: *et qui* Weber

<19:17 *shall be slain by Jehu* D-R/C: *him Iehu shal kil* D-R; *shall be slain by Elisha* D-R/C: *him shal Eliseus kil* D-R>

19:18 *virorum quorum genua*: *universorum genua quae* Weber; *ante Baal*: *Baal* Weber; *manus*: *manum* Weber

19:19 *inde Helias*: *inde* Weber; *arantem*: *arantem in* S-C; *iugis boum arantibus*: *arantibus* Weber

<19:19 *up* D-R/C: omitted in D-R>

19:20 *oro te*: *oro* Weber

20:1 *et duos*: *duos* S-C

<20:6 *houses* KJV: *house* D-R>

20:9   *in initio: initio* Weber

20:12 *audisset Banadad: audisset* Weber

20:13 *ait ei: ait* Weber; *nimiam?* *D-R: *nimiam;* S-C

20:15 *duum: duorum* S-C

20:18 *Et: at* Weber

20:20 *venerat: veniebat* S-C; *equitibus suis: equitibus* Weber

20:21 *Nec non: nec non et* Weber

20:24 *tuo: suo* Weber

<20:26 *Wherefore* D-R/C *at the return of the year* KJV: *Therfore after a yeare was passed* D-R>

20:27 *profecti sunt* $\Lambda^{H_2}\Pi^F E\theta^{HS}KI\Omega^J$ [Quentin's sigla]: *profecti* S-C, Weber; *metati sunt: metati* Weber

20:28 *Deus* [both times] *D-R: *deus* S-C, Weber

20:29 *Dirigebantque: dirigebant* Weber

<20:29 *both* D-R/C: *these, and they* D-R>

20:32 *funes in capitibus: funiculos in capitibus suis* S-C; *dixerunt ei: dixerunt* Weber

<20:32 *let me have my life* D-R/C: *Let my soule liue* D-R>

20:33 *eum ad me: eum* Weber

20:37 *inveniens: conveniens* Weber

<20:38 *disguised himself by sprinkling dust on his face and his eyes* KJV (*disguised himselfe with ashes vpon his face*): *with sprinkling of dust changed his face and his eies* D-R>

20:39 *transiret: transisset* S-C

20:43 *venit in: venit* Weber

21:1   *tempore illo vinea: vinea* Weber

21:4   *dabo: do* Weber

<21:4   *would eat no* KJV: *did not eate* D-R>

21:6   *vineam meliorem: vineam* Weber; *Non dabo: non do* Weber

<21:7   *good cheer* D-R: literally, *contented mind*>

21:8   *optimates: ad optimates* Weber

21:10 *quod benedixit* Frede AU c men 24 500.8, JUL-T ars 1.204 (*benedixerit* for *benedixit*): *benedixit* S-C, Weber

<21:10 *blasphemed* D-Rn: *blessed* D-R; *then* KJV: omitted in D-R>

<21:13 *saying* KJV: omitted in D-R; *blasphemed* D-Rn at 21:10: *blessed* D-R>

21:13   *Deo et regi*: *Deum et regem* S-C

21:15   *Surge, et*: *surge* Weber

<21:15   *for* KJV: *taking* D-R>

21:20   *inimicum tibi*: *inimice mee* Weber

21:25   *talis ut*: *talis sicut* S-C

21:26   *effectus*: *factus* S-C

21:27   *vestimenta sua*: *vestem suam* Weber; *ambulabat*: *ambulavit* S-C

22:5   *mei*: *mei et* Weber

22:8   *possimus*: *possumus* S-C

22:9   *adducere*: *et adduce* *D-R

<22:12   *prosper, for* KJV: *goe prosperousely, &* D-R>

22:12   *manus*: *manu* Weber

22:13   *ergo*: *ergo et* S-C

<22:15   *prosper* KJV: *goe prosperousely* D-R>

22:15   *manus*: *manu* Weber

22:30   *Dixit itaque*: *dixitque* Weber; *habitum suum*: *habitum* Weber

22:31   *aut* C [Quentin's siglum]: *et* S-C, Weber

22:34   *Vir*: *unus* Weber

<22:34   *at a venture* KJV: *the arrow at al aduenture* D-R, literally, *an arrow at random*>

22:35   *vesperi*: *vespere* S-C

<22:35   *blood ran out of the wound* KJV: *bloud of the wounde ranne* D-R>

22:36   *personuit*: *insonuit* S-C

22:37   *est in*: *est* Weber

22:38   *currum eius*: *currum* Weber

22:39   *eburneae*: *eburnea* S-C; *Verborum*: *sermonum* S-C

22:41   *Iosaphat vero*: *Iosaphat* Weber

22:42   *et quinque annos*: *quinque annis* S-C

22:43   *erat*: *est* Weber

<22:49   *but* KJV: *and* D-R>

22:51   *Dormivitque Iosaphat*: *dormivitque* Weber

4 Kings

<1:1   *the death of Ahab* KJV: *Achab was dead* D-R>

<1:2   *shall* KJV: *may* D-R>

1:3　*dicens, "Surge, et*: *surge* Weber

<1:3　*say* KJV: *thou shal say* D-R>

1:6　*Ite, et*: *ite* Weber

<1:6　*to* D-R/C: *to consult* D-R>

1:7　*habitus est vir ille*: *habitu est vir* Weber

<1:7　*manner of man was he* KJV [*was he* in roman type]: *shape and habite*
　　　had that man D-R>

1:8　*accinctus*: *accinctis* Weber

<1:8　*with* D-R/C: *and girded . . . with* D-R>

1:10　*e* [both times]: *de* S-C

1:11　*Rursumque*: *rursum* Weber

<1:11　*and* D-R/C: omitted in D-R>

1:12　*e* [both times]: *de* S-C; *ergo ignis*: *ergo ignis Dei* Weber

<1:13　*fell upon* KJV: *bowed* D-R>

1:13　*et animas*: *et animam* Weber

<1:14　*spare* D-R/C: *haue mercie on* D-R>

1:16　*possis*: *posses* S-C

2:2　*usque*: *usque in* S-C

2:3　*in Bethel*: *Bethel* Weber; *tollet*: *tollat* Weber

2:4　*Hierichum*: *Iericho* S-C

2:6　*usque ad*: *ad* Weber

2:7　*eos qui*: *qui* Weber

<2:7　*and stood in sight* KJVn: *who also stood ouer agaynst* D-R>

2:10　*tollar a te, erit tibi*: *tollor a te erit* Weber

<2:10　*am* KJV [in roman type]: *shal be* D-R>

<2:11　*walking and talking* D-R/C: *and going talked* D-R>

<2:13　*from* KJV: *to* D-R>

<2:14　*from* KJV: *to* D-R>

2:14　*aquas, et non sunt divisae*: *aquas* Weber

<2:15　*at* S: *that were in* D-R>

2:15　*de contra*: *econtra* S-C

2:16　*possint*: *possunt* S-C; *eum in*: *in* Weber; *uno*: *unum* S-C; *unam*: *una*
　　　Weber

<2:16　*some* [both times] KJV: *one of the* D-R>

<2:17　*But* D-R/C: *And* D-R; *and . . . but* KJV: *Who when* D-R>

<2:18　*for* KJV: *but* D-R>

2:18   *mittere*: *ire* Weber

2:20   *Quod*: *qui* Weber

2:22   *ad*: *in* S-C

2:23   *inde in*: *inde* Weber

2:24   *cum*: *cum se* Weber

2:25   *est in*: *est* Weber

3:7   *eum*: *Moab* Weber; *et equi*: *equi* Weber

3:10   *Eheu! Eheu! Eheu*: *Heu, heu, heu* S-C; *manus*: *manu* Weber

3:12   *rex Iuda, et*: *et* Weber

3:13   *manus*: *manu* Weber

3:14   *ad eum Heliseus*: *Heliseus* Weber; *ne*: *non* S-C

<3:16   *full of ditches* KJV: *diches and diches* D-R>

<3:17   *yet* KJV: omitted in D-R>

3:18   *manus vestras*: *manu vestra* Weber

<3:20   *that* KJV: *and* D-R>

3:22   *contra*: *e contra* S-C

<3:24   *who* D-R/C: *but they* D-R; *And they being conquerors* D-R/C: *They therfore that had ouercome* D-R>

3:26   *inrumperet*: *inrumperent* S-C

<3:26   *but* KJV: *and* D-R>

4:2   *unguear*: *ungar* S-C

4:4   *ostium tuum*: *ostium* Weber

<4:6   *no more* KJV: *none* D-R>

4:8   *devertebat*: *divertebat* S-C

<4:8   *there was a day when* KJVn: *there came a certayne day* D-R; *her house* D-R/C: *her* D-R>

4:10   *ergo ei*: *ergo* Weber

4:11   *devertit*: *divertit* S-C

<4:11   *there was* D-R/C: *there came* D-R; *when* D-R/C: *and* D-R>

4:12   *Sunamitin*: *Sunamitidem* S-C

4:13   *puerum suum*: *puerum* Weber

4:15   *ante*: *ad* Weber

4:17   *quam*: *qua* S-C

4:18   *cum esset quaedam dies et*: *quadam die cum* *D-R

4:19   *doleo; caput meum doleo*: *caput meum* Weber

4:20   *adduxisset*: *duxisset* S-C

<4:20 *then* KJV [in roman type]: omitted in D-R>

  4:23 *Vadam*: *vale* Weber

  4:24 *ne mihi*: *ne* *D-R

  4:25 *de contra*: *e contra* S-C

<4:25 *coming towards* S: *ouer against him* D-R>

  4:27 *montem*: *monte* Weber; *a me*: *me* Weber

<4:29 *any* KJV: *a* D-R; *lay* KJV: *thou shalt put* D-R>

  4:31 *eos*: *ante eos* S-C

  4:33 *et super*: *et* Weber

  4:35 *huc et*: *huc atque* S-C

  4:36 *At*: *Et* Weber; *Sunamitin*: *Sunamitidem* S-C

  4:40 *exclamaverunt*: *clamaverunt* S-C

  4:41 *Cumque tulissent*: *et* Weber; *ut comedant*: *et comedat* Weber

<4:41 *some* D-R/C: omitted in D-R; *now no* S: *no more* D-R>

  4:43 *coram centum*: *centum* Weber

<5:5 *And he* KJV: *Who when* D-R>

<5:6 *and* KJV: *he* D-R>

<5:7 *how* KJV: *that* D-R>

  5:13 *et si*: *si* Weber

<5:13 *if* KJV [in roman type in KJV]: *& if* D-R; *what* D-R/C: *wheras*
      D-R>

<5:14 *Then* KJV: omitted in D-R>

  5:15 *sit alius*: *sit* Weber

<5:15 *take* KJV: *to take* D-R>

<5:16 *pressed him he still refused* D-R/C: *would haue forced him, he did in no-*
      wise agree D-R>

<5:17 *from hence* D-R/C: omitted in D-R>

  5:18 *ingredietur*: *ingreditur* Weber; *illo*: *illi* S-C [probably typographical
      error]; *eo*: *me* Weber

<5:18 *goeth* KJV: *shal goe* D-R>

<5:19 *spring* D-R: literally, *choice*>

<5:20 *But* KJV: *And* D-R; *in not receiving* KJV: *that he tooke not* D-R>

  5:22 *me ad te*: *me* Weber

<5:23 *two changes of garments* KJV: *the duble rayment* D-R>

<5:24 *and* D-R/C: omitted in D-R; *hands* S: *hand* D-R>

  5:26 *vineta*: *vineas* S-C

5:27　　*in*: *usque in* S-C

<5:27　　*as white as* KJV [in roman type]: *as it were* D-R>

<6:1　　*with thee is too* KJV: *before thee is* D-R>

6:5　　*materiem*: *materiam* S-C; *Eheu! Eheu! Eheu*: *Heu, heu, heu* S-C

<6:5　　*some* D-R/C: omitted in D-R; *for* KJV: omitted in D-R; *was bor-rowed* KJV: *I did borow* D-R>

6:9　　*locum illum*: *loco illo* Weber

6:10　　*Misit itaque*: *misit* Wber

6:11　　*indicatis*: *indicastis* Weber

6:13　　*Dixitque*: *dixit* Weber

<6:14　　*and . . . and* KJV: *who when . . . they* D-R>

6:15　　*est viditque*: *vidit* S-C; *Eheu! Eheu! Eheu*: *Heu, heu, heu* S-C; *eheu eheu* Weber

<6:17　　*And . . . and* KJV: *And when . . . he* D-R>

6:18　　*oravit ad*: *oravit* Weber

<6:18　　*with blindness* KJV: *that they saw not* D-R>

6:20　　*Samariam*: *Samaria* Weber

6:22　　*sed pone*: *pone* Weber

<6:25　　*did the siege continue* D-R/C: *it was besieged* S-R>

6:26　　*mulier quaedam*: *mulier* Weber

6:27　　*salvet*: *salvat* S-C

<6:27　　*If the Lord doth not save* KJV [*If* in italics in D-R/C]: *No, our Lord saue* D-R; *What aileth thee* D-R: literally, *What do you want for yourself*>

6:30　　*per*: *super* Weber

<6:30　　*upon* KJV: omitted in D-R>

6:31　　*ait rex*: *ait* Weber

6:33　　*Adhuc*: *et adhuc* Weber

<7:1　　*about* KJV: *At* D-R>

<7:7　　*Wherefore* KJV: *therfor* D-R; *desiring to save their lives* D-R/C: *des-rous to saue their liues only* D-R>

<7:10　　*So . . . and* KJV: *And when* D-R/C>

7:10　　*hominem*: *hominum* Weber

7:12　　*fame*: *fame magna* *D-R; *viventes*: *vivos* S-C

<7:13　　*let us send and see* KJV: *sending, we may trie* D-R>

7:14　　*in*: *ad* Weber; *Ite, et*: *ite* Weber

<7:15 *in their fright* KJV (*haste* for *fright*): *when they were amased* D-R>
<7:16 *was sold for* KJV [*sold* in roman type in KJV]: *became at* D-R>
  7:17 *incubuerat*: *incumbebat* S-C; *introitu portae*: *introitu* Weber
  7:20 *erat*: *fuerat* S-C
<8:1 *and* KJV: omitted in D-R>
  8:3 *et pro*: *et* Weber
<8:8 *recover* KJV: *escape* D-R>
<8:9 *taking* KJV (*and tooke*): *hauing* D-R>
  8:12 *dixit*: *respondit* Weber
  8:14 *Recipies*: *recipiet* Weber
<8:15 *on the next day* KJV (*morrow* for *next day*): *when the next day was come*
       D-R>
  8:15 *stragulum*: *sagulum* Weber; *aquam*: *aqua* Weber
  8:18 *coram Domino*: *in conspectu Domini* S-C
  8:21 *omnes*: *omnis* S-C
<8:22 *the same* KJV: *that* D-R>
  8:29 *Rama*: *Ramoth* S-C; *aegrotabat ibi*: *aegrotabat* Weber
  9:2 *in interius*: *interius* Weber
  9:4 *in Ramoth*: *Ramoth* Weber
  9:5 *est illuc*: *est* Weber; *ad te, O*: *ad te* Weber
  9:7 *et ulciscar*: *ut ulciscar* Weber
<9:15 *or flee* KJV (*nor escape*): *fugitiue* D-R>
  9:18 *Pacatane*: *pacata* Weber; *Dixitque*: *dixitque ei* Weber
<9:18 *in* D-R/C: *that was gotten vp into* D-R; *behind* KJV: omitted in D-R;
       And KJV: *also* D-R; *but* KJV: *&* D-R>
  9:19 *Num*: *Numquid* S-C
<9:20 *but* D-R/C: *&* D-R; *drives furiously* KJV: *goeth amayne* D-R>
<9:21 *met* KJV: *found* D-R>
<9:25 *his* KJV: omitted in D-R; *and* KJV [in roman type]: omitted in
       D-R>
  9:26 *et proice*: *proice* Weber; *agrum*: *agro* Weber
  9:27 *Et percusserunt eum in*: *in* Weber
  9:28 *tulerunt in*: *tulerunt* Weber; *sepelieruntque*: *sepelieruntque eum* S-C
  9:29 *regnavit*: *rege* Weber
  9:30 *venitque Hieu in*: *venit Hieu* Weber
  9:33 *ungulae*: *ungulae qui* Weber

9:34   *ingressus: introgressus* S-C; *ut: et* Weber; *biberetque: bibissetque* Weber;
        Ite, et: ite Weber

<9:34   *see after* S: *see* D-R>

<9:37   *same* D-R: literally would be omitted>

<10:1   *them that brought up Ahab's children* D-R: literally, *Ahab's tutors*>

<10:3   *most* D-R/C: omitted in D-R>

10:5   *praepositi: praepositus* Weber; *praefecti: praefectus* Weber; *nobis regem:*
        regem Weber; *Quodcumque tibi placet: quaecumque tibi placent* S-C

<10:6   *by* KJV: omitted in D-R>

<10:8   *said* KJV: *answered* D-R>

10:8   *ea in* Σ [Weber's siglum]: *ea ad* S-C; *ea* Weber

<10:10   *any* D-R/C: omitted in D-R>

10:12   *camaram: Cameram* S-C; *Camaram* Weber

<10:13   *met with* KJV: *found* D-R>

10:13   *Qui: at illi* Weber

<10:14   *And they . . . and* KJV: *Who when* D-R>

10:14   *camaram: Cameram* S-C; *Camaram* Weber

10:15   *da mihi* Ψ[D]*re* [Quentin's sigla]: *da* S-C, Weber; *dedit ei: dedit* Weber;
        currum: curru Weber

10:16   *in curru: currui* Weber

<10:16   *So he made him ride* KJV: *And being sette* D-R>

<10:19   *wanting* KJV: *but that he come* D-R; *to offer* KJV [in roman type; *doe*
        for *offer*]: omitted in D-R>

10:20   *Et dixit: dixit* Weber

<10:20   *Proclaim* KJV: *Sanctifie* D-R>

10:23   *ait: et ait* Weber

<10:23   *that there be not* KJV: *lest perhaps there be* D-R>

<10:24   *If any* KJV: *Whosoeuer* D-R; *he that letteth him go* KJV: omitted in
        D-R; *shall answer life for life* D-R/C: *his life shal be for the life of him*
        D-R>

10:25   *autem: ergo* Weber; *in ore: ore* Weber

<10:25   *saying* D-R/C: omitted in D-R>

10:27   *ad: in* S-C

10:29   *fecerat: fecit* S-C

10:30   *fecisti: egisti* S-C

<10:30 *according to* KJV: omitted in D-R>

<10:36 *time . . . was* KJV [*was* in roman type]: *dayes . . . be* D-R>

11:2 *triclinio*: *cubiculo* *D-R

11:6 *excubitum* [both times]: *excubias* S-C

11:7 *circum*: *circa* S-C

11:9 *e sabbato*: *sabbato* S-C

<11:11 *hands* D-R/C: *hand* D-R>

<11:12 *their hands* KJV: *with the hand* D-R>

11:13 *Audivit autem*: *audivit* Weber

11:14 *propter*: *prope* S-C

11:15 *consepta*: *septa* S-C

12:1 *et quadraginta*: *quadraginta* Weber

12:3 *adhuc enim*: *adhuc* Weber

<12:4 *of their own free heart* D-R: literally, *according to their heart's decision*>

12:7 *instauratis*: *instaurastis* Weber

<12:9 *bored* KJV: *opened* D-R>

<12:11 *hands* KJV: *hand* D-R>

<12:12 *and wheresoever* D-R/C [*and* in italics]: *in al thinges, which* D-R>

12:13 *et omne*: *omne* S-C

<12:13 *or* [all four times] D-R/C: *and* D-R; *any* KJV: *euerie* D-R>

<12:15 *they reckoned not* KJV: *there was no account made* D-R>

<12:18 *dedicated to holy uses* D-Rn: *consecrated* D-R>

13:2 *et non*: *non* Weber

13:4 *quia*: *qua* Weber

13:5 *manu regis*: *manu* Weber

13:6 *sed in*: *in* Weber

13:8 *fecit*: *fecit sed* Weber

13:11 *sed in*: *in* Weber

13:12 *fecit et*: *fecit / sed et* Weber; *Dierum Regum*: *regum* Weber

<13:12 *wherewith* KJV: *how* D-R>

<13:14 *whereof* KJV: *wherof also* D-R>

<13:18 *them* KJV [in roman type in KJV]: *them agayne* D-R; *upon* KJV: omitted in D-R; *And* KJV: *And when* D-R>

<13:19 *And* KJV: omitted in D-R>

13:19 *consumptionem*: *consummationem* Weber

13:20   *autem: quoque* Weber; *terram: terra* Weber
13:21   *cum tetigisset ossa Helisei: ambulavit et tetigit ossa Helisei / et* Weber
<13:23 *made* D-R/C: omitted in D-R>
13:23   *et Isaac: Isaac* Weber
<13:25 *war* KJV: *the right of warre* D-R>
14:1   *Anno: In anno* S-C
14:4   *incensum in: in* Weber
<14:6   *children of the murderers* KJV: *their children that killed him* D-R;
        wherein KJV: *as* D-R; *for his own sins* KJV: *in his owne sinne* D-R>
14:8   *videamus* Frede SED-S misc 67.11 (270.29): *et videamus* S-C, Weber
<14:11 *But* KJV: *And* D-R; *did not rest satisfied* D-R/C: *agreed not* D-R>
<14:12 *put to the worse* KJV: *strooken* D-R>
14:14   *in Samariam: Samariam* D-R
14:17   *quindecim: viginti quinque* Weber
<14:21 *who was* KJV (*which was*): omitted in D-R>
<14:26 *that it was* KJV [in roman type in KJV]: omitted in D-R>
14:27   *de sub: sub* Weber
<15:5   *so that* KJV: *and* D-R>
15:12   *Iste: ipse* Weber; *tui usque: usque* Weber; *super: de te super* Weber
<15:12 *was* KJV [in roman type]: *is* D-R>
<15:13 *began to reign* KJV: *reigned* D-R>
15:14   *in Samariam: Samariam* Weber
<15:15 *which he made* KJV: *wherwith he wrought treason* D-R>
<15:19 *him in the* D-R/C: *his* D-R>
15:29   *et universam: universam* Weber
<15:29 *captives* KJV: omitted in D-R>
<15:34 *right* KJV: *liked* D-R; *so* D-R/C: omitted in D-R>
<16:4   *and* KJV: *victimes, and* D-R; *green tree* KJV: *tree greene leaues* D-R>
<16:5   *and . . . but* KJV: *and when . . . they* D-R>
16:8   *inveniri: invenire* Weber
<16:8   *it for a present* KJV [*it for* in roman type in KJV]: *giftes* D-R>
16:10   *regis: regi* S-C
16:14   *aeneum: aereum* S-C
16:15   *aeneum: aereum* S-C
<16:17 *of* KJV: *paued with* D-R>

16:18   *templum*: *templo* Weber

<17:4   *had done* KJV [in roman type]: *was accustomed* D-R>

<17:7   *so it was that* KJV: *it came to passe, when* D-R; *and* KJV: omitted in D-R>

17:9   *offenderunt*: *operuerunt* Weber

<17:14   *necks* KJV: *necke* D-R>

17:17   *consecrabant*: *consecraverunt* S-C, *consecrabant ei* Weber; *ut inritarent*: *et inritarent* Weber

17:18   *de*: *a* S-C

17:22   *et non*: *non* Weber

17:25   *eis*: *in eos* S-C

<17:28   *one . . . and* KJV: *when one . . . he* D-R>

<17:29   *gods of their own* KJV: *their owne god* D-R; *temples of the high places* KJV (*houses* for *temples*): *highe temples* D-R; *every nation* KJV: *Nation and Nation* D-R>

17:29   *habitabant*: *habitabat* S-C

<17:32   *temples of the high places* KJV (*houses* for *temples*): *highe temples* D-R>

17:34   *eius et*: *eius* S-C

<17:35   *with whom* KJV: *and . . . with them* D-R>

17:35   *colatis*: *colatis eos* S-C

17:36   *et illum*: *illum* Weber

17:38   *percussit*: *percussi* Weber

<17:41   *Their* KJV: *for . . . their* D-R>

17:41   *patres*: *parentes* Weber

18:2   *et novem*: *novem* S-C

18:4   *nomen eius*: *eum* Weber

<18:5   *nor any* KJV [*any* in roman type]: *yea neither* D-R>

<18:6   *but kept* KJV: *and he did* D-R>

18:8   *usque*: *usque ad* S-C; *muratam*: *Munitam* S-C

18:9   *in Samariam*: *Samariam* Weber

<18:13   *the* S: *all the* D-R>

18:14   *in Lachis*: *Lachis* Weber

18:17   *venerunt*: *venerunt in* Weber; *fullonis*: *Fullonis* S-C, Weber

<18:17   *they . . . and* KJV: *who when they . . . they* D-R>

18:21   *ingredietur*: *ingreditur* Weber

<18:26 *speak* KJV: *that thou speake* D-R>

18:27 *Rabsaces, dicens: Rabsaces* Weber; *potius ad: ad* Weber

18:28 *clamavit: exclamavit* S-C

<18:30 *surely* KJV: *deliuering* D-R>

<18:33 *any of* KJV: omitted in D-R>

19:3 *dixerunt ei* Θ^GIr cum Rab. Mauro in 4 Reg. 4, 19 [Quentin's sigla]: *dixerunt* S-C, Weber

<19:4 *It may be* KJV: *If perhaps* D-R>

<19:9 *say . . . Ethiopia* KJV: *Æthiopia, saying* D-R>

19:10 *manus: manu* Weber

19:11 *fecerint: fecerunt* S-C; *vastaverint: vastaverunt* S-C

<19:11 *Behold* KJV: *For* D-R>

<19:12 *any of* D-R/C: *al* D-R>

19:16 *Et audi: audi* S-C

<19:20 *the prayer thou hast made to* KJV: *That which thou hast besought* D-R>

19:21 *te virgo: virgo* Weber

<19:21 *laughed thee to scorn* KJV: *scorned thee* D-R>

19:23 *et electas: electas* Weber; *et saltum: saltum* Weber

<19:25 *that* KJV: *and* D-R; *should* KJV: *shal* D-R; *turned* D-R/C: omitted in D-R>

19:26 *quasi: velut* S-C

19:27 *et introitum tuum et: et* Weber

19:28 *labris: labiis* S-C

19:29 *quod: quae* S-C

<19:32 *come before it with shield nor cast a trench about* KJV (*banke against* for *trench about*): *shal shield occupie it, nor munition compasse* D-R>

19:35 *in castris: castra* Weber

20:1 *prophetes: propheta* S-C

20:3 *memento quaeso: memento* Weber

<20:3 *remember* KJV: *remember I pray thee* D-R>

20:5 *et vidi lacrimas tuas: vidi lacrimam tuam* Weber

<20:6 *and* KJV: *yea &* D-R>

20:8 *tertio: tertia* S-C

20:9 *accedat: ascendat* S-C

<20:10 *let* KJV: *that* D-R>

20:13 *adventum: adventu* S-C; *possidebat: habere poterat* S-C, *habere potuerat* Weber

<20:13 *precious odours* D-R: literally, *dyes*>

20:14 *venerunt ad me: venerunt* Weber

20:15 *quaecumque: quae* Weber

<20:15 *said* KJV: *answered* D-R; *that: whatsoeuer* D-R>

<20:17 *that* KJV: *&* D-R>

20:17 *Babylonem: Babylone* Weber

20:19 *es: est* Weber

21:7 *quo: quod* S-C

21:8 *sic tamen si: si tamen* S-C; *universam* D²Ψᴮ* [Quentin's sigla]; *et universam* S-C, Weber

<21:8 *feet* KJV: *foot* D-R; *only* KJV: *yet so* D-R; *according to* KJV (*according to all*): *al* D-R>

<21:12 *of them* D-R/C: *it* D-R>

21:13 *et delens: delens* Weber

21:14 *manus: manu* Weber; *vastitatem et in rapinam: vastitate et rapina* Weber

<21:14 *prey* KJV: *waste* D-R>

21:19 *et duo: duorum* S-C; *duobus quoque: duobusque* Weber

<21:23 *plotted* Heb: *lay in wayte* D-R>

22:1 *Triginta et: et triginta* Weber

22:4 *templi a: a* Weber

22:5 *domus: in domo* Weber; *distribuent: distribuant* S-C

<22:5 *and let them* KJV: *who also shal* D-R>

22:6 *lapidicinis: lapicidinis* S-C

22:10 *Narravit quoque: narravitque* Weber

22:11 *legis* Ψᴮ* [Quentin's siglum]: *libri legis* S-C, Weber

22:14 *propheten: prophetidem* S-C

22:19 *quod: quo* Weber

23:2 *habitabant: habitant* Weber

<23:2 *the inhabitants* KJV: *that dwelt* D-R; *both . . . and* KJV: *from . . . to* D-R>

<23:4 *for* KJV: *in* D-R>

23:6   *sepulchra*: *sepulchrum* Weber

<23:10   *there* D-R/C: omitted in D-R>

23:15   *Bethel et*: *Bethel* Weber

<23:15   *grove* KJV: *groue also* D-R>

<23:23   *was this phase that was* D-R/C: *this Phase was* D-R>

23:24   *Hierusalem*: *in Hierusalem* Weber

<23:25   *any like* KJV [*any* in roman type]: *the like to* D-R>

23:28   *verba*: *sermonum* S-C

23:34   *Aegyptum, et mortuus est ibi*: *Aegyptum* Weber

23:35   *secundum*: *iuxta* S-C

24:2   *Syriae et*: *Syriae* Weber; *erat*: *fuerat* S-C

<24:3   *them* KJV [in roman type]: *it* D-R; *from* S?: omitted in D-R>

<24:4   *filling* D-R/C: *& filled* D-R>

24:11   *servis suis ut*: *servi eius* Weber

<24:14   *to the number of* D-R/C: omitted in D-R>

25:4   *Sedicias per*: *per* Weber

<25:4   *between* D-R/C: *by the way of the gate, which is betwen* D-R>

25:8   *in Hierusalem*: *Hierusalem* Weber

25:11   *qui*: *quae* S-C

<25:12   *But* KJV: *And* D-R>

25:13   *omne*: *omnium* Weber

<25:13   *of them* KJV: omitted in D-R>

25:14   *et mortariola et*: *et* Weber

25:15   *Nec non et*: *nec non* Weber; *aurea* Λ^{H}*Σ^{O2}DE [Quentin's sigla]: *aurea aurea* S-C, Weber; *argentea* Σ^{T}*DEΘ^{S}*: *argentea argentea* S-C, Weber

<25:15   *such as were of gold in gold and such as were of silver in silver* KJV [without second *such as*; *in* both times in roman type]: *those that were of gold: and that were of siluer* D-R>

25:17   *reticulum*: *retiaculum* S-C

<25:17   *which was* D-R/C: omitted in D-R; *that were* D-R/C: omitted in D-R>

25:19   *sexaginta*: *sex* Weber

25:25   *qui et*: *qui* Weber

<25:25   *so that he* KJV (without *so*): *who also* D-R>

25:26   *Consurgens autem*: *Consurgensque* S-C

<25:26   *both . . . and* KJV: *from . . . to* D-R>

25:27   *vero*: *vero in* S-C

25:28   *benigne*: *benigna* Weber

<25:29   *before him* KJV: *in his sight* D-R>

<25:30   *continual* KJV: *without intermission* D-R>

Alternate Spellings

In general, the translators of the Douay-Rheims edition of the Bible preserved the transliterations of Hebrew names (and words based on those names) found throughout the textual tradition of the Sixto-Clementine edition of the Vulgate Bible. While these transliterations do reflect the Latin sources for the English presented in this edition, they do not represent what is currently thought to be the likely pronunciation of the Hebrew words or, in some books, words from other ancient languages: for example, the name we see in the New Revised Standard Version (NRSV) as "Ahuzzath" (Gen 26:26) was transliterated by the authors and revisers of the Latin text as "Ochozath." This sort of transliteration renders a few well-known characters harder to recognize, such as Noah, or "Noe" in the Latin tradition. Furthermore, there are frequent inconsistencies in the Douay-Rheims translation as to the spellings of names.

Another quirk of the Douay-Rheims and Vulgate Bibles is that they often identify locations by the names they were understood to have had at the time of the Vulgate's composition rather than the names found in Hebrew scripture. For example, "Mesopotamia of Syria" (Gen 28:2) represents a place referred to in the NRSV as "Paddan-aram."

In presenting the Latin text and the Douay-Rheims transla-

tion, the transliterations in the English have been updated for the sake of accuracy and ease of reference. The Latin has been preserved to reflect its own textual tradition in accordance with the principles stated in the Introduction. However, when names given are not simply a matter of representing vowel and consonant sounds, the Douay-Rheims translation has been left intact so that it remains a genuine translation of the facing text.

There are moments in the Bible where the anachronistic place-names are of significance: at the end of Balaam's last prophetic blessing of Israel, he declares, "They shall come in galleys from Italy; they shall overcome the Assyrians and shall waste the Hebrews, and at the last they themselves also shall perish" (Nm 24:24). The Hebrew word rendered as "Italy" is transliterated in the NRSV as "Kittim," and though the meaning is obscure, it is almost certainly not Italy, for reasons outlined by Milgrom (1990), ad loc. Nevertheless, it is fascinating and important to realize that in the Western European tradition from the fourth century CE until the twentieth century, many read, wrote, and learned that Italians would "waste the Hebrews." Because of this and other instances in which the place-names, however unrepresentative of the Hebrew tradition they may be, are important in terms of what readers of these versions of the Bible may have believed, the Vulgate words have been retained.

Below is a list of the names in the English translation of the Historical Books. The names are followed by an alternate spelling (or, in some cases, an alternate word) if there is one. An entry presented in italic text signifies a word retained from the Douay-Rheims translation; all other words are the spellings given by the NRSV. An entry in roman text with no alternative

spelling means that the spellings are identical in the two editions; one in italic text with no alternative spelling means that the name is in the Douay-Rheims translation but no parallel was found in the NRSV. In a few cases, words have been based on the spellings of the NRSV and the form in the Douay-Rheims text. For example, the Douay-Rheims text reads "the Sichemites" (Gen 33:18), where the NRSV has "Shechem." To illustrate the translation of the Douay-Rheims while providing an up-to-date transliteration of the Hebrew word, "the Shechemites" has been printed; similarly, in cases where Jerome translated parts of a Hebrew place-name into Latin where the NRSV left the whole name in Hebrew (such as the "temple of Phogor," as opposed to "Beth-peor" at Dt 3:29), the transliterated part of the name has been updated in this edition, but the Latin and English translations have not been changed, yielding "temple of Peor."

Aaron

Aaronites

Abagtha [Abgatha]

Abana

Abda

Abdeel

Abdi

Abdon

Abel

Abel [Abela]

Abel-beth-maacah [Abel-
   beth-maacha]

Abel-meholah [Abelmahula]

Abel-meholah [Abelmehula]

Abel-meholah [Abelmeula]

Abenboen

Abi

Abi-albon [Abialbon]

Abiathar

Abida

Abiel

Abiezer

Abiezer [Ezri]

*Abigabaon [Gibeon, the father
   of]*

Abigail

Abihail

Abihu [Abiu]

Abihud [Abiud]
Abijah [Abia]
Abijam [Abiam]
Abimael
Abimelech
Abinadab
Abinoam [Abinoem]
Abiram
Abishag [Abisag]
Abishai [Abisai]
Abishalom [Abessalom]
Abishua [Abisue]
Abishur [Abisur]
Abital
Abitub [Abitob]
Abner
Abraham
Abram
Absalom
Acco [Accho]
Achan
Achar
Achbor [Achobor]
Achish [Achis]
Achor, Valley of
Achsah [Achsa]
Achsah [Axa]
Achshaph [Achsaph]
Achshaph [Axaph]
Achzib
Achzib [Achazib]

Achzib [Achziba]
Adadah [Adada]
Adaiah [Adaia]
Adaiah [Adaias]
Adaiah [Hadaia]
Adalia
Adam
Adam [Adom]
Adam [Arba]
Adam, law of [instruction for
the people]
Adamah [Edema]
Adami
Adar
Addan [Adon]
Addar
Addon
Adeodatus [Elhanan]
Adiel
Adin
Adithaim
Adlai [Adali]
Adlai [Adli]
Admatha
Adna [Edna]
Adnah [Ednas]
Adonai
Adoni-bezek [Adonibezec]
Adoni-zedek [Adonisedec]
Adonijah [Adonia]
Adonijah [Adonias]

Adonikam [Adonicam]

Adoniram

Adoraim [Aduram]

Adoram [Aduram]

Adrammelech [Adramelech]

Adriel [Hadriel]

Adullam

Adullam [Odollam]

Adullam [Odullam]

Adummim [Adommim]

Adummim [Adommin]

Agag

Agag, of the race of [Agagite]

Agagite

Agee [Age]

Ahab [Achab]

Aharah [Ahara]

Aharhel [Aharehel]

Ahasbai [Aasbai]

Ahasuerus [Assuerus]

Ahava

Ahaz

Ahaz [Achaz]

Ahban [Ahobban]

Aher

Ahi

Ahiah [Echaia]

Ahiam

Ahiam [Aliam]

Ahian [Ahiu]

Ahihud [Ahiud]

Ahijah [Achia]

Ahijah [Achias]

Ahijah [Ahia]

Ahijah [Ahias]

Ahikam [Ahicam]

Ahilud

Ahimaaz [Achimaas]

Ahiman

Ahimelech [Achimelech]

Ahimoth [Achimoth]

Ahinadab [Abinadab]

Ahinoam [Achinoam]

Ahio

Ahishahar [Ahisahar]

Ahishar [Ahisar]

Ahithophel [Achitophel]

Ahitub [Achitob]

Ahlab [Ahalab]

Ahlai [Oholai]

Ahlai [Oholi]

Ahoah [Ahoe]

Ahohite

Ahumai

Ahuzzam [Ozam]

Ahzai [Ahazi]

Ai [Hai]

Aiah [Aia]

Aija [Hai]

Aijalon [Aialon]

Aijalon [Ailon]

Aijalon [Ajalon]

Aijalon [Helon]
Ain [Aen]
Akihar [Achior]
Akkub [Accub]
Alemeth [Alamath]
Alemeth [Almath]
Alian
Allammelech [Elmelech]
Allon
Almodad [Elmodad]
Almon
Alvah [Alva]
Amad [Amaad]
Amal
Amalek [Amalec]
Amalek [Amalech]
Amalekite [Amalecite]
Amalekites [Amalecites]
Amam
Amariah [Amaria]
Amariah [Amarias]
Amasa
Amasai
Amashsai [Amassai]
Amasiah [Amasias]
Amaziah [Amasai]
Amaziah [Amasias]
Amelech [the king]
Ami
Amittai [Amathi]
Ammiel

Ammiel [Amihel]
Ammihud [Ammiud]
Amminadab [Aminadab]
Ammizabad [Amizabad]
Ammon
Ammon [Ammoni]
Ammoni [Emona]
Ammonite
Ammonites
Amnon
Amok [Amoc]
Amon
Amorite [Amorrhite]
Amorites [Amorrhites]
Amos
Amoz [Amos]
Amthar
Amzi [Amasai]
Amzi [Amsi]
Anab
Anah [Ana]
Anaharath
Anaiah [Anaia]
Anaiah [Ania]
Anak [Enac]
Anakim [Enacims]
Anamim
Anammelech [Anamelech]
Anan
Anani
Ananiah [Anania]

Ananiah [Ananias]
Anath
Anathoth
Anathothite
Anem
Aner
Ange
Aniam
Anim
Anna
Anthothijah [Anathothia]
Anub [Anob]
Apamea
Apharsites
Aphek [Aphec]
Aphek [Apheca]
Aphekah [Apheca]
Aphiah [Aphia]
Aphik [Aphec]
Appaim [Apphaim]
Ara
Arab
Arab [Arbi]
Arabia
Arad
Arad [Arod]
Arad [Hered]
Arah [Area]
Arah [Aree]
Aram
Aran

Arapha [giants]
Araunah [Areuna]
Arba [Arbe]
Arbathite
Arbi, of [the Arbite]
Archi [the Archites]
Archite [Arachite]
Ardon
Argob
Aridai
Aridatha
Ariel
Arisai
Arkite [Aracite]
Armenians, the [Ararat]
Armoni
Arnan
Arnon
Aroer
Aroerite [Arorite]
Arpachshad [Arphaxad]
Arpad [Arphad]
Arphasachites [envoys]
Arphaxad
Artaxerxes
*Artificers, Valley of the [Ge-har-
     ashim]*
Arubboth [Aruboth]
Arumah [Ruma]
Arvadite [Aradian]
Arza [Arsa]

Asa
Asahel
Asahel [Asael]
Asahel [Azahel]
Asaiah [Asaa]
Asaiah [Asaia]
Asaph
Asarel [Asrael]
Asarelah [Asarela]
Asedoth
Asedoth [the hill country]
Asedoth [the slopes]
Ash-baal [Esbaal]
Ashan [Asan]
Ashbel [Asbel]
Ashdod [Azotus]
Ashdodians [Azotians]
Ashdodites [Azotians]
Asher [Aser]
Asherah [Astaroth]
Ashhur [Ashur]
Ashima [Asima]
Ashkelon [Ascalon]
Ashkelonites [Ascalonites]
Ashkenaz [Ascenez]
Ashnah [Asena]
Ashnah [Esna]
Ashtaroth [Astaroth]
Ashtaroth [Astharoth]
Ashterathite [Astarothite]

Ashvath [Asoth]
Asiel
Asir [the captive]
Asmodeus
Asnah [Asena]
Aspatha [Esphatha]
Asriel [Esriel]
Asriel [Ezriel]
Asshur [Asur]
Assir [Asir]
Assurim
Assyria [Assur]
Assyrians
Astarte [Astaroth]
Astarte [Astarthe]
Atarah [Atara]
Ataroth
Ataroth-addar
Ater
Ater [Ather]
Athach
Athaiah [Athaias]
Athaliah [Athalia]
Athaliah [Athalias]
Athaliah [Otholia]
Athersatha [the governor]
Athlai [Athalai]
Attai [Ethai]
Attai [Ethei]
Attai [Ethi]

Avith

Avva [Avah]

Avvim [Avim]

Avvites [Hevites]

Ayya [Asa]

Azaliah [Assia]

Azaniah [Azanias]

Azanoth-tabor [Azanottha-
bor]

Azarel [Azareel]

Azarel [Azreel]

Azarel [Ezrel]

Azarel [Ezrihel]

Azariah

Azariah [Azaria]

Azariah [Azarias]

Azaz

Azaziah [Ozazie]

Azaziah [Ozaziu]

Azbuk [Azboc]

Azekah [Azeca]

Azekah [Azecha]

Azel [Asel]

Azgad

Aziza

Azmaveth

Azmaveth [Azmoth]

Azmon [Asmona]

Azriel [Esriel]

Azriel [Ozriel]

Azrikam [Azaricam]

Azrikam [Ezricam]

Azubah [Azuba]

Azzur [Azur]

Baal

Baal Perazim [Baal Pharisim]

Baal-berith [Baalberith]

Baal-gad [Baalgad]

Baal-hanan [Balanam]

Baal-hanan [Balanan]

Baal-hazor [Baalhasor]

Baal-hermon [Baal Hermon]

Baal-meon [Baalmaon, town
of]

Baal-meon [Beelmeon]

Baal-perazim [Baalpharasim]

Baal-shalishah [Baalsalisa]

Baal-tamar [Baalthamar]

Baal-zebub [Beelzebub]

Baalah [Baala]

Baalah, Mount [Mount Baala]

Baalath

Baalath [Balaath]

*Baalath Beer Ramath [Baalath-
beer, Ramah]*

Baalim [the Baals]

Baana

Baana [Bana]

Baanah [Baana]

Baara [Bara]
Baaseiah [Basaia]
Baasha [Baasa]
Bagoas [Vagao]
Baharumite [Bauramite]
Bahurim [Baromi]
Bakbakkar [Bacbacar]
Bakbuk [Bacbuc]
Bakbukiah [Becbecia]
Balaam
Baladan
Balah [Bala]
Balak [Balac]
Bale
Bamoth-baal [Bamothbaal]
Bani
Bani [Benni]
Bani [Boni]
Bani [Bonni]
Barak [Barac]
Bariah [Baria]
Barkos [Bercos]
Baruch
Barzillai [Berzellai]
Basemath
Bashan [Basan]
Bathsheba [Bethsabee]
Bavvai [Bavai]
Bazlith [Besloth]
Bazluth [Besluth]

Bealiah [Baalia]
Bealoth [Baloth]
Bebai
Bebai [Babai]
Becher [Bechor]
Becorath [Bechorath]
Bedad [Badad]
Bedan [Badan]
Bedan [Baden]
Bedeiah [Badaias]
Beeliada [Baaliada]
Beelteem [the royal deputy]
Beer [Bera]
Beer-sheba [Bersabee]
Beera [Bera]
Beerah [Beera]
Beeroth [Beroth]
Beerothite [Berothite]
Bela
Bela [Bala]
Bela [Bale]
Belial, son of [scoundrel; worthless or ill-tempered person]
Ben
Ben-abinadab [Benabinadab]
Ben-deker [Bendecar]
Ben-hadad [Benadad]
Ben-hesed [Benesed]
Ben-hur [Benhur]
Ben-zoheth [Benzoheth]

Benaiah [Banai]
Benaiah [Banaia]
Benaiah [Banaias]
Benaiah [Banea]
Benaiah [Baneas]
Bene [Bane]
Benennom [son of Hinnom]
Benjamin
*Benjamin, children of [Benja-
  minites]*
Beno [Benno]
Beor
Beracah [Beracha]
Beraiah [Baraia]
Berak [Barach]
Berechiah [Barachia]
Berechiah [Barachias]
Bered [Bared]
Beri
Beriah [Baria]
Beriah [Beria]
Berith
Berothai [Beroth]
Berzaith [Barsaith]
Besai
Besodeiah [Besodia]
Besor
Betah [Bete]
Beten
Beth-anath [Bethanath]

Beth-anites [Bethanites]
Beth-anoth [Bethanoth]
Beth-arabah [Batharaba]
Beth-arabah [Beth-Araba]
Beth-aven [Bethaven]
Beth-azmaveth [Beth-
  azmoth]
Beth-barah [Bethbara]
Beth-biri [Bethberai]
Beth-dagon [Bethdagon]
Beth-emek [Bethemec]
Beth-gader [Bethgader]
Beth-haccherem [Bethhacha-
  ram]
Beth-hanan [Bethanan]
Beth-haram [Betharan]
Beth-hoglah [Beth-Haglah]
Beth-hoglah [Bethhagla]
Beth-horon
Beth-horon [Bethoron]
Beth-jeshimoth [Bethiesim-
  oth]
Beth-jeshimoth [Bethsimoth]
Beth-lebaoth [Bethlebaoth]
Beth-maacah
Beth-marcaboth [Bethmar-
  chaboth]
Beth-nimrah [Bethnemra]
Beth-pazzez [Bethpheses]
Beth-pelet [Bethphelet]

Beth-rapha [Bethrapha]
Beth-shan [Bethsan]
Beth-shean [Bethsan]
Beth-shemesh [Bethsames]
Beth-shemites [Bethsamites]
Beth-shittah [Bethsetta]
Beth-tappuah [Beththaphua]
Beth-zur [Bessur]
Beth-zur [Bethsur]
Bethcar [Bethchar]
Bethel
Bethlehem
Bethlehemite [Lahmi]
Bethuel [Bathuel]
Bethul
Betonim
Bezai [Besai]
Bezalel [Beseleel]
Bezalel [Bezeleel]
Bezek [Bezec]
Bezer [Bosor]
Bichri [Bochri]
Bidkar [Badacer]
Bigtha
Bigthan [Bagathan]
Bigthana [Bagathan]
Bigvai [Begoai]
Bigvai [Beguai]
Bileam [Baalam]
Bilgah [Belga]
Bilgai [Belgia]

Bilhah [Bala]
Bilhan [Balaan]
Bilhan [Balan]
Bilsan [Belsan]
Bilshan [Belsam]
Binea [Banaa]
Binnui [Bannui]
Binnui [Bennui]
Binnui [Benoi]
Bishlam
Bithiah [Bethia]
Bizatha [Bazatha]
Biziothiah [Baziothia]
Blessing, Valley of [Valley of Be-
 racah]
Boaz [Booz]
Bocheru [Bochru]
Bohan [Boen]
Bohan, Stone of [Stone of
 Boen]
Bosra [Beeshterah]
Bougean [Bugite]
Bozez [Boses]
Bozkath [Bascath]
Bozkath [Besecath]
Bozrah [Bosra]
Bukki [Bocci]
Bukkiah [Bocciae]
Bul
Bunni [Baninu]
Bunni [Boni]

Bunni [Bonni]
Burning [Saraph]
Buz

Cabbon [Chebbon]
Cabul
Cadumim, torrent of [onrushing torrent]
Calcol
Calcol [Chalchal]
Caleb
Calor
Camp of Dan [Mahaneh-dan]
Canaan [Chanaan]
Canaan [Charan]
Canaanite [Chanaanite]
Canaanites [Chanaanites]
Canaanitess [Chanaanitess]
Caphtorim
Carchemish [Charcamis]
Carehim [Korahites]
Carkas [Charcas]
Carmel
Carmel [Carmelus]
Carmel [the fertile lands]
Carmel, Mount
Carmelite
Carmelitess
Carmi [Charmi]
Carshena [Charsena]
Casiphia [Chasphia]

Casluhim [Casluim]
Cedar [Gilead]
Ceni [the Kenites]
Cerethi [Carites]
Chabris [Chabri]
Chabul [Cabul]
Chaldeans [Babylon]
Chaldeans [Chaldees]
Challdeans
Charmis [Charmi]
Chelal [Chalal]
Chellon, land of [country of the Chelleans]
Chelub
Chelub [Caleb]
Chelubi [Calubi]
Cheluhi [Cheliau]
Chemosh [Chamos]
Chenaanah [Chanaana]
Chenaanah [Chanana]
Chenani [Chanani]
Chenaniah [Chonenias]
Chephirah [Caphara]
Chephirah [Caphira]
Chephirah [Cephira]
Cheran [Charan]
Cherethites [Cherethi]
Cherith [Carith]
Cherub
Chesalon [Cheslon]
Chesil [Cesil]

Chesulloth [Casaloth]
Chidon
Chileab [Cheleab]
Chilion [Chelion]
Chimham [Chamaam]
Chinnereth [Cenereth]
Chinneroth [Ceneroth]
Chinneroth [Cenneroth]
Chiseloth-tabor [Ceseleth-
    thabor]
Chislev [Casleu]
Chitlish [Cethlisa]
Christ
Cilicia
Cleopatra
Col-hozeh [Cholhoza]
Conanniah [Chonenias]
Cun [Chun]
Cush [Chus]
Cushan Rishathaim [Chusan
    Rasathaim]
Cuthah [Cutha]
Cuthites
Cyamon [Chelmon]
Cyrene [Kir]
Cyrus

Dabbesheth [Debbaseth]
Daberath [Dabereth]
Dagon

Dalphon [Delphon]
Damascus
Dammim [Dommim]
Dan
Danah [Danna]
Daniel
Dara
Darda
Darkon [Darcon]
Darkon [Dercon]
David
Dead Sea
Debir [Dabir]
Debir [Debara]
Deborah [Debbora]
Dedan [Dadan]
Delaiah [Dalaia]
Delaiah [Dalaiau]
Delaiah [Delaia]
Delilah [Dalila]
Dibon
Dievites
Diklah [Decla]
Dilan [Delean]
Dimnah [Damna]
Dimonah [Dimona]
Dinhabah [Denaba]
Diphath [Riphath]
Dishan [Disan]
Dishon [Dison]

Dodai [Dudia]
Dodavahu [Dodau]
Dodo
Doeg
Dor
Dor, countries of [Naphoth-dor]
Dor, province of [Naphath-dor]
Dositheus
Dothan
Dothan [Dothain]
Dumah [Duma]
Dumah [Ruma]

Ebal
Ebal [Hebal]
Ebed [Abed]
Ebed [Obed]
Eber [Heber]
Ebez [Ades]
Ebiasaph [Abiasaph]
Ebron [Abaran]
Ecbatana
Eden
Eder
Eder [Heder]
Edna [Anna]
Edom
Edomite
Edomites
Edomites [Idumeans]

Edrei [Edrai]
Edrei [Edri]
Eglah [Egla]
Eglon
Egypt
Egyptians
Ehud [Ahod]
Ehud [Aod]
Eker [Achar]
Ekron [Accaron]
Ekron [Acron]
Ekronites [Accronites]
Ela
Elah [Ela]
Elasah [Elasa]
Elath [Aila]
Eldaah [Eldaa]
Elead [Elad]
Eleadah [Elada]
Eleasah [Elasa]
Eleash [Elasa]
Eleazar
Eleazar [Eliezer]
Elhanan [Elchanan]
Elhanan [Elehanan]
Eli [Heli]
Eliab
Eliada
Eliada [Elioda]
Eliahba [Eliaba]

Eliakim

Eliakim [Eliachim]

Eliakim [Eliacim]

Eliam

Eliashib [Eliasub]

Eliathah [Eliatha]

Eliehoenai [Eleoenai]

Eliehoenai [Elioenai]

Eliel

Eliel [Elial]

Elienai [Elioenai]

Eliezer

Elihoreph

Elihu [Eliu]

Elijah [Elia]

Elijah [Elias]

Elika [Elica]

Elimelech

Elioenai

Eliphal

Eliphaz

Eliphelehu [Eliphalu]

Eliphelet

Eliphelet [Eliphalet]

Eliphelet [Eliphaleth]

Eliphelet [Elipheleth]

Elisha [Eliseus]

Elishah [Elisa]

Elishama [Elisama]

Elishaphat [Elisaphat]

Elishua [Elisua]

Elizaphan [Elisaphan]

Elkanah [Elcana]

Elkiah [Elai]

Elnaam [Elnaim]

Elnathan

Elon

Elon

Elon [Ahialon]

Eloth [Ailath]

Elpaal [Elphaal]

Elpelet [Eliphalet]

Elteke [Eltheco]

Eltekeh [Elthece]

Eltekon [Eltexon]

Eltolad [Eltholad]

Elul

Eluzai

Elymeans [Elicians]

Elzabad [Elizabad]

Elzabad [Elzebad]

Emath, tower of [Tower of the Hundred]

En-dor [Endor]

En-gannim [Engannim]

En-gedi [Engaddi]

En-hazor [Enhasor]

En-rimmon [Remmon]

En-shemesh [Ensemes]

Enam [Enaim]

Enan

Endor

Enoch [Henoc]
Enosh [Enos]
Ephah [Epha]
Epher
Ephlal [Ophlal]
Ephraim
Ephraim, Mount
Ephraimite [Ephrathite]
Ephrath [Ephrata]
Ephrathah [Ephrata]
Ephrathah [Ephratha]
Ephrathah [Ephratta]
Ephrathites
Ephron
Ephron, Mount
Er [Her]
Erchuites
Esar-haddon [Asarhaddon]
Esar-haddon [Asor Haddan]
Esau
Esdraelon [Asdrelon]
Esdraelon [Esdrelon]
Eshan [Esaan]
Eshban [Eseban]
Eshek [Esec]
Eshtaol [Estaol]
Eshtaol [Esthaol]
Eshtaolites [Esthaolites]
Eshtemoa [Estemo]
Eshtemoa [Esthemo]
Eshtemoh [Istemo]

Esthon
Etam
Eth-kazin [Thacasin]
Ethan
Ethanim
Ethbaal
Ether
Ether [Athor]
Ethiopia
Ethiopian
Ethiopians
Ethnan
Ethni [Athanai]
Euphrates
Euphrates [river]
Eve
Evi [Hevi]
Evil-merodach [Evilmero-
dach]
Ezbai [Azbai]
Ezbon [Esbon]
Ezel
Ezem [Asem]
Ezem [Asom]
Ezem [Esem]
Ezer
Ezer [Eser]
Ezer [Ezar]
Ezion-geber [Asiongaber]
Ezra [Esdras]
Ezrah [Esra]

Ezrahite
Ezri

Foreskins, Hill of the
  [Gibeath-haaraloth]
Forrest, an embroiderer, the
  [Jaareoregim]
Foundation

Gaal
Gaash [Gaas]
Gaash, Mount [Mount Gaas]
Gabaa
Gabael [Gabelus]
Gabatha
Gabbai [Gebbai]
Gad
Gadi
Gadites
Gadites [Gaddi]
Gahar
Gahar [Gaher]
Galal
Galilee
Gallim [Gallium]
Gamul
Gareb
Garmi [the Garmite]
Gatam [Gathan]
Gath [Geth]
Gath-hepher [Gethhepher]

Gath-rimmon [Gethrem-
  mon]
Gaza
Gaza [Gazan]
Gazabar
Gazez [Gezez]
Gazites
Gazzam [Gazam]
Gazzam [Gezem]
Geba
Geba [Gabaa]
Geba [Gabae]
Geba [Gabee]
Geber [Gaber]
Gedaliah [Godolias]
Gedaliah [Golodia]
Geder [Gader]
Gederah [Gaderoth]
Gederah [Gedera]
Gederite
Gederoth [Gaderoth]
Gederoth [Gideroth]
Gederothaim
Gedor
Gedor [Gador]
Gehazi [Giezi]
Gentiles
Gentiles [nations]
Gentiles, of the [-ha-goiim]
Gentiles, the [these nations]
Genubath

Gera

Gerar [Gerara]

Geri

Gerizim [Garizim]

Gershom [Gersam]

Gershom [Gersom]

Gershom [Gerson]

Gershon [Gerson]

Gershonite [Gersonite]

Gershonites [Gersonni]

Gerzi [Girzites]

Geshan [Gesan]

Geshem [Gossem]

Geshur [Gessur]

Geshur [Gessuri]

Gessuri [Ashurites]

Gether

Gezer [Gazer]

Gezer [Gazera]

Gibbar [Gebbar]

Gibbethon [Gabathon]

Gibbethon [Gebbethon]

Gibea [Gabaa]

Gibeah [Gabaa]

Gibeah [Gabaath]

Gibeah [Gabam]

Gibeon [Gabaon]

Gibeonite [Gabaonite]

Gibeonites [Gabaonites]

Giblites [Giblians]

Giddalti [Geddelthi]

Giddel [Geddel]

Giddel [Jeddel]

Gideon [Gedeon]

Gihon

Gilalai [Galalai]

Gilboa [Gelboe]

Gilboa, Mount [Mount Gelboe]

Gilead [Galaad]

Gileadite [Galaadite]

Gileadites [Galaadites]

Gilgal [Galgal]

Gilgal [Galilee]

Gilgal, house of [Beth-gilgal]

Giloh [Gilo]

Gilonite

Gilonite [Gelonite]

Gimzo [Gamzo]

Ginath [Gineth]

Ginnethoi [Genthon]

Ginnethon [Genthon]

Girgashite [Gergesite]

Gishpa [Gaspha]

Gittaim [Gethaim]

Gittite [Gethite]

Gittites [Gethites]

Gizonite [Gezonite]

Gob

Gog

Golan [Gaulon]

Goliath

Gomer

Goodlyman [Ishod]

Goshen [Gosen]

Gothoniel

Gozan

Great Sea

Guni

Haahashtari [Ahasthari]

Habaiah [Hobia]

Habor

Hacaliah [Hachelai]

Hacaliah [Helchias]

Hachilah [Hachila]

Hachmoni [Hachamoni]

Hadad

Hadad [Adad]

Hadadezer [Adarezer]

Hadashah [Hadassa]

Hadassah [Edissa]

Hadid

Hadoram [Adoram]

Hadoram [Aduram]

Haeleph [Eleph]

Hagab

Hagabah [Hegaba]

Haggai [Aggeus]

Haggiah [Haggia]

Haggith

Haggith [Aggith]

Hagri [Agarai]

Hagrite [Agarene]

Hagrites [Agarites]

Hakkatan [Eccetan]

Hakkoz [Accos]

Hakkoz [Accus]

Hakkoz [Haccus]

Hakupha [Hacupha]

Halah [Hala]

Halah [Lahela]

Halhul

Hali [Chali]

Hallohesh [Alohes]

Ham [Cham]

Haman [Aman]

Hamath [Emath]

Hamath [Hemath]

Hamathite

Hammath [Chamath]

Hammedatha [Amadethi]

Hammon [Hamon]

Hammoth-dor [Hammoth Dor]

Hammuel [Hamuel]

Hamon

Hamor [Emor]

Hamor [Hemor]

Hamran [Hamram]

Hamul

Hamutal [Amital]

Hanan

Hananaiah [Hananias]

Hananel [Hananeel]
Hanani
Hananiah [Ananias]
Hananiah [Hanania]
Hananiah [Hananias]
Hananiah [Henanias]
Hannah [Anna]
Hannathon [Hanathon]
Hanniel [Haniel]
Hanoch [Enoch]
Hanoch [Henoch]
Hanun
Hanun [Hanon]
Hapharaim
Hara [Ara]
Haran
Haran [Aran]
Harar [Arari]
Harar [Orori]
Hararite [Ararite]
Harbona
Hareph [Hariph]
Harhaiah [Araia]
Harhas [Araas]
Harheres [Hares]
Harhur
Harim
Harim [Arem]
Harim [Haram]
Harim [Harem]
Harim [Herem]

Hariph
Harnepher [Hernapher]
Harod [Harad]
Harod [Harodi]
Harorite [Arorite]
Harosheth [Haroseth]
Harsha [Harsa]
Harum [Arum]
Harumaph [Haromaph]
Haruphite
Haruz [Harus]
Hasadiah [Hasadias]
Hashabiah [Hasabia]
Hashabiah [Hasabias]
Hashabiah [Hasebia]
Hashabnah [Hasebna]
Hashabneiah [Hasebnia]
Hashabneiah [Hasebonia]
Hashbaddanah [Hasbadana]
Hashebiah [Hasebias]
Hashem [Assem]
Hashubah [Hasaba]
Hashum [Hasem]
Hashum [Hasom]
Hashum [Hasum]
Hasrah [Hasra]
Hassenaah [Asnaa]
Hassenuah [Asana]
Hassenuah [Senua]
Hasshub [Hassub]
Hasshub [Hasub]

Hassophereth [Sopheret]

Hasupha

Hathach [Athach]

Hathath

Hatipha

Hatita

Hattil [Hatil]

Hattush [Hattus]

Havilah [Hevila]

Havvoth Jair [Havoth Jair]

Hazael

Hazaiah [Hazia]

Hazar-gaddah [Asergadda]

Hazar-shual [Hasarsuhal]

Hazar-shual [Hasersual]

Hazar-susah [Hazersusa]

Hazar-susim [Hasarsusim]

Hazarmaveth [Asarmoth]

Hazazon-tamar [Asason-thamar]

Haziel [Hosiel]

Hazor [Asor]

Hazor [Hasor]

Hazor [Heser]

Hazzebaim [Asebaim]

Hazzelelponi [Asalelphuni]

Heber

Heber [Haber]

Hebrews

Hebron

Hebronites

Hedges [Gederah]

Hegai [Egeus]

Helah [Halaa]

Helam

Helbah [Helba]

Heldai [Holdai]

Heleb [Heled]

Heled

Helek [Helec]

Helem

Heleph

Helez [Heles]

Helez [Helles]

Helkai [Helci]

Helkath [Halcath]

Helkath [Helcath]

Heman

Heman [Eman]

Heman [Hemam]

Hemath

Hena [Ana]

Henadad

Henadad [Hanadad]

Hepher

Hepher [Epher]

Hepher [Opher]

Hephzibah [Haphsiba]

Heppizzez [Aphses]

Hereth [Haret]

Hermon

Hermon, Mount

Heshbon [Hesebon]

Heshmon [Hassemon]

Hethim [the Hittites]

Hezekiah [Ezechias]

Hezekiah [Hezechias]

Hezekiah [Hezecia]

Hezion

Hezir

Hezir [Hazir]

Hezrai [Hesrai]

Hezro [Hesro]

Hezron [Esron]

Hezron [Hesron]

Hiddai [Heddai]

Hiel

Hilen [Helon]

Hilkiah [Helchias]

Hilkiah [Helcia]

Hilkiah [Helcias]

Hillel [Illel]

Hinnom [Ennom]

Hinnom, Valley of [Valley of
    Ennom]

Hinnom, Valley of the Chil-
    dren of [Valley of the Chil-
    dren of Ennom]

Hinnom, Valley of the Son of
    [Valley of the Son of En-
    nom]

Hiram

Hittite [Hethite]

Hittites [Hethites]

Hivite [Hevite]

Hivites [Hevites]

Hizki [Hezeci]

Hizkiah [Ezechias]

Hobaiah [Habia]

Hod

Hodaviah [Odoia]

Hodaviah [Odovia]

Hodaviah [Oduia]

Hodesh [Hodes]

Hodevah [Oduia]

Hodiah [Odaia]

Hodiah [Odia]

Hodiah [Oduia]

Hodshi [Hodsi]

Hoglah [Hegla]

Hoham [Oham]

Holofernes

Holon

Holon [Olon]

Homam

Hophni [Ophni]

Horam

Horeb

Horem [Herem]

Hori

Hormah [Arama]

Hormah [Harma]

Hormah [Herma]

Hormah [Horma]

Horonite
Hosah [Hosa]
Hoshaiah [Osaias]
Hoshama [Sama]
Hoshea [Osee]
Hotham
Hothir [Othir]
Hozai
Hubbah [Haba]
Hukkok [Hucuca]
Hukok [Hucac]
Hul
Huldah [Holda]
Huldah [Olda]
Humtah [Athmatha]
Huppah [Hoppha]
Huppim [Hapham]
Huppim [Happhim]
Hur
Hurai
Huram
Huri
Hushah [Hosa]
Hushah [Husati]
Hushai [Chusai]
Hushai [Husi]
Husham [Husam]
Hushath [Husathi]
Hushathite [Husathite]
Hushim [Hasim]

Hushim [Husim]
Hushim [Mehusim]

Ibhar [Jebaar]
Ibhar [Jebahar]
Ibleam [Jeblaam]
Ibneiah [Jobania]
Ibnijah [Jebania]
Ibsam [Jebsem]
Ibzan [Abesan]
Ichabod
Idalah [Jedala]
Idbash [Jedebos]
Iddo [Adaia]
Iddo [Addo]
Iddo [Jaddo]
Igal [Igaal]
Igal [Jegaal]
Iim [Jim]
Ijon [Ahion]
Ijon [Aion]
Ikkesh [Acces]
Ilai
Imlah [Jemla]
Immer [Emmer]
Imna [Jemna]
Imnah [Jemna]
Imrah [Jamra]
Imri [Amri]
Imri [Omrai]

Iphdeiah [Jephdaia]
Iphtah [Jephtha]
Iphtah-el, Valley of [Valley of Jephtael]
Iphtah-el, Valley of [Valley of Jephtahel]
Ir [Hir]
Ir-shemesh [Hirsemes]
Ira
Ira [Hira]
Iram [Hiram]
Iri [Urai]
Iron [Jeron]
Irpeel [Jarephel]
Iru [Hir]
Isaac
Isaiah [Isaias]
Ish-bosheth [Isboseth]
Ishbah [Jesba]
Ishbak [Jesboc]
Ishbi-benob [Jesbibenob]
Ishi [Jesi]
Ishiah [Jesia]
Ishma [Jesema]
Ishmael
Ishmael [Ismael]
Ishmael [Ismahel]
Ishmaelite [Ishmahelite]
Ishmaelite [Ismahelite]
Ishmaelites [Ismaelites]

Ishmaiah [Jesmaias]
Ishmaiah [Samaias]
Ishmerai [Jesamari]
Ishpah [Jespha]
Ishpan [Jespham]
Ishvah [Jesua]
Ishvi [Jessui]
Ismachiah [Jesmachias]
Israel
Issachar
Isshiah [Jesia]
Isshiah [Jesias]
Isshijah [Josue]
Ithai [Ethai]
Ithamar
Ithiel [Etheel]
Ithlah [Jethela]
Ithmah [Jethma]
Ithnan [Jethnam]
Ithra [Jethra]
Ithran [Jethran]
Ithream [Jethraam]
Ithream [Jethrahem]
Ithrite [Jethrite]
Ithrites [Jethrites]
Ittai [Ethai]
Ittai [Ithai]
Ivvah [Ava]
Izhar [Isaar]
Izharites [Isaarites]

Izliah [Jezlia]
Izrahiah [Izrahia]
Izrahite [Jezerite]
Izri [Isari]
Izziah [Jezia]

Jaakan [Jacan]
Jaakobah [Jacoba]
Jaala [Jahala]
Jaalah [Jala]
Jaareshiah [Jersia]
Jaasiel [Jasiel]
Jaasu [Jasi]
Jaazaniah [Jezonias]
Jaaziah [Oziau]
Jaaziel [Jaziel]
Jabbok [Jaboc]
Jabesh [Jabes]
Jabesh Gilead [Jabes Galaad]
Jabez [Jabes]
Jabin
Jabin [Jaban]
Jabneel [Jebnael]
Jabneel [Jebneel]
Jabneh [Jabnia]
Jacan
Jachin
Jacob
Jada
Jadason [Hydaspes]

Jaddai [Jeddu]
Jaddua [Jeddoa]
Jaddua [Jeddua]
Jadon
Jael [Jahel]
Jagur
Jahath
Jahath [Jeth]
Jahath [Leheth]
Jahaz [Jasa]
Jahaz [Jassa]
Jahaziel
Jahaziel [Ezechiel]
Jahaziel [Jaziel]
Jahaziel [Jeheziel]
Jahdai [Jahaddai]
Jahdiel [Jediel]
Jahdo [Jeddo]
Jahmai [Jemai]
Jahzah [Jaser]
Jahzah [Jassa]
Jahzeiah [Jaasia]
Jahzerah [Jezra]
Jahziel [Jasiel]
Jair
Jair, towns of [Havvoth-jair]
Jairite
Jakim [Jacim]
Jalam [Ihelom]
Jalon

Jamin

Jamlech [Jemlech]

Jamnor

Janai

Janim [Janum]

Janoah [Janoe]

Japheth

Japhia

Japhia [Japhie]

Japhlet [Jephlat]

Jarah [Jara]

Jared

Jarha [Jeraa]

Jarib

Jarmuth [Jaramoth]

Jarmuth [Jerimoth]

Jarmuth [Jerimuth]

Jaroah [Jara]

Jashen [Jassen]

Jashobeam [Jebsaam]

Jashobeam [Jesbaam]

Jashobeam [Jesboam]

Jashub [Jasub]

Jathniel [Jathanael]

Jattir [Jether]

Javan

Jawbone, place of the [Lehi]

Jazer

Jazer [Jaser]

Jaziz

Jearim, Mount [Mount Jarim]

Jeatherai [Jethrai]

Jebus

Jebusite

Jebusites

Jecoliah [Jechelia]

Jeconiah [Jechonias]

Jedaiah [Idaia]

Jedaiah [Jadaia]

Jedaiah [Jedaia]

Jedaiah [Jedei]

Jedaiah [Jodaia]

Jediael [Jadihel]

Jediael [Jedihel]

Jedidah [Idida]

Jeduthun [Idithum]

Jeduthun [Idithun]

Jehallelel [Jalaleel]

Jehallelel [Jaleleel]

Jehdeiah [Jadias]

Jehdeiah [Jehedeia]

Jehezkel [Hezechiel]

Jehiah [Jehias]

Jehiel

Jehiel [Jahiel]

Jehieli

Jehizkiah [Ezechias]

Jehoaddah [Joada]

Jehoaddan [Joadan]

Jehoaddin [Joadan]

Jehoahaz [Joachaz]
Jehoash [Joas]
Jehohanan [Johanan]
Jehoiachin [Joachin]
Jehoiada [Joiada]
Jehoiakim [Joakim]
Jehoiarib [Joiarib]
Jehonathan [Jonathan]
Jehoram [Joram]
Jehoshabeath [Josabeth]
Jehoshaphat [Josaphat]
Jehosheba [Josaba]
Jehozabad [Jozabad]
Jehozadak [Josedec]
Jehu
Jehud [Jud]
Jehuel [Jahiel]
Jeiel [Jehiel]
Jekabzeel [Cabseel]
Jekameam [Jecmaan]
Jekamiah [Icamia]
Jekamiah [Jecemia]
Jekuthiel [Icuthiel]
Jemini [Benjamin]
Jemini, children of [Benja-
 minites]
Jemini, of the race of [Benja-
 minite]
Jemini, of the sons of [a Benja-
 minite]
Jemini, son of [Benjaminite]

Jemini, son of a man of [Benja-
 minite]
Jemini, sons of [Benjaminites]
Jephleti [the Japhletites]
Jephthah [Jephte]
Jephunneh [Jephone]
Jerah [Jare]
Jerahmeel [Jerameel]
Jered [Jared]
Jeremai [Jermai]
Jeremiah [Jeremia]
Jeremiah [Jeremias]
Jeremiah [Jerenias]
Jeremoth [Jerimoth]
Jeremoth [Ramoth]
Jeriah [Jeriau]
Jeribai
Jericho
Jeriel
Jerijah [Jeria]
Jerimoth
Jerimoth [Jerimuth]
Jerioth
Jeroboam
Jeroham
Jerubbaal [Jerobaal]
Jeruel
Jerusalem
Jerusha [Jerusa]
Jerushah [Jerusa]
Jesarelah [Isreela]

*Jesbaham sitting in a chair
[Josheb-basshebeth a Tah-
chemonite]*
Jeshaiah [Isaia]
Jeshaiah [Isaias]
Jeshaiah [Jesaia]
Jeshaiah [Jeseias]
Jeshanah [Jesana]
Jeshebeab [Isbaab]
Jesher [Jaser]
Jeshimon [Jesimon]
Jeshishai [Jesisi]
Jeshohaiah [Isuhaia]
Jeshua [Jesue]
Jeshua [Josue]
Jesimiel [Ismiel]
Jesse
Jesse [Isai]
Jether
Jetheth
Jethson
Jetur
Jeturites [Itureans]
Jeuel [Jahiel]
Jeuel [Jehiel]
Jeush [Jaus]
Jeush [Jehus]
Jeuz [Jehus]
Jews [Judeans]
Jews' [of Judah]
Jezebel [Jezabel]

Jezer
Jeziel [Jaziel]
Jezrael [Israel]
Jezrahiah [Jezraia]
Jezreel [Jezrael]
Jezreel [Jezrahel]
Jezreel, Valley of [Valley of
    Jezrael]
Jezreelite [Jezrahelite]
Jezreelitess [Jezrahelitess]
Joab
*Joab, crowns of the house of
    [Atroth-beth-joab]*
Joah
Joah [Joaha]
Joah [Joahe]
Joakim
Joakim [Joachim]
Joash [Joas]
Jobab
Joed
Joel
Joel [Johel]
Joelah [Joela]
Joezer
Jogbehah [Jegbaa]
Joha
Johanan
Johanan [Joanan]
Johanan [Jonathan]
Joiada

Joiakim [Joacim]
Joiarib
Jokdeam [Jucadam]
Jokmeam [Jecmaan]
Jokneam [Jachanan]
Jokneam [Jecnam]
Jokneam [Jeconam]
Jokshan [Jecsan]
Joktan [Jectan]
Jokte-el [Jectehel]
Jokthe-el [Jecthel]
Jonadab
Jonah [Jonas]
Jonathan
Joppa [Joppe]
Jorah [Jora]
Jorai
Joram
Jordan
Jorkeam [Jercaam]
Joseph
Joshah [Josa]
Joshaphat [Josaphat]
Joshaviah [Josaia]
Joshbekashah [Jesbacassa]
Joshibiah [Josabia]
Joshua [Josue]
Josiah [Josias]
Jotbah [Jeteba]
Jotham [Joatham]
Jotham [Joathan]

Jozabad
Jozabad [Jezabad]
Jozabad [Jozabed]
Jozacar [Josachar]
Jozadak [Josedec]
Judah [Juda]
Judah [Judas]
Judah, children of [Judahites]
Judaia [Judean (adj.)]
Judea [Judah]
Jushab-hesed [Josabhesed]
Just, Book of the [Jashar, Book of]
Juttah [Jeta]
Juttah [Jota]

Kabzeel [Cabseel]
Kadesh [Cades]
Kadesh-barnea [Cadesbarne]
Kadmiel [Cedmihel]
Kain [Accain]
Kallai [Celai]
Kamon [Camon]
Kanah [Cana]
Kareah [Caree]
Karka [Carcaa]
Kartah [Cartha]
Kartan [Carthan]
Kaserin [Charan]
Kattath [Cateth]
Kedar [Cedar]

Kedemah [Cedma]
Kedemoth [Cademoth]
Kedemoth [Cidimoth]
Kedesh [Cades]
Kedesh [Cedes]
Keilah [Ceila]
Kelaiah [Celaia]
Kelita [Celita]
Kemuel [Camuel]
Kenan [Cainan]
Kenath [Canath]
Kenaz [Cenez]
Kenite [Cinite]
Kenites [Cinites]
Kenizzite [Cenezite]
Kerioth
Keros [Ceros]
Keshion [Cesion]
Keturah [Cetura]
Kibzaim [Cibsaim]
Kidron [Cedron]
Kinah [Cina]
Kiriath [Cariath]
Kiriath-arba [Cariath-Arbe]
Kiriath-baal [Cariathbaal]
Kiriath-jearim [Cariathaim]
Kiriath-sannah [Cariath-
    senna]
Kiriath-sepher [Cariath-
    Sepher]
Kiriathaim [Cariathaim]

Kiriatharim [Cariathiarim]
Kish [Cis]
Kishi [Cusi]
Kishion [Cesion]
Kishon [Cison]
Kitron [Cetron]
Kittim [Cethim]
Kohath [Caath]
Kohathites [Caathites]
Kolaiah [Colaia]
Korah [Core]
Kore [Core]
Koz [Cos]
Kue [Coa]
Kushaiah [Casaia]

Laadah [Laada]
Lachish [Lachis]
Ladan [Laadan]
Ladan [Ledan]
Ladan [Leedan]
Lahad [Laad]
Lahmam [Leheman]
Laish [Lais]
Lakkum [Lecum]
Lamech
Lamentations [Laments]
Laomin
Lappidoth [Lapidoth]
Lasharon [Saron]
Latussim

Leah [Lia]
Lebanah [Lebana]
Lebaoth
Lebonah [Lebona]
Lecah [Lecha]
Lehabim [Laabim]
Lehem [Lahem]
Lehi [Lechi]
Leshem [Lesem]
Letters, The City of
Levi
Levite
Levites
Levitical
Libanus [Lebanon]
Libanus [the Lebanon]
Libnah [Labana]
Libnah [Lebna]
Libnah [Lobna]
Libni [Lobni]
Libya
Libyans
Likhi [Leci]
Linath [Labanath]
Lo-debar [Lodabar]
Lod
Lod [Led]
Lotan
Lud
Ludim
Luz [Luza]

Lying [Cozeba]
Lysimachus

Maacah [Maacha]
Maacah [Machathi]
Maacah [Machati]
Maachathi [Maacathite]
Maadai [Maaddi]
Maadiah [Madia]
Maai
Maarath [Mareth]
Maasai
Maaseiah [Maasia]
Maaseiah [Maasias]
Maaseiah [Masia]
Maaz [Moos]
Maaziah [Maazia]
Maaziah [Maaziau]
Macedonian
Macedonians
Machbannai [Machbani]
Machbenah [Machbena]
Machir
Machnadebai [Mechnedebai]
Madai
Madmannah [Madmena]
Madmannah [Medemena]
Madon
Magala, place of [encampment]
Magbish [Megbis]
Magdiel

Magog
Magpiash [Megphias]
Mahalalel [Malaleel]
Mahanaim [Manaim]
Maharai
Maharai [Marai]
Mahath
Mahavite [Mahumite]
Mahazioth
Mahlah [Maala]
Mahlah [Mohola]
Mahli [Moholi]
Mahlon [Mahalon]
Mahol
Makaz [Macces]
Makkedah [Maceda]
Malcam [Molchom]
Malchiajah [Melchias]
Malchiel [Melchiel]
Malchijah [Melchia]
Malchijah [Melchias]
Malchiram [Melchiram]
Malchishua [Melchisua]
Mallothi [Mellothi]
Malluch [Maloch]
Malluch [Melluch]
Malluch [Meloch]
Malluchi [Milicho]
Mambre
Manahath
Manasseh [Manasse]

Manasseh [Manasses]
Manoah [Manue]
Maoch
Maon
Mara
Maralah [Merala]
Mareshah [Maresa]
Marsana [Marsena]
Mashal [Masal]
Massa
Matred
Matri [Metri]
Mattan [Mathan]
Mattaniah [Mathanaias]
Mattaniah [Mathania]
Mattaniah [Mathanias]
Mattaniah [Mathaniau]
Mattaniah [Matthanias]
Mattattah [Mathatha]
Mattenai [Mathanai]
Mattenai [Mathania]
Mattithiah [Mathathias]
Me-jarkon [Mejarcon]
Mearah [Maara]
Mebunnai [Mobonnai]
Mecherathite
Meconah [Mochona]
Medan [Madan]
Medeba [Medaba]
Medes
Media

Megiddo [Mageddo]
Mehetabel [Meetabel]
Mehetabel [Metabeel]
Mehida [Mahida]
Mehir [Mahir]
Meholath [Molathi]
Meholathite [Molathite]
Mehuman [Mauman]
Melatiah [Meltias]
Melech
Melehias
Melothus
Memucan [Mamuchan]
Menahem [Manaham]
Meonothai [Maonathi]
Mephaath
Mephibosheth [Miphi-
boseth]
Merab [Merob]
Meraiah [Maraia]
Meraioth
Meraioth [Maraioth]
Merari
Mered
Meremoth
Meremoth [Marimuth]
Meremoth [Merimuth]
Meres [Mares]
Merib-baal [Meribbaal]
Merodach Baladan [Berodach
Baladan]

Merom
*Merome, region of [heights of the
field]*
Meronothite [Meronathite]
Meroz
Mesha [Mosa]
Meshech [Mosoch]
Meshelemiah [Meselemia]
Meshelemiah [Mosollamia]
Meshezabel [Merezebel]
Meshezabel [Mesezabel]
Meshezabel [Mesizabel]
Meshillemith [Mosollamith]
Meshillemoth [Mosollamoth]
Meshobab [Mosabab]
Meshullam [Mesollam]
Meshullam [Messulam]
Meshullam [Mosollam]
Meshullemeth *[Messalemeth]*
Mesopotamia
Mesopotamia [Aram-naharaim]
Mesopotamia [beyond the River]
Mesrai [Egypt]
Mesraim [Egypt]
Messa
Methuselah [Mathusale]
Meunim [Munim]
Mezahab [Mezaab]
Mezoba [Masobia]
Mibhar [Mibahar]
Mibsam [Mabsam]

Mibsam [Mapsam]
Mibshan [Nebsan]
Mibzar [Mabsar]
Mica [Micha]
Micah [Melcha]
Micah [Micha]
Micah [Michas]
Micaiah [Michaia]
Micaiah [Michea]
Micaiah [Micheas]
Michael
Michal [Michol]
Michmas [Machmas]
Michmash [Machmas]
Michmash [Mechmas]
Michmethath [Mach-
methath]
Michri [Mochori]
Middin [Meddin]
Midian [Madian]
Midianites [Madianites]
Migdal-el [Magdalel]
Migdal-gad [Magdalgad]
Mijamin [Miamin]
Mikloth [Macelloth]
Mikneiah [Macenias]
Milalai [Malalai]
Milcom [Melchom]
Millo [Mello]
Miniamin [Miamin]
Minnith [Mennith]

Miriam [Mariam]
Miriam [Mary]
Mirmah [Marma]
Mishael [Misael]
Mishal [Masal]
Mishal [Messal]
Misham [Misaam]
Mishma [Masma]
Mishmannah [Masmana]
Mishraites [Maserites]
Misor
Mispar [Mesphar]
Mispereth [Mespharath]
Misrephoth [Maserephoth]
Misrephoth [Maserophot]
Mithnite [Mathanite]
Mithredath [Mithridates]
Mizpah [Maspha]
Mizpah [Masphath]
Mizpeh [Masepha]
Mizpeh [Masphe]
Mizpeh [Mesphe]
Mizzah [Meza]
Moab
Moabite
Moabites
Moabitess
Moadiah [Moadia]
Moladah [Molada]
Molech [Moloch]
Molid

Mordecai [Mardochai]
Moriah, Mount [Mount
    Moria]
Moses
Most Salt Sea [Dead Sea]
Moza [Mosa]
Mozah [Amosa]
Musach [covered portal]
Mushi [Musi]

Naam [Naham]
Naamah [Naama]
Naaman
Naarah [Naara]
Naarah [Naaratha]
Naarai
Naaran [Noran]
Naasson
Nabal
Naboth
Nacon [Nachon]
Nadab [Nabath]
Nahalal [Naalol]
Nahalol [Naalol]
Naham
Nahamani
Naharai
Nahash [Daas]
Nahash [Naas]
Nahath
Nahor [Nachor]

Nahshon [Nahasson]
Naioth [Najoth]
Naomi [Noemi]
Naphath [Nopheth]
Naphath-dor [Nephath-Dor]
Naphish [Naphis]
Naphtali [Nephtali]
Naphtalites [Nephtalites]
Naphtuhim [Nephtuim]
Nathan
Nathan-melech [Na-
    thanmelech]
Nathanael [Nathanias]
Nathineans [temple servants]
Nazirite [Nazarite]
Neah [Noa]
Neariah [Naaria]
Nebai
Nebaioth [Nabajoth]
Neballat
Nebat [Nabat]
Nebo
Nebuchadnezzar [Nabu-
    chodonosor]
Nebuzaradan [Nabuzardan]
Neco [Nechao]
Nedabiah [Nadabia]
Nehemiah [Nehemia]
Nehemiah [Nehemias]
Nehum [Nahum]
Nehushta [Nohesta]

Neiel [Nehiel]

Nekeb [Neceb]

Nekoda [Necoda]

Nemuel [Namuel]

Nepheg

Nepheg [Napheg]

Nephisim [Nephusim]

Nephtoah [Nephtoa]

Nephtoah, Water of [Water
   of Nephtoa]

Nephushesim [Nephussim]

Ner

Nergal [Nergel]

Nethanel [Nathanael]

Nethaniah [Nathaias]

Nethaniah [Nathanias]

Nethinites [temple servants]

Netophah [Netupha]

Netophahite [Netophathite]

Netophathite

Netophathites [Netophathi]

Netophathites [Netophati]

New Hazor [New Asor]

Neziah [Nasia]

Nezib [Nesib]

Nibhaz [Nebahaz]

Nimrod [Nemrod]

Nimshi [Namsi]

Nineveh [Ninive]

Nisan

Nisroch [Nesroch]

Noadiah [Noadaia]

Noadiah [Noadias]

Noah [Noa]

Noah [Noe]

Nob

Nob [Nobe]

Nobah [Nobe]

Nodab

Nogah [Noga]

Nogah [Noge]

Nohah [Nohaa]

Nun

oath, House of [Beth-ashbea]

Obadiah [Abdias]

Obadiah [Adias]

Obadiah [Obadia]

Obadiah [Obdia]

Obadiah [Obdias]

Obed

Obed-edom [Obededom]

Obediah [Obedia]

Obil [Ubil]

Oded

*Offence, Mount of [Mount of
   Destruction]*

Og

Ohel [Ohol]

Oholibamah [Oolibama]

Olivet, Mount [Mount of Olives]

Omar

Omri [Amai]

Omri [Amri]

Onam

Onan

Ono

Ophel

Ophir

Ophni

Ophrah [Ephra]

Ophrah [Ophera]

Ophrah [Ophra]

Oreb

Oren [Aram]

Orientals [east]

Ornan

Osnappar [Asenaphar]

Othni

Othniel [Othoniel]

Our Testimony that the Lord is God [Witness]

Ox [Idox]

Ozem [Asom]

Oziel [Ozias]

Paarai [Pharai]

Padon [Phadon]

Pahath-moab [Phahath Moab]

Pahath-moab [Phahathmoab]

Pai [Phau]

Palal [Phalel]

Pallu [Phallu]

Palmira [Tadmor]

Palmira [Tamar]

Palti [Phalti]

Paltiel [Phaltiel]

Parah [Aphara]

Paran [Pharan]

Parmashta [Phermesta]

Paros

Parosh [Pharos]

Parshandatha [Pharsandatha]

Paruah [Pharue]

Pasach [Phosech]

Pasdammim [Phesdomim]

Paseah [Phasea]

Paseah [Phesse]

Pashhur [Phashur]

Pashhur [Pheshur]

Passhur [Phassur]

Pathrusim [Phetrusim]

Peaceable [Solomon]

Pedaiah [Phadai]

Pedaiah [Phadaia]

Pekah [Phacee]

Pekahiah [Phaceia]

Pelaiah [Phalaia]

Pelaiah [Pheleia]

Pelaliah [Phelelia]

Pelatiah [Phaltias]

Pelatiah [Pheltia]

Peleg [Phaleg]

Pelet [Phalet]
Pelet [Phallet]
Peleth [Phaleth]
Pelethites [Phelethi]
Pelonite [Phallonite]
Pelonite [Phelonite]
Peninnah [Phenenna]
Penuel [Phanuel]
Peresh [Phares]
Perez [Phares]
Perida [Pharida]
Perizites [Pherezites]
Perizzite [Pherezite]
Perizzites [Pherezites]
Persia
Persians
Peruda [Pharuda]
Pethahiah [Phataia]
Pethahiah [Phathahia]
Pethahiah [Pheteia]
Peullethai [Phollathi]
Pharaoh [Pharao]
Pharpar [Pharphar]
Pharurim [precincts]
Phelethi
Philistia
Philistine
Philistines
Phinehas [Phinees]
Pilati [Phelti]
Pilha [Phalea]

Pinon [Phinon]
Piram [Pharam]
Pirathon [Pharathon]
Pirathonite [Pharathonite]
Pisgah [Phasga]
Pispa [Phaspha]
Pithon [Phithon]
Plantations [Netaim]
Pochereth [Phochereth]
Poratha [Phoratha]
Priapus [Asherah]
Ptolemy
Puah [Phua]
Pul [Phul]
Pur [Phur]
Purah [Phara]
Put [Phut]
Puthites [Aphuthites]

Queen [Hammolecheth]

Raama [Regma]
Raamiah [Raamias]
Rab-saris [Rabsaris]
Rabbah [Arebba]
Rabbah [Rabba]
Rabbah [Rabbath]
Rabbith [Rabboth]
Rabshakeh [Rabseces]
Racal [Rachal]
Rachel

Raddai
Ragau [Ragua]
Rages
Raguel
Rahab
Raham
Rakkath [Reccath]
Rakkon [Arecon]
Ram
Ram [Aram]
Rama
Ramah [Arama]
Ramah [Horma]
Ramah [Rama]
Ramah [Ramatha]
Ramah [Ramoth]
Ramath [Ramoth]
Ramath-lehi [Ramathlechi]
Ramathaim-zophim [Rama-
    thaimsophim]
Ramathite [Romathite]
Ramiah [Remeia]
Ramoth
Ramoth Gilead [Ramoth Ga-
    laad]
Rapha
Rapha [giants]
Raphah [Rapha]
Raphain [Raphaim]
Reaiah [Raaia]
Reaiah [Raia]

Reba [Rebe]
Recah [Recha]
Rechab
Red Sea
Red Sea [sea]
Reeds, Valley of the [Wadi
    Kanah]
Reelaiah [Rahelaia]
Regem [Rogom]
Rehabiah [Rohobia]
Rehob [Rohob]
Rehob [Rohol]
Rehoboam [Roboam]
Rehoboth [Rohoboth]
Rehum
Rehum [Reum]
Rehum [Rheum]
Rei
Rekem [Recem]
Rekem [Recen]
Remaliah [Romelia]
Remeth
Rephael [Raphael]
Rephah [Rapha]
Rephaiah [Raphaia]
Rephaim (Raphaim) [giants]
Rephaim [Raphaim]
Rephaim [Raphaims]
Rephaim, Valley of [Valley of
    Raphaim]
Resheph [Reseph]

rest, he that saw half of the places of [Haroeh, half of the Menuhoth]
Reu [Ragau]
Reuben [Ruben]
Reubenites [Rubenites]
Reuel [Rahuel]
Rezeph [Reseph]
Rezin [Rasin]
Rezon [Razon]
Ribai
Riblah [Rebla]
Riblah [Reblatha]
Rimmon [Remmon]
Rimmono [Remmono]
Rinnah [Rinna]
Rizia [Resia]
Rizpah [Respha]
Rock, The [Sela]
Rodanim [Dodanim]
Rogel
Rogelim
Rohgah [Roaga]
Romamti-ezer
   [Romemthiezer]
Ruben
Rumah [Ruma]
Ruth

Sabta [Sabatha]
Sabteca [Sabathaca]

Sachar
Sachia [Sechia]
Salamiel [Salathiel]
Salebim [Shaalbim]
Salecah [Salecha]
Salecah [Selcha]
Sallai [Sellai]
Sallu [Salo]
Sallu [Shellum]
Salma
Salmon
Salt, City of
Saltpits, Valley of [Valley of Salt]
Saltus [Jair]
Samaria
Samaritans
Samlah [Semla]
Sammuel [Samuel]
Samson
Samuel
Sanballat [Sanaballat]
Sanir
Sansannah [Sensenna]
Saph
*Sarai, half of the place of rest of
   [half of the Manahathites,
   the Zorites]*
Sarid
Satan
Saul
Scorpion [Akrabim]

Scorpion, the [Akrabbim]
Seba [Saba]
Secacah [Sachacha]
Secure [Joash]
Segub
Seir
Seir, Mount
Seirah [Seirath]
Seled [Saled]
Selmon [Zalmon]
Semachiah [Samachias]
Senaah [Senaa]
Seneh [Sene]
Sennacherib
Seorim
Sepharvaim
Sephet
Serah [Sara]
Seraiah [Saraias]
Seraiah [Saraia]
Seraiah [Seraias]
Serug
Seth
Shaalabbin [Selebin]
Shaalbim [Salebim]
Shaalbon [Salaboni]
Shaalbonite [Salabonite]
Shaalim [Salim]
Shaaph [Saaph]
Shaaraim [Saraim]
Shaashgaz [Susagaz]

Shabbethai [Sabathai]
Shabbethai [Sebethai]
Shabbethai [Sephtai]
Shagee [Sage]
Shaharim [Saharim]
Shahazumah [Sehesima]
Shalishah [Salisa]
Shallum [Sellum]
Shalmai [Selmai]
Shalmaneser [Salmanasar]
Shama [Samma]
Shamgar [Samgar]
Shamhuth [Samaoth]
Shamir [Samir]
Shamlai [Semlai]
Shamma [Samma]
Shammah [Samma]
Shammah [Semma]
Shammai [Sammai]
Shammai [Semei]
Shammoth [Sammoth]
Shammua [Sammua]
Shammua [Samua]
Shamsherai [Samsari]
Shapham [Saphan]
Shaphan [Saphan]
Shaphat [Saphat]
Sharai [Sarai]
Sharar [Sarar]
Sharezer [Sarasar]
Sharon [Saaron]

Sharon [Saron]
Sharonite [Saronite]
Sharuhen [Sarohen]
Shashai [Sisai]
Shashak [Sesac]
Shaul [Saul]
Sheal [Saal]
Shealtiel [Salathiel]
Sheariah [Saria]
Sheba [Saba]
Sheba [Sabee]
Sheba [Seba]
Sheba [Sebe]
Shebaniah [Sabania]
Shebaniah [Sebenia]
Shebaniah [Sebenias]
Shebaniah [Sebnia]
Shebarim [Sabarim]
Sheber [Saber]
Shebnah [Sobna]
Shebuel [Subael]
Shebuel [Subduel]
Shebuel [Subuel]
Shecaniah [Sebenias]
Shecaniah [Sechenia]
Shecaniah [Sechenias]
Shechem [Sechem]
Shechem [Sichem]
Shechemites [Sichemites]
Sheerah [Sara]
Shehariah [Sohoria]

Shelah [Sale]
Shelah [Sela]
Shelah [Siloe]
Shelemiah [Salmias]
Shelemiah [Selemaia]
Shelemiah [Selemias]
Shelemiah [Selemiau]
Sheleph [Saleph]
Shelesh [Selles]
Shelomith [Salomith]
Shelomoth [Salemoth]
Shelomoth [Salomith]
Shelomoth [Selemith]
Shem [Sem]
Shema [Sama]
Shema [Samma]
Shema [Semeia]
Shemaah [Samaa]
Shemaiah [Samaia]
Shemaiah [Semei]
Shemaiah [Semeia]
Shemaiah [Semeias]
Shemariah [Samaria]
Shemariah [Samarias]
Shemariah [Semeria]
Shemariah [Somorias]
Shemed [Samad]
Shemer [Semer]
Shemer [Somer]
Shemida [Semida]
Shemiramoth [Semiramoth]

Shemuel [Samuel]
Shen [Sen]
Shenazzar [Senneser]
Shephatiah [Saphathia]
Shephatiah [Saphatia]
Shephatiah [Saphatias]
Shephatiah [Sephatia]
Shephi [Sephi]
Shephuphan [Sephuphan]
Sherebiah [Sarabias]
Sherebiah [Sarebia]
Sherebiah [Sarebias]
Sheresh [Sares]
Sheshai [Sesai]
Sheshan [Sesan]
Sheshbazzar [Sassabasar]
Shethar [Sethar]
Shethar-bozenai [Stharbuza-
nai]
Sheva [Siva]
Sheva [Sue]
Shibboleth [Scibboleth]
Shihor [Sihor]
Shikkeron [Sechrona]
Shilhi [Salai]
Shilhi [Selahi]
Shilhim [Selim]
Shiloh [Silo]
Shilonite [Silonite]
Shilonites [Siloni]
Shilshah [Salusa]

Shimea [Samaa]
Shimea [Simmaa]
Shimeah [Samaa]
Shimeah [Semmaa]
Shimeam [Samaan]
Shimeath [Semaath]
Shimei [Samae]
Shimei [Semei]
Shimei [Semeias]
Shimeon [Simeon]
Shimon [Simon]
Shimrath [Samareth]
Shimri [Samri]
Shimri [Semri]
Shimri [Zamri]
Shimrith [Semarith]
Shimron [Simeron]
Shimron [Zemaraim]
Shimron-meron [Zemaraim]
Shimshai [Samsai]
Shion [Seon]
Shiphi [Sephei]
Shiphmite [Aphonite]
Shisha [Sisa]
Shishak [Sesac]
Shitrai [Setrai]
Shittim [Setim]
Shobab [Sobab]
Shobach [Sobach]
Shobai [Sobai]
Shobal [Sobal]

Shobek [Sobec]
Shobi [Sobi]
Shoham [Soam]
Shomer [Somer]
Shophach [Sophach]
Shua [Suaa]
Shua [Sue]
Shuah [Sue]
Shual [Sual]
Shubael [Subael]
Shuhah [Sua]
Shumathites [Semathites]
Shunammitess [Sunamitess]
Shunem [Sunem]
Shuppim [Saphan]
Shuppim [Sepham]
Shuppim [Sephim]
Shur [Sur]
Shuthelah [Suthala]
Sia [Siaa]
Siaha [Sia]
Sibbecai [Sabachai]
Sibbecai [Sobbochai]
Sibbecai [Sobochai]
Sibboleth
Sibmah [Sabama]
Sidon
Sidon, the Great
Sidonians
Sihon [Sehon]
Silla [Sella]

Simeon
Simeonites
Sinai [Sina]
Sinite
Sippai [Saphai]
Sirah [Sira]
Sisera [Sisara]
Sismai [Sisamoi]
Sivan [Siban]
So [Sua]
Soco [Socho]
Socoh [Socho]
Socoh [Socoth]
Solomon
Sopher [the secretary]
Sophereth
Sotai
Stone of Help [Ebenezer]
Suah [Sue]
Succoth [Soccoth]
Succoth [Sochot]
Succoth [Socoth]
Succoth-benoth [Sochoth-
    benoth]
*sun to stand, he that made the
    [Jokim]*
Sun, City of the
Sur
Susa [Susan]
Susanechites [Susa, people of]
Syria [Aram]

Syria [Edom]
Syria Sobal
Syriac [Aramaic]
Syrian [Aramean]
Syrians [Arameans]

Taanach [Thanac]
Taanach [Thanach]
Taanach [Thenac]
Taanath-shiloh [Thanath-
    selo]
Tabbaoth
Tabbaoth [Tebbaoth]
Tabbath [Tebbath]
Tabeel
Tabor [Thabor]
Tabrimmon [Tabremon]
Tahan [Thaan]
Tahath [Thahath]
Tahath [Thanath]
Tahpenes [Taphnes]
Tahrea [Tharaa]
Talami [Tolmai]
Talmai [Tholmai]
Talmai [Tholomai]
Talmon [Telmon]
Tamar [Thamar]
Tanhumeth [Thanehumeth]
Taphath [Tapheth]
Tappuah [Taphua]
Tappuah [Thaphua]

Taralah [Tharela]
Tarea [Tharaa]
Tarshish [Tharsis]
Tartak [Tharthac]
Tartan [Tharthan]
Tattenai [Thathanai]
Tebaliah [Tabelias]
Tebeth
Tehinnah [Tehinna]
Tekoa [Thecua]
Tekoite [Thecuite]
Tekoites [Thecuites]
Tel-harsha [Thelharsa]
Tel-melah [Thelmela]
Telah [Thale]
Telassar [Thelassar]
Telem
Tema [Thema]
Temah [Thema]
Teman [Theman]
Temanites [Themanites]
Temeni [Themani]
Terah [Thare]
Terebinth [Elah]
Teresh [Thares]
Tharra
Tharsis
the carpenter [Heresh]
The Spring of him that Invoked
    from the Jawbone [En-
    hakkore]

Thebez [Thebes]
Therphalites
Thohu [Tohu]
Tibhath [Thebath]
Tibni [Thebni]
Tiglath-pileser [Thaglath-
  phalasar]
Tigris
Tikvah [Thecua]
Tilgath-pilneser [Thelgath-
  phalnasar]
Tilon [Thilon]
Timna [Thamna]
Timnah [Thamna]
Timnah [Thamnan]
Timnah [Thamnatha]
Timnah [Themna]
Timnath Serah [Thamnath
  Saraa]
Timnath-heres [Thamnath-
  sare]
Timnath-serah [Thamnath-
  sare]
Tiphsa [Thapsa]
Tiphsah [Thaphsa]
Tiras [Thiras]
Tirhakah [Theraca]
Tirhanah [Tharana]
Tiria [Thiria]
Tirshatha [the governor]
Tirzah [Thersa]

Tishbite [Thesbite]
Titan [the Titans]
Tizite [Thosaite]
Toah [Thohu]
Tob
Tob [Istob]
Tob-adonijah [Thobadonias]
Tobiah [Tobia]
Tobiah [Tobias]
Tobias
Tobijah [Tobias]
Tobit [Tobias]
Tochen [Thochen]
Togarmah [Thogorma]
Toi [Thou]
Tokhath [Thecuath]
Tola [Thola]
Tolad [Tholad]
Topheth
Tou [Thou]
Troglodites [Sukkiim]
Tubal [Thubal]
Tyre
Tyrian
Tyrians

Uel
Ulam
Ulla [Olla]
Ummah [Amma]
Unno [Hanni]

Ur
Uri
Uriah [Uria]
Uriah [Urias]
Uriel
Uthai
Uthai [Othei]
Uz [Hus]
Uzai [Ozi]
Uzal [Usal]
Uzza [Asa]
Uzza [Oza]
Uzzah (Oza), Breach of [Perez-
    uzzah]
Uzzah [Oza]
Uzzah, Striking of [Perez-uzzah]
Uzzen-sheerah [Ozensara]
Uzzi [Azzi]
Uzzi [Ozi]
Uzzia [Ozia]
Uzziah [Aziam]
Uzziah [Ozias]
Uzziel [Eziel]
Uzziel [Ozial]
Uzziel [Oziel]
Uzzielites [Ozielites]

Vaizatha [Jezatha]
Vale-Casis [Emek-keziz]
Vaniah [Vania]

Vashni [Vasseni]
Vashti [Vasthi]

Weepers, Place of [Bochim]
Wilderness, Sea of the [sea of the
    Arabah]
Woods, The City of the

Zaanannim [Saananim]
Zaanannim [Sennim]
Zaavan [Zavan]
Zabad
Zabbai
Zabbai [Zachai]
Zabdi
Zabdi [Zabdias]
Zabdi [Zebedei]
Zabdiel
Zabud
Zaccai [Zachai]
Zaccur [Zacchur]
Zaccur [Zachur]
Zadok [Sadoc]
Zaham [Zoom]
Zair [Seira]
Zalaph [Seleph]
Zalmon [Selmon]
Zalmunna [Salmana]
Zanoah [Zanoa]
Zanoah [Zanoe]

Zaphon [Saphon]
Zarephath [Sarephta]
Zarethan [Sartham]
Zarethan [Sarthan]
Zarethan [Sarthana]
Zattu [Zethu]
Zattu [Zethua]
Zaza [Ziza]
Zebadiah [Zabadia]
Zebadiah [Zabadias]
Zebadiah [Zebedia]
Zebah [Zebee]
Zebidah [Zebida]
Zebina [Zabina]
Zeboim [Seboim]
Zebul
Zebulun [Zabulon]
Zebulunite [Zabulonite]
Zebulunites [Zabulonties]
Zechariah [Zacharia]
Zechariah [Zacharias]
Zecher [Zacher]
Zedekiah [Sedecias]
Zeeb [Zeb]
Zela [Sela]
Zelek [Selec]
Zelophehad [Salphaad]
Zemaraim [Samaraim]
Zemaraim, Mount [Mount
    Semeron]

Zemarite [Samarite]
Zemirah [Zamira]
Zenan [Sanan]
Zephaiah [Sophonias]
Zephaniah [Sophonias]
Zephath [Sephaath]
Zephathah [Sephata]
Zephi [Sephi]
Zer [Ser]
Zerah [Zara]
Zerah [Zare]
Zerahiah [Zarahia]
Zerahiah [Zaraias]
Zerahiah [Zareha]
Zerahites [Zarahi]
Zerahites [Zarai]
Zeredah [Sareda]
Zeredah [Saredatha]
Zeresh [Zares]
Zereth [Sereth]
Zereth-shahar [Sarathasar]
Zeri [Sori]
Zeror [Seror]
Zeruah [Sarua]
Zerubbabel [Zorobabel]
Zeruiah [Sarvia]
Zetham [Zathan]
Zetham [Zethan]
Zethan
Zethar

Zia [Zie]

Ziba [Siba]

Zibeon [Sebeon]

Zibia [Sebia]

Zibiah [Sebia]

Zichri [Zechri]

Ziddim [Assedim]

Ziha [Siaha]

Ziha [Siha]

Ziha [Soha]

Ziklag [Siceleg]

Zillethai [Salathi]

Zillethai [Selethai]

Zimmah [Zamma]

Zimmah [Zemma]

Zimran [Zamran]

Zimri [Zambri]

Zimri [Zamri]

Zin [Sin]

Zin [Sina]

Zina [Ziza]

Zion [Sion]

Zion, Mount [Mount Sion]

Zior [Sior]

Ziph

Ziph [Siph]

Ziphites

Zippor [Sephor]

Ziv [Zio]

Ziz [Sis]

Ziza

Zobah [Soba]

Zobah [Suba]

Zobebah [Soboba]

Zoheleth

Zoheth

Zophah [Supha]

Zophai [Sophai]

Zorah [Saraa]

Zorah [Sarea]

Zorathites [Saraites]

Zorathites [Sarathi]

Zuph [Suph]

Zur [Sur]

Bibliography

Carleton, J. G. *The Part of Rheims in the Making of the English Bible.* Oxford: Clarendon, 1902.

Cartmell, J. "English Spiritual Writers: x. Richard Challoner." *Clergy Review* n.s. 44, no. 10 (October 1959): 577–587.

A Catholic. "A new Version of the Four Gospels, with Notes, Critical and Explanatory." *Dublin Review* 2, no. 2 (April 1837): 475–492.

Biblia Sacra: Vulgatae Editionis Sixti V Pont. Max. iussu recognita et Clementis VIII auctoritate edita. Vatican City: Marietti, 1959.

Challoner, R. "The Touchstone of the New Religion: or, Sixty Assertions of Protestants, try'd by their own Rule of Scripture alone, and condemned by clear and express Texts of their own Bible." London, n.p.: 1735.

———. ed. *The Holy Bible translated from the Latin Vulgat: Diligently compared With the Hebrew, Greek, and other Editions in divers Languages. And first published by The English College at Doway, Anno 1609. Newly revised, and corrected, according to the Clementine Edition of the Scriptures with Annotations for clearing up the principal Difficulties of Holy Writ.* 4 vols. Dublin(?): 1752.

———., ed. *The Holy Bible, translated from the Latin Vulgate, Diligently compared with the Hebrew, Greek, and other editions in divers languages. The Old Testament, First published by the English College at Douay, A.D. 1609 and The New Testament, First published by the English College at Rheims, A.D. 1582. With annotations, references, and an historical and chronological index. The whole revised and diligently compared with the Latin Vulgate Published with the approbation of His Eminence James Cardinal Gibbons Archbishop of Baltimore.* Baltimore: John Murphy, 1899.

———., ed. *The New Testament of Our LORD and SAVIOUR JESUS*

CHRIST. Translated out of the Latin Vulgat; diligently compared with the original Greek: and first published by English *College at* Rhemes, *Anno 1582. Newly revised and corrected according to the* Clementin *Edition of the Scriptures. With Annotations, for Clearing up modern Controversies in Religion; and other Difficulties of Holy Writ.* 2 vols. Dublin(?): 1752.

Cotton, H. *Rhemes and Doway: An Attempt to shew what has been done by Roman Catholics for the Diffusion of the Holy Scriptures in English.* Oxford: University Press, 1855.

de Hamel, C. *The Book: A History of the Bible.* London: Phaidon, 2001.

Dodd, C. [H. Tootell]. *The Church History of England, From The Year 1500, to The Year 1688. Chiefly with regard to Catholicks.* 8 vols. Brussels [London], 1737–1742.

Duffy, E., ed. *Challoner and His Church: A Catholic Bishop in Georgian England.* London: Darton, Longman & Todd, 1981.

English College of Doway. *The Holie Bible Faithfully Translated into English, out of the Authentical Latin. Diligently conferred with the Hebrew, Greeke, and other Editions in diuers languages. With Arguments of the Bookes, and Chapters: Annotations. Tables: and other helpes, for better understanding of the text: for discoueirie of corruptions in some late translations: and for clearing Controversies in Religion.* 2 vols. Doway: Lavrence Kellam, at the signe of the holie Lambe, 1609–1610.

English College of Rhemes. *The Nevv Testament of Iesvs Christ, Translated Faithfully into English, out of the authentical Latin, according to the best corrected copies of the same, diligently conferred vvithe the Greeke and other editions in diuers languages: Vvith Argvments of bookes and chapters, Annotations, and other necessarie helpes, for the better vnderstanding of the text, and specially for the discouerie of the Corrvptions of diuers late translations, and for cleering the Controversies in religion, of these daies.* Rhemes: Iohn Fogny, 1582.

Frede, H. J. *Kirchenschriftsteller: Verzeichnis und Sigel.* Freiburg: Herder, 1995.

Gilley, S. "Challoner as Controvertionalist." In E. Duffy, ed., *Challoner and His Church: A Catholic Bishop in Georgian England.* London: Darton, Longman & Todd, 1981, pp. 90–111.

Greenslade, S. L., ed. *The Cambridge History of the Bible: The West, from the Reformation to the Present Day.* Rev. ed. Cambridge: Cambridge University Press, 1975.

Gryson, R. *Altlateinische Handschriften: Manuscrits Vieux Latins.* Freiburg: Herder, 1999.

The Holy Bible, Conteyning the Old Testament, and the New: Newly Translated out of the Originall tongues: & with the former Translations diligently compared and reuised: by his Maiesties speciall Comandement Appointed to be read in Churches. London: Robert Barker, Printer to the Kings most Excellent Maiestie, 1611; rpr. Thomas Nelson, 1990.

Kaske, R. E. *Medieval Chirstian Literary Imagery: A Guide to Interpretation.* Toronto: University of Toronto Press, ca. 1988.

Knox, T. F. Introduction. In *The First and Second Diaries of the English College, Douay, and an Appendix of Unpublished Documents, Edited by Fathers of the Congregation of the London Oratory, with an Historical Introduction.* Records of the English Catholics under the Penal Laws. Chiefly from the Archives of the See of Westinster 1. London: David Nutt, 1878.

Metzger, B. M., and R. E. Murphy. *The New Oxford Annotated Bible: New Revised Standard Version.* New York: Oxford University Press, 1991.

Milgrom, J., comm. *The JPS Torah Commentary: Numbers.* Philadelphia: The Jewish Publication Society.

Pope, H., and S. Bullough. *English Versions of the Bible.* St. Louis: Herder, 1952.

Quentin, H. *Biblia sacra: iuxta Latinam Vulgatam versionem.* Typis Polyglottis Vaticanis, 1926–[1995].

———. *Mémoire sur l'établissement du texte de la Vulgate.* Collectanea Biblica Latina 6, 1922.

Rahlfs, A., ed., and R. Hanhart, rev. *Septuaginta: Id est Vetus Testamentum graece iuxta LXX interpretes, Editio altera.* Stuttgart: Deutsche Bibelgesellschaft, 2006.

Sabatier, P. *Bibliorum Sacrorum Latinae versiones antiquae, seu Vetus Italica, et Ceterae quaecunque in Codicibus Mss. & antiquorum libris reperiri poterunt: Quae cum Vulgata Latina, & cum Textu Graeco comparantur. Accedunt Praefationes, Observationes, ac Notae, Indexque novus ad Vulgatam è regione editam, idemque locupletissimus.* 3 vols. Rheims: Apud Reginaldum Florentain, Regis Typographicum & Bibliopolam, sub signo Bibliorum aureorum, 1743–1749.

Weber, R., ed. *Biblia Sacra Vulgata.* 5th ed. Stuttgart: Deutsche Bibelgesellschaft, 2007.